Reconstruction Era Fashions

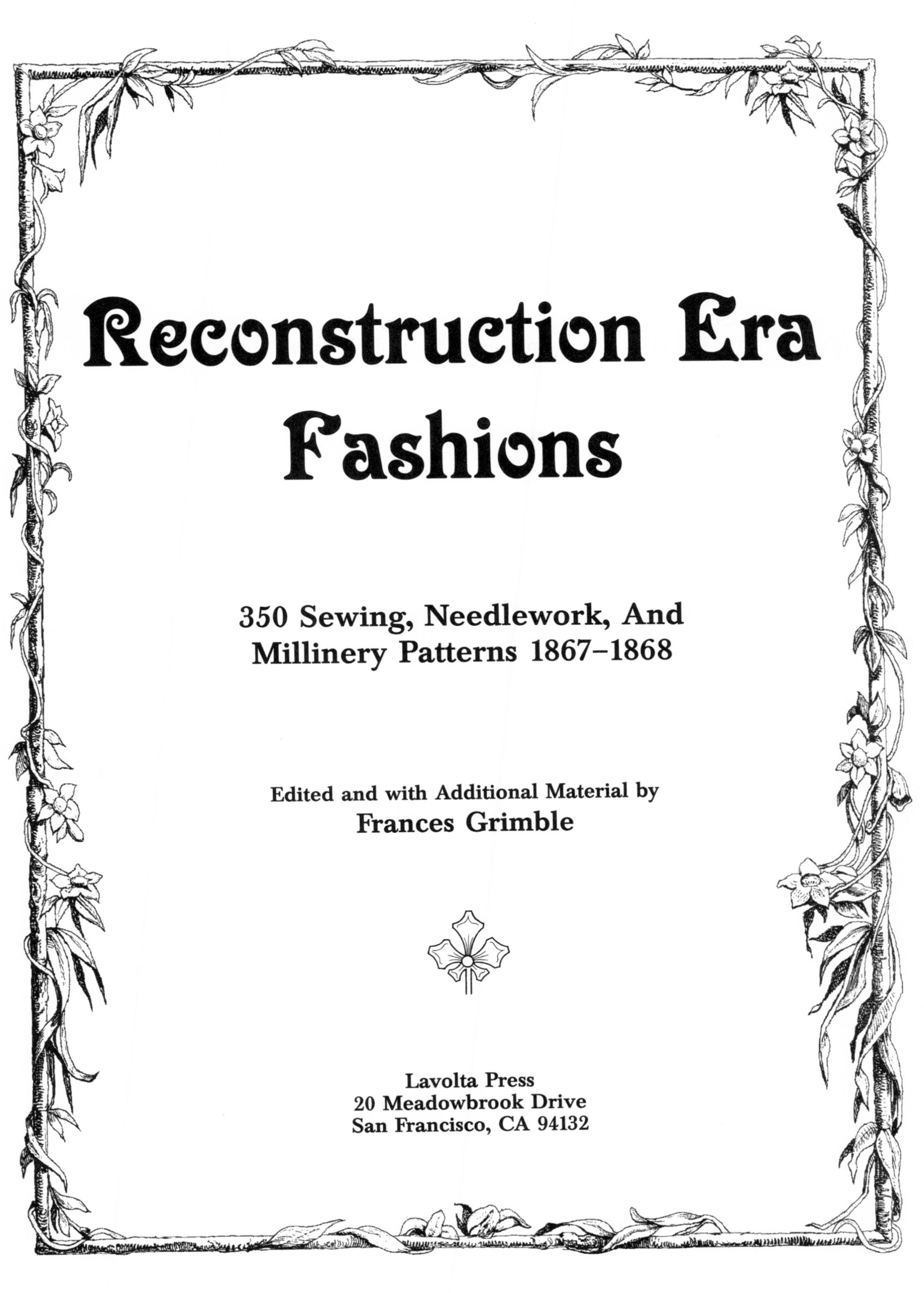

Reconstruction Era Fashions

350 Sewing, Needlework, And Millinery Patterns 1867–1868

Edited and with Additional Material by

Frances Grimble

Lavolta Press
20 Meadowbrook Drive
San Francisco, CA 94132

First edition

ISBN: 0-9636517-4-9

Published by
Lavolta Press
20 Meadowbrook Drive
San Francisco, CA 94132
http://www.lavoltapress.com

Book design, cover design, scanning, scan editing and coloring, page layout, and production management by Frances Grimble and Allan Terry

Printed and bound in the United States of America

Publisher's Cataloging-in-Publication
(Provided by Quality Books, Inc.)

Reconstruction era fashions : 350 sewing, needlework, and millinery patterns 1867-1868 / edited and with additional material by Frances Grimble.
p. cm.
Includes bibliographical references and index.
LCCN 2001088460
ISBN 0-9636517-4-9
1. Dressmaking--United States--Patterns. 2. Costume --United States--History--19th century. 3. Fashion--United States--History--19th century. I. Grimble, Frances. II. Title: Harper's bazar.

TT520.R43 2001 646.4'07
QB101-700621

Acknowledgments

I'd like to thank a number of people who have not only contributed to this book, but provided consistent support. My husband, Allan Terry, engineered the technical process for bringing the original materials into book form. He helped to design the cover and interior, and edited and colored the cover scans. He also programmed a database, kept my computer running, and performed countless other tasks.

My brother, Robert Grimble, was always ready to donate legal advice. Our printer, McNaughton & Gunn, did their usual high-quality job. Charles Arkebauer of Typemasters provided prepress services and advice. San Leandro Investment Company warehoused our books.

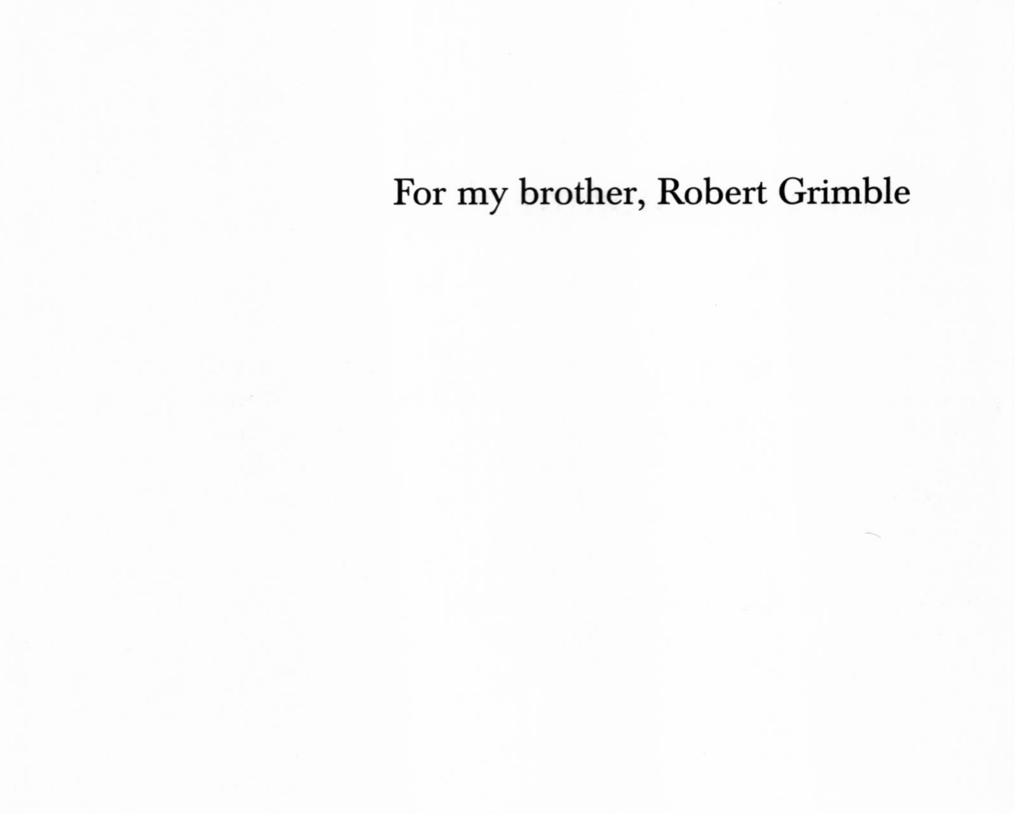

For my brother, Robert Grimble

Contents

Contents

Contents

Contents

Contents

Contents

Contents

Introduction

When researching this book, I was struck by the dearth of detailed information, or even illustrations, on women's styles of the late 1860s. Most costuming books treat them as a mere interval between the extreme crinoline styles of the early to mid 1860s, and the extreme bustle styles of the early to mid 1870s.

Late 1860s Fashions

Yet this "early bustle period" has considerable charm. Late in 1867 the basic dress style had a slightly high-waisted, close-fitting bodice (which *Harper's Bazar* generally called a "waist" or "corsage"; the term "bodice" was more often applied to peasant style waists). The skirt was gored, often trained, and sometimes cut in one with the waist. A day dress in this style, with the typical high cut at the throat and two-piece "coat sleeves," is shown in the November 30, 1867 *Harper's Bazar* by the Brown Irish Poplin Dress. Instead of the high-waisted bodice, some day dresses had a jacket, like the Morning Dress with Jacket in the December 14, 1867 issue. The evening bodice usually had a lower neckline and shorter sleeves. The neckline could be a wide oval or V, as shown by the March 28, 1868 Low-Necked Evening Waist. Or it could be cut in a deep rectangle partly filled in with a chemisette, like the October 24, 1868 Maria Theresa Dress Waist.

Another popular waist was the separate waist or "chemise Russe" (what we would call a blouse) worn with a contrasting skirt. Depending on its dressiness, it was suitable either for day (like the Waist with Simulated Bodice in the June 20, 1868 issue) or evening (the Pompadour Basque Waist and the Pompadour Waist with Bretelles in the January 25, 1868 issue).

The skirt could be looped up over an underskirt to produce the fashionable "polonaise" silhouette—a conscious imitation of the 18th century—or for ease in walking. One method is shown by the Tirettes for Looping Up Skirts in the October 17, 1868 issue. Another way to create an overskirt and/or bustle effect was to wear the longer, more fitted versions of an upper garment called the "paletot." The paletot could be worn either instead of a dress waist, or over it as an outer garment. Its skirt functioned as an overskirt, which was often bunched up. This style is seen in the November 14, 1868 Camargo Paletot and Adeline Paletot. *Harper's Bazar* advised women to make a paletot in a color and fabric that would coordinate with several different skirts.

Outer garments also included loose, flowing coats like the November 16, 1867 Alexandra Paletot. A sacque style could be worn as a jacket, like the Don Caesar Paletot in the same issue. Capes were worn, especially for evening, like the January 25, 1868 Bedouin and Talma.

The dress was supported by a crinoline, such as the one in the December 14, 1867 issue. The crinoline could have a built-in bustle, like the Hoopskirt in the December 12, 1868 issue. Or a separate bustle might be worn over it, like the Horsehair Bustle or the Pannier Bustle in the same issue. The figure was supported and defined by a corset, like the four in the September 5, 1868 issue.

Under the corset a woman wore a chemise. Although the chemise was a simple, loose garment, its neckline and sleeves had to be concealable under the dress. For example, the Pompadour Chemise in the September 26, 1868 issue is cut to be worn with the "Pompadour" rectangular neckline. A woman also needed to wear drawers, such as the Drawers with Round Belt in the same issue. The term "underskirt" was applied to a concealed petticoat (as well as to a dress skirt partly revealed by a looped-up overskirt). The petticoat was styled to accommodate the size of the bustle and the length

of the train. One example is the Underskirt with Train and Bustle in the December 12, 1868 issue. Undergarments also included the under waist and the corset cover, both seen in the January 11, 1868 issue.

The fashion columns in *Harper's Bazar* indicate that although some trimmings could be bought, many were homemade. Trimmings included ruches, flounces, and bows that involved ribbon work techniques (whether using ribbon or silk fabric), such as those in the October 17, 1868 "Trimmings for Dresses and Skirts." Trimmings for separate waists and "lingerie" (the term included some accessories as well as undergarments) used what we call today heirloom sewing techniques. These included hand and purchased embroidery, lace piecing, appliqué, crocheting, tatting, knitting, and netting. Often multiple techniques were combined in one trimming. Examples are described in "Waist and Lingerie Trimmings" in the June 20, 1868 issue. Beaded trimming was also popular, for example the "Dress and Outerwear Trimmings" in the June 27, 1868 issue. Sashes and paletots were adorned with handmade fringes, like the ones in the July 25, 1868 issue.

Many accessories were used to vary a wardrobe. Detachable collar-and-cuff sets, cravats, jabots, and chemisettes were embellished with heirloom sewing techniques. They might even be entirely hand crocheted or tatted (for example the Cravat of Tatting and Velvet Ribbon in the December 21, 1867 issue). Evening berthas were similarly trimmed. A particularly popular accessory was the Marie Antoinette fichu (see the March 28, 1868 issue). This had a capelike point hanging over the back. The long ends came around the shoulders to cross in front, then were passed around to fasten in back, the remainder hanging like sash ends. Elaborate sashes of satin, silk, or ribbon, with long hanging ends, were also popular. Even parasols were covered at home, as evidenced by instructions for "Parasols and Trimmings" in the May 9, 1868 issue.

A bonnet, hat, cap, or evening headdress was a necessary component of many outfits (although the plates do not show a head covering being worn at all times). Some caps for home wear, such as the August 8, 1868 Net Breakfast Cap with Cape, could easily be made using ordinary sewing skills. This is also true of the veils worn with bonnets, like the Mantilla Veil in the January 25, 1868 issue. Women frequently trimmed their own bonnets. Sometimes they even made the foundations, as instructed by the article "Making Bonnet Frames and Bonnets" in the May 9, 1868 issue. The evening headdress was usually a wreath or bandeau of artificial flowers and/or leaves and/or lace, with a long hanging "tail," as shown by the headdresses in the February 29, 1868 issue.

Hairstyles relied heavily on the unabashed use of "additional hair." One common component was the chignon, a large hairpiece braided or coiled in any of many ways, then attached to the back of the head. Some styles had long back curls, like the Josephine Coiffure and the Sévigné Coiffure in the March 7, 1868 issue. These could be built into the hairpiece or pinned on separately.

The Advent of Harper's Bazar

Fashions evolved even during the fourteen months covered by this book. One way to keep up with them was to subscribe to a fashion magazine. From its premier issue of November 2, 1867, *Harper's Bazar* proved to be far more informative than its American competitors *Godey's Lady's Book* and *Peterson's Magazine.* For one thing it was published weekly rather than monthly. For another, it had a higher proportion of fashion information. As a November 2 editorial explained, the magazine was "intended largely for ladies." It would "devote a considerable space to the matters which fall particularly under their jurisdiction, such as dress, and household affairs. … We shall also give in each alternate number of our journal numerous patterns, accompanied by plain and practical directions, readily understood, which will enable every lady, if she chooses, to cut and make her own and her children's entire wardrobe, with much of that of her husband. Beautiful colored fashion plates will likewise be presented from time to time. … Fancy work of all kinds will also find room in our columns. … In a word, we propose to make the *Bazar* a first-class weekly newspaper of fashion–the only one in existence in this country."

Patterns in This Book

Each issue of *Harper's Bazar* had 16 pages, measuring about 11 3/8 by 16 inches. About half consisted of fashion plates, needlework instructions, and fashion columns. In addition, two issues per month (the "alternate numbers") featured a separate oversized pattern supplement. This contained full-sized sewing and sometimes embroidery patterns for 20 or more garments and accessories. (If color plates were published in 1867 or 1868 I do not have them; the cover illustration is from the November 22, 1868 *L'Illustrateur des Dames.*) The patterns were among the highest quality of their day. In contrast, the 1868 issues of the monthly *Peterson's Magazine* each contained one in-text sewing pattern, if any; and the scaling down of these was not particularly accurate.

The fashion information in *Harper's Bazar* was also up-to-date. The November 2 editorial explained, "We have perfected special arrangements with the leading European fashion journals, especially with the celebrated *Der Bazar* of Berlin, which supplies the fashions to the newspapers of Paris, whereby we receive the same fashions in advance, and publish them weekly, simultaneously with their appearance in Paris and Berlin. ... This advantage is shared by no other newspaper in the country. Our readers will thus be sure of obtaining the genuine Paris fashions simultaneously with the Parisians themselves, instead of from stray journals three or four weeks old."

Although an examination of the 1867 *Der Bazar* shows publication of the same material to be not quite simultaneous, it was often close. The paletots in the November 16 *Harper's Bazar* were published in the November 1 *Der Bazar.* The Crocheted Corset in the December 28 issue was published in the December 15 *Der Bazar.* Sometimes the interval was longer; for example the Skirt Trimming in the February 15, 1868 *Harper's Bazar* is from the October 15, 1867 *Der Bazar.* The 1868 *Godey's Lady's Book* was far less timely in its publication of some of the same plates, whether their source was *Der Bazar* or *Harper's Bazar.* For example, redrawn plates of the Pompadour Waist with Bretelles and the Bodice with Lappets in the January 25, 1868 *Harper's Bazar* were printed in the September 1868 *Godey's Lady's Book*, without in-text patterns.

Although *Harper's Bazar* was very similar to *Der Bazar* in its format and type of content, it was by no means a translated reprint. Much of its fashion material was original or drawn from other sources. This included a substantial regular column titled "New York Fashions." It described the latest trends in styles, colors, fabrics, trimmings, accessories, shoes, and jewelry, plus specific outfits seen for sale. It served as a glossary of the season's new fashion terms. Sometimes it included hints on wardrobe planning or sewing. This book includes edited selections from most "New York Fashions" columns, chosen for their relevance to reproducing or accessorizing period outfits. Columns that dealt entirely with matters not covered in this book have been omitted.

The Patterns in This Book

The material in this book is drawn from a bound volume containing the complete 1867–1868 issues of *Harper's Bazar,* including all but one of the pattern supplements. The number of sewing and needlework patterns was staggering, and choosing among them was difficult. I decided to focus only on women's fashions, rather than children's, men's, or home furnishings and knickknacks. Some patterns stated to be for girls in their late teens are given. (Any information on age appropriateness is in the text. The models in most plates portray a stylized youthful ideal, even for fashions described as "elderly.") I omitted fashion plates not associated with any pattern or instructions. I did my best to represent the entire ladies' wardrobe promised by the magazine's editors. I selected at least one pattern for every style given, skipping others that seemed too similar. I included most examples of special-occasion garments, such as sports outfits and bridal wear. Most foundation garments are also included.

The original needlework patterns consisted of one or more engraved plates in the magazine, text instructions, and sometimes a printed pattern on the supplement sheet. I transcribed all the instructions, editing them for clarity. I also included any

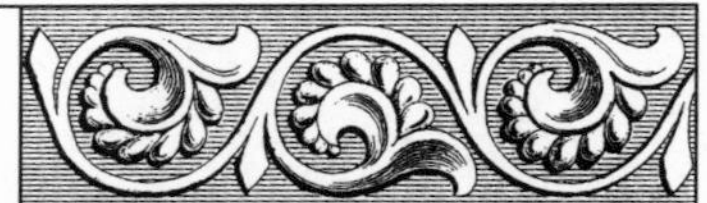

pattern pieces. Most of the original crocheting, knitting, tatting, and netting instructions are step-by-step. This is not always true of instructions for embroidery, ribbon work, beading, and other decorative techniques. The needleworker was expected to understand how to complete such projects largely by examining the engraved plates. Some were given at a specified scale to aid the process; so I have not rescaled any without stating the scale.

Each sewing pattern is accompanied by one or more fashion plates. I edited all the plates to correct damage caused by time and printer's errors. Some plates had a double-page format that was too large for this book. These illustrated some garments for which no pattern was ever given, and others with patterns I had omitted. I cropped these plates. Where necessary I erased or redrew parts of backgrounds and garments. Some other fashion plates were resized to fit the available space.

Each pattern also includes a description of the finished garment and assembly instructions. I edited this text while mentally performing garment construction. I compared it to the fashion plates and pattern pieces. However, a few original instructions or patterns contained ambiguities that I was unable to resolve.

Some instructions include measurements in 5ths, 10ths, 3rds, or 6ths of inches. I did not try to convert these to English units. Instead I recommend using an engineer's ruler (available at drafting supply and art stores). This is triangular in cross section, giving faces for six scales from 10 divisions per inch to 60. The major units of the 30-division ruler are 3rds of inches, the major units of the 50-division ruler are 5ths, and so on.

Although the pattern instructions are quite useful, they assume knowledge of basic sewing techniques. *Harper's Bazar* occasionally published articles describing these. Some excellent material on period pattern alterations and dressmaking was published in the September 4, 1869 issue and is included in Appendix A of this book. Helpful articles were published in conjunction with related patterns. Examples are "Making Corsets" in the September 5, 1868 issue and "Buttonholes for Underclothing" in the September 26, 1868 issue.

The original pattern supplements measured about 21 1/2 by 30 1/2 inches (though the size varied) and were printed on both sides. Each side contained many overlapping pattern pieces. (See Figure 1.) These were distinguished by different line types and figure numbers. *Harper's Bazar* explained, "As to cut out a single pattern would destroy all the others on the supplement, the patterns desired must be transferred to separate sheets of paper. This can be done with the greatest ease by the newly invented copying wheel [the illustration looks like a modern tracing wheel]. ... Lay the supplement over a sheet of brown or white paper ... and roll the wheel over the pattern desired; the outline will thus be punctured on the paper beneath, and the pattern can then be cut from the same."

Because the original patterns were full size, they had to be scaled down for inclusion in an 8 1/2-by-11-inch book. All scaling was accurately done by computer. The scales are 1/16, 1/8, 1/4, 1/2, and occasionally 1:1. My choice of scale was based on whether the pattern piece was small enough to fit on the page and large enough to contain its labels. I labeled each pattern piece with the scale used. Where possible I kept all pieces for a garment to the same scale.

Some original pattern pieces were too large even for the supplements. *Harper's Bazar* solved this problem by printing some parts as if they were folded over. Even larger pieces were broken into two sections (which might themselves have foldovers) to be put together after tracing. All pattern pieces in this book are as complete as they were given; I have already done all necessary unfolding and piecing. For some skirts only part of the length was given. Sewers were told to lengthen the pattern to fit the wearer, in the instructions or by downward-pointing arrows on the pattern. I suggest determining the skirt width by that of other, full-length patterns and the guidelines in the fashion columns; and the length by your height plus the fashion guidelines and plates.

Occasionally pattern pieces were given as measurements rather than on the supplement. I drafted some that fit in the book. Others turned out to be very long and narrow, or otherwise

Patterns in This Book

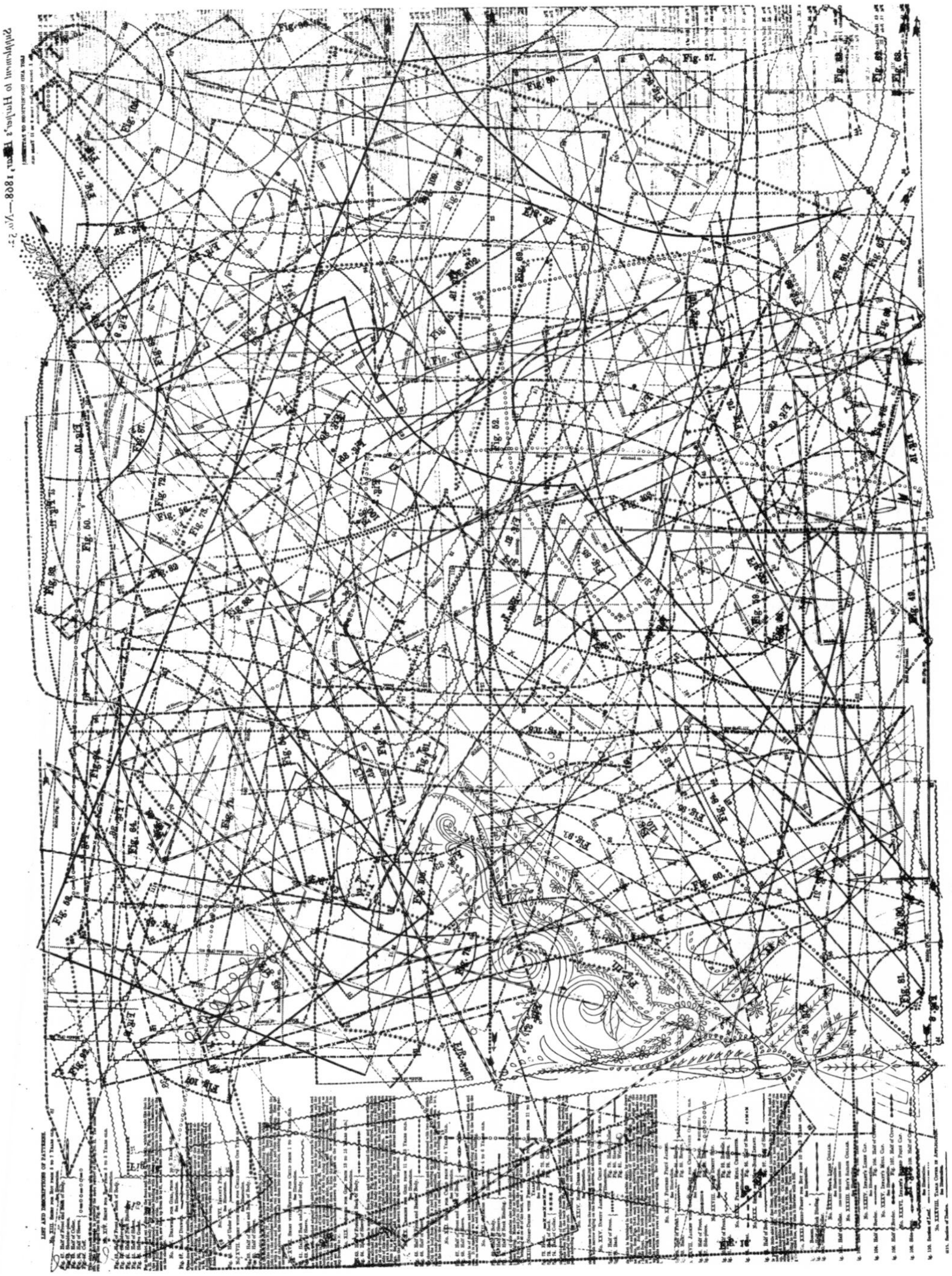

Figure 1. One side of the original pattern supplement for October 24, 1868

proportionally peculiar. However, most are simple shapes that can easily be drafted using the measurements.

A few small but curved pieces, such as some collars, are given neither as patterns nor measurements. In these cases I suggest borrowing from another pattern. As the instructions indicate, often pieces were recycled from one pattern to another. Some styles were even the identical pattern with different trimmings. For example, the skirt of the Norderney Walking Dress in the May 23, 1868 issue was used for several other dresses. Given the size of this book, I elected to retain the cross-references rather than repeating these patterns.

Occasionally most of a pattern was published in one issue, but trimmings or alternate pattern pieces were published later. I collected all related parts of a pattern together. I laid out the pattern pieces the way they are sewn together, as well as the page size allowed.

I transferred the construction labels printed on the patterns. Numbers tell you how seams were sewn together. Bullets, asterisks, and *x*s mark joins other than seams, such as pleats and "bosom pleats" (darts). A dashed line labeled "middle" usually means "cut on fold." Other dashed lines mark the turnover of a revers (lapel), the middle front of an asymmetrical garment, or simply the middle of a pattern piece. Most narrow lines indicate where something is placed. What is placed is explained by a text label or the instructions. It can be shirring, a pleat, trimming, a pocket, millinery wire, or a corset whalebone. Trimming lines are not always given full length, probably due to conflicting lines on the pattern supplement. Marks that look like buttonholes, buttons, and eyelets are used to mark their placement; sometimes only part of a row is given. Sometimes text instructions are used instead of pattern labels; for example the sewer is told to make pleats of a certain size in a bertha rather than every pleat being marked.

Harper's Bazar advised sewers to make "due allowances for seams, for which none is made on the patterns in the supplement." Some instructions give hem measurements. However, to facilitate scaling up and fitting I have not added any seam or hem allowances. Some grain lines are labeled "straight way of stuff." Others are clarified by the "middle" labels. Still others are likely the straight center fronts and backs of pieces. Where no indication of grain was given, I have not provided it.

How to Enlarge the Patterns

The patterns in this book can be enlarged by projection, by gridding, and in some cases by photocopying. Projection is the most flexible method, because it enables you to enlarge the pattern to any desired size. Gridding allows you to scale up the pattern to its original size (and make fitting alterations later). Photocopying works best for pattern pieces small enough to fit on one sheet of paper after enlargement. It is the easiest method for patterns with embroidery transfers or many trimming placement marks.

Before projecting a pattern, decide whether to enlarge it to the key measurements for the finished garment or to the original size. Although enlarging to key measurements is convenient, it is less accurate. Body shapes do not enlarge proportionally. If you enlarge the pattern to its original size, proportions will be preserved. However, you will have to adjust the key measurements after enlargement. For very loose garments such as capes, which require little fitting, this might be the wisest course.

The key measurements are the bust for most pieces of waists, one-piece dresses, and paletots, and the sleeve length for sleeves. The usual key measurement for a skirt without fitted hips is the waistline. However, if there is enough fullness at the skirt waist, you may be able to enlarge to the skirt length and adjust the waistline in the fitting muslin.

Put the pattern on the projector. Tape a large sheet of dotted or gridded pattern paper to a wall. Or, enlarge the pattern onto pattern-tracing cloth (a gridded lightweight interfacing) and use this later as the muslin. Because the key measurement is the entire distance around the bust (for example) the measurements of all relevant pattern pieces must be added up. Note that most pieces are cut twice and others are cut on the fold. Be sure to allow

How to Enlarge the Patterns

wearing and style ease. Adjust the distance of the projector from the wall until the key measurement is correct.

If you are enlarging to the original size, add a graph before projection using transparent graph paper. A gridded mylar is sold in art stores, or you can make your own by copying graph paper onto transparency film. (If you cannot find mylar or graph paper with an appropriate grid, Appendix C lists a freeware program that enables you to create your own.) Place the pattern on the transparent graph and photocopy it onto transparency film. Put the gridded pattern on the projector. Adjust the distance of the projector from the wall until the grids align.

Draw the projected pattern using clear plastic rulers and French curves (clear tools do not block projection). Or draw freehand and clean up the lines later. Projected lines look thick. You need to decide whether to trace the outsides or the insides. Transfer numbers, asterisks, bullets, trimming placement lines, and other internal pattern marks.

To enlarge a pattern by gridding, first add a grid by photocopying as described above. Lay an ample piece of dotted pattern paper or pattern-tracing cloth on your worktable. Put the gridded pattern beside it. Plot points from the grid onto the pattern paper. Start at the center front, center back, or a straight line of the pattern piece. On the pattern paper, pencil a mark that represents one end of this line. If the line is perfectly straight, count the squares to the other end on the grid. Count the same number of squares on your pattern paper and pencil another mark. If the line is curved count the squares, or portions thereof, up (or down) and across to the next point. Mark that point on your pattern paper. Continue counting and marking till you finish the section.

Then connect the points to draw the pattern. Use a yardstick or L-square for straight lines. Fit French curves against a curved area till you find the best match. Sometimes you'll need to use more than one curve for an area, or draw it freehand or with a flexible spline.

Before enlarging a pattern piece by photocopying, calculate its final size by measuring its length and width and multiplying them by the amount to be enlarged. You may have to enlarge the piece in sections. The sections should overlap slightly, and the overlap area should include one or two distinctive marks. After copying align the sections at the marks and tape. An alternative is to find a copy shop with a large-format copier. Most photocopiers can enlarge up to 150% or 175%. You can enlarge a pattern further by passing it through multiple times.

No matter what enlargement method you used, you need to proof and finish the pattern. Measure edges that will be seamed together. If they're different lengths, check the original measurements and redraw as necessary. True seam lines where fabric will be folded into darts, pleats, or facings. Fold the pattern like the fabric and redraw nonmatching lines.

Add seam and hem allowances by measuring out from the pattern edge with the plastic ruler. For straight edges measure each end and connect the lines. For curved edges draw short lines at such frequent intervals that they connect. Or use a double tracing wheel to indent the paper, then pencil over the indents. I suggest adding seam allowances of 1 to 2 inches on side seams, 1 inch on tight-fitting sections, and 1/2 inch on loose-fitting ones.

Draw a grain line following a long row of pattern-paper dots. Label the pieces with the pattern source, garment type, and style date. Indicate how many times each piece will be cut from fashion fabric, lining, underlining, and/or interfacing. Where necessary mark the right, left, top, and/or bottom.

Make a muslin (with extra-large seam allowances) and adjust it till the fit is correct. Transfer all corrections to a final version of the pattern for later use.

— Frances Grimble

November 2, 1867

Bonnets

The "airy fairy" fanchon, so long popular, is gradually being deposed by the much more stately Marie Antoinette bonnet, more in keeping with the picturesque costumes now worn. The Marie Antoinette, with all its variations of Mousquetaire, Marquise, and Princess Caroline, has a narrow brim, short ears, and a broad, flat crown without the least semblance of a curtain. It is worn further on the top and front of the head than the shapes of last season, and fits closely over the chignon. Broad bandeaux of gilt or velvet, and wreaths of flowers, forming an elaborate diadem, are placed over the forehead. This diadem is the most noticeable characteristic of the new shape, and gives it the stately appearance requisite. The strings are also an important feature. There are usually two or three pairs, intended for service as well as ornament, as they are really required to hold the short ears in proper position. The narrow ribbons that serve to tie the bonnet at the throat are fringed or ornamented with embroidery and lace. The overstrings are of real lace with velvet ribbon insertion, or wide scarves of colored tulle beaded with jet and gilt or dewdropped with crystal, arranged in the Spanish fashion over the back of the bonnet.

The fanchon still lingers with us in a slightly changed form. It used to be a matter of some doubt which was the front and which the rear of this bonnet. But as now worn the Marie Stuart point still remains in front, while the back is shorn of its point, being entirely straight on the chignon.

The Trianon, a cross between the fanchon and Marie Antoinette, will be a favorite with those who dislike to be the first by whom the new style is tried.

Trimmings

In trimmings there is great variety. Feathers are not so much used as they will be later in the season. Flowers are in profusion everywhere. Many bonnets are simply frames covered with velvet heartsease or daisies. There are new designs in flowers of gilt and velvet. There are many novelties in leaves and berries–wreaths of leaves of all the varied shades of the autumn forest–metallic berries, bronzed, red, and fire color, with clusters of golden wheat, grapes, acorns, and thistles of downy marabou. Gilt ornaments of every description are in high favor; jet and pearl are used abundantly; amber has disappeared. Ribbons are but little used for trimming, and only in narrow widths. There are, however, some pretty shaded and fringed ribbons very effectively introduced as scarves on the new bonnets.

Round Hats

In round hats white felt is the favorite material. Bronzed straws are worn with Bismarck suits. It is useless to name a hat, as each milliner has a different name of her own. One pretty style has a shallow crown and narrow brim; another has a half-high crown and turned-up brim. Wreaths of leaves and bandeaux of shirred velvet, with a rosette or an aigrette at the side, are the trimmings. Ostrich feathers and willow plumes are too large for these tiny chapeaux, and are superseded by small tufts of marabou and cock's feathers.

Dresses

The picturesque gored dress continues to be the approved style. This is not only a graceful but a sensible fashion, as it does away with the absurd practice of gathering into a few inches at the waist the same quantity of material that is made to cover a large space on the floor.

The Corsage

There is a return to the short waists of the Empire. The corsage is short on the shoulder and under the arm, and rounded at the waist to be worn with a wide belt. Small reversed collars are worn with chemisettes half high at the throat. Many dresses are cut away square *à la Pompadour.* But the high standing collar vandyked, or scalloped and bound, to match the trimming on sleeves and skirt is more stylish. For evening dress the neck is cut square and very low indeed.

The Marie Antoinette fichu, which crosses in front of the corsage and falls into long rounded streamers tied negligently at the back, is made of the same material as the dress. It is decidedly an ornamental addition. Waist belts are wide and much trimmed with tasseled fringe and jet pendants. Wide sashes of lace or ribbon are tied behind in a large bow.

Sleeves

Coat sleeves are still worn and are gradually narrowing to the tight sleeve of the Empire. Flowing sleeves are only suitable for full dress. In their proper sphere they are graceful and becoming, but are in bad taste for home dress, where comfort and convenience are the great considerations. They are cut quite short on the forearm, sloping gradually away to a point at the back, and are very much trimmed inside. Puffs and caps at the top of the coat sleeves are but little used.

Skirts

Gored skirts are made with long trains for full dress. They are gored to fit plain in front and at the sides. The two back widths are left entire and pleated or gathered at the waist to give the proper fullness to the train. In very long trains these back widths are sometimes cut off square to prevent them from curling up as pointed trains are apt to do. The front and sides are quite short–gradually sloping longer toward the back, giving a graceful sweep to the train. When two skirts are used the upper one is looped up at the sides or caught up in a loose knot behind, *à la benoiton.*

Indoor dresses for demitoilette have plain gored skirts just long enough to escape the floor.

Walking Dresses

Short dresses for walking have become indispensable articles in a lady's wardrobe. They are short enough to escape the rubbish on the sidewalk, yet sufficiently long to be modest. They relieve the hands of the onerous task of holding up voluminous skirts, and dispense with the trouble of looping, and are withal trim and jaunty.

The double skirt has found a rival in single skirts with trimming arranged to simulate an upper skirt. The handsomest designs are the costumes in two colors–the embroidered petticoat of blue, green, or Bismarck, with black pardessus over it–a combination of the Swiss peasant bodice and peplum.

Sacques and Paletots

Short paletots are worn with walking dresses, and are variations of last winter's styles. The mantilla paletot has long lappets in front resembling a mantle, but the back is straight and short. A long loose sacque called the Gabrielle is worn with suits. It reaches to the knee, and is confined at the waist by a wide belt fastened behind with a large bow and ends. A tight-fitting pelisse with cape is also worn.

Cloaks

Cloaks are to be longer and looser than those of last year. In many the added length is entirely confined to the front. The long tabs and points that reach almost to the floor slope upward in the back until they barely conceal the waist. Very few circulars are imported–the gored sacque with flowing sleeves being the genus of which there are innumerable species.

Tufted cloths are not so popular as last winter, and have given place to smooth surfaces on which immense quantities of trimming are lavished. The favorite colors are black, brown, and purple; gray has lost favor. Cloth is trimmed with a heavy silk braid, varying from 1/8 to 1 1/2 inches wide. Velvet is profusely ornamented with embroidery and lace.

November 2, 1867

The Breton Jacket

The Breton jacket introduced last season is still a favorite. It is a piquante little garment specially intended for morning wear, made of scarlet, black, or blue cloth embroidered in bright colors. Jet and gilt beads and tinsel braid are also introduced into the trimming. It was this coquettish little garment that first brought about the rage for colored embroidery that is now so universal.

Colors

Bismarck, or gold-brown, is the prevailing shade, and reappears in some guise almost everywhere. The new shades of green are its only formidable rivals. The deep green known as "invisible," now called "mermaid," is in great favor. There are a variety of lighter shades for evening wear–yellowish greens, prettier than one would imagine, and really beautiful by gaslight. These are "pistache," "frog," "butter," and "chou" (cabbage), names certainly not very attractive in the abstract, but which will on examination commend themselves as perfectly appropriate.

Silk Dress Goods

Decided contrast is the rule in brocades. Black and Bismarck grounds are strewn with flowers of brilliant hues–half-blown roses, heather bells, daisies, and convolvulus. Autumn leaves are scattered on a Marie Louise blue; gilt and blue flowers on a white ground; and a white or amber design on black.

Handsomer and more expensive than the brocades are the embroidered robes. Heavy corded silks, Bismarck or black grounds, are worked with the needle on the front, back, and two side breadths, in pyramids of flowers, so beautiful and lifelike that a perfume is only needed to persuade one that they are real.

In plain colors there is a novelty called poult-de-soie antique, a thick corded silk with the luster of satin. This is brought out in the quaint old colors worn by our grandmothers–blue-black, dead-brown, invisible green, or mermaid, and of course the inevitable Bismarck. The quiet colors of this elegant material make it particularly desirable for handsome walking dresses.

An appropriate name for another novelty is the chameleon, a revival of the changeable silks, that take new tints in different lights. The combination of color is most exquisite. "Sunrise" is a pearly gray combined with rose color; "sunset," a golden hue in one light, purple and azure in another; and "moonlight," whose glimmering is too intangible to admit of description.

Among other new fabrics is the magnificent Antwerp silk, thick enough to stand alone, 1 1/2 yards wide. Another novelty is Holland satin, a reversible material, satin upon one side and silk on the other. *Drap de la reine* is corded diagonally on one surface only.

Woolens

In woolen goods brown and Russian gray predominate. Merchants say they are selling ten pieces of Bismarck to one of any other color.

There has been imported a larger assortment of bright plaids than at any previous season. Knotted velours, with a raised white dash, are pretty and durable. Shaded velours are a welcome change from the plain velours so long worn. Empress cloth is brought out in cashmere patterns, and is preferable to the real cashmere, as it is thicker and warmer. A new article of twilled winsey, a mixed gray and black, is well adapted to walking suits, and is perfectly waterproof. Blue serge, and gold color with black, are much admired.

There is considerable variety in poplins. The chiné is in grave shades of purple, green, and brown with white, while the plaids are in every color of the rainbow. In solid colors there is a French poplin that many consider superior to the best Irish. It has smoother threads, is softer, and falls into more graceful folds.

Trimmings

Crosscut folds of satin with a heading of lace, or a narrow piping of the dress material placed in the center, are a fashionable trimming. These folds are put on straight with pointed leaves at intervals on either side. Pipings of silk are braided together 1 inch wide. Vandyked and castellated points of silk neatly bound are sewn around sacques and on sleeves. Elegant jet fringes and gimp are among the novelties. Amber has disappeared, but gold ornaments are used profusely.

Embroidery is, however, the ruling passion of the hour. The Oriental patterns are in all colors. The work is beautifully executed, and the colors are selected with artistic skill, yet the effect is not good. A French mixture of crochet work and embroidery in fine jet and black silk, or in silk of any one shade, is in better taste.

Laces

A love for beautiful laces is becoming a mania. Nothing tells more in a lady's costume than the lace she wears. Let it be inferior, and the richest velvets and jewels will not shield her from criticism; while real lace, no matter how small a quantity, gives a better tone to the most ordinary material. Point de gaze, the handsomest of all laces, is beautifully brought out in patterns of fern leaves and medallions.

The Shakespeare style is most popular for collars of fine lace. Standing collars, embroidered in vandykes and edged with Valenciennes, are pretty and stylish. A small chemisette, worn inside the dress, is attached to hold them in position.

Veils of real lace are small and square, with the lower edge deeply pointed. Long barbes are tied at the back with bow and streamers, or merely fastened with ornaments of jet or pearl.

Gloves

Gloves are longer at the wrist, and ornamented on the back with embroidered crests and ciphers in contrasting colors, and stitching in a Grecian pattern. Substantial studs and hooks are used as fastenings, but the handsomest are drawn together by tasseled tirettes. Tiny eyelets of gilt or silver are laced together on the back of the glove by a silk cord with tassels. "Etna" and "Vesuvius" browns, redder tints than Bismarck, are the favorite shades. White gloves, hitherto so plain, are ornamented with tirettes and tassels to match the lacing on the back. Gloves for evening wear extend halfway to the elbow, and are fastened with several studs.

Crinolines

The crinoline has grown beautifully less until it is as small as can possibly be worn. The standard skirt for ordinary toilette measures only 2 yards round the bottom. Those for ceremonious occasions measure only 3 yards, which, of course, affords but little assistance in managing a train.

Underskirts, even those of fine muslin, should be gored. Any gathers about the hips spoil the effect of the gored dress. The Boulevard skirt, entirely seamless and shaped on a frame, is an improvement on the full Balmoral.

Peplum

This peplum is of lilac silk, lined with thin silk of the same color, with an interlining. Cut the upper part, under part, and interlining from the front festoon, lappet, and both parts of the belt, of the stuff double. Run the belt together, on the wrong side, around the top and sides. Turn it over and put on the lappet in pleats, as on the pattern, *x* to •. Join the loops in front to correspond with the numbers on the pattern. Put on the hooks and eyes and trimming.

Peplum

November 2, 1867

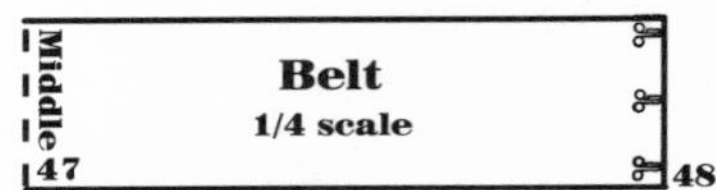

Belt

1/4 scale

50 49

Middle

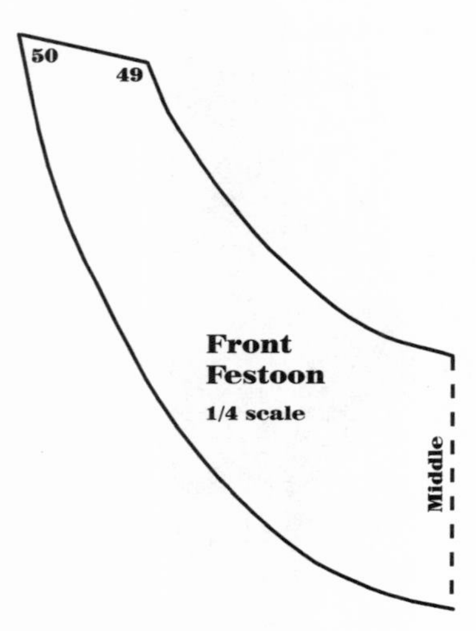

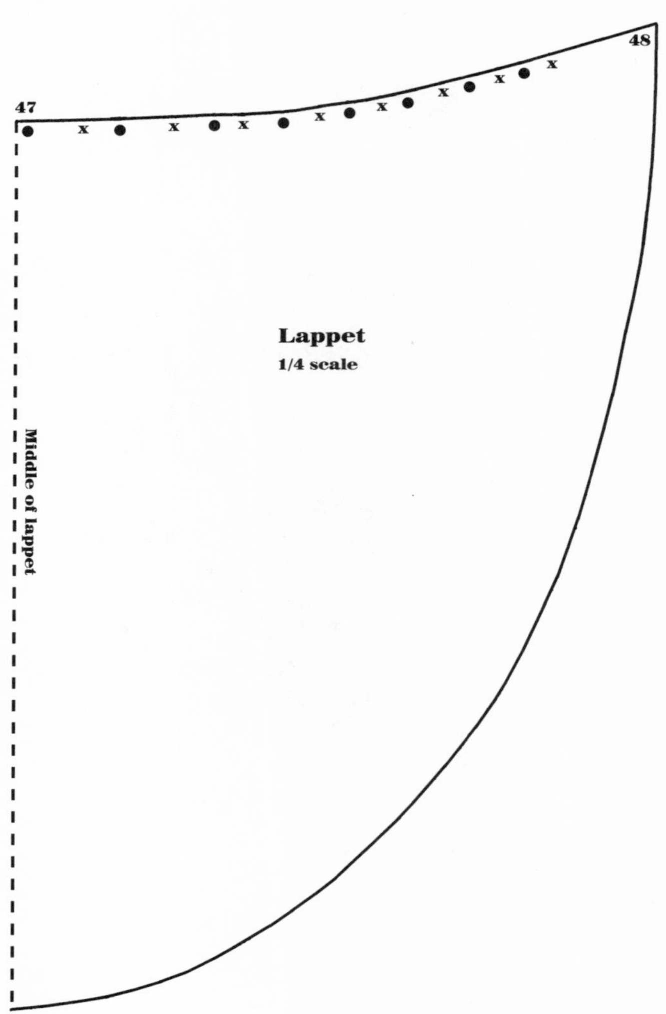

November 9, 1867

New Styles and Colors

The new costumes being made up for the approaching season display a mixture of the antique and modern–the styles of the Empire combined with the Swiss peasant dress of today, the Scotch burnoose, the Greek sleeve, and the Sultana jacket.

The catalog of colors increases. Among the new marine greens, besides frog and mermaid, there is "sea foam" and "undine." A dark shade of brown is "noisette," or nut brown; another is "Egyptian," a dead brown, mummylike and somber. "Etna" and "Vesuvius" are redder shades, said to resemble burning lava, and a bright tint, like flame, is called "feu." A beautiful glimmering gray is distinguished as "moon on the desert."

Materials

Silks brocaded in small patterns can be bought. As the figures increase in size, so in proportion do the figures asked for them.

For evening dresses there are moirés in all the delicate gaslight greens; white poult-de-soie, French gray, and pearl color, brocaded with clusters of rosebuds; embroidered satins, blue with a design in silver, green with gold, and amber with white. There are thin gauzy fabrics, striped cerise and white, or polka dots and spangles, to be worn as tunics over trains of solid colors.

In plainer goods there is a handsome silk velour, an extra-heavy reps, which is very much like Irish poplin. Norwegian poplin is a serviceable article, which is taking the place of alpaca. It is more durable, and will bear any amount of crushing without seeming rumpled. A novelty among poplins is the Japanese–a dark ground, often tea color, strewn with Japanese figures in bright shades. By way of variety these will make pretty breakfast dresses. Elegant embroidered poplin robes are sold. Crêpe poplin is soft and fine, with none of the harsh feel and stiffness so often found in poplins. It is in Scotch plaids, 1 1/2 yards wide. Broché poplin in small blocks of gold and black, or blue and brown, is a desirable article.

Empress cloths are brought out in stripes–a black or garnet ground with stripes of gilt leaves. Palm leaves and Oriental figures look well on a Bismarck ground. Foulards in contrasting colors, with patterns in imitation of brocade, are pretty for house dresses. Velveteen is much used for short suits, but it is not durable, and soon looks shabby. Winsey, jasper silk, serge, and poplin are more desirable.

Street Dresses

Handsome short dresses are made of silks in two colors. A scant gored dress with high bodice, tight sleeves, and skirt just escaping the ground, has over it a shorter dress of another color made with a fourreau, low bodice, and long hanging sleeves. A mauve dress may have a black fourreau, or a black dress a mauve fourreau. We have seen a blue silk with Bismarck fourreau, and another of apple green with both a black and a gray fourreau. An economical variety may be given to a lady's wardrobe by having different fourreaux for the same dress. The fourreaux are short and scant, requiring but little material; and if the colors are judiciously blended the variety is pleasant. A wide sash is worn with these dresses. It is made of the silk of the overdress trimmed with ruches of the underskirt.

Another style of walking dress has a plain skirt simply fastened at the waist, over which is worn a gored dress; waist, sleeves, and skirt in one, reaching below the knee, and buttoned down before. When tight fitting these pelisses are worn with a small round cape falling to the waist. When left loose they are called Gabrielles and are worn with a sash.

November 9, 1867

Bias ruffles 2 inches wide are worn on the lower skirt of short dresses. They should be neatly bound, and are usually in uneven numbers–three, five, or seven.

Marie Antoinette fichus large enough to serve as mantles are added to walking dresses–an agreeable variety now that short sacques are so common. These are usually of the dress material, but are occasionally made of black silk to be worn with any dress. The lappets with which they are tied at the back are long and rounded.

Indoor Toilettes

House dresses, if made with trains, must be very short in front and at the sides. Nothing more completely destroys the effect of a train than holding the skirt up in front, nor can anything be more awkward than for a lady to constantly trip herself by stepping on her dress. If long dresses are worn in the street they can be stylishly fastened up in the *blanchisseuse* fashion, so as to have precisely the effect of a short dress.

The redingote style is introduced in dresses intended entirely for the house. These have surplice waists lapped on the breast and worn with a belt. The skirt also crosses over and has two rows of large buttons down the front. Chemisettes worn with these waists and with the Pompadours are now left open instead of closed, and are made of Cluny and guipure lace.

Morning Dresses

Marseilles and muslin for morning wear have disappeared, but we find white dresses in thicker materials such as alpaca, foulard, and mohair. Satin folds edged with white fringe, Cluny lace over colored ribbon, or black guipure and jet, trim them handsomely. Elegant white robes de chambre are embroidered in Turkish designs in brilliant colors. Palm leaves of velvet and Japanese figures are also used by way of ornament. Roman scarves of gay colors are worn with these. Cashmere robes are brought out in new patterns, the border extending up each width describing the gores.

A low bodice, or corselet of black grosgrain, with epaulets and long lappets at the back, trimmed with crosscut folds studded with jet, is prettily worn over woolen dresses.

Trimmings

High bodices are very much trimmed on the neck and shoulders. Velvet ribbon or folds of silk or satin form a kind of collar or necklace, in points graduating longer toward the back. Jet or silk pendants are attached to each point. Lower down on the bodice a peasant waist is simulated by the trimming. Crocheted fringe is arranged about the shoulders as a bertha. Wide belts *à la Africaine* have deep fringe or silk vandykes and silk pendants to correspond with the collar or bertha.

Folds for trimming are now sewn on in the center instead of the top of the band. Beaded braid and narrow pipings of the dress material are used to conceal the sewing. Points and scallops are bound or corded with white satin.

Steel-bead fringe trims black dresses very prettily.

Jackets

Sleeveless jackets of scarlet cloth, cut rounding in front in the Zouave style and pointed at the back, are worn over white waists. The trimming is narrow strips of white fur or embroidery in jardinière patterns. Bullion ornaments that look like small coins are strung together, overlapping each other, and are placed on either side of the front.

The jaunty sailor's jacket is piquant and becoming. It may be made of white serge, trimmed with blue folds, or blue serge trimmed with white. A wide square collar either lies on the shoulders, or when raised fastens closely around the neck.

Caps

Caps, or rather coiffures, a most graceful accessory to morning toilettes, are now made so coquettishly that the youngest married lady need not be frightened at the idea of wearing a cap. These fancy lappets display instead of concealing fine hair, as they occupy no more space on the head than the bands of ribbon so long worn. A Marie Stuart point forms the front, while the ends fall over the chignon.

Bonnets

Black and gold is a favorite combination for fall bonnets. Fanchons of black tulle with gold ornaments are popular. Fur will be much used later in the season. Grebe bonnets are already worn. These are in the fanchon shape, and are tied with gay velvet strings. The much-talked-of toquet is only a more elegant name for the porkpie hat. Colored veils to match the bonnet are worn over the chignon instead of the face. Crinoline straw, both black and white, is a favorite material for traveling and plain bonnets.

Dress Looped Up à la Blanchisseuse

The accompanying arrangement for looping up trailed dresses is both simple and convenient, and is far superior to any yet adopted. The long robe is at once converted into a graceful walking dress, and the whole contour of the bottom is preserved.

Take up the front part (which is gored and perfectly plain) about 14 inches below the waist. Fold it and bring the edge of the fold close to the waistband. Fasten the side breadths in the center of the back by a button and loop, or hook and loop, as seen in the first illustration. Then draw up the upper part of the back breadth through the opening, and let it fall over in a puff, as seen in the second illustration. When fastened up, the skirt should be short enough to show the border of the underskirt.

November 16, 1867

Cloakings

Among cloakings the standard cloth is smooth beaver. Tricot beaver, with a scarcely perceptible rib, is a handsome material, and admits of elaborate trimming. Chinchilla beaver, gray and black, is a serviceable article, suitable for traveling cloaks. Velour is a light material used for fall garments. In shaggy cloths we have the Astrakhan of last winter, an excellent imitation of the lambskin. It has short, knobby tufts, black and white mixed, and plain black or white, 1 1/2 yards wide. Sealskin is among the novelties of the season. The real article is very expensive; but there is an imitation that can scarcely be told from the genuine.

The Alpine and camel's-hair cloths are beautifully fine and soft, and make elegant evening wrappings. The original camel's-hair is pure white; but there are now scarlet grounds, with a long white silky fleece, or striped blue and white, or gilt and black.

Plush is brought out in great variety; and is really becoming a formidable rival to velvet. It is made up in short loose paletots and tight-fitting jackets. Large buttons and a cable cord at the edge are the only trimming. It is in all colors; brown, purple, and dark blue are the favorites, as they are in all wrappings. One pattern is an imitation of ermine–white, with black tufts. Another is shot with silk, and has large mauve and blue spots.

Scarlet chinchilla beaver is used for extra carriage wrappings. A beautiful cloth, thick and warm, is made of the fleece of the Angora goat. Lamb's wool, 1 inch thick, is sold double fold. These cloths are expensive, but they are nearly all 1 1/2 or 2 yards wide, hence it does not take many yards to make a cloak.

Colored velvets are very much worn in Paris. The preference here still continues in favor of black, though a few colored cloaks–blue, purple, and Bismarck–are worn. There is also velveteen with a silk finish.

Modes

It is scarcely possible to find two cloaks alike, yet radically there is but little difference. The great variety is in the trimming. The gored sacque is the standard shape, longer and looser than those of last season. Most of the added length claimed for the new styles is found in the scarflike mantilla front. The peplum points on the side have disappeared, but there are occasionally long square tabs under the arms, that make the cloak retain something of the appearance of a peplum. Circulars are seldom seen; a few large talmas are brought out, as some ladies always prefer them.

The bottom of the sacque is cut into dents of every conceivable shape–squares, tabs, pendants, and castellated points. Many ladies are reluctant to have handsome material cut up in this reckless manner, and have instead satin vandykes bound or piped and sewn on the plain edge of the sacque. Another plan is to arrange the passementerie to simulate squares and points. This is quite stylish, and wears better; the indented edges curl up, and are apt to be frayed and jagged before the season is half over.

Another part of the cloak that admits of great variety is the sleeve. The choice lies between the coat sleeve, the flowing sleeve, and a medium between the two, or a combination of both. All are admissible, and the decision is left to the taste or convenience of the wearer. There is a sleeve that folds up inside of the arm, protecting it like a coat sleeve. On the outside it is cut into a pointed fall that perfectly simulates a flowing sleeve, most admirably combining style and comfort.

Pockets are frequently concealed in the long tabs and trimmings instead of being placed in conspicuous positions. Sashes sewn in with the side seams are tied loosely behind with broad flowing ends. Rosettes, tassels, and fringes adorn the pointed ends of the sash.

The Redingote and Killarney

A novelty among fall wrappings is the long redingote, which resembles the old-fashioned great-coat without its cape, but with a rolling collar and worn with a vest. It is buttoned all the way down before.

The Killarney cloak in brown waterproof is an agreeable change from the monotonous black and gray. It is quite long, with sleeves and a cape that can be worn with or without the cloak, and is fastened by a cord passing through the trimming. A snap fastening allows the cape to be easily removed.

Burnooses are again worn. They are usually in Scotch plaids, and we have seen some in gray and Bismarck cashmere with palm-leaf borders.

Embroidery

Embroidery in silk, chenille, and jet is used in lavish profusion. The original fabric of the cloak is sometimes a matter of conjecture, so heavily is it laden with needlework.

The Oriental and jardinière patterns in several colors, with jet and amber beads intermingled, are not so popular as plain black, or any one subdued color in all its different shades. The eye soon wearies of the conspicuous patterns, and the fashion will scarcely be permanent. In view of this a good plan is to have bands of satin needleworked and sewn lightly on the cloak, removing them at pleasure, and without destroying the pile of the material.

Lace, Rouleaux, Appliqué, Etc.

Lace is the most elegant garniture of velvet cloaks. Barbes are sewn down the seams, and wide flounces on the skirt. Thread is the favorite lace; guipure has lost favor.

Rouleaux of satin, made by braiding together narrow pipings, are much used. Many imported cloaks, both cloth and velvet, are trimmed with silk braid 1 inch wide. An appliqué trimming of vines, with large leaves, is very handsome. On smooth cloths the appliqué is of velvet, or of Astrakhan fur; grosgrain is used on materials with heavy pile. Chinchilla fur and plush trim velvet handsomely for midwinter.

There are several different kinds of fringe—ball fringe, crocheted, moss, knotted, twisted, corded, and beaded fringe. Almost every garment has some part of it ornamented by one of these varieties.

Buttons are still large, and are of crocheted silk, jet, or gilt. Cable cords and camel's-hair fringe are the only trimmings suitable for the shaggy cloths.

It is not an offense against good taste to trim opera cloaks in the most gorgeous manner. Hence embroidery in brilliant colors, and bullion braids and fringes, are appropriate for the trimming of evening wrappings.

Varieties

Shot silks are coming into favor again. A pretty pattern with a black ground, shot with blue, is reversible, blue shot with black on the other side. Both sides are beautifully wrought up. This silk is 3/4 yard wide.

Imported walking dresses may be bought with the skirt and paletot ready made and trimmed. Material for the body is furnished.

Circassian ceintures are very much worn. A ribbon belting encircles the waist. Two rings of jet or gilt are attached to the belt. From these falls a chain, in which another ring is placed, and this ring holds the ends of the sash.

Bonnets of Bismarck should be relieved by a face trimming of a becoming shade, as no color is so trying to the complexion as the reddish brown now worn. "Tying the bonnet under the chin" is out of fashion. Bows are dispensed with. Ornaments of jet, pearl, and gilt, or sprays of flowers, are used instead. Square veils with long barbes fastened behind are worn with round hats. Lace the color of the hat is used for trimming.

November 16, 1867

Paletot with Flowing Sleeves

Paletot of dark blue cloth. Three and 3/4 yards of cloth 1 1/2 yards wide are required. It is trimmed with black silk, crocheted and bead buttons, bead fringe, and cord and tassels. Cut out the fronts and side pieces, the back whole, and the sleeves. Join the back, sides, and fronts according to the figures on the pattern. Put on the trimming. Sew in the sleeves. Finish with buttons and buttonholes.

Paletot with Flowing Sleeves

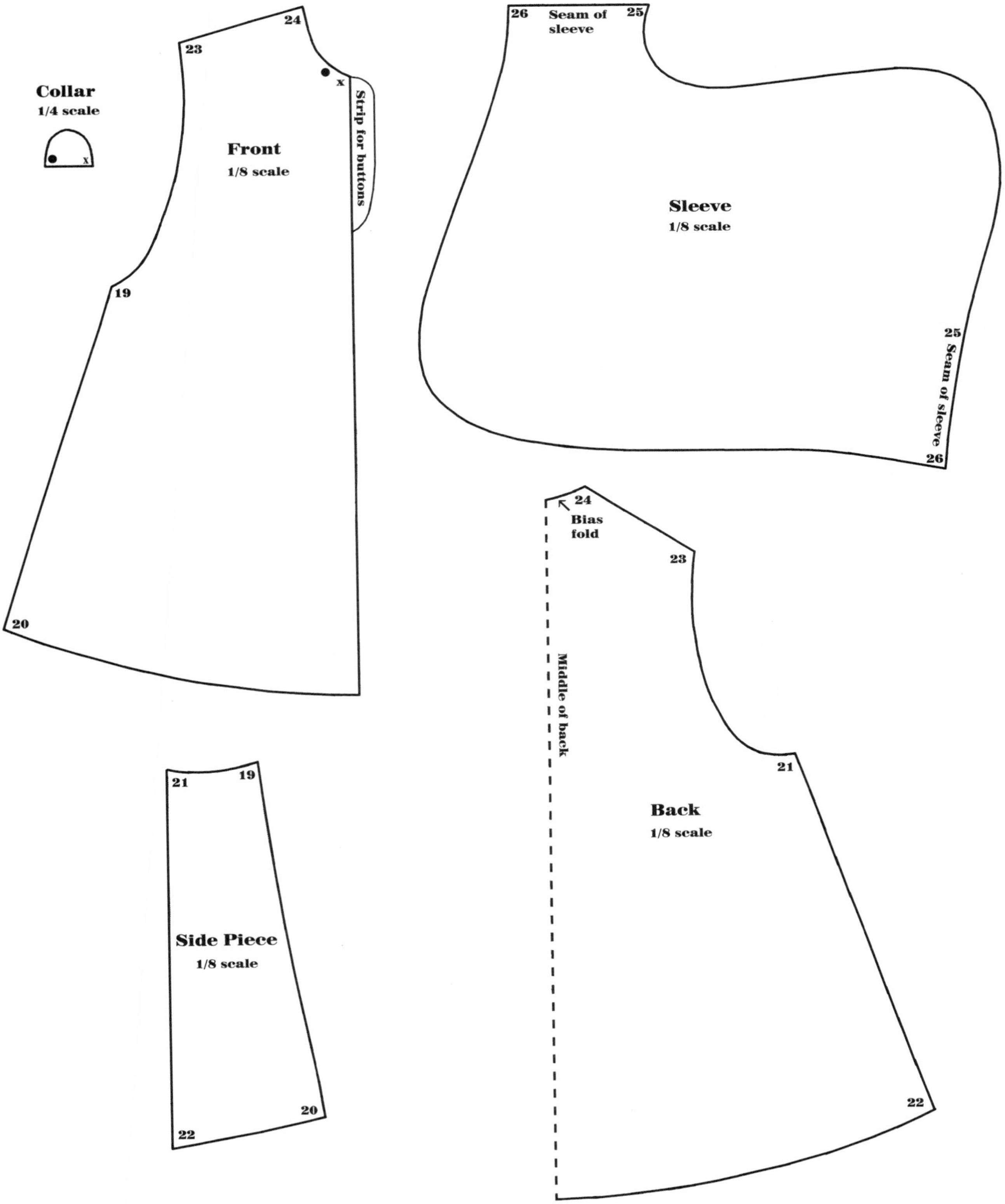

Collar
1/4 scale

x

Front
1/8 scale

23
24
x
Strip for buttons
19
20

Sleeve
1/8 scale

26
Seam of sleeve
25
25
Seam of sleeve
26

Side Piece
1/8 scale

21
19
20
22

Back
1/8 scale

24
Bias fold
23
Middle of back
21
22

Alexandra Paletot

This paletot is of blue velour, with long flowing sleeves, and small standing collar. The right side buttons over the left, which is straight on the edge (sides are seen reversed in the illustration). Three yards of cloth 1 1/2 yards wide are required. The paletot is simply bound with satin, 1 inch wide, and trimmed with satin buttons.

Cut the right and left fronts. Cut the back whole, and the collar. Cut two pieces each for the pocket lapels and sleeves.

Face the fronts with a strip of silk 4 inches wide. Stitch on the satin binding as illustrated. Sew on the buttons and make the buttonholes. Put in the pockets. Join the fronts and back together, and bind the whole round the bottom. Bind the sleeves in the same manner and sew them in. Put on the collar, and finish with hook and eye, or button and loop.

Alexandra Paletot

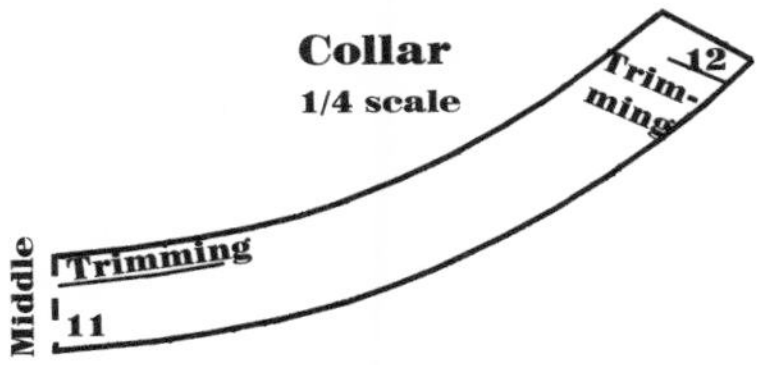

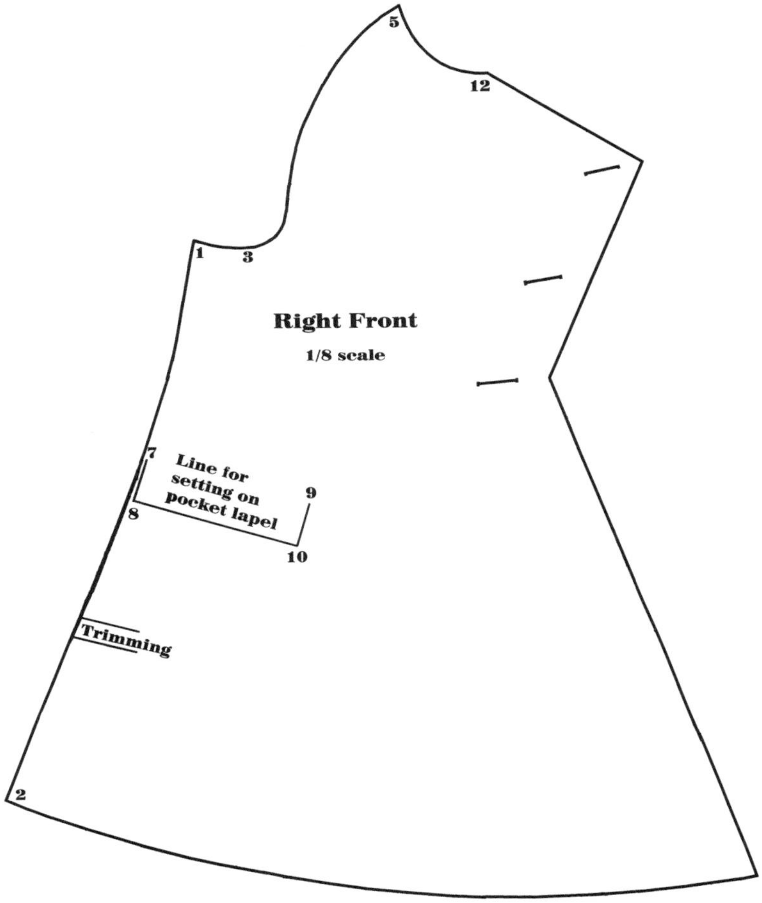

Collar
1/4 scale
Trim-ming 12
Middle Trimming 11

Right Front
1/8 scale
5 12 1 3
7 Line for setting on pocket lapel 9
8 10
Trimming
2

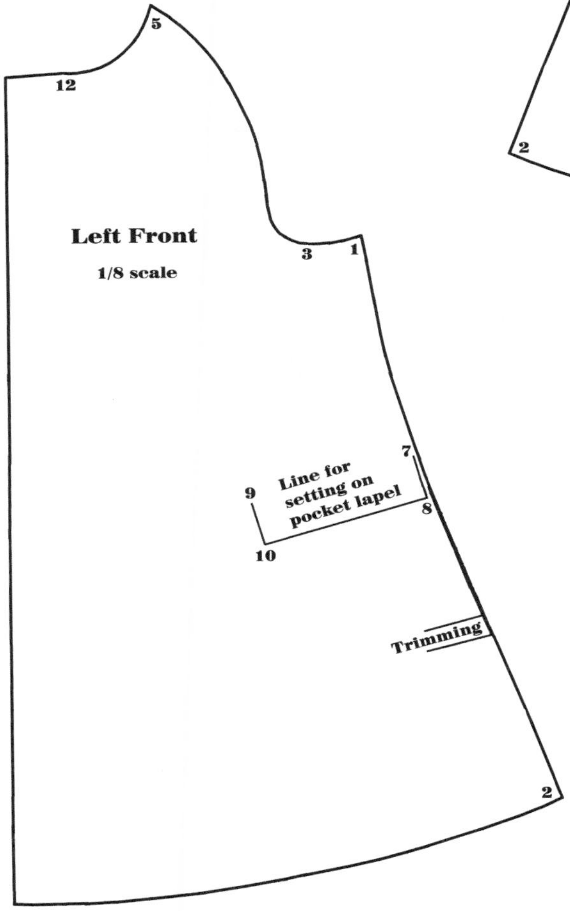

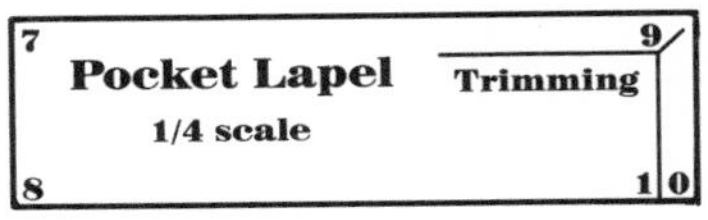

Left Front
1/8 scale
5 12 3 1
9 Line for setting on pocket lapel 7
8 10
Trimming
2

Pocket Lapel
1/4 scale
7 Trimming 9
8 10

November 16, 1867

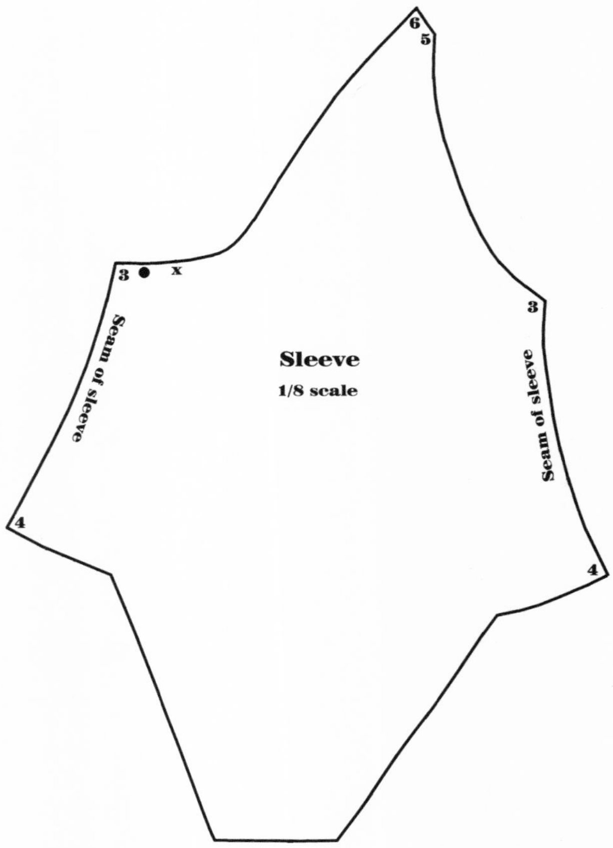

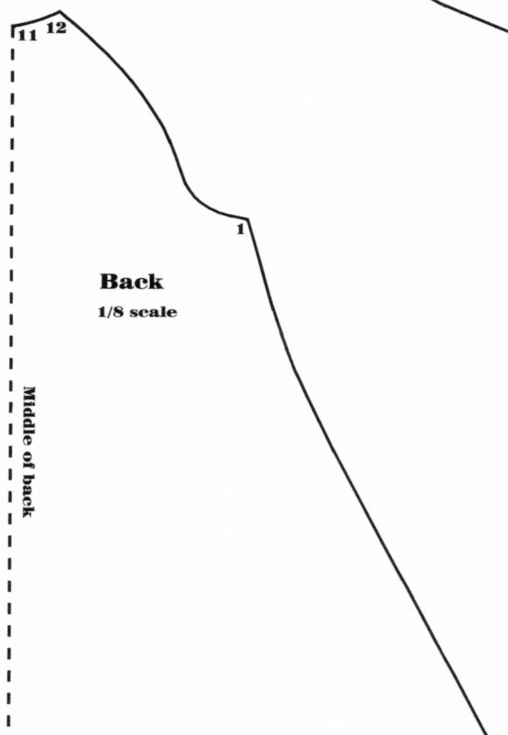

Don Caesar Paletot

Don Caesar Paletot

Paletot of light brown lambskin. Two and 1/4 yards of cloth 1 1/2 yards wide are required. Cut two pieces each of the front, epaulet, and cuff. Cut the sleeves, each in two pieces. Cut the back and collar whole.

Sew up the paletot. Put on the collar. Set on the sleeves to correspond with the figures on the pattern, covering the seams on the wrong side with braid.

November 16, 1867

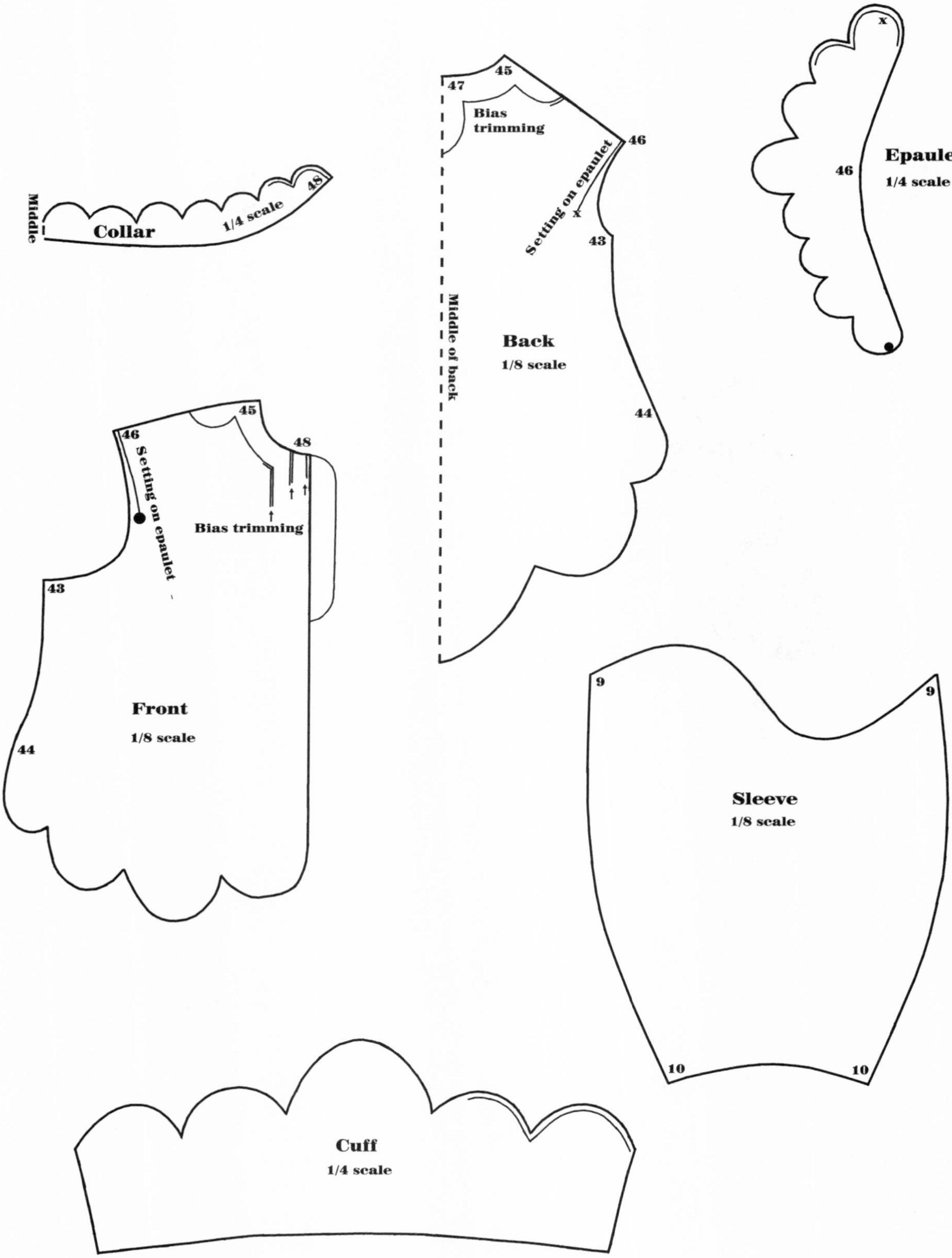

Elegant Paletot

Paletot of purple velour, descending in a long point on the side. The small standing collar and sleeves are scalloped on the edge. Two and 1/4 yards of cloth 1 1/2 yards wide are required. This paletot is richly trimmed with passementerie ornaments, bead gimp, and jet fringe. The front is fastened with large crocheted and jet buttons.

Cut both fronts, and the back whole. Cut the collar, and both pieces for each sleeve.

Face the fronts about 4 inches wide with silk. Put on the buttons and buttonholes. Join the back and fronts together. Line the collar with silk, bind it, and set it on, covering the seam with bead gimp. Trim with passementerie ornaments and three rows of bead gimp round the bottom and armholes, finishing the bottom with fringe. Sew up the sleeves from 49 to 50, and from 51 to 52. Scallop, face, and trim the bottoms. Sew them in the armholes as marked on the pattern.

November 16, 1867

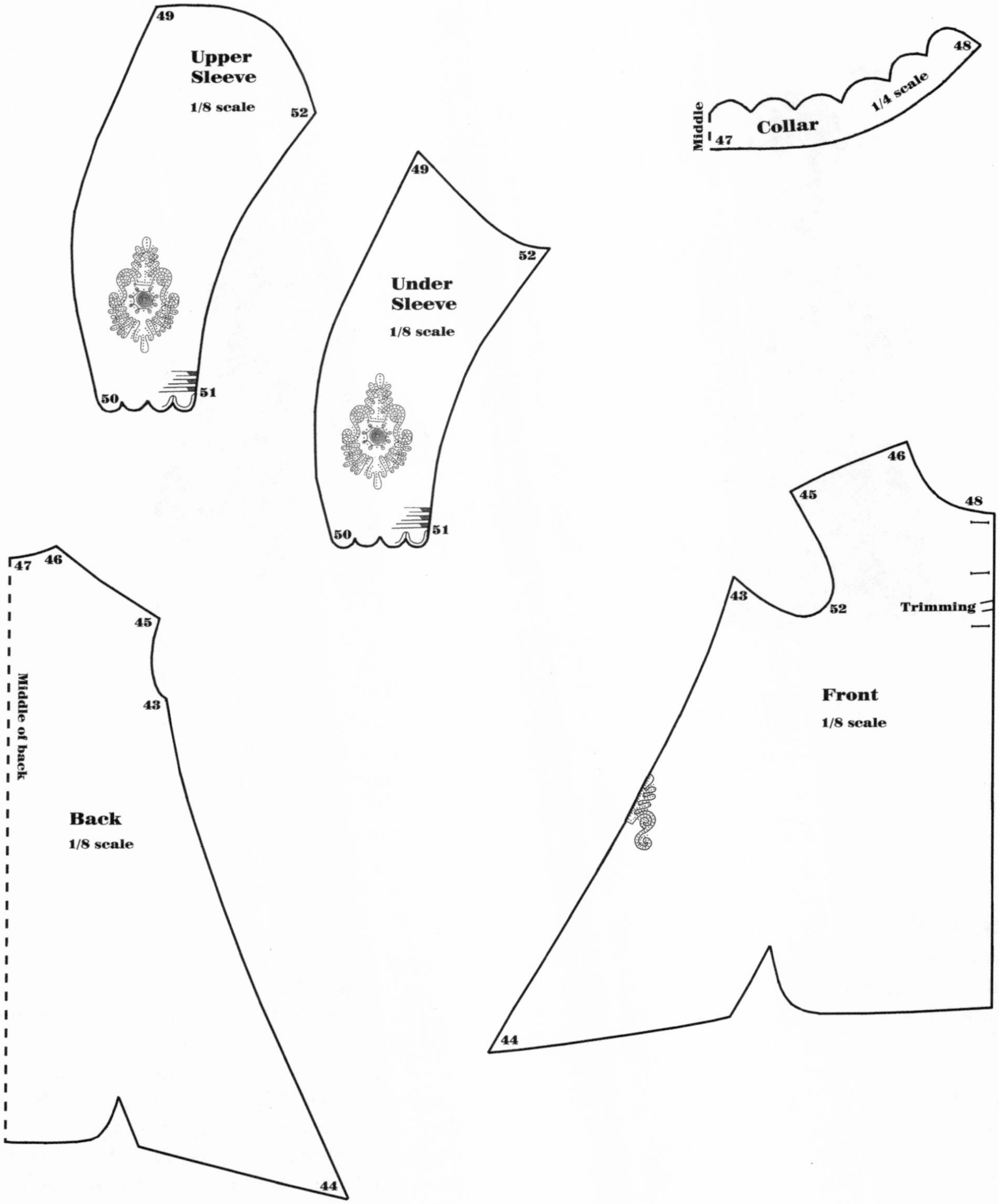

49
Upper Sleeve
1/8 scale
52
50
51

49
52
Under Sleeve
1/8 scale
50
51

48
1/4 scale
Middle
47
Collar

47 46
45
43
Middle of back
Back
1/8 scale
44

46
45
48
43
52
Trimming
Front
1/8 scale
44

November 23, 1867

Bonnets

The foundation of the bonnet is still very small. It is the profusion of ornament that gives the impression of increased size.

The fanchon is so universally becoming that all efforts to displace it have failed. It has, however, undergone some modifications. The front is much improved by a coronet. The back, shorn of its point, passes straight over the chignon, and is finished by the graceful Spanish veil.

The Marie Antoinette style has a more legitimate claim to be called a bonnet, as it has a regularly defined crown and brim. The brim is usually pointed on the forehead, surmounted by a diadem, and flaring at the temples.

Another shape, intended for very young ladies, fits close to the head with a straight front. It is pointed over the chignon, and is precisely the reverse of the remodeled fanchon.

Fabrics

Velvet and satin are the principal fabrics. A union of the two is seen in almost every bonnet. Velvet bonnets are trimmed with pipings or folds of satin, and those of satin with rosettes and scarves of velvet. Uncut and royal velvet is brought out in all the favorite shades, Bismarck, "capucine," "sarde," or pearl color, "celadon," and blue-purple. There was a time when purple was sacred to our grandmothers. It is now worn by the gayest belle. A few bronzed and Italian straws of open pattern are seen, lined with a warm rich color of silk.

Wide lapels of velvet, lined with satin and bound with a narrow bias satin or fringed at the ends, are handsome strings for velvet bonnets. An edge of blonde sometimes borders the strings. A gilt spray fastens them under the chin, relieving the wearer from the necessity of tying a bow of stiff ribbon that refuses to be graceful. When narrow strings are worn they are of satin or grosgrain ribbon, 2 inches wide.

Squares of fine lace are thrown over velvet bonnets, and long barbes fall over the chignon. Blonde and point lace are used with the delicate shades of green and pearl color. Chantilly supplies the drapery to the deep rich colors.

Round Hats

The shape is as small as can be worn, and the light trimming does not detract from its jaunty appearance. Low crowns and rolling brims prevail, shaped in a variety of ways. The brim may be depressed in front and back, or turned up at one side or behind, or reversed alike all around. High crowns, square and slanting, are displayed, but one seldom meets them on the street.

Velvet, plush, and felt are the best materials. A few black and bronzed straws are worn, but leghorn and crinoline are laid aside for the present. Astrakhan, sealskin, and chinchilla hats are made to wear with paletots of those furs. Scarves of velvet and satin, trimmed with narrow pipings or folds, and fringed at the ends, depend from the back. Black velvet is rimmed with white satin piping, and white with black. In others there is a tendency to preserve one tone throughout the whole hat, all the materials–velvets, feathers, and lace–agreeing in color. Skating toquets are made of Astrakhan, otter, and chinchilla. For the promenade we have Hungarian hats of ermine and grebe. The turned-up brims of turbans are quite broad in front, sloping narrower toward the back. A pompon of feathers or a gilt spray is the only ornament.

Trimmings

There are new feathers; new flowers; new laces; and new ornaments of jet, gold, and Roman pearl. Instead of willow feathers and long ostrich plumes, we have short ostrich tufts, silver heron feathers, the Swiss bird grebe, pheasant's plumes, and prettier than all others, the delicate marabous in tufts and fringes tipped with gilt and jet. The new velvet flowers are tastefully mingled with gilt. Velvet leaves are veined with gold, and thistles of downy marabou are covered with a filigree network. Scarlet berries with bronzed autumn leaves make graceful diadems. Sprays of coral are effectively introduced into evening hats. Parma violets, marguerites, pansies, and wreaths of hawthorn and clematis are exquisitely modeled.

The attempt to have materials and trimmings of a uniform color has led to the introduction of lace of various colors. These laces have a tawdry appearance, and are as much to be deprecated as the profuse use of gilt. We advise that gilt be sparingly and judiciously used. A small gilt spray or leaf, a gilt-tipped marabou fringe, or pendants of gilt lilies on a coronet, are pretty and in good taste. But the broad bandeaux of yellow gilt, the clusters of grapes and berries, and fringes of bullion, are coarse and objectionable.

Jet is carved, and formed into bandeaux and pendants. Seed jet is not used except on illusion. Small ornaments of Roman pearl fasten white lace overstrings. A drop trimming to correspond surrounds the edge of the bonnet.

Veils

The Spanish veil is especially suited to the fanchon, but is worn with bonnets of all shapes. It was originally a straight scarf falling over the chignon, and fastened at the throat with long, flowing strings. Now several forms are given it. Some are cut in a direct line from shoulder to shoulder, while others are pointed at the back.

Tulle, dotted with chenille or embroidered with beads, is used for square veils. Colored net and blonde veils are worn long. Guipure and Chantilly are suitable laces for heavy falls over the chignon. The mantilla veil has long tabs in the front, hanging loose, or caught together by a spray or small bow of ribbon. Another style laps in front, like the Marie Antoinette fichu. Round blonde veils, to match the color of the bonnet, are fastened near the front and thrown backward. These are graceful, and serve for drapery, which the new shapes require. The stiff brim and flat crown need to be softened and relieved by tulle and lace.

Round veils, with long tabs fastened behind, are worn with hats. Of colored lace veils the Bismarck is prettiest. Puffed trimmings of tulle and blonde on round hats have long ends that serve for veils.

Miscellaneous Items

Low-necked bodices or corselets of grosgrain, with epaulets, and long lappets at the back, are trimmed with bias folds of the same material, studded with jet nail heads. They are worn over empress cloths and self-colored merinos.

Gored aprons of colored silk are pretty additions to home toilettes. They are embroidered in narrow vines in gay colors, or braided with mottled braid. Two narrow fluted ruffles, bias and bound, are also used for trimming.

Two colors of ribbon sewn together make becoming cravats for morning wear. Capucine and black contrast prettily. Two narrow ribbons are sewn together at the edges to pass round the neck. The ends in front are finished by knotted silk fringe. They may be tied in a bow or fastened with a brooch.

Sashes of satin, tied in large bows behind, with ends reaching almost to the bottom of train skirts, are much worn with evening toilettes. They are 2 1/2 or 3 yards long, and are loosely knotted at the waist. Velvet ribbon, 1/4 yard wide, and satin, with a vine of velvet leaves in the center, are used for sashes. They may be of the most delicate or the most brilliant hues, and are ornamented with lace and pearl passementerie. When white they are embroidered with bouquets of bright colors. The Venetian sash has a brocaded landscape on each streamer, and is heavily fringed.

Black Lace Fichu

Black Lace Fichu

This fichu is made of black lace. Fold shawl fashion. The under part falls about 3 inches below the upper, and makes a pleat at the top of the back, as illustrated. The ends are crossed in front, and fastened with a bow or rosette.

Fichu
1/8 scale

Lace Cravat

This cravat is made of lace insertion, 5/8 yard long and 3/4 inch wide, laid over violet ribbon, 2 inches wide, and bordered on each side with a fall of Valenciennes edging. Small pansies embroidered in muslin are then sewn on the insertion, about 1 inch apart. A large pansy is placed in the middle, where the ends cross each other.

November 30, 1867

Knitting

Among those pretty knitted garments that afford such graceful employment for leisure hours and add so much to one's comfort as the cold weather advances, we have seen some beautiful afghans, shawls, hoods, and jackets. The Berlin zephyr wools, split, single, double fold, and triple, are principally used in their manufacture. The black and white Shetland wools, formerly preferred for shawls, have given place to the various zephyrs.

Lingerie

Cluny, guipure, and Maltese laces are the most serviceable laces for trimming. Valenciennes and thread are very frail, but nothing else looks so handsome in conjunction with very sheer linen, lawn, and cambric.

Tucks that have the effect of being cut on the bias are pretty and durable trimming. They should be stitched lengthwise of the linen, and inserted diagonally. If cut bias they will not iron smoothly. Puffs and ruffles of cambric are also arranged diagonally.

Embroidery on linen does not wear so well as that done on thick cambric. It is always best to select a pattern without herringbone, as the strain on the thread in open work is too great, and it breaks easily. The machine embroidery is in pretty patterns, but we cannot recommend it, as it frays easily.

Sets of linen made up for sale consist of five pieces. These are the nightdress, trimmed petticoat, plain underskirt, chemise, and drawers, all of the same material and trimmed to match. They can, of course, be made up at home at much less expense, and with more attention to the nice details, such as rolled ruffles, overseamed selvages, and neatly scraped gathers. It is too much the practice in our lingerie establishments to use the sewing machine for all kinds of seams.

Petticoats, like skirts of dresses, are now gored to fit the figure below the waist.

A pretty trimming for flannel skirts is a braiding pattern chain stitched by hand or machine with silk floss. It washes better than embroidery or braiding, and is very ornamental.

Embroidered corsets are not so much worn as those stitched with white satin twist. The French coutil corsets are expensive, but are of the best material and shape, and wear well. The colored prunella and silk corsets are convenient for ladies when traveling, as it is a difficult matter to get white corsets properly washed.

Novelties

Cloaks and muffs are worn to correspond. A black velvet sacque, half-adjusted to the figure, is short in back, and long and scarflike in front. A border of sable fur constitutes the trimming. Velvet muff with band of sable near each end. Sacques of sealskin and Astrakhan have muffs and toques to match made of the same material.

Satin rouleaux of all colors may be bought by the yard. This trimming is made of satin pipings plaited together. It is newer than folds and bands, and does not fray so easily. It is a suitable trimming for all fine woolens, as velour, empress cloth, etc.

Ten yards of velveteen will make a short gored dress, single skirt, and short jacket. The spotted English velvet with silk finish is the newest. Black ground with tiny white or blue spots.

French cloth is much worn for dresses. It is not so lustrous as English cloth, and will not spot with rain. It is 1 1/2 yards wide. Six yards are sufficient for a gored dress. Napoleon blue and Bismarck are the prettiest colors. Black worsted braid 1 inch wide, arranged *à la militaire,* is a suitable trimming. It may also be bordered with fur.

Crochet Stitches

These stitches are for hoods, capes, etc.

The victoria stitch in Figure 1 is seen crocheted backward and forward, two rows making one complete row. On a foundation of the requisite length crochet the first row, from right to left. In every stitch 1 stitch remains as a loop on the needle. Second row from left to right. Loop the thread over the needle and knit 2 stitches of the last row together, as illustrated.

Figure 1. Victoria stitch

The waved stitch in Figure 2 differs but little from the victoria stitch, which forms its foundation.

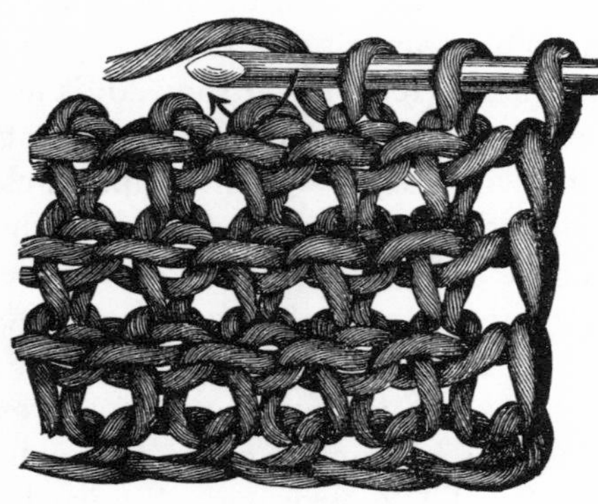

Figure 2. Waved stitch

Figures 3, 4, and 5 show the method of making the net stitch, which is represented the original size.

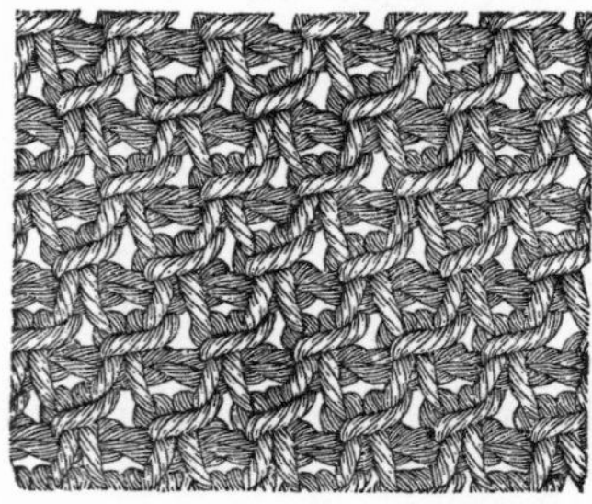

Figure 3. Net stitch

Figure 4. Making net stitch

Figure 5. Making net stitch

The scale stitch in Figure 6 is crocheted from right to left, wholly on one side, beginning with the thread anew for every row. Begin with a foundation as usual. Crochet the first row as follows. Miss the last stitch of the foundation, and take up a loop from the 4 following stitches. Then draw the needle through the whole 5 together. Follow with 1 chain which forms the whole figure. For the next figure, crochet * 1 stitch with the thread looped under the chain; 1 with the thread looped behind the 5 stitches of the figure; then 1 stitch in the next 2 stitches of the foundation. The needle is drawn through the whole 5 stitches as before, and 1 chain is made. Repeat from *, and cut off the thread at the end of the row.

Figure 6. Scale stitch

To begin the next row fasten the thread in the superfluous stitch of the preceding row. Crochet 3 chain, miss the last of the same, take a loop from the next 2 stitches, and continue as in the first row.

Trimmings for Hoods and Capes

To make the border in Figure 1, take a splinter of wood or strip of pasteboard 1/4 inch wide. Wind it from the right to the left with four strands of split zephyr. Crochet a foundation on both sides with one strand of split zephyr, making alternately 1 single crochet and 1 chain in four strands of the wound thread together. Having knitted together the thread on the splints, roll the thick part under.

Figure 1. Border

Make a second strip in a similar manner, winding the wool from left to right. Both strips lie with their edges against each other, and are crocheted together with 1 single crochet in the 2 corresponding chain, between which make 1 chain. This row, which is on the left side of the trimming, must be quite loose.

The trimming is finished by two rows of gray double zephyr crocheted on each of the free edges of the strips knit together. For these, crochet in gray double zephyr, 1 double crochet in every chain of the edge, with 3 chain between.

To make the clasp trimming in Figure 2, make a foundation of white single zephyr of the requisite length, on which knit two rows in victoria stitch. Then make the first row. Crochet alternately in each stitch of the preceding row 1 single crochet and 1 loop as follows. Draw the crochet needle through the loop of the single crochet; make in single crochet in the next stitch of the preceding row, make a loop in the same stitch, put the thread over the needle, and draw it through both loops; *x* a loop on the aforesaid loops, and again draw the needle through both together. Repeat five times from *x*. Then draw the needle again through the loop, take the loop of the single crochet in front of the figure on the needle, and afterward the loop of the figure, and knit both together.

Figure 2. Clasp trimming

Finish the row of loops with a row of victoria stitch (1 stitch in every stitch of the preceding row). Make another row of loops in the manner before described. The loops must set one above another. Lastly, crochet a chain with scarlet zephyr on both sides of the trimming.

The border in Figure 3 is crocheted lengthwise, with a foundation of white zephyr in double crochet, continued with shells of black and white zephyr as follows. Make a foundation of the requisite length. Crochet thereon * 3 double crochet on

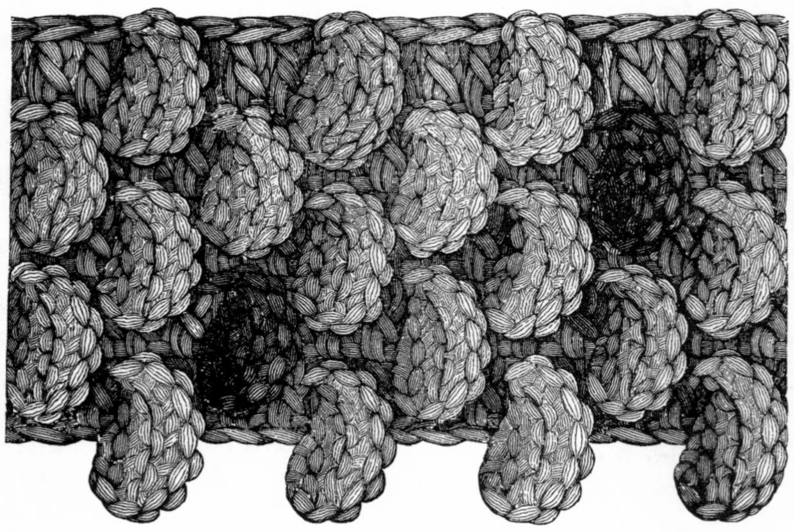

Figure 3. Crocheted border

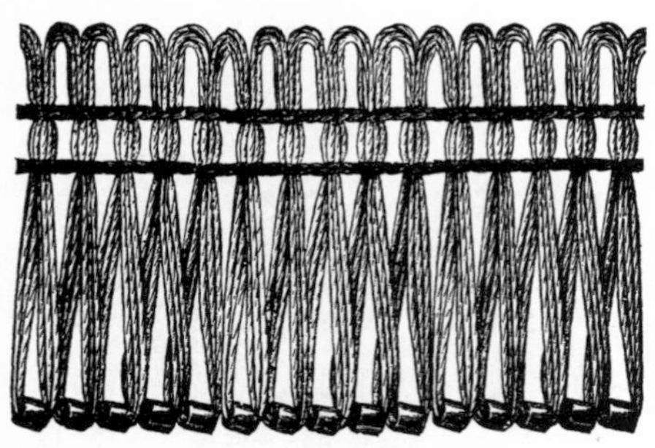

Figure 4. Woolen fringe

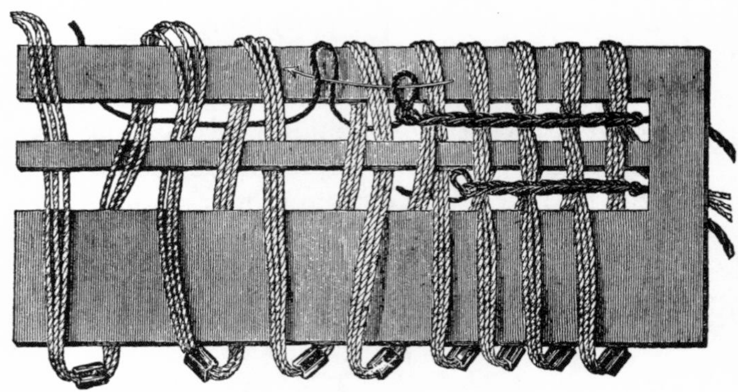

Figure 5. Making woolen fringe

the next 3 stitches. Follow with two rows of shells. Put the thread once over the needle, and take up 3 loops in the next stitches of the foundation, putting the thread over the needle between each. On the stitches thus formed crochet two rows of shells.

Repeat from *, knit three rows of white shells and one of black. In the following rows, which are knit in the same manner, make alternately one row with and one without black shells.

Figures 4 and 5 show this woolen fringe finished and in the process of execution. First prepare a piece of pasteboard (see illustration). Wind it with three strands of drab split worsted, which has first been strung with jet beads, letting one bead come at the bottom of every turn. This done, crochet the threads together with black worsted, as shown, with 1 single and 1 chain alternately. Care must be taken to keep the thread on the under side.

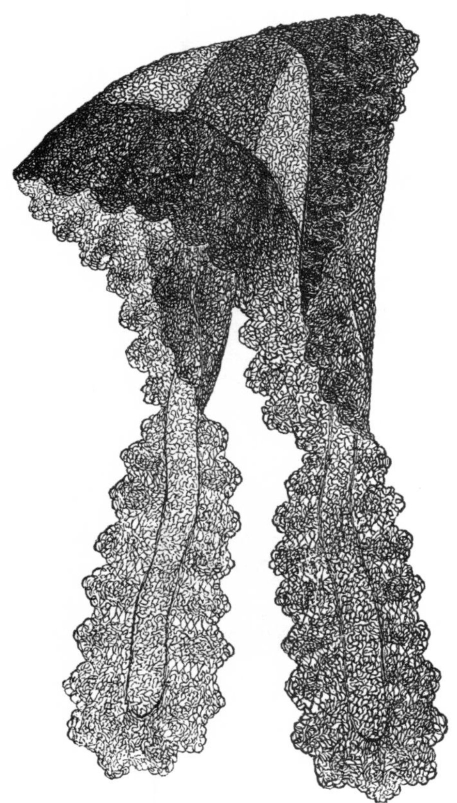

Knitted Fanchon

The materials required are 1 1/2 oz. black fleecy wool and two fine wooden needles.

This fanchon is knitted throughout on the right side, to fit the pattern. It is widened and narrowed on the outer edge alone. The lace border that forms the edge is made of the same wool, in the following manner.

Make a foundation the length of the edge. Then knit the first row: 1 stitch with the thread over the needle, 1 stitch in the same manner, 1 slip stitch, 2 knitted together, and the slip stitch drawn over the last, thus narrowing 2; 1 knitted. Repeat from * to end.

Second row: Purl, the thread over the needle being always knitted as a stitch. Repeat these two rows nine times, and cast off the stitches. Sew on the lace.

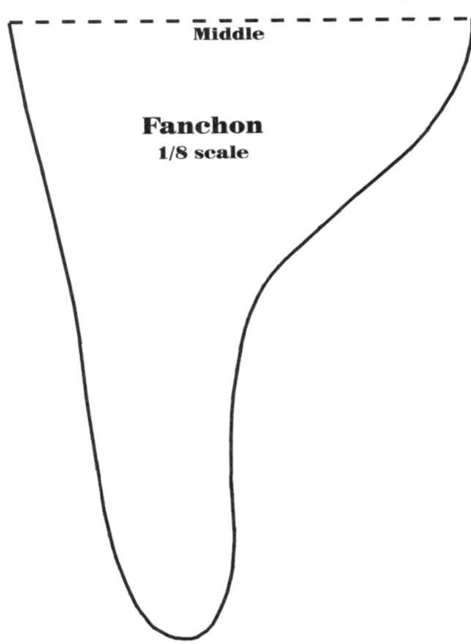

Gored Morning Dress

This elegant morning dress is wholly gored. The right side, which laps over the left, is bias on the edge. The original is of soft red, black, and white woolen. It is trimmed with black velvet, 2 inches wide, edged with red silk cord and white silk piping. The small standing collar and belt are likewise of black velvet. It may also be made of gray or white flannel, trimmed with velvet.

Cut both fronts. Lengthen or shorten at the bottom, as may be required. Cut two side gores, and for the back and collar one piece each. Cut a piece for the pocket. Cut from the sleeve pattern two pieces each of black silk, and the outside material for the sleeves.

Each front is faced on the edge about 4 inches wide with black silk. A false hem for buttonholes, about 2 inches wide, is set under the edge of the right front. Black buttons are put on the opposite side. Sew up the skirt according to the figures on the pattern. Face the bottom about 4 inches wide with the same material as the outside. Set on the trimming. Trim the pocket welt with silk and cord, as illustrated, and set on the left side, making Figures 9 and 10 on the front and side come together. Sew up the sleeves from 11 to 12 and from 13 to 14. Trim them, and sew them in the armholes from 14 to 14. A strip of velvet 3 1/2 inches wide, lined with silk, with an interlining, serves as a belt.

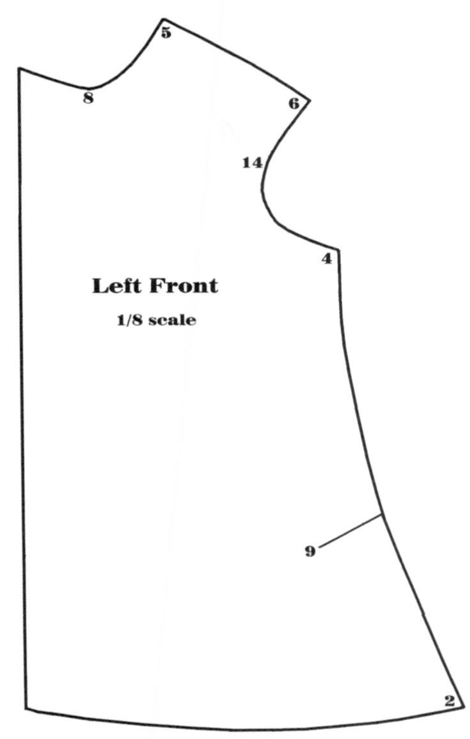

5
8
6
14
4
Left Front
1/8 scale
9
2

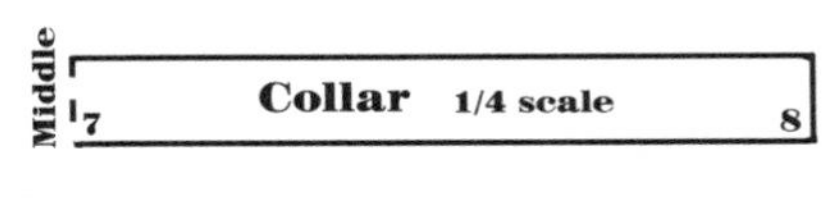

Middle
7
Collar 1/4 scale
8

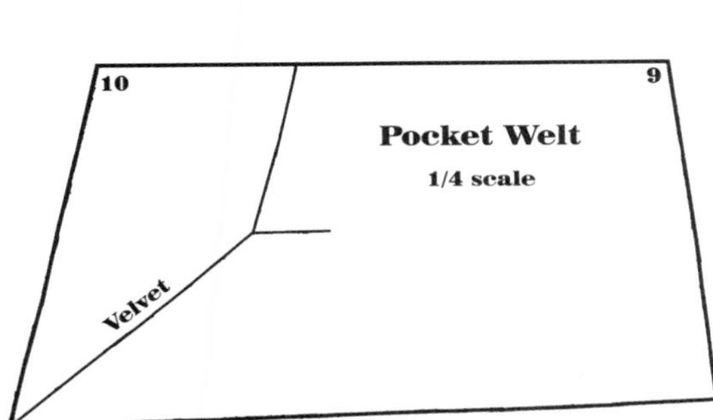

10
9
Pocket Welt
1/4 scale
Velvet

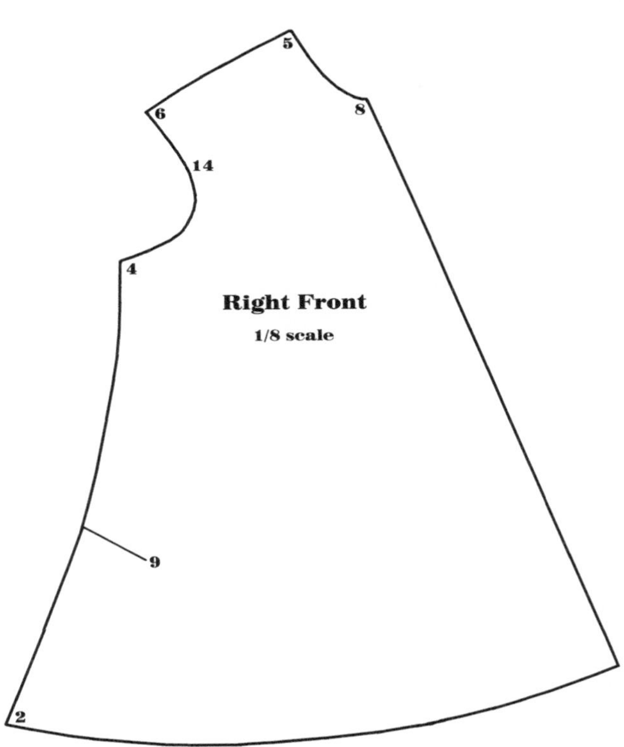

5
6
8
14
4
Right Front
1/8 scale
9
2

November 30, 1867

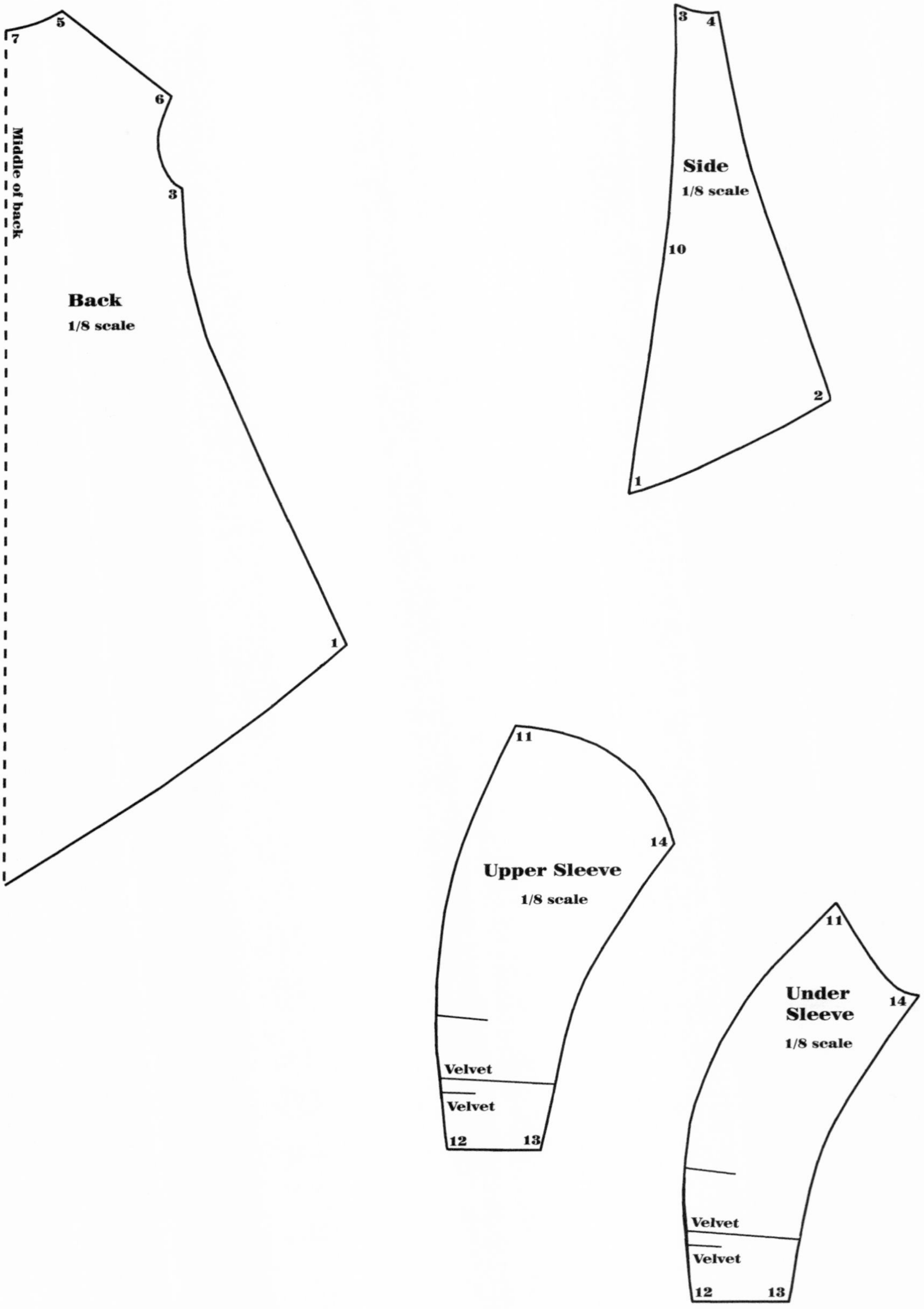

Gray Grosgrain Silk Dress

Gray Grosgrain Silk Dress

This dress and the following four are all gored, the waist and skirt being cut together. The waist lining must be cut about 2 inches larger than the outside.

The gray grosgrain silk dress is trimmed round the bottom with an Empire flounce of the same material, and with pieces set up both sides of the front breadth. Bias folds of the dress material, 2 inches wide, bound with narrow lilac ribbon, with a heading of very narrow black velvet, complete the trimming. This dress is fastened up the front with smoked pearl buttons.

Cut from the front, side front, side back, and trimming each two pieces. Cut from the back and belt each one piece. Cut both parts of the sleeves.

Baste the outside of the waist on the lining and lay the bosom pleats. Then hem the fronts, and put on the buttons and buttonholes. Join the front, side front, side back, and back according to the figures, sewing together the two front breadths to the *. The right front laps over the left about 1 inch, in imitation of a pleat, on which the buttons are placed. Cord the neck with lilac silk. Face the bottom about 1/2 yard wide and bind it with braid. Set on the flounce, which is hemmed narrow around the bottom. Trim the trimming pieces with the bias folds. Set them up the front according to the figures on the pattern. Cover the seam where they are set on, as well as that of the flounce, with the same bias folds.

Sew up the sleeves. Face them with the same stuff as the dress. Put on the trimming, of bias folds of grosgrain, bound with lilac silk, with a heading of narrow velvet. Sew them in the armholes, with lilac silk cord, from 16 to 16. The belt is trimmed with folds to match the dress.

November 30, 1867

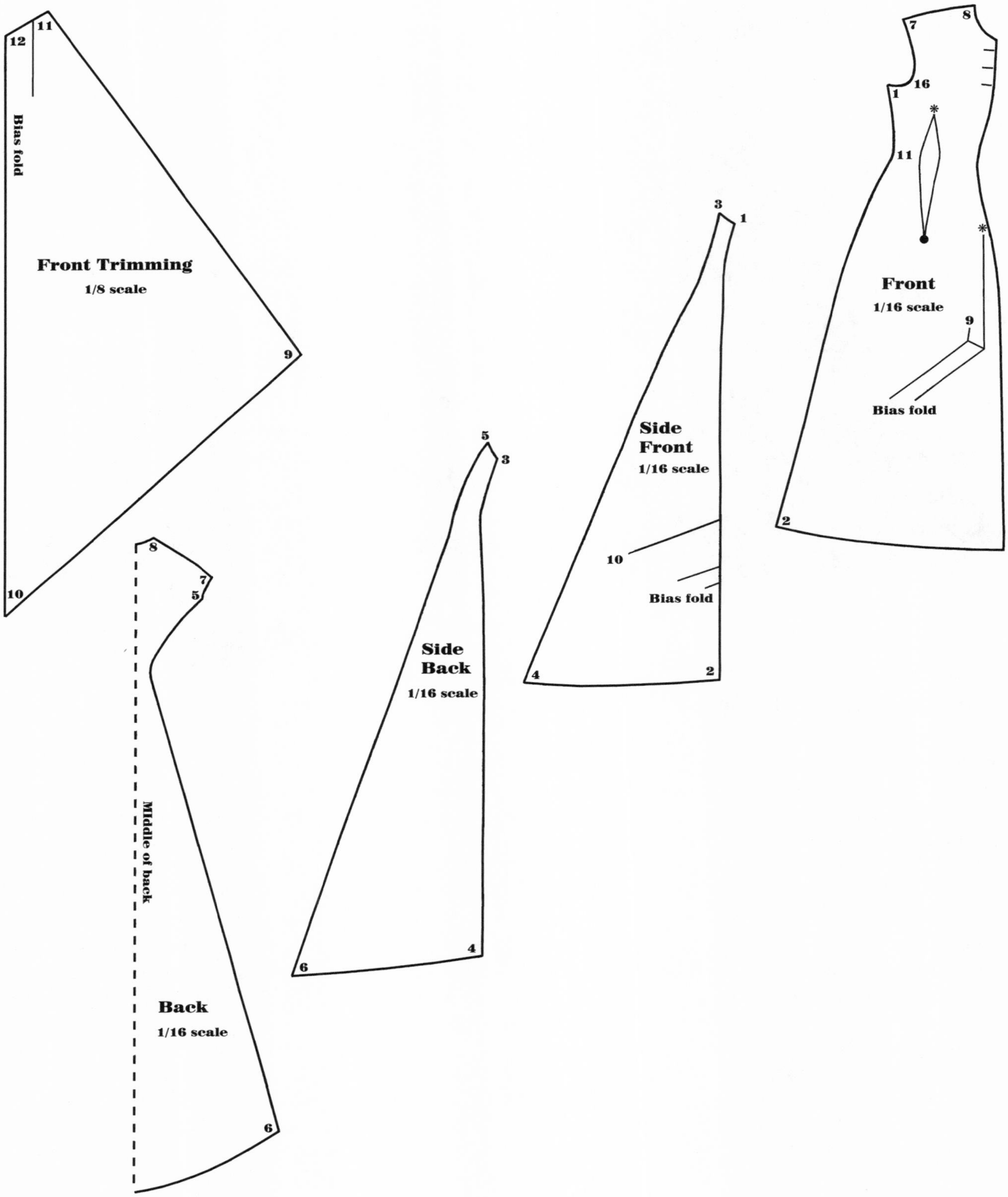
Front Trimming
1/8 scale
Bias fold
12
11
9
10
Back
1/16 scale
Middle of back
8
7
5
6
Side Back
1/16 scale
5
3
4
6
Side Front
1/16 scale
3
1
10
Bias fold
4
2
Front
1/16 scale
7
8
16
1
11
9
Bias fold
2

Peplum

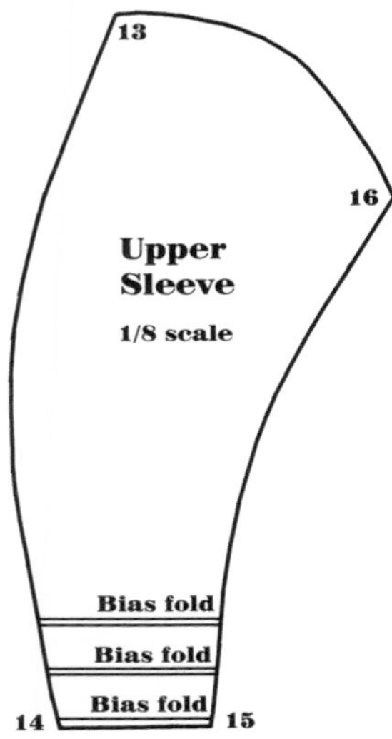

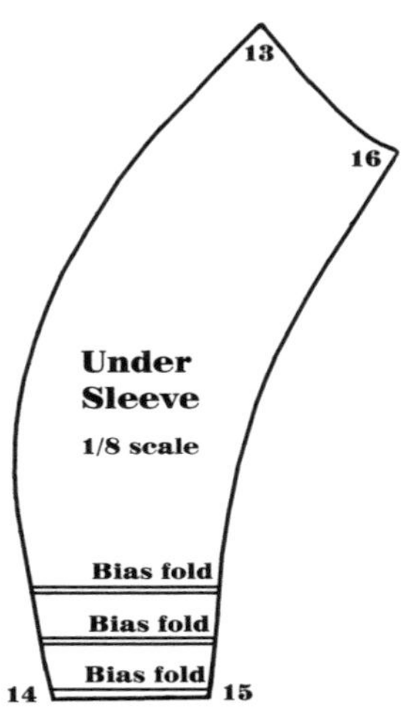

Peplum for Gray Grosgrain Silk Dress

Cut two pieces for the peplum. Sew it together in the back. Trim it round the edge with the bias folds described. Put it on the belt, according to the figures on the pattern.

Middle 17 **Belt** 1/4 scale 18

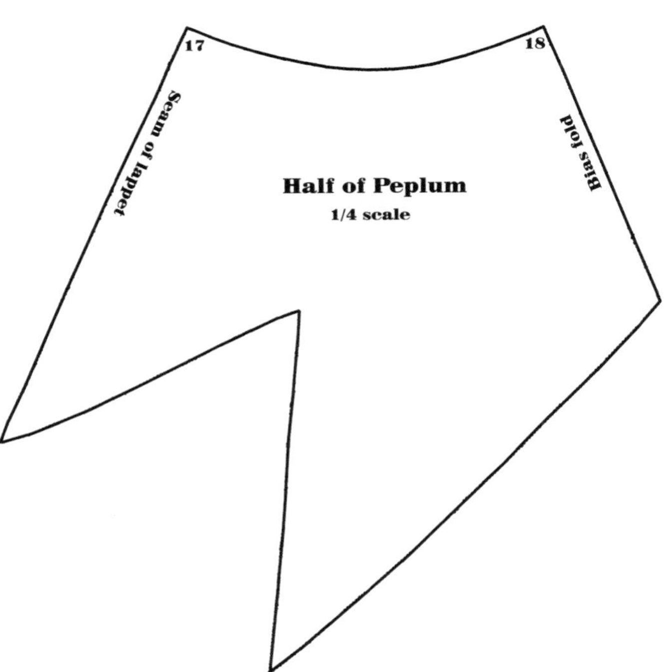

Bismarck Poult-de-Soie Dress

This dress is trimmed round the bottom with three rows of satin piping and fringe in scallops. The waist and sleeves are trimmed to match the skirt. Satin belt.

Lilac Taffeta Dress

This dress is trimmed with bias folds of violet silk. The fichu is of the same material as the dress, and trimmed in the same manner.

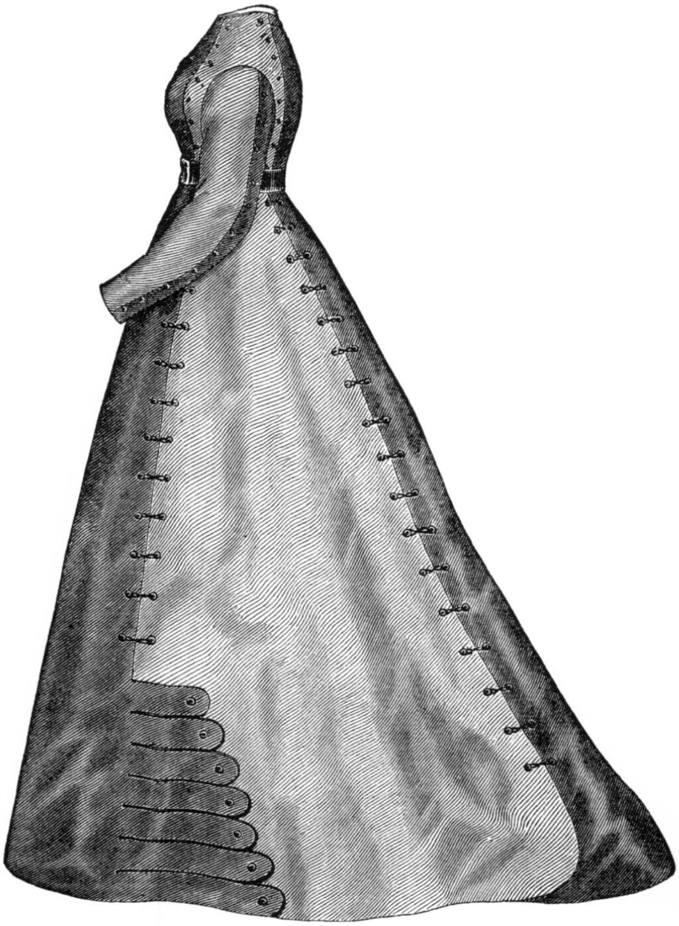

Brown Irish Poplin Dress

This dress is of light and dark brown Irish poplin. The back and front breadths are corded with dark brown satin up the sides. The side breadths are apparently fastened together with brown satin buttons and loops of cord.

Green Taffeta Dress

This dress is trimmed with bias folds and pipings of light green satin, and narrow and wide lace, with crocheted and jet buttons and grelots.

December 7, 1867

Furs

Fashions in furs are not capricious. Until within the past year or two there has been so little variety in these comfortable wrappings that they began to be considered unsusceptible of change. Now there are new shapes and new materials.

The long victorine and tippet are old fashioned. Cuffs are out of use. A set consists of collar and muff. Collars are small, and pointed behind. Short tabs in front are finished with fur tassels. Muffs are also smaller. Tips or tassels of fur instead of silk adorn the ends of the muff. The head of the animal from which the fur is taken is also used for ornament. Pockets and portmonnaies are placed on the back of flat muffs for shopping and skating. Boas are worn of mink and sable, but are oftener seen in ermine for evening wear than in the dark furs suitable for the promenade.

The greatest change of all is in the cloaks. Large unwieldy capes are superseded by graceful paletot cloaks and half-adjusted sacques. These loose paletots admit of more ornament than the circular garments. A wide angora fringe surrounds them, and furs of a different shade from the body of the sacque are inserted in braiding patterns.

Russian and Hudson Bay sable are the most valuable furs, and are handsome enough to defy all novelty and change. Mink, always neat and durable, is a standard medium article, its value depending on the number of dark stripes in the garment. The gray Siberian squirrel is less expensive, soft and silky. These furs will still be sought after, notwithstanding the presence of the more novel sealskin, Astrakhan, Persiani, Russian lambskin, and krimmer.

Sealskin in its natural state is "cuir" color, approaching very nearly to the fashionable Bismarck brown. It is more admired, however, when colored a dark rich maroon. The Persiani, Russian lamb, and krimmer are erroneously spoken of by ladies under the general name of Astrakhan. They are found in different localities in southern Europe, and when placed beside each other a very perceptible difference is observed. Astrakhan has short knobby tufts, and may be white, black, or gray. Persiani is more silky, and has longer fleece. Russian lambskin is always black, and has a peculiar wavy appearance. Krimmer is either gray or black. The hair is short and curly, looking more like cloth than fur. The Swiss grebe and canary down are from the birds known by those names. They are smoother and more glossy than ermine, and are intended for evening wrappings, but will not, of course, supplant ermine.

Ermine is the standard fur used for evening. Circulars and sacques with separate collar and muff are made to order. The muff and collar are worn with handsome street costumes.

Shoes

Boots this season combine utility and beauty. Thick soles that support the instep, half-rounded toes, heels of medium size, and high ankles, are all the requisites for comfort. The most fastidious cannot fail to find some pleasing style among the various trimmings of lace, embroidery, stitching, appliqué, and fur.

Tips of patent leather are not worn. Toes are neither round nor square, but something between the two. Heels are high, narrow, and curved. Buttons are the favorite fastening.

Kid boots are worn for the street instead of bronze or prunella. Walking boots are fastened with twenty jet buttons. The soles are heavy and slender. Appliqué straps and leaves of patent leather and colored morocco ornament the ankle and instep. With suits of one color boots are made of the dress material, and elaborately stitched and embroidered. High Polish walking boots of Russian leather have gay tassels at the ankle. Colored kid and bronze boots with thin soles are suitable for the house or carriage, but are too *prononcée* for the promenade.

Silk and satin quilted slippers with low broad heels are warm and pretty for invalids. Sandals of velvet lined and bordered with fur are comfortable for chamber wear.

Collar for Young Lady

This collar is made of puffings of tulle, on a foundation of lace, with three loops of rose-colored ribbon between each puff, and a rosette of the same ribbon in front. Crystal grelots set under the loops complete the trimming.

December 14, 1867

Evening Toilettes

Corsages of evening dresses are merely corselet ceintures, or girdles of silk, over lace or tulle chemisettes. When an overskirt of silk is worn the girdle and skirt are cut in the Gabrielle style, without shoulder straps. When separated from the skirt the corsage extends over the shoulders, and is exceedingly low and square in front and back. Puffs of tulle fill out the squares to a proper height. Belts and sashes have entirely done away with pointed waists. Some dresses just imported, instead of being laced, are buttoned behind with large flat button molds covered with the dress material.

Sleeves are either very short and puffed, or long lapels hanging under the arm, not behind it, with merely a rosette or flower over the shoulder.

Skirts of all kinds of material are gored with long trains. The front and sides are flat and close fitting. A handsome train of medium length is formed by sloping the skirt gradually until the back widths are 1 yard longer than the front. An imported bridal dress measures 3 yards from the belt to the edge of the train, and the back widths of a white Antwerp silk are 4 yards long. Trained skirts are not pointed, but rounded gradually, or cut off square. Double skirts are made of two materials. The under one is of rich silk with an overskirt or tunic of lace looped at the sides, the front forming an apron. Or a gauze or tulle trained skirt with long peplum or tunic of silk. The underskirt is not trimmed.

Marie Antoinette fichus of real lace and of tulle are worn over colored silks, and are very becoming to slender figures. They are crossed in front, with long flowing ends at the back.

Sashes are worn either at the back or side, and are short or long according to fancy. They are always broad, cut on the bias, and heavily trimmed at the ends. When made of the dress material they are lined with white satin, and bordered with lace or piped with thick cords. Knotted fringe is sewn on the bias ends, or they are caught together with a chenille tassel. Waistbands with ornamental rings for sashes are very much worn. The rings are now made of wooden molds covered with velvet or satin.

Gaze de Chambray, Tulle, Etc.

First among thin materials is the beautiful gaze de chambray. This gossamer tissue is brocaded with gilt and silver threads in bouquets and in robes. Thick satin stripes alternate with delicate gauze in a most effective way. Plain white chambray is trimmed with puffing and pleated ruffles or with tinsel ribbons. Tunics and overdresses of colored silk are worn over trained chambray skirts. Sleeves and high bodice of gauze puffed, with silk ruches or small flowers between the puffs. Overdress low, and rounded at the top, the skirt slashed at the side with long sashes between.

Lyons tulle is spangled with colors or gilt and beaded with crystal. No material is so universally becoming. It is prettily embroidered with gay colors and with straw.

Velvet, Satin, and Brocade

Ten yards of colored Lyons velvet makes a trained gored dress. Capucine and purple satins with tunics of Chantilly lace, and Mexican blue with point lace tunic are very handsome. Chiné silks with bouquets of flowers artistically grouped on white grounds, brocades, glacé silks in new shades, grosgrain in plain colors, and the shaded chameleons complete the list of thick materials for evening dresses.

Trousseaux

Trousseaux of point appliqué and point d'aiguille are imported. They only form a small part of the bridal toilette. They consist usually of a lace shawl, veil, wide flounce for wedding dress, narrower lace for garniture, monchoir, and fan cover all in the same pattern. The fan is mounted with white silk and mother-of-pearl.

White satin, the traditional bridal dress, is at length rivaled by the magnificent Antwerp silk, heavily corded, 1 1/2 yards wide. This silk is handsome enough to dispense with all trimming. The lustrous poult-de-soie antique, and a silk with thick satin cords, are also sold for wedding dresses.

Tarlatan, grenadine, and tulle are selected for bridesmaids. Several skirts of tulle and tarlatan alternately, often five or seven, produce a beautiful effect, each differently trimmed with puffs, ruches, lace, and satin folds. Moss fringe and tinsel passementerie are suitable trimmings. Flowers are, however, prettier for bridesmaids. They are arranged round the bertha and as a girdle.

Opera Cloaks and Hats

A new style of opera cloak, or rather scarf, is straight, with a fold pointed in the back, forming a hood like the Arab cloaks. It crosses in front, one end being thrown over the shoulder in the Spanish fashion.

Opera hoods, knitted in a loose stitch of split zephyr, are overshot with silk floss and crystal beads. Cashmere baschliks and ermine hoods are becoming and comfortable for extra carriage wrappings.

Coiffures

Wreaths of small flowers, with but little foliage, are worn for headdresses. Coronets are arranged entirely without leaves. Trailing vines fall on the shoulders, or are twined around the chignon. Hawthorn wreaths, verbenas, clematis, and marguerites, with gilt stamens, and glittering with crystal dewdrops, are favorite coiffures. Chrysanthemums and china asters of velvet and crêpe form pretty bandeaux between rows of puffs, or above the short curls on the forehead.

White lilac and orange blossoms are mingled together for bridal garnitures. Cape jessamine and apple blossoms of wax are mingled in the same tiara. A set for a bride consists of wreath for the hair, shoulder knots, bouquet for corsage, and vines for bertha and girdle. Necklace and wristlets are added for very youthful brides.

Varieties

Purple, it is predicted, is to be the leading color, now that Bismarck is on the wane.

A novelty, called the Russian gored knitted skirt, has just been introduced, which is designed to supersede the ordinary flannel skirt. It is made of merino, is warm and clinging, does not shrink, and is a serviceable garment for cold weather.

Morning Dress with Jacket

This morning dress and jacket are made of gray flannel, embroidered in chain stitch with black crochet silk as illustrated. Velvet ribbon or braid may also be used. The jacket and dress are fastened in front with black crocheted buttons and loops.

For the jacket, cut the outside, interlining, and silk lining, from the front and side patterns, each two pieces. Cut from the back one piece. Cut the sleeves.

Baste the outside on the interlining. Embroider with the silk. Put in the lining, and join the whole. Then bind the edge with braid, and finish with buttons and buttonholes.

Morning Dress with Jacket

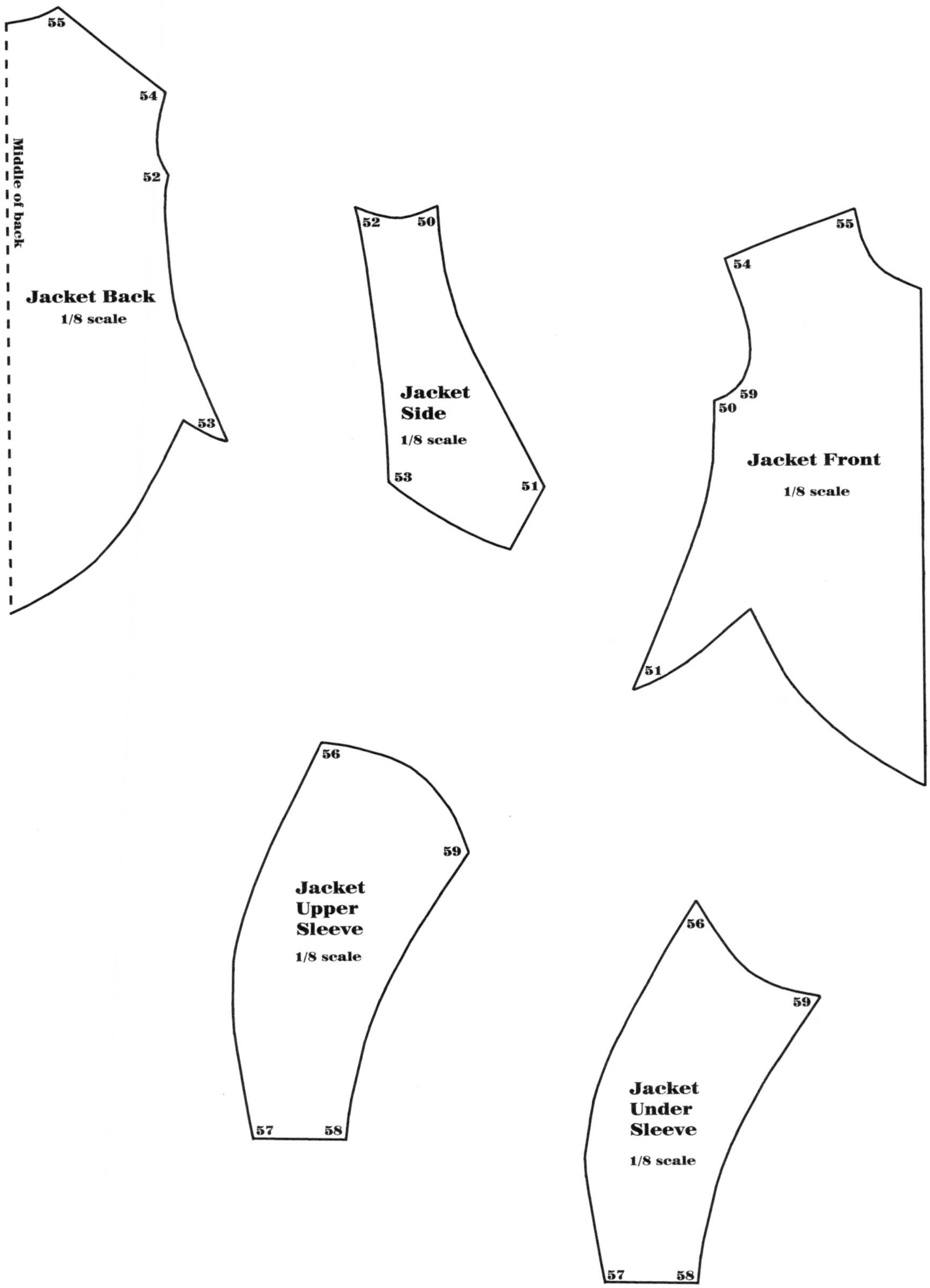

December 14, 1867

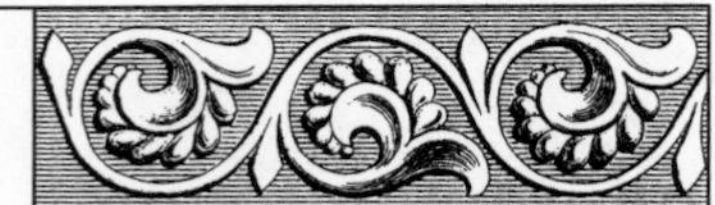

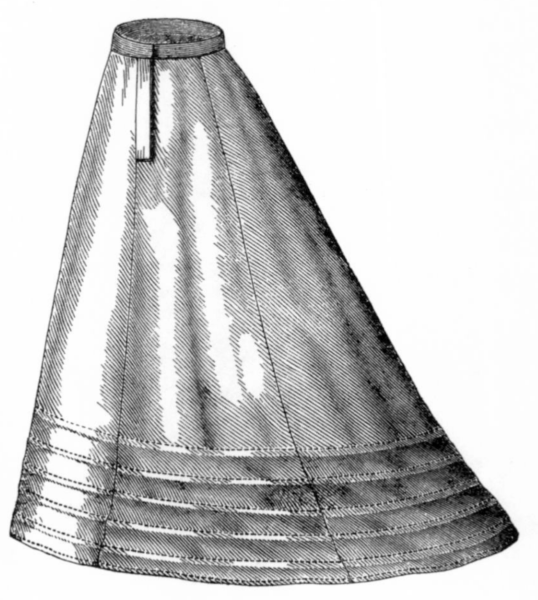

Crinoline

This crinoline may be made of muslin or woolen stuff. It has six small hoops around the bottom. Cut from the front one piece, and from the first side breadth, second side breadth, and back each two pieces. Cut double from the front and back belt.

Join the parts to correspond with the figures on the pattern. Hem the bottom. Put on tapes for the hoops, on the wrong side. Hem the edges of the slit, which is left open between the front and first side breadth from 1 to the top. On the left side of the skirt lay a single pleat in the top of the skirt from *x* to •. Put on the binding.

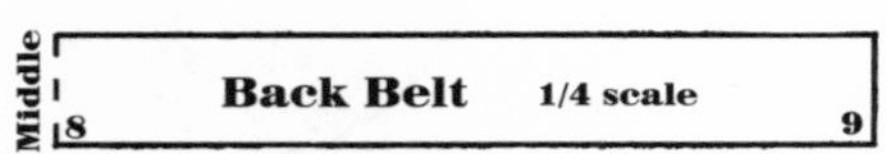

False Hem
1/4 scale
7
x
1

Crinoline

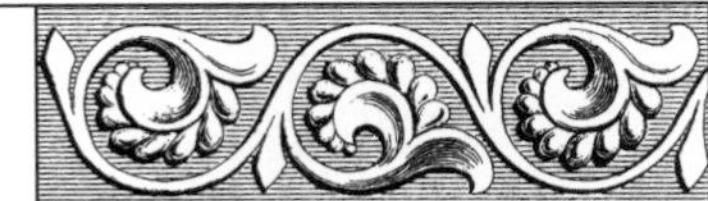

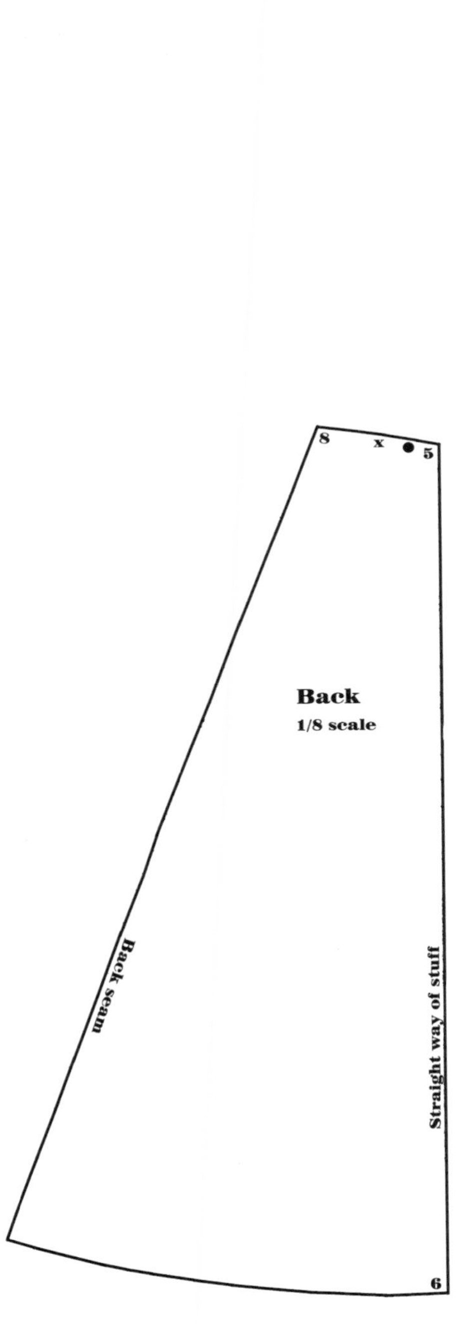

8
x
5
Back
1/8 scale
Back seam
Straight way of stuff
6

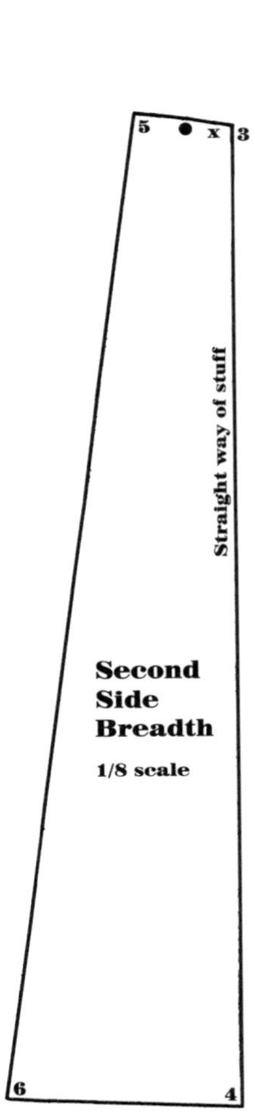

5
x
3
Straight way of stuff
Second Side Breadth
1/8 scale
6
4

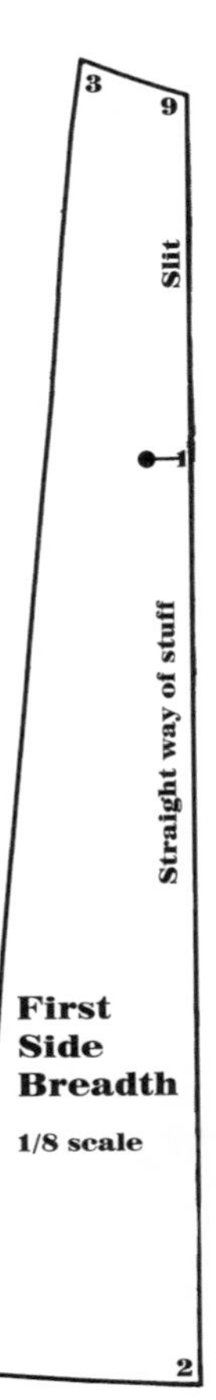

3
9
Slit
1
Straight way of stuff
First Side Breadth
1/8 scale
4
2

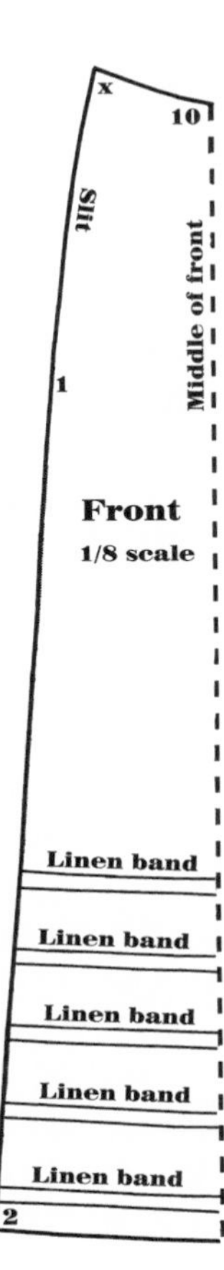

x
10
Slit
Middle of front
1
Front
1/8 scale
Linen band
Linen band
Linen band
Linen band
Linen band
2

December 21, 1867

Coiffures and Chignons

Chignons are again worn higher and more voluminous, spreading nearly over the entire back of the head. We give several illustrations of coiffures and chignons as arranged by some of the most celebrated hairdressers of Paris, together with descriptions whereby any lady can dress her own hair, or instruct others how to do so.

Except a large, curly loop behind and at the side, the coiffure in Figures 1 and 2 is entirely composed of torsades, well crisped to give them suppleness. The parting of the hair is left to the taste of the hairdresser, who, however, should be careful always to comb up the hair on the temples straight from the roots, and to well conceal the beginning and end of the torsades. The ornament consists of a cluster of volubilis.

Figure 1. Coiffure–front

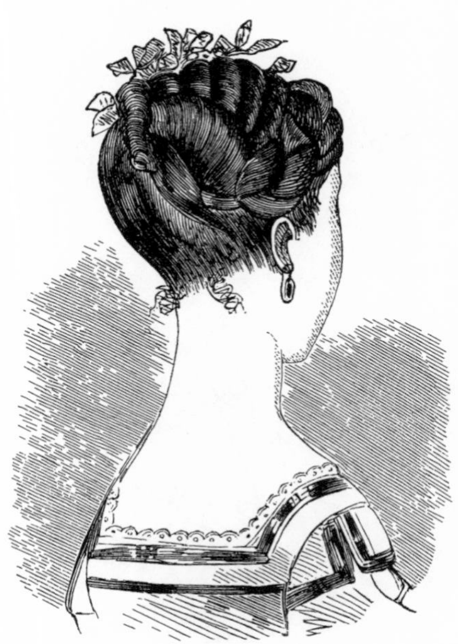

Figure 2. Coiffure–back

The coiffure in Figure 3 is a half peruke mounted on silk ribbon and springs, without hooks. It is fastened with pins just like a chignon. It may be dressed at the artist's residence and placed on the lady's head in an instant. The ornaments may also be changed as preferred.

Figure 3. Half peruke

To make the coiffure in Figure 4, after parting the hair, make two small raised bandeaux. The upper one must be tightly crisped. The chignon, of which only one side is seen, is quadrilled with large loops very slightly crisped. A loose torsade is put round the chignon. Add some light curls, an aigrette of wheatears, and some daisies.

Figure 4. Coiffure

To make the coiffure in Figure 5, separate a lock on the temples. Comb it up well after having crisped it to make it look voluminous. Make the parting very far backward. Then tress a loose plait to be placed on the top of the forehead, taking care to spread the branches. Behind, a chignon raised from below, accompanied by three or four curls. Place the ribbons as illustrated.

Figure 5. Coiffure

For the chignon in Figure 6, prepare a round shape made of wire or thin steel springs, and cover it with coarse net. Take a little more than 2 ounces of frizzed hair, 22 inches long. Make it into quadrilled tresses. Arrange them as in the illustration. That is, by turning the hair from the point to the end, and making a cluster of irregular loops, completing the whole by a few very light curls.

Figure 6. Chignon

Figure 7 is mounted on a shape made of wire, tulle, and ribbon, and is rather elongated in form. It requires 1 1/2 ounces of smooth hair and 1 ounce of crisped. The execution consists in rolling the branches on themselves and interlacing them.

Figure 7. Chignon

Figure 8 takes only 1 1/2 ounces of hair 1/2 yard long. This must be formed into a large roll, and a bow that can be easily completed with the lady's own hair, so as to imitate nature to perfection. The shape on which this chignon is mounted is triangular.

Figure 8. Chignon

The chignon in Figure 9 is mounted on a square shape. Make two torsades, one above the other, with hair 24 inches long, slightly crisped. Finish with a bow with two loops.

Figure 9. Chignon

Figure 10 is mounted on a round shape of ribbon wire. It requires 2 ounces of hair about 3/4 yard long, in tresses. The coiffure consists of five interlaced loops, and a torsade going round them.

Figure 10. Chignon

For the coiffure in Figures 11 and 12, part the hair from one ear to the other about 4 inches from the forehead. Divide it into five portions on each side by one horizontal and two vertical partings. With the front lock, touching the forehead, make a Mary Stuart bandeau, and a rolled bandeau over it. Form three bandeaux rolled under, the last of them meeting the loops of the chignon. These loops are rolled on the fingers from the end to the roots.

Make a large bow resting on the nape, but not covering it, also a few irregular loops on top of the head. Then place the ornaments as illustrated.

Figure 11. Coiffure–front

Figure 12. Coiffure–back

Figure 13 represents an ingenious method of lengthening the braids of one's own hair. Fasten tresses to the end of crêpés a little shorter than the former, then braid them in the hair. The hair thus covers the crêpés to the end, when the added hair is plaited in turn, forming a continuous braid that exhibits no break to the eye.

Figure 13. Braids

The curls in Figure 14 are designed to be worn behind the ears. They are confined with ribbons, as illustrated. They are concealed by short curls fastened on in like manner, or by the lady's own hair, suitably arranged.

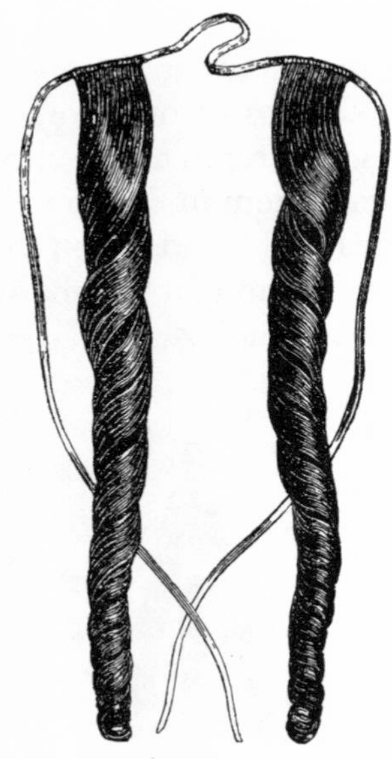

Figure 14. Curls

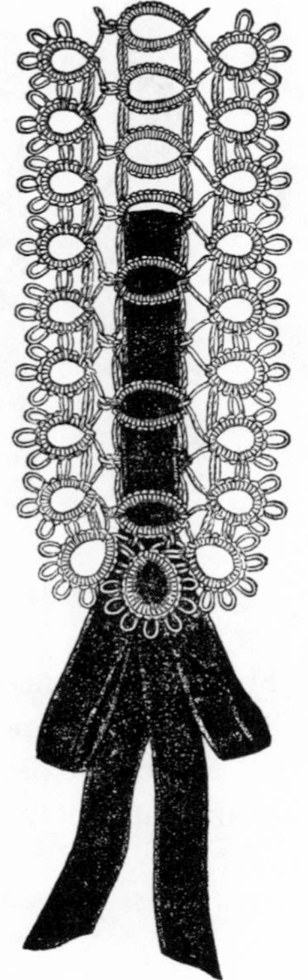

Cravat of Tatting and Velvet Ribbon

This cravat, one end of which is shown, is worked with tatting cotton No. 60.

Begin one end of the cravat with a large loop; first, 2 double stitches (1 to the right, 1 to the left). Work 1 picot or purl stitch, 4 double stitches, 1 picot, 5 double stitches, 1 picot, 2 double stitches, 1 picot, 2 double stitches, 1 picot, 9 double stitches, 1 picot, 2 double stitches. * Leave about 1/5 inch thread between the loops, which must stand opposite each other. Work 2 double stitches, 1 picot, 3 double stitches, 1 picot. Make 2 double stitches and 1 picot four times, 3 double stitches, 1 picot, 2 double stitches. After finishing the second loop, again leave 1/5 inch of thread.

Turn the work so that the large ring that is finished will be turned upward. Work 2 double stitches, fasten to the 1st picot of the first loop 9 double stitches, and attach to the picot in the first loop that follows the 9 double stitches, 2 double stitches, 1 picot, 2 double stitches, 1 picot, 9 double stitches, 1 picot, 2 double stitches. Form into a loop; turn the little loop upward.

Cravat

Repeat from * till the work is as long as you wish the cravat to be. However, in the little loops, instead of working the 2 picots, attach to the last and the one before the last picot of the preceding loop. The last large loop on the other end of the cravat must be like the loop described first on the outside, between the 2 picots, instead of making 9 stitches work 4 double, 1 picot, 5 double.

After finishing this last large loop work for the border of the cravat, leaving again 1/5 inch space, a smaller loop which is to be attached to the picot of the former little loop in the corresponding place. Fasten the thread to the next picot of the large loop. Make a little loop like the former, only instead of 2 double, 1 picot repeated four times, make 2 double, 1 picot and repeat five times. Attach to the next picot of the large loop one loop like the former, only make 2 double and 1 picot eight times instead of five times. Attach to the last picot of the last large loop.

Then after having worked the end of the border, work the long side of the border all in little loops, as described in the beginning, and after finishing each loop, attach the working thread to the free picot in the middle of each large loop.

After finishing this row, work the other end like the first. Finally, run through the middle row of loops a narrow velvet ribbon of any desired color. Finish the ends of the cravat with a loop and ends of the ribbon.

December 28, 1867

Diamonds and Pearls

Beginning with jewelry, diamonds and pearls, of course, take precedence. A diamond brooch, larger than the palm of the hand, attracts special admiration. It is a floral design; the rose, leaves, and stem made of innumerable small diamonds. The setting nowhere obtrudes itself. The jewels are placed on fine projecting points, almost invisible, beneath which is a spiral coil or spring that vibrates with the slightest motion, keeping the diamonds in a constant quiver, and displaying their brilliancy to the greatest advantage.

A bridal parure of pearls consists of brooch, earrings, necklace, and bracelet. Twenty of the rose pearls are as large as a good-sized pea, and several pear-shaped pendants are still larger. This is said to be the most valuable set of pearls for sale in the United States.

Opals, Emeralds, Etc.

Among colored stones opals and emeralds are always fashionable for full evening dress. Sapphires and rubies are in high favor. Amethysts, garnets, and malachite are passé. Turquoise, coral, and topaz are in vogue; carbuncles are obsolete.

Neapolitan Coral

The delicate rose-pink coral is more desirable than the deep red. The designs are after the antique, classical, and Egyptian. Coral cameos represent the full face instead of profile. Semicircular brooches have a rose coral in the center, with conical pieces radiating above and beside it, and long pendants beneath. Very little gold is visible in these styles.

A full parure of Naples coral contains a brooch, eardrops, comb, necklace, bracelet, and buttons for sleeves and corsage. It is of the rare mottled coral. Shells of Etruscan gold hold large rose corals in the center. Long pendants of coral, tipped with gold.

A coral cameo of rich peachblossom tint is a bacchante crowned with vine leaves and clusters of grapes. The veins of the leaves and the luxuriant hair are cut with marvelous accuracy. The set includes earrings and pin. A less expensive set is a bunch of roses and buds. The coral is fine and exquisitely carved, but the flowers are formed of small bits of little value. The petals of the rose are transparent, and consequently very fragile.

Byzantine Mosaics

The Byzantine mosaics are far more beautiful than the Roman and Florentine. They are made of smaller stones, and are of more varied and brilliant colors. This is a reproduction of an art known to the ancients, but which was lost for a long time. The aid of the microscope is necessary to appreciate the perfection of these artistic gems. Birds of brilliant plumage and flowers of richest color and luster are formed of tiny stones, with all the accuracy of painting. They are mounted with Etruscan gold, and fashioned in quaint medieval styles and after Egyptian models. An emblematic cross, a peculiarly Catholic gift, is made in commemoration of the late conclave of bishops. A miniature locket has a cherub in mosaics on one side, and the word "eros" on the other. Satyrs, sphinxes, scarabaei, doves, and groups of cherubs are favorite mosaic designs.

Enameled Painting and Etruscan Gold

The process of burning enamel into gold is a secret known only to a few. A mythological set represents the chase of the fleet-footed Atalanta, an elaborate design carefully carried out. It includes brooch and earrings.

There are many pretty devices in a simple style of enameling that are less expensive. Flowers, feathers, beetles, dragonflies, and scorpions are imitated to the life. A handsome set is a wreath of bluebells enameled on gold. The stamens are gold tipped with diamonds. A concealed spring keeps the flowers in constant motion. Clusters of violets, a single pansy, and lilies of the valley, a pure white spray on a dark green leaf, are made up in sets. A silver brooch represents a brown ostrich feather, enameled in all the Bismarck shades. A bonnet pin is a butterfly with ruby eyes and diamond-tipped wings. The antennae and wings are found to be perfect when examined through a microscope.

Plain Etruscan jewelry, or dead gold as it is sometimes called, is intended for morning wear. There are some new designs–heavy, massive bars of gold, scallop shells, and emblematic insignia, always with pendants or fringe.

Cameos, Onyx, and Sardonyx

Cameos are again becoming fashionable. The Madonna, Psyche, Ceres, and allegorical scenes are cut in white on a dark ground. Sardonyx is a favorite stone for cameos. The value of the stone depends on the number of different parallel strata of various colors. The settings are of finely wrought gold, inlaid with diamonds, pearls, and rubies.

A sardonyx pin is cut to show three layers of different color in the same stone. The background is dark brown, the profile pure white, and over the abundant curls is drapery of the clearest amber. The setting is studded with pearls.

Another brooch represents a Madonna. The head and bust are exquisitely cut in immaculate white on a dark ground. The setting is of diamonds and black enamel. Earrings to match. Still another is a square pink onyx with a fancy scene in clear white. The design is of little value, but the workmanship is excellent. The mounting is of white roses made of pearls, and leaves of fine diamonds in Etruscan gold twining about the branches. Beneath is a fringe of gold, tipped with diamonds. Mythological subjects are in good taste for cameos. One set represents on the pin Music, and on the earrings the muses of Painting and Literature. Orpheus with his lyre, Neptune with his trident riding the waves, and many other designs are displayed.

Ebony onyx, in solid pieces like coral, has taken the place of jet for mourning jewelry.

Necklaces, Lockets, Etc.

Flexible gold necklaces are formed of massive yellow links, which nevertheless are as pliant and light as a silk ribbon. Lockets of Etruscan gold, or clasps with long pendants, ornament them in front. Some of the devices for these lockets are beautiful and original. Cameos cut in opals set with diamonds, lattice of turquoise with diamonds set in the interstices, squares of pink onyx with Etruscan beaded borders, amethysts with monograms and flowers in pearls or diamonds, enameled pictures and mosaics dazzle the eye.

Handsome glove clasps are of emerald and amethyst with diamond initials. Filigree chains connect them, to which little jingling bells are attached.

Jeweled buttons for sleeves and corsage, and girdle ornaments, are made of Etruscan gold with centers of pearl, amethyst, or emerald, to suit the dress color. Solid malachite, coral, and turquoise are left plain without any gold setting.

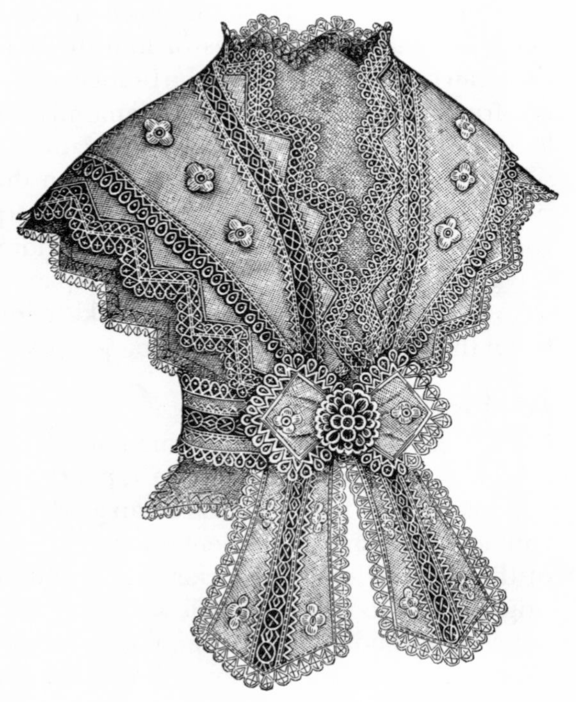

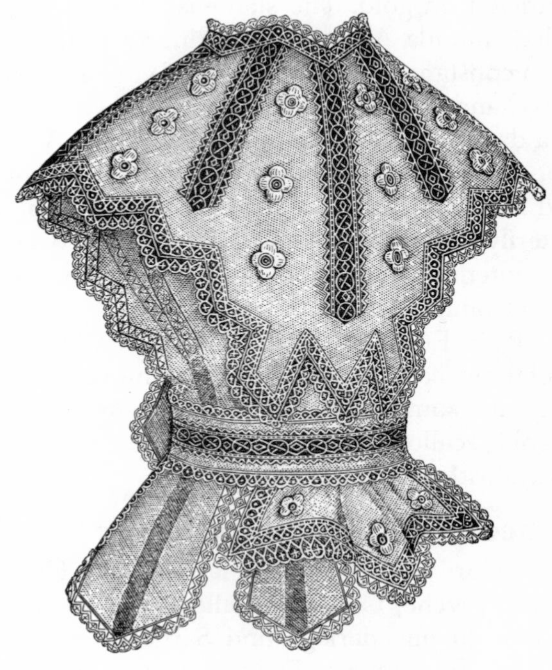

Fichu with Belt

This elegant fichu is set on a belt, and furnished with a small lappet behind. The principal material is fine muslin. The trimming consists of guipure insertion and edging, with needlework application figures over pink silk.

Cut the two fronts of muslin, and the back and lappet, each whole. Sew on the embroidery shown in Figures 1 and 2. Join the back and fronts to correspond with the figures on the pattern. Put on the insertion, hem the fronts, and set on the edging. Lay the lappet in pleats from *x* to •. Put on the trimming as shown. Finish with a bow, for which cut two pieces. Edge them with lace, lay in pleats from * to ••, and loop them. Finish in the center with a circular needlework figure edged with lace.

Figure 1. Embroidery

Figure 2. Embroidery

Fichu with Belt

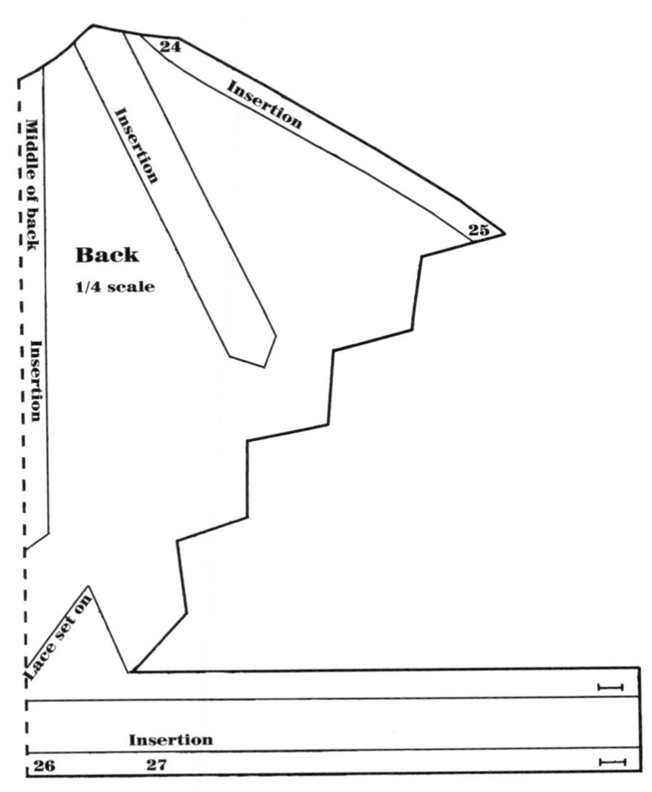

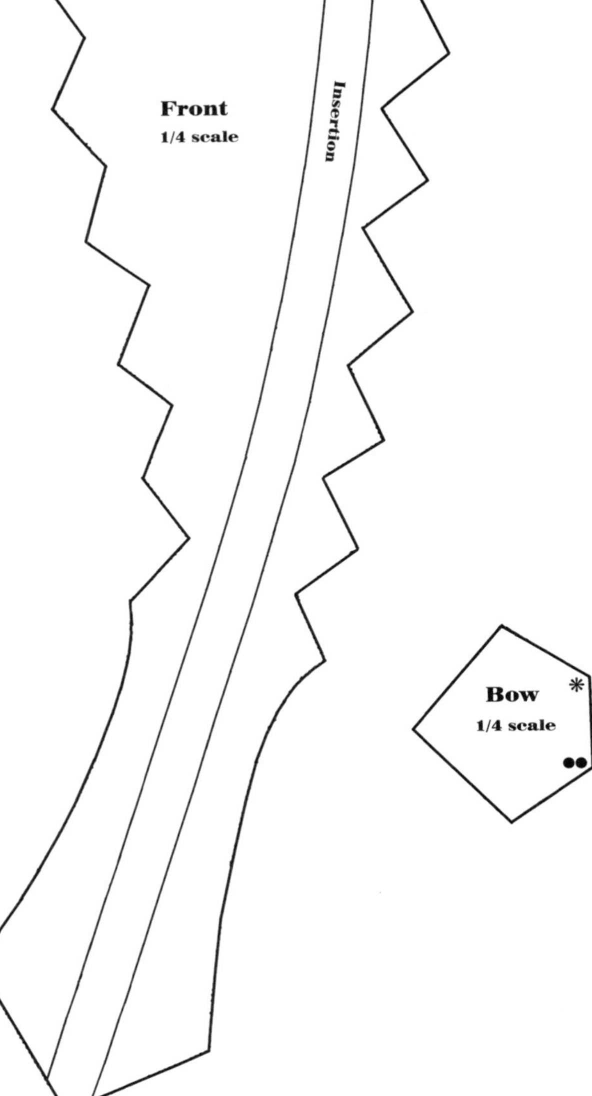

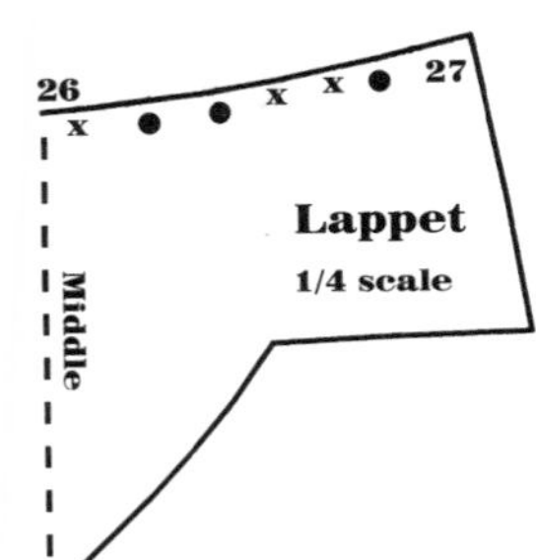

Bow
1/4 scale

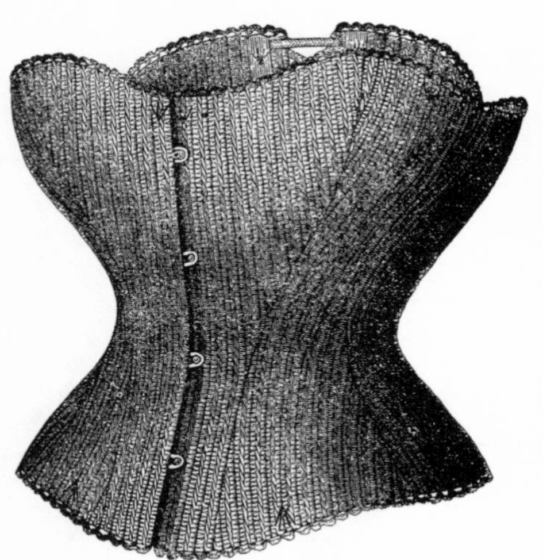

Crocheted Corset

This corset is of yarn or worsted, worked in single crochet backward and forward, making ribbed crochet–two rows make a ridge. It must be worked very tight, taking up both loops of the stitch. Half the corset is given. Before beginning the work the parts of the pattern must be cut in thin muslin, or some kind of lining stuff. Put them together according to the numbers, then take it as a measuring pattern for the crochet work. After having the given shape it will be easy to make such a corset larger or smaller.

Begin at the back of the corset. Make a chain of 134 stitches; crochet two rows. In the third row the eyelet holes are made–after every 8 stitches make 2 chain; miss 2 stitches of the former row. In the fourth row crochet over these 2 chain stitches in single crochet. Then make 38 rows, and on the upper edge narrow according to the pattern.

With the forty-third row begin on the lower edge the hip gore. Crochet only on the first 54 stitches two rows. To make the bias side of the gore, in every first ribbed row of the following 14 rows leave off 6 stitches at the upper end of these 54 stitches. There will be only 12 stitches left. Then lengthen the rows in the same way they were shortened, by adding the same number of stitches at the upper end of the following sixteen rows. With thirty-two rows the gore is finished. Then work over the whole row of stitches, narrowing at the upper edge and increasing at the lower, according to the pattern shape.

The second and third hip gores are crocheted in a similar manner. Between the second and third gore work two rows three times on the lower edge to give it sufficient width. Crochet up to 46 or 48 stitches on the lower edge. The same is done on the upper edge.

From the front and back patterns crochet the waist on about 60 stitches, counting from the upper edge; first sixteen rows, and again for the bias side of the gore a sufficient number of stitches must be left off till only 10 remain on the upper edge. The same thing must be done on the lower edge of the corset to correspond with the pattern.

Then crochet the breast gore like the hip gore, adding as many stitches in the second row as have before been left off. But as this gore becomes much larger there are more rows to crochet, and these forty rows must correspond to the sixteen rows before crocheted. All the front parts are finished according to the pattern.

When both parts of the corset are finished, crochet on the upper edge little scallops as follows. * Work 1 single crochet in 1 stitch of the edge, and a little picot which consists of 4 chain, 1 single crochet in the 1st of the chain. With this picot skip a sufficient number of stitches. Repeat from *.

As shown on the pattern, put on the back worsted tape for holding the whalebones and for the clasps in front. Through the holes lace crossways woolen cord.

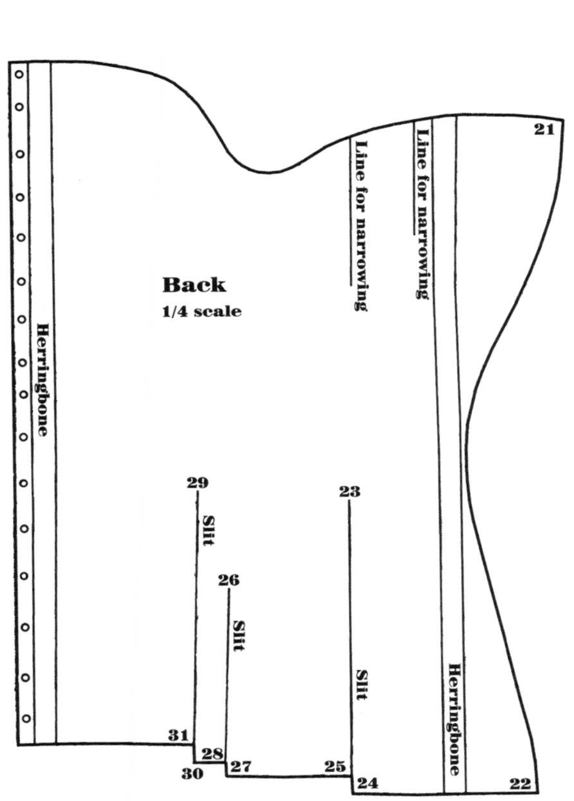

21
Line for narrowing
Line for narrowing
Back
1/4 scale
Herringbone
29
Slit
26
Slit
23
Slit
Herringbone
31
28
30
27
25
24
22

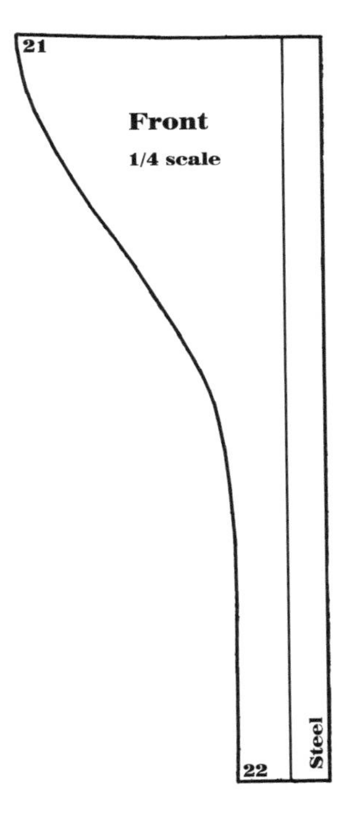

21
Front
1/4 scale
22
Steel

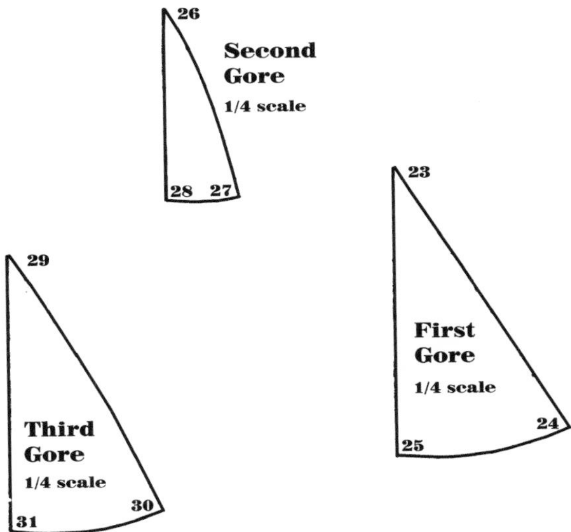

26
Second
Gore
1/4 scale
28
27
23
First
Gore
1/4 scale
24
25
29
Third
Gore
1/4 scale
30
31

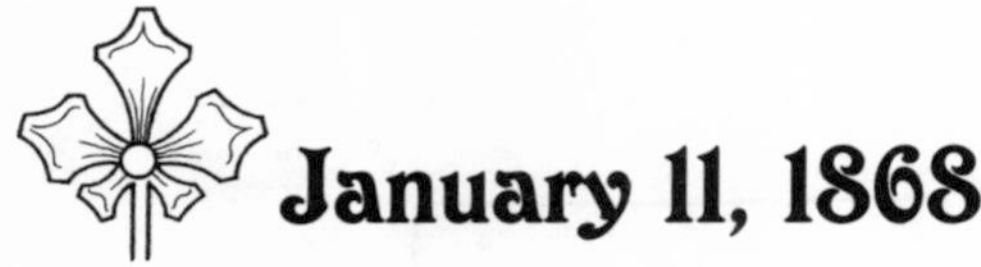

January 11, 1868

Swansdown Opera Cloaks

Some opera cloaks just imported are made of swansdown. They are as warm as ermine. They hang more gracefully, as they have not the stiff skin of the animal beneath them, and are far more light and fleecy in appearance. Tufts of the down are sewn on muslin so closely together that it has the appearance of a woven fabric. They are circular shaped, and ornamented with insertions of the down dyed a Bismarck color, arranged in diamonds and in vines. Lining of cherry-colored silk, wadded and quilted. White silk cord, with camel's hair tassels.

Skating Costumes

Toilettes Russe, or fur-trimmed costumes in imitation of the Russians, are fashionable for skating suits. A pretty one of Bismarck ottoman reps has a plain skirt reaching to the ankle. A loose redingote, falling below the knee, is lapped diagonally from throat to hem. Coat sleeves and belt with long sash. A 2-inch border of mink fur, a lighter brown than the dress, surrounds the redingote and the edge of the skirt. Brown velvet toquet with band of fur. Brown cloth boots bordered with mink at the ankle, and gloves of undressed kid with fur wristlets.

Another fur-trimmed suit is of maroon velour. A high, round corsage and gored skirt just escaping the ground. Plain waist. Tight sleeves and skirt bordered by a wide band of sealskin, dyed maroon. There is a sealskin belt, to which is attached a monchoir bag of the same material. A jaunty, short basque of the fur is sufficiently tight fitting to display the figure. Sealskin toquet with a short, ostrich tuft on the side and brown lace veil merely covering the face. Black boots with sealskin gaiters reaching to the knee. No crinoline. Gloves with back and gauntlet of seal.

Very gay colors in contrast with dark shades are chosen for skating dresses. Gray with scarlet or blue is popular. Bright plaid poplins with plush jackets are pretty, but should be worn only by experienced skaters, who are not liable to accidents, as they are easily soiled. Cloth is the most fashionable material for these suits. Embroidery is sometimes used for trimming them, but is not so appropriate as fur or bands of plain velvet or plush. Heavy corded fringes are also used. Blue and green cloths are handsomely and inexpensively trimmed with bands of gray plush imitating chinchilla fur. Hats of the plush with aigrette of feathers.

Dress with Double-Breasted Waist

This gored dress is well suited for home or street wear. The skirt is straight at the bottom, without a train, and pleated in back. The original is of winsey, effectively trimmed with broad and narrow black worsted braid and passementerie buttons. The waist is closed in front with similar buttons, with the upper part of the right side rolling over.

For the skirt, cut the front breadth, the two side breadths, and the two back breadths. Sew up the breadths, making the figures on the pattern correspond. Leave a slit on the left side from 11 to the top. Hem the latter narrow. Set on a false hem of double stuff. Face the bottom of the skirt about 4 inches wide with the same material. If this is not sufficiently heavy, face the skirt with a strip of buckram 1/4 yard wide. Pleat the back breadths, and set on a binding of double stuff. In the slit remaining from * to • set a muslin pocket, faced with the dress material, and trim it as illustrated.

For the waist, cut the right front. Cut the left allowing for a hem 1 1/4 inches wide. Cut the two side pieces. Cut the back and collar, the last of double stuff. Cut the sleeves from the pattern for the Waist with Rolling Collar.

Lay the bosom pleats and hem the left front. Then join the parts, making the figures on the pattern correspond. Put on the standing collar. Hem the bottom of the waist narrow. Put on the trimming as illustrated. The dotted line marks where the right side rolls over, which must be noticed in setting on the trimming. In sewing the braid on the front edge of the right front, the latter is fastened to

January 11, 1868

the stuff beneath, and a loop of braid is put on to correspond with a button on the left side.

Sew up the sleeves from 13 to 14 and from 15 to 16. Face the bottom about 4 inches wide with the same material. Put on the trimming. Lay a pleat in the top of the under part. Set them in the armholes, covering the seam with narrow braid sewn on flat.

The belt is 2 1/2 inches wide. It is made of the dress material, with a stiff interlining. It is trimmed with wide braid.

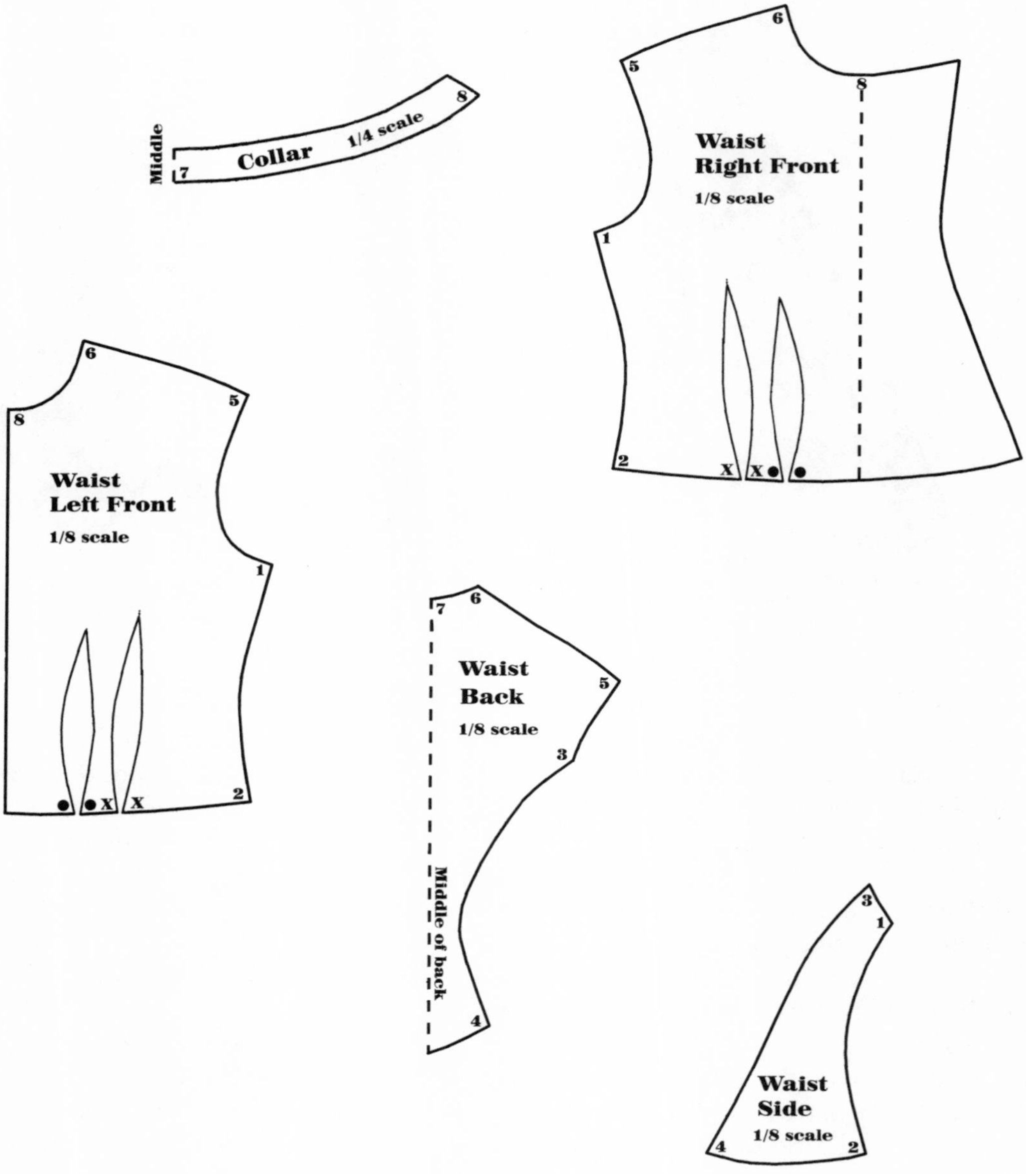

Collar 1/4 scale

Waist Right Front 1/8 scale

Waist Left Front 1/8 scale

Waist Back 1/8 scale

Middle of back

Waist Side 1/8 scale

Dress

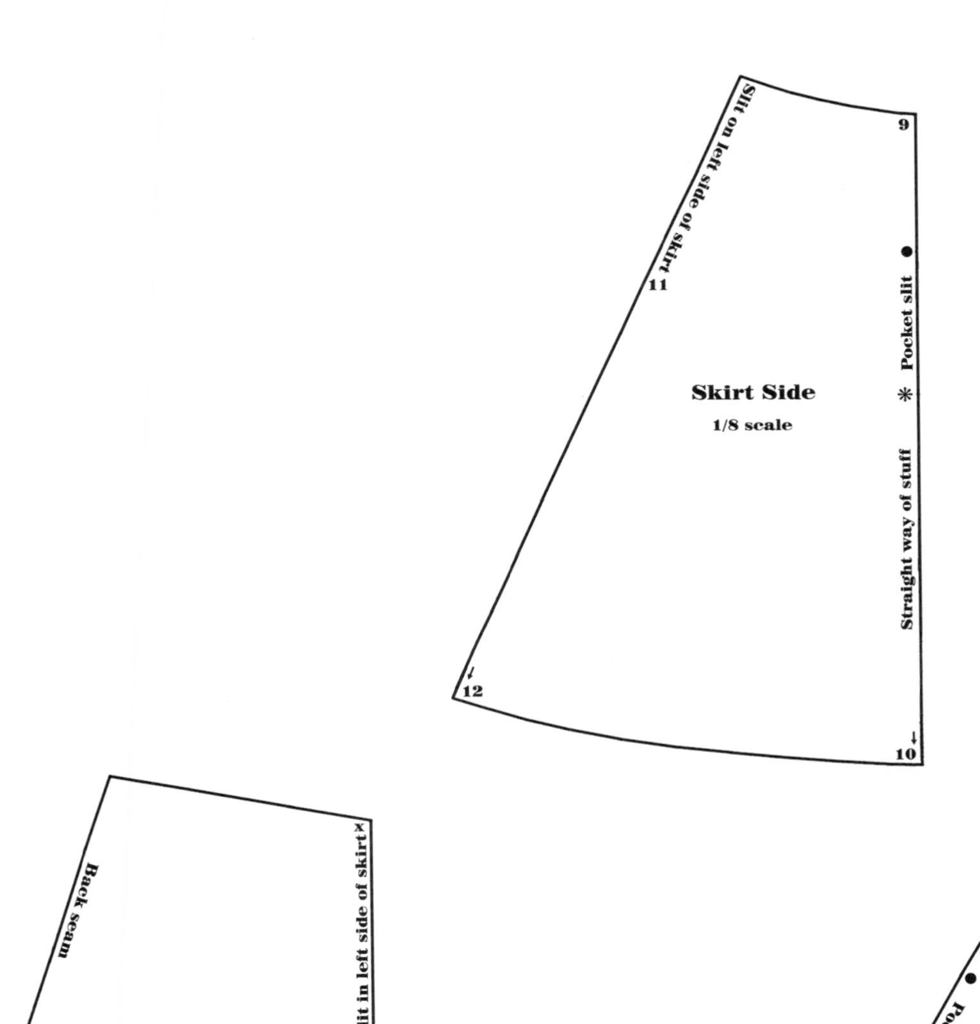

Skirt Side
1/8 scale
Slit on left side of skirt
Pocket slit
Straight way of stuff
9
11
12
10

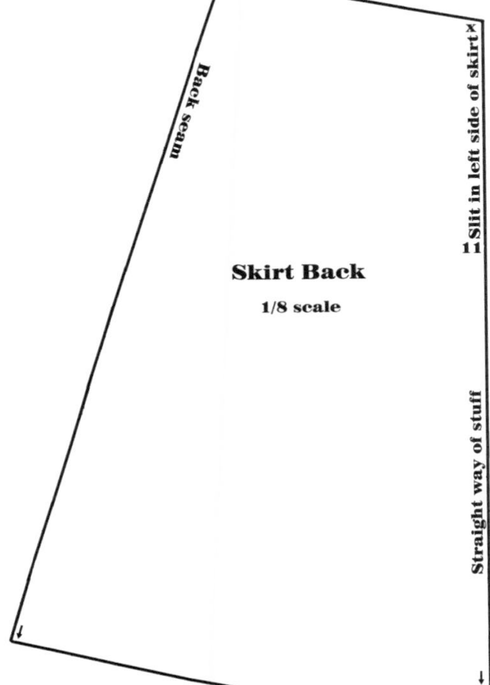

Skirt Back
1/8 scale
Back seam
Slit in left side of skirt
Straight way of stuff
11
12

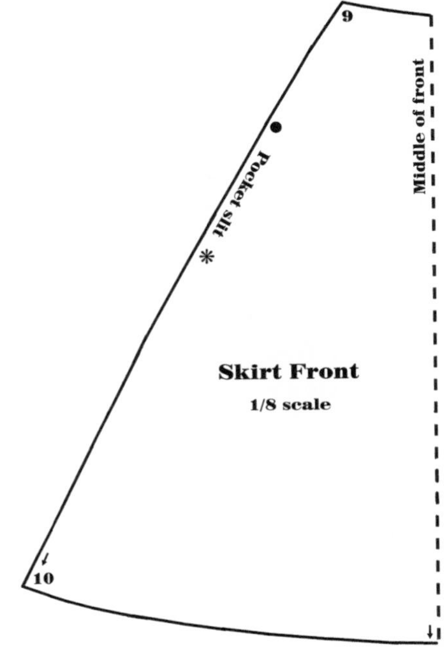

Skirt Front
1/8 scale
Pocket slit
Middle of front
9
10

January 11, 1868

Waist with Rolling Collar

This waist is of white cashmere, with a rolling collar faced with red silk. It is trimmed with bias folds of red silk, cashmere, silk cord, and red and white crocheted buttons.

Cut the fronts, the back whole, and both parts of the sleeves. From the collar and sleeve trimming cut each two pieces of red silk, cashmere, and interlining. Join the back and fronts. Sew the collar together in the back and set it on. Make a narrow hem round the edge of the waist. Sew up the sleeves from 13 to 14 and from 15 to 16. Set on the trimming, and sew them in the armholes.

Waist with Rolling Collar

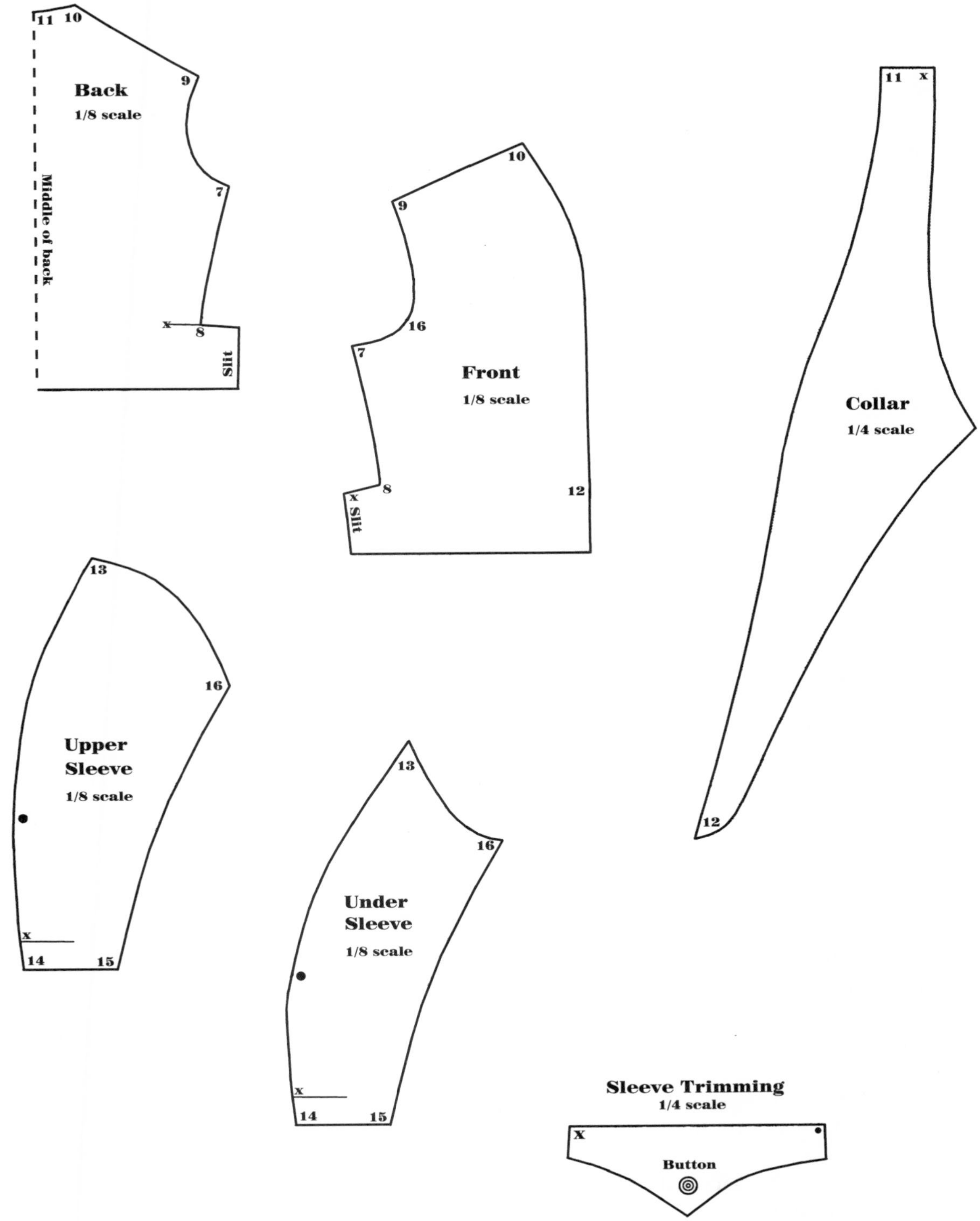

11 10

Back

1/8 scale

9

7

Middle of back

x 8

Slit

10

9

16

7

Front

1/8 scale

x 8

Slit

12

11 x

Collar

1/4 scale

12

13

16

Upper Sleeve

1/8 scale

x

14 15

13

16

Under Sleeve

1/8 scale

x

14 15

Sleeve Trimming

1/4 scale

X

Button

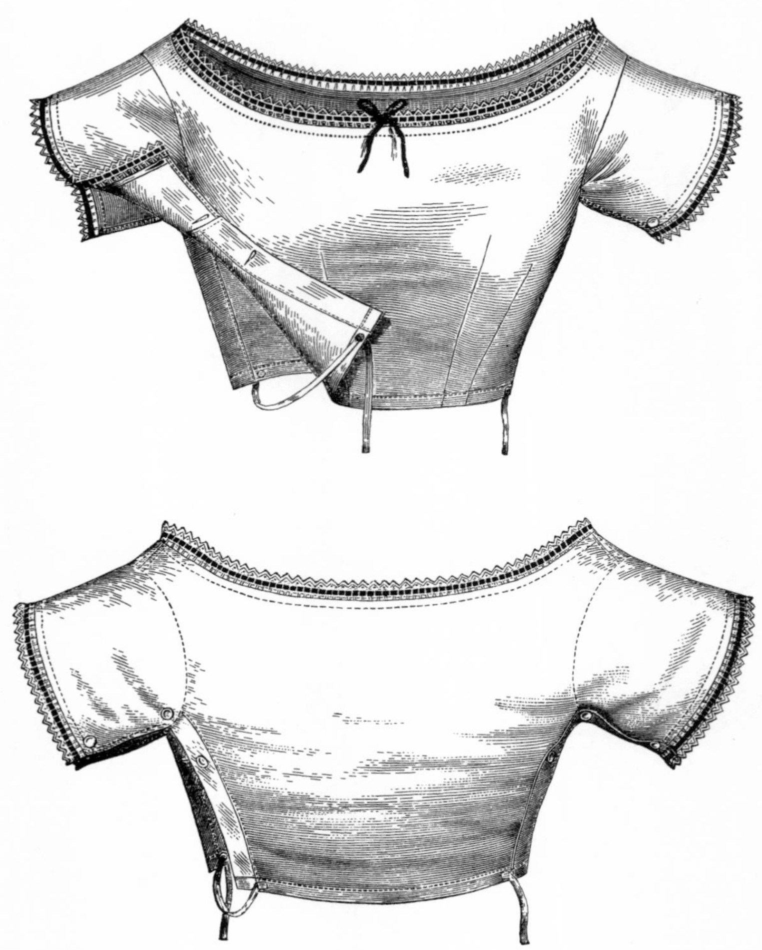

Under Waist

This waist, which buttons at the side, is designed to be worn under thin dresses, which show so plainly the buttons on under waists that fasten in front. It must be drawn on over the head. It is made of muslin or linen.

Cut the front and back, each in one piece, allowing on each 1 inch for a hem at the sides. Cut the sleeves.

Lay the bosom pleats in front. Also lay a pleat as marked in the middle of the back. Hem the sides. Put on the buttons and buttonholes as marked on the front. Sew up the shoulders from 23 to 24. Hem the sleeves on the bottom and sides, and set on buttons and buttonholes as illustrated. Sew the sleeves on the waist to correspond with the figures on the pattern. Bind the bottom of the waist with a strip of muslin or linen about 1 inch wide. Run through a piece of tape, which passes through an eyelet hole in front to tie the waist. Trim the neck and sleeves with lace, through which run a narrow velvet ribbon.

Under Waist

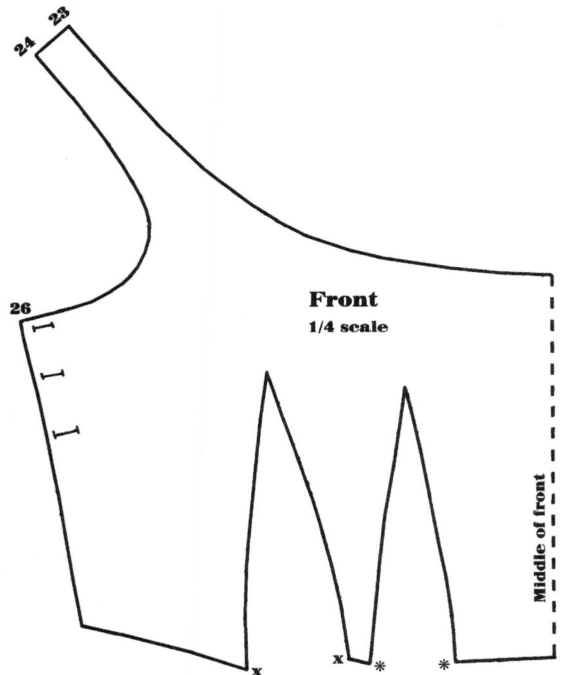

24
23
26
Front
1/4 scale
Middle of front
x
x
*
*

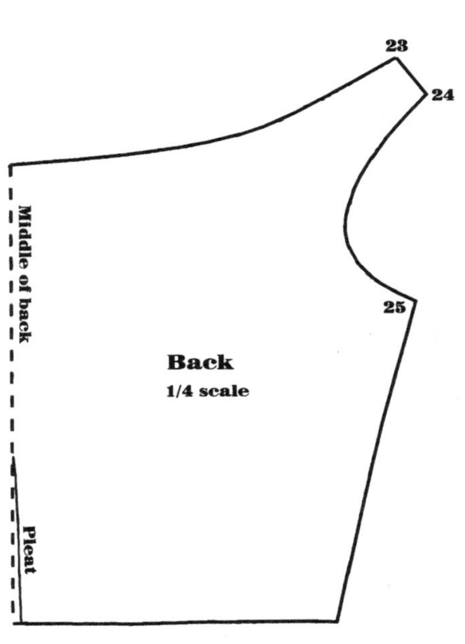

23
24
Middle of back
25
Back
1/4 scale
Pleat

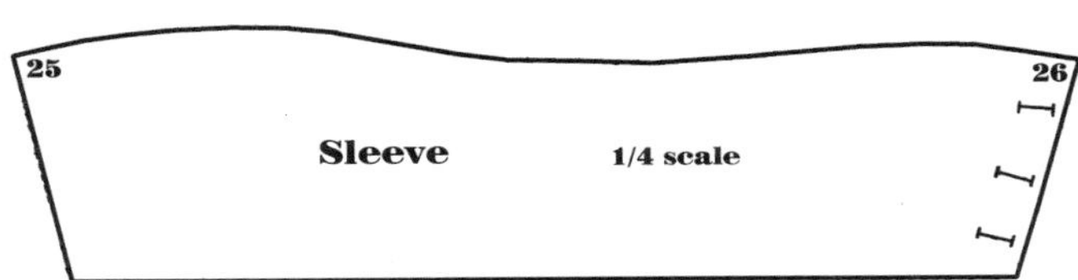

25
26
Sleeve
1/4 scale

January 11, 1868

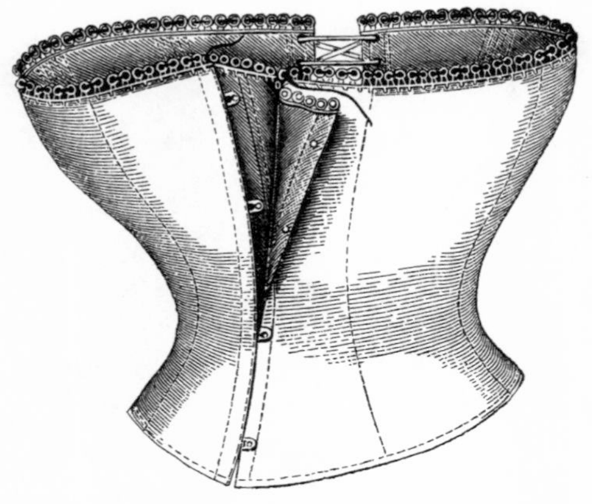

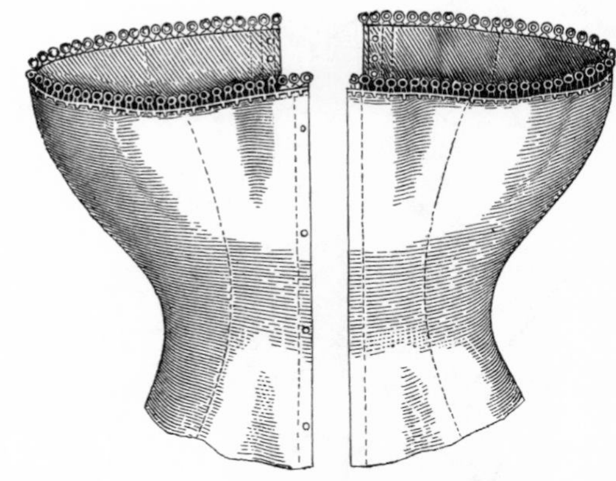

Corset Cover

This cover is an excellent protection for corsets, which lose their shape by being often washed. The illustrations show the cover separate, and fitted on the corset. The original is of linen, trimmed round the neck with tatted lace, the corset being trimmed in a similar manner. A narrow band is run through both edges. The cover is fastened in front with buttons and cord loops. The back is laced with the corset.

Cut from all four pattern pieces each two pieces, allowing for the seam. In the front and back allow besides 1 inch for the hem. Make the hem. Work the eyelets as illustrated. Stitch the parts together, making the figures on the pattern correspond. Hem the top and bottom.

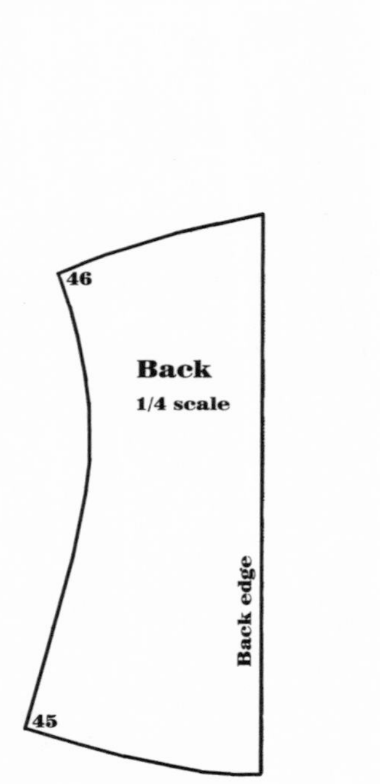

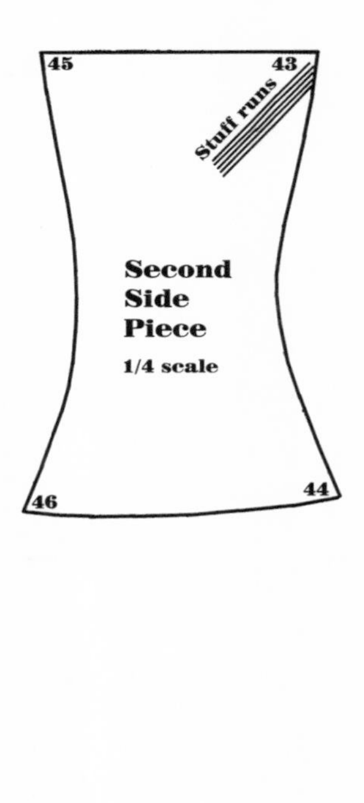

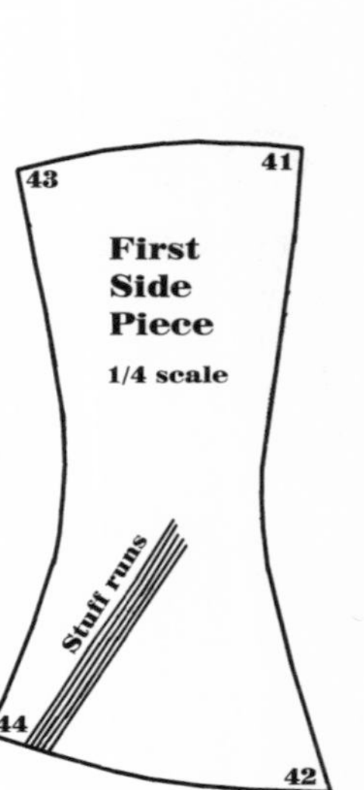

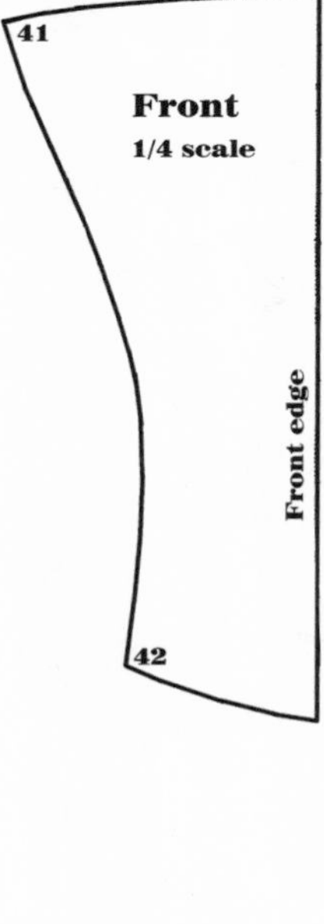

January 18, 1868

Bonnets

The fanchon is exceedingly small, and is still a favorite. The Marie Antoinette, shorn of some of its disagreeable features, is also worn; but the most popular hat is a medium between these. It is short at the ears like the Empire bonnet, is fitted snugly to the head, has a brim and the upper half of a crown, and is exceedingly comfortable. Black velvet bonnets of this shape, the material laid plain on the frame, trimmed with folds of the same or of satin, are neat and stylish. A band of scarlet velvet is over the forehead, with a cluster of rosebuds on the left. Narrow satin strings and Spanish veils are worn with these shapes as well as the fanchon.

A few of the feather and fur bonnets, now so fashionable in Europe, have just been imported. The feathers used are those of the grebe and pheasant. The white and pearl gray grebes are bound with green, scarlet, or blue velvet. Bonnets of dark pheasant's feathers have a fall of brown lace, and are trimmed with ornaments of gold and cut steel.

Sealskin is the handsomest fur for bonnets. When the best quality is used it rivals velvet in elegance, and is warm and comfortable without being heavy. Chinchilla is another smooth, light fur much used. Some Astrakhan and Persiani bonnets are imported, with cloaks and muffs to correspond; but they look clumsy and heavy.

Flat round toquets and turbans, both of fur and feathers, are worn with short promenade suits. They are also well adapted for skating costumes.

Street Suits

Suits of black satin and of silk velvet are used for church and visiting. Very little material is required, and this is sufficiently handsome to dispense with elaborate trimming. On satin dresses folds of the same arranged in Greek blocks, or crocheted passementerie without jet, is a handsome trimming. Belts over the paletot or redingote are formed of folds, to which are attached three large jet rings. A wide satin sash, ornamented with passementerie, is looped through the rings. Bands of fur are most suitable for velvet. Gray and black Astrakhan, sealskin, or chinchilla are preferred.

The new figured velveteens are much admired, and are much less expensive than velvet. Dark shades of purple and brown are striped with satin of the same shade. Others are spotted with small dots, and again there is a latticed pattern. Maroon is a favorite color in these goods, but we see more purple costumes at present than any other color.

For plainer suits cloth and serge are the most acceptable material. Sailor's blue, "Humboldt" purple, and olive green are fashionably worn. The trimming is embroidery in silk, or a wide black worsted braid. These costumes are suitable for shopping and morning walks, and should be made plainly, without any effort at display. The bonnet and gloves should be of the same shade.

Miscellaneous Items

For the convenience of dancers short ball dresses are coming into favor. The trains now so necessary for full dress are objects of censure to gentlemen, and occasion a good deal of annoyance to their wearers. The new Pompadour trains are more easily managed, as they are left open in front and may be thrown over the arm in a crowd.

Dresses for demitoilette are lapped at the waist in the redingote style. A velvet ribbon or the fashionable jeweled collar with a locket is worn around the neck.

Bretelles of black velvet and guipure lace are fashionably worn with self-colored dresses of empress cloth or velour. Sailor collars of fine linen, deeply pointed at the sides, are pretty for morning wear.

Crocheted Garter

This garter is made of red worsted, in a kind of afghan stitch, worked lengthwise. Red silk elastic is run through each broken row. Buttons and loops are used for fastening. The place where it is fastened is covered with a crocheted rosette.

Make of the red worsted a chain of the required length. Upon this work the first part of the first pattern row as follows. Out of the 5 last chain make a stitch by inserting the needle into the 6th chain, putting the thread once around the needle and drawing it through. Then make 3 chain; these 3 chain form a long stitch. Make 1 of these long stitches in every 2nd chain. As in the afghan stitch, the last loop of every long stitch must remain on the needle. Now work back, dropping each loop, making 1 chain between. Make three of these rows, and the garter will be wide enough. At the beginning of the second and third rows 3 chain must be made, and the long stitches must always be directly over one another.

The elastic must not be quite as long as the garter, so that the work will be a little full. Run it through the loops, between the long stitches in front and the single threads at the back, as shown in Figure 1. Fasten the ends carefully.

Figure 1. Part of garter–full size

For the rosette, make with the red worsted a chain of 6 stitches; form it into a round with a slip stitch. * Take up the next chain, put the thread once around the needle and make 1 stitch. Make 9 similar single crochet stitches in the same chain stitch. To give these 10 single crochet stitches the form of a loop, take up the next chain and make in it 1 slip stitch, not putting the thread around the needle. Repeat from * five times.

Second row of the rosette: Between every 2 loops make 1 single crochet; after every single crochet 1 chain. The third row is a row of loops like the first, but the loops must always be made in the chain stitches of the former row. Make, by turns, in 1 chain 1 loop, and in the next chain 2 loops. This row will now contain 9 loops.

Having worked so far, the rosette is easily finished. The original contains four rows of loops, in which the number of loops is increased as much as necessary. A row like the second row must be worked between every row of loops.

Sew the rosette, when finished, to the garter in its proper place.

January 25, 1868

Mourning Goods

Bombazine has long been considered the most suitable dress for deep mourning. The English bombazine, a dead black without gloss, is preferable to the lustrous French goods with silk warp. Bias folds of the same, or of English crêpe, are appropriate trimming. Very little jet is used. Good taste demands a nunlike simplicity and absence of ornament.

French serge, a new material this season, is very much sought after. It is a mixture of silk and wool, heavier than bombazine, and a trifle wider, measuring 38 inches. The double twill is very distinct. This goods is far superior to the colored English serge now worn for street suits. It is soft and fine, falling into graceful folds. Nine yards are sufficient for a lady of medium height.

A similar material is called Henrietta cloth. It differs from serge in having an almost invisible twill, and is heavier and wider than bombazine.

Corded Materials

An extra-heavy goods for midwinter is found in the ottoman reps. Heavily corded, and not so lustrous as poplin, this is used in the deepest mourning for street suits. Ten yards makes the short dress and paletot. French poplins are also used for street dresses. Empress and Biarritz cloths are soft, pliant, corded materials. In empress cloth the cord is horizontal, in the Biarritz perpendicular. The average quantity for a dress is 10 yards. Black Irish poplin is sold; the tabrinette or double-corded poplin is the heaviest and best of all.

Crêpe Cloths

A handsome dress goods resembling crêpe is called Eugenie crêpe at some establishments, at others Balmoral crêpe. As it is 2 yards wide, only 4 yards are required for a dress. Australian crêpe is narrower, measuring 40 inches. Eight yards is the average quantity sold for a dress. Barathea is a beautiful wavy fabric 1 1/4 yards wide.

English Serge and Mohair Fabrics

The fashionable English serge is all wool, but feels so harsh to the touch one would suppose it part cotton. It has a broad twill, is waterproof, and is suitable for street dresses. It is trimmed for mourning and colors alike with wide woolen braid. Fourteen yards make a dress and redingote.

A double-width delaine, called tamise cloth, is a soft, smooth material, intended for house dresses. This is the only form in which the once popular delaines are now used, and the soft velvety merinos are left on the shelves uncalled for. They are disliked because it is impossible to brush them without making the surface rough. Queen's cloth is a mohair fabric of wool and cotton mixed. It is 1 1/2 yards wide. Cotton cloth is very similar, but is more suitable for deep mourning, as it has less luster.

Poplin and mohair alpacas are of different quality and prices. For ordinary use they are the most serviceable of all black materials, as they wear well, retain their color, and may be brushed without becoming rough. French calico, black ground with white stripes and figures, is sold, as is English calico of the same description.

Underskirts of melton cloth are shaped like the Boulevard skirts. A very handsome one is of black melton, with a purple Greek border of Amozine braid; another is steel gray with black border.

Mourning Silks

For handsome dresses there are heavy corded silks, suitable for the deepest mourning when trimmed with bands of fluted crêpe. There are taffetas and grosgrains without luster, and soft poult-de-soie. Widow's silk is entirely lusterless: a soft, rich fabric, without the usual noisy rustle of silk. Among some handsome novelties at one of our leading houses is an elegant black goods called Eugénie satin, a repped satin, falling in heavy folds, producing the effect of uncut velvet. Another new and beautiful fabric is called imperial satin serge. It has the bright gloss of satin, but is as soft as merino, making rich folds without creasing. Still another novelty, and rarer than all, is a cobweb moiré. The watered figure, instead of being thrown on the silk in irregular dashes, forms at intervals a beautiful representation of a spider's web.

Second Mourning

For second mourning all the materials we have described are used, with more elaborate trimmings of jet, and purple, and white. It is very fashionable this winter to trim black with white. Occasionally a black passementerie or a velvet appliqué is laid on a white fold. Among suitable materials are the French poplins, black striped with gray, white, or purple. There is a good quality of silk, with lavender and gray stripes on a black ground. Twelve yards make the dress.

Gray serge, with satin face, 7/8 wide, is shot, chiné, and striped diagonally. Scotch winsey is a most serviceable article, of mingled purple and black.

Bonnets and Veils

Bonnets of English crêpe are worn in all seasons for deep mourning. Only very old ladies wear bombazine. The most tasteful bonnets are the plainest, made by laying three thicknesses of crêpe over the frame without folds. The strings are of corded ribbon or wide crêpe, bound. Widow's ruches, of white tarlatan bouillonnée, are made with two or three puffs. Large bows of tarlatan for fastening the bonnet are tucked at the ends, or bordered with a ruche. Corded silk without gloss is used for second mourning, with soft blonde puffs, jet ornaments. Since purple has become so fashionable in colors it is not so suitable for half mourning. White and black are used in conjunction.

Square veils of English crêpe with deep borders are fastened on each side by jet pins. Long crêpe veils are 1 5/8 yards long, worn with a string through the top. For lighter mourning there are veils of Brussels blonde, trimmed with folds of crêpe, and with feathers. These have three long points beneath the chin, or are round masks with lappets falling over the chignon.

Shawls and Cloaks

Camel's-hair cloth, fine and soft, is sold in squares for shawls. It is 2 yards wide. Tibet cloth and cashmeres are sold by the yard for long or square shawls. Long double shawls of merino with fringed ends are priced according to quality. A square shawl of a new sergelike material has a wide crêpe fold for trimming.

Cloaks of beaver, frosted or plain, are appropriately trimmed for mourning. Astrakhan and Russian lambskin paletots are the most suitable for wrappings. A very handsome Astrakhan cloth, with diamond figures, is sold for cloaks. It is 1 1/2 yards wide. Muffs are made of Astrakhan and of English crêpe.

Trimmings, Collars, Etc.

Bands of fluted crêpe with scalloped edges are made in a variety of patterns for trimming dresses, and sold by the yard. Crocheted passementerie without jet, and plain galloons, are used for mourning silks.

White organdy collars and undersleeves of narrow folds and shell pipings are pointed in the Shakespeare style. Tarlatan ruches, like widow's caps, are worn standing around the neck, with lappets in front. Folds of English crêpe in scalloped patterns are the deepest mourning collars. French crêpe is flimsy and soon becomes brown; it is therefore poor economy to use it.

Linen lawn handkerchiefs with black hems 2 inches wide, are warranted to wash without mixing the black and white. For lighter mourning there are cambric handkerchiefs with plain broad hem and monogram embroidered in black. Others are of French lawn with black Greek borders above the hem.

Varieties

Onyx jewelry is preferred to jet for deep mourning. It is not highly polished, and is in medieval designs, solid pieces radiating from balls in the center, with long pendants. Very little gold is visible.

Varieties

The new "Mantua" red, so fashionable in Paris, and which, it is predicted, will be the ruling color for the rest of the season, is a brilliant shade like ruby. We have seen it in the elegant imperial serge before alluded to, a repped material with satin face; said to be in favor for Parisian court trains. The new red, with Metternich green, the green of mignonette, and the intense marigold and capucine, are the colors most in vogue for rich evening dress.

Double skirts are very much worn. When gracefully made they take away the stiffness of a gored dress. They are bordered around the edge when short. When left long, following the train of the lower skirt, they are only scalloped at the front seams, and looped up, forming an apron.

Pelisses and redingotes require 5 yards of material, 7/8 yard wide. They are lined with flannel or cloth, and occasionally with fur, and are worn without other wrapping.

The neat-fitting, seamless kid gloves have become very popular. The advantage of having but one long seam, that in which the thumb is set, is highly appreciated. They are handsomely stitched on the back, or laced together with cord and tassels through tiny silvered eyelets. All the fashionable shades of brown and red are made for street dress, and a long white glove with fine buttons for evening wear. There are dogskin, beaver, and castor gloves, double stitched, with undressed kid gauntlets for riding, all fitting well, yet with no outside seams.

A graceful new veil called the chignon partially covers the bonnet, droops over the chignon, and is tied beneath the chin. It is made of Chantilly net, with appliqué border.

January 25, 1868

Pompadour Gored Dress

This tasteful dress is of light gray velour, trimmed with gray silk rouleaux and silk fringe. It is worn over a chemisette of puffed lace. Gray silk buttons up the front.

Cut from the front, first side piece, and second side piece, each two similar pieces. Cut the back and both parts of the sleeves. The breadths of the dress must be lengthened at the bottom as much as may be required, taking care to preserve the contour.

For the waist, cut the lining somewhat larger than the outside. Face the fronts with velour. Sew the bosom pleats, and put on the buttons and buttonholes. Then join the parts to correspond with the figures on the pattern. Cord the neck. Face the bottom of the skirt. Sew in the sleeves, and finish with the trimming.

Pompadour Gored Dress

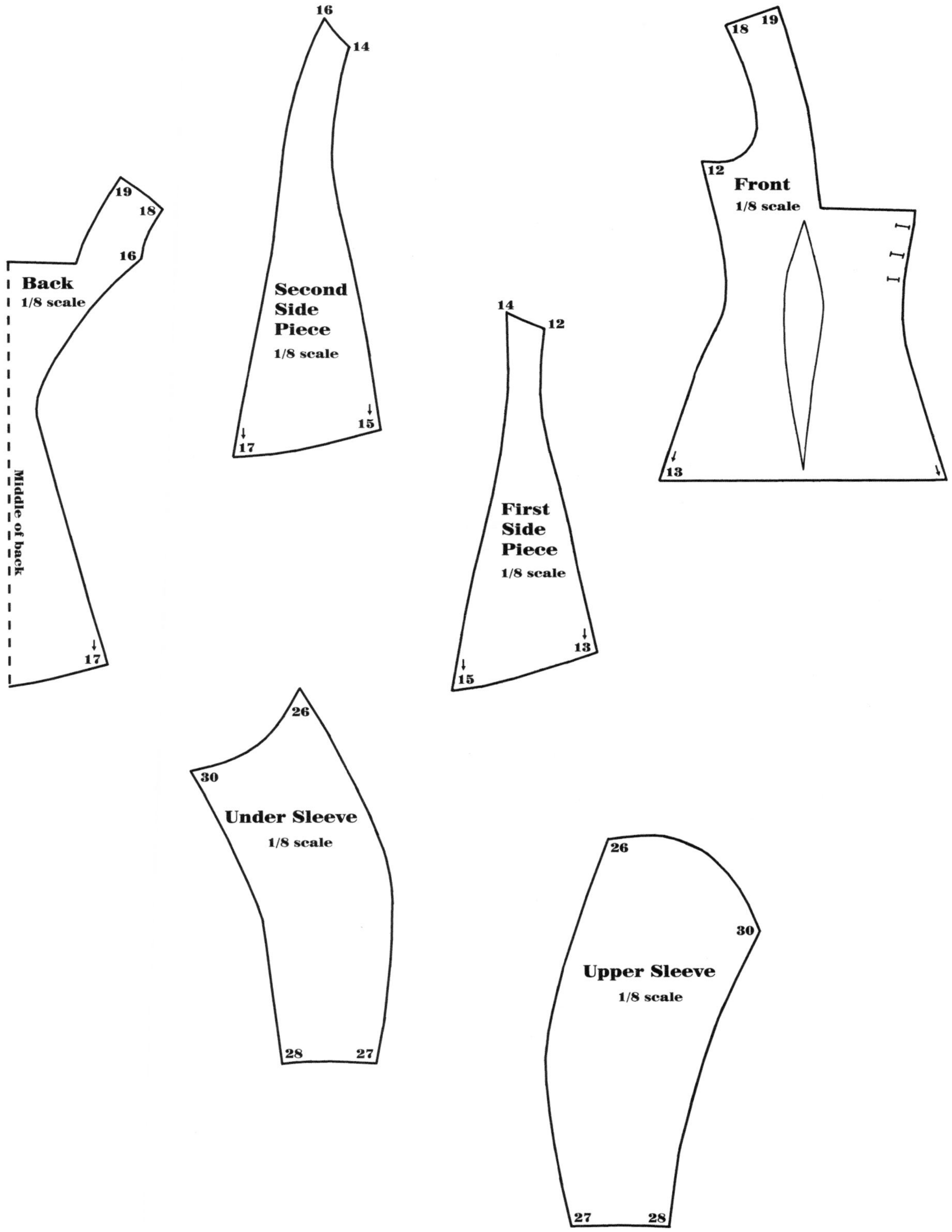

16
14

Second
Side
Piece
1/8 scale

17
15

19
18
16

Back
1/8 scale

Middle of back

17

18 19

12

Front
1/8 scale

13

14
12

First
Side
Piece
1/8 scale

15
13

26
30

Under Sleeve
1/8 scale

28 27

26
30

Upper Sleeve
1/8 scale

27 28

Bodice for Young Lady

The original dress is of gray poplin, trimmed with black velvet, and fringed as illustrated. The belt is also of black velvet. The pattern of the bodice, which is lined with white muslin, is the same as the Bodice with Lappets. It is worn over a high-necked white waist.

Bodice with Lappets

Bodice with Lappets

This bodice is made of narrow silk braid, notched on the edges and studded with beads, black watered ribbon 1 1/2 inches wide, black lace 2 and 4 inches wide, studded with beads, jet buttons, and jet grelots.

For the bodice, first cut a foundation of stiff lace from the front pattern, two pieces for the fronts, and one piece for the back. Join the back and fronts to correspond with the figures on the pattern. Lay the bosom pleats.

Having thus obtained the shape, arrange the braid thereon as illustrated. Fasten the pieces where they intersect each other. Bind the upper part with narrow watered ribbon edged with narrow lace. Cover the seam with the bead braid. Finish the armholes in a similar manner, and set on broad lace.

Set the bottom in a double belt of watered ribbon 1 1/2 inches wide, covered with broad black lace, and sew the bead braid over the seam. Fasten to the belt lappets of watered ribbon, 1/2 yard long and 1 1/2 inches wide. Point the ends and trim them with grelots. Sew the bead braid along the edges. Set jet buttons at the top of the lappets and at the place where they cross each other. Fasten the belt with hooks and eyes, covered with a rosette of the watered ribbon, 1 inch wide, dotted on the edge with beads.

January 25, 1868

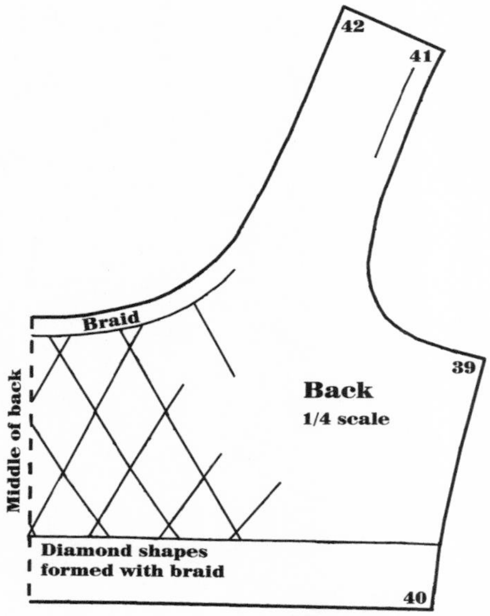

42
41
Braid
Back
1/4 scale
39
Middle of back
Diamond shapes formed with braid
40

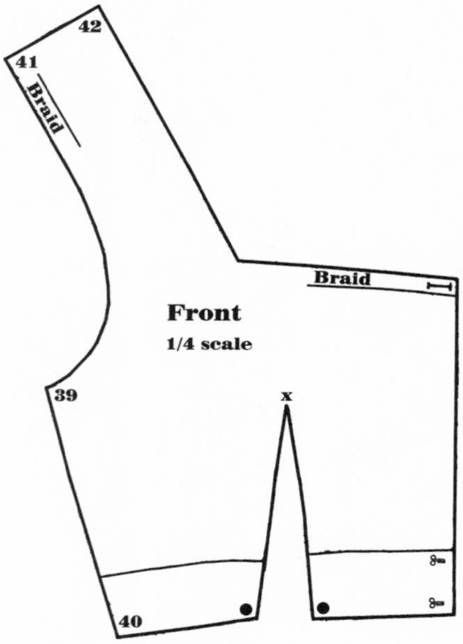

42
41
Braid
Braid
Front
1/4 scale
39
x
40

Pompadour Waist with Yoke

Pompadour Waist with Yoke

This waist must be worn with a white or light skirt, which must match the trimming of the waist in color. The original is of mull, trimmed with needlework insertion 1 inch wide, Valenciennes insertion 2/5 and 4/5 inch wide, and Valenciennes edging 3/5 and 4/5 inch wide. A black velvet ribbon is run through the narrowest insertion. Black velvet ribbon 2 inches wide, and small embroidered rosettes, complete the trimming.

For the waist, cut the two fronts and the back. Arrange of the needlework insertion and the broader Valenciennes insertion, two pieces after the front yoke and one piece after the back yoke. Lay the pleats as marked from *x* to • in the front and back. Join these parts to correspond with the figures on the pattern, with the front and back yokes, pleating the muslin in front as marked on the pattern from 21 to 22, and 24 to 25. Set a double strip of muslin up the fronts, for buttons and buttonholes. Cover the same on the right with the broad Valenciennes insertion, bordered on both sides with narrow edging, and laid over black velvet ribbon. Join the back and fronts to correspond with the figures on the pattern. Trim the neck with the narrow Valenciennes insertion and edging. Run a narrow black velvet ribbon through the former, leaving the ends hanging about 1/4 yard. Hem the bottom and side slit narrow. Face the same with double muslin, about 3 inches wide.

Cut the sleeves. Trim as illustrated. Run black velvet ribbon through the narrow insertion at the bottom of the sleeve, and tie the ends in a bow. Cord the armholes, sew in the sleeves, and put black velvet ribbon over the shoulders. The ends of this ribbon are formed into a loop about 4 inches long, confined by a needlework rosette edged with lace. Finish with a rosette of black velvet in front of the waist.

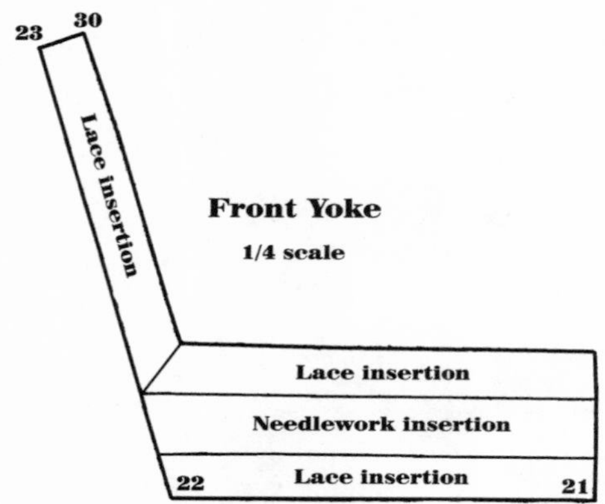

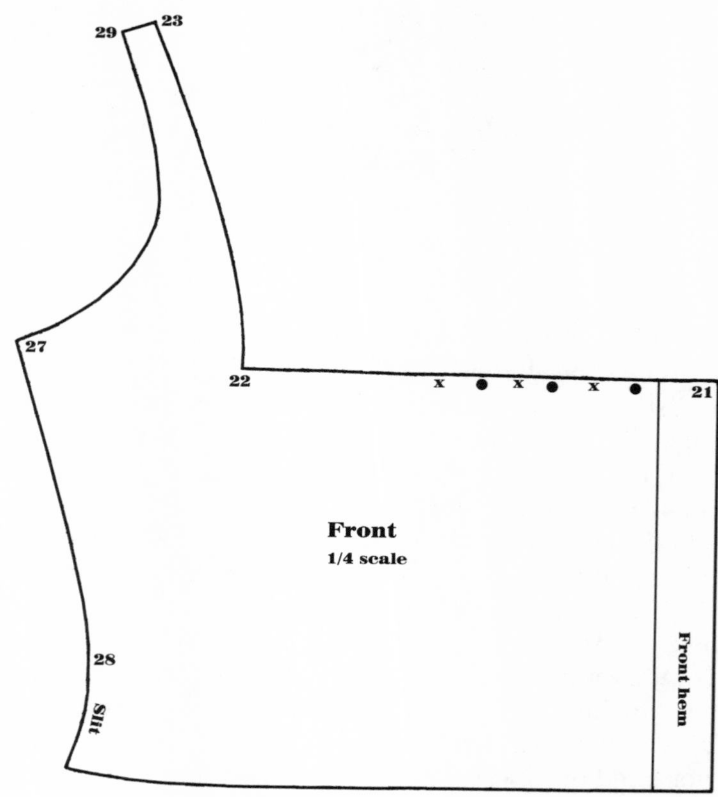

Pompadour Waist with Yoke

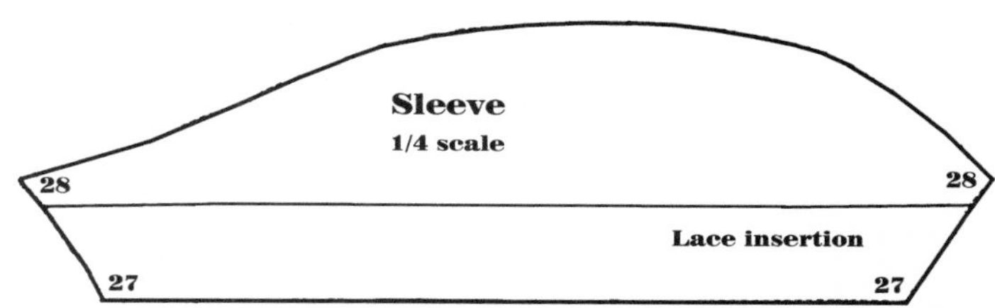

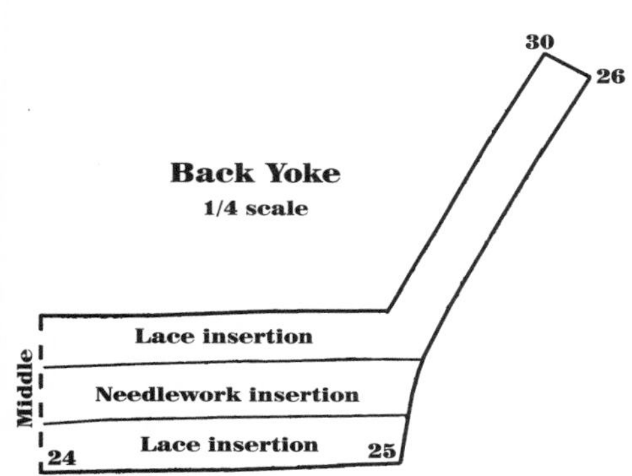

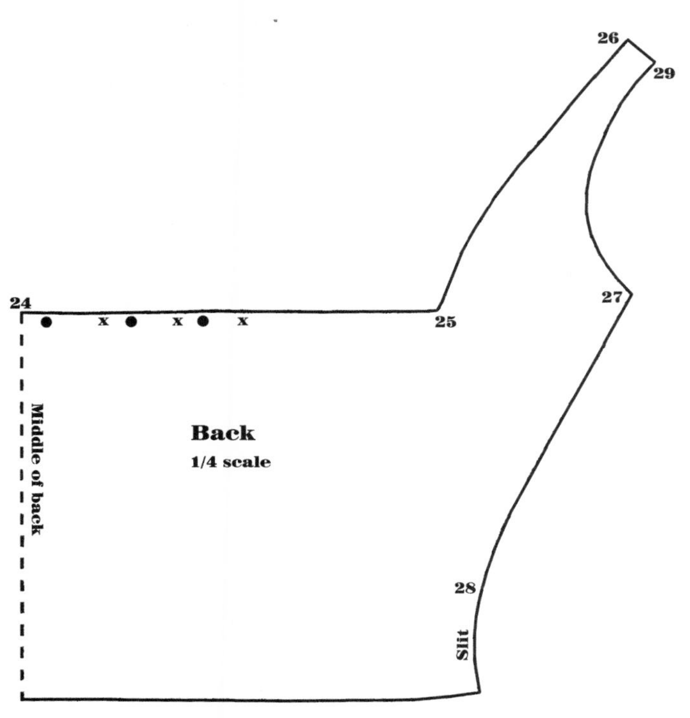

January 25, 1868

Pompadour Waist with Bretelles

This waist is of muslin, Valenciennes edging 1 inch and 1 1/2 inches wide, and needlework insertion. It is finished in front with a bow of pink ribbon.

Cut the two fronts, allowing 1 inch for the hem. Cut the back. Hem the fronts, and put on the buttons and buttonholes. Sew the bosom pleats. Make a seam in the back from 31 to 32. Join the back and fronts on the shoulders from 35 to 36. Arrange the Valenciennes lace, which must be whole on the shoulders, as illustrated. Hem the neck narrow. Trim the front with a strip of narrow lace, sewn together in the middle, and slightly frilled. Cover this seam with needlework insertion. The back is trimmed down the middle in the same manner.

The bretelles are made of lace, bordered on one side with small, and on the other with narrow edging, with needlework insertion covering the seams through the middle. Join the back and fronts from 33 to 34. Set a double band on the bottom of the waist. Cover this waistband with pink satin ribbon, with a bow of the same on the front and back.

The sleeves are cut from the pattern for the Pompadour Waist with Yoke. They are trimmed with narrow lace and needlework insertion as illustrated. The muslin is cut away under the lace.

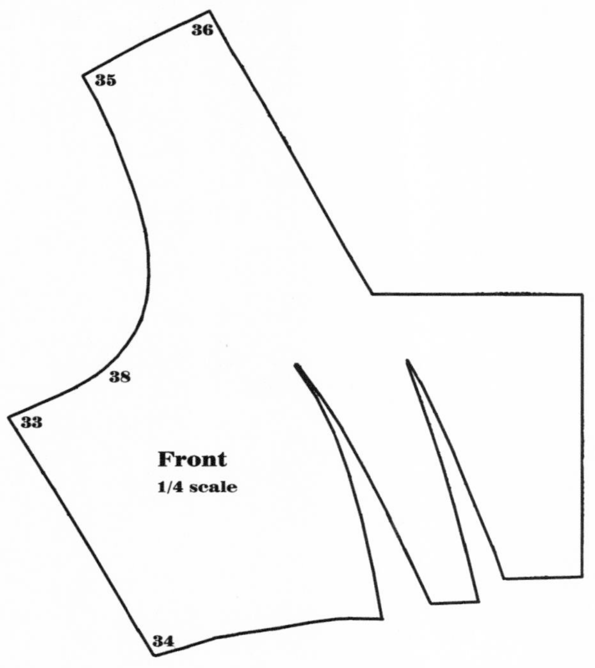

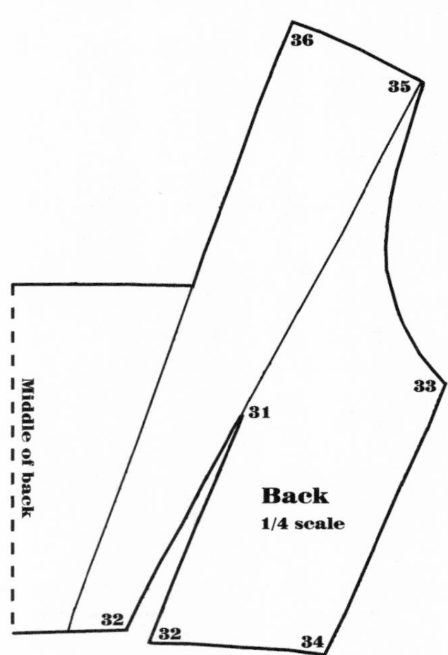

Pompadour Basque Waist

This waist is of muslin, guipure insertion 4/5 inch wide, guipure edging 3/5 inch wide, small needlework rosettes edged with lace, and blue ribbon 1 and 2 inches wide.

Cut from the muslin from the front middle one piece, from the front two pieces, from the back one piece, and the sleeve lappets. Lay the bosom pleats in the front. Join the fronts and back to correspond with the figures on the pattern. Arrange the insertion and ribbon as illustrated, taking care to fasten the insertion so that the muslin can be cut away from under it. With the ribbon make short loops at the top, and long loops with ends at the bottom of the waist. Put on the frilled edging, the rosettes, and the bows of narrow ribbon. Lay a strip of muslin doubled along the edge of the left front. Sew small buttons thereon. Cover it with blue ribbon, making corresponding loops on the right side.

The sleeves consist of a strip of muslin, about 3/4 yard long and 4 inches wide. This is puffed and confined by a band of insertion and edging, with a lappet, similarly trimmed, and a ribbon bow on the top.

January 25, 1868

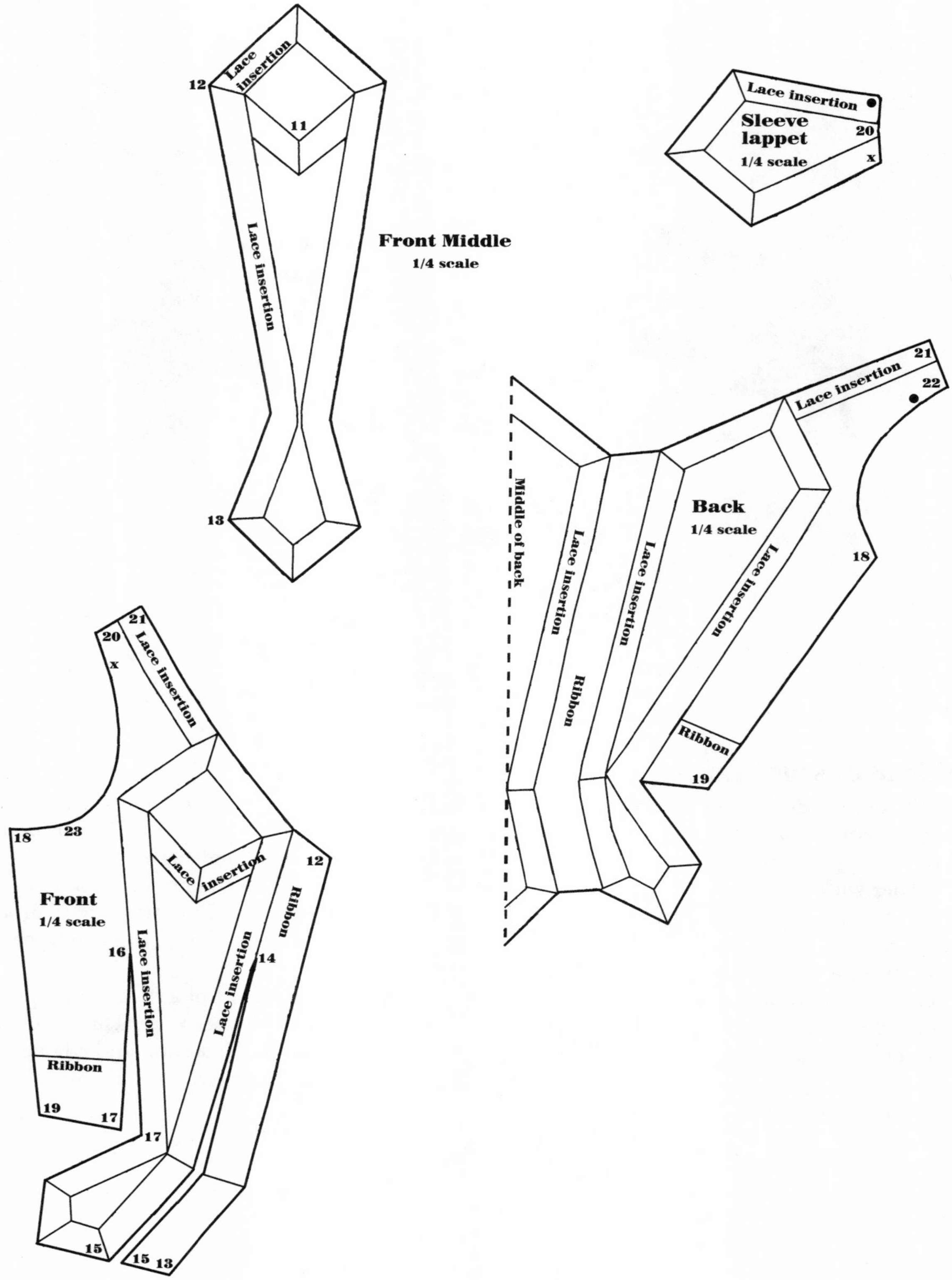

Front Middle
1/4 scale
Lace insertion
Lace insertion
11
12
13
Sleeve lappet
1/4 scale
Lace insertion
20
x
Back
1/4 scale
Middle of back
Lace insertion
Lace insertion
Lace insertion
Lace insertion
Ribbon
Ribbon
21
22
18
19
Front
1/4 scale
Lace insertion
Lace insertion
Lace insertion
Lace insertion
Ribbon
Ribbon
20
21
x
18
23
16
12
14
19
17
17
15
15
13

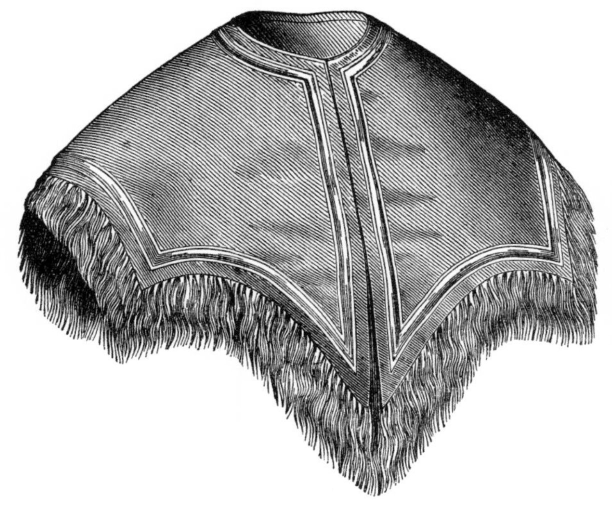

White Poplin Pelerine

This pelerine is of white poplin, trimmed as illustrated with satin piping and angora fringe 1 1/2 inches wide. It is lined with silk, and thinly wadded.

Cut of the outside, lining, wadding, and interlining from the front each two pieces, and from the back one piece. Lay the wadding between the lining and interlining. Quilt the whole. Then baste on the outside. Join the fronts and back from 35 to 36, thinning the wadding somewhat along the seams. Run the edges together. Cord the neck. Trim the bottom with narrow satin piping and angora fringe.

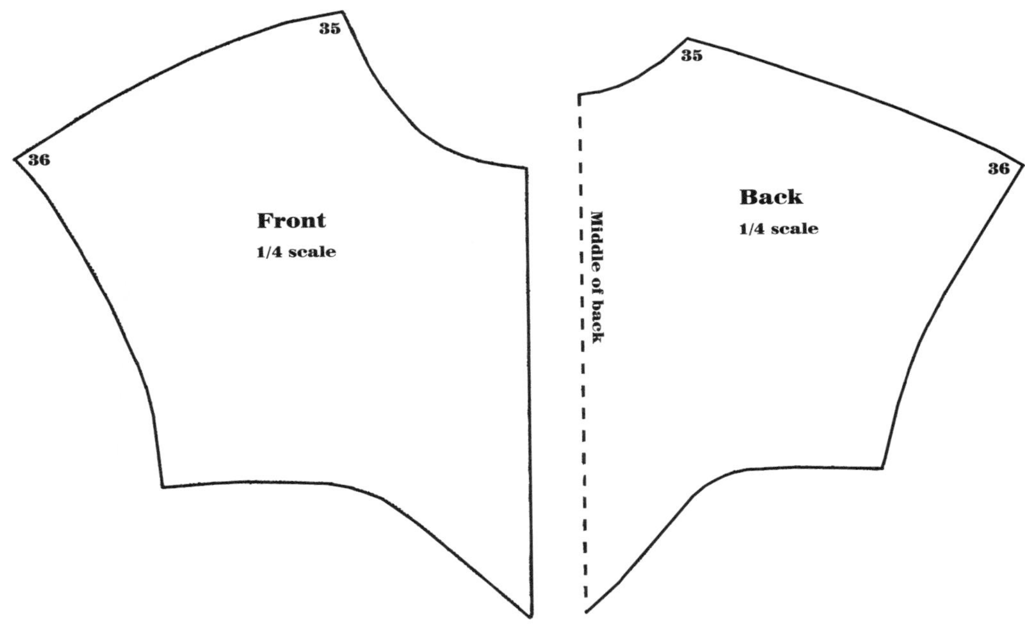

January 25, 1868

Low-Necked Under Waist

This waist is of silk, lined with muslin. It is completed with a Russian chemise, formed of pleated muslin, bordered with guipure insertion and edging. A narrow black velvet ribbon is run through the insertion and tied in a bow. The waist may also be made of plain muslin.

Cut the fronts and side pieces, the back, and the sleeves. Baste the outside and lining together. Lay the bosom pleats. Join the back, side pieces, and fronts. Put on the hooks and eyes. Cord the waist round the edge. Sew up the sleeves from 53 to 54, and set them in the armholes with a cord. Lastly, trim the waist with guipure edging.

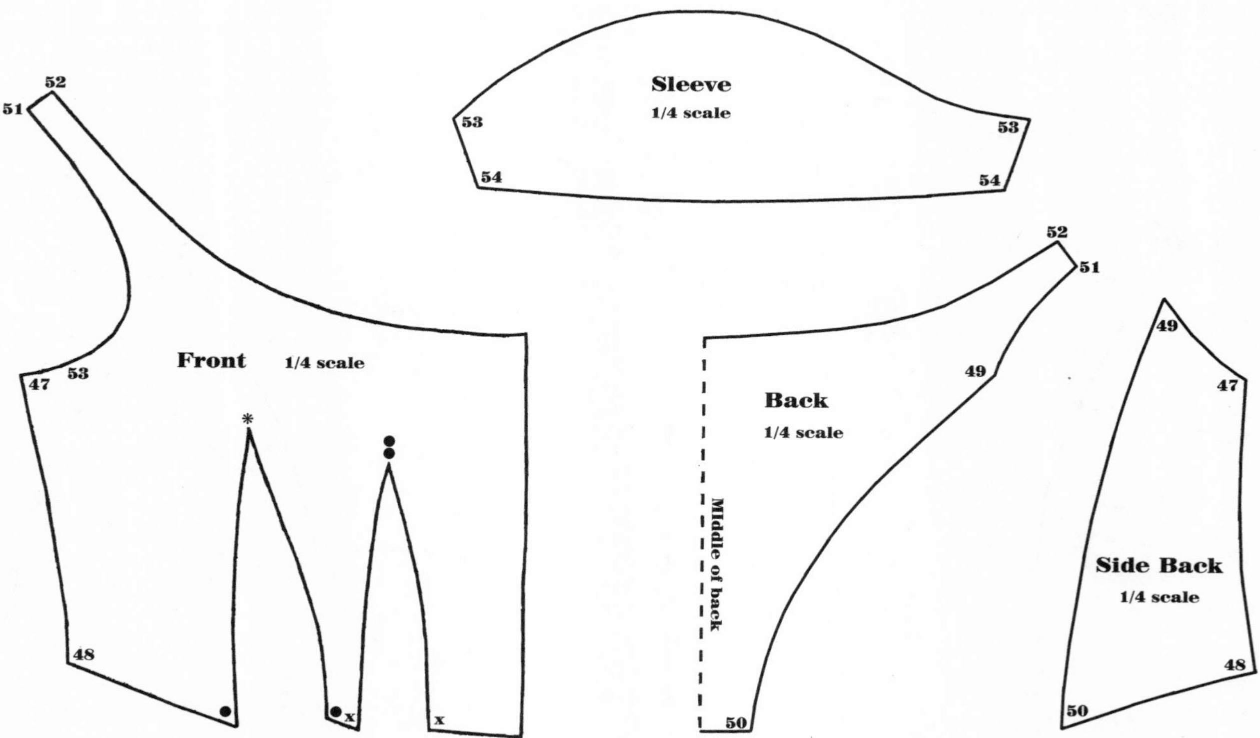

Gored Flannel Underskirt

Gored Flannel Underskirt

This underskirt is of white flannel, scalloped round the bottom with red worsted, and embroidered in point Russe with the same material.

Cut from the front and back each one breadth, and the two side breadths. Cut the double muslin belt.

Sew up the breadths to correspond with the figures on the pattern. Face the bottom with a strip of flannel 2 inches wide, and embroider as illustrated. Make a slit in the middle of the back from 6 to *x* along the solid line. Face the edges with muslin. Gather the top from the middle of the back to 3 on each side. Set it in the belt. A button and buttonhole complete the skirt.

Belt 1/4 scale

6

5

Middle

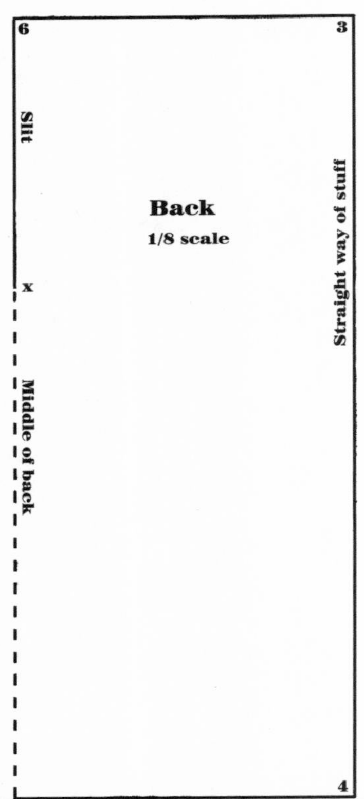

6
3
Slit
Back
1/8 scale
Straight way of stuff
x
Middle of back
4

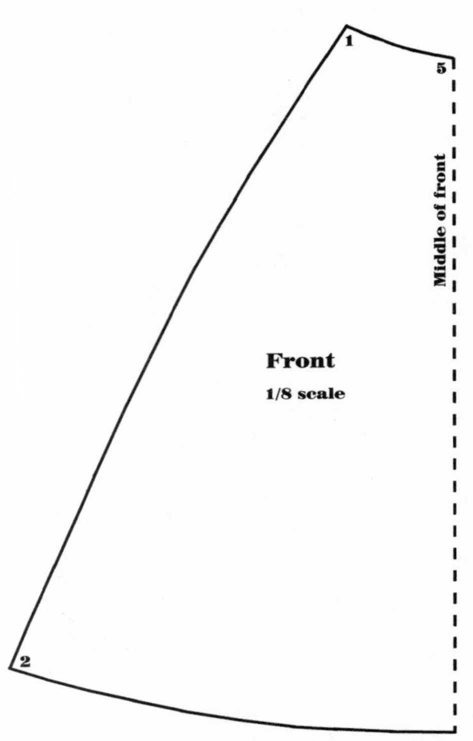

1
5
Middle of front
Front
1/8 scale
2

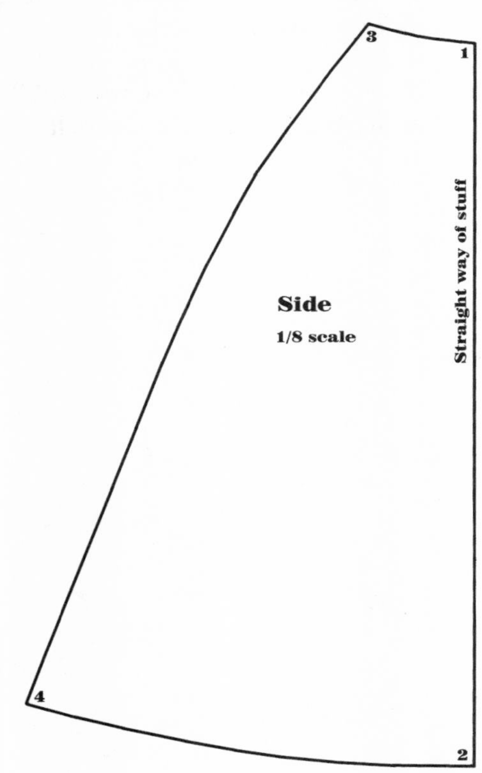

3
1
Straight way of stuff
Side
1/8 scale
4
2

Bedouin

The original of this opera cloak is of white silk, trimmed with blue velvet ribbon 1 inch wide and broad angora fringe.

Cut one piece 1 yard long (the middle of the back) and 1 1/2 yards wide, which is rounded at the bottom, in the shape shown (which is given at 1/16 size). Face the bottom with a strip of white silk, 2 inches wide, and cord the edge with white silk. Cut the lappet for the back double. Sew angora fringe, 3 inches wide, between the edges. Set it on the Bedouin. Then put the velvet trimming round the neck to form a triangle 5 inches long and 4 inches wide (which is given in miniature). Trim this with velvet ribbon and cross-stitch of blue silk. Lastly, set the velvet ribbon round the edge of the Bedouin.

January 25, 1868

Triangle
1/8 scale

Middle

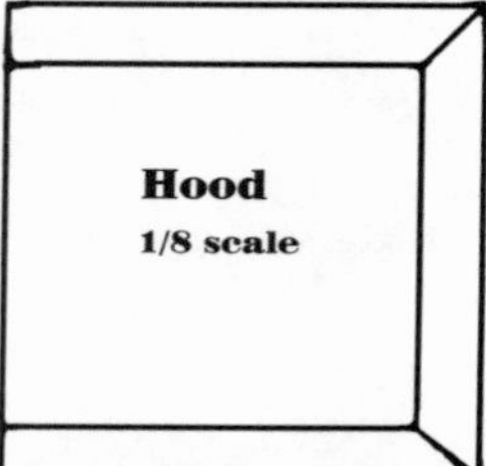

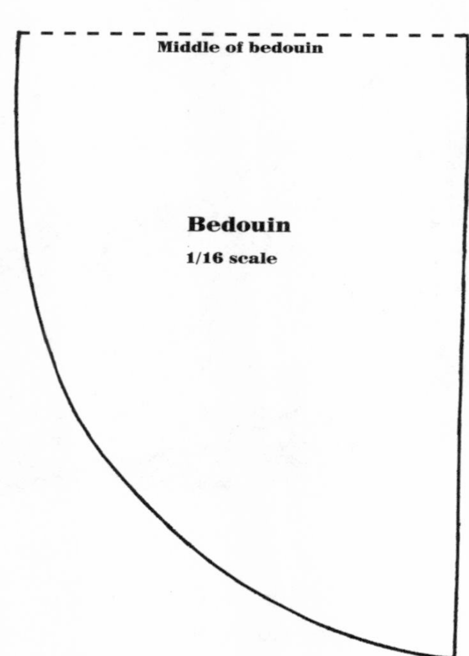

Scarf Bedouin

The original of this opera cloak is of white cashmere, trimmed with a bias strip of white silk 2 inches wide, white silk braid, rosettes of white silk cord, and angora fringe 3 inches wide. The small standing collar is scalloped.

Cut from the front and back, which give one half, each two equal pieces, having first taken care to lengthen the back. Having joined the two parts of the back from 3 to 4 and from 4 to 5, lay the shoulder pleat from 1 to 2. Turn the edges down narrow on the right side on the fronts and back. Cover with the bias strip of white silk, and trim this on each side with braid. This bias trimming only reaches about halfway up the front, the edge of which is turned in, and bound with a narrow strip of silk. Lay three pleats in the middle of the back, which are marked by *x* and •. Join the fronts and back to correspond with the figures on the pattern. Lastly, put on the collar and the remaining trimming.

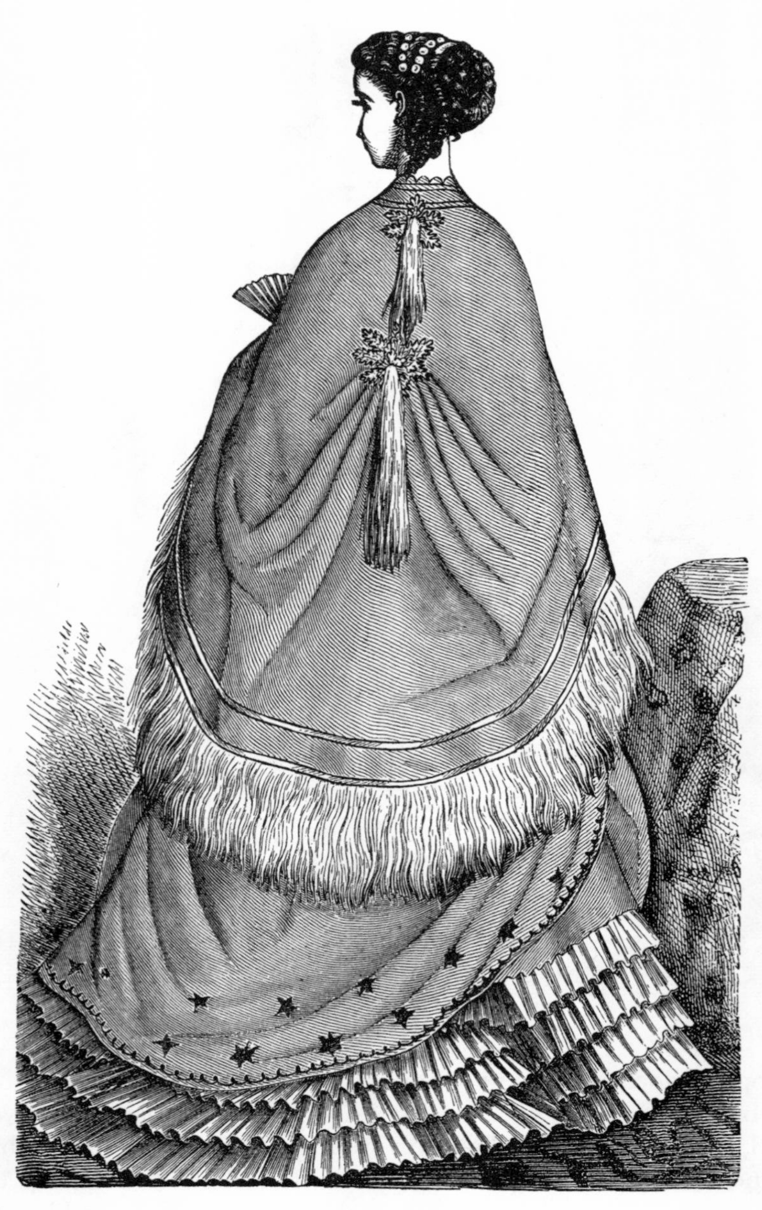

Scarf Bedouin

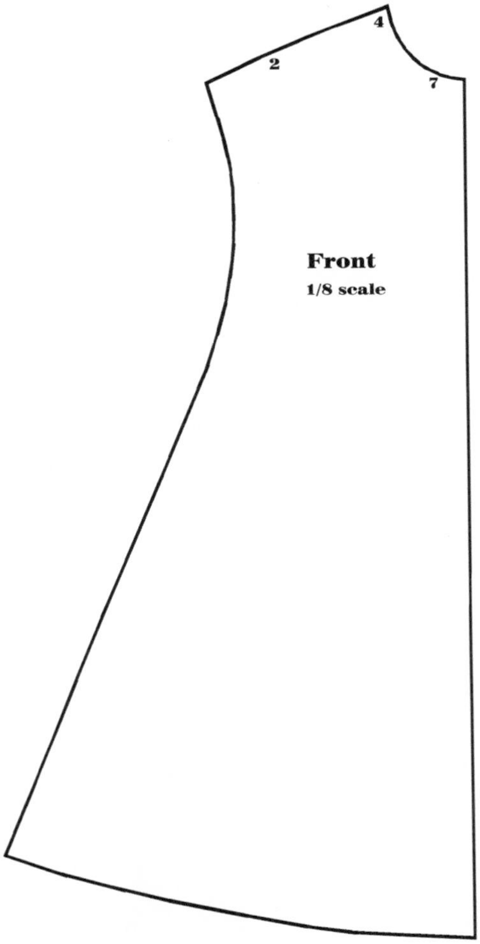

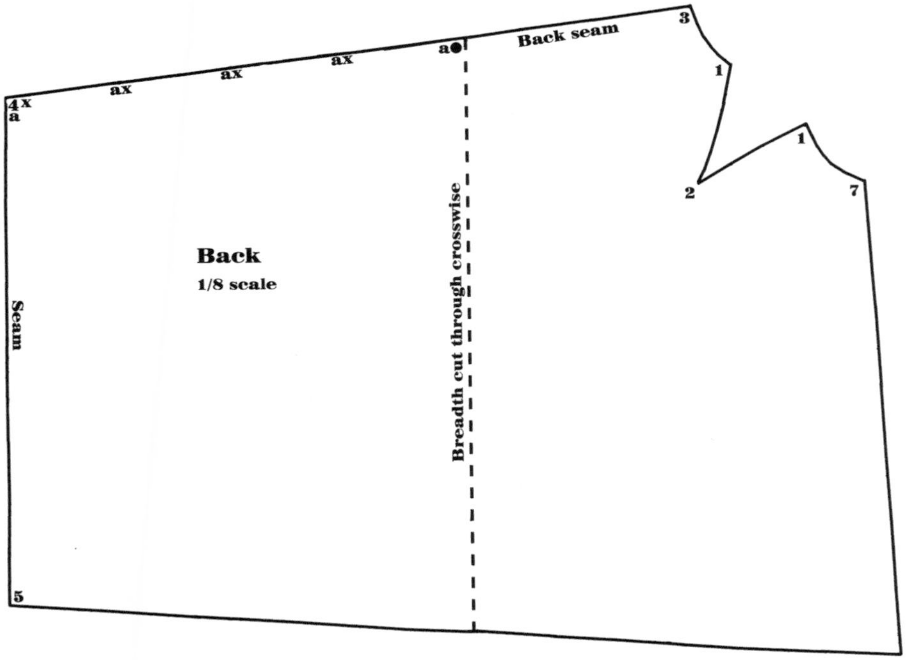

Front

1/8 scale

2 4 7

Back seam

3 1 2 1 7

4 x a ax ax ax a

Back

1/8 scale

Seam

Breadth cut through crosswise

5

Talma

This opera talma is of Irish poplin, lined with silk. It is scalloped round the bottom and bound with satin. Satin rouleaux simulate scallops up the front. The bottom is trimmed besides with angora fringe, 6 inches deep, which is set on underneath so as to leave the scallops loose. Guipure lace, 2 inches wide, laid over a bias fold of satin, and satin buttons complete the trimming.

Scallop the bottom, making each scallop 1 3/5 inches deep and 2 2/5 inches wide. Baste the outside and lining together. Sew up the seam in the middle of the back. Lay the shoulder pleats. Then bind the talma with satin. The standing collar consists of lappets of poplin, lined with silk and bound with satin to correspond with the rest of the garment. These lappets lie over each other, and are set on underneath the neck. Finish with trimming, as illustrated.

Talma

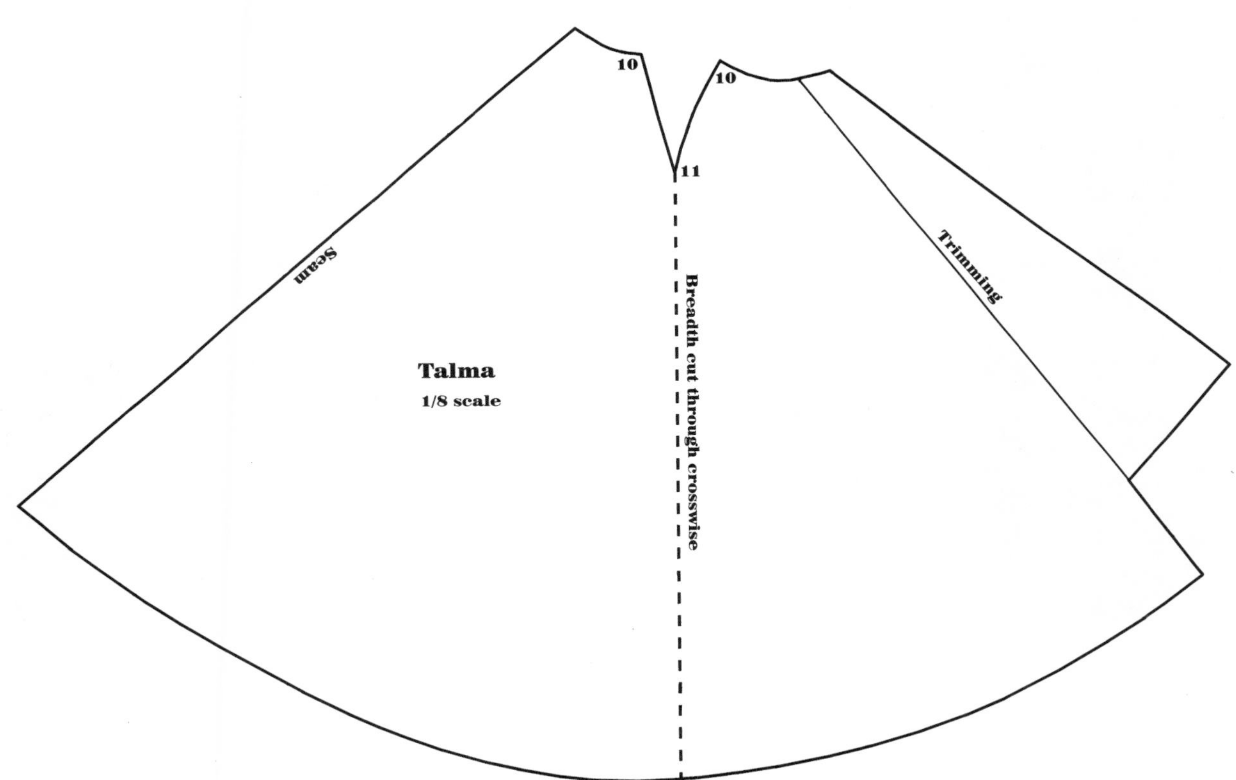
10
10
11
Seam
Trimming
Breadth cut through crosswise
Talma
1/8 scale

Cashmere Baschlik

This baschlik can be worn over a bonnet or round hat, as a protection against cold and rain. The illustrations show it covering a fur hat. The original is of gray cashmere, lined with gray silk, and trimmed with white silk braid and white beads. A very pretty one can be made of black cashmere, lined with black or colored silk, and trimmed with black cord.

The pattern of half the baschlik is given. Cut of the outside and lining each two pieces of the same size. Sew the outside and lining together from 7 to 8 and from 8 to 9. Put on the trimming as illustrated and cord the edge. Finish the point behind with a tassel of gray and white silk.

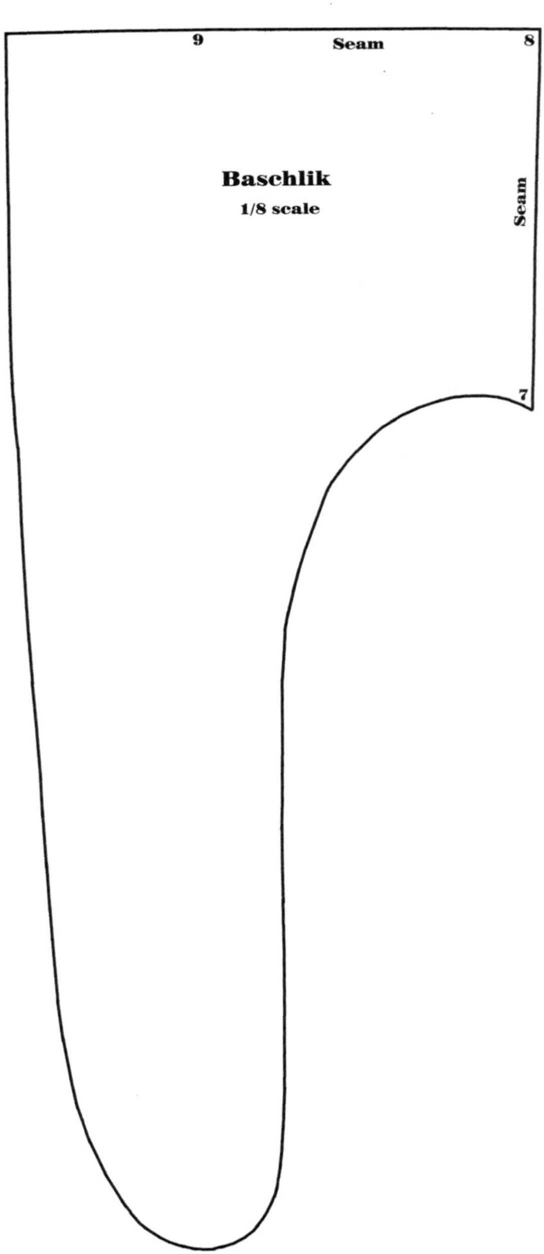
9
Seam
8
Baschlik
1/8 scale
Seam
7

Mantilla Veil

This graceful and elegant veil, which somewhat resembles the Spanish mantilla, is an excellent adjunct to the small bonnets, protecting the face and neck from the frosty air. The veil is in two pieces. A pattern is given for the larger, and the smaller can readily be seen in the first illustration. The original is of black dotted lace, the larger part being bordered with edging 2 inches wide, and the smaller with edging 1 inch wide. To the upper corners of the latter is fastened an elastic cord about 7 inches long, which is passed beneath the chignon to confine the veil. The ends of the larger part are fastened in front as illustrated.

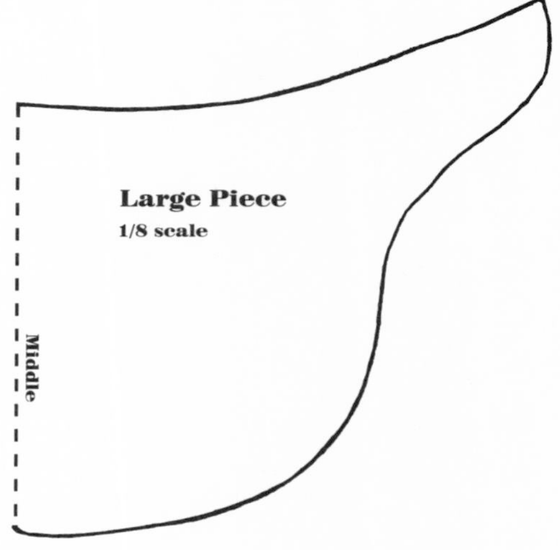

February 1, 1868

Evening Attire

The Pompadour colors, blue and pink together, are in vogue for evening dress.

Satin is very much used in conjunction with tulle, not only beneath it as transparent, but as peplum overskirts, as tabliers or aprons, and as open trains over two or three tulle skirts. It is made into berthas and sashes, and Marie Antoinette fichus. It is also arranged in folds with pearl trimming and blonde lace to form braces or bretelles for low-necked dresses of gauze and self-colored silk.

White crêpe is used for trimming ball dresses. It is scarcely so becoming as tulle, but is preferred on account of its novelty and its peculiar glistening, like hoarfrost, in the gaslight.

The Parisiennes have a new invention for looping ball dresses, called a *porte-jupe.* Two jeweled brooches united by a gold chain are placed, one at the waist and the other near the edge of the skirt, looping gracefully the long material between them.

Another French caprice is a jeweled chatelaine. A gold hook, set with precious stones, is fastened to the belt. Suspended from this hook are chains to which are attached a locket, a pencil, tablets, and a vinaigrette.

Enameled hummingbirds, peacocks, butterflies, bees, and even spiders, are fashionable French ornaments. Collars of scarabaei and of Brazilian beetles, with long pendants, are linked together by gold chains.

Baschliks

Baschliks, or hood-bonnets, are worn for driving and evening parties. They are warm and comfortable and exceedingly becoming. Young ladies wear them of blue or rose-colored satin, quilted in diamonds and bordered with swansdown, or of white cashmere or silk, with quilted lining, and embroidery of floss and seed pearls. They are fastened by buttons and loops, or silk cords and tassels of camel's-hair. Very elegant ones are made of lace, lined with silk. Chantilly is worn over crimson, and point lace over blue silk. Elderly ladies prefer them of black velvet or satin, trimmed with lace or fur.

A kind of baschlik is also worn in Europe by skaters. It is of the material of the dress and redingote, and trimmed to match. A square headpiece is continued in long lappets down the front, crossed under the chin, again at the back, and fastened upon the breast with a brooch.

Belt with Sash

This belt is a tasteful adjunct to a ball or evening dress, and is made of the dress material. The original is of brown silk, the ends of the bow being trimmed with brown silk fringe.

The belt is of double silk, corded on the edges with satin, and trimmed around the bottom with corded loops of silk. The belt is fastened with hooks and eyes, over which the bow is placed.

For the bow cut from the silk double, and stiff lace for interlining two each from the patterns for the larger and smaller pieces. Lay the interlining between the silk. Cord each of these four pieces with brown satin across the ends and on one side. Then lay the other side in pleats in the form of a fan. Put the four pieces together as shown, letting the smaller pieces lie over the larger ones. Cover the seam with a loop of brown silk, corded on each side with brown satin. The ends of the bow are made of brown silk double, with an interlining of stiff lace. They are corded on the edges with brown satin, and trimmed across the bottom with heavy brown silk fringe. The top is pleated and set under the bow.

Either of the other bows illustrated can be substituted for the fan-shaped bow. The first illustration shows a bow made of a bias strip of doubled silk, 2 inches wide, with an interlining. This is formed into a rosette with loops, the longest of which is 1/4 yard long.

In the second illustration is a bow with ribbon loops, 2 inches wide and 1/8 yard long, laid in three pleats at the ends. It is finished in the middle, where the loops are joined together, with a piece of ribbon pleated three times as shown.

End of Bow
1/4 scale

Smaller Piece of Bow
1/4 scale

Larger Piece of Bow
1/4 scale

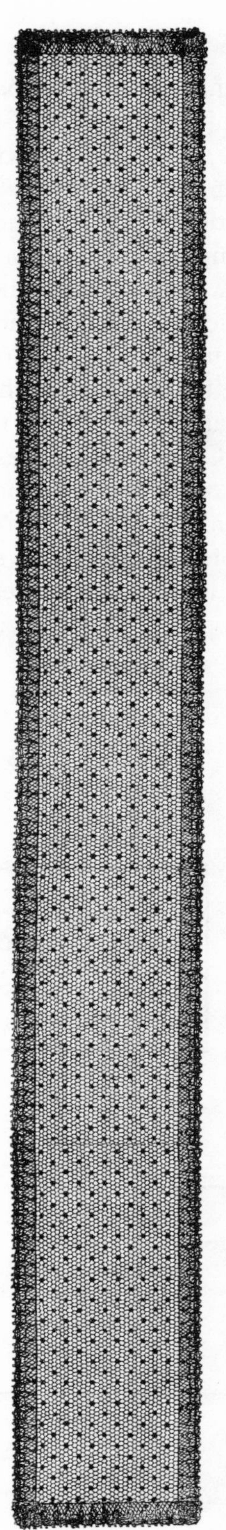

Lace Scarf

This scarf is made of dotted black lace, bordered with lace edging. This is pleated lengthwise through the middle, and arranged in the different styles shown.

For bretelles, fasten the middle in front to the belt with a lace rosette, brooch, or bow. Pass the ends over the shoulders in the form of bretelles, tie them behind in a bow, and fasten the same to the belt.

For a sash, fasten the middle of the scarf with a ribbon bow on the right shoulder. Tie the ends under the left arm in a bow. It can also be tied as a sash round the waist.

For a fichu, fasten the middle to the belt behind. Pass the ends over the shoulders, cross them in front, and tie them in a knot behind.

Lace Scarf

Scarf
1/8 scale

Knitted Corset

Knitted Corset

This corset is knitted of heavy unbleached cotton, and almost entirely in common garter stitch. It is very warm, worn without whalebones, and commendable for its pliability. The original is fastened in front by buttons and buttonholes. Materials: Coarse unbleached cotton; two fine steel knitting needles.

Begin the corset on the front row by casting on 115 stitches. Knit twelve rounds as above, slipping the 1st stitch of every round.

Then purl one round, knit one round, purl one round; which three rounds form a plain stripe on one side (the right) of the work; then knit twenty rounds plain. In the following round (thirty-sixth) purl the first 49 stitches (the slip stitch in the beginning of each round is not counted); the remaining stitches of the round, as also all the stitches of the following round, are knitted plain. The wide, smooth stripe of three rounds, which, by so doing, comes upon the right side in the upper part of the corset, forms a part of the border of the first gore. This last requires thirty-seven rounds to complete, and is knitted plain backward and forward. For the first round knit the first 14 stitches, and leave the remaining stitches of the last round without knitting. Every second round of the following fifteen is lengthened 4 stitches by knitting with it 4 stitches from the row that was left. For the next round (seventeenth) of the gore knit the entire row of stitches the full length of the corset–the first 47 plain, then 2 purled, and the remainder plain. For the eighteenth to the twentieth rounds knit also the entire length of the corset, but in the nineteenth, the first 42 stitches plain, then 7 purled, and the remainder plain. For the twenty-first round of the gore knit 38 stitches, purl 4, and leave the remainder without knitting. The twenty-third, twenty-fifth, twenty-seventh, twenty-ninth, thirty-first, and thirty-third rounds are knitted like the twenty-first. However, each must be shortened by 4 plain stitches immediately before the 4 purled, so the thirty-third round counts only 14 plain stitches and 4 purled. It is understood that the preceding rounds, for which no special directions have been given, must be knitted plain. Now knit one round on the whole 115 stitches, the first 49 purled and the remainder plain, *x* the return round plain, which forms the stripe on the other side of the finished gore. Now knit fourteen rounds, then the second gore, which is formed precisely as the first.

After the completion of the second gore, knit three rounds entire. Then begin the hip gore, which is formed like the other gores, with the exception of being longer and broader. Without counting the plain stripe that surrounds it, and which is knit like those of the other gores, this hip gore counts thirty-eight rounds. The first round includes 14 stitches; every second round of the next eighteen is lengthened by 5 stitches; every second round of the remaining nineteen shortened by 5 stitches.

Having finished the hip gore, knit eighteen rounds the entire length of the corset. In the beginning of the following round (nineteenth), in the upper part of the corset, cast off 8 stitches, and in the beginning of the twenty-first 2 stitches, to form the armhole. Knit thirty rounds on the shortened row, then form the second hip gore.

Having completed this, knit twelve rounds, casting on 1 stitch at the end of the last (at the armhole); besides this cast on 1 stitch at the end of the second round following, and 20 in the second following that. On the round thus lengthened knit eighty rounds.

Then form in the middle of the back two gores, one in the upper, and one in the lower part of the corset. In forming these two gores only the 12 middle stitches are left without knitting. Knit first the upper gore, of which the first (longest) round reaches from the top to the 12 middle stitches. Thenceforth shorten every second following round of the gore by the 4 stitches next the 12 middle stitches. Proceed in this manner till the shortest row of the corset, which must count 20 stitches, is reached. On this knit one return round, and the gore is half finished.

Knit now one round the entire length of the corset, all the stitches of the upper gore and the 12 middle stitches being purled, and the remainder (which form the first round of the lower gore) plain. The next round is knitted from the lower edge to the 12 middle stitches. Every second following of the next sixteen rounds must be shortened by 2 stitches, and every second of those following that by 3 stitches, till the shortest row of the gore (which must count 20 stitches) is reached. Having knitted the return round, knit one round the entire length of the corset (the right side being on the right side of the corset). This finishes the half of the lower gore, and, at the same time, the half of the corset.

The second half is knitted in the same manner, except that the order of the rounds is reversed. Knit first the second half of the upper gore, which must be begun with the shortest round of 20 stitches. Lengthen every following second round by the same number of stitches taken off in the first half. Having finished the upper gore, knit one round the entire length of the corset (the right side being on the right side of the corset). Then knit the second half of the lower gore, lengthening every second round in the same proportion in which the first half was shortened. Having finished these two back gores, the corset can be completed by the directions already given.

A row of buttonholes must be formed in the front, twelve rounds before taking off, the corresponding buttons being on the other side. Now collect the 11 stitches lying next the armhole on the front, and knit garter stitch as follows, to form the shoulder band. The first three rounds knit the entire row, then every second following of the next three rounds narrow by 2 stitches, thus forming a little gore next the armhole. Then knit fifty rounds, and again a little gore, of which the first round counts 2 stitches with the third and fifth rounds following lengthened each by 2 stitches, and the seventh and ninth rounds narrowed by 2 stitches. Then knit forty-four rounds, after which knit the 11 stitches still on the needle with the 11 stitches on the back edge next the armhole.

Having knit the second shoulder band in the same manner, collect on needles the side stitches on the upper edge of the corset, and knit two rounds backward and forward as usual. Then one eyelet row, and finally two rounds plain, after which the work is cast off. Through the eyelet row draw a band, by means of which the corset can be drawn together.

February 8, 1868

Lingerie

The word "lingerie" is used by our furnishing houses to comprise all those white garments of lace, linen, and muslin necessary for a lady's complete outfit, including muslin dresses for morning and evening, fichus, canezous, camisoles, peignoirs, and sets of underlinen.

Ladies who do not wear linen use percale for handsome underclothing.

Chemise bands are worn very wide. Two rows of cambric insertion 1 inch wide, with a puff of the same width between, and a lace edge, form a pretty band. Double, or box pleats, made narrow, fit neatly, and are easily ironed if stitched lengthwise of the linen. A new feature is to cut yoke and sleeves in one piece. Trimmings are arranged diagonally and in medallions. Tucks, puffs, and insertions slant in points toward the front. Lace, appliqué embroidery, and bunches of tucks are cut into oval medallions, squares, diamonds, or hexagons, and strapped around with narrow bands of linen to strengthen them. Drawers, very wide at the ankle, are trimmed to match the chemise.

Gowns with yokes are more frequently called for than sacques and circular shapes. Handsome peignoirs are loose Gabrielles. Yokes, pointed or straight according to fancy, are formed entirely of trimming, and made without shoulder seams. A band of trimming down the front of the garment is very ornamental. Standing collars are preferred, as they do not rumple easily. Full sleeves are clumsy. A better style is a loose coat sleeve with pointed cuff large enough for the hand to pass through. Valenciennes is the favorite lace for these garments. Cluny is also desirable, as it is very strong and washes well.

Muslin petticoats are gored. Those intended to be worn under short dresses have but four gored breaths without gathers at the belt. Long trained skirts have six widths, and are frequently cut by the same pattern as the outside dress. Nine yards of 4-quarter muslin is required for a trained skirt, 62 inches long in the back. Ruffles are again fashionably worn around the skirt, and tucked bands are inserted, as it is difficult to tuck the sloping widths smoothly. Diagonal tucks, or those perpendicularly arranged, are prettiest.

Corset covers are cut to extend over the hips. For slender figures it is best to make them very full, and gather into a belt, with basques attached.

Woolen embroidery is recommended for flannel as it keeps the same color as the flannel after washing.

Collar with Lappets

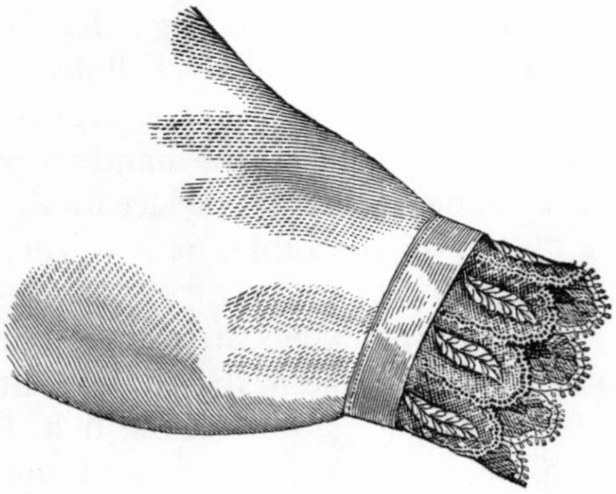

This collar, with sleeves and cuffs to match, is made of lappets or leaves of Swiss muslin, embroidered and edged with Valenciennes lace, which overlap each other and form the articles. The illustrations show the collar, the sleeve, and a full-size section of the cuff. The leaves forming the collar are somewhat larger in front than behind. They are set into a double band, care being taken to make the three front leaves slant a little to either side as shown.

Cravat Collar with Lappets

This collar is made of muslin lappets or leaves, embroidered in satin stitch and edged with Valenciennes lace, which are set into a narrow band overlapping each other a little. The pattern is the same as that of the Collar with Lappets. The band is covered with blue ribbon, over which Valenciennes lace is pleated. Long ends of blue ribbon fall from the back of the collar.

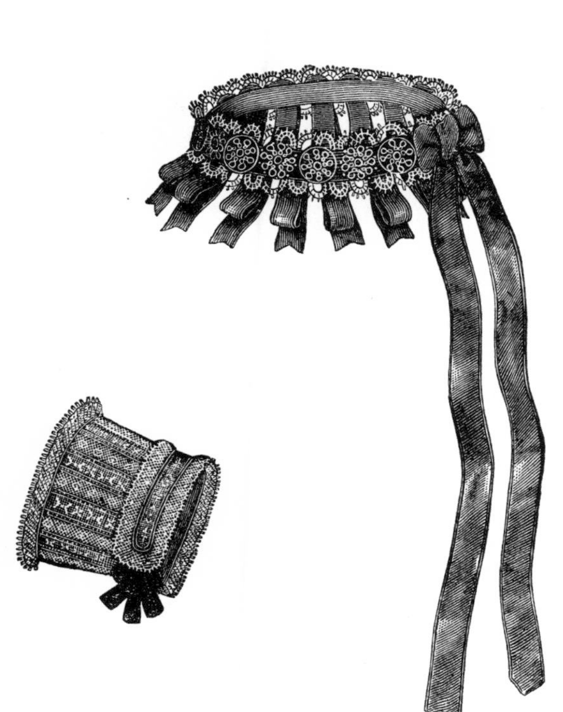

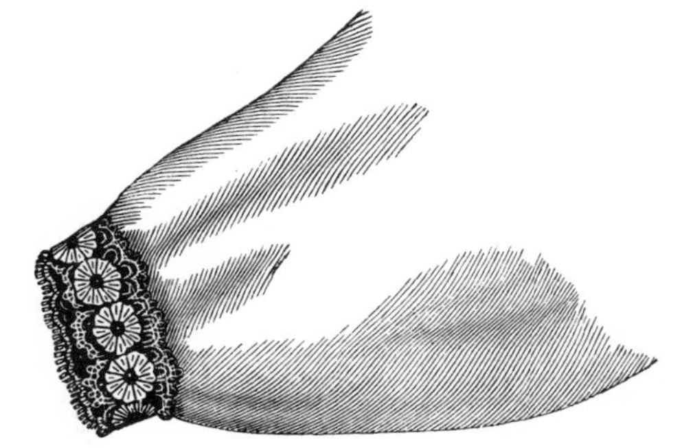

Cravat Collar with Ribbon Loops

This collar, with matching cuffs, consists of a strip of muslin, on which needlework rosettes are sewn. The muslin is cut in scallops along the lower edge, and a frill of Valenciennes lace is set thereon. Pink ribbon is laid underneath. Loops and ends of pink ribbon complete the collar, as shown. The design is the same as the Collar with Tabs. An accompanying illustration shows matching cuffs.

Collar with Tabs

This collar, with matching sleeves, is made of a strip of Swiss muslin, 21 inches long, on which needlework rosettes are sewn. The muslin is then cut out in scallops on the under edge along the rosettes, and edged with a frill of Valenciennes lace. The ends are scalloped and edged with lace on both sides. The illustrations show the collar on the chemisette, the sleeve, and a full-size section of the end of the collar. The collar is set into a double band. The sleeve is trimmed round the bottom with needlework rosettes applied on muslin to match the collar. Pink ribbon is laid under both sleeves and collar.

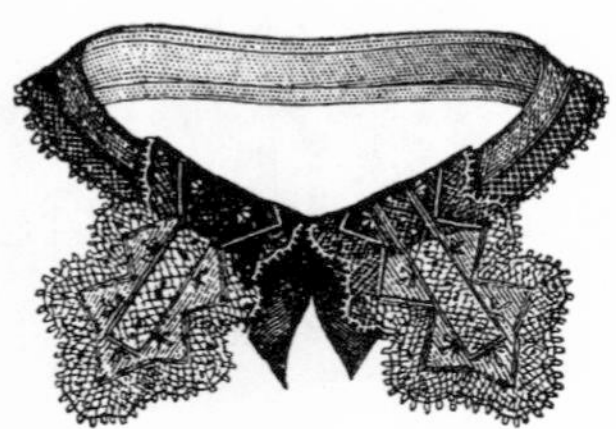

Bavette Collar

This collar, with matching cuffs, is set on a small band of needlework insertion, which is trimmed on the lower edge with narrow Valenciennes lace set on full. Two ends or bavettes, made of Valenciennes insertion and points of needlework, edged with Valenciennes lace, are set on the front of the collar. The illustrations show the collar complete and a full-size section of the cuff to be worn with it, made like the bavettes.

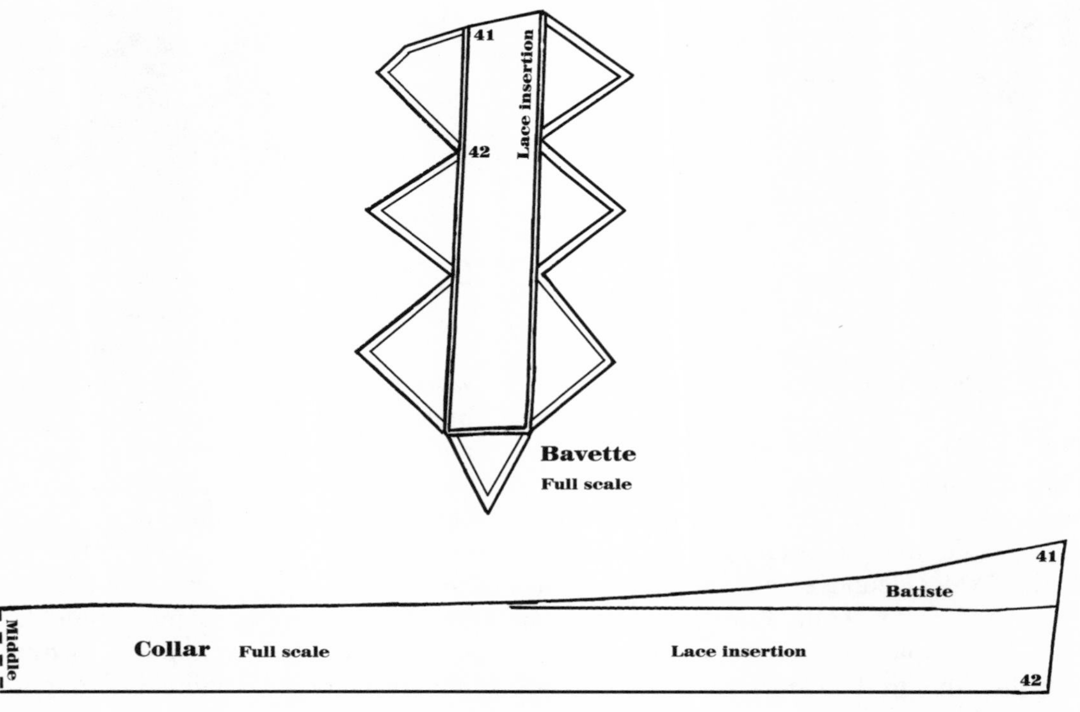

Bavette Collar with Chemisette

Bavette Collar with Chemisette

This collar, with matching chemisette and cuffs, is made of narrow Valenciennes insertion, 2/5 inch wide, and fine needlework squares. The pattern for half of it is given. It is edged with Valenciennes lace 1/2 inch wide. The design for the squares is worked in satin stitch on Swiss muslin. Having set the collar on a small band, join it to the chemisette.

The chemisette is made of fine linen, double, Valenciennes insertion, and needlework squares. It is bordered with narrow needlework insertion and a frill of Valenciennes edging. Two bows of blue ribbon finish the chemisette in front, as shown. The illustration shows the chemisette arranged on the figure.

February 8, 1868

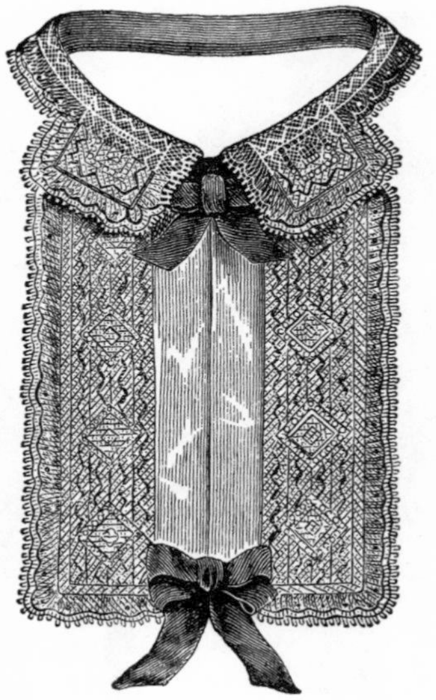

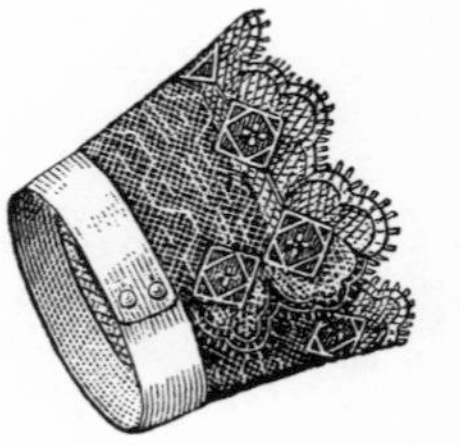

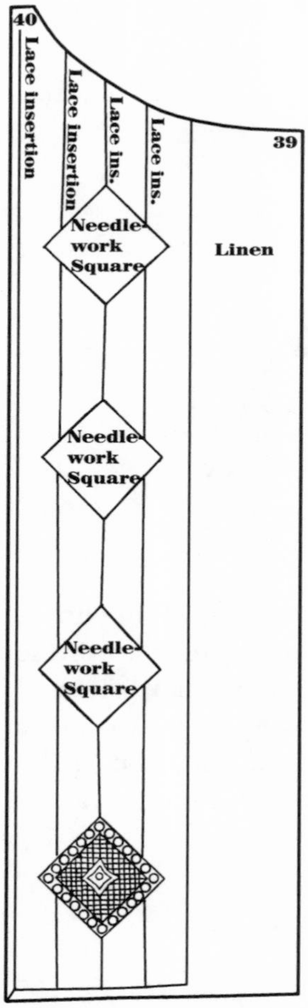
40
Lace insertion
Lace insertion
Lace ins.
Lace ins.
39
Linen
Needle-work Square
Needle-work Square
Needle-work Square

Chemisette
1/2 scale

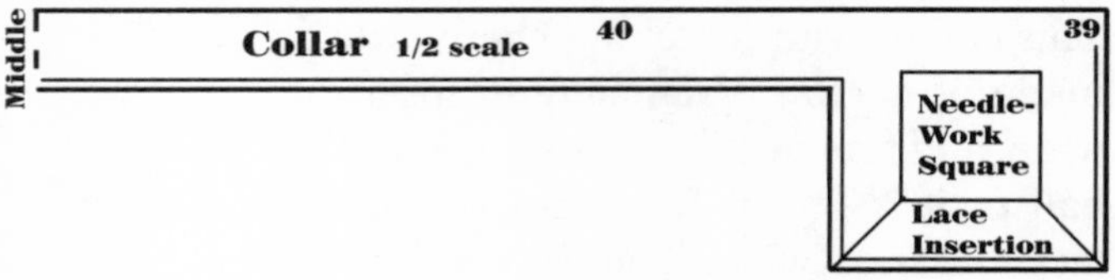
Middle
Collar 1/2 scale
40
39
Needle-Work Square
Lace Insertion

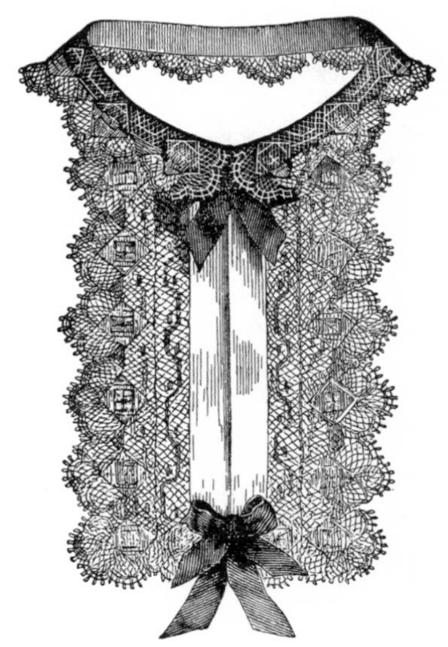

Collar and Chemisette

This collar and chemisette is made of narrow Valenciennes insertion and small needlework squares. The pattern for half the collar is given, as well as the design for the squares, which is worked in satin stitch on nainsook. The collar is bordered with narrow Valenciennes edging, and is set into a double band. The chemisette is cut from the same pattern as the chemisette for the Bavette Collar above. It is made of fine linen, double, insertion, and needlework squares. It is bordered with Valenciennes edging. Two bows of ribbon finish the front. The cuffs match the collar.

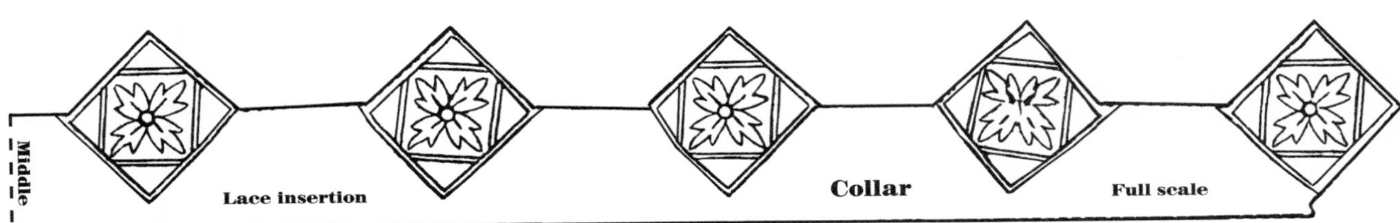

February 8, 1868

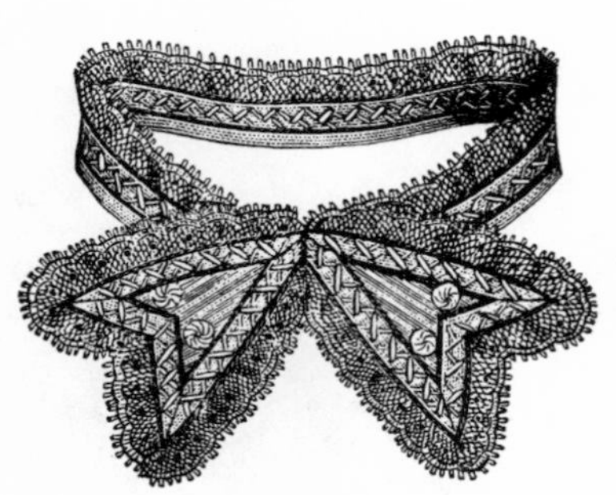

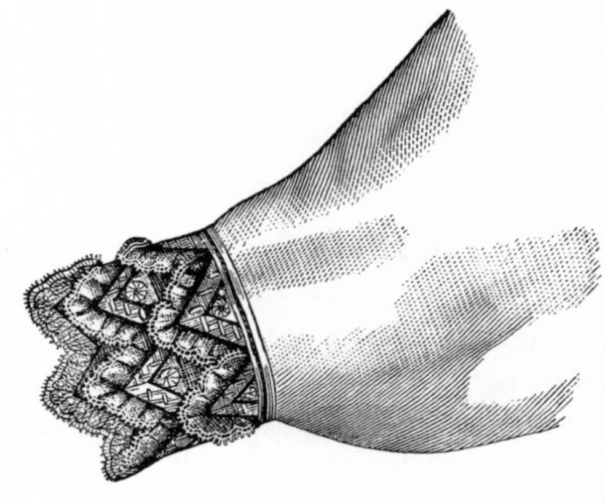

Cravat Collar

This collar, with matching cuffs, is made of needlework insertion, edged with Valenciennes lace. Cravat ends of pleated Swiss muslin, bordered with needlework insertion and Valenciennes lace, with two small figures in the corners, are set on the front of the collar. The collar is sewn in a band.

The cuff is made of a strip of Swiss muslin, 1/4 yard long and 1 1/2 inches wide, sewn together at the ends. It is laid in small pleats, on which are sewn points of Swiss muslin (see pattern), bordered with narrow needlework insertion and Valenciennes edging, and ornamented with application figures of needlework.

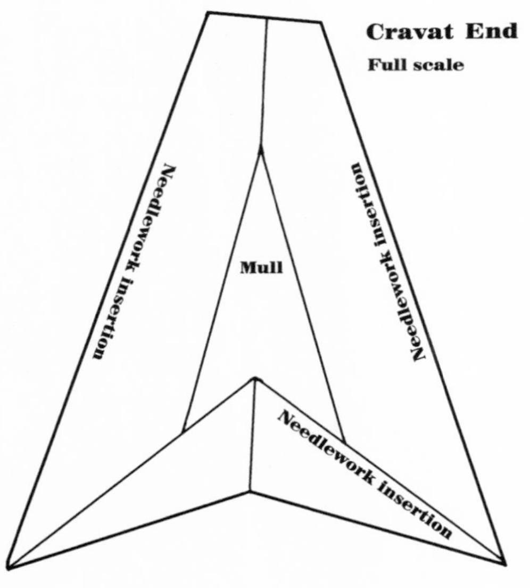

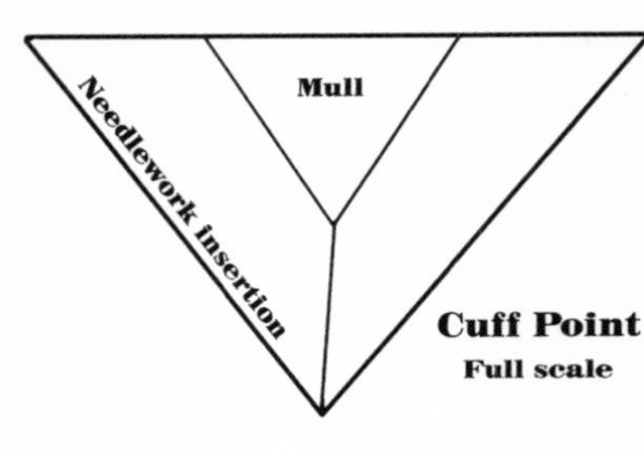

February 15, 1868

Skating Suits

Materials for skating suits should be chosen for service and durability, as the most experienced skaters are liable to accidents on a crowded rink. Cloth, serge, velveteen, and poplin are more appropriate than the handsome velvet and plush dresses in vogue this winter. The skirt of the dress should be shorter than the usual walking dress, and not so full. Tight-fitting basquines are the most jaunty wrappings. Loose redingotes and paletots of the same material as the dress are preferred for slender figures. A belt with short sash ends is worn with loose garments.

Gray felt cloth, entirely waterproof, makes an appropriate skating costume. It is 1 7/8 yards wide. Six yards make the short dress and jacket. Skirts of real Scotch woolen plaid are bright and pretty, with dark velvet jackets and turbans. We have seen some very beautiful suits of English corduroy, light gray skirts, and short basques, worn with a longer skirt of blue poplin, or over green ottoman reps.

Very pretty skating sets are of Siberian squirrel, short boas, and pocket muffs, ornamented with the head of the animal. Similar sets of black Astrakhan or ermine are sold. Round muffs and capes require almost twice as much fur as the flat pocket muffs and boa, and are consequently double the price. Skating turbans of sealskin and of krimmer are adorned with wings of gay plumage or clusters of metallic leaves. Those of Astrakhan and Persiani have long tassels of the fur.

Borders of fur for trimming are sold by the yard. These include Astrakhan bands 2 inches wide, real ermine, and mink.

Varieties

Among the latest importations are some dress silks of beautiful quality, in new colors and strange combinations. The patterns are simple narrow stripes, solid and even, only a few threads in each. The colors are most brilliant, often contrasting widely, yet so prettily blended that each softens the other. Fancy alternate stripes of the gay marigold and rich capucine toned down to a quiet and tasteful shade. Another pattern has a purple stripe on a chameleon ground of pink and gray; still another is apple green with mauve; again there are tiny threads of cuir color on Bismarck, and two shades of lavender on white. These silks are 3/4 yard wide.

The becoming Duchesse cravat, or collar, is easily made by forming a puff of white net over blue ribbon. A narrow lace on either side. The puff laps at the brooch. Wider lace and appliqué embroidery are sewn at each end, forming tabs.

The fashionable feather trimming is seen on imported veils. A square of Brussels net pointed below the chin, has a border of delicate white and black feathers, and tiny pearl beads.

Sashes are worn wider, and not so long. Rosettes or bows are placed near each end. Lace sashes are worn for evening full toilette. Those of black velvet are lined with scarlet or capucine, or with white satin. Heavy net fringe and jet pendants on the pointed ends.

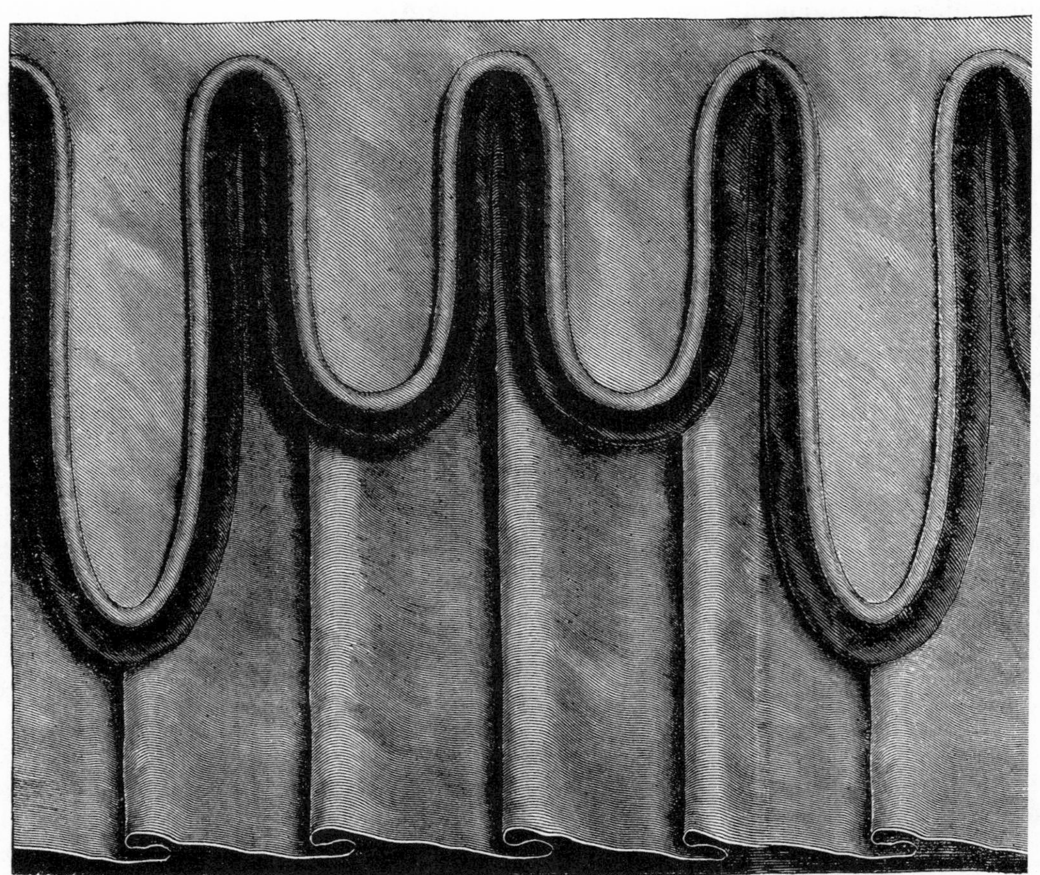

Skirt Trimming

This simple trimming for underskirts is easily made by pleating a strip of cloth. Then set flat on it, at a little distance from the bottom, a scalloped strip of some bright color, bound with braid as shown.

February 22, 1868

Kid Gloves

Late importations of kid gloves display some new and graceful designs. The handsomest style has a wristband fastened with two studs of gilt or silver. A dozen similar studs and a silk cord with tassels of crimped silk headed with gilt ornament the back. The stitching and embroidery are neatly done in a contrasting color. The wristband is welted and bound with kid to match the embroidery.

Brown gloves are still fashionable, ranging from light tan to *buerre* and cream color for evening and full dress, through all the yellow shades to the golden Bismarck and Vesuvius. Lavender, mauve, church purple, and "mentana" red are stitched on the back with black silk in a Greek pattern and bound with black kid. Gilt ornaments. Black is bound with white and fastened with silver studs. Straw color, pistache, and a rosy, fleshlike tint are embroidered with black and drawn together by tirettes and tassels.

A pretty fashion among the seamless gloves is a white kid with puffed cuffs fitted to the wrist by elastic cords. A scalloped edge falls on the arm. Rows of tiny gilt eyelets on the puff are interlaced with silk cords. On others are embroidered monograms, truelove knots, bows, butterflies, birds, and bees. Rows of feathered stitching on the back.

Dark kid gauntlets for traveling and morning dress are neatly made with bias cuffs, welted with white tirettes inside, and three silver buttons on the back of the cuff.

Varieties

A Merrimac print of an ingenious and intricate design is called the Devil's Dream. At the first glance you see only a plain purple calico of an ordinary pattern, spotted with white and black. On looking at it longer a transformation takes place. Innumerable figures appear–beasts, birds, clowns, skeletons, harlequins, fiends, goblins, and all the demons of Pandemonium are before you.

A pretty lace camisole is made of black guipure, with rows of scarlet velvet ribbon, inserted at intervals of 1 inch down the whole garment. Wide guipure lace around the sacque and sleeves, under which is scarlet fringe of crimped silk.

Striped silks and satins are in vogue for evening dresses–rose color or blue, with white in alternate stripes 1 inch wide. They are usually made with double skirts, the upper one trimmed with a silk ruche and festooned. Lace fichus are worn with them. Wide sashes of lace form a pretty addition.

Crocheted Tatting

Hitherto tatting has been done only with a shuttle. We give herewith descriptions and illustrations by means of which it can be done with a crochet needle. The use of the latter is so generally understood that the new method will be more quickly and easily learned. It is also less trouble than tying the knots with a shuttle, and requires less time and labor. The work is firmer and more even, and is more easily washed. The principal superiority, however, is that it can be used in a much greater number of designs and arrangements. It is adapted to making lace, rosettes, insertion, pieces for figured designs, etc., all of which are in precisely the same style as ordinary tatting. It can also be unraveled and worked over if there is any imperfection in the work, which, as is known, is impossible in tatting.

The materials consist of a crochet hook and cotton–either the twisted crochet cotton, or spool thread of a size corresponding to the work. The work can, of course, be made in any quality of cotton desired. The hook must be about half as coarse as the cotton. The whole length of the needle must be of equal size, and either fastened to a wooden or bone handle or screwed into a holder. The hook must be smooth and blunt at the point, and from 1 to 2 inches long, as the entire row of loops is taken on it at once. To make the instructions clear, the stitches in Figures 1, 5, 11, and 12 are magnified.

Begin by tying a loop as for crochet work and taking it on the needle. Then take the hook in the right hand. Lay the thread in a loop between the thumb and forefinger of the left hand, bringing the end of the working thread above. Take this loop on the needle and pull the thread till it is firm. (This makes a plain loop.) In making the next (purled loop) the end of the thread must be brought under. These two loops form a double stitch. Continue till the number of double stitches on the needle is sufficient to form a ring.

Figure 1. Double knot

Then throw the thread around the needle about 1 inch from the end of the row. Hold the stitches between the thumb and forefinger of the left hand, and draw the thread through all the stitches, holding the hook of the needle downward and forward (see Figure 3).

Figure 2. Beginning of ring

Figure 3. Rounding of ring

Next make the thread firm, so the loop on the needle lies close to the other row of stitches, and fasten it into a ring by drawing the thread through the loop. Then crochet a slip stitch, putting the needle through the upper part of the last double stitch (Figure 4 shows this point by an arrow).

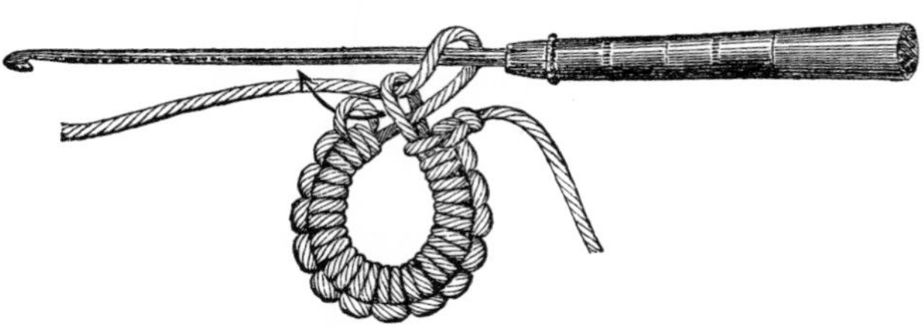

Figure 4. Closing of ring

Crochet a few chain stitches to connect the rings, and proceed with the next precisely in the same manner as the first. The picots are made by leaving the thread of any length desired between any 2 double stitches. The rings are also joined by the picots. Put the hook through the picot, draw the thread through into a loop, and retain this on the needle.

Figure 5. Execution of picot

The lace in Figure 6 is made of rings, connected by 5 ch. (chain stitches) between each. Each ring consists of 5 ds. (double stitches), 1 p. (picot), 8 ds., 1p., 5 ds. The picots serve only as a means of joining the rings.

Figure 6. Crocheted tatting edging

The rings in the lace in Figure 7 are joined like those of the edging previously described. Each ring consists of 6 ds., then 7 p., each separated from the next by 2 ds., 6 ds. In every ring except the first take up in place of the 1st p. the last p. of the former ring.

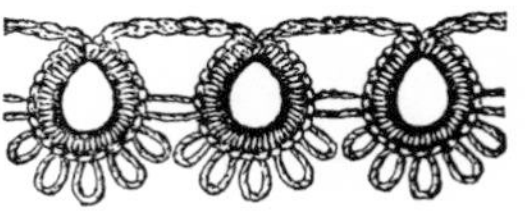

Figure 7. Crocheted tatting edging

To work the edging in Figure 8, * make 21 ds.; join into a ring; crochet 5 ch. Then follows a figure composed of 8 plain loops, joined like the stitches of the large rings; crochet again 5 ch. Repeat from *. Each following ring is joined to the preceding after the first 5 ds. Finish above by a row of 6 ch. alternately with 1 sc. (single crochet) in the connecting stitches of the figures.

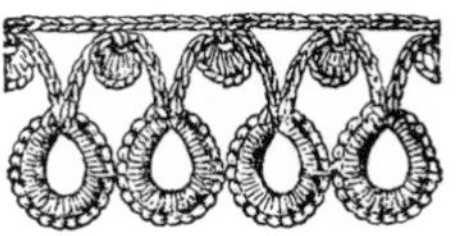

Figure 8. Crocheted tatting edging

To work the insertion in Figure 9, crochet a ring as follows. Make 5 ds. 7p., each separated from the next by 2 ds.; 5 ds.; then 17 ch. At the end of this a ring like the first. 7 ch; then a figure consisting of 9 plain stitches. Turn the work. Fasten to the 11th stitch of the first 17 ch. by putting the needle through the upper part of the stitch. Close the figure

February 22, 1868

by drawing a loop through the 11 loops on the needle. Make 7 ch; 1 sc. in the 4th stitch of the same chain row; 3 ch.; a ring like the first, fastening it to the former ring after making 5 ds.; 7 ch. Turn the work. Make one figure like the former small figures, fastened to the 8th ch. (this is the chain row preceding the last ring). 7 ch., which are fastened to the 4th ch., counting from the next ring; 3 ch. Repeat from *.

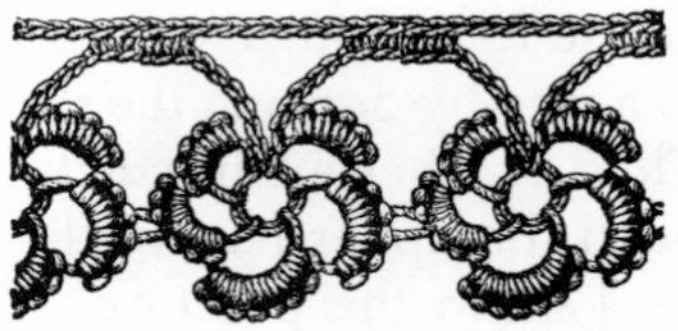

Figure 10. Crocheted tatting edging

Figure 9. Crocheted tatting insertion

Figure 11. Beginning of star

Figures 10, 11, and 12 show another crocheted tatting edging. For this crochet * 5ds.; draw the thread through without joining the stitches into a ring. Retain the loop on the needle and crochet 6 ds; draw the thread through these 6 stitches, and again retain the loop on the needle. Crochet 8 ds. in the same manner; then 5 ds., 1 p., 1 ds., and last 5 ds., so that there are altogether 5 loops on the needle (see Figure 11). Then throw the thread around the needle as usual, and draw it through the 5 loops. Join the ring by 1 sc., taken under the connecting thread as shown by a point in Figure 12, thus forming a figure similar to a star. Then follow 18 ch. Repeat from *, joining each following figure to the one preceding by taking up the picot after the first 3 of the 6 ds. The next row consists of 5 sc. in the 7th to 11th stitches of the 18 ch. of the last row; alternate with 6 ch.

Figure 12. Finishing of star

The edging in Figure 13 consists of rings linked into each other. Crochet 30 ds. and draw the thread through *. Join in a ring by pulling the needle under the working thread, which is thrown around and drawn through in a loop. The working thread must now lie inside the ring. Then crochet 6 ch., putting the needle through the loop above the finished ring on the needle so that it lies back of the chain stitches. Make 30 ds.; draw the thread through all the loops on the needle. Then draw half the length of the row of loops through the first ring, and repeat from *. The next row consists of 1 dc. (double crochet stitch) in the middle of the 5 ch. of the preceding row; alternate with 4 ch.

Figure 13. Crocheted tatting edging

Figure 14. Crocheted tatting edging

The lace in Figure 14 is finished in one round. Crochet a ring consisting of 5 ds.; 7 p., each separated from the next by 2 ds.; 5 ds. Close to this a second ring: 6 ds; take up the last p. of the former ring; 5 p., each separated from the next by 2 ds.; 1 p.; 6 ds. Finally a third ring like the first. Instead of the 1st p., however, take up the last p. of the second ring. Crochet now 8 ch.; take up the last p. of the second ring; 2 ch.; take up the p. before the last of the second ring; 6 ch.; 1 ch. p., the same length as the other picot stitches. This chain picot is made by drawing the loop on the needle somewhat longer than usual, then taking the needle out and inserting it in the previous stitch, and continuing to crochet so that the loop is fastened and forms a picot. After this 3 ch.; again 1 ch. p., 8 ch; then three leaf figures like the former. In the first ring, however, instead of forming the first 4 picots, take up the 2 ch. p. and then the 2 p. of the third ring of the former figure. Having finished the figure, work 5 ch., and join to the chain stitches preceding the first leaf.

For the lace in Figure 15, which is worked in three rounds, crochet for the first round the three-leaved figures as follows. * A ring of 16 double stitches (ds.); a second ring of 20 ds.; a third ring of 16 ds.; then 10 chain stitches (ch.); a figure of 9 plain stitches (see Figure 15); 10 ch. Repeat from *. The first ring of the next figure must be fastened to the middle side stitch of the last ring. Second round: 1 single crochet stitch (sc.) in the 4th chain stitch of the former round, *; 6 ch.; one figure of 9 plain stitches; 6 ch; sc. around the thread that joins the little figure of the last round. Repeat from *. Third round: Alternately 1 sc. around the joining thread of the next figure; 9 ch.

Figure 15. Crocheted tatting edging

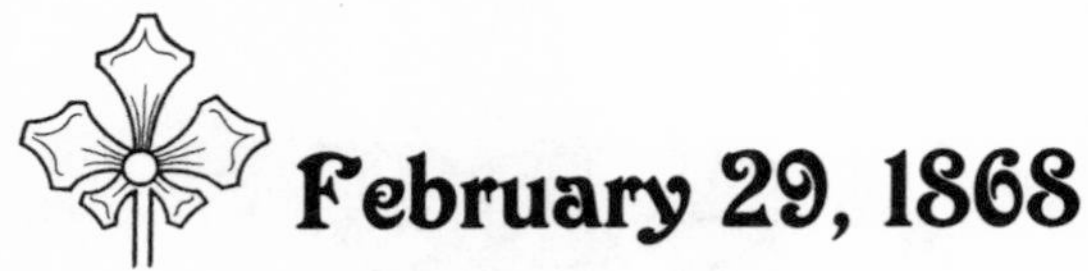

February 29, 1868

Bonnets

The evening bonnets made by our leading milliners are of lace, of feathers, and of beaded tulle, made in very simple styles. Rows of point lace, with a cluster of flowers in front, are mounted on small frames. Lace medallions of various shapes, oval, diamond, and triangular, are prettily displayed over velvet of any light shade, such as pearl gray, pink, and lavender. Ornaments are placed directly over the forehead in the point formed by the curved diadem that is added to the fanchon. Velvet and lace bows with ends are arranged high up on the back of the bonnet.

Velvet and Satin Hoods

Fur-trimmed hoods are prettily made up. Those for evening wear are of white or blue or amber satin, quilted in small diamonds, with pearls introduced in the stitching, and bordered with ermine or swansdown. Traveling hoods of black velvet are usually made in the fanchon shape, with long lapels at the throat. They may be trimmed with Astrakhan, chinchilla, or mink. A pretty one of gray satin is bordered with gray Persiani. These are found at the furriers instead of the milliners.

Fur gauntlets are now worn by ladies, resembling those used by gentlemen when driving; and are large enough to be drawn over a kid glove. Sealskin and white otter are most in favor for these. A hood, gloves, and boa of chinchilla are pretty suits for sleighing and traveling.

Walking Dresses

Walking suits, with a single skirt simulating two, have given place to those with double skirts. Imported suits have the upper skirt formed into a small train that is to be looped up disclosing a gay petticoat beneath. The loops make heavy puffed festoons. Four buttons and loops are the simple accessories, or machinery, if you please, for festooning the long upper skirt.

Black velvet dresses are worn over scarlet, blue, or green satin petticoats. Passementerie, jet, fringe, and satin piping ornament the velvet skirt. The satin may be either left plain or bound with velvet of the same shade, cut bias. Two or three narrow ruffles of satin are also used. Striped petticoats of very handsome materials, grosgrain alternating with velvet stripes, are fashionably worn. They are without trimming. Full suits of velvet are trimmed with fur.

Parisian ladies loop the velvet skirts of their walking dresses with a sash fastened at the middle of the back. Very gay colored sashes are worn, but those of black velvet are in better taste.

The Marie Antoinette mantle is the newest style of wrapping. The redingote or polonaise is still very popular. Short loose paletots have wide flowing sleeves, lined with satin like the underskirt.

Varieties

A pretty domino, worn at one of the masquerades now so fashionable, is of blue satin. A square yoke is made to fit smoothly over the evening dress worn beneath. The rest of the garment falling from this yoke is gored in such a manner that it may afterward be worn as the skirt of a dress. It is loose, with a slight train, and is confined at the waist by a belt and sash. A ruche of white satin surrounds the yoke, sleeves, and skirt. A white satin hood attached to the neck is large enough to disguise the wearer most effectually.

A new sash worn in Paris is made of gimp in which jet beads are interwoven. This sash hangs from the sides, is festooned into a sort of basque, and then falls almost to the edge of the skirt, where the ends cross and form a bow with long tassels. Bretelles for the shoulder accompany the sash.

Loose, square breakfast jackets are giving place to bodices with tight-fitting sleeves and a sash worn at the side. Another style has a small basque attached to the waist instead of a sash.

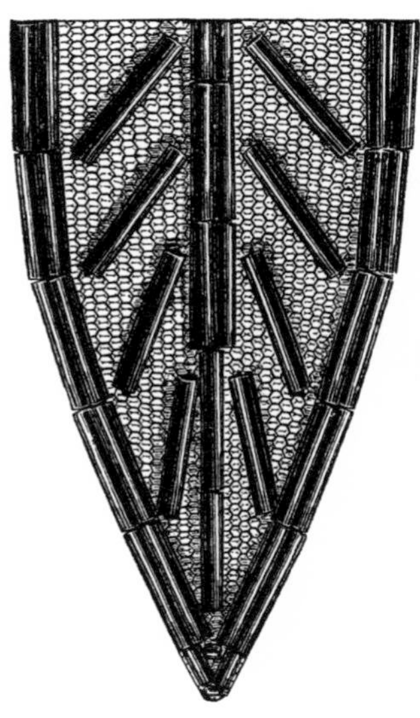

Rush Headdress

This headdress is composed of leaves designed to simulate rushes. The leaves are made of black silk lace, on a foundation of stiff lace, and are wired round the edge and through the middle. An accompanying illustration shows a leaf full size, ornamented with jet bugles. The five long leaves are graduated in length. The top of each is fastened to a piece of stiff lace, on which smaller leaves are set in the form of a bow. The headdress is worn a considerable distance in front, so that the long leaves fall over the chignon.

February 29, 1868

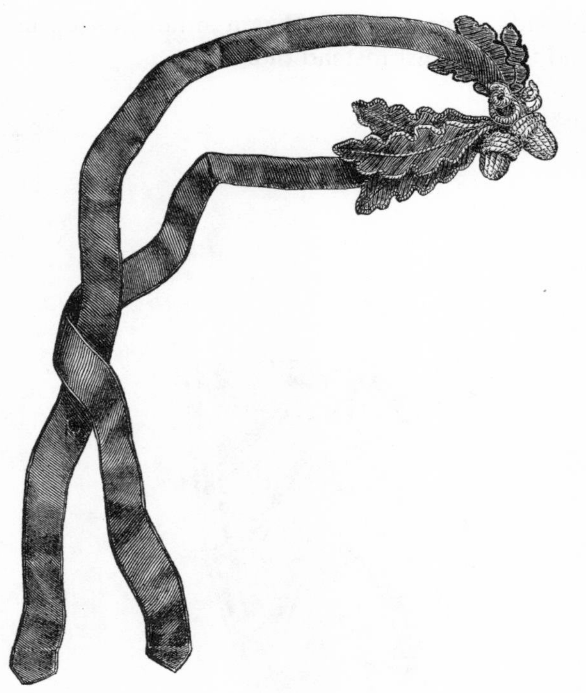

Blackberry Wreath

This headdress is formed of a small wreath of blackberry blossoms, blackberries, and leaves. It encircles the head, with a long spray depending behind.

Oak Leaf Bandeau

This bandeau is made of brown ribbon, trimmed with oak leaves of brown silk and gold cord, and bronze acorns. Take a straight foundation, about 13 inches long and 1 inch wide. Cover it with brown silk. Set on the ends two long brown ribbons, to be tied under the chignon. Trim the bandeau in front with leaves and acorns, as shown. The accompanying illustration shows a leaf full size. This is made of double stiff lace. It is covered with brown silk, wired round the edge, and finished with fine gold cord.

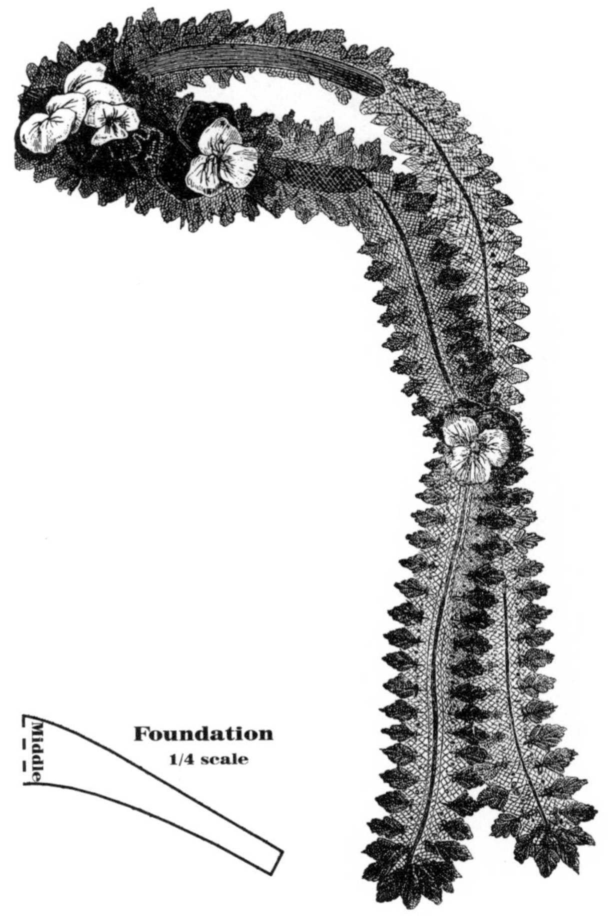

Black Velvet Headdress

The foundation of this headdress is made of a hoop of ribbon wire 20 inches in circumference, covered with black velvet. On the left side set short ends of black velvet ribbon 1 1/2 inches wide, a cluster of green and bronze leaves, and a ribbon 2 yards long. Then fasten the other end of the ribbon to the right side of the bandeau, winding it twice obliquely around the foundation. Finish the bandeau in front by a thick cluster of brown and bronze leaves, alternating with each other.

Headdress of Lace and Pansies

This headdress is intended for middle-aged ladies. It is composed of black lace 1 1/2 inches wide, narrow black insertion with black velvet ribbon run through it, jet grelots, and pansies.

The foundation is cut from the pattern, and covered with velvet. The lace is then sewn together in the middle, and closely box pleated on the foundation as illustrated. Clusters of pansies are laid in the pleats in front and on one side. To each end of the foundation fasten a barbe 3/4 long. This is formed by sewing the lace on each side of the insertion, and running a velvet ribbon through the latter. Then attach these ends together with a single pansy.

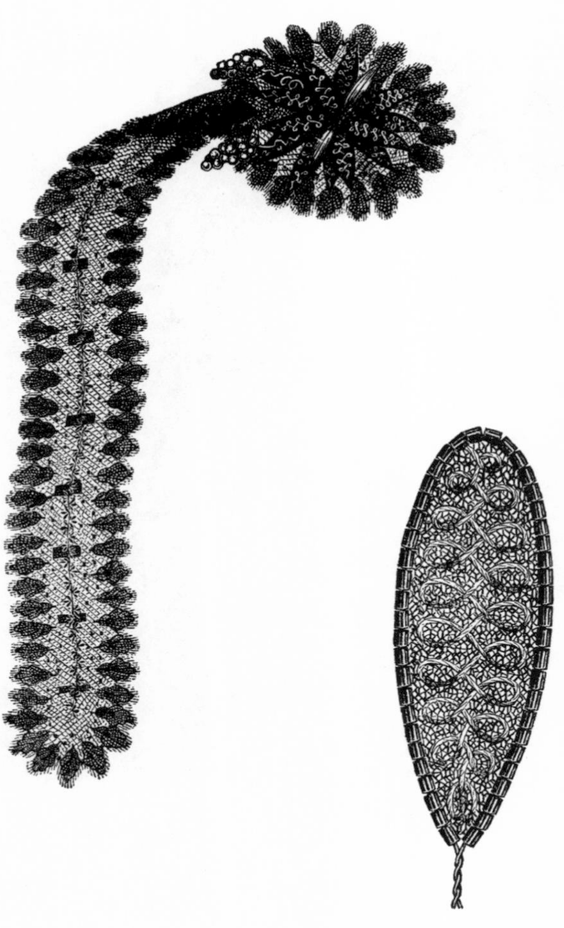

Rosette Headdress

This headdress is formed of a black lace barbe, black leaves, bronze leaves, and clusters of grapes. Cut a circular piece of stiff lace from the pattern. Cover it with silk lace. Pleat black lace 2 inches wide a little way from the edge, so it covers the latter. Put the leaves and grapes in the center.

The black leaves can be made of stiff lace, covered with silk lace. The illustration shows one full size. These leaves are wired round the edge, studded with black beads, and veined in the middle with fine gold cord. Black velvet leaves may be used instead.

A barbe, made by sewing two pieces of lace together, and barring it at regular intervals with velvet, is fastened at the back. A ready-made barbe may be substituted.

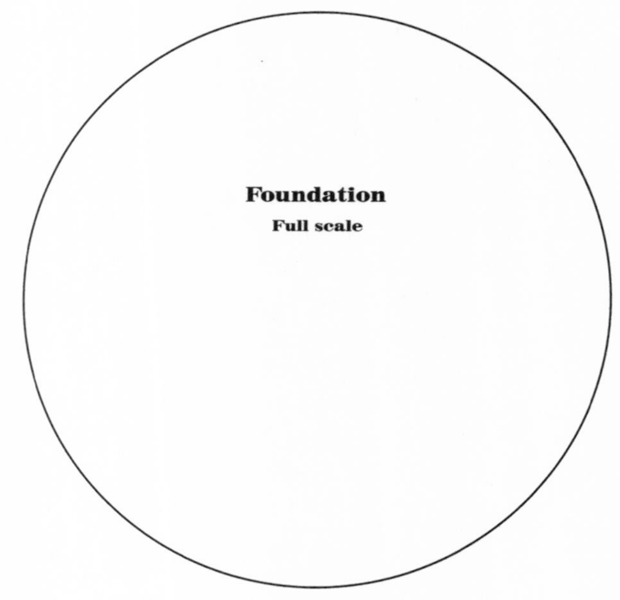

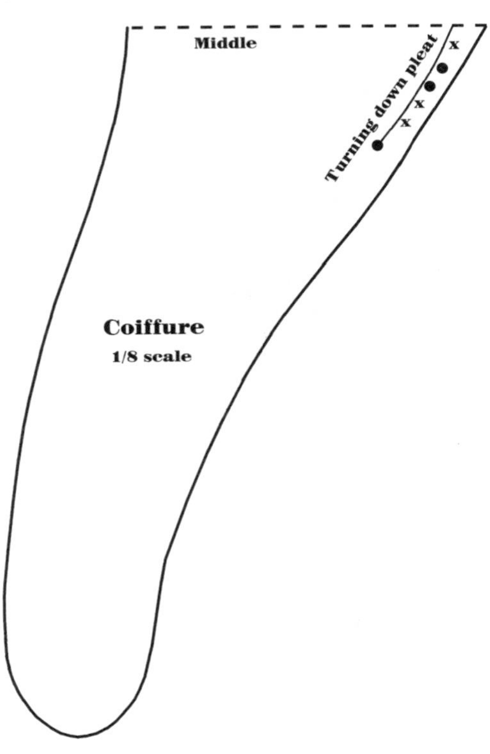

Opera Coiffure

This headdress is simple and effective. It is composed of figured silk lace, edging, and colored velvet ribbon. Cut of black figured lace one piece from the pattern. Trim it round the edge with lace 1 1/2 inches wide, and pleat it from *x* to •. Finish with two bows with loops and ends.

Spanish Mantilla

The original is of black figured lace, edged with a frill of black lace 2 inches wide. A crimson rose with leaves and buds confines the mantilla.

Cut the mantilla. Set the aforesaid frill of lace around the edge, as well as along the slit in the middle of the back from the bottom to *x*. Cover the seam with narrow lace insertion, through which run a narrow black velvet ribbon. With this ribbon the mantilla is gathered along the front edge, and from the middle to * on either side. Finish with rose.

Spanish Mantilla

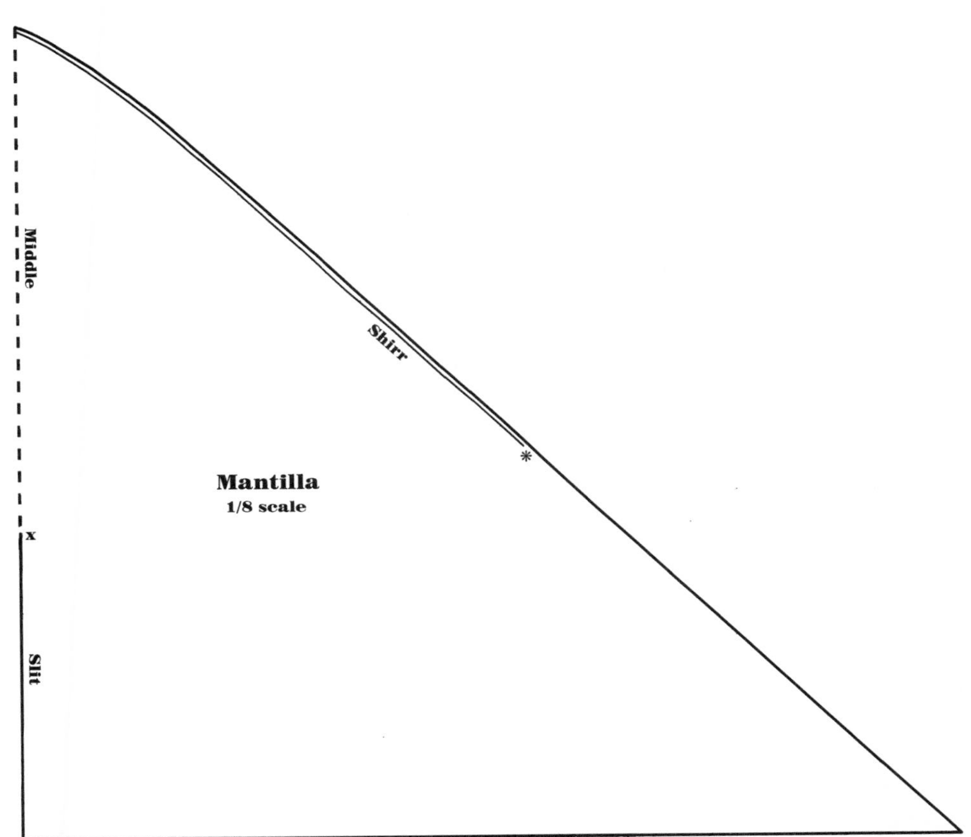

Bretelles with Belt

These bretelles are made of blue satin ribbon, 2 1/2 and 1 1/2 inches wide, and white blonde 2 inches wide, laid on a foundation of Swiss muslin, and fastened to a similar belt.

Cut of the muslin two pieces each from the front and back. Cover them with the broad ribbon, making a small pleat along the middle. Make a cross pleat in each of the front bretelles, along the narrow line. Set the blonde along the straight line on the cut piece, making a fullness at the point. Then sew the front bretelles fast at the back from 27 to 28, letting the back bretelles hang loose from the seam in imitation of a lappet. Now sew two pieces of the narrow blue ribbon on the front of the bretelles, as marked by * and •• on the front, so as to cross each other. Cover the place where they are sewn on with a bow without ends of the same ribbon.

Set the bretelles on a belt. This consists of black satin ribbon, 1 1/2 inches wide, and of the necessary length, covered with double Swiss muslin, which is again covered with blonde. The belt closes at the back and sides. Finish with a bow with long ends of broad blue ribbon, edged on one side with blonde.

Bretelles with Belt

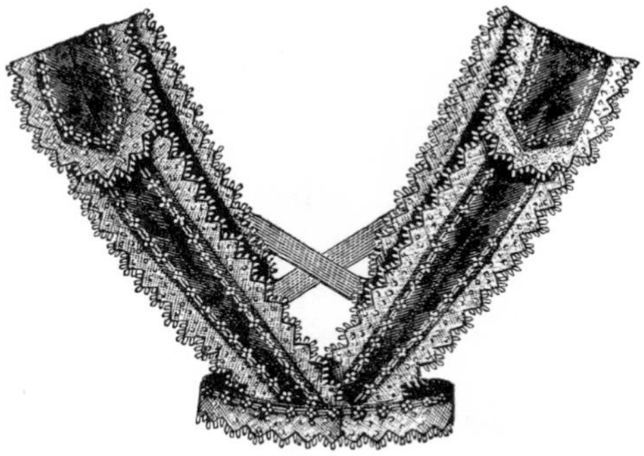

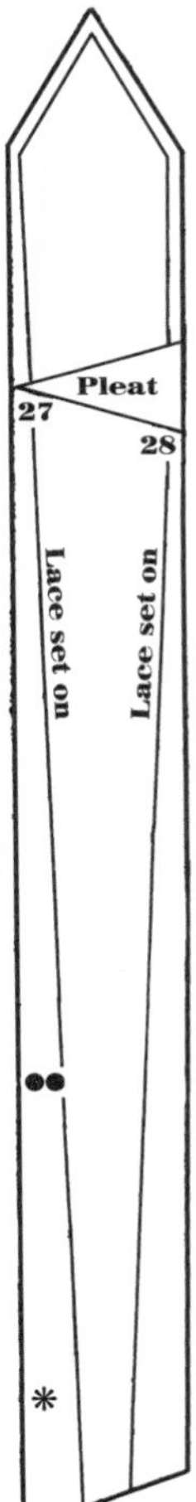

Front Bretelle
1/4 scale

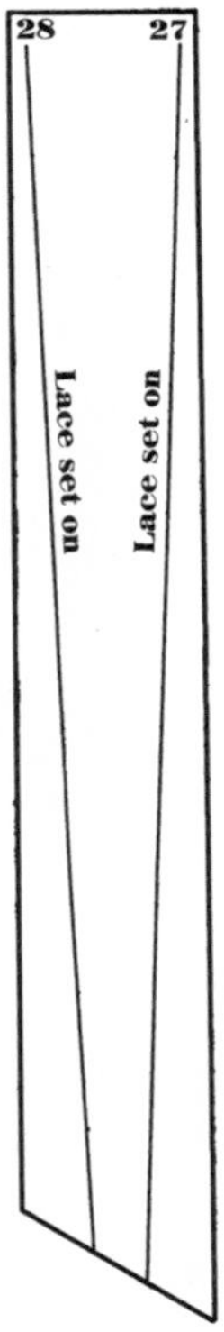

Pleat
27
28
Lace set on
Lace set on

Back Bretelle
1/4 scale

28
27
Lace set on
Lace set on

Peasant Waist with Bretelles

Blue satin ribbon 1 1/2 inches wide and waved, black velvet points with white edges, arranged on a foundation of Swiss muslin, form this pretty waist.

Cut from Swiss muslin, allowing for turning down, two pieces from the bretelle, from the front and back crossbands each two pieces, and from the long band one piece of double stuff.

Bind the upper part of the muslin with satin ribbon. Quill the ribbon on the edge as illustrated. Cover the muslin with three rows of the velvet points. One row covers the binding, one the setting on of the quilled ribbon, while the third row lies between the two, and reaches from the middle to * on either side in the bretelle.

The front crossband is arranged in the same manner. But the long band is first covered with ribbon, then trimmed on the edge with the quilled ribbon and points. Join the parts to correspond with the figures on the pattern.

Set on the belt, which consists of a strip of double muslin 1 1/2 inches wide, covered with ribbon and a row of pointed velvet. The belt fastens behind, and is covered with a bow with long ends of satin ribbon 3 inches wide.

Peasant Waist with Bretelles

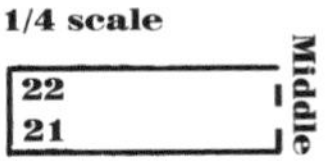

Back Crossband
1/4 scale

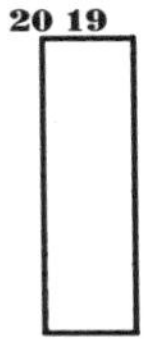

22
21
Middle

Long Band
1/4 scale

20 19

Bretelle
1/4 scale

*
22
21
17
18
*

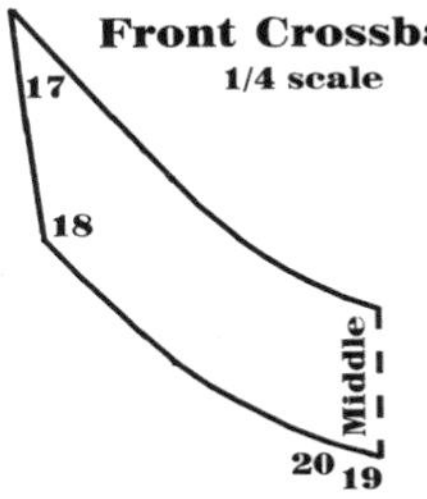

Front Crossband
1/4 scale

17
18
Middle
20 19

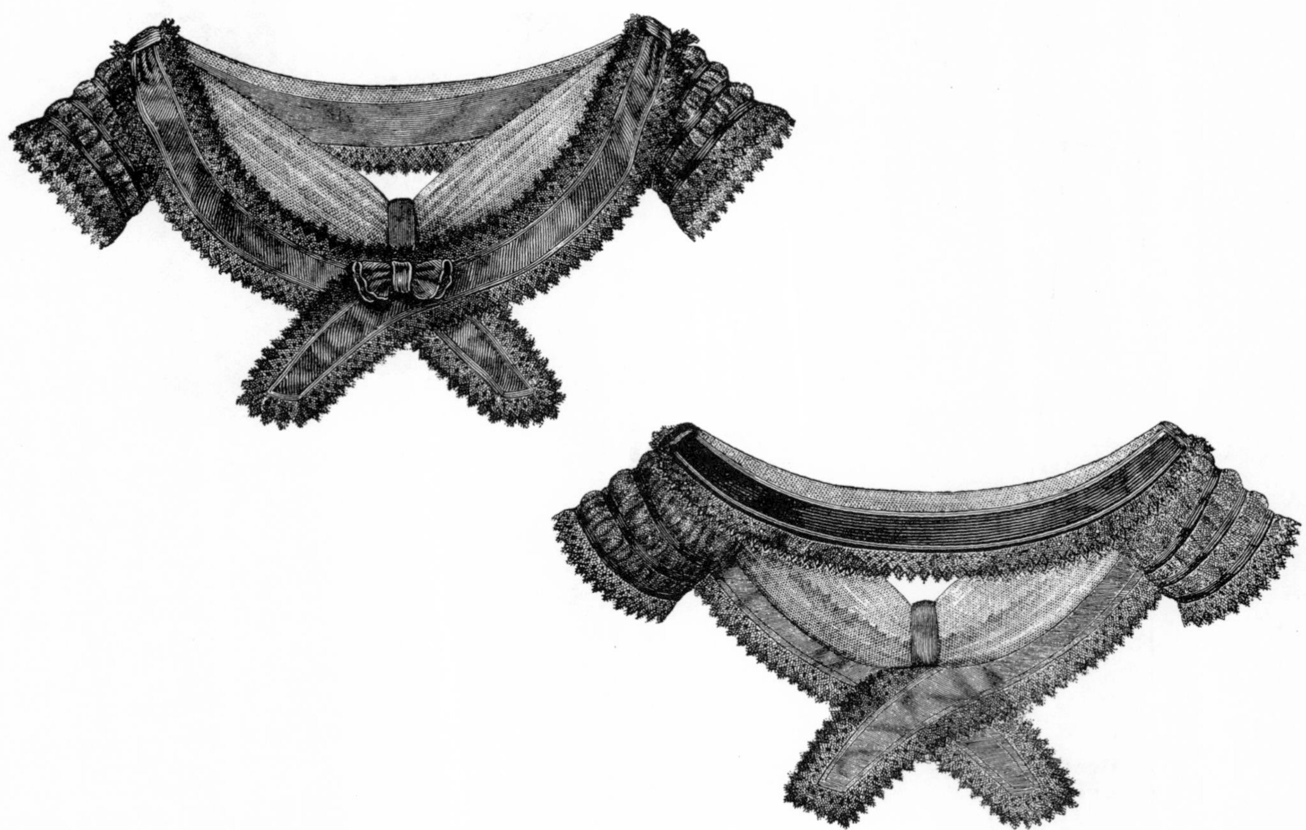

Black Satin and Lace Bertha

This bertha is designed to be worn over a black or colored dress. The original is of black satin, black silk lace, narrow black satin piping, and bead lace 1 1/4 inches wide. Short sleeves, of puffed lace, are worn with this bertha, but are fastened over the short sleeves of the dress before the bertha is put on.

Cut from satin, the bias way of the stuff, cotton lace, and muslin interlining, two pieces each from the front. Bind the edges with ribbon, and trim with piping and lace. Cross and fasten the ends at 25. Cover the place with the bow of satin, lace, and bead fringe shown in the illustration. Finish the front by the addition of pleated lace. For this, first cut for the foundation of cotton lace two pieces from the lining for the front. Lay the pleats therein as marked. Cover it with a straight strip of silk lace, closely pleated, and a little larger than the foundation, so as to completely conceal it. Join the pieces in the middle of the front. Cover the seam with a loop of satin. Sew the whole on the satin to correspond with the figures on the pattern. This completes the front of the bertha.

The back is of double satin cut bias. Edge it with piping, and trim the bottom with lace. Then set on it the pleated lace, which comes above it at the top, as illustrated. Join the fronts and back to correspond with the figures on the pattern. Cover the seams with a loop of satin.

For each sleeve take a strip of cotton lace, 14 inches long and 4 inches wide in the middle, narrowing down to 2 inches at the ends. On this arrange three small puffs of silk lace. Separate the puffs with satin piping, and trim the bottom of the sleeves with lace. Sew up the sleeves, and set the top into a double band.

Black Satin and Lace Bertha

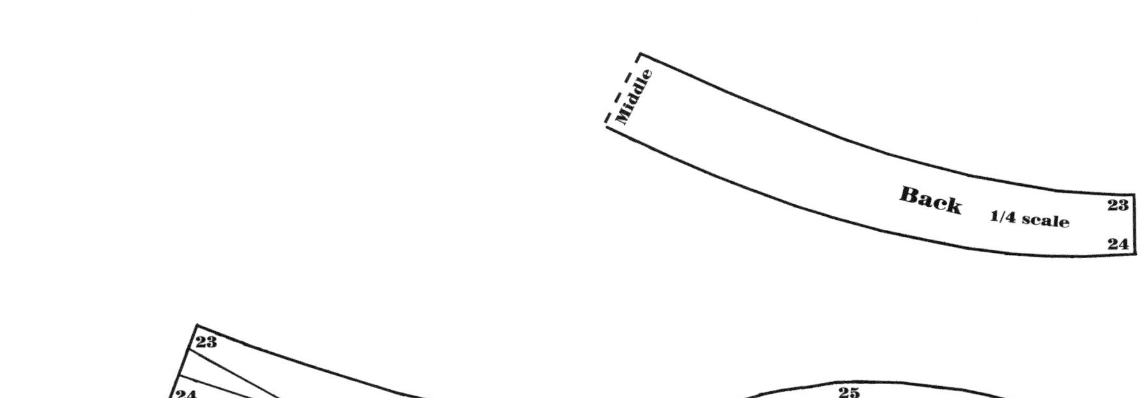

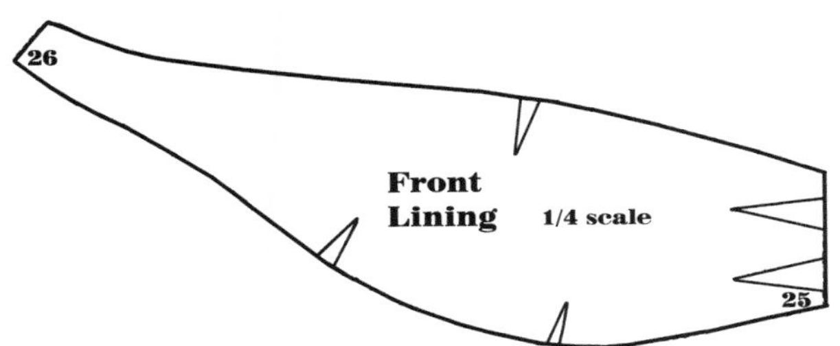

White Lace and Pink Satin Bertha

The peculiarity of this bertha consists of two rouleaux of pink satin, which are festooned from the middle of the back, and are fastened in front under a bow. The original is of white lace, pleated over a foundation of white silk lace. It is trimmed with white blonde 3 inches and 1 inch wide, the aforesaid rouleaux, satin piping, and bows of pink satin ribbon 1 1/2 inches wide.

The front and back patterns give half the bertha. Cut the stiff lace after these patterns. Cover it with the lace, laid in pleats 3/4 inch wide. Join the back and fronts on the shoulders from 15 to 16. Trim the bottom with the wide blonde, surmounted by satin piping, which is surmounted in turn by the narrow blonde. To mark the points at the top the lace is laid in a pleat at the middle of each, and trimmed to match the bottom. The rouleaux is 2 1/2 yards long. The ends are sewn together in the middle of the back, and carried round as illustrated. Finish with bows with long ends on the shoulders. Cut away the stiff lace on the wrong side.

White and Pink Bertha

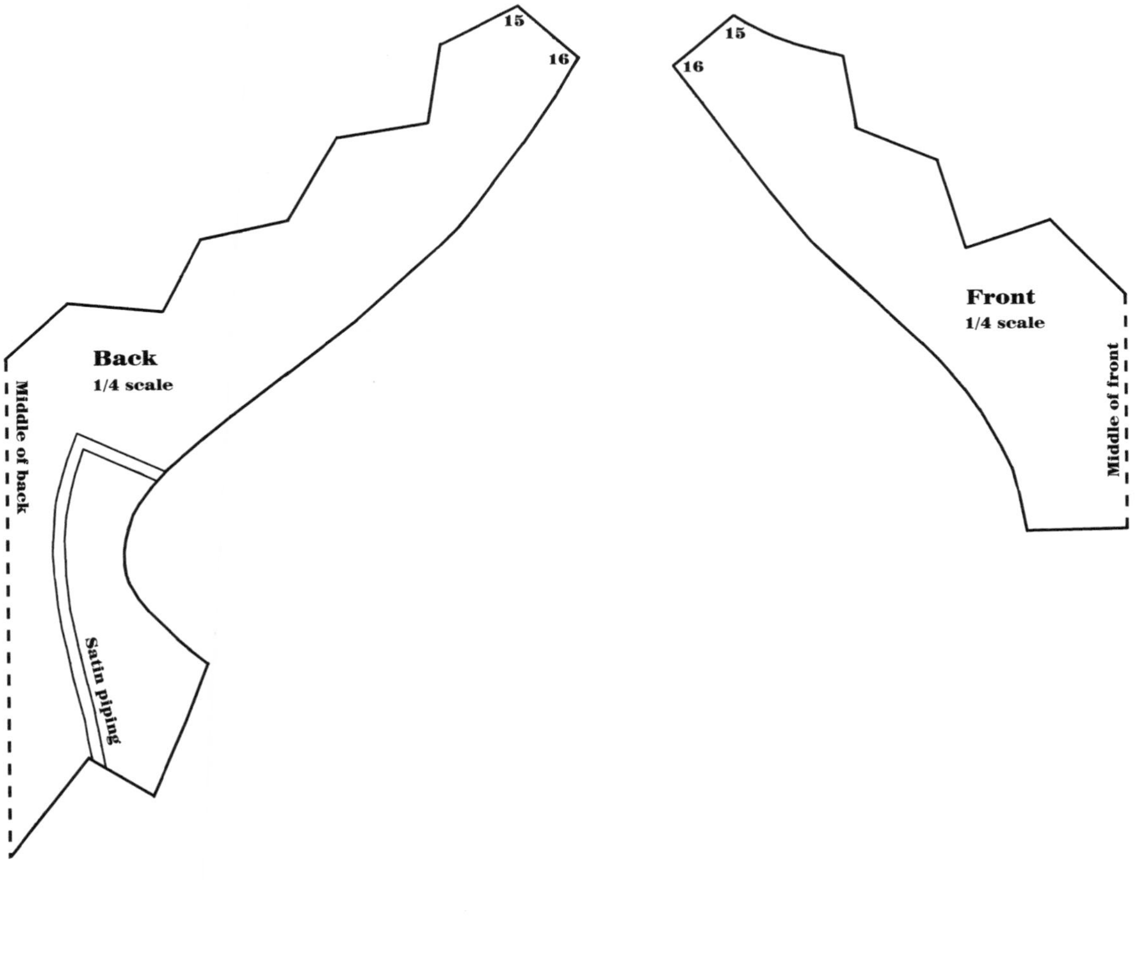

15
16
Back
1/4 scale
Middle of back
Satin piping

15
16
Front
1/4 scale
Middle of front

White Lace and White Satin Bertha

This bertha is made of a trimming of satin, satin ribbon, and white blonde on a foundation of white silk tulle. The last is puffed in front and pleated in the back of the bertha.

Cut of white stiff lace, from the front and back each one piece. Sew them together from 24 to 25. Cover them with tulle, puffed in front and pleated in back, as before described. Edge the neck with blonde 1 inch wide. Edge the bottom with blonde 3 inches wide, with a heading of satin piping. Trim the back with a bias fold of satin. Finish with two satin rouleaux in front, and bows of satin ribbon on the back and shoulders.

White Bertha

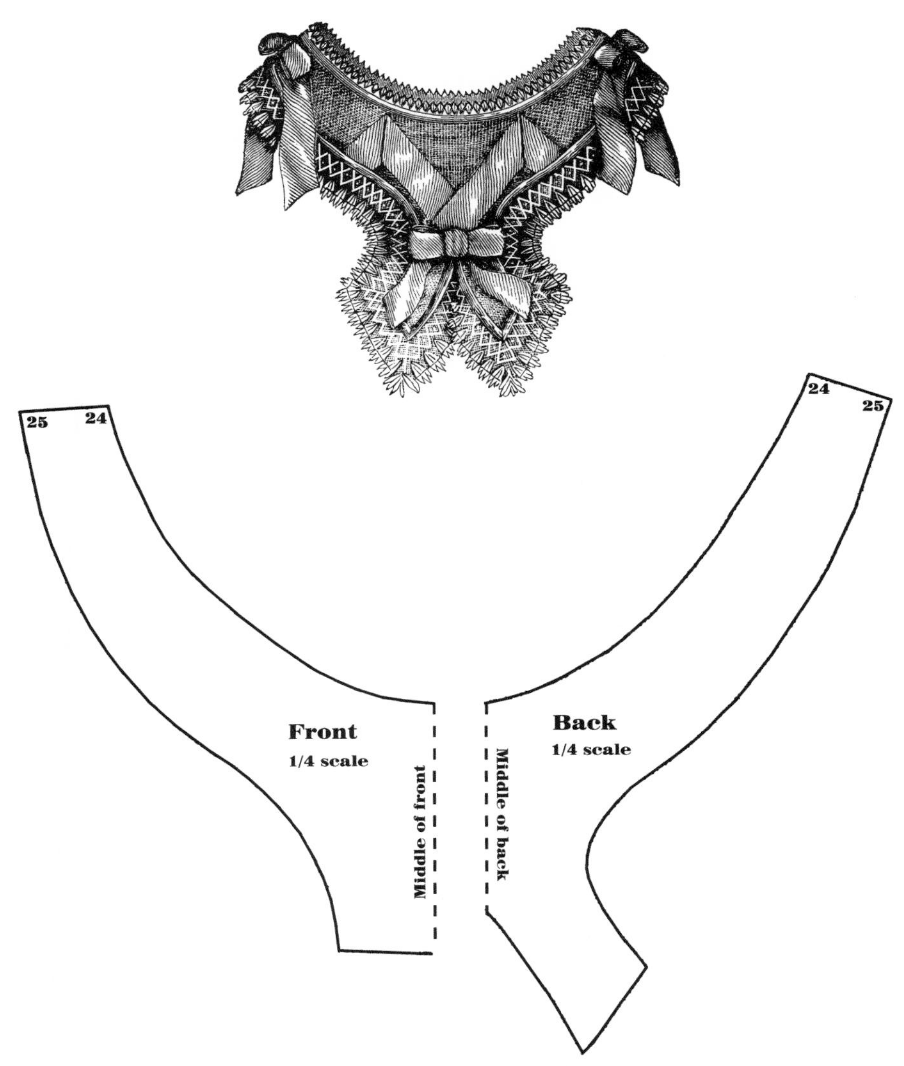

Low-Necked Waist

This elegant waist is made of white mull. It is trimmed with narrow guipure insertion, guipure edging of different widths, application figures, and pink ribbon 1 inch wide, which is set in points around the top and bottom of the waist. A bow and ends of the same ribbon trims the back.

Arrange the fronts out of the mull and insertion according to the pattern, allowing 1 inch in front for a hem. Arrange the back according to the illustration. Cut away the mull under the insertion, and lay a pleat in the corners of the latter. Make the bosom pleats and hem the fronts. Join the fronts and back. Set the bottom into a double belt 1 1/2 inches wide.

For the sleeves take a strip of mull 3/4 yard long and 5 inches wide in the middle, but gradually narrowing to 3 1/2 inches at the ends. Gather this strip through the middle and along each side, to form two puffs. Sew the ends together and bind the bottom. Trim it with narrow edging and ribbon laid in points and surmounted by very narrow lace. Cord the armholes with mull, and sew in the sleeves.

Lastly, put on the application figures, with the rest of the trimming. Finish the front with small buttons and loops.

Low-Necked Waist

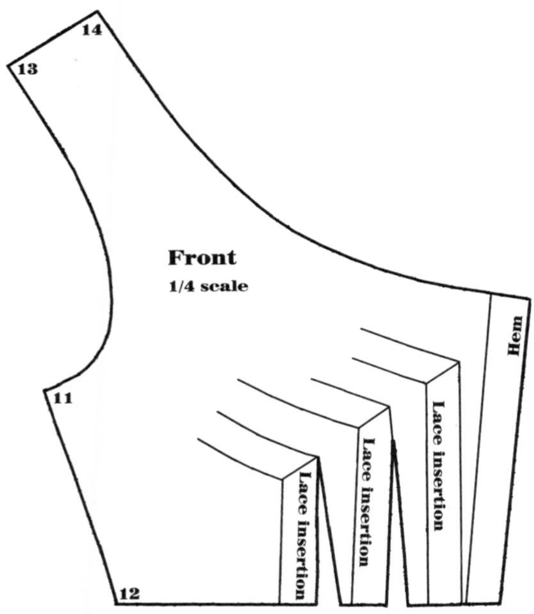

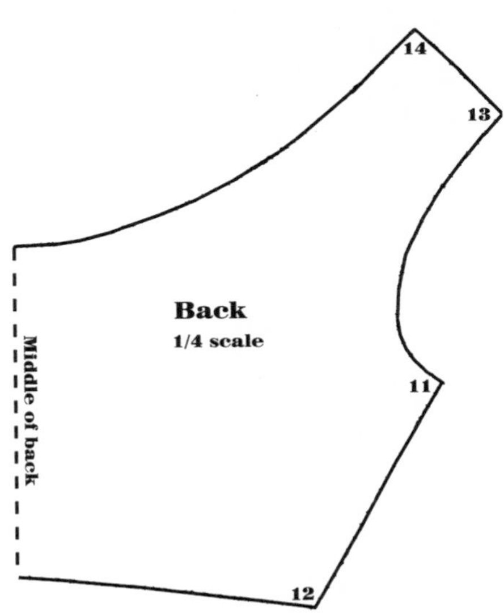

February 29, 1868

Jacket with Fur Trimming

This is a very pretty street jacket for a young girl; it can also be worn in the house. The original is of steel-colored tricot beaver. It is trimmed with chinchilla, jet buttons, and black cord, as illustrated.

Cut from the front, side front, side back, and back each two pieces. Cut the sleeves. Lay the bosom pleats. Put on the buttons and buttonholes. Then join the parts together. Face the edge with a strip of silk about 1 1/2 inches wide, and set on the trimming. Sew up the sleeves from 13 to 14 and from 15 to 16. Face them round the bottom with silk. Trim them with fur. Set them into the armhole from 16 to 16, covering the seam with a strip of fur.

Jacket with Fur Trimming

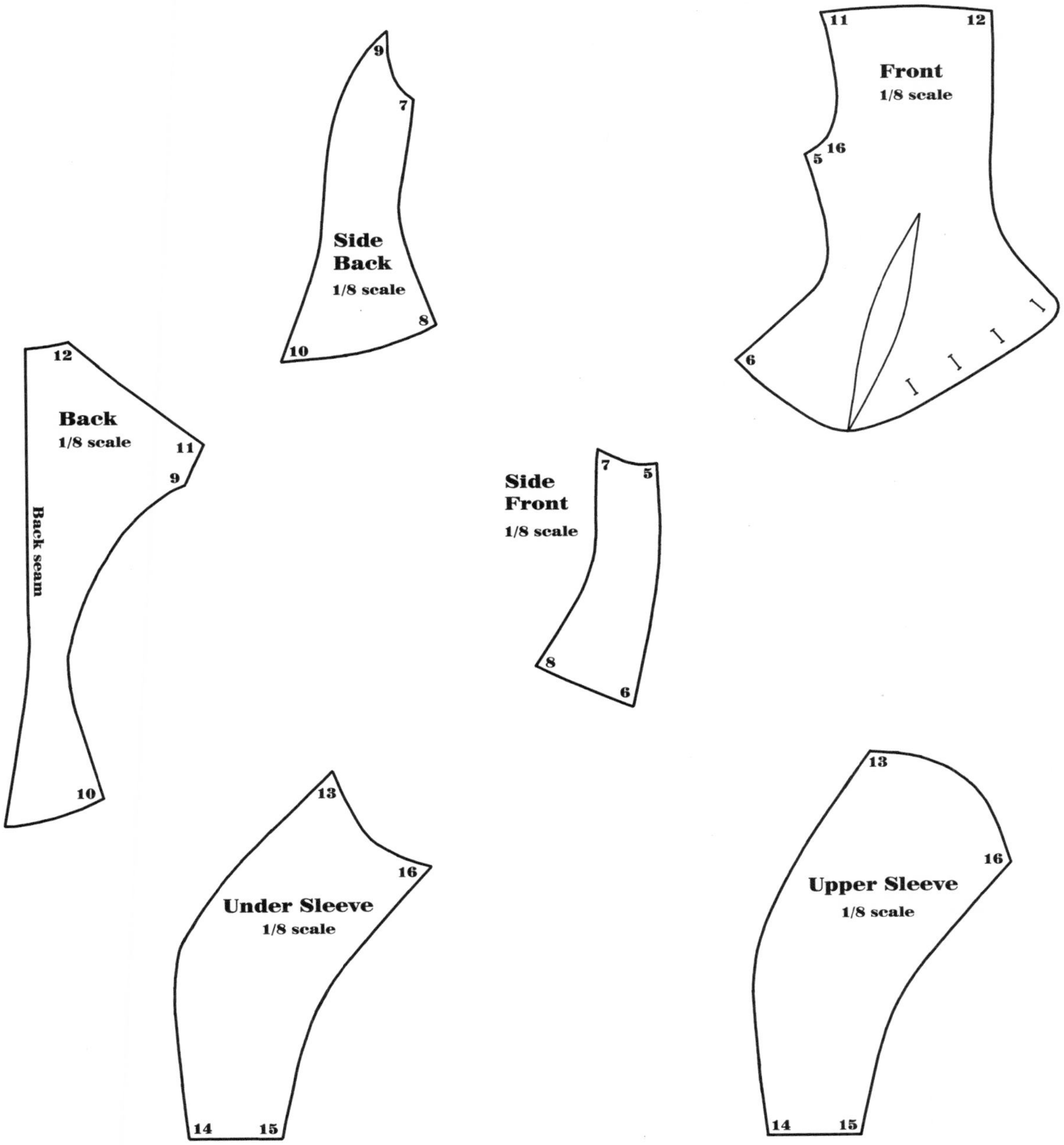

Side Back
1/8 scale
9 7 8 10

Front
1/8 scale
11 12 5 16 6

Back
1/8 scale
12 11 9 10
Back seam

Side Front
1/8 scale
7 5 8 6

Under Sleeve
1/8 scale
13 16 14 15

Upper Sleeve
1/8 scale
13 16 14 15

Talma

This opera cloak is well suited to a middle-aged lady. It can be made of black, gray, or light brown silk, poplin, cashmere, or other material. The original is of silver-gray poplin, lined with gray silk. It is trimmed round the edge with a bias strip of darker gray silk, on which white braid is stitched to simulate a border. The bottom of the talma is cut in large points. On these are sewn application figures of the same silk used for the border, and edged with white braid. A similar figure is placed in the middle of the back and the upper corners of the front. The talma is fastened in front with passementerie buttons and loops of gray silk cord.

Cut two pieces each for the front and back. Join them according to the figures on the pattern, felling the lining over the seams. Set on the trimming as illustrated.

Talma

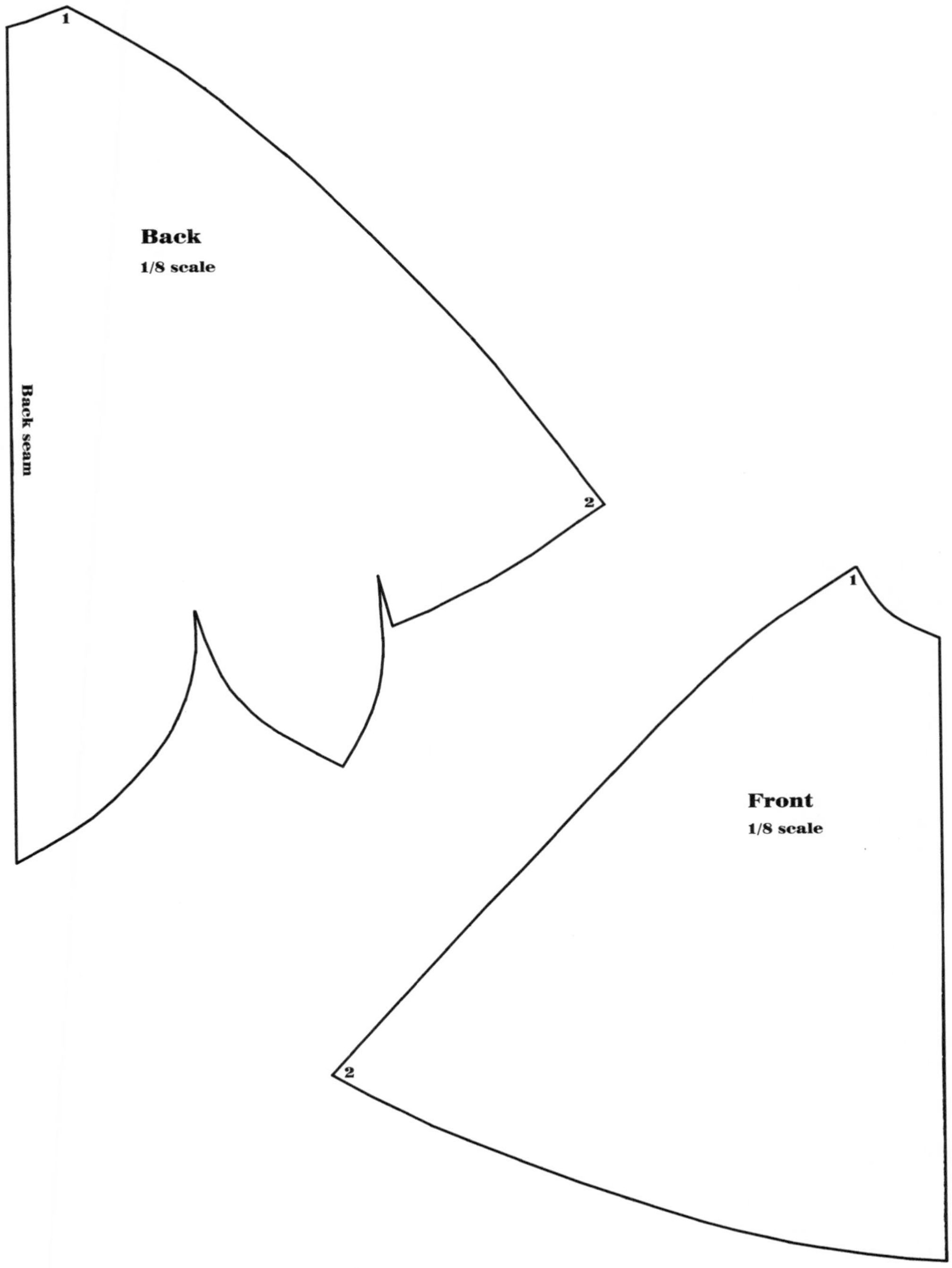

Back

1/8 scale

Back seam

1

2

Front

1/8 scale

1

2

March 7, 1868

Among the Jewels

The display of diamonds at the jewelers is now more magnificent than it was during the holidays. One set is made up of large stones of marvelous brilliancy. The oval pendants in the eardrops are of extraordinary size, and the necklace contains some very large stones, graduating smaller toward the back. A solitaire ring at another house is set in a massive gold hoop. A set includes brooch and eardrops. The brooch is a cross formed by six large diamonds set in silver. The setting is simple and pure, without effort to display the beauty of the stones, which are able to rest on their own merits. A necklace is mounted in the graceful fashion known as knife-edge setting. The diamonds are suspended on golden filaments, very strong, yet slender as a hair, and almost invisible, and the stones seem to rest on the flesh without support. A brooch made up of small diamonds represents a feather. Another is a bird of paradise with rubies and emeralds in the gorgeous plumage. A hummingbird and butterfly, with opal wings and ruby and emerald eyes, are among the ornaments for the hair.

There are quaint barbaric designs–a Moorish set with long, square pendants constantly in motion; stars with ruby centers flashing forth a blaze of light; crescents with pendants in the Byzantine style; and doves, insects, and other emblems. One most exquisite brooch is a flower cup enclosing a circle of diamonds quivering about an opal of such varied colors that all the beauties of the rainbow seem imprisoned in it.

Lapis Lazuli and Cameos

A choice set of lapis lazuli has a diamond marguerite encrusted on the brooch and earrings, and is mounted in solid Etruscan gold.

Among the cameos we were especially pleased with a set of opals–pin, eardrops, and buttons–a different Greek profile on each, surrounded with diamonds. On a Siberian topaz of rare size was cut a full face and bust of Cleopatra. Another in glazed jasper was a turbaned head, grave and majestic, in an enameled border. An emerald sphinx displayed a tiara and necklace of tiny diamonds. The setting was a gold and white enameled rope with diamond drops of water dripping from the ends. There were heads in chalcedony, and rare intaglios, and mythological subjects in sardonyx. One set, most beautifully carved, represented Orpheus searching for Euridyce, a lyre in one hand and a torch in the other.

Mosaics and Enamel

A case of jewels just received from Geneva contains a Byzantine mosaic set in the Egyptian style, with hieroglyphics and symbols of Faith, swans, peafowls, and bees.

An antique set of enamel, the subject virgin priestesses at the altar of Vesta, with diamonds and pearls encrusted, was set in Roman gold. Another of black enamel and pearls and diamonds, suitable for half mourning, was in a light setting of frosted gold. In a third was a lovely face with diamond ornaments at the throat and in the hair.

In the floral designs was a bunch of lilacs enameled on gold, with green leaves. A diamond dewdrop in the center of each flower. Another was a cluster of violets with diamonds in the heart that vibrated with the slightest motion. Again there were tiny forget-me-nots in a souvenir pin.

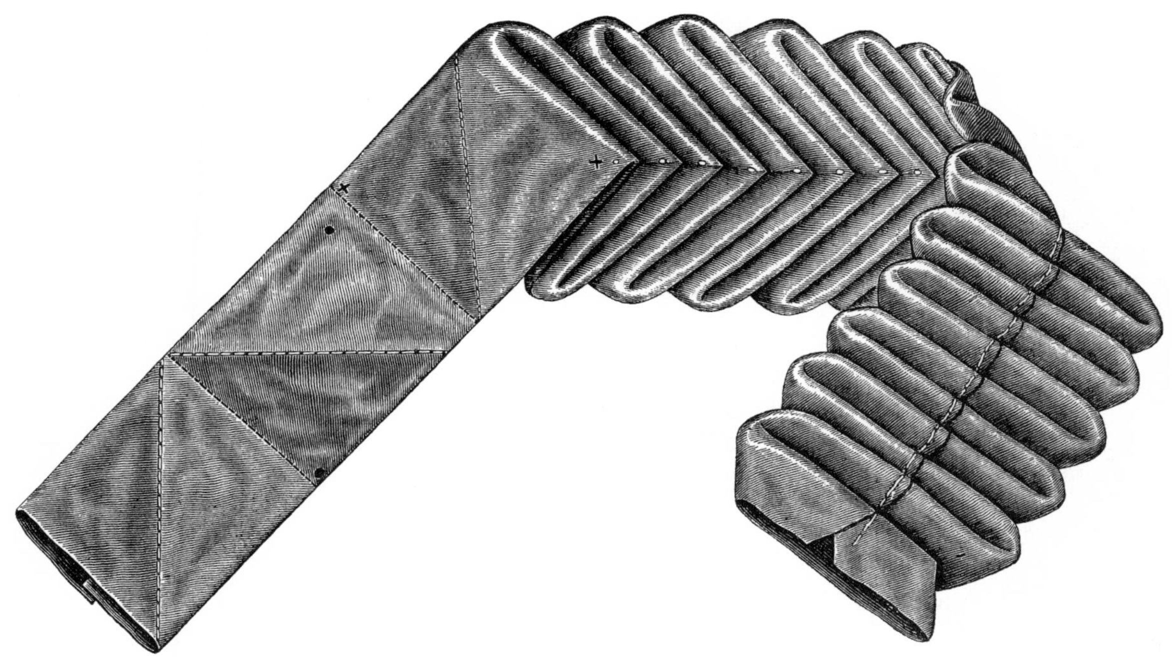

Simulated Braid Trimming

This trimming is for dresses, etc. It can be made of ribbon, or bias folds of silk or satin. The original is of bias folds of green satin 2 1/2 inches wide. The edges are laid over each other as shown. These folds are then laid in pleats, as shown, the black dotted line denoting the outer fold, and the white dotted line the inner fold. Lastly, the pleats are fastened from *x* to *x* and from • to •.

Cravat End with Rosette

A brown silk ribbon 2 or more inches wide is ornamented at both ends with brown twisted silk, in worked guipure, and then finished by a fringe 2 inches wide, of the same silk. The illustration represents one end of the cravat full size.

The rosette is worked on a cardboard foundation. Take for the middle bars four threads; that is, two bars of two threads each, crossing in the middle, and form a little wheel of plain stitches in the center. These crossbars are then worked in point de reprise. Make, then, without working, two diagonal bars, composed each of two threads crossing the central wheel. Now draw the thread twice around through the eight bars already formed, to form the middle circle of the rosette. Work these in point de reprise, and finish this circle with scallops as shown. After this, work the larger outside row, which borders the terminations of the central bars, and to which the last row of scallops is worked. In executing this the threads of the bars must of course be worked in in their proper places. The rosette can be completed without further description by reference to the illustration.

Next carefully cut away the cardboard from the under side without cutting through the thread. Fasten the rosette from the wrong side to the stuff, which must be cut away as closely as possible. Lastly tie the fringe, as in the illustration. Each bunch of this consists of six threads, each 4 inches long, which are laid together at half their length.

Hairdressing

These tasteful and becoming styles are easily executed. Though they all require a considerable quantity of hair, any natural deficiency may readily be supplied by artistically made braids, curls, and chignons, which form the most elegant of all headdresses, and which can be easily made to look precisely like one's own hair.

In the Marie Antoinette Coiffure, as in all the other styles we give, a small braid is made of the back hair, which serves to fasten the chignon. Part the hair in a line from ear to ear. Tie the back hair low on the neck. Brush the front hair upward, and confine it with a hoop of shell, jet, or gold. Then arrange it in a puff, passing the ends underneath the same. Knot the back hair low on the neck. Then carry it loosely upward, and finish with a bow on the crown. Two long curls, falling behind, and short curls on the neck complete the coiffure.

Figure 1. Marie Antoinette Coiffure–front

Figure 2. Marie Antoinette Coiffure–back

For the Josephine Coiffure, make of a strand of the back hair a braid on the crown from 1 1/2 to 2 inches long. Then wind the back hair over a crêpé that covers the entire back of the head, as shown, taking care to hide the crêpé completely. The ends of the hair are concealed under the chignon. The chignon comb is fastened in the small braid we have mentioned, which holds it more firmly. The front hair is waved, brushed upward, and arranged as shown. A long curl, with short curls on the neck, finishes the coiffure.

Figure 3. Josephine Coiffure–front

The Ambassadress Coiffure consists of a chignon of heavy braids and twisted strands. The front hair is arranged as shown, with short curls and a Josephine lock. A velvet bandeau with bow and ends is placed on the hair.

Figure 5. Ambassadress Coiffure–front

Figure 4. Josephine Coiffure–back

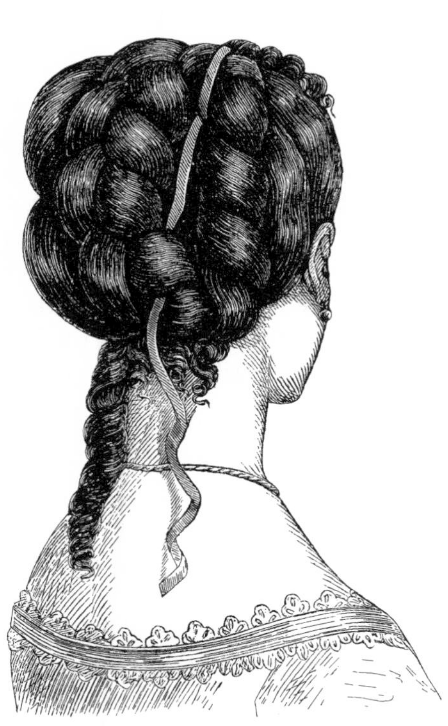

Figure 6. Ambassadress Coiffure–back

Figure 7. Sévigné Coiffure–front

The Sévigné Coiffure is well suited to evening dress. The back hair falls in long curls from the crown low on the neck. If the hair is not long enough a chignon of curls can be used over another of braids or twists. The front hair is waved and arranged as shown. A coronet, formed of leaves, ribbons, and a bow, completes the coiffure.

Figure 8. Sévigné Coiffure–back

March 21, 1868

Spring Bonnets

We are inclined to think that the appearance of increased size is given by the high coronet and rolling brim that in many cases extends around the sides and back of the bonnet. Flaring fronts and a broad roll surrounding the bonnet are found on both the fanchon and Marie Antoinette shapes when a mantilla veil is not worn. If the veil is used the roll extends only down the front and sides.

Straw, silk, Malines lace, and illusion with satin polka dots are the materials that will be most used. Yellow straws will be very much worn as well as a black straw, thin but not so transparent as the Neapolitan, and sprinkled with steel beads. There are bonnets formed of round leghorn cords. Others are rouleaux of interwoven straw and satin. A dark brown straw is made of thick rolls like piping. Gray and black, and black and white braids are mixed together. Bands of chip and of yellow straw are alternated with points and blocks of silk.

Malines lace is a new powdered tulle that has the appearance of being covered with frost. It is very pretty and gossamerlike, and is used for overstrings, and as a transparent over satin and silk. This beautiful novelty was shown us in all the old colors and in two new shades, the "caroubier," or cranberry, very similar to mentana red, and a flamelike tint called "sultan."

Mantilla Veils

The mantilla veil is worn long, falling over the shoulders, and crossing in front like a fichu. It is caught together low down on the breast by flowers or a rosette, and is often so embodied in the bonnet that it really forms the bonnet, instead of being a mere accessory. The frames of such bonnets are made of steel wire, slight but firm, and fitting closely to the head. A bandeau of velvet and flowers surmounts the forehead. To this is attached a tulle drapery that constitutes at once the veil and the bonnet, flowing gracefully over the chignon, beneath which it is held in place by a velvet band. The steel frame is almost invisible, and there is but one thickness of tulle over the head. This is a fashion that cannot fail to be popular, as it will display to advantage the present elaborate styles of dressing the hair. On other bonnets the veil is fastened at the back of the frame beneath a bow of ribbon or cluster of flowers.

Ornaments

Gilt will be little worn except in conjunction with steel. Very pretty ornaments, such as butterflies and medallions, are made of cut steel. Small jet beads are intermingled with straw in the bandeaux, and acorns are pendant from them. Similar bands are made with steel beads and with garnets, while others are formed entirely of beads without straw. Pearl leaves have cut-steel stars on them that glitter like jewels, and there are steel veins in bunches of straw leaves.

Straw fringes are headed with jet, and acorns of pearl and of satin are bursting from a straw shell. There are feather flowers with beetles and butterflies among them, and agrafes formed of myriads of tiny enameled insects. Very narrow poult-de-soie ribbons are used. Transparent metallic grasses, crimson berries, pine burrs, and forest leaves of autumn tints are among the ornaments. Colored blonde edges and feathery fringes surround the mantilla veils.

Cloth and Silk Wrappings

The spring garments will be very similar to those worn in the fall. There are probably more tight-fitting basques, and a greater number are lapped in the redingote style. Light gray cloths, tan color, and a mottled black and white will be most worn. Tan color is trimmed with a darker shade of brown. Black is used on everything else. Wide military braid, bullion fringe, and a variety of handmade trimmings are seen.

In silk garments the sash is the newest feature. Of fifty specimens shown us, not one was without a long, loosely tied sash, or a rosette at the side from which long streamers depended.

Fichus and capes of lace and of silk are worn over loose sacques and basques. Simple polonaises or redingotes of black silk velvet, with belt and sash, are designed to be worn with dresses of any color.

Trimmings

Jet has almost entirely disappeared as a trimming for mantles. Gross after gross of tiny satin buttons adorn a single garment. Guipure lace is revived again in new pointed feathery patterns. Several rows of thick military braid, or silk galloon without beads, is considered stylish. Netted and bullion and chenille fringes, and ruffles of quilled silk, surround capes and sacques. Pleated ruffles of silk, the small pleats all running one way, are bound on the edge with satin, and a tiny button is placed on each fold. Satin pipings, bias bands of silk with satin cord at either side, and satin rouleaux will be in vogue. So will flowers made of silk and satin, representing stem, leaf, and flower, and many intricate trimmings made by hand.

Spring Silks

Later importations are in stripes, with chiné figures, very small checks, and larger square blocks. For the present intermediate season there are alternate black and white stripes, varying from the hairlines of white to stripes 1 inch wide. These silks are 3/4 yard wide. In lighter colors there are 1/2-inch stripes of mauve, green, and blue, besides a black and white chiné stripe of the same width on a white ground. Pearl color and cherry are pretty together, and apple green with a chameleon of pink and gray. The chiné patterns are in various shades of gray and brown on white, or a gayer combination of several colors, mottled together, yet prettily blended. They are 5/8 wide. There are tiny stripes of blue, green, and purple with white, and small checks of the same colors. A tasteful and inexpensive material for evening dresses is called tinseled tarlatan. It is 1 1/4 yards wide. There are threads of silver and of gilt on white, on apple green, and on the brown shade of red called "Bismarck's court color." Dewdrops of crystal on white are pretty but frail. Scarlet blooddrops on black are more serviceable.

Percales and Cambrics

Piqués, percales, and French cambrics are either striped or in small figures. Buff grounds strewn with black or purple are in good taste. There are solid stripes of black, bouquets, scroll-like figures, and a pattern imitating lace.

A novelty in cambrics is a robe dress of small figures with a border for trimming, the whole length of the cloth. A plate accompanies each dress, showing the way the border should be placed on the gored skirt. Double rows of wheatears border a dress of narrow stripes. Another has small rosebuds scattered over the dress, with a vine and leaves for trimming. A dress pattern is 11 yards.

Novelties in Lace

Among late importations are some evening dresses of lama lace. This is a machine lace usually made in the same patterns as thread lace, which it closely resembles. The dresses are woven in the shape of a princess robe, with demitrain. The corsage is low necked with sleeves scarcely 1 inch long, and is woven to fit the bust without a seam. They should be made up over silk. The white one shown us was displayed over lavender.

There is a variety of patterns in black. A polonaise or redingote of black lama is graceful and new. A lace belt and sash confines it at the waist. A white routade or talma is suitable for receptions. There are short jackets with open flowing sleeves, and a new sacque called the Castellan, with long square Greek sleeves.

Besides these are mantilla coiffures worn in the Spanish fashion without a bonnet, covering the head and fastening loosely under the chin, or thrown over the bonnet, forming a coquettish mask-veil that conceals the upper part of the face. Wide lace sashes with bows and loops, or rings, are also imported, and a variety of Marie Antoinette fichus of lama, Valenciennes, and guipure.

March 28, 1868

The Marie Antoinette Dress

Radical changes in dress are usually introduced in the fall. Modistes tax their ingenuity to devise novelties and variety for the gay winter season. In the spring the most successful features of the fall modes are remodeled and adapted with the necessary variations to lighter materials. For instance, the Marie Antoinette type of dress has been worn during the winter, but more particularly for full dress. It will now be more generally adopted, and made up in all kinds of material.

The Marie Antoinette fichu, cape, or scarf, as it is variously called, made to cross on the breast with long sash ends loosely tied behind, will be used as a wrapping for short suits. It will be of the same material as the dress, and in black silk. It is especially becoming to slender figures, as the effect is to enlarge the bust and display a tapering waist. When intended for the street it is deep in the back, reaching to the belt. It is trimmed with fringe, lace, or a double ruffle of silk sewn on in box pleats. Smaller fichus, mere scarves, indeed, are made of lace or silk to be worn over basquines of black silk. Very pretty ones of clear muslin and lace are arranged to suit a variety of toilettes, by changing the ribbons under the puffs with which they are trimmed.

The Corsage

The style of corsage prevalent during the winter, with short shoulders and round waist, will be used with slight modifications for spring dresses. Our best modistes, however, never go into extremes. At present fashion does not exact either a very short or a very long waist, but one fitted in accordance with the figure. Broad shoulders that need to be contracted are shaped with short seams, and the sleeve is placed very high. But if the figure is too slight, it is amplified in appearance by cutting the corsage long on the shoulders. It was formerly considered necessary, to make the back sufficiently narrow, to place the shoulder seam 2 or 3 inches behind the line of the shoulders. Now it exactly describes that line, and may be seen from the front. Side bodies are made quite narrow. The waist is not so high at the throat as has been the fashion lately, but is still finished by a bias band, or a fold scalloped, or pointed and bound.

The Pompadour corsage is still in favor, together with revers, or rolling collars. The old-fashioned surplice waist open to the belt, and held together with a brooch, is revived for thin materials that are made full and gathered into a belt. Double-breasted garments are lapped in a deep point or sloped on the bias in the redingote style. Bretelles are also used.

The Sleeve

We are compelled to say the coat sleeve has as yet no formidable rival. True, it has been worn a long time; but it is graceful and convenient, and susceptible of great variety of trimming. Four bands of bias satin, 1 inch wide, make a stylish trimming. They are placed horizontally on the upper half of the sleeve from seam to seam, one band at the armhole, the lowest at the wrist, and the other two at regular intervals between. This is exceedingly becoming to a long arm, as it shortens it in appearance. Another pretty style is to put a puff of silk around the elbow.

Cuffs are pointed and very deep. Tight sleeves are being made for spring walking dresses. Very broad cuffs are worn with these, and a slight heading like an epaulet. Wide, open sleeves cut square at the end are worn over tight-fitting sleeves of the same material, or full puffs of muslin or lace. The Moyen-Age sleeve is closed to the elbow, where it opens and hangs in a straight line below. It is sometimes caught together at the end. The Marie Antoinette sleeves are puffed to the elbow, and finished by a wide ruffle of the material, fringe, or lace.

The Skirt

Skirts of walking dresses are made slightly longer, almost touching the ground. They consist of eight gored widths similar to those used for trained skirts, but not so wide. Short overskirts are looped at the sides, or left open, the front forming a rounded apron and connected with the back by bands or clusters of ornaments. Black silk is in favor for spring suits.

Narrow ruffles bound on each edge and gathered near the top to form a heading are arranged in waves around the skirt, or sewn on plain. Blue, green, and Bismarck silk are sometimes used for binding the frills by way of enlivening the dress. Silk, it is said, will take the place of satin for folds and bindings. Satin looks heavy and frays easily, but it is still preferred for piping. Bias bands of silk would look exceedingly plain unrelieved by the jet that is now passé, were it not for the crocheted beads and buttons that are strung on the folds in great quantities.

We are not informed of any decided change in trained dresses. There is a tendency to greater amplitude, but the fullness is still confined to the back of the dress. Usually there are seven gored widths in the front and sides, and a full one gathered in at the back. With very stout figures two full widths are used. A small pleat laid over on the gored seams adjusts the skirt into the waist. The plain width is gauged. The lap at the fastening should be over the second seam on the left. The pocket is concealed beneath the opposite seam on the right side. Small fancy pouches for the handkerchief are attached to the belt, or made to hook on the corsage.

The plainest dress is scarcely considered complete without a sash or belt. Belts are not very wide. They are formed of narrow folds of the dress material alternating with others of the silk or satin used for trimming. A rosette finishes the front. The newest sashes have a rosette, and are fastened beneath each of the second seams on the side, and loosely caught together low down on the skirt. They should be 1/4 yard wide, and bound and lined with satin. French dresses and sacques have the sash at the sides, under the arm, with a bow or rosette for heading.

Trimmings are placed on the front width, simulating aprons, or in military folds of graduated length, and long sashes are sewn down the front seams. Ruffles on trained skirts are wider than those used for short dresses. They are often scalloped on each side and bound. This is a great deal of labor, and now that jet is out of fashion we are to have a variety of handmade trimmings that require skillful and patient needlewomen.

The Chemise Russe and Robes

The chemise Russe for morning wear is prettily brought out in cashmere and delaines of rich-colored grounds, with gay Parisian patterns stamped on them for trimming. Gay Turkish jackets are in white delaine, and in black spotted with gilt or with crimson, with bright borders.

There are new fancies in cashmere and delaine robed dresses for early spring. The garment is of some light, delicate tint–a blue, pea green, or peachblossom, or the soft shade of tan that is almost white, with stripes up each gored seam of wreaths of field flowers or tiny palm leaves. A diagram with each garment shows the way of placing the trimming.

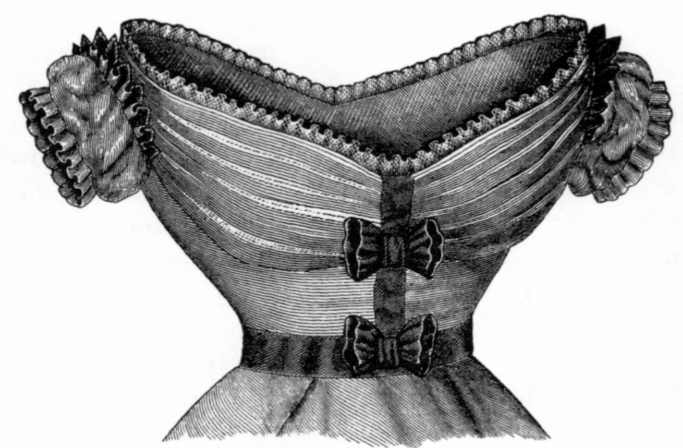

Low-Necked Evening Waist

The original of this waist is of gray silk gauze. The trimming consists of folds of the same material, arranged in the form of a bertha, bordered with gray satin, and ornamented with gray satin bandeaux. The waist is trimmed, besides, with bows of blue satin and epaulets of gray and blue satin. The same pattern may be used for making waists of other materials, such as light wash goods, silk, or other light stuffs, the trimming being chosen to suit the dress.

Cut of fine muslin, as lining, and the outside, two pieces each from the front and side back. Allow 1 1/2 inches for the hem at center front. Cut the back in one piece. Hem the fronts. Sew the hooks on the right side and the eyes on the left. Stitch up the bosom pleats. Then join the fronts and back. Put small whalebones in the bosom pleats and the seams under the arms. Cord the waist on the upper and lower edge.

For the sleeve cut a muslin piece, and cover it with a puffing. This consists of a bias piece 6 inches wide and 27 inches long. It is cut on the upper side from the middle, sloping toward the ends, where it should be only 4 inches wide. Fold this in pleats in the length of the material, according to the muslin sleeve. Finish on the under edge with a band 1/2 inch wide. Sew up the sleeve from 36 to 37. Set it in the armhole, so that 36 lies opposite 36 on the front. Fasten the epaulet in with this seam.

A pattern of part of the epaulet is given. According to this, prepare a strip of blue satin, 22 inches long, and a similar strip of gray satin. Join the two on the outer sloping border. Lay the pleats on the straight side, fastening *x* on •, as shown on the pattern, so that the length is reduced to 10 inches. Sew it in with the sleeve, taking care that the * is opposite the * in front, so that the blue satin lies next the waist.

For the simulated bertha trimming, cut from the front and back pleated pieces each two pieces. The fronts are arranged in seven folds lying upward, each 1 inch wide and 1/3 inch apart. The pleated part will be about 4 inches wide, and half this wide on the shoulders. A lower fold of the same material must be added, which will appear like a broad band. The front is ornamented with a band of blue satin 1 1/2 inches wide. The folds for the back are similarly arranged, and are composed of six folds 1 inch wide. This trimming is sewn together on the shoulder from 38 to 39, and arranged on the waist.

The bows, which are set on as illustrated, finish the trimming of the waist.

Low-Necked Evening Waist

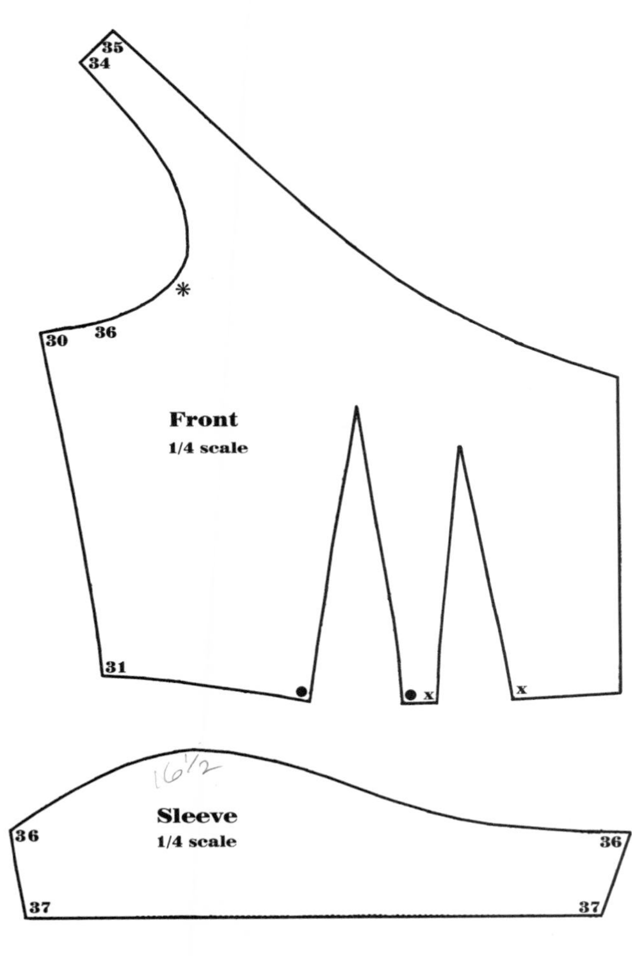

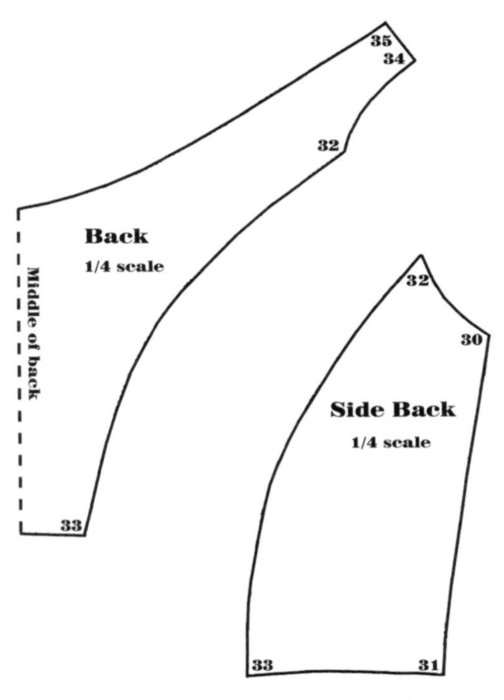

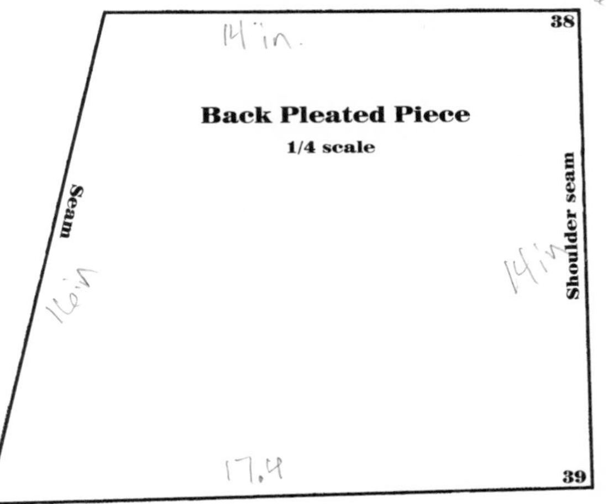

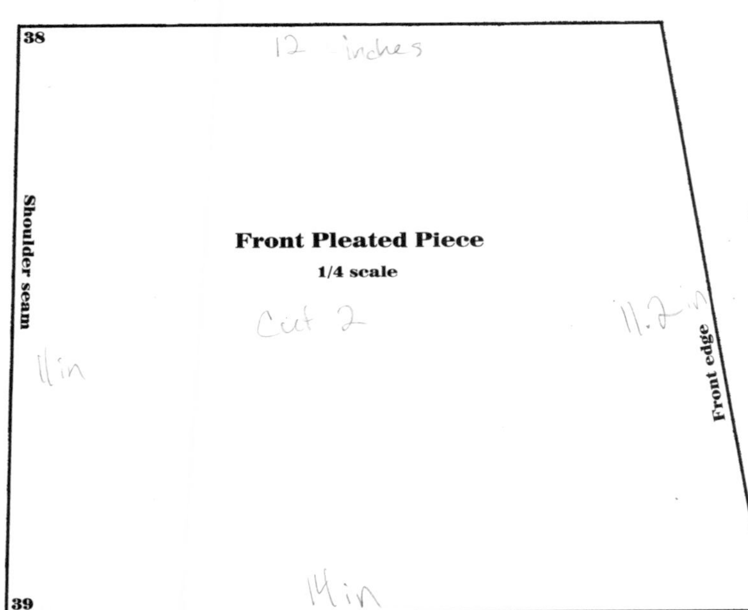

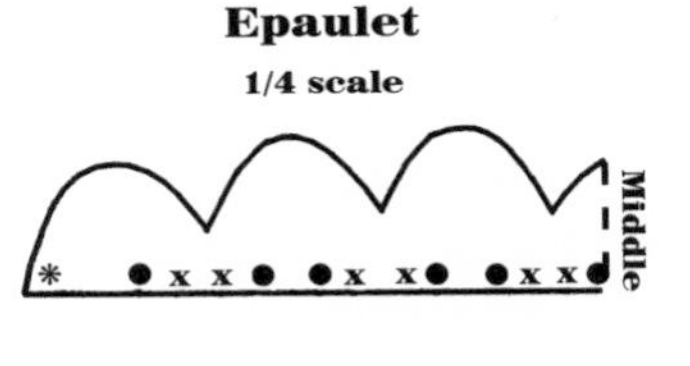

March 28, 1868

Marie Antoinette Fichu

This fichu is made of white figured lace, and has lappets of guipure insertion, with lilac ribbon laid underneath. The fichu is trimmed round the edge with guipure lace 1/2 inch and 1 inch wide, and with loops of lilac ribbon.

Cut from the back one piece, and from the lower part two pieces. Join the parts according to the figures on the pattern. Set on the lappets along the lines marked. The ribbon that is laid underneath the lappets reaches to the edge of the fichu and forms a loop with end. Then trim the fichu around the top and across the bottom with wide and narrow lace, with the wide lace pointing inward and the narrow lace outward. Trim the bottom with lilac ribbon 1 inch wide, set on in points, and covered with narrow lace.

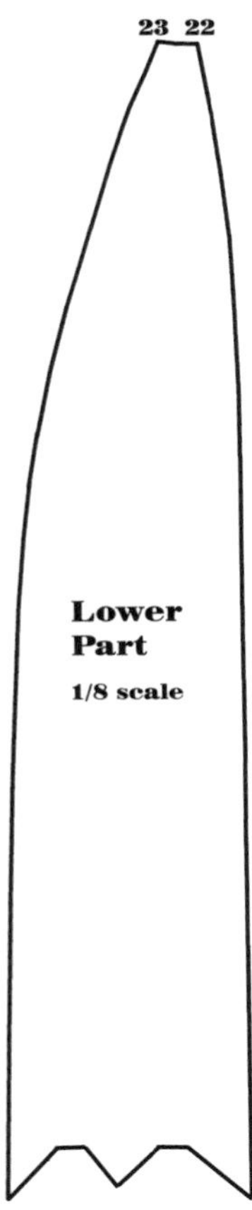
23 22
Lower
Part
1/8 scale

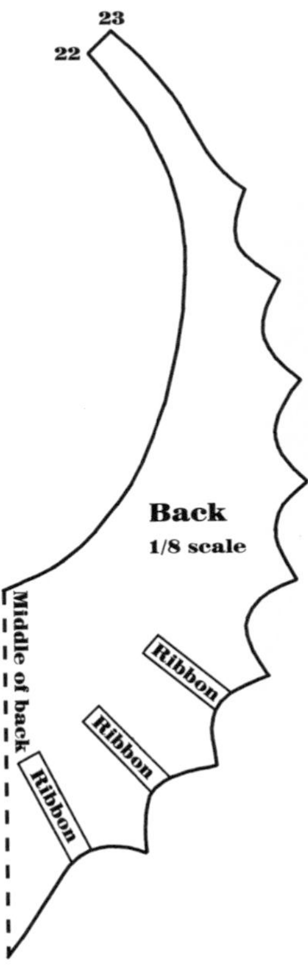
23
22
Back
1/8 scale
Middle of back
Ribbon
Ribbon
Ribbon

March 28, 1868

Styrian Jacket

This is a tight jacket of an entirely new design. It is made of white and blue cloth, trimmed with blue ribbon, colored silk embroidery, and blue silk tassels. The jacket can also be made of light and dark brown silk–the embroidery being in brown silk, and the trimming and tassels of the same color. Black silk and velvet, embroidered in either black or colored silk, is also pretty. The jacket must be lined with suitable material.

Cut of white cloth, with white lutestring as lining, both fronts. Cut from the side front and side back each two pieces. Cut the back in one piece. Cut the pieces for the sleeves. The back part of the skirt is to be cut out in the middle according to the pattern, along the narrow line, and in its place a piece of blue cloth is set on under the other.

Embroider the outside. Lay it on the lining. Sew the parts together according to the numbers on the pattern. Sew in the sleeves. Finish with the trimming and tassels. Add three flaps of blue cloth, which are fastened at the neck behind; these are also trimmed with tassels. A belt of the same material is fastened by hooks and eyes. To this are added two ends of blue and three flaps of white cloth, which are joined by a rosette of blue cloth.

Styrian Jacket

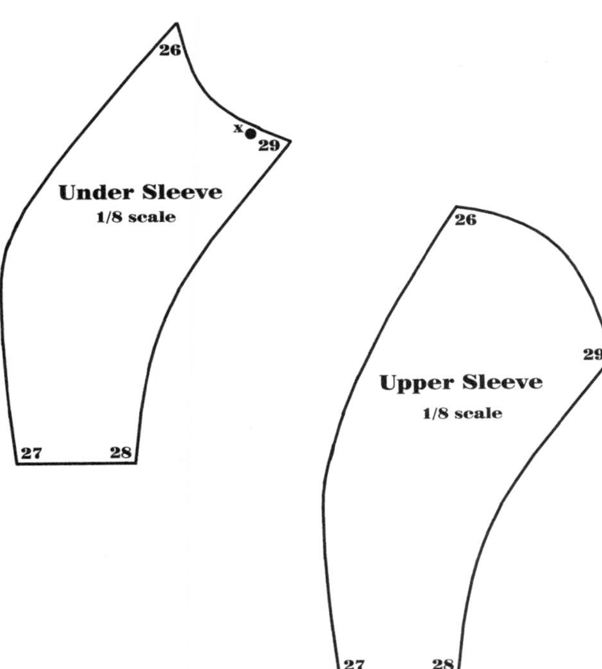

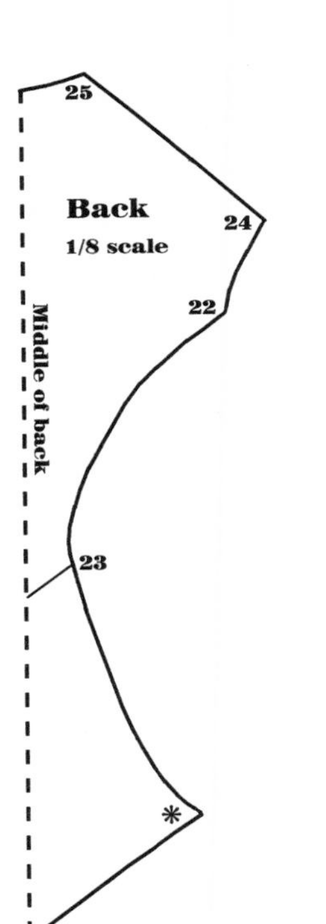

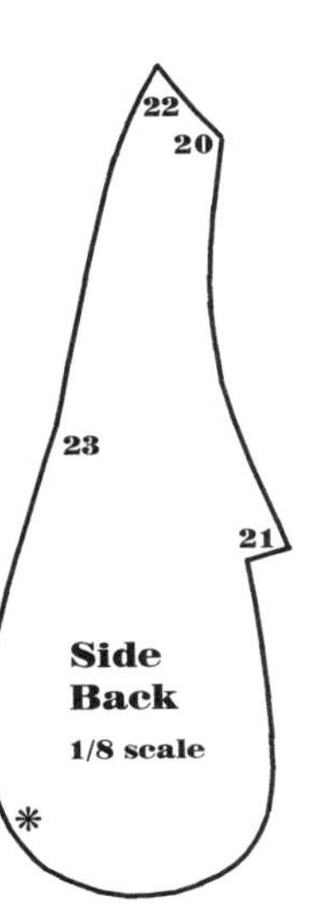

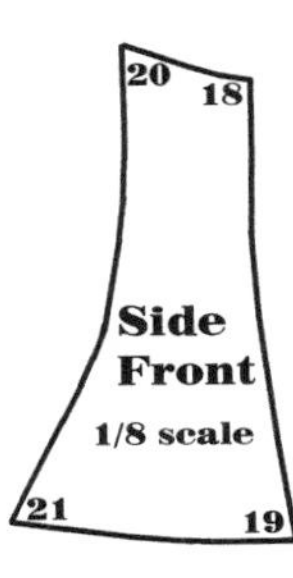

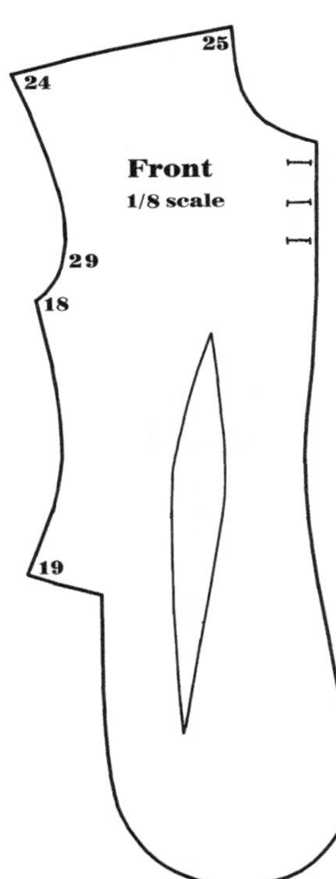

April 4, 1868

Suits

During the summer it will be found a comfortable plan to dispense with the regular dress corsage, and wear white waists under blouse wrappings. Let the skirt of the dress, however, be ample and perfect. It is poor economy and bad taste to scant the dress material in order that there may be a greater abundance of trimming. We deprecate the idea adopted by some of sewing a band of the same goods as the redingote around an old skirt, or one made of cambric. At every breath of wind that moves the redingote, the wearer fears the sham will be discovered.

The handsomest and most novel fabric for suits this season is silk serge. It is in great demand. It has diagonal reps, is all silk, soft and pliant, will not rumple easily, and is 7/8 yard wide. It is in quiet colors; some of them very quaint, indeed. There are dark browns and grays, and the dismal yellow frog greens, distinguished as "living frog" and "dying frog." Another shade is called "piecrust." Thirteen yards makes the skirt and redingote, or a basquine.

There is but little variety of pattern in the goods used for suits. Solid colors, chinés, and mottled grounds cover the whole range. Stripes are not well adapted to short dresses. Black seems to be in greater favor than ever. Black, green, and a very light shade of tan, with gray chinés and pongee, will be most worn.

Poplin alpaca, a fabric with thick, coarse threads, is stylish and serviceable for ordinary street dresses. It will not retain the dust, nor does it lose its gloss and shrink when wet. Pongee poplins are not new, but are much sought after. They are very desirable for traveling dresses, and it is almost impossible to wrinkle them. The fabric is silk and linen; black or brown mixed with white are the usual colors. There are pretty chinés, and white grounds with a colored dash on them that look nearly as handsome as an all-silk poplin.

There is a variety of other goods, such as mohair, challis, pineapple cloth, and goat's hair, all suitable for spring wear. Mohair is exceedingly pretty when made with narrow frills on the skirt, redingote, and fichu.

Parasols

The handles of parasols this season are in rustic styles, broad and flat. Some are inlaid with woods of different shades. Others have medallions of gilt with a profile on them or a beetle or fly, while small mirrors are inserted in the handles of others. Massive sticks of yellow ivory are displayed ready to be mounted with silk and lace covers.

The jet embroidery so profusely used last summer is entirely out of style. Rosettes of lace, small butterfly bows of silk or satin, pinked ruffles, marabou feathers, leaves of gilt, and bullion fringes are the fashionable ornaments. On very light, delicate colors clusters of flowers are painted, a different group on each division of the parasol. A stuffed hummingbird with outstretched wings is poised on one, while butterflies and mother-of-pearl flowers are found on others.

The useful pongees are lined with delicate and becoming colors. Black satin is lined with crimson and "Mazarine blue." A novelty is black satin speckled with yellow as if powdered with gold. Black silk without luster is used for mourning, surrounded with deep bands of crêpe.

Lace Collars, Fichus, Etc.

Short barbes of real point lace and point appliqué are brought out for collars. These are preferred to round collars, as they can be adjusted by a brooch to fit neatly. The Shakespeare points are not so long as formerly, and are rounded. A newer shape has the points diverging from the brooch. The five sharp points worn last season have now two tabs hanging down behind. A pretty fashion in thread lace is a narrow standing collar with points turned over at the throat, like those worn by gentlemen. Linen collars are made with deep points on the shoulders, or are plain bands hemstitched, or trimmed with Cluny insertion and edging.

The Empress has revived the old-fashioned velvet band, or dog's collar, worn smooth over the throat and fastened by a small brooch. Our American empresses cannot all afford to stud these bands with emeralds and diamonds as her Majesty does, but they have already adopted this pretty little device to make a white throat look fairer still. With the Pompadour and revers waists this black velvet collar is preferred to the heavy India necklaces, long strings of gilt filigree beads, that fall sometimes almost to the belt.

White organdy fichus are inexpensive and graceful additions to home toilettes, and can easily be made at home. The fichu and sash ends should be cut lengthwise of the muslin without a seam in the whole affair. The prettiest trimming is a fluted ruffle 3 inches wide, with a narrow hem and two tucks on one edge, and merely hemmed on the other. A fine cord gathers it to leave a narrow frill at the top. Another easily made is of illusion puffs covering the whole foundation. A narrow box-pleated ruffle of the same surrounds it.

April 4, 1868

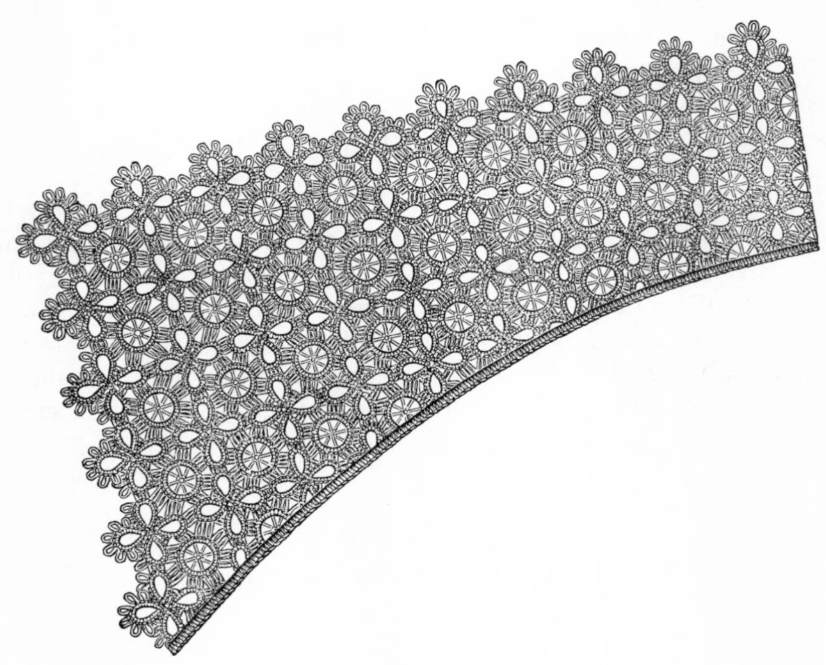

Tatted Collar

This collar, part of which is shown full size, is worked with very fine twisted thread. It is composed of four-leaved tatted figures and single tatted rings, which are joined as shown.

The four-leaved figures are worked as follows: Work 3 ds. (double stitches), 1 p. (picot). Alternate seven times 2 ds., 1 p., then 3 ds., and join the row. Close on this leaf of the figure work three similar leaflets. But in working these, join the last picot of the last leaf instead of forming the 1st picot of the new leaf. And in working the last of the four leaves, join to the 1st picot of the first leaf instead of forming the last picot. Having finished the figure tie together the beginning and end of the threads, and cut them off.

Join these figures in a row by joining the 2 middle picots of a leaf of the former figure instead of working the 2 middle picots of the last leaf. Every two rows of these four-leaved figures are joined by the tatted rings already spoken of, and which are composed each of 32 ds., which are joined between the four-leaved figures as shown. Begin each ring with 2 ds., take up the picot of the four-leaved figure, work again 2 ds., and take up the next picot. Continue in this manner, paying attention to the illustration, until the ring has reached the required size.

Each ring is worked in the center in lace stitch, as shown. Work the collar round the neck in close buttonhole stitch.

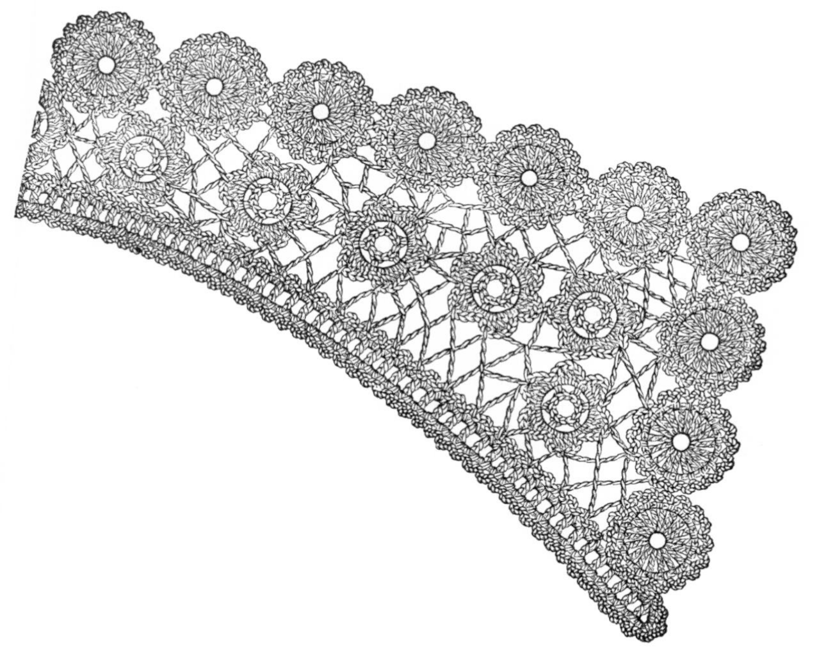

Crocheted Collar

This collar is worked with fine crochet cotton. It is composed of single crochet rosettes and flowerlike figures, which are joined by sewn bars.

Work first the rosettes, which are always begun in the center. Make a foundation of 9 chain, join in a ring with a slip stitch, then crochet the first round. First 5 chain, of which the first 4 serve as 1 treble; after which alternate in the ring seventeen times 1 treble and 1 chain.

Second round: 1 single crochet in each chain of the last round, between which always 4 chain. After this fasten the thread. Every following rosette is fastened to the preceding, as shown.

The flowerlike figures are also begun in the center. Make a foundation of 12 chain, join in a ring with a slip stitch and crochet. First round: 2 chain, which serve as a short double stitch; * 3 chain, passing over 1 stitch; 1 short double in the following stitch. From * repeat four times. Then follow 3 chain.

Second round: In every 3 chain between 2 short double of the last round always 1 single crochet; 1 short double; 3 double; 1 short double; 1 single crochet.

Having prepared the requisite number of rosettes and figures, make the border round the neck as follows. On a foundation chain of suitable length crochet one round alternating 1 double; 1 chain passing over 1 stitch. Then on this round, as also on the other edge of the foundation row, each one round composed of 2 single crochet in every chain, followed by 3 chain.

Now arrange the finished figures on a foundation of pasteboard or oilcloth cut to the shape of the collar. Fasten them together with sewn bars of fine crochet cotton.

April 11, 1868

Milliners' Openings

Some of our most exclusive milliners have displayed at their early openings a variety of beautiful bonnets, designed to be worn when the first spring days arrive. The new bonnets are not larger than those of last season, the diadem is the leading feature, and the fanchon still prevails. A graceful new shape, called the Metternich, consists of a large round crown entirely without a brim, except such as is formed by the diadem. This crown bonnet is worn very far forward, the diadem being placed over the forehead, and the crown covering the top of the head, leaving the back hair without drapery.

Black Lace

Black lace promises to be a favorite material for spring bonnets. A single piece of Chantilly covers the frame. Many bonnets are entirely made of lace; the headpiece, the fall at the back, and the barbes being all in one. It is sometimes embossed with steel or straw.

Another elegant and expensive style is silk embroidery of tiny flowers, forget-me-nots, and heliotropes, on the coiffure and barbes. A thread of steel or gilt, so fine as to be almost invisible, glistens unexpectedly amidst the fine meshes of a gossamer barbe. Black Malines, of smaller meshes, and thinner, if possible, than tulle, is powdered with steel that glitters like gems.

We notice also that black lace, either thread or blonde, is used for trimming bonnets of every description–white straws, chips, and Neapolitans, both gray and black, and also forms a part of colored tulle and crêpe hats. It is quilled on the diadem, is made into rosettes and bows, with long barbe ends over the back, and covers the narrow ribbon strings that fall in the front solely for ornament. A great deal of colored lace is used, but it does not supersede the black, because it is not brought out of such handsome quality. Although it is desirable to have all the trimmings of a bonnet harmonize, yet colored lace is not looked upon with favor by people of taste.

An elastic cord, passing under the chignon, is necessary to keep the new bonnets in proper position. If preferred, narrow strings of poult-de-soie ribbon are used to tie at the throat, but it is considered more stylish to dispense with them altogether, or fasten them at the back. The lace overstrings that accompany almost every bonnet hang loose almost to the belt, where they are caught by a rosette, bow, a spray of flowers, or an ornament of steel or pearl. The throat is thus left bare, a fashion that we will appreciate more highly when the heat of summer sets in. A fall of lace, or a scarf, is attached to nearly all bonnets.

The delicate Malines lace is brought out in every shade of color, and is preferred to the coarser dotted nets. It is used for scarves and mantilla veils, and frequently forms the whole bonnet. It is very much admired when sprinkled with tiny specks like diamond dust or frost.

A brilliant shade of yellow is called "buttercup." A dark rich shade of red is called "sultan." Garnets are used with this color. The Metternich green, so much in favor for evening, is found to be very trying to the complexion by daylight unless relieved by lace. In conjunction with black lace it makes a suitable bonnet for spring, and is so pretty that means will be found to make it becoming.

Ornaments and Flowers

Among the prettiest ornaments are those of pearl, not white alone, but light shaded tints and rich colors as dark as maroon. There are flowers with pearl petals and gilt stamens, and butterflies with quivering rings of colors as varied as an opal. Pendants of pearl and of straw droop from the diadem and the crown of bonnets. Garnets are introduced among the trimmings. They look too conspicuous to be popular; but we have seen a few tastefully arranged and softened by lace. Steel and gilt are used together with very good effect, and the steel is desirable alone, but not the gilt. Occasionally a little jet is seen. Handsome crystal flowers vibrate on slender stems among metallic leaves. Drooping sprays of velvet and feather flowers on gilt tendrils, buttercups with long, trailing grasses, and clusters of the smallest flowers without foliage, such as mignonette and verbenas, are displayed in every window. The small flowers are used on coronets, while the bonnet is trimmed at the crown and sides with a large scarlet poppy, a white lily, the brilliant cactus, or a tulip. Daisy wreaths are also still in favor, and autumn leaves, especially those purpled by the frost.

French Bonnets

Close-fitting Neapolitans, studded with steel or jet, may be bought. With the addition of a little lace and a few flowers, and some straw ornaments, any lady of taste can make for herself a spring bonnet at very trifling expense. If white straws are preferred, violet and Metternich green ribbons are arranged in loops over the crown and coronet, together with a few straw leaves and large pendant ornaments at the ends of the long strings. A ruffle of black lace is a pretty finish to ribbon strings.

Round Hats

Very few round hats have been displayed at the openings. It is rather early for them, as they are more especially adapted to the seaside and country. The Spanish and Marie Antoinette styles, with high sloping crowns, are the newest shapes, and are pretty for watering places and riding hats. But another shape, with a lower crown and turned-up brim, will be more popular for the city. The rims are rolling or caught up at the sides, and faced with colored satin or velvet. Straw cords and tassels and straw passementerie form the trimmings. A few turbans, sloping downward from the front, are seen. A regular cap with visor is made of leaves or shells of silk. Lace strings more than 1 yard long fall from the sides, are lapped in front, and tied behind like a fichu.

Dressmakers' Openings

The redingote or polonaise is in such favor that it will not be abandoned this season. It is no longer cut so full as the original pattern, but is half adjusted to the figure by side bodies, and is worn with a fichu or scarf.

All the short suits exhibited had two skirts, the under one bordered with a flounce or with three narrow frills. The upper skirt is gored flat in front, with the back widths fulled in at the sides, and puffed or festooned to give a very full appearance, as of the tournure or bustle. There is no longer any doubt that the pannier style is about to be revived, or that it will generally be worn, since it is precisely the opposite of the scant drapery over small crinoline that has so long been in favor.

There were graceful burnooses for evening wear, with folded hoods and openings for the arms. A light material of silk and wool was chain stitched in delicate colors and fringed. Others were of black cashmere embroidered or braided with gilt, and fringed.

April 11, 1868

Collar of Watered Ribbon

This pretty and stylish collar is made of black watered ribbon 1 inch wide, and jet beads and grelots. Cut a piece of ribbon just long enough to reach round the neck. Sew on it two rows of beads lengthwise. Set on the bottom seventeen pieces of ribbon, each 5 inches long. The ends of these are pointed by turning the corners over on the wrong side and sewing them fast, and trimmed each with a large bead and a grelot. The seam where the ends are set on is likewise ornamented with a bead and grelot. A chain formed of jet rings and beads, of the requisite length, is set on the ribbon ends, halfway from the top, as shown. The collar is tied behind with two ribbons, each 1 yard long, which are likewise pointed at the ends, and ornamented with beads and grelots.

Black Satin and Lace Waist

Black Satin and Lace Waist

This waist is made of black satin and black figured lace. It is trimmed with bias folds of black satin, 2/5 inch wide, lace insertion, and lace edging 2/5 inch wide, embroidered with jet beads and bugles.

Cut of satin and Swiss muslin for lining from the front and side back each two pieces, and from the back and neck binding each one piece. The neck binding is double, and bias at the top. Cut of lace from the lace pattern one piece. Cut the sleeves. In these the satin reaches from the bottom to the narrow line; the rest is of lace.

Face the front edges with a strip of black satin 1 1/4 inches wide. Set thereon the buttons and buttonholes. Join the front, side back, and back to correspond with the figures on the pattern. Bind the top and bottom with satin. Put on the trimming with the help of the illustration.

April 11, 1868

Sew on the lace piece according to the figures on the pattern. This lace piece is hemmed up the front and furnished with buttons and buttonholes as illustrated. Sew the band on the neck and trim it with lace.

Sew up the sleeves from 31 to 32, and from 33 to 34. Trim the bottom and sew them in the armholes with a cord.

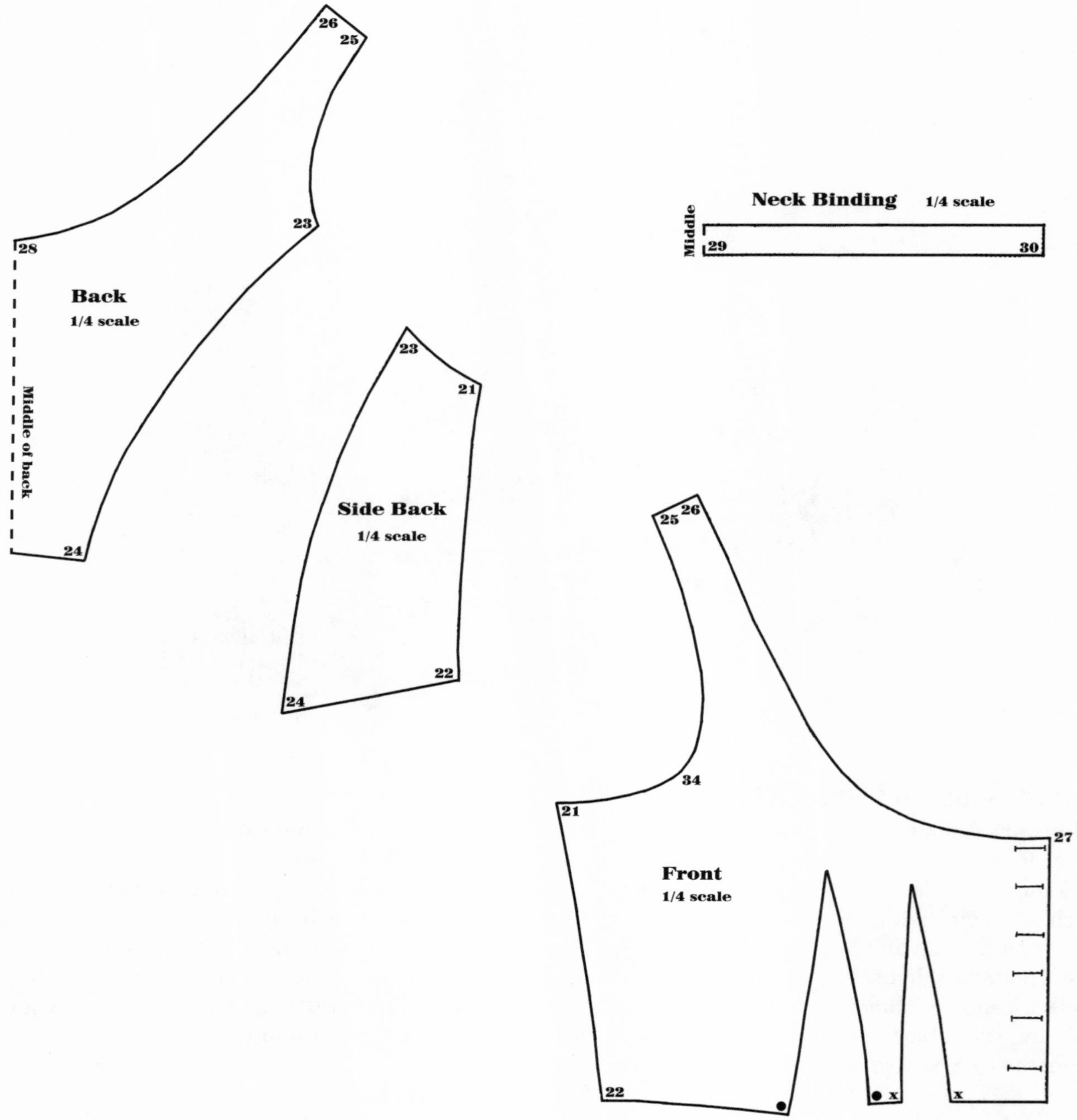

Back 1/4 scale

26 25 23 28 24 Middle of back

Side Back 1/4 scale

23 21 22 24

Neck Binding 1/4 scale

Middle 29 30

Front 1/4 scale

25 26 34 21 27 22 x x

Black Satin and Lace Waist

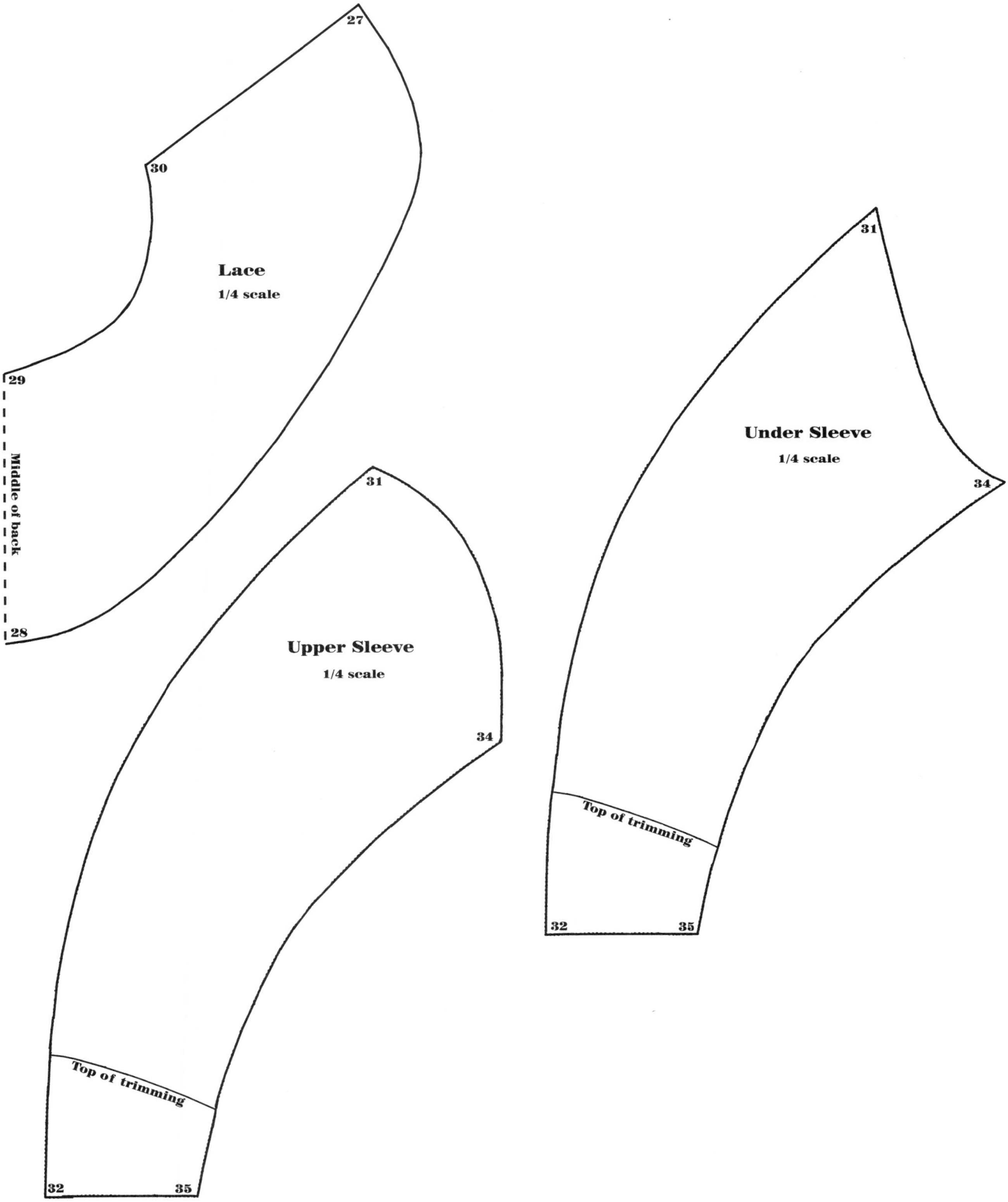

27

30

Lace

1/4 scale

29

Middle of back

28

31

Upper Sleeve

1/4 scale

34

Top of trimming

32 35

31

Under Sleeve

1/4 scale

34

Top of trimming

32 35

Polonaise or Redingote

This sleeveless polonaise or redingote must be of the same color as the dress, although the material may be different. Sleeves can be added and the front cut straight, if preferred. The suit in the illustration consists of a short dress of brown poplin, trimmed with brown silk rouleaux. The paletot is of brown taffeta, lined with silk, and trimmed with bias silk folds of the same color. The waist is confined by a narrow belt, with loops and ends behind.

Polonaise or Redingote

Cut the fronts, outside, and lining from the front patterns. Cut the back whole. Lengthen the polonaise on the bottom as much as desired.

Baste the outside and lining together. Sew up the bosom pleats in the waist. Join the back and fronts, making the figures on the pattern correspond with each other. Run the edges together. Cord the neck and armholes. Then set on the trimming and belt. The latter is fastened behind with loops and ends. The polonaise is closed at the neck with a hook and eye.

April 11, 1868

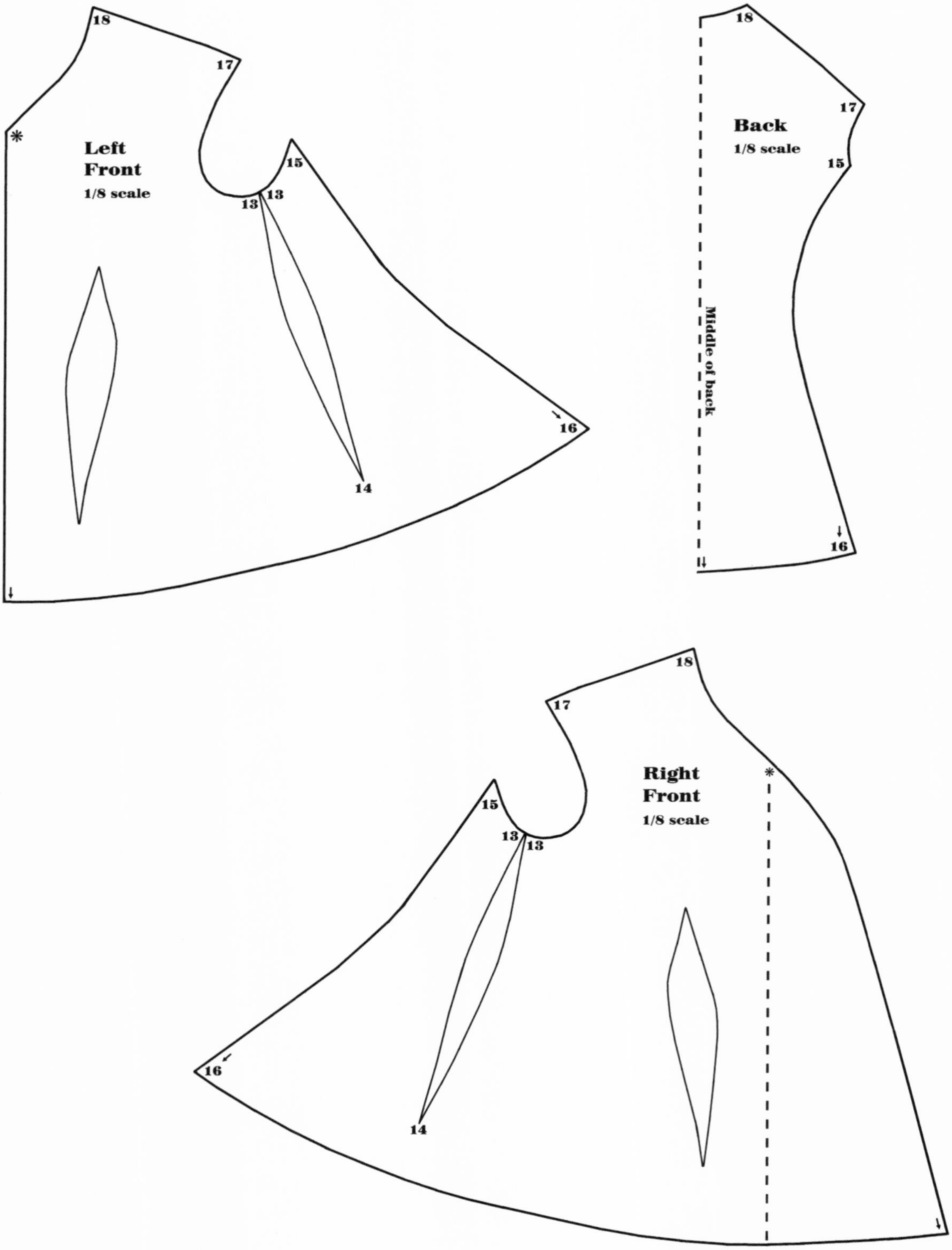

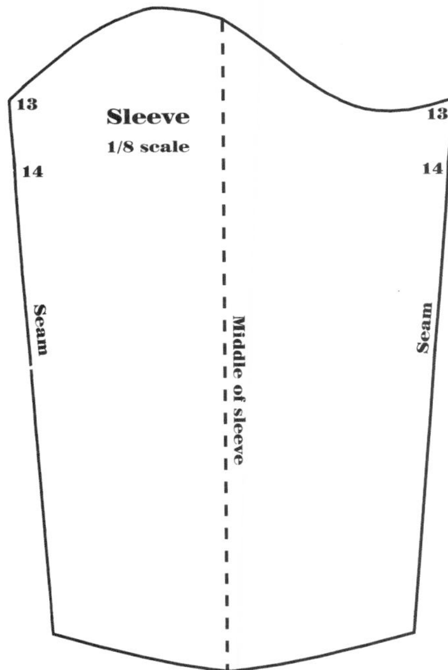

Polonaise Paletot

This paletot is of black silk, with black silk lining. The left front fastens diagonally over the right (sides are seen reversed in the illustration). It is trimmed with bows of black satin ribbon 2 1/2 inches wide, which are set down the front and also on the long Grecian sleeves. The last are joined by the bows. The paletot is cut, except for the sleeves, from the Polonaise or Redingote pattern above.

Cut the sleeves, both silk and lining, from the pattern. Sew them up from 13 to 14, and join them beyond with the trimming. Then set them in the armholes and trim with bows as illustrated.

If it is desired to wear the sleeves tight instead of hanging, sew them together the entire length. Then turn over the under edge to the distance of 4 inches as a cuff on the right side. Trim this cuff with black satin.

April 18, 1868

Dress Goods

During the present intermediate season when winter wrappings have become too heavy and unlined silks and laces are too light, the short street suits, with an extra lining that may be used or removed at pleasure, become indispensable.

The fancy woolen serge imported for spring has a diagonal silk reps that gives it a bright luster, and a much more dressy appearance than the all-wool serge worn during the winter. We have seen it in pinhead checks and small oval-like globules, but the plain gray twills are preferred.

Granite poplin is very well described by the name it bears. It is, however, of several qualities. The ordinary granite is a dark gray mottled goods, very much in appearance like the rock for which it is named. This is serviceable but not attractive. A finer quality is lustrous and smooth, and will rank favorably among the materials for walking suits.

A new mixture of wool and lisle thread, which reminds one of winsey, is called wash poplin. It is in mottled and chiné patterns and plain grounds, in which a white thread crosses a brown or black. All the requisites for a serviceable traveling dress are found in this goods. It is reversible, not easily torn, and will wash without fading or shrinking. It is 3/4 yard wide.

A pretty combination of silk and linen is called poplinette. It resembles the summer silks in luster and in its patterns of small checks and blocks, but is more durable and does not wrinkle so easily. Seven-eighths of a yard is the usual width. Plain colored poplinettes, or silvery-gray grounds with black or white penciled stripes, are brought out in a wider goods of a trifle better quality, almost as handsome as an Irish poplin. Dressmakers, however, prefer to use material 7/8 wide, as it cuts to better advantage.

Epingleine, an all-wool poplin of heavy reps, is not new, but is displayed in all the fashionable shades of light brown, gray, and green. The robed mohairs are prettily brocaded in wreaths around the skirt with smaller vines for sleeves and corsage. Seaside poplin is a suggestive name for a quiet pretty material that has a wiry stiffness about it that makes it hang well, and which it is said moisture will not destroy. Of the same order of goods is China cloth, a new mohair with a glazed surface that looks like enamel. The colors, dove and buff, are too light for the present season, and too delicate to make a very serviceable dress at any time.

Thin Goods

A few organdies are shown in striped patterns, and in wreaths and clusters of flowers on a white ground. A dark sultan red stripe is beside a white one on which are cashmere figures. Or a white ground is striped with black relieved by brilliantly colored palm leaves, or wreaths of wood violets, or squares and blocks of the fashionable tint of pale amber.

Robes of gossamer grenadine are sold. A lovely pattern has the principal part of the dress of solid blue and white stripes 1 inch wide, bordered at the sides and bottom of the skirt with a vine of flowers of most gorgeous hues on a white ground. Narrower vines are provided for the sleeves and waist. Another dress has violet stripes instead of blue. A different style is a dark ground with a wide stripe of gay colors down the center of each width.

Among the grenadines sold by the yard those with black grounds are most admired. On many of these there is merely a white satin stripe. On others, strewn at intervals, are bunches of rose geranium, or a cluster of small flowers of every shade, forming a tiny nosegay, tied together with a cordon of gilt. Again there are wood-colored stripes with pale yellow primroses or buttercups between. In all these there are thick satin stripes. There is a plainer quality with small set figures.

Chambray gauze for evening dresses is brought out in solid colors. The popular shades are all represented, buttercup, sultan, Metternich green, and violet. This is one of the most beautiful transparents that can be worn over silk or satin. The white grounds are also very attractive with thick medallions and dashes of rich colors. One specially admired has a white velvet square on which is a beautifully shaded moss rosebud.

Chameleons

Chameleon silks for evening dresses display most beautifully blended colors, forming soft neutral tints that require gaslight to bring out their beauty. The pure azure called "Mexico" and a pale amber when together enter into a perfect unison, forming a harmony of shade widely different from that made by attempting to combine two colors in positive contrast, such as Mazarine blue and gold. Straw color and green assimilate naturally, making pistache when viewed in front, presenting each shade distinct yet slightly modified by the other when a side view is taken. Lilac and maize combine prettily; dove color and green form a grayish hue; blondine and white make the merest shadow of rose color on white; and orange shaded with pink forms salmon.

Illusion, tulle, and the merest films of lace are appropriate trimmings for these delicate silks. There are fichus and barbes and sashes of fairylike texture that might have been designed for them.

Morning Dresses

A pretty style of morning dress is a princess robe buttoned slanting from the throat to the hem in the redingote fashion. Coat sleeves with a deep cuff turned back, simulated by trimming. Large flat linen buttons. Narrow pocket flaps are placed lengthwise of the skirt.

An appliqué vine of blue or pink leaves of French chambray, braided at the edge, or featherstitched with white, is a pretty trimming for plain white piqué. Rows of points formed by folding a square of muslin are also used on either side of bias folds and bands. If the folds are cut perfectly on the bias, and the points folded smoothly, this trimming is easily ironed and will be found well adapted to wash materials. With a little practice ladies can make these new handmade trimmings at home.

Solid colored brilliants, figured cambrics, and the cool, white linens with narrow stripes of black are loosely gored with body and skirt in one, and surrounded with a deep flounce beginning at the knee. A cord and tassel is worn at the waist, or a belt of same. Instead of the rosette so long worn in front of the belt, a pretty fashion is to point the end that laps, and place a strap of the material over the front of the belt, giving the appearance of a buckle.

Petticoats

Muslin skirts to be worn under short dresses are gored flat at the front and sides, and trimmed with three fluted ruffles, or with a group of tucks and one ruffle. With trained dresses the petticoat worn next the dress should be trained also, and be but little shorter than the dress. A wide flounce set on at the knee, with the skirt proper gored plain, makes a graceful skirt. A better trimming is three ruffles of graduated widths, narrow in front, and deep behind.

Pretty Balmorals of thick white serge have dark blue and brown medallion borders. The gored design is marked on the widths. Very heavy piqué is also stamped for petticoats, with a vine of flowers and leaves in black, or a broad Greek border.

Collars, Collarettes, and Cuffs

Medallions of needlework and Valenciennes are attached to the front of linen collars, and hang pendant like a locket. Cuffs to match have similar medallions that are to be fastened over on the outside of a coat sleeve. Sets of this kind are exceedingly pretty for demitoilettes, and suit especially the neat summer silks and poplinettes used for home dresses.

Another style of morning collar has alternate points of narrow Valenciennes and of linen, with wide square cuffs, on which are as many as eight rows of Valenciennes, forming a deep vandyke between plain linen points. Tiny bows of embroidery and lace, with blue ribbon beneath them, are worn at the throat. Straight bands, exquisitely needleworked on one side, are to be worn either as standing or turndown collars. Some of the handsomest sets have collarettes with them, long falls of lace, to be worn with the open surplice and revers dresses now fashionable.

Varieties

A new *sortie de bal* or evening wrapping is a round cloak of cashmere called, in honor of a classic garment, the chlamys. It resembles the talma in shape, and is of the finest cashmere. A white and blue ground or a dark rich color is bordered with palm leaves and other Oriental designs in gay and brilliant colors. The garment is surrounded by a fringe made of the fleece of the cashmere goat, in which is blended all the varied colors of the border. It is lined with soft silk.

April 25, 1868

Sacques, Pelisses, and Mantillas

Black faille, or unwatered moiré, is an elegant fabric much used for sacques and mantles. It is more lustrous than grosgrain, and thicker and richer. A better gloss is given to grosgrain this season, which not only improves its appearance, but will, it is said, prevent it from turning rusty and brown, as black corded silks are so apt to do. Plain taffeta, with a glistening smooth surface, is not used.

Fancy pleated trimmings are displayed in new arrangements. There are reversed pleats with a button on each end; quilled pleats with piping in the center; and frills with the narrow pleats all turned one way and secured at both edges. Bias folds, inserted points, crosscut bands, piping, flutings, ruffles, rosettes, and butterfly bows, and an endless variety of handmade ornaments have been provided to take the place of passementerie and the longtime favorite jet. Laces, fringe, tassels, and a small bead of crocheted silk are also used in profusion.

It is scarcely possible to find any two garments shaped precisely alike–but basquines and half-fitting jackets predominate. Very few loose paletots are seen. French garments are either fitted to the form or left slightly loose and confined at the waist with a belt and sash. The fronts are longer than the back, with square mantilla ends, or they are rounded and crossed on the waist like a fichu. The back is made short, to disclose the skirt *en paniers,* and the sides are frequently open and filled in with lace. Another pretty style has the fronts pointed and lapped, with both points visible.

Pelisses are buttoned down the entire front in a straight row, or are double-breasted, with a pointed lap on the left, and fastened diagonally down the skirt. They are smooth at the shoulders, and belted in at the waist. The skirts are looped up at the sides. The coat sleeve is almost the only one used.

The scarf mantilla without sleeves is a most novel garment. It is light and cool, and peculiarly appropriate for muslin and grenadine dresses that are easily rumpled. It can be cut with square fronts or lapped scarf ends like a fichu.

Of all the new styles introduced this season the Watteau seems to have met with most favor. The peculiarity of this stylish wrapping consists in the fold at the back, which may be either one wide box pleat, or two or even three smaller ones.

The old-fashioned mantilla falling low off the shoulders, with long, square, scarflike fronts, is again revived. This is graceful and cool for summer wear, and may be made of the dress material for short suits.

Graceful burnoose scarves with mantilla fronts, all wool, are worn in honeycomb patterns in gay solid colors and in cashmere stripes on a white ground for evening mantles. A deep fringe surrounds them, and a silk cord and tassel, in which all the colors of the burnoose are blended, is tied at the throat. Plain checks, black and white, or blue and black, are shown for morning wear and for extra carriage wrappings.

India Cashmere Shawls

The one article of feminine apparel that is in no danger of ever being discarded by fashion is an India shawl. In our fickle climate there is scarcely a month of the year in which they may not be called into requisition, and as an heirloom they are as much prized as gems. The most elegant velvets are cut up into cloaks that will only present a stylish appearance one season. Or else they are made into circulars or loose shapes with an eye to remodeling them, so that when the velvet is new the style is bad, and only when the material is worn are they made into the prevailing mode. But an India cashmere is always fashionable.

April 25, 1868

Notwithstanding the popular conviction, there is no such material as camel's hair made into shawls. The fleece of the cashmere goat is the material used, and the embroidery is done in small scraps so beautifully needleworked together that it is difficult to find the joins. The handsomest shawls are of course those that are most nearly covered with embroidery. A small, plain center is, however, necessary, as the embroidered part is too thick to fold pleasantly about the neck. Calcutta shawls are preferred to those made in Delhi and Bombay, as the colors are better blended, and the cashmere surface more thoroughly worked up. The surface should be perfectly smooth.

Plain shawls with India borders are often arranged in America by cutting long shawls that are found to be unsalable into borders for squares of cashmere. In this case the figures of the border run around the shawls, while in those made in India the palm leaves are pointed toward the center, the figures at the corners are symmetrical, and the colors are delicately but gradually shaded from the outer to the inner edge of the border. This may also be easily detected from the fact that American borders are chain stitched or embroidered onto the centers, while those from India are connected by needlework so well done and intricate that it seems to be woven.

The brilliantly colored shawls with a great deal of bright magenta in them are favorites in Paris, but have never been admired here.

Cloak and Dress Trimmings

These trimmings are for cloaks and dresses. Figures 1 and 2 show how to make piping.

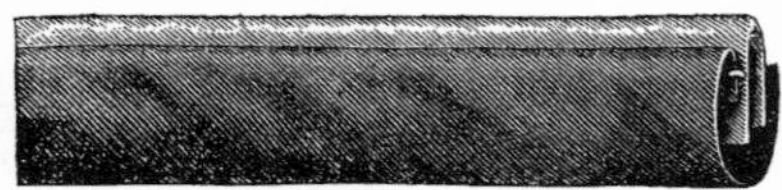

Figure 1. Piping

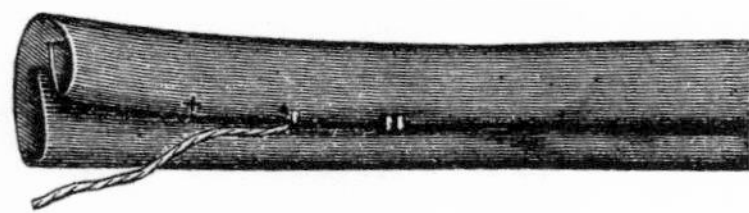

Figure 2. Making piping

Figure 3 shows how to make folds of silk, satin, or cloth.

Figure 3. Bias fold

The silk bows in Figures 4 and 5 are especially adapted for trimming pocket lapels, sleeves, and epaulets. They can be made of black or colored silk, or the garment material.

Figure 4 is of black silk reps. It consists of six loops, each 3 inches wide, edged with satin piping and a bias fold 1/4 inch wide. These are laid in two pleats at the end, and arranged on a piece of stiff lace, as shown. The center consists of a passementerie figure in the shape of a leaf with grelots.

Figure 5 consists of a strip of silk 5 inches long and 1 inch wide, edged with narrow satin piping. The ends are pointed and finished with passementerie buttons. Beneath the sides and under part of this are sewn nine loops, each 2 inches long and 1 inch wide, also edged with satin piping.

Figure 4. Silk bow

Figure 5. Silk bow

The middle of the rosette in Figure 6 is of gray satin, and the outer part of gray cloth. The nine outer pieces are each 2 1/2 inches wide and 1 4/5 inches long. They are stitched round with gray silk, box pleated at the end, and set on a circular piece of stiff lace. The four satin loops in the middle are each 1 4/5 inches and 1 2/5 inches long, with interlining between and box pleated at the end. A satin knot is placed in the middle of the rosette, which is 4 inches in diameter.

Figure 6. Rosette

The rosette in Figure 7 is designed for a belt or sash. It is made of a circular piece of pasteboard, 2 inches in diameter, covered with grosgrain. On this four satin loops are laid crosswise, to form a star, and a small satin button is set on each end. A large satin button confines the loops in the center. The edge of the rosette is finished with small satin points.

Figure 7. Silk rosette for sash

The trimming in Figure 8, and the following five, are especially adapted to sleeves, pockets, standing collars, etc. This simple and elegant trimming consists of upright loops of satin ribbon 1/4 inch wide. The setting on of them is concealed by silk cord wound round them as shown.

Figure 8. Loop and cord trimming

The trimming in Figure 9 is made of small bias folds of satin. The ends are folded crosswise, to form points. They are then sewn together at the bottom, and a bias fold of satin is stitched over the seam.

Figure 9. Pointed trimming

Figure 10 shows a strip of the garment material, bound on the bottom with bias satin, then closely pleated, and set under a satin piping. To keep the pleats in place a strip of buckram is set under them, to which they are caught. Figure 11 shows how this is done.

Figure 10. Pleated trimming–right side

Figure 11. Pleated trimming–wrong side

For the trimming in Figure 12 a bias fold of satin is folded lengthwise, and box pleated at the bottom. Points of cloth, bound with satin, are then set over this, leaving the ends of the points free. A bias satin fold is stitched across the bottom.

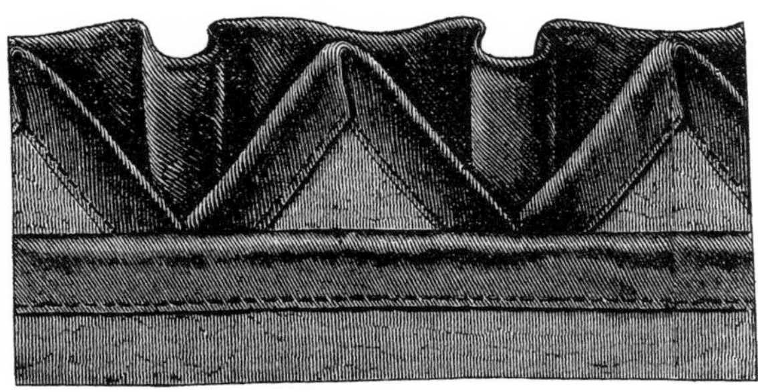

Figure 12. Pleated and pointed trimming

The trimming in Figure 13 consists of bias satin folded to form upright points. It is covered at the bottom with satin piping.

Figure 13. Pointed trimming

Looping Up Garments

Long cloaks are now often looped up to show more of the dress; and paletots and dresses are looped up in the same manner. The illustrations show the back of a traveling paletot, looped up, and a simple and easy way of doing this with buttons.

In sewing up the seams that join the breadths of the dress skirt or paletot, leave open a portion of the seam to form the buttonholes. Afterward open the seam and stitch it down on the right side. Then sew on the required buttons as shown, so that two buttonholes will lie under each button (see Figure 1).

Looping Up Garments

In buttoning up the dress, put the button marked I backward through the buttonhole marked 1 and forward through the buttonhole marked 2. In the same manner button II is brought through buttonholes 3 and 4, and button III through buttonholes 5 and 6. This forms the three folds shown in Figure 2. Additional buttons and buttonholes may of course be furnished each seam if desired.

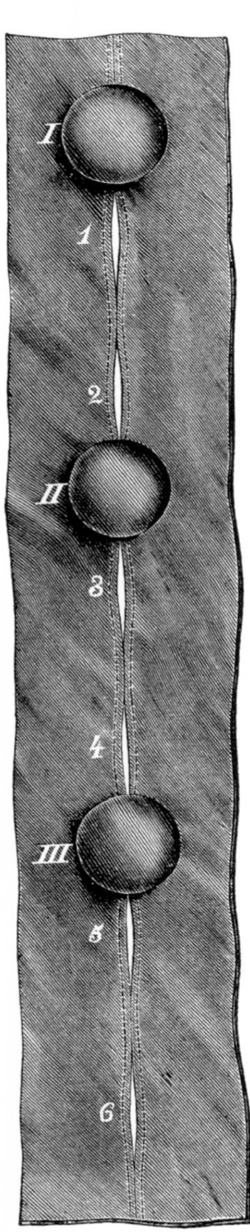

Figure 1. Button strip before looping up

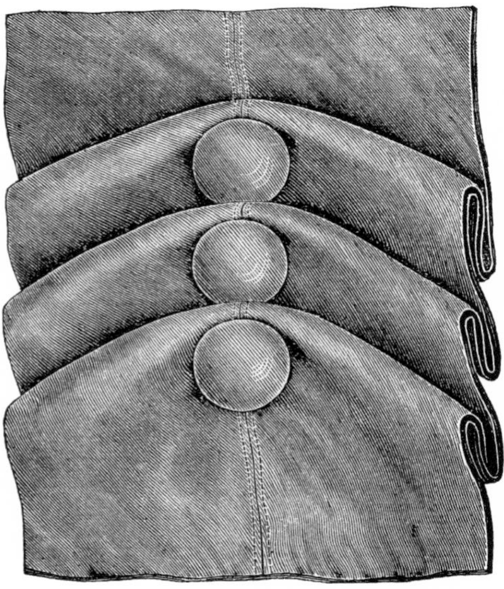

Figure 2. Button strip after looping up

Sash End

This sash end is worn with a belt, either behind or at the side. It is made of black silk reps. The upper part consists of eight loops of different sizes, four of which overlie the others. A pleated loop confines them in the middle. The sash ends are trimmed and edged with bias folds and satin cord, and finished with heavy tasseled fringe.

Sash End

Larger Under Loop
1/2 scale

Smaller Under Loop
1/2 scale

Sash End
1/4 scale

Larger Upper Loop
1/2 scale

Smaller Upper Loop
1/2 scale

Upright Loop

1/2 scale

Sash End

1/4 scale

x

Pendant Loop

1/2 scale

Sash End

This sash end is worn with a belt, either behind or at the side. It is made of black silk reps. It consists of four upright loops and one large pendant loop. The loops are of the same material as the ends, interlined with stiff muslin, and confined by a knot of silk reps. The sash ends are lined with marcelline and interlined with stiff muslin, and are edged with a heavy silk cord. Each one is adorned with a rosette, composed of seven loops of the same material, with a simulated button in the center. The ends are pleated at the top from *x* to •.

Belt with Tabs

Belt with Tabs

This pretty belt is made of grosgrain, lined with same, and furnished with an interlining. It is trimmed with tabs, whereof the pattern is given. These tabs are bordered with points of narrow satin ribbon. The points are made by notching the ribbon, then turning down the corners on the wrong side and tacking them together.

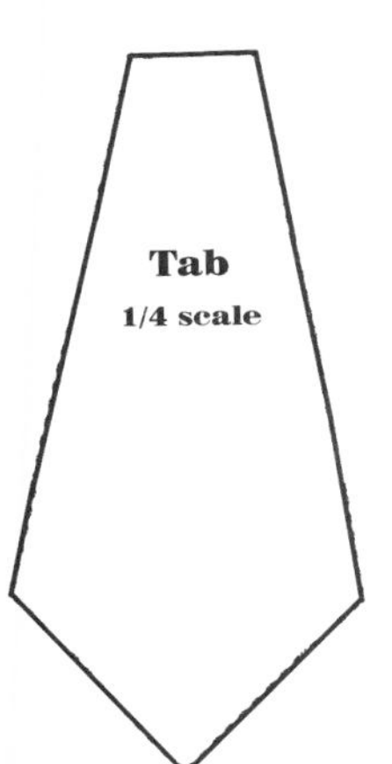

Undine Paletot

This simple and tasteful paletot is of light gray cloth. The ends overlap each other in the fashion of a fichu. A yard and 3/4 of cloth, 1 1/2 yards wide, is required. The trimming is a binding of light brown satin, 2/5 inch wide, and small lappets of the paletot material, likewise bound with satin. A heavy brown silk cord and tassels is fastened at the back of the waist, wound round, and knotted at the side.

Cut from the front, first side piece, second side piece, and back each two pieces. Sew up the seam in the back. Join the back, side pieces, and front. Stitch on the binding. The lappets are of the same material as the outside, lined with silk and bound with satin. Set the lappets on the neck and up the front, between the outside and facing of the paletot. The facing is a strip of silk, 1 1/2 inches wide. Hooks and eyes are set on the front. The sleeves are trimmed as illustrated.

April 25, 1868

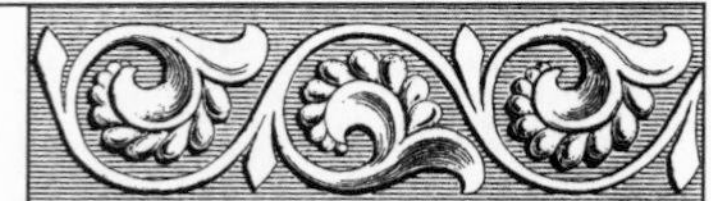

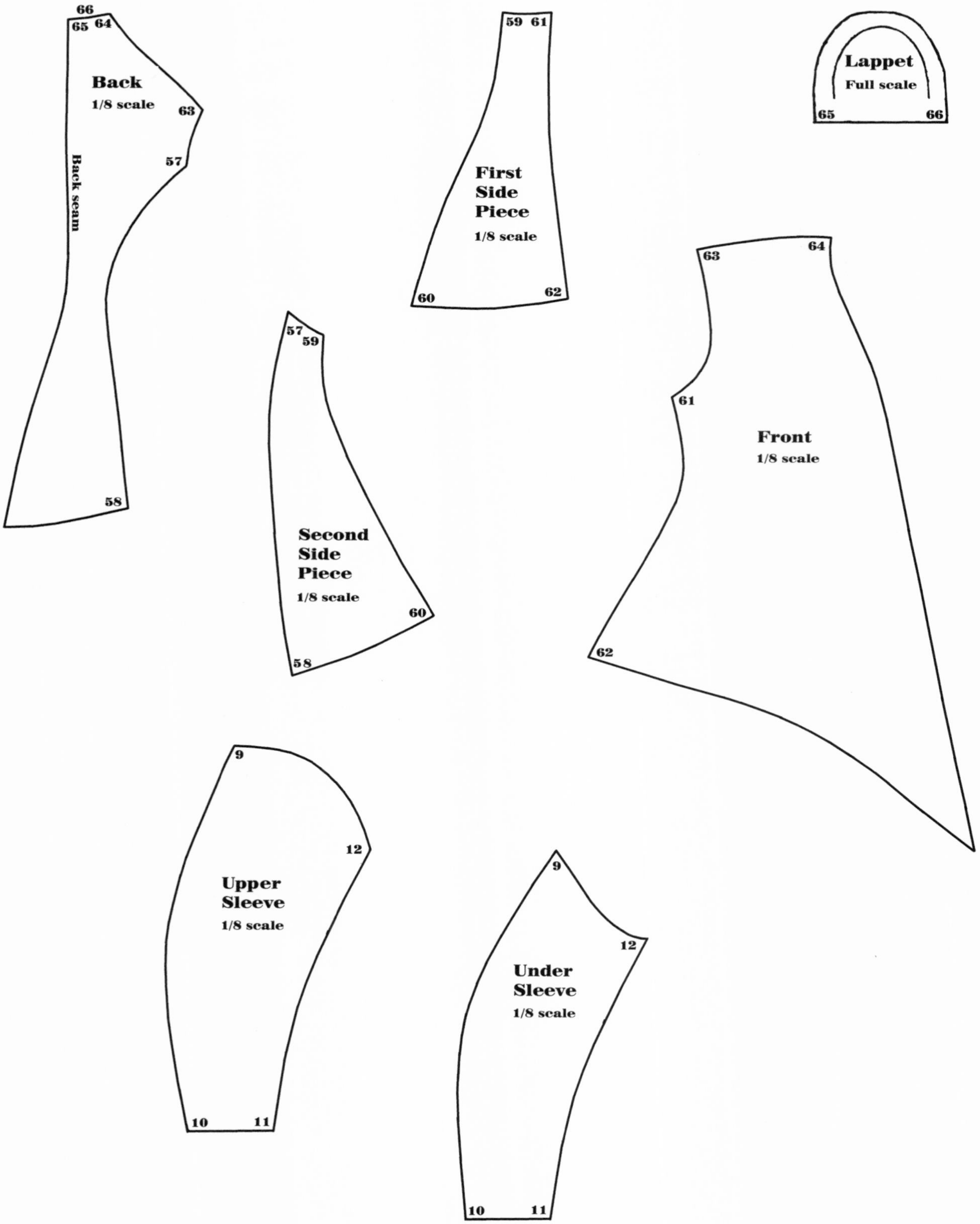

66
65 64

Back
1/8 scale

63

57

Back seam

58

59 61

First Side Piece
1/8 scale

60 62

Lappet
Full scale

65 66

57
59

Second Side Piece
1/8 scale

60

58

63 64

61

Front
1/8 scale

62

9

12

Upper Sleeve
1/8 scale

10 11

9

12

Under Sleeve
1/8 scale

10 11

Watteau Paletot

This graceful paletot is of black grosgrain. Five yards of silk 3/4 yard wide are required. The back is laid in pleats, under which a belt is passed. The trimming consists of black lace, 2 1/2 inches wide, with a heading of passementerie braid.

Cut from the front and back each two pieces, and two pieces for each sleeve. Make the bosom pleats. Sew up the seam in the back. Arrange the latter in box pleats, bringing *x* and • together. From the neck to the straight line on the back the pleats are sewn inside along the inner fold. Join the back and fronts. Face the edge with a strip of silk 1 1/2 inches wide. Put on the trimming. The neck is finished with a small standing collar. Sew the two parts of the sleeves together. Face the bottom with a bias strip of silk. Trim the sleeves, and sew them in the armholes. Lastly, put a belt 2 inches wide under the back pleats.

April 25, 1868

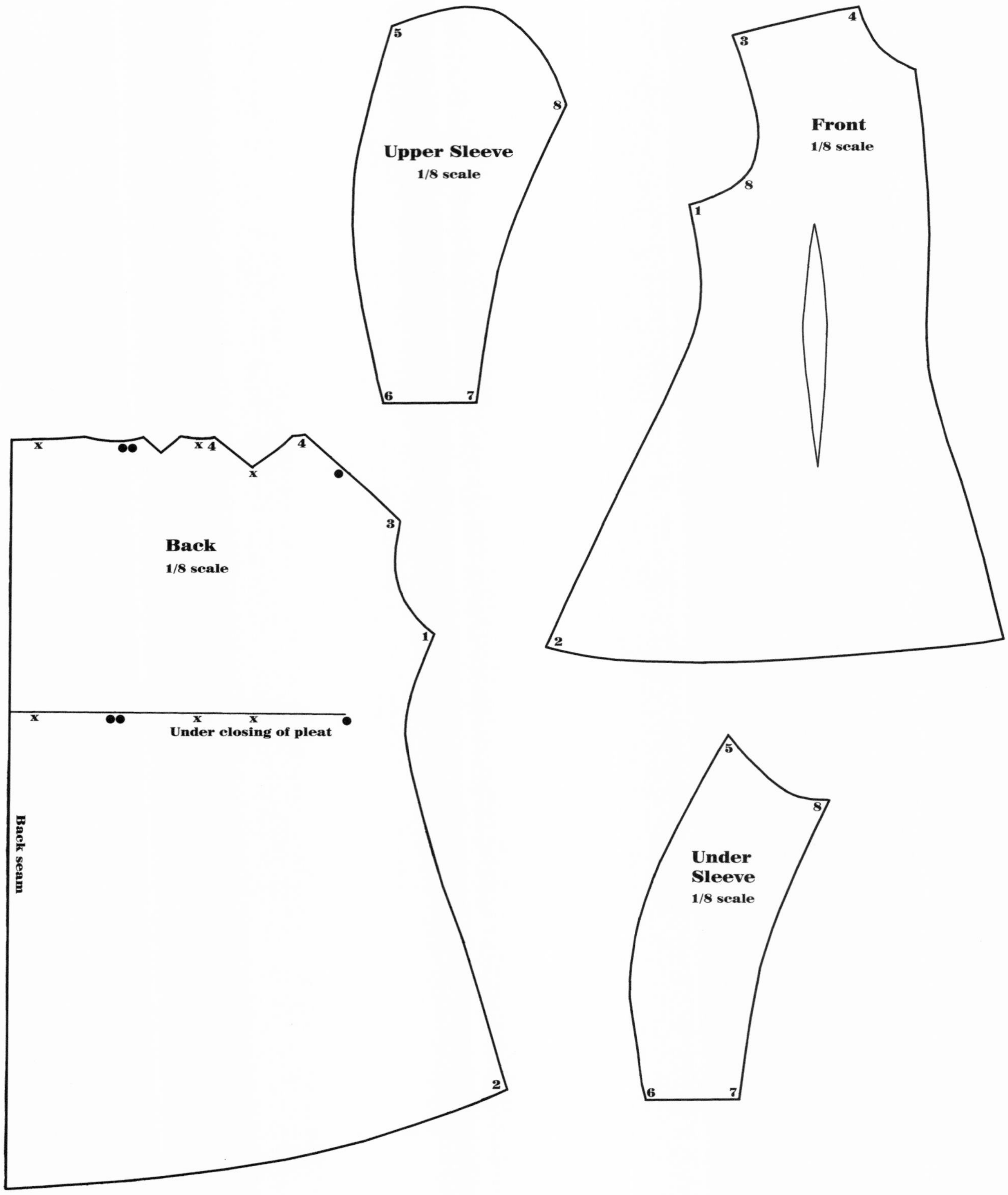

Upper Sleeve
1/8 scale
5
8
6
7

Front
1/8 scale
4
3
8
1
2

Back
1/8 scale
x
●●
x 4
x
4
●
3
1
x
●●
x
x
●
Under closing of pleat
Back seam
2

Under
Sleeve
1/8 scale
5
8
6
7

Polonaise Paletot

This paletot is of black grosgrain. Four and 1/4 yards of silk 3/4 yard wide are required. It is closed in front and furnished with revers. The trimming consists of bias folds of grosgrain, black lace, and crocheted buttons. The buttonholes are simulated with black braid. A belt with bow completes the paletot.

Cut from the waist front, skirt front, skirt back, and front of revers each two pieces. Cut from the waist back and back of the revers each one piece. The sleeves are made from the pattern for the Undine Paletot. Lay the bosom pleats, join the waist, and sew on the skirt. Face the edge of the paletot with a strip of silk. Put on the bias folds and lace. Trim the sleeves, and sew them in the armholes.

April 25, 1868

The revers are interlined with stiff muslin and lined with silk. Cut through one piece of the front of the revers along the dotted line. Put the trimming on the lower part, as illustrated. Set it on the right side of the skirt along the narrow line. Then join the remaining piece, put on the trimming, and set it on the left side of the waist. Set the other whole piece on the right side of the waist and skirt as far as 53 on the skirt front, sewing the overplus the whole width on the left side of the skirt. Loops are placed along the latter at a distance of 4 inches from each other, the corresponding hooks being set on the revers.

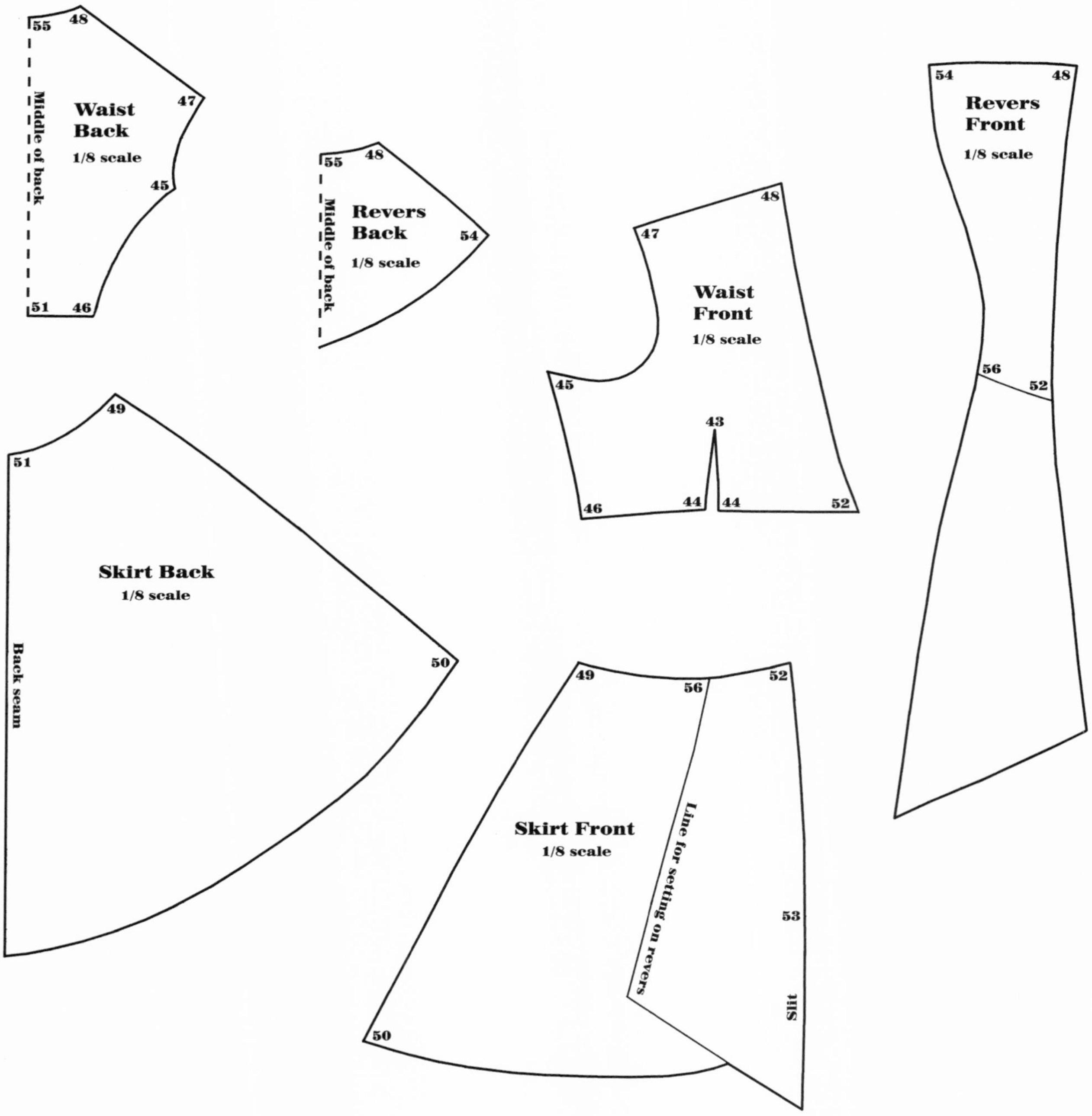

May 9, 1868

Parasols and Trimmings

The present styles of parasols do not differ in shape from those of last year. They are mostly covered with silk or poult-de-soie, and lined with white marcelline, though the lining is sometimes the same color as the outside. The styles of trimming are numerous. They consist of bias folds, points, flaps, and puffs, either of the same material as the parasol or satin; fringe; embroidery in satin stitch, point Russe, etc. The trimming is usually the same shade as the parasol, though a darker or lighter shade is sometimes used.

Wooden handles are much in vogue, some being carved and etched in light or dark colors, and some white, smooth, and polished. Bone and ivory handles are also used. Elegant imported parasols are made, covered with point lace, with handles formed of solid pieces of goldstone, onyx, amber, and carnelian; but these are very expensive.

Mode Poult-de-Soie Parasol

This parasol is lined with white marcelline. About 1/2 inch from the outer edge sew on a frill of poult-de-soie 2 1/2 inches wide, with the pleats some distance apart. Cut into points on the outer edge 1 inch deep by 1 1/2 inches wide, with a strip 1 inch wide of the same material set under along this pointed edge. The place where the trimming is sewn on is covered by velvet ribbon 1/4 inch wide.

Above the frill small points of the poult-de-soie are sewn on (see Figure 1). For each point take a piece of the material 2 inches square. Fold it to form a triangle; then fold it again to bring the three corners together. Having prepared the points sew them on as shown, taking care to put the slit at the middle of the upper point. The places where these are fastened on the parasol are covered by velvet ribbon which is sewn on. In addition a straight row of the velvet is sewn on above. The handle is of bone.

Figure 1. Trimming for mode poult-de-soie parasol

May 9, 1868

Light Green Parasol

This poult-de-soie parasol is ornamented with small crescent figures embroidered in silk twist and finished with bugles. Figure 1 shows this full size. The star design illustrated in Figure 2 may be substituted.

Above this is a row of puffs of the poult-de-soie. These puffs are arranged together from a piece of stuff 2 1/2 inches wide. This is pleated across at regular distances, and sewn on the parasol, so the part lying between each point of pleating stands out in a loose puff. Between every two puffs is a little band of black satin.

The lining is of white marcelline. The handle is of polished whitewood.

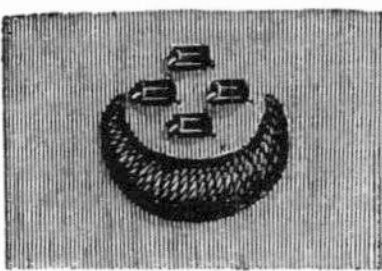

Figure 1. Embroidery pattern for parasol

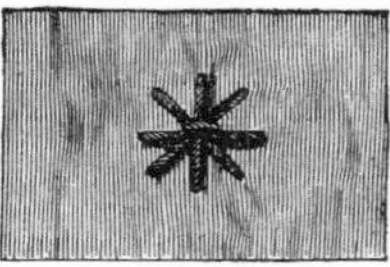

Figure 2. Embroidery pattern for parasol

Black Silk Parasol

This parasol is ornamented on the edge with black silk fringe 3 inches wide, and tabs of the same material as the parasol. These tabs are each 2 1/2 inches long and 2 inches wide. They are bound around the edges with a satin binding 1/4 inch wide, and are sewn close to each other on the parasol. Those tabs that fall over a rib of the frame must be laid on in a pleat on the upper edge, so that it will not stretch. The place where the tabs are sewn on is covered by a row of puffs of the silk fastened by small silk bands, like those for the Light Green Parasol.

The lining is of white marcelline. The handle is of black quaintly etched wood.

The closed parasol is fastened together by a braided ring of black silk cord (see Figure 1). For making this six cords are needed. These are laid together at half their length and then divided into three strands, each consisting of four cords, and are braided together as shown by Figure 2. The under end of the braid is wound firmly with black cord and then fastened under the upper end, where the cords are fastened together. On the ring thus formed fasten two tassels. Then draw a black silk cord through the braid of the ring. Fasten one end of this cord to the upper point of the parasol, and the other to the under end of one rib.

Figure 1. Ring for closing parasol–full size

Figure 2. Section of braid for ring

A crocheted ring, such as is shown in Figure 3, may be substituted for the braided one. The pattern is worked of black silk twist. On a foundation of the requisite length crochet three rounds sc. (single crochet), putting the needle through both the upper veins of the stitches. This forms the thick middle strip.

Figure 3. Section of crocheted ring for parasol

Then work on both sides, and across one end of this strip, the interlacing scallops. In the 1st stitch of the last round work 1 sc., 10 ch. (chain stitches), 1 sc. on the 4th following stitch. Then having turned the work crochet back on the chain stitches 1 sl. (slip stitch) in each ch., 1 sl. in that stitch of the thick strip in which was worked the 1st sc. before the chain row. Then, returning, 15 sc. on the scallop; 1 sl. in that stitch of the strip in which was worked the sc. after the chain row; 2 ch. * Now take the needle out of the loop and put it through the 2nd of the 3 stitches of the thick strip that were passed over by the chain row. Again take up the loop that was dropped from the needle–in doing which the needle must be put under the scallop–and crochet together with one thread the loop and stitch on the needle. Then work a scallop composed of 3 ch., 1 sl. in the 4th from the last sc. of the former scallop and 6 ch. In working the first 3 ch. of this row the working thread always lies behind the scallop just finished. In forming this scallop pass over 4 stitches of the thick strip, taking 1 sc. in the following stitch. Then, turning the work, crochet a row of sl. back on the scallop; 1 sl. in the sc. of the strip before the chain row; then 15 sc. on the scallop, 1 sl. in the next sc. that was worked in the thick strip; 2 ch.

Repeat from * until the thick strip is bordered with scallops as shown. The scallops may be worked on one end as shown in the full-size figure. Having finished the crochet work, join the strip in a ring by sewing the scalloped end over the other.

Figure 2. Embroidered border for parasol

Parasol Trimmings

Each of these styles represents 1/8 of a parasol cover.

This parasol is a foundation of gray and black silk. The edges are cut in scallops and worked in buttonhole stitch with gray silk twist, as shown in Figure 1. Above the black border runs a vine embroidered in satin stitch with black silk twist. Figure 2 shows a section full size. On each side of the embroidery is worked a row of chain stitch, and outside of these a row in herringbone. These rows are worked with black on the gray silk, and with gray on the black silk. A pattern of 1/8 of the cover is given.

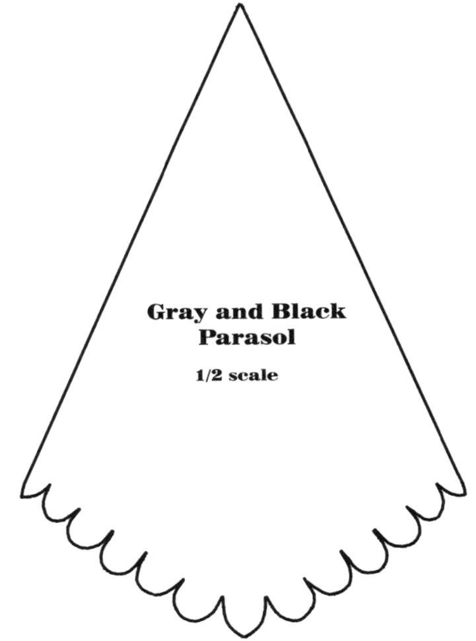

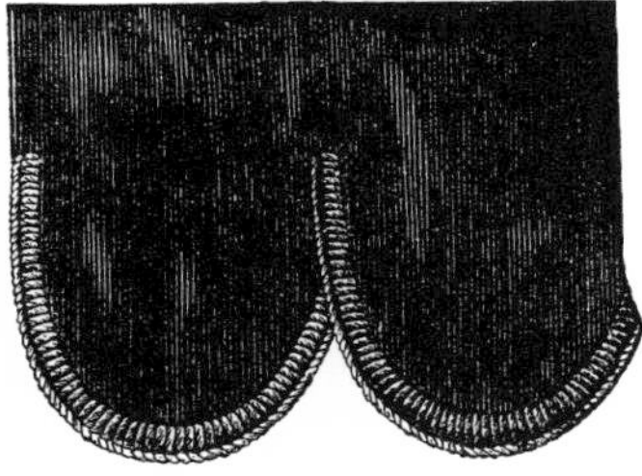

Figure 1. Trimming for parasol

This parasol is a cover of lilac silk, embroidered in satin stitch and point Russe, and finished on each side by a border of chain stitch and one of herringbone, worked in violet silk. A section is shown full size.

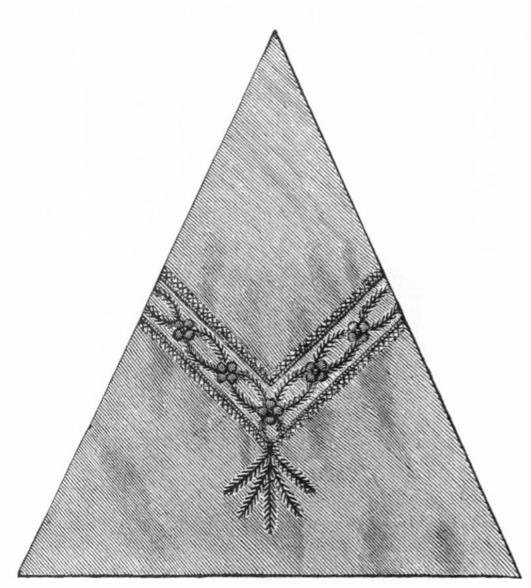

Parasol Trimmings

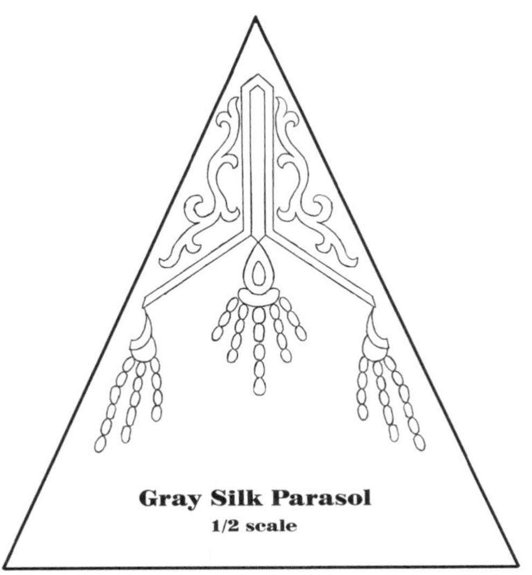

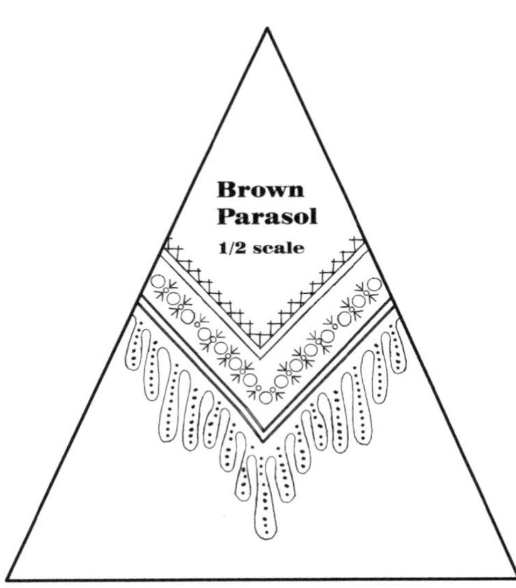

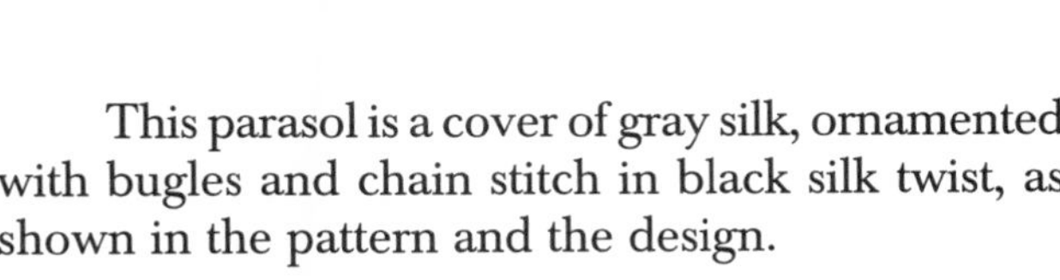

This parasol is a cover of gray silk, ornamented with bugles and chain stitch in black silk twist, as shown in the pattern and the design.

This parasol is a cover of light and dark brown silk. It is worked as shown by the pattern and the design. The stitches are chain and herringbone stitch, satin stitch, and point Russe. The embroidery is done with dark silk on the light, and with light silk on the dark foundation.

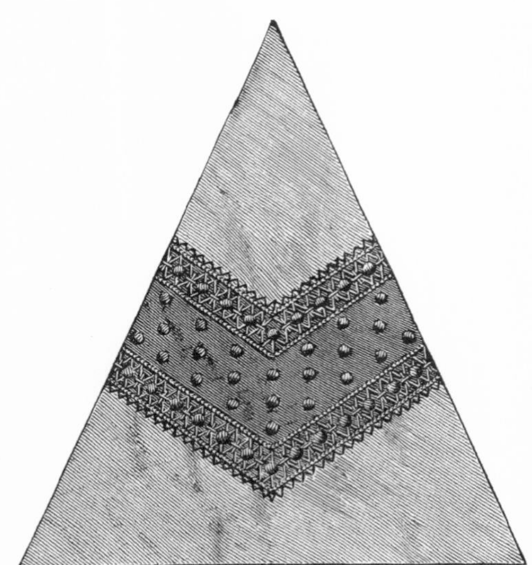

This parasol is a cover of light brown poult-de-soie, bordered with dark brown. This is embroidered in satin stitch and point Russe, and finished with chain stitches of light brown silk twist. The outer edges of the border are finished by a row of herringbone stitch in light brown silk.

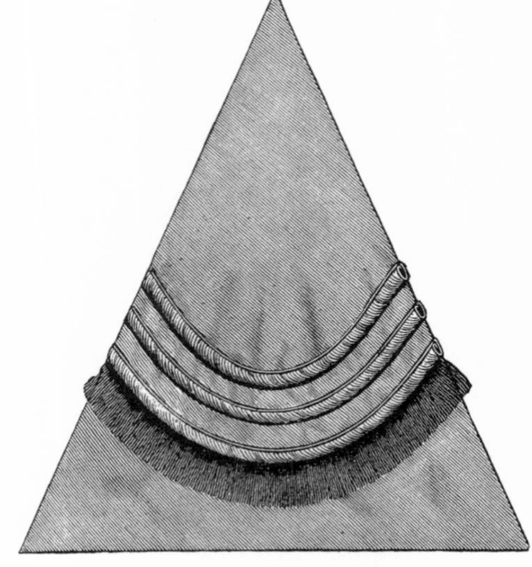

This parasol is a cover of light brown silk, trimmed with bias folds of the same material and brown fringe. The bias folds are sewn on with brown satin cord.

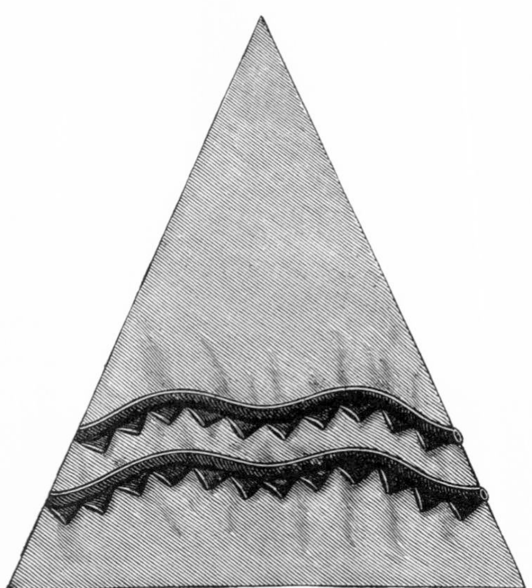

This parasol is a cover of gray poult-de-soie, trimmed as shown with bias folds and points of black satin. The bias folds are bordered on one side with white and black satin cord.

Parasol Trimmings

Figure 1 is a parasol trimming made of coarse silk twist. The threads are stretched across each other and fastened at the crossing points by two crystal beads. A bias fold of the stuff is sewn on at each side of these threads with satin cord.

Figure 1. Trimming for parasol

The trimming in Figure 2 is used on a cover of light and dark silk. It consists of long straight stitches of silk twist, every five of which are drawn together and fastened by a cross-stitch. Two rows of chain and one of herringbone stitch complete the trimming.

Figure 2. Embroidery pattern for parasol

Making Bonnet Frames and Bonnets

With the aid of the accompanying figures, our readers will be enabled to make their own bonnet frames, cheaply and easily. We also give patterns of the latest styles of bonnets.

The making of a bonnet frame is very simple. The material needed is foundation muslin, coarse and fine wire, and for some styles, also silk. For the frame of a black bonnet use black foundation and black wire, and for a white bonnet white material. For a lace or crêpe bonnet in colors wind the frame with narrow bias strips of the same material, and cover the foundation with several thicknesses of the same, so that it may not show through. Pliers are used for cutting the wire. If these are not at hand make an oblique cut with the scissors, after which it is easily broken.

For the simple forms, shape first the outer edge of the frame of coarse wire, allowing the ends to lap over about 1 inch. Fasten them together as shown in Figures 1 and 2, with fine wire such as is used in making flowers. Instead of this, fine bonnet wire may be used, which is easily taken out. The so-formed wire circle (see Figure 1), the size of which is according to the size and form of the frame, and is designated in the descriptions accompanying each, must now be bent into the requisite form as shown in the pattern. The ends that are fastened together must always come in the middle of the back of the frame.

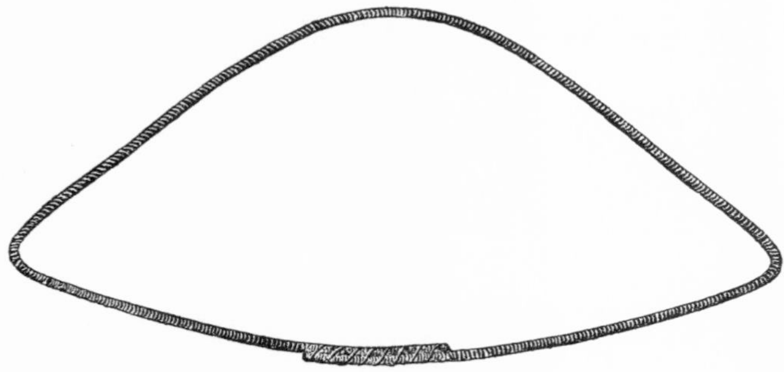

Figure 1. Outer wire of bonnet frame–reduced

Figure 2. Joining the wires–full size

The cross wires, of fine wire, must next be fastened to this, as shown in the patterns and accompanying descriptions. Each piece should be cut about 1/2 inch longer than is given in the cut. The ends of these cross wires are wound around the outer edge of the framework as shown in Figure 4. It is well to use scissors or a knife to make the fastening firm. The points where the wire crosses are fastened by threads, the ends of which are tied. Having finished the framework, stretch the foundation muslin lightly over it, fastening only on the outer border.

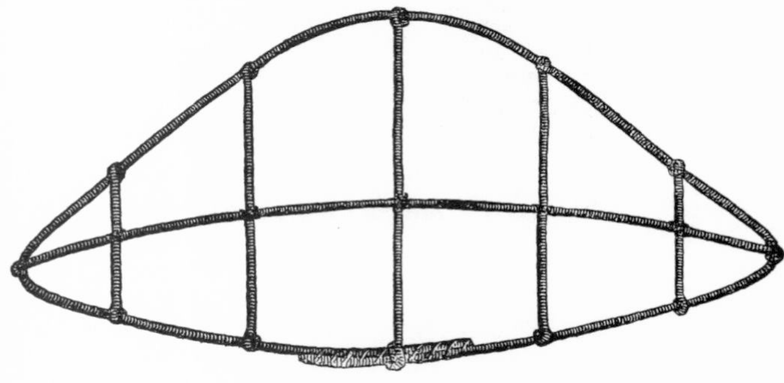

Figure 3. Wire of bonnet frame–reduced

Figure 4. Fastening cross wire to outer wire–full size

The most simple style given here is the Metternich, Figure 5. In making the frame, fashion the outer part of the framework from a wire 25 inches long, after the pattern, as shown in Figure 1. The cross wires are placed as shown in the pattern and the accompanying illustrations. Over the prepared framework stretch tightly a piece of foundation. Hemstitch it over the outer wire, cut the edges away 1/4 inch from the edge of the wire, and sew this down on the inside of the frame.

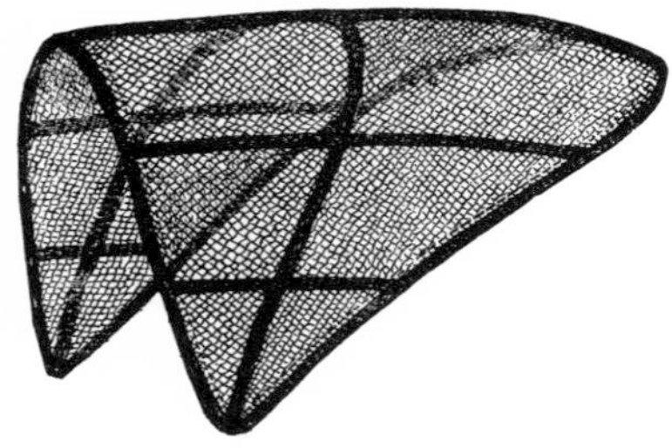

Figure 5. Frame of Metternich

Figure 6 is the Marie Antoinette. Begin this by fastening the ends of a wire 24 inches long as shown in Figure 2. Bend it in the shape given by the pattern. Fasten to this the middle long wire and the cross wires as shown in Figures 3 and 4. On this lay the doubled stuff bias along the middle line. Cut the sides, leaving 1/2 inch of the material beyond the edge. In the front part lay the pleat as shown and sew the foundation to the outer wire.

The Augusta bonnet is made after the same pattern as the Marie Antoinette.

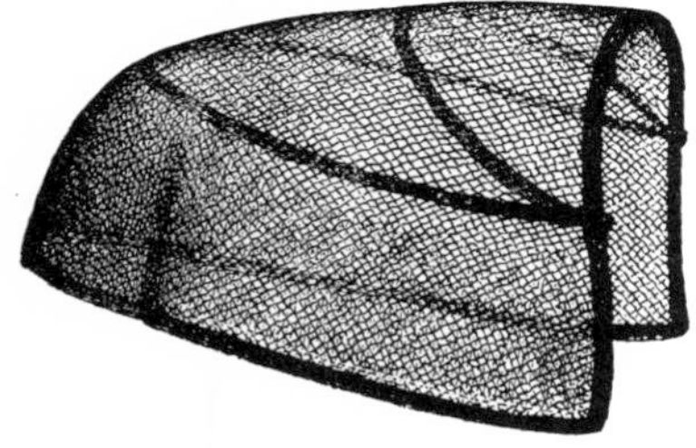

Figure 6. Frame of Marie Antoinette

The Pompadour bonnet, Figure 7, consists of three bands and a headpiece of the foundation muslin. Cut first of any silk at hand–it is immaterial whether it be old or new–two bias bandeaux, each 2 1/2 inches wide, the one 11 and the other 12 inches long. In addition cut a straight piece of foundation muslin 12 1/2 inches long, for the front band. The material of the bandeaux is to be laid over on both sides 3/4 inch from the edge, so that each finished band will be 1 inch wide. In each seam made by thus folding the material, lay a fine wire and backstitch it fast. The upper edge of the stuff may be laid under in a narrow hem and then hemmed to the under edge as shown in Figure 8. To give the silk bands the shape shown by the back and middle bandeaux, the outer side of the stuff must be stretched and the wire bent as shown. The finished bandeaux are fastened together at the points designated by the numbers. Then cut according to the crown pattern a piece of foundation muslin, bias along the middle, and extending 1/4 inch beyond the edges. This must be sewn to the bands on the under side, holding the material in as required between the numbers 56 and 57.

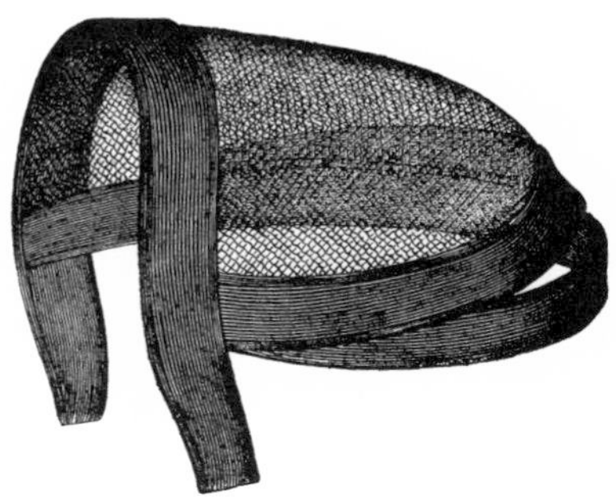

Figure 7. Frame of Pompadour

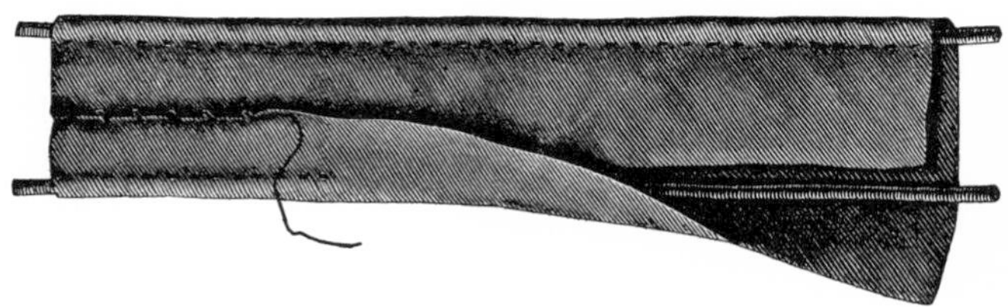

Figure 8. Making bandeau for Pompadour–full size

The Pompadour and Watteau bonnets are made in this manner. Having completed the frame, cover it with the material chosen. The manner of doing this, as also the arrangement of bows, flowers, lace, feathers, etc., can scarcely be described.

It must be learned from illustration, and will depend on individual taste and the skill of the maker. It only remains to mention that the material must always be put on bias, so that it can be stretched at will, whether it be plain, pleated, or puffed over the frame. In putting on the outside material–if it be plain it must be tightly stretched–lay it over the frame, cut it at 1/2 inch beyond the edge of the bonnet, and sew it fast to the foundation on the inner side, taking care not to let the stitches be visible on the outside. Line with tulle or material like the bonnet.

The borders may be made in different ways. Take either a piece of the bonnet material, or, in case that be light, silk or velvet of the same color. Figures 9 to 11 show a rounded border. Take a bias strip 2 inches wide, as shown by Figure 9. Sew it on the bonnet, taking care to sew through the double material, and to draw the thread tight. Lay the stuff over the edge and hem down on the under side so the stitches will not show on the outside.

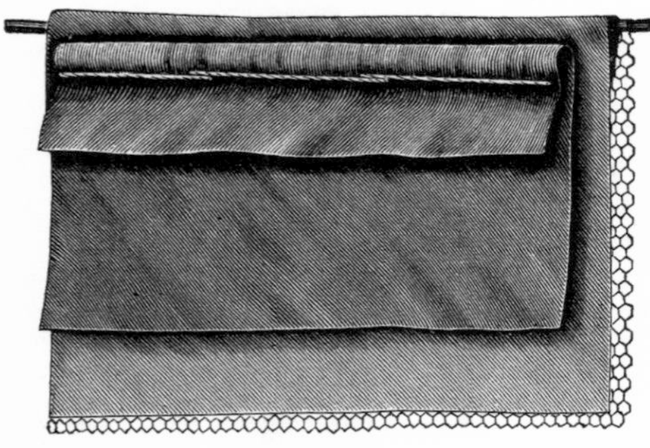

Figure 9. Binding of bonnet–full size

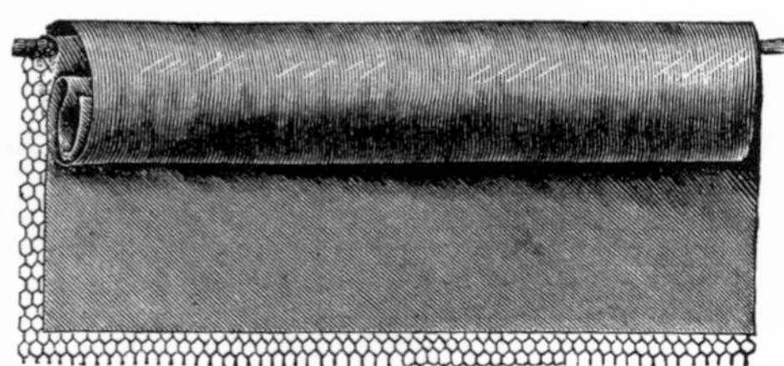

Figure 10. Binding of bonnet–full size

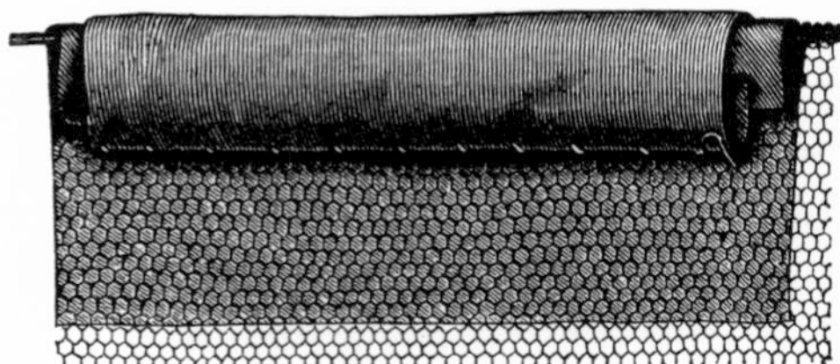

Figure 11. Binding of bonnet–full size

The border shown by Figure 12 is made in a similar manner, but in this a fold without a cord is laid on the right side. This may be a different color from the bonnet.

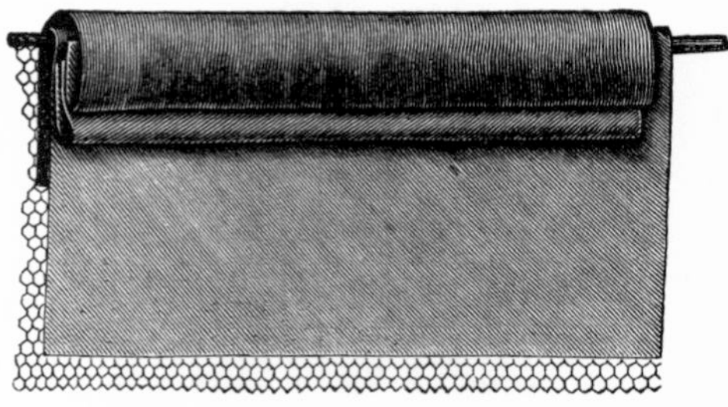

Figure 12. Binding of bonnet–full size

Still another border is made by a bias strip of stuff 1 1/2 inches wide. Lay the edges over at the width of 1/4 inch (see Figure 13). Fold the strip together at half its width, and fasten one end to a corner of the bonnet. Lay it so the middle seam made by doubling will lie exactly on the front edge of the bonnet. Stretch the strip along the edge till it exactly fits. Then fasten it on the other corner and hem down on the inside. On the outside the border will lie smooth, and does not need to be fastened.

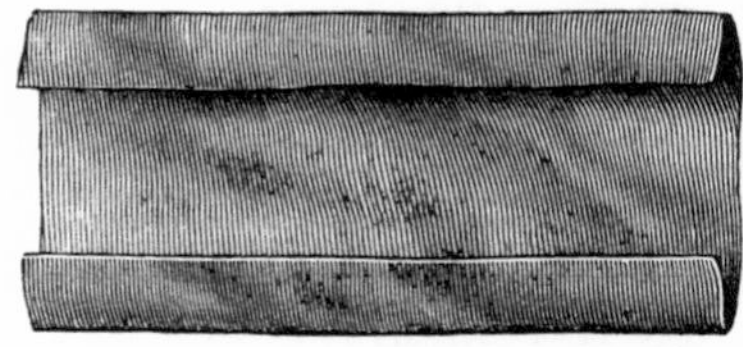

Figure 13. Bias strip for binding–full size

For the band simulating a diadem, which is sewn on the front of many bonnets, sew together two widths of wire bonnet, each 9 inches long. Cover them with a strip of bias material, 5 inches wide, laying in a piece of stiff muslin. Figure 14 shows a finished band. The ends must be fastened inside near the front edge of the bonnet. The remainder is left loose.

Figure 14. Bandeau for bonnet–reduced

Figure 15. Joining wire for bandeau

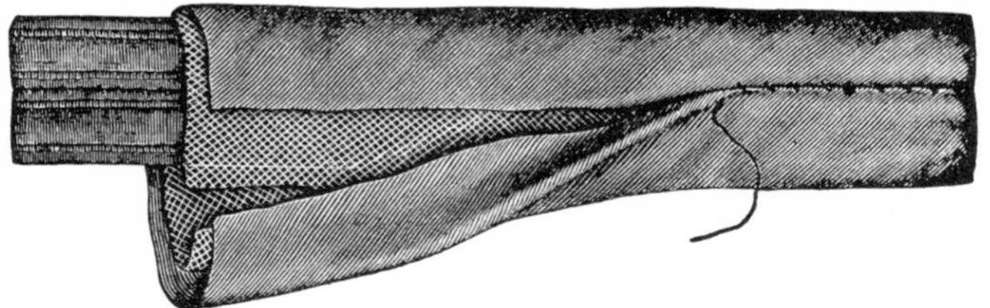

Figure 16. Making bandeau–full size

As the bonnets are mostly fastened under the chin by tulle or crêpe, the ribbons are usually narrow. They are sewn on the corners of the bonnet, and tied back under the hair. The ribbon is folded down to the width of 1 inch by making two pleats, and is then sewn on as shown in Figure 17.

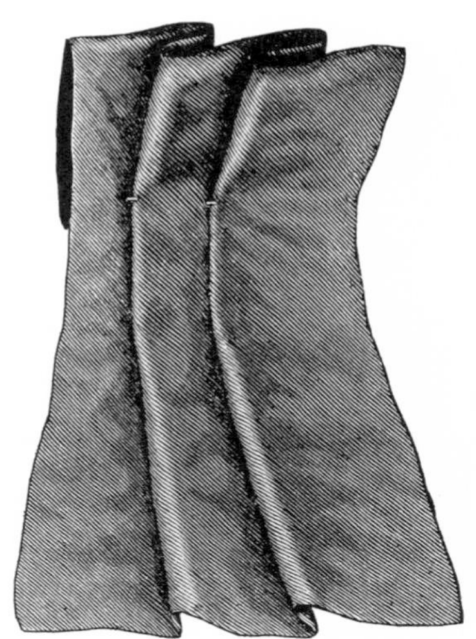

Figure 17. Sewing on strings

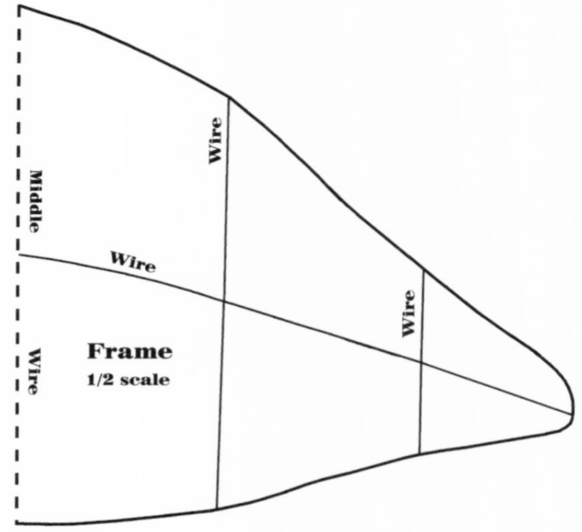

Metternich Bonnet

This stylish bonnet is made entirely of gray crêpe. The pattern of the frame is given. This is covered with several thicknesses of crêpe, laid on plain, and finally with a single thickness gathered to form two high puffs in front. Three fan-shaped bows of gray ribbon, one of which is shown half size, and a lace edge 1 1/2 inches wide, together with blackberry blossoms set on a black silk band, form the diadem. A pleated scarf of gray crêpe, edged with lace 1 1/2 inches wide, passes over the back of the bonnet. It is brought forward and fastened under the chin with a spray of blackberry blossoms. A bow of gray ribbon, 2 1/2 inches wide, with short ends, is set on the back of the bonnet. Strings of narrow ribbon tie it behind under the chignon. A single blackberry blossom is set on the left side of the front.

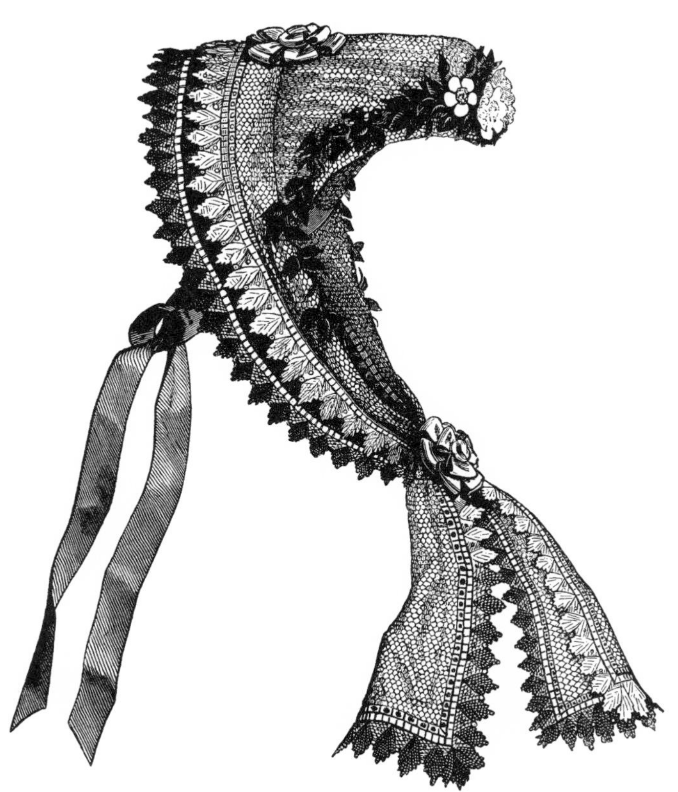

Augusta Bonnet

This tasteful bonnet is of white lace trimmed with broad white blonde and watered ribbon 1 1/2 inches wide. A wreath of sweetbrier with buds and leaves forms a diadem in front, with the ends extending down on the strings. The pattern of the frame is the same as for the Metternich Bonnet. It is cut of white stiff lace, and bound with a narrow strip of satin. It is then covered with several thicknesses of tulle, laid on smooth, and finally with a single thickness of tulle gathered to form two high puffs in front. The back of the bonnet is covered with watered ribbon, 1 1/2 inches wide, the long ends of which are tied under the chignon. This is covered again with a scarf made of a strip of tulle, 1 5/8 yard long and 5 inches wide, edged with blonde 2 inches wide. The scarf is doubled, as shown, so the lower edge of one row of blonde just reaches to the upper edge of the other, and laid in pleats across the back of the bonnet. A rosette of watered ribbon is set in the middle of the scarf, on the top, and another confines the ends under the chin. A satin band, covered with pleated lace, is fastened in front, and covered with the sweetbrier wreath.

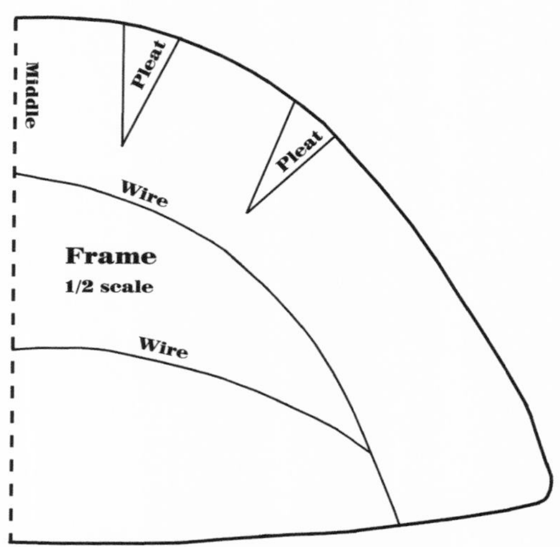

Marie Antoinette Bonnet

The frame is cut of black stiff lace. It is covered with several thicknesses of black lace laid on smooth, and lastly with one thickness of pleated, beaded lace. Lace edging, beaded leaves, and a pink rose complete the trimming. A frill of two rows of lace is set round the edge of the bonnet, and is surmounted in front with a satin piping. A wreath of beaded leaves forms the heading behind. The rose is placed on the left side. A lace scarf, bordered with a lace edging, is confined with a rose under the chin. Strings of black watered ribbon.

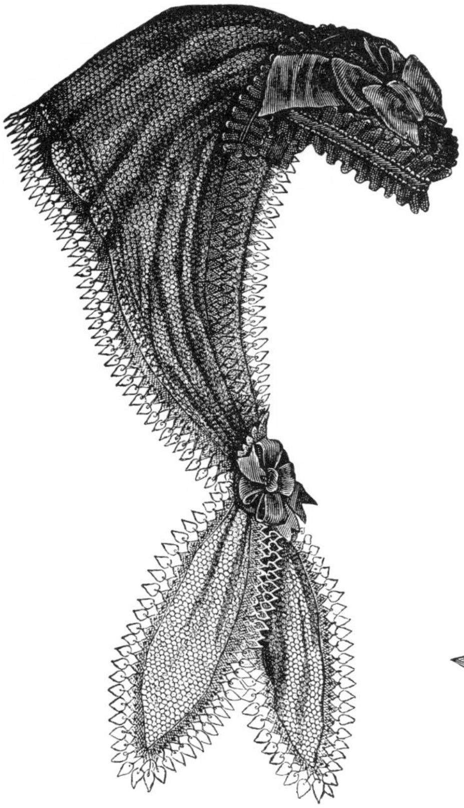

Pompadour Bonnet

Pompadour Bonnet

This bonnet is made of black figured lace, black silk blonde, and black ribbon. The diadem is formed of a bronze band inlaid with steel. A roll of colored velvet or satin, or a half wreath of fine flowers can be substituted. A wide lace scarf falls over the back of the bonnet in the form of a veil, and is brought forward for strings, which are fastened with a rosette under the chin. The pattern of the frame is given, in four pieces. The front of this frame is covered with a puffing made of a straight piece of lace. The edge of the bonnet is trimmed in front and behind with a quilling formed of two pieces of blonde, 3/4 inch wide, the straight edges of which are sewn together. A similar quilling is set on the band in front. The lace scarf that forms the veil is 1 5/8 yard long and 1/4 yard wide. This is pointed at the ends and bordered with edging 3/4 inch wide. The veil is pleated on the back of the bonnet. A ribbon rosette bow, shown half size, fastens the ends together in front. A double bow with short ends is set on top of the bonnet, which is completed by the bronze and steel band.

May 9, 1868

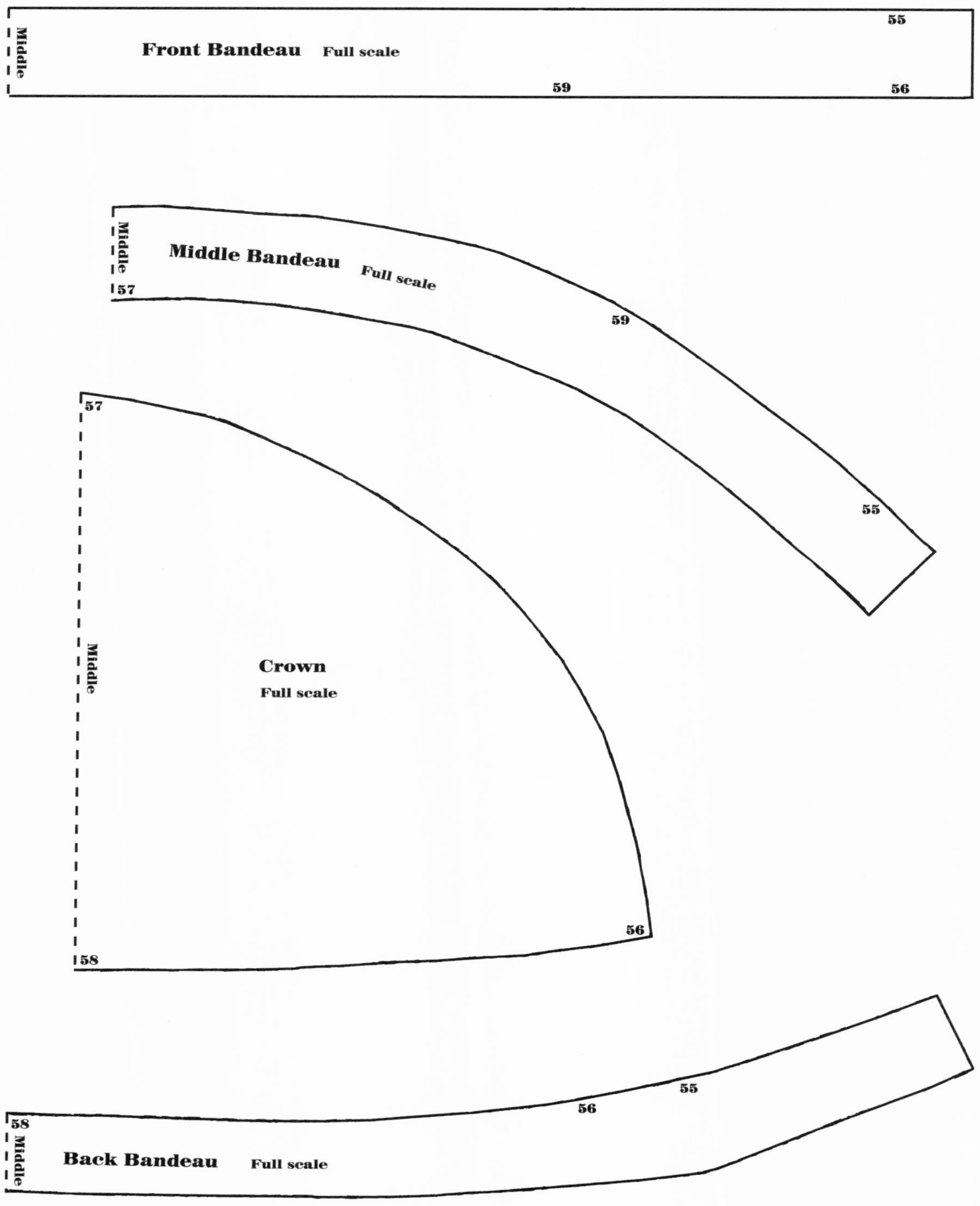

Middle

Front Bandeau Full scale

55

59

56

Middle

Middle Bandeau Full scale

57

59

55

57

Middle

Crown

Full scale

56

58

58

Middle

Back Bandeau Full scale

56

55

Watteau Bonnet

Watteau Bonnet

This bonnet, which is a very good accompaniment to the Watteau paletot, is of black figured lace. The trimming consists of blue satin puffing, a black feather, and a steel butterfly. The pattern of the frame is the same as for the Pompadour Bonnet. This is covered with pleated lace. A lace edge, 2 inches wide, is set round the bonnet. A scarf made of a straight strip of lace, 1 1/2 yards long and 4 inches wide, bordered with an edge 2 inches wide, is fastened on the back of the bonnet. The puffing on the front consists of a bias strip of satin, 20 inches long and 5 inches wide, sloping gradually to a width of 3 inches at the ends, and arranged in the same manner as that of the Trianon Hat. A somewhat narrower puffing is set on the back of the hat, to cover the setting on of the scarf, which falls over the puff as illustrated. The ends of the scarf are confined by a blue satin bow, shown half size. A feather and steel band, with two narrow ends of ribbon, completes the trimming.

Trianon Hat

This pretty hat is made entirely of blue crêpe. Bows of blue satin and a spray of blue satin flowers with moss green leaves complete the trimming. It is made on a foundation of straw. An old straw bonnet can be ripped up and made to answer very well for the purpose. The crown is soft and oblong; the rim is 2 inches high.

Having prepared the foundation, cover it with six thicknesses of crêpe, laid on plain. Bind with a bias fold of blue satin, and put in a white silk lining. The hat is trimmed round the edge with a puffing. For this take a strip of double crêpe, 5 inches wide, and hem the edges 1/2 inch wide. Gather it on both sides just above the hem, and fasten it to a strip of double crêpe, so the hem may form a frill on either side of the puff thus made. Sew narrow blue ribbons on each side of the hat, to be tied under the chignon.

The scarf consists of a strip of crêpe, 1 1/2 yards long and 5 inches wide, hemmed round the edge, and pleated on the hat. The ends of the scarf are fastened under the chin with a double bow of satin ribbon, as for the Watteau Bonnet. A similar bow is set on the front of the hat, over which the spray of flowers is placed, and is carried over the top of the hat, with the end hanging loose behind.

May 16, 1868

Summer Bonnets

An opening of summer millinery at a leading house discloses to us bonnets of new shapes entirely different from those displayed at the early openings. One style is simply a flat crown, differing from the Metternich of the spring in that it is shaped to the head, and fits over the chignon. A quilling of lace, ribbon, and flowers forms a tiara that projects like the visor of a cap. Another style has a fanchon front and sides with deep Marie Stuart point on the forehead, but fits squarely over the chignon. This is exceedingly stylish when made in chip, which promises to be in high favor this summer. Still another style is the Watteau. It is intended to accompany street suits, and is made of the suit material, or of silk and ribbon of one color. It is a regular bonnet, with everything that appertains thereto except a curtain. Lace drapery is only used with very dressy suits.

A French model from which the Watteaus are copied is silk of pale Mexican blue, a shade very fashionable in Paris. The foundation is concealed by ruches of silk, notched at the edges. The coronet is flat, and made of loops of ribbon caught up to form shells. A bandeau of gilt, studded with steel in a Greek pattern, is over the coronet. An aigrette of black and white feathers is directly in the center. This bonnet is worn very far forward, and with a high chignon. The strings are covered with ruches and held together low down on the breast by a half-moon bow.

A lovely chip bonnet all black and white is flat and round. Loops of thick white satin form a visor, with a band of cut jet between. Tufts of black and white ostrich feathers are on the left side. A fold of white satin as thick as piping is covered with black lace, which forms a drapery at the back, falling into strings in front. A rosette bow of satin with fringed ends holds the strings. An elastic cord under the chignon keeps the bonnet secure. This stylish coiffure is worn with colors, but is also suitable for light mourning.

Another chip bonnet, suitable for half mourning, is of the fanchon and Marie Stuart shape. Large violets of the deepest purple shade in which that flower is seen are massed together in front on the deep point over the forehead. The drapery at the back is of the finest Chantilly lace, and is in one piece with the long barbes that form strings. A cluster of violets at the throat.

Carriage bonnets of transparent Malines and frosted crêpe, so aerial and light that they are scarcely tangible enough for description, are made for midsummer and watering-place wear. One is of white Malines with a trimming of delicate pearl leaves on a gilt stem. The tiara and lace strings are covered with a slender vine of these fragile ornaments. Another is of white crêpe flecked with tiny specks that glitter like diamonds. The material is laid on the foundation in narrow folds or tucks from the back to the front. The diadem is of blonde lace arranged in shells, over which are branches of white hyacinth made of wax, and a marvelous imitation of nature. The blonde lace fall at the back is brought forward to form strings.

On bridal bonnets the clematis and spirae are heaped in masses on the front. Apple and cherry blossoms, sparkling with moisture as if just washed by a shower, nestle amidst snowy flakes of downy marabou. Tiny stalks of lily of the valley droop gracefully over the coronet.

The French bonnet, after which the new round shapes are modeled, is of chip with a quilling of corn-colored satin in front. A fall of satin covered with black lace 6 inches deep drapes the chignon. It is brought forward for strings, crossed over on the breast like a fichu, and is knotted behind below the waist, where it falls into long sash ends.

May 16, 1868

A buttercup-colored crêpe is almost covered on top with long thin grasses of Metternich green, while scarlet poppies droop over the back hair. That this may not look gaudy the whole bonnet is covered with a coiffure of very thin black Chantilly lace, which softens the bright colors that it half conceals, half discloses. Small ornaments of cut steel and gilt are pendant from every point of the lace. Innumerable loops of ribbon form a tiara, in the center of which is a butterfly of steel and gilt. The lace barbes of the coiffure form strings.

An attractive bonnet is a Marie Antoinette of English straw. The face trimming is a quilling of thick black silk, above a Metternich green silk band, on which is a Greek border of gilt. On the outside, along the rim, are branches of metallic leaves of a light yellow-green that look very frail, but will bend without breaking. A large crimson rose, with buds and tendrils, droops from the left side. The peculiarity of this stylish bonnet consists in a bag crown of black tulle, in which the chignon is to be placed. Below this crown is a wide lace drapery, open in the center.

Mourning Bonnets

Simplicity and plainness are studied for mourning bonnets. For fresh mourning we were shown English crêpe fitted plainly over the frame, with narrow folds or quilling for a tiara. Two wider folds fall from the back and extend along the sides, forming strings. A kind of bag for the waterfall, which entirely conceals the hair, is made for those who desire it.

Veils are made double of the crêpe 1 1/4 yards long, and gathered with a string at one end. If long veils are preferred they are pinned on at the sides with jet ornaments, and each end is finished with a hem 3/8 yard deep. For a veil it is best to get the crêpe that comes in rolls. That folded in boxes has a crease formed in the middle that comes directly in the center of the face.

Widow's caps do not surround the whole face, but form a tiara over the forehead.

May 23, 1868

Japanese Foulards

Among some novelties just arrived are the Japanese silks, or foulards, for suits. The overdress and petticoat are different colors, but are imported together in a wooden box, covered with Japanese letters. The design after which they are to be made is traced on colored paper with Japanese symbols, and altogether they present a decidedly Oriental appearance. They are all of solid colors, well selected. The handsomest shown us had the overskirts of a clear shade of gray, with a petticoat of blue, brown, or violet. There were cheaper patterns in two shades of brown.

Satin and Serge

Another novelty is the linen-back satin for petticoats. It is in 1/4- and 1-inch stripes of gold and black; or pink and gray; and green, scarlet, or purple, with white.

In another set of boxes are smoothly folded patterns of summer serge, the dress and petticoat unlike. This fabric is all silk, thin and wiry, and is a kind of twilled foulard. A serge overdress of the fashionable nankeen color accompanies a blue or green skirt. The petticoat of cuir-colored serge is striped satin, pink and white. A more quiet suit is of brown satin, under cream-colored foulard. A violet dress of soft Turk satin is over the same shade of repped silk.

We find in other boxes four beautiful costumes. French plates accompany them, exhibiting the design. The lower skirt of one is Turk satin, with 1-inch stripes of purple and gold. The overdress is purple satin. A long fringed sash has three broad stripes like those of the petticoat. Material like the overdress is furnished for bonnet, gaiters, and parasol. The outside dresses of the other three patterns are steel gray. The petticoats are, first, gold and Mentana red stripes; second, pink and green; and third, bronze and gilt.

Country Suits

In anticipation of the usual hegira to the seaside and watering places country suits, as they are called, are in active preparation. The Parisian models are in the Watteau or Pompadour style, or *à la Marie Antoinette.*

The Watteau is an imitation of the pastoral dress worn by court shepherdesses in the days of Louis XV. It is a close copy of the original costume, with its square Pompadour neck, its velvet necklace and cross, the merest atom of sleeve, a belt and sash looped with eglantine, and a festooned overdress with striped petticoat, short enough to display clocked stockings and slippers with rosettes. This fanciful attire is surmounted by a Louis Quinze hat turned up at the left side, and a Cardinal pelerine with long pointed hood.

Differing from this is the Marie Antoinette, with its high-necked fichu folded over the breast, sleeves puffed to the elbow and frilled, slender waist and panniers, with skirts trimmed with innumerable ruffles and ruches. The broad-rimmed garden hat of chip is trimmed with field flowers, and completes a costume peculiarly becoming to youthful faces and slender figures. The Watteau is better suited to maturity and embonpoint; but like everything else, they are worn indiscriminately.

Dress Materials

Twilled mohair, soft light cashmere, chambray gauze, alpaca, and the Japanese foulards are selected for summer suits, in delicate shades of buff, fawn color, drab, and pea green. Glossy white alpaca and mohair are trimmed with the clear light blue now so fashionable in Europe. Chambray gauze or goat's-hair, a thicker fabric than that worn for evening dresses, is in narrow stripes of any bright color, with white. Green, blue, and mauve are much admired. It is 7/8 wide. Marseilles and piqué suits consist merely of the polonaise and gored skirt, without a tight-fitting corsage. They are braided in rich patterns, with medallions on each width and vines up the seams. The sleeves and collar are finished with narrow fringe. Cool and pretty costumes for midsummer are made of white organdy with two skirts, a low full waist, and wide fichu. These are worn without the fichu for short dancing dresses. Valenciennes lace, goffered ruffles, and gay ribbons are the trimmings.

Hints About Dressmaking

French dresses, when buttoned in front of the corsage, are no longer very high at the throat. The neck is disclosed as far down as the slope of the shoulders. Vandyked and scalloped bands are universally worn. They fit more neatly when cut bias, and should match the trimming in color. Another plan is to stitch a row of points on a narrow band. The points are formed by doubling small squares of silk, then folding toward the center.

Underskirts of imported costumes have a belt defined on the skirt, plain and smooth in front, but are gathered in back with a drawstring.

The best plan for finishing the edge of a skirt is to sew the material of the dress and facing together on the wrong side, making a broad seam, then turn over evenly, and press smoothly. The seam may be from 1/4 to 1 inch wide, and if sewn without puckering, serves to make the edge of the skirt stand out firmly. The old practice of turning up the material of the dress on the facing is objectionable, as the skirt is apt to cut out at the edge. An excellent modiste advises us that skirt braid for binding is no longer considered essential. The material of the braid is so different from that of the dress that they will not shrink alike, and all worsted braids shrink slightly, even though dipped in scalding water before they are used.

The Cardinal Pelerine And Sleeveless Jackets

The most novel wrapping of the season is called the Cardinal pelerine. It is made either of black faille or of the dress silk. It is also shown in black cashmere. The shape is similar to the scarf burnoose. It has a pointed hood folded in the back, long mantilla fronts, and is fitted into the waist by a concealed belt.

Sleeveless jackets have been worn for two seasons, but they still find favor. They are jaunty little garments that give a tone to the simplest toilette, and are equally suitable for morning and evening.

Lingerie

Linen cambric collars and undersleeves are displayed for afternoon toilettes. The collars are standing, fastened with a bow and ends of lace and cambric. The sheerest cambric is laid in tiny cordlike folds, held securely at each side, and vandyked at the top. The vandykes are filled out with Valenciennes and embroidery. On others Valenciennes insertion is laid in pleats and trimmed with appliqué needlework. Again, there are sprays of flowers and leaves of real point d'Alencon inserted in cambric. Medallions of tucks rest amidst the filmiest laces, sewn in with seams so small that they are scarcely perceptible. Valenciennes and even point lace bows are attached to ribbon cravats to be worn with standing linen collars. Plain sets for morning are of linen, with three or four cords stitched in the pointed edges. Rows of pin stitching separate the thick cords.

Beautiful paper collars of all styles are made in lace patterns, so elaborate as to be mistaken at a little distance for needlework or guipure. They are especially convenient for traveling.

Spring Shoes

Walking boots for this season are lower on the ankle than those worn during the winter. The half-high, or three-quarter Polish boot, is cooler and looks better with short dresses. Kid is preferred to prunella or the satin Français. Grison's kid is the least liable to crack and turn brown, but even this is not infallible. An excellent dressing is now prepared that restores the polish and does not soil the skirts when moist.

Half-high Polish gaiters with medium rounded toes without tips, and buttoned with jet, are the favorite boots for walking. Heels are slightly lower, very little curved, and are much broader than the sloping heels lately in vogue. Fancy boots are stitched with white. A carriage or evening shoe is laced in front and trimmed over the instep with braiding and jet. A pretty light gaiter is made of prunella uppers finished with kid. Bronze boots are still seen on the street. All bronze is defaced by moisture. There is a bronze dressing that will restore the color, but not permanently.

The white satin of the wedding dress is made into bridal slippers and gaiters. The ornaments are blonde lace and seed pearl embroidery. The gaiters are buttoned with Roman pearls. Dancing boots, with slightly concave heels, are of colored kid, or of the dress material, with colored heels.

Bows for slippers are made of colored velvet cut bias, and of kid leaves bound with silk and held together by steel buckles. Bronze bows have gilt buckles. Large Pompadour rosettes that cover the entire instep are admired for morning use. They are put on ordinary black kid slippers, with curved heels, covered with cloth the color of the rosette. Toilette slippers without heels have kid facings 1/2 inch deep around the top, and chain stitched with violet or blue silk.

Buttons for Trimming

Figures 1 to 9 show six buttons suitable for trimming dresses, cloaks, etc., and which are easily made. All these buttons consist of a round piece of wood, which is covered with stuff and ornamented partly with embroidery, and partly with silk braid and cord.

Figure 1 is a button covered with brown silk, and corded crosswise with fine brown silk cord and gimp. The center is formed by a knot of silk cord.

Figure 1. Brown silk button

Figure 2 is a button covered with violet cassimere. The figure in the center is worked with violet silk twist over a foundation of pasteboard. This figure is surrounded with a row of knots, worked with the same silk.

Figure 2. Violet cassimere button

Figure 3 is a button of gray silk. The starlike figure is worked in point Russe with dark gray silk twist.

Figure 3. Gray silk button

This is a button of brown silk worked in buttonhole stitch with brown silk twist, as shown in Figures 4 and 5. Make, first, at regular distances of 1/3 inch apart, 9 stitches. Then fasten each stitch with a buttonhole stitch, working from left to right, and always so that the point of the needle is directed toward the middle of the button. Continuing in this manner, work around the thread of the former round in each new round.

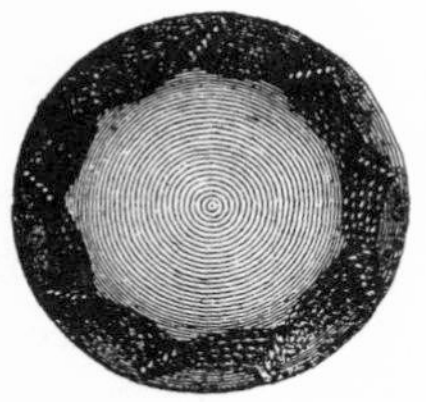

Figure 4. Making brown silk button

Figure 5. Making brown silk button

Figure 6 is a button of gray alpaca. The star is formed of fine gray silk. First stretch, as in Figure 7, eight threads across the button at regular intervals. Wind these as shown with gray silk, which must not be too fine. Having covered almost the entire upper part of the button with the silk, fasten the threads with silk threads between every two of the eight stretched threads. These drawn close form the starlike figure shown in Figure 6.

Figure 6. Gray alpaca button

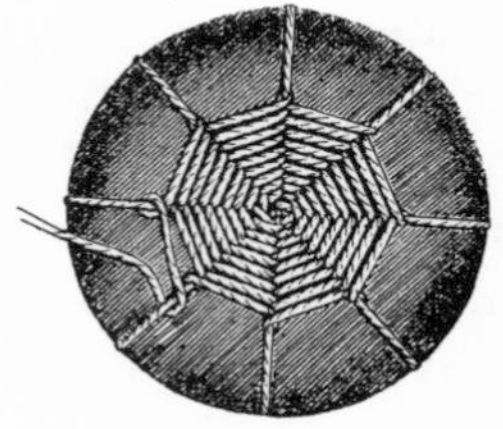

Figure 7. Making gray alpaca button

Figure 8 is very similar to the former. In this also eight threads are stretched over the button. These are covered as shown in Figure 9, so that the eight threads finally appear as raised ribs.

Figure 8. Ribbed button

Figure 9. Making ribbed button

Georgine Walking Dress

This costume consists of a double skirt and paletot of Panama cloth. It is trimmed with small rounded lappets of brown silk, double, and bias folds of the same material. Belt and sash of brown silk, with rosette. The skirt is like that of the Norderney Walking Dress. The paletot is cut from the Undine Paletot pattern in the April 25 issue.

Norderney Walking Dress

This suit is made of gray serge, stitched with gray silk. It is trimmed up the front with two rows of gray buttons.

For the skirt cut from the front one piece. Cut from the first side breadth, the second side breadth, the back, and the pocket welt each two pieces, the pocket welt being double and lengthwise of the stuff.

Sew the back breadths together. Set a strip of serge 4 inches wide under the front breadth. Stitch it fast on the outside along the top and bottom. Trim the front breadth with buttons. Then join the breadths according to the figures on the pattern. Leave openings for the pockets between the side breadths and front breadth from * to ••. Leave an opening between the left side breadth and the back breadth for the skirt slit. Sew a muslin pocket to the edges of the pocket slit. Cover it with a double interlined welt, trimmed with buttons as illustrated. Hem the edges of the skirt slit narrow. Face the bottom of the skirt with a strip of wigging, 12 inches wide, covered on the lower edge with a strip of bias serge, 3 inches wide. The latter simulates a cord at the bottom, and is fastened with two rows of stitching on the right side. Lay a pleat on either side of the front breadth from *x* to •. Gather the breadths and lay two pleats on each side of the gathers from *x* to •.

Set on the belt, which is fastened with a hook and eye. Finish the belt at the back with a sash of the dress material. Cut two loops and two ends from their respective patterns. The edges of the ends are turned down and finished with a row of stitching. A loop covers the seam where the sash is set on the belt.

Norderney Walking Dress

For the waist cut the fronts, allowing 2 inches for a hem on the front edge of each. Cut the back and collar whole, the latter double. Cut the sleeves.

Hem the fronts with two rows of stitching on the right side to match the skirt bottom. Set on the buttons, and make the buttonholes. Make the bosom pleats. Join the back and fronts according to the figures on the pattern. Set the collar on the neck, finishing the last with two rows of stitching and a hook and eye in front. Hem the bottom of the waist.

Sew up the sleeves from 13 to 14 and from 15 to 16. Face them on the bottom and along the seam to the elbow with a strip of serge. Finish with two rows of stitching, and trim with buttons as illustrated. Then lay a pleat in the top from *x* to •. Sew them in the armholes, making 16 on the sleeve correspond with 16 on the front.

For the fichu cut from the front two pieces, and from the back one piece. Join the fronts and back on the shoulder from 17 to 18. Face the edge of the fichu with a bias strip of serge 2 inches wide, standing out from under the edge to simulate a cord. Fasten it with two rows of stitching on the right side.

17
Middle of back
18
Fichu Back
1/8 scale

17
18
Fichu Front
1/8 scale

12
Middle
11
Collar
1/4 scale

13
Upper Sleeve
1/8 scale
16
14 15

13
x 16
Under Sleeve
1/8 scale
14 15

11 10
9
Waist Back
1/8 scale
7
Middle of back
8
Slit

10
9
12
Waist Front
1/8 scale
16
7
8
Slit
x x

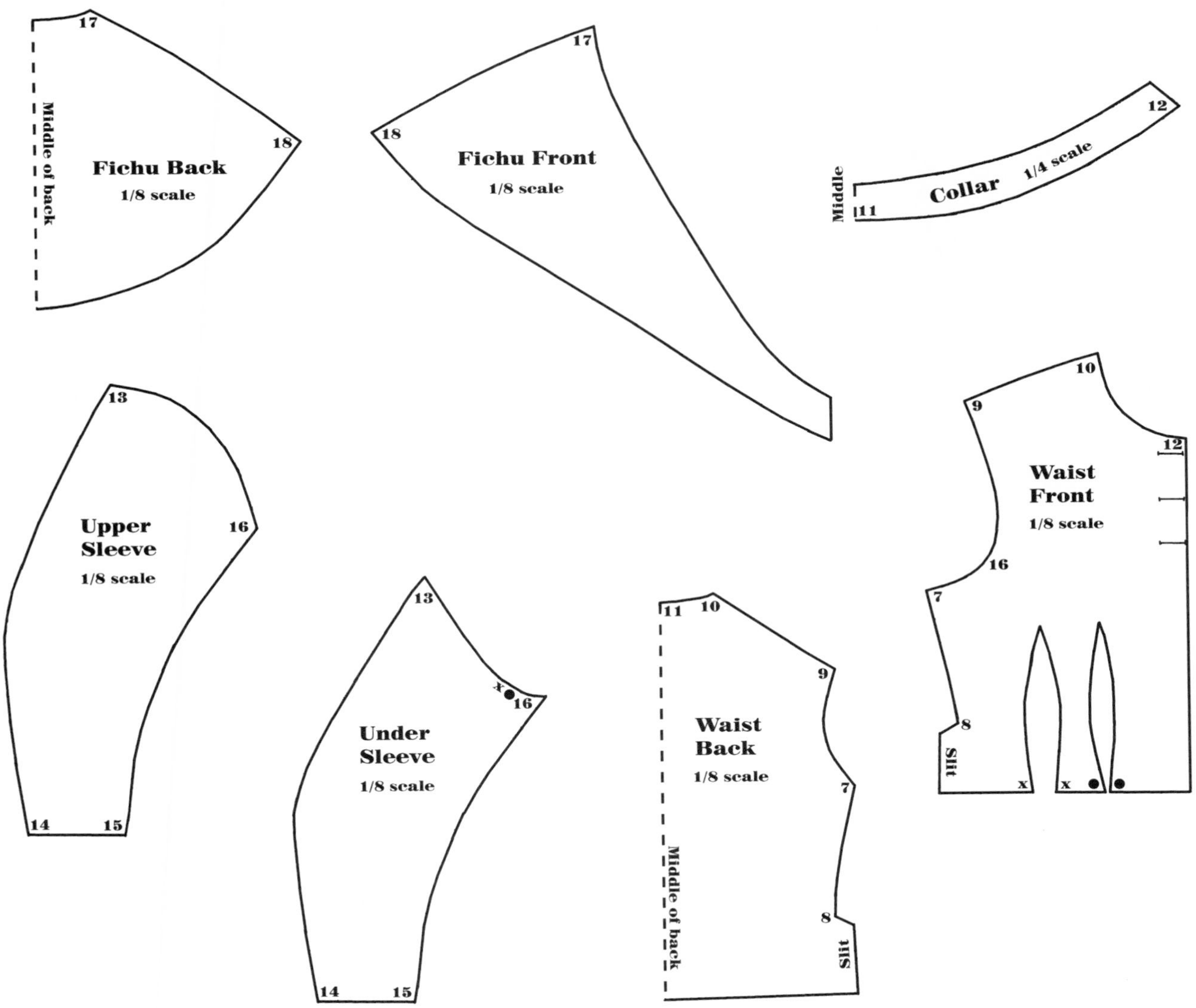

May 23, 1868

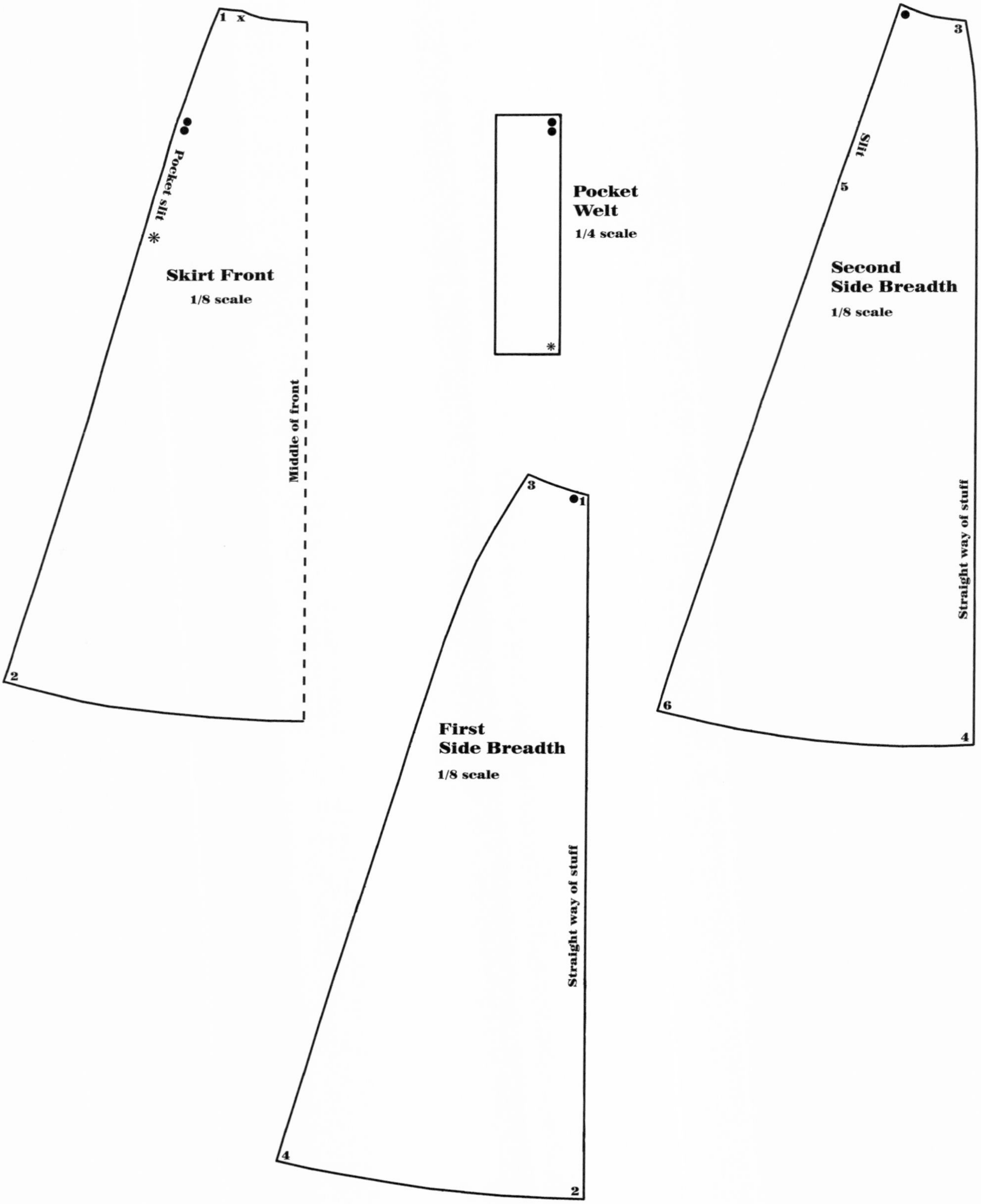

1
x
2
Pocket slit
Skirt Front
1/8 scale
Middle of front
Pocket
Welt
1/4 scale
3
1
First
Side Breadth
1/8 scale
Straight way of stuff
4
2
3
Slit
5
Second
Side Breadth
1/8 scale
Straight way of stuff
6
4

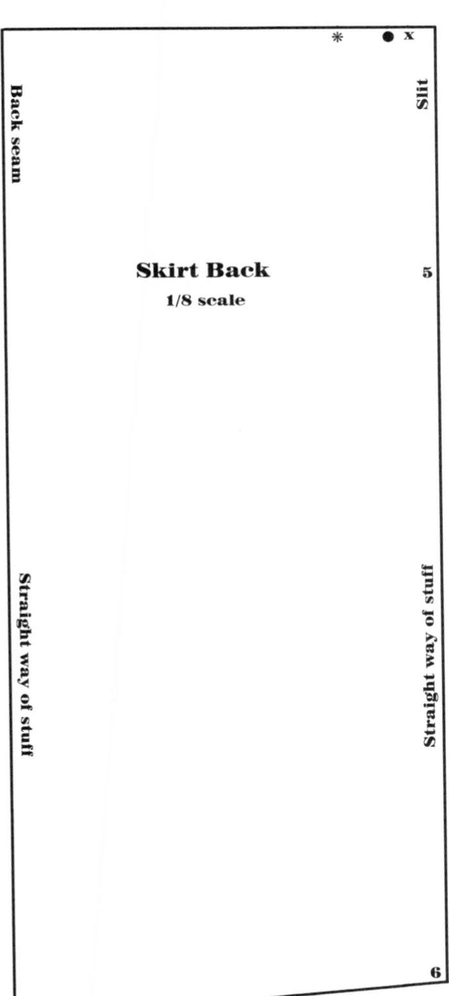

Sash Loop
1/4 scale

Sash End
1/8 scale

Vienna Walking Dress

This suit is of gray poplin, and consists of a skirt and paletot. The trimming consists of bias folds of the same, with a stiff muslin lining, bound round the edge with a narrow strip of black silk. On the bottom of this is set small lappets of double poplin, with a stiff lining, bound with black, and of different sizes. The skirt is made like that of the Norderney Walking Dress. It is trimmed with a flounce 6 inches wide.

Cut from the front, side front, side back, and back each two pieces. The sleeves are like those of the Norderney Walking Dress. Sew the backs together. Join the backs, fronts, and side pieces according to the figures on the pattern. Turn the edge of the paletot down on the right side. Set on the trimming as illustrated. Make the sleeves and trim the bottom. Sew them in the armholes, which are also trimmed. The belt is 1 1/2 inches wide, interlined with stiff muslin and bound round the edge. It fastens behind, and is finished with a bow and sash ends of poplin.

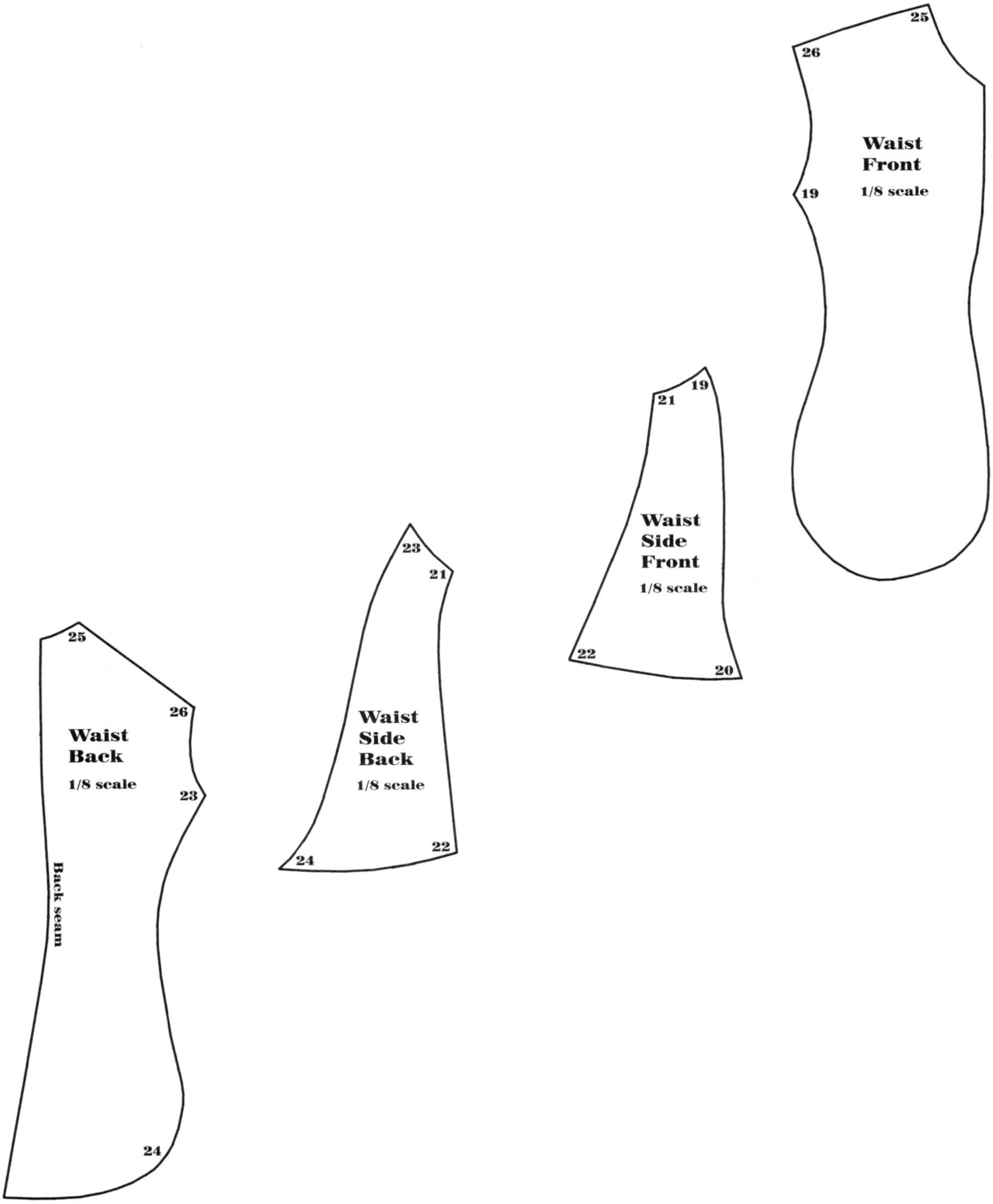

25
26
Waist
Front
19
1/8 scale
19
21
Waist
Side
Front
1/8 scale
22
20
23
21
Waist
Side
Back
1/8 scale
22
24
25
26
Waist
Back
1/8 scale
23
Back seam
24

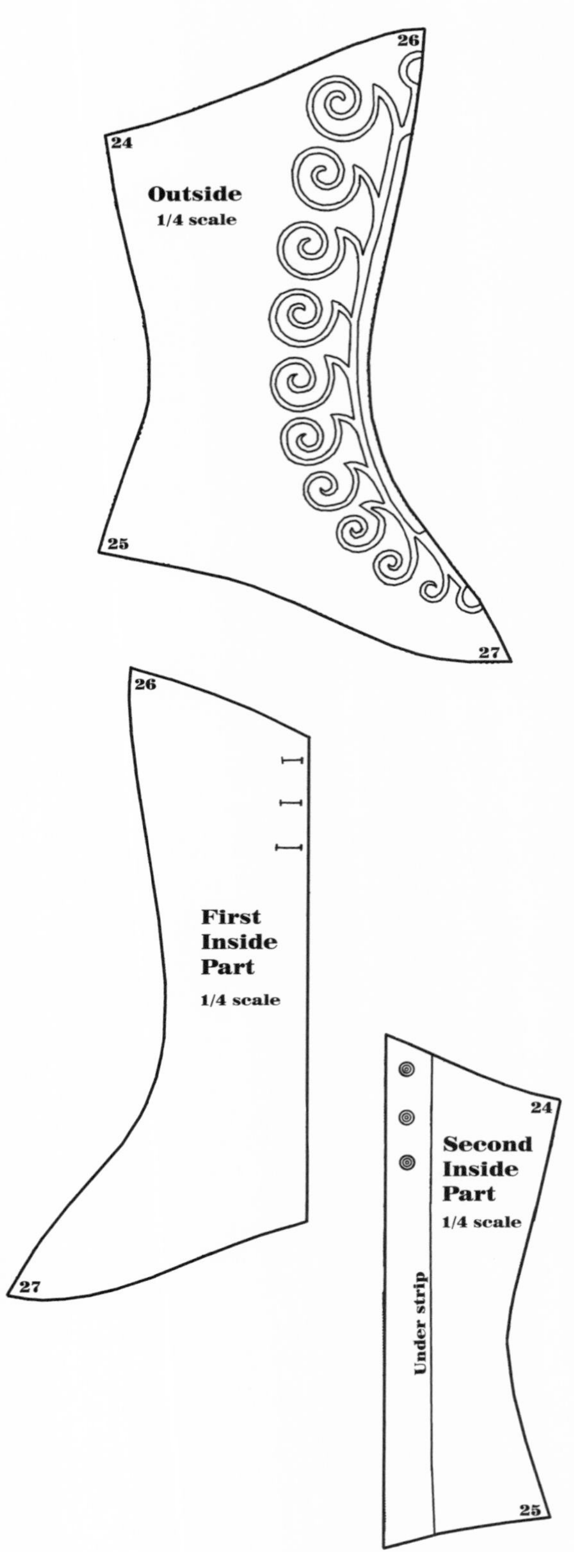

Brown Linen Legging

This legging for ladies is of brown linen, trimmed with brown braid. It is fastened with buttons and buttonholes on the inside or outside of the foot, as may be preferred.

Cut for each legging from the outside part and the two inside parts each one piece. Allow a little less than 1 inch for turning in on the inside parts. Hem this over on the wrong side. Set on the buttons and buttonholes. Trim with braid as marked on the pattern. Join the parts as shown by the figures. Bind the top and bottom of the legging with narrow brown braid, which is stitched on with silk of the same color. Lastly, set a strap of enameled cloth on the bottom, as illustrated.

Plaid Linen Legging

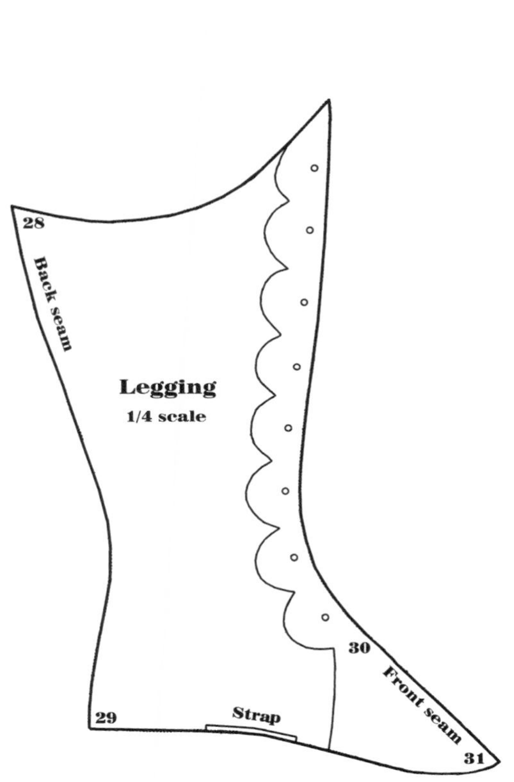

Plaid Linen Legging

This legging for ladies is of black and white plaid linen. It is trimmed up the front with a scalloped strip of black silk, stitched on with white silk.

Cut from the bias stuff two pieces from the pattern. Set on the scalloped trimming. Sew the legging together in the back from 28 to 29, and in front from 30 to 31. Set the eyelets up the front. Face the top and bottom of the legging with a bias strip 1 inch wide, of the same material as the outside, which is stitched fast on the right side. Put a strap of enameled cloth on the bottom. This is somewhat sloping at the ends, the front edge being 3 and the back 3 1/2 inches long. The lacing is laced with black and white silk braid, and finished at the top with a black and white tassel.

May 30, 1868

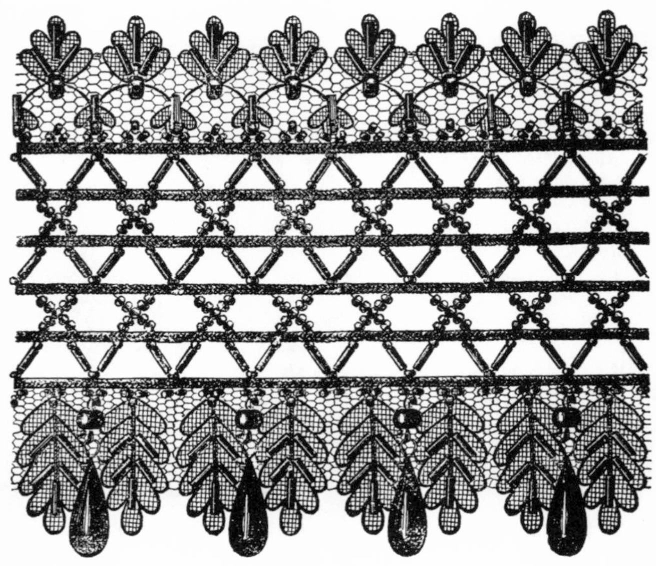

Beaded Border

This border forms an exceedingly tasteful trimming for bodices and waists. It is made of black silk braid and lace, on which jet beads and bugles are sewn as shown. The bottom is finished with jet grelots between the leaves of the edge, the latter of which are veined with bugles.

June 6, 1868

Riding Habits

Black is the favorite color for habits, because the least conspicuous. Ladies' cloth is the material selected, and 7 yards the necessary quantity. When a lady has more than one habit, she usually selects the second of dark blue or invisible green melton. Serviceable habits, for constant use and for country wear, are made of brown waterproof and the light mixed tweeds in shades of pale gray and dust color.

The Corsage

The regular habit corsage, with a blunt point in front, slight spring over the hips, and short basque behind, is preferred to the fancy jackets that are cut straight around the hips. The waist should be only moderately long. Care should be taken that it is the natural length under the arms, as if made too long it is apt to wrinkle and turn up, and is very uncomfortable. Two bosom pleats should be taken in front, instead of the one seam advised by many tailors. One seam ends abruptly, and two are necessary to give proper fullness to the bust. Thin horsehair and a little wadding increase the round appearance. The back should be amply broad at the top, but very narrow at the bottom, with gracefully curved side bodies. The basque at the back is 8 or 10 inches long, sloping from the hips. A pleat is laid on each side, simulating a continuation of the seams of the side body. The pleat is pressed flat, and finished with a button at each end. The basque is lined with the habit material. Tailors advise that the waist be lined with thick silk, as it fits more smoothly than linen, and does not stretch. Ball buttons, either crocheted silk or solid jet, are fashionable. They should be put very close together, to prevent gaping between the buttonholes.

The Sleeve

The coat sleeve should fit easily to the arm. When worn with gauntlets it is closed at the wrist, but is left slightly loose when designed for the linen cuffs and wristband gloves now in vogue. A kind of chevron of silk braid sometimes ornaments the sleeve. On others the only trimming is the outline of a deep cuff defined by two rows of braid or silk cord. A row of buttons, smaller than those on the corsage, extends up the sleeve from the wrist.

Trains, Trousers, Etc.

Skirts are not so full and long as were formerly worn. They are gored flatly in front and at the sides, with a slight fullness at the back, which should be gathered in, as pleats are difficult to adjust gracefully in the saddle. The proper length of a riding skirt is 1/4 yard longer than the ordinary walking dress, yet many ladies have them 1 1/2 or 1 3/4 yards long. Something depends, of course, on the height of the horse; but long trains to habits are very unsafe, and are not now considered stylish.

Riding trousers of the cloth of the habit are worn with the present style of short skirts. They may be made either in the bloomer style, gathered into a band at the ankle, or cut small with straps sewn on.

Narrow linen collars, either standing or turndown, are worn with habits. The cuffs should match, and all must be of immaculate whiteness.

The hat selected by equestriennes for riding in Central Park is a glossy beaver with low crown and curved rolling brim. A veil of grenadine, or of black or colored net, surrounds the hat and streams at the side. Caps with visors and Spanish hats with high, sloping crowns made of fancy yellow straws are shown for summer wear.

The best modistes refuse to make habits, as they say it is a man's work. When their customers order a habit in their summer outfits, the modiste employs a professional tailor.

Summer Dresses

American ladies, loath to part with what they have cherished against so much opposition, are having their summer dresses made with the graceful, sweeping trains worn during the past season. The skirts, however, are not gored to fit so plainly over the hips as they have been of late. Many ladies prefer to have the front widths plain and all the breadths slightly sloped. But the very newest dresses have three front widths alone gored, while the others are straight and gathered at the back.

We hear many objections made by ladies who do their own sewing to goring thin dresses. But modistes say that by taking a little care not to stretch the bias edges of the goods, or to pucker the sewing, the gored seams will hang as well in thin materials as in the thickest silks. It is said also that the bias seams of muslin skirts cannot be ironed properly. This is the fault of the laundress who attempts to smooth the seams by pulling them on the bias instead of the way of the thread.

Double skirts, such as are seen on walking dresses, are worn with thin trained dresses. The upper skirts are made with apron fronts and looped up with immense puffs at the back. It is especially stylish to catch them up directly behind almost to the waist, a grotesque fashion that we thought at first sight was certainly a ludicrous mistake of the modiste. Short sashes with four broad loops and two fringed ends hanging very little below the loops are worn with these skirts. The long sash is already passé. Sometimes a long tunic or a kind of court train is formed by leaving the upper skirt open in front and gathering the fullness in from the hips backward.

Box-pleated quilling and narrow ruffles are worn on all kinds of thin material. The ruffles vary in number from three to fifteen. An odd number it is said has the prettiest effect. Grenadine and chambray ruffles must always be cut bias and bound. Wash muslins have straight ruffles cut crossways of the goods and hemmed. White materials are scalloped and needleworked at the lower edge and put on in box pleats. One wide flounce around the bottom of the skirt is more distingué than the narrow frills that have already become common. It is made in a variety of ways. The easiest plan is to bind both edges and put on in box pleats, wide apart from each other, but lapped so deep that the pleat is distinctly defined without being held securely at the lower edge. Sometimes the edges are vandyked, a pleat being laid in each vandyke. A silk button or a tiny shell bow ornaments each pleat. Occasionally a narrow quilling is added to the upper edge of the flounce. It is pleated in with the flounce and gives the appearance of a full ruche heading. French flounces have the pleats all running one way and reversed about 2 inches below the heading. This produces a pleated puff that is very much admired.

Waists are plain blouses gathered into a belt, or with shirred yokes. A pretty design for solid-colored organdies is to make the puffs of the yoke run diagonally from right to left. The old-fashioned surplice waist is again in vogue. This is the simplest form of waist, and is becoming alike to stout and slender figures. It is easily made by the blouse pattern. The back is precisely the same. The fullness in front is made by gathering at the shoulder the piece that is usually cut out at the neck. The front is then left in a straight line and fits true.

Grenadines and chambray gauze are made with a tight-fitting corsage over silk of the same shade. These materials are so thin and gauzelike that many shades of gray, blue, and Metternich green cannot be worn over white without losing almost every semblance of color. A silk petticoat of the same shade must therefore be worn beneath them. This adds to the expense, but improves the appearance greatly. Black iron grenadine is always lined throughout with silk.

French dresses imported for summer have invariably the coat sleeve so long worn. It is elaborately trimmed up the outer seam, or with innumerable horizontal folds from the wrist to the shoulder. The ruffled Marie Antoinette sleeve is being made here, and is appropriate with the present costume.

The Marie Antoinette fichu is universally worn and admired.

Organdy Robes And Embroidered Muslin

Among the summer importations are some elegant organdy robes. The waist, sleeves, and upper part of the skirt are in solid colors, a deep blue, fawn color, or light green. The lower part of each skirt width has gay borders of field flowers, wide enough to reach to the knee, narrower in front, and widening over the train. The same flowers in smaller borders are furnished as garniture for sleeves and sash.

Corded organdies have small figures on a white ground. Piqué, the least heavy of thick muslins, and most desirable, is sold in pretty patterns with a band of trimming at each selvage. For ordinary house dresses we have the Japanese linen, a kind of lisle thread, thin, wiry, and cool. It is of mixed white and black and gray, and is prettily trimmed with frills or box-pleated flounces, bound with black ribbon, or with blue, cherry, or green.

White will be more worn this summer than for several years, and occupies a prominent place in summer outfits for the seaside and watering place. It is chosen alike for morning robes, afternoon toilettes, croquet dresses, street suits, and dancing dresses. Some beautifully embroidered dress patterns have been imported. They are of Victoria lawn and sheer Swiss muslin. The lower part of the skirt is ornamented with the finest French needlework. Ladies say, however, that they do not make up stylishly without destroying so much of the embroidery that they prefer to select a design among the many shown at the furnishing houses, and order a dress appropriate to their height and figure. Many of these are expensively trimmed with Valenciennes lace. Others, equally well and tastefully made, are ornamented with the low-priced Hamburg insertion and box-pleated ruffling.

A useful novelty is a chemise and corset cover combined. It consists of a regular chemise skirt gathered into a waist to cover the corsets. It is fitted closely, with bosom pleats in front and considerable spring over the hips. One shown us was of Richardson's linen, trimmed with a puff of linen cambric at the shoulders, with a band of Irish insertion of eyelets, and a Valenciennes edge. The very short sleeve was formed by a tiny puff and fluted lace.

Varieties in Lace

Among the many pretty things that add variety to summer toilettes, we are shown fancy aprons of black lace with bretelles and sash. They are looped at the sides with large rosettes of ribbon the color of the dress with which they are worn. They are made only in the French woven laces, that imitate admirably real thread lace. Most fastidious ladies consider it admissible to wear fancy jackets and aprons of imitation laces, since they are only a transitory fashion.

Coiffure mantillas, worn in the Spanish style, draping the head and bust, promise to supersede hats and bonnets at the watering places. They are combinations of the hood and mantilla scarf, and are exceedingly graceful. Pretty ones are of Brussels net and embroidered with colored flowers.

Among veils a new shape is of embroidered tulle falling over the face like a mask, with long wide barbes that cross under the chignon and tie loosely in front, or are held together with a flower, bud, or bow below the chin.

Another style crosses in front as a fichu, and ties at the back of the waist, forming a sash. A novelty worn abroad is half veil and half fichu, and may be worn as an opera mantle. The veil falls over the face, but may be thrown back like the coiffure mantilla.

Waist with Fichu

This waist of Swiss muslin is rendered very stylish and beautiful by the addition of a Marie Antoinette fichu. The fichu is bordered with points of lilac satin, edged with lace, and trimmed with guipure edging and insertion. The waist is trimmed round the neck, down the front, and on the sleeves with a similar row of points.

Cut the fronts, allowing 1 inch for a hem on the front edge. Cut the side pieces. Cut the back, collar, belt, and fichu whole, the collar and belt double. Cut two pieces for each sleeve.

Make the bosom pleats. Hem the fronts, and furnish them with buttons and buttonholes. Join the waist according to the figures on the pattern. Set on the standing collar and belt. The latter has a frill about 3 inches wide on the bottom, which is covered by the skirt. Sew up the sleeves from 43 to 44 and from 45 to 46. Trim with the satin points,

Waist with Fichu

insertion, and edging. Sew them with a cord in the armholes. Trim the standing collar with points and lace.

Set on the corners of the fichu two sash ends, 1 1/8 yard long, and 8 inches wide at the bottom, sloping upward to fit the fichu. Trim the fichu as illustrated. Sew it to the waist. The points turning upward are each held fast to the waist by a stitch.

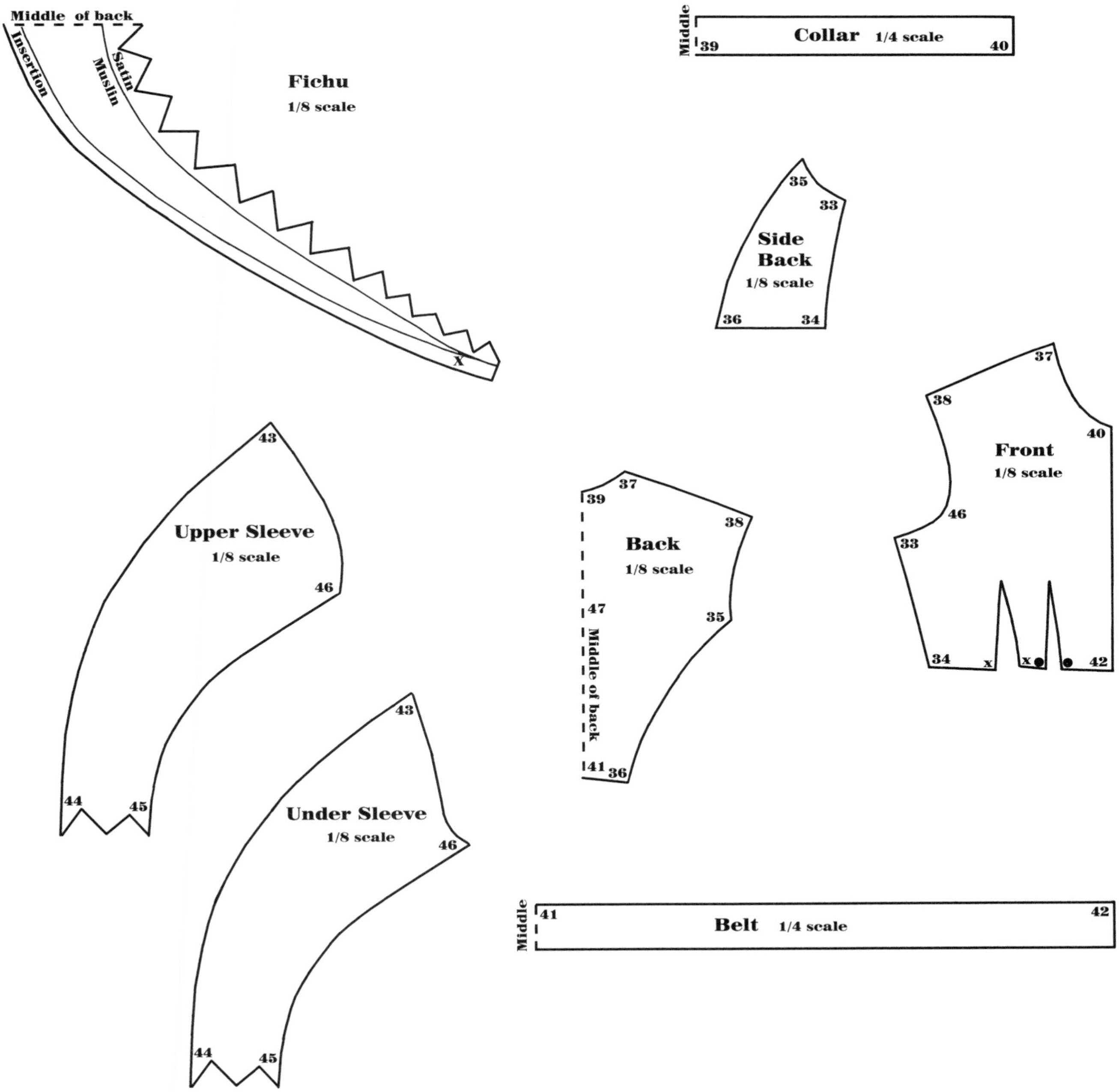

Middle of back
Insertion
Muslin
Satin
Fichu
1/8 scale
x

Middle 39 **Collar** 1/4 scale 40

35 33
Side Back
1/8 scale
36 34

37
38
40
Front
1/8 scale
46
33
34 x x 42

43
Upper Sleeve
1/8 scale
46
44 45

39 37
38
Back
1/8 scale
47
35
Middle of back
41 36

43
Under Sleeve
1/8 scale
46
44 45

Middle 41 **Belt** 1/4 scale 42

Waist with Simulated Fichu

The trimming of this waist imitates a fichu, which is completed with sash ends. The original is of Swiss muslin. The trimming consists of guipure insertion and edging 1 inch wide, and application needlework figures.

Cut the fronts, allowing 1 inch on the front edge of each for a hem. Cut the back and sleeves.

Hem the fronts. Set on small buttons and buttonhole-stitch loops. Join them to the back with a cord. Set a double band on the neck. Sew on the trimming as shown in the illustration and marked on the pattern. The narrow lines on the front and back show the setting on of the lace that simulates the fichu. The foundation is cut out underneath the insertion and needlework figures.

Sew up the sleeves from 17 to 18 and from 19 to 20. Hem the bottom and trim with lace. Set them in the armholes with a cord.

The sash ends are set on the waist from *x* to •. They are 1 yard long and 7 inches wide, sloping to 3 inches at the top and rounded at the end. They are edged with lace, and ornamented with insertion and needlework figures.

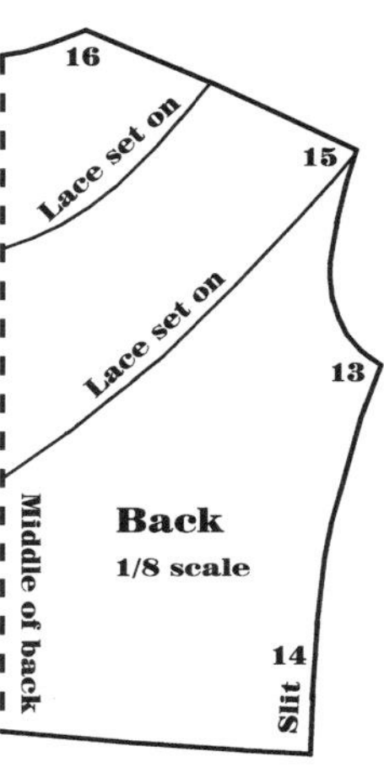

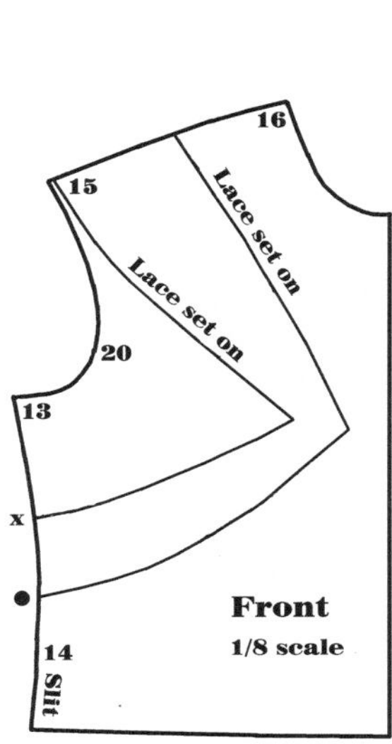

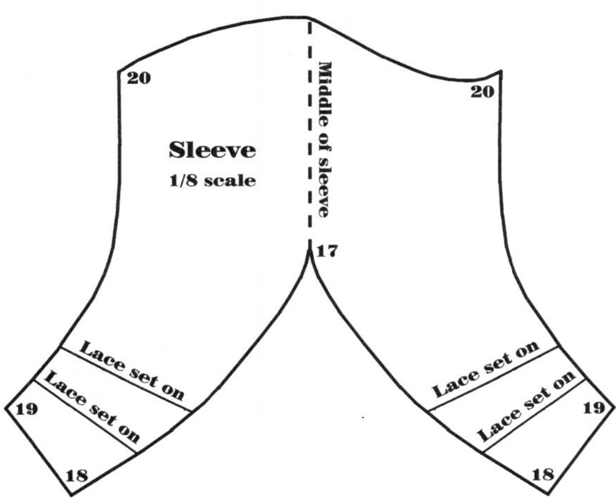

White Cashmere Baschlik

This pretty baschlik is of white cashmere. It is trimmed as illustrated with black velvet ribbon 1 inch wide, very narrow black lace, and white angora tassels.

Cut the baschlik whole. Sew up the seam from 11 to 12. Turn the edge down all round on the right side about 1/5 inch. Sew on the lace. Cover the setting on of the latter and the turned-down edge with the velvet ribbon. Put on the tassels. Lastly, lay the baschlik together in the back so the *x*s lie the one above the other, and fasten the double stuff together.

White Cashmere Baschlik

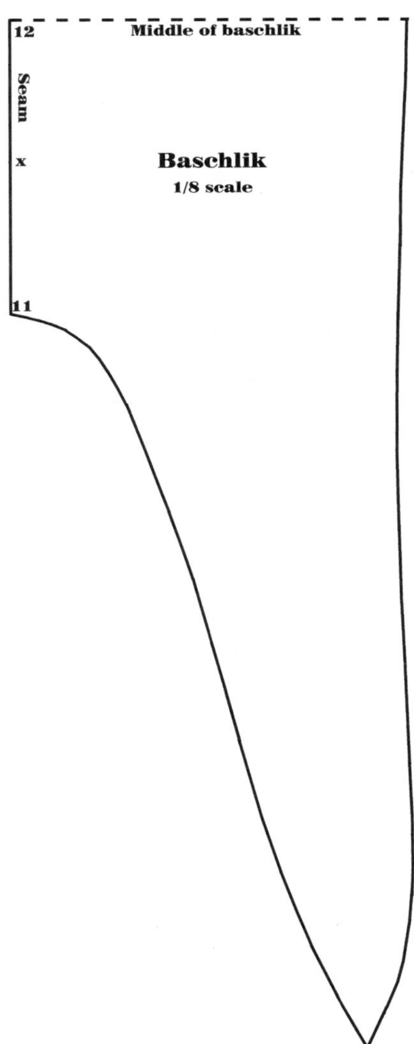

June 6, 1868

Summer Sun Bonnet

This garden hat is tasteful and easily made, and will be found useful in the coming season. It is made of figured Swiss muslin, lined with blue linen.

Cut the outside and lining from the front, crown, and cape. Baste the outside on the lining. Stitch with white silk the double material cut from the front. Run through the shirr thus made a whalebone or a cane of the length given in the pattern. On the front side of the crown lay the double material over on the right side 1/4 inch. Hem it down with the whalebone or cane inside. On the other side (the back) lay the material underneath in the same manner, with the whalebone or cane inside. Fasten the ends of each whalebone carefully on the bias ends of the piece. Then bind the piece with a bias strip of the Swiss muslin.

The gathered crown is now fastened, according to the figures on the pattern, to the foundation of the hood. This last is first pleated, always bringing *x* on •. The double material of the cape is trimmed on the outer edge. On the upper edge lay it in pleats, bringing *x* on •, and fasten it to the front and crown. The seam thus made between the crown and cape is covered on the inside of the bonnet with a strip of Swiss muslin.

On the front and back edges of the crown, and on the outer edge of the cape, set a pointed ruche as illustrated, and on the middle of the back a Swiss muslin bow. The strings are of Swiss muslin. They are laid in a few pleats on the upper ends.

Summer Sun Bonnet

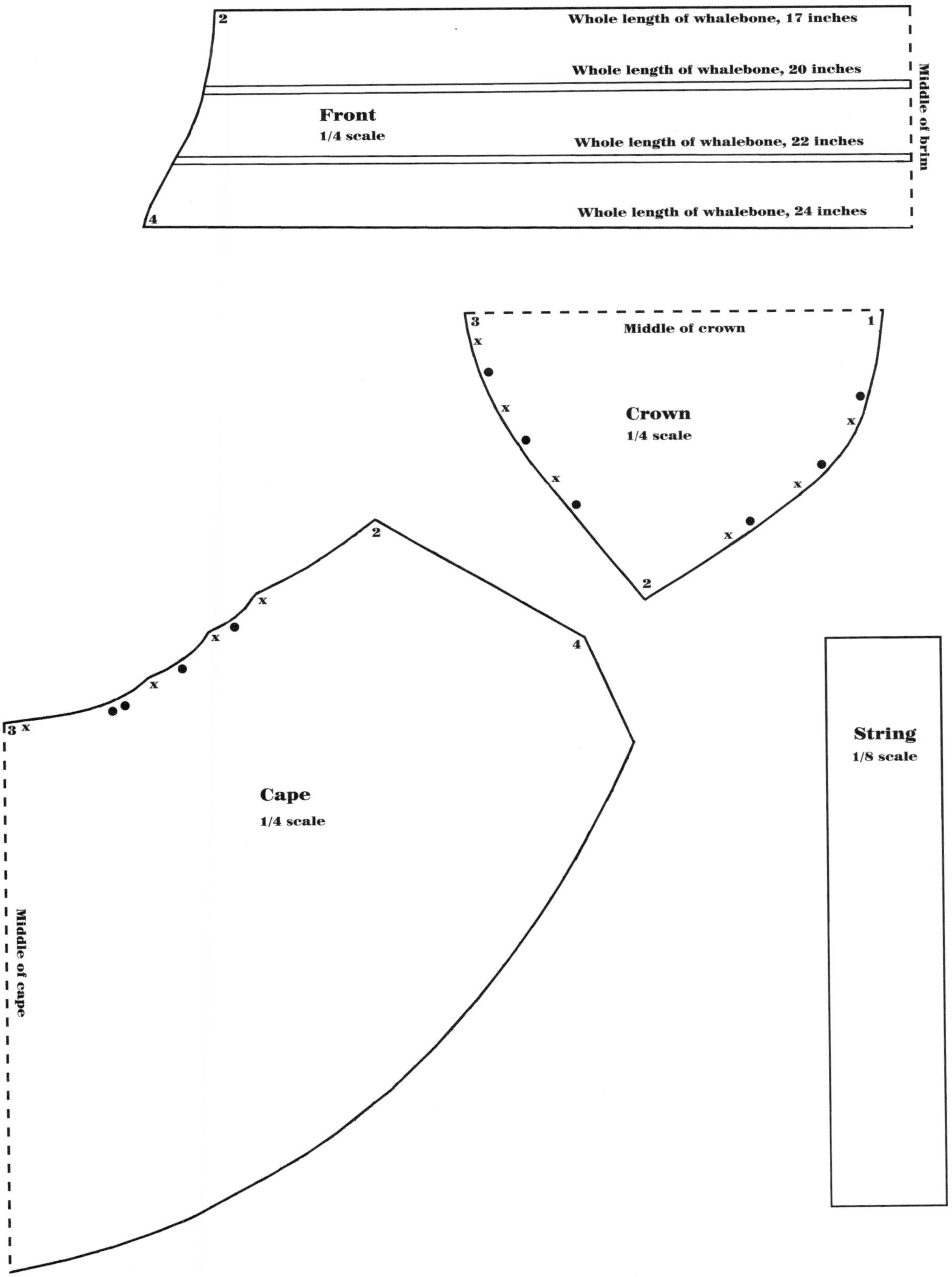

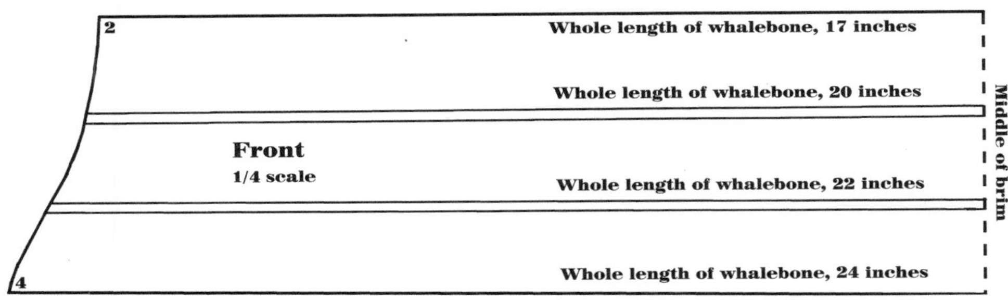

3
Middle of crown
1
x
x
Crown
1/4 scale
x
x
x
x
2

2
x
x
4
x
3 x
Cape
1/4 scale
Middle of cape

String
1/8 scale

June 6, 1868

Garden Hat

This round garden hat is of white and pink linen, the latter being the lining. Cut of the outside and lining one piece each from the crown and brim, and one piece of the lining from the crown.

This last is laid in pleats, always bringing *x* on •. A covered wire is run in on the outer edge. Then cover the outside with pink and white linen. Line the crown with white linen. Lay the piece of white linen cut from the brim on the pink linen. Then backstitch the double material with white silk, following the lines given. Run into each of the shirrs thus formed a thin round whalebone or cane of the length given in the pattern. On the under side of the brim the stuff is laid over on the right side 1/4 inch, and hemmed down with the whalebone or cane run in. The other side of the brim is fastened in the same manner, except the hem must be laid on the under side. The ends of every whalebone or cane are lapped over about 1 inch and carefully fastened. Hemstitch the double material across the ends from 5 to 7. Cover the seam, as illustrated, with small bows of white linen. Then sew the brim, according to the figures on the pattern, to the outer edge of the crown.

Border the hat with a pinked ruche of linen 2 inches wide. The strings are made of white linen. They are hemmed on the sides and the under end 1/2 inch wide. The top is pleated where it is sewn on the hat.

Garden Hat

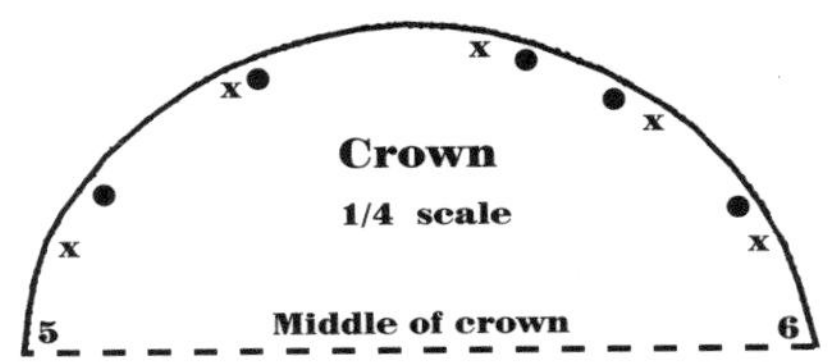

6 5

Whole length of whalebone, 20 inches

Brim
1/4 scale

Whole length of whalebone, 25 inches

Middle of brim

Whole length of whalebone, 34 inches

Whole length of whalebone, 42 inches

Whole length of whalebone, 49 inches

7

String
1/8 scale

June 13, 1868

Bridal Toilettes

We are reminded by our readers that a few hints about wedding toilettes and the selection of a trousseau are timely at all seasons of the year. The suggestion is made also that we relate what is attainable by people in that golden mediocrity, neither very rich nor very poor, rather than the elaborate and extravagant outfits selected for wealthy brides.

What will the wedding dress be is the first question. With those who can afford it satin is the usual choice. A white satin dress has hitherto required considerable expenditure for lace and jewelry. But a pretty fashion coming into vogue in Europe dictates that the bride be simply dressed, with little lace, and no ornaments but orange flowers. Unless very fine lace is used it is better to dispense with it altogether, and trim with soft illusion and handmade satin trimmings.

The popular quality of satin is 27 inches wide. A very good article, all pure silk, measures only 22 inches. Faille and soft poult-de-soie are the next choice after satin. Very handsome corded silks may be bought. Plain taffetas require an overskirt of illusion that adds considerably to the outlay.

Skirts of wedding dresses are seldom looped in the pannier fashion. Simplicity of style is affected almost to severity. Long trains gored flatly in front, with fullness at the back, are more appropriate.

It is a matter of fancy as to whether the corsage is high or low. Grecian folds of tulle are made into berthas for both styles, and thick quillings of the dress material surround the shoulders. A tiny fichu, not more than 3 inches wide, is formed of folds and lace, and is sewn on the dress instead of the bretelles so much worn during the winter. This is only suitable for dresses that open in front, as most evening dresses are now made.

If the corsage is low the sleeve is merely a fold of satin or fall of lace caught together with a bouquet. Narrow coat sleeves accompany the high corsage.

It is scarcely necessary to speak of the tulle and illusion dresses over taffeta skirts sometimes worn by brides, as they do not differ materially from many evening dresses.

Very pretty veils are made of soft illusion, entirely untrimmed, but cut in graceful style. The selvage edges of the tulle, with a wide hem, fall from the top and bottom of the veil, which should fall almost to the end of the train. The short veil over the face reaches nearly to the waist. This simple illusion veil is very much admired. Lace, satin pipings, and wide ruches of tulle add greatly to the expense of the veil. Clematis, jasmine, and white lilies occasionally take the place of the traditional orange flower for bridal wreaths.

The bridal dress should be worn frequently during the honeymoon, and not often afterward. It is then a compliment to the hostess. But as it is the dress worn on the most conspicuous occasion of the wearer's life it attracts attention, and soon becomes familiar.

Trousseau Dresses

A novelty silk, suitable for the reception dresses that form part of the trousseau, is called moiré serge. It is as thick as satin, but soft and pliant like poult-de-soie, has a thick diagonal reps, and is beautifully watered. It is brought out in a delicate shade of lavender, Metternich green, flesh color, and blue. There are 10 yards in each pattern.

We think also that it is safe to select one of the silk chameleons. The lilacs and gray shot with white are especially appropriate for brides.

A correspondent asks if there is any prescribed street costume for a bride. We answer in the negative. There never was a time when such matters were left so entirely to the taste of the wearer. Even the conventional white bonnet gives place to one appropriate to the dress with which it is worn. The most approved toilettes are ones in which the dress, wrapping, bonnet, parasol, shoes, and gloves are of one color, and as nearly as possible of one material.

A morning dress of cashmere is always seasonable in our changeable climate. It is better to have this of a delicate color, lavender, light blue, or pale amber, as it gives variety to the bridal wardrobe in which white is always apt to predominate. It should be made loosely, falling in large pleats from the shoulder. Shell puffs of silk and the new worsted guipures are suitable trimming.

Alpaca frays easily, and is no longer in favor. Morning Gabrielles of white muslin are included in the trousseaux furnished at first-class houses. They are of nainsook, of Swiss muslin, and of piqué. When only one is made it is best to have it of nainsook, as it is not so thin as Swiss, and washes better than piqué. Striped linens, the pretty French jaconets with colored figures, and the American cambrics, make neat breakfast dresses, and seem to have entirely superseded the sheer lawns once so much worn.

For afternoon dresses there are the poplinettes, a silk and linen mixture; the grenadines; and the light silks, stripes, checks, and chinés. A stylishly made black silk is also serviceable on many occasions, and is always ladylike and in good taste.

A gored skirt and polonaise, plainly trimmed, is all that is required for the traveling dress. There is a perplexing variety of material offered. Silk serge is considered the most distingué, but is expensive. Instead we choose a serviceable poplin or woolen serge, that costs only half the money, and will better endure the hard usage of travel.

Underlinen

We cannot, of course, prescribe the number of garments necessary. Much depends on the supply already on hand. Orders given at the furnishing houses usually include a dozen linen and a dozen cotton of the principal articles of underclothing. Half of each dozen should be handsomely trimmed. The others are intended for constant use, and should be simply made.

Lace and linen cambric are soon worn out or torn out in washing. Very sheer linen cambric is expensive, and is so frail it is not worth the tedious needlework required for puffs and ruffles. Richardson's linen is selected for the best outfits. In muslins it is requisite that the threads be closely woven, and the selvage even. French percale and New York Mills are serviceable for articles that require a heavy material, such as gowns and drawers. Jones's cambric and French nainsook make the more handsome gowns. Jaconet is but little used.

Valenciennes lace is the most suitable for trimming, but a fine thin lace thickens up in washing, and looks no better than a coarser and more durable article. Appliqué embroidery, or transferring as it is sometimes called, must be sewn on very securely, or it will be roughened and torn off by the smoothing iron. Thick needlework is the most substantial of all trimmings. The eyelets and compass work, once so fashionable, are seldom seen now. Hamburg embroidery is inexpensive, as it is done by machinery, and is always in pretty designs. It is best to choose patterns without any revere work or herringbone.

The chemise and drawers should be trimmed to match and worn en suite. Chemise bands are very wide. Many ladies prefer them closed all around. A deep fall of trimming is sometimes attached to the band, reaching to the waist to form a corset cover. The sleeves are merely a row of lace and embroidery.

Half-a-dozen low bodices with short sleeves are provided for corset covers. Some are entirely formed of puffs and gathered into a belt, while others are made of pleats, or are tight fitting.

Petticoats of different lengths must be arranged to suit the skirts of street dresses, demitrains, and trains. They should be gored almost flat in front, and gathered at the sides and back. Tucks and ruffles are the trimmings for short petticoats. Embroidery and lace and elaborate trimming are lavished on trained petticoats, as they are often worn with short jackets for breakfast dresses.

Several petticoats to be worn under the crinoline are also essential. These are short and narrow, containing only three widths of muslin, and are gored to fit the figure about the hips. Flannel skirts should not be made too full. Half-a-dozen at least are necessary.

It is necessary that two crinoline skirts be provided–a short one for street dresses, and a trained one for full dress. If steel skeletons are worn there should be half-a-dozen muslin covers for the bottoms. These are made of thick white muslin, 1/2 yard wide, covering the crinoline inside and out, and buttoned together at the upper edge. They are prettily trimmed with a fluted ruffle. The Lace Imperial Skirt lately introduced does away with the necessity for these covers, as the mesh of the lace is woven thickly toward the bottom. The whole skirt may be put in the water and washed without injuring the steel hoops.

Ladies contrive devices of their own for giving the full appearance now in vogue, such as puffs of horsehair, or crinoline worn beneath the hoops.

A dozen nightdresses is considered a sufficient number. The favorite pattern is a deep yoke, pointed before and behind, with three widths in the skirt. Bands around the neck look neater than turndown collars. Coat sleeves are used altogether. The best half-dozen gowns are of linen or nainsook. If Valenciennes is used for trimming it should be stitched in with a narrow band of the material.

Short dressing sacques are convenient to dress the hair in. They are made of percale or cambric, and are ruffled, or plainly trimmed. Long dressing gowns are made with body and skirt in one. The fullness is laid in pleats and held by a cord and tassel at the waist.

The supply of handkerchiefs should be very liberal. The neatest style for morning use is of sheer linen with a wide hem, and the initials, monogram, or given name embroidered in a corner. Two or three tucks above a hem are also pretty. Ladies can make their own evening handkerchiefs at much less expense than they can be bought ready-made. A 12-inch square of linen cambric is rolled at the edges, and bordered with Valenciennes insertion and lace. The cambric should be thin and sheer, and the lace very fine. The material should be basted on paper to keep the proper shape.

Plain cuffs, collars, and undersleeves of linen and cambric may also be abundantly provided. It is best, however, to have but a few lace collars. The shape changes, and they are very expensive.

Beaded Bandeau

This bandeau, the middle section of which is shown full size, consists of a straight strip of stiff white lining, about 1/2 inch wide. This is covered with wax and crystal beads, and ornamented in the middle with a butterfly worked in the same manner.

First, arrange the wax beads on the lining as follows. Fasten on one side of the strip a fine wire on which wax beads have been strung. Then wind the wire around the lining, in doing which arrange the beads on the right side, and leave the bare wire on the inside. Having covered the lining, finish the edge with a row of crystal beads that have been previously strung on a fine wire.

Next set on the butterfly, for which first cut a piece of lining of the shape shown. Cover this as shown with wax beads, and crystal beads and bugles. However, only the small crystal beads are to be strung on wire. The remaining bugles are sewn on with silk.

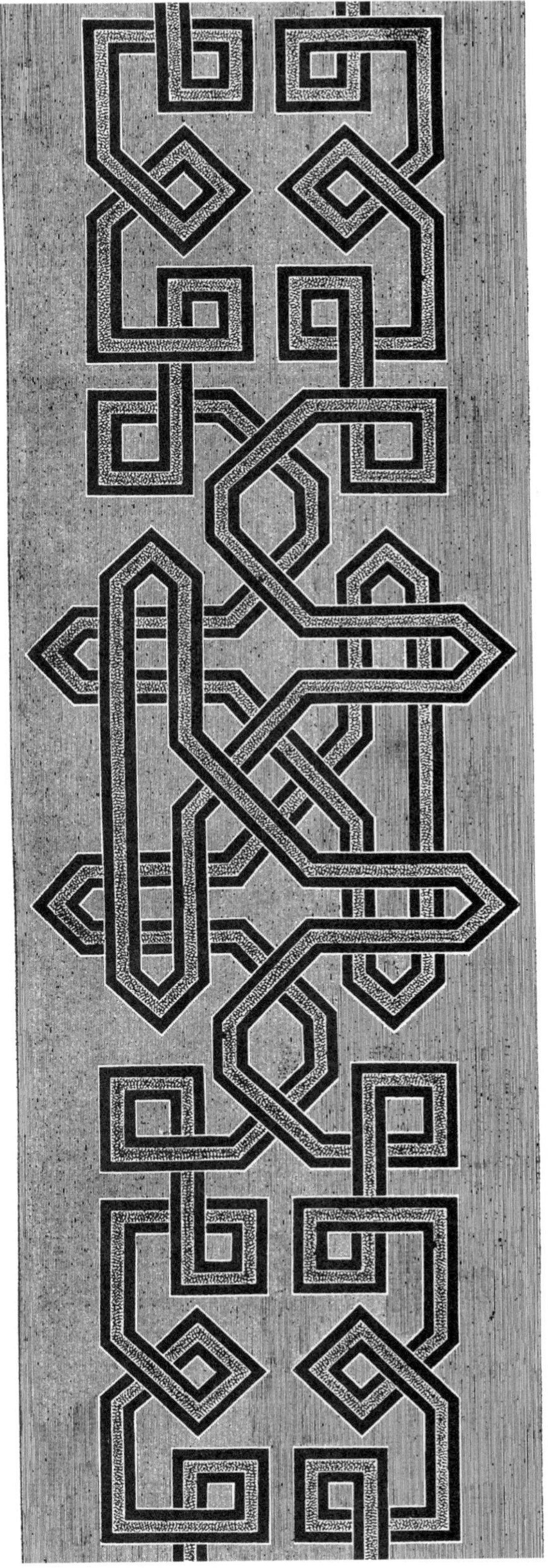

Border
This border is especially designed for covers, though it may be used as the border of a skirt. The design is worked in braid, ribbon, or velvet ribbon, bordered on each side by a narrower braid.

June 20, 1868

Mourning Dress Goods

A new material for mourning dresses is called byzantine, a capricious name that conveys no idea of the goods. It resembles challis in appearance, but is thinner and is not too glossy for fresh mourning. It is 2 yards wide; from 4 to 6 yards are bought for a dress. A kind of silk grenadine introduced this season is called florentine. It is very thin and lustrous, and is stronger than ordinary grenadine. A good quality is 3/4 yard wide; but the best quality is 8 quarters wide. Hernani is another name for the popular iron grenadine. It has square meshes, is all pure silk, and is commendable for its durability and soft black color. Canvas grenadine is similar, but the meshes are larger, and there is some wool in the fabric. It is 3/4 yard wide. Crêpe morette is a thin material with crêpe finish. It is not new, but is stylish, and much sought after.

Ladies wearing mourning have objected to purchasing thin black goods, saying they found them of most perishable fabric and but little cooler than thick materials. This was true of the old-fashioned bareges. But the wiry grenadines with open meshes are very durable, and make cool and pleasant dresses. They are now the staple article for summer wear, both in mourning and in colors.

Materials for Suits

French bombazine has a silk warp, and is consequently much lighter than the all-wool English goods, and is preferred for warm weather. Street suits for fresh mourning are made of it, trimmed with folds of crêpe or a thick cord covered with bombazine. Parisienne and tamise cloth are soft woolen materials of light quality suitable for short dresses. Woolen serge is very much admired, but difficult to obtain. The lusterless silk serge is the newest fabric for street suits, and is preferred by many to the more expensive grosgrains.

House Dresses

Solid black foulard silks are shown for house dresses. For lighter mourning the grounds are varied with white stars, crosses, dots, stripes, and sprays of flowers. Since English mixtures of wool and cotton have become so cheap, black lawns and calicos are but little used. It is customary to sell the Balmoral goods and Australian cloths in dress patterns. Scotch ginghams of clear white, crossed with black bars or gray and black mottled grounds, make neat house dresses. Many ladies are buying them for short traveling dresses.

Lighter Mourning

Black grenadines with gray dashes on the surface, or with white set figures, are selected for half mourning. At one house are grenadine bareges, black with white satin stripes, varying from 1/8 to 2 inches wide. Solid black iron grenadines are trimmed with white or lavender, producing a beautiful effect. Lavender foulards with deep purple spots are admired. A white foulard has large polka dots in black. Silver-gray pongees and poplins of silk and linen, or silk and worsted, are serviceable for street dresses trimmed with folds of black grosgrain and thick fringe. Chiné serge of mottled black and white is a novelty. Dark granites and gray mohairs look well with black binding and braid. A kind of winsey, a white ground with rough black cords, makes up well.

Underskirts

Petticoats of black moreen and of mohair are useful, as they may be worn with a variety of dresses or used as the lower skirt of a suit. They should be trimmed simply with wide braid and a pleated flounce. After the first mourning is laid aside, striped skirts are admissible. Black and lavender or lead-colored stripes are more suitable than the black and white now so much used by ladies not in mourning. White cambric skirts with fluted ruffles edged with black are sold. Lavender mohair striped with white is worn for half mourning.

Styles and Trimmings

The goods we have mentioned are made into both trained dresses and short suits. The styles are similar to those for colors. Good taste always suggests simplicity of attire for mourning. Such trimmings as gathered ruffles and puffs are too fanciful. Box-pleated flounces, ruffles with the pleats all turned one way, quillings, fluting, folds, worsted braid, and heavy cord fringes are the most appropriate trimmings. All trimmings are now sewn on straight around the skirt and near the edge, instead of being arranged in curves and squares. A single fold of the material, 2 inches wide and piped with grosgrain, is used for suits. For widow's mourning a thick cord at the edge of the skirts and mantle is sufficient ornament. A stylish fit, good material, and the absence of superfluous ornament combine to make black a tasteful and becoming dress.

Shawls and Mantles

Suits are so universally worn that but few mantles are imported. Square grenadine shawls, with fringe, or hemmed, or bordered with crêpe, are chosen for elderly ladies. Tibet cloth and grenadine are made into mantles. A pretty fashion for both these materials is a loose sleeveless sacque, with a deep cape in front, falling into long scarves at the back, loosely tied together. Another is merely a large double talma, trimmed with a wide quilling of the grenadine.

Bonnets and Veils

English crêpe bonnets are made at all seasons of the year for the deepest mourning. The favorite shape is a large fanchon, covered with two thicknesses of the crêpe. The trimming consists of folds and pleats at the back and on the diadem. The fall over the chignon, now so fashionable, is made of crêpe folds that extend toward the front, forming strings. On other bonnets the crêpe strings are wide, and edged with a notched ruche. A mantilla veil of Brussels net, trimmed with crêpe folds, draping the chignon and shoulders, is very effective.

Only widows wear white caps inside the bonnet. These should at first be made of tarlatan, reaching merely across the forehead, without framing the face. At the end of a year the tarlatan puff may be exchanged for a white tulle ruche. The strings should be of black crêpe. Silk ribbon is not considered deep mourning. A crêpe bag for concealing the hair is sometimes attached to the bonnet.

Black tulle and Brussels net are worn by ladies who wish to lay aside crêpe, but are not willing to put on lace. Very young ladies wear white flowers on black bonnets. Purple is more becoming to older persons. Lavender and black lace bonnets are the lightest mourning. A few jet and steel ornaments are still worn.

English crêpe, 40 inches wide, is required for veils. Take 2 yards of the crêpe, and turn up the hem 1/4 yard deep at each end. This veil is thrown over the bonnet, and pinned with jet pins. If the gathered veil is preferred, 1 3/4 yards is required. At one end 1/2 yard is turned up for a hem. This style is now made for widows, instead of doubling the crêpe. It is cooler for summer. For very slight mourning a round veil, with long tabs, is made of Brussels net, trimmed with crêpe folds.

Widow's caps for young ladies are small squares of white tarlatan, worn with a point over the forehead, like the Marie Stuart cap. The headpiece has four small tucks each way through the center. A narrow quilling or plain folds form the border. They are held on by an elastic under the back hair, or with tarlatan strings tied in a bow under the chin. After the first year Lyons tulle is substituted for tarlatan. Ladies more advanced in years wear the regular cap with the bag crown.

Collars, Etc.

Collars are made double of the crêpe, slightly pointed in front, and bordered with a 1/2-inch band of crêpe ornamented with four rows of stitching. Many persons prefer black grenadine for collars instead of crêpe, as it does not turn brown, and is cooler. It is arranged in shell-shaped scallops and folds. Undersleeves have wide, square cuffs very large at the wrist, trimmed to match the collar. Tarlatan and organdy are the materials for white collars. A plain, folded tie of white tarlatan or muslin, similar to those worn by gentlemen, is selected for widows. Linen collars with black borders stitched on are suitable for morning. The sailor shape, deeply pointed at the sides, is pretty for young ladies, with a grenadine necktie held by a jet ring.

Handkerchiefs of sheer linen are bordered with black 2 inches deep, covering the whole hem. This is newer than the black band above the hem. Lavender borders are shown for half mourning.

Marie Antoinette fichus of white tarlatan and of organdy are trimmed with two narrow folds, or a pleated ruffle or ruche. These are inexpensive, and exceedingly pretty with a black dress. They are also made of tulle, of Brussels net, and of guipure, to be worn over lavender and purple. Sleeveless jackets with sashes made of these materials make the plainest toilettes look dressy. Lace bows at the throat, the chemise Russe, guipure paletots, and bretelles serve to break the monotony of mourning clothing, and are not expensive when made at home by skillful fingers.

Parasols, Gloves, and Shoes

Parasols of Turk satin and of soft, dead-black poult-de-soie are lined with black and trimmed with three folds of English crêpe set on as a border. The carved ebony handles are flat and broad. For lighter mourning three quilled ruffles surround the edge, and the lining is white and lavender.

Kid gloves with two buttons at the wrist are selected for fresh mourning. Silk gloves with a kid finish are sometimes preferred. They are neatly made, and ornamented on the back with a silk lacing, at the end of which are tassels capped with silver. Black and purple kids are embroidered on the back with white for light mourning.

Cloth and glove-kid gaiters without tips are buttoned with onyx and jet. The heels are concave, and sometimes covered with cloth.

Jewelry

The handsomest mourning jewelry is of onyx, made in the styles now fashionable for coral, formed of solid balls and bars, arranged in circles and crescents with pear-shaped pendants. Tiny diamonds and pearls are sometimes set in the center of the balls. Another style is a plain flat surface of onyx made round, with a monogram or initial carved in the center. The surface is left a dead black without luster, and the Old English letters are brightly polished. The monogram is sometimes made in gold. A deep gray stratum of the onyx is shown at the edge as a border. For half mourning, gold, onyx, and black enamel together are made in Oriental patterns. Shell cameos are massively set in jet. An elegant set consists of a pin, earrings, and bracelet. The unpolished jet center represents a beautiful female head set in a glossy jet border.

Onyx buttons for sleeves and dress fronts are made to match. Chatelaines are made of large jet links. Wide jet necklaces and crosses, to be worn around the neck with a lutestring ribbon, are admired for young ladies. Bandeaux and combs of carved jet are shown.

Waist and Lingerie Trimmings

These trimmings are for chemises Russe, fichus, lingerie, etc.

Figure 1 shows a bow of rounded tabs of Valenciennes insertion, 1/2 inch wide, bordered with pleated lace a little narrower. Between the tabs arrange points made of green satin ribbon 3/4 inch wide. The place where the tabs are sewn on is covered by a rosette, which is also edged with lace. This bow is seen on the Tucked Waist.

Figure 1. Bow for Tucked Waist–half size

Figure 2 shows a bow of red ribbon 1/3 inch wide, bordered with lace on one side and pointed at the ends. The ends are pointed by laying back the outer edges of the ribbon and lace and sewing them down on the back. In the center three loops of ribbon are arranged.

Figure 2. Ribbon and lace bow

Figure 3 shows a bow of embroidered lappets, pleated on the outer edge, and Valenciennes lace 1/3 inch wide. These lappets are fastened on a muslin foundation, as shown. They partly cover the loops of blue satin ribbon that have been previously arranged on the foundation. This bow is seen on the Waist with Bretelle Trimming.

Figure 3. Bow–half size

Figure 4 shows a simulated braid trimming, composed of two pieces of pink satin ribbon, which are wound with Valenciennes insertion as shown. On the edge of this run pleated Valenciennes lace. The Waist with Simulated Braid Trimming is ornamented with this pretty and easily made trimming.

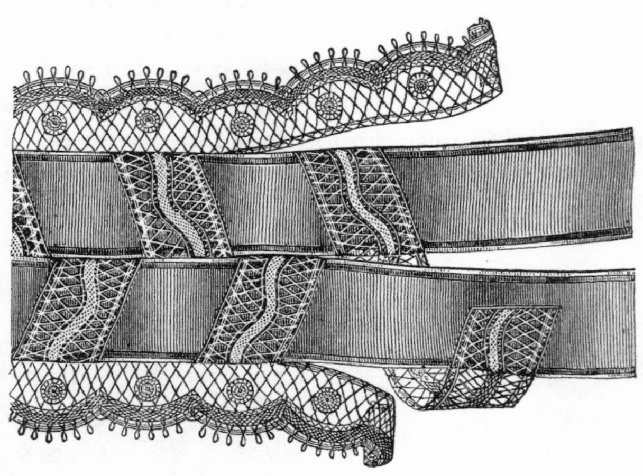

Figure 4. Making simulated braid trimming–full size

The trimming in Figure 5 consists of narrow green satin ribbon, which is crossed on a straight piece of muslin as shown. It is ornamented with two sizes of circular figures, embroidered in point de minute. The muslin is cut away from the outside of the ribbon.

Figure 6 shows a needlework rosette. It is worked in back stitch, straight half-polka stitch, and satin stitch. The openwork center is formed of fine guipure cord, after which the foundation is cut away.

Figure 6. Needlework rosette

Figure 7 shows an embroidered rosette. It is worked in straight half-polka and satin stitch. The inside of each large hole is finished by a guipure wheel. This rosette is used on the Waist with Simulated Bodice.

Figure 5. Swiss muslin, ribbon, and needlework trimming

Figure 7. Embroidered rosette

Figures 8 and 9 show two trimmings, embroidered with white cotton in French stitch, as illustrated. These serve for trimming chemises Russe, standing collars, etc.

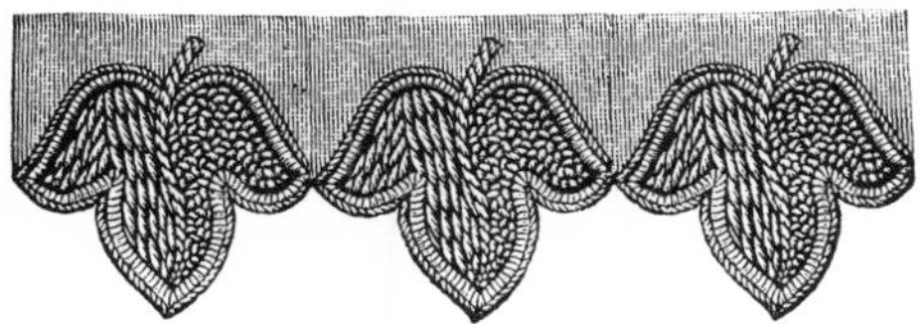

Figure 8. Needlework trimming

Figure 9. Needlework trimming

Figure 10 shows a pointed edging. This serves as trimming for chemises Russe, standing collars, cuffs, etc. The edge consists of green satin points of double material, to which are also fastened buttonhole-stitch scallops arranged in points. The embroidered scallops are fastened on a piece of muslin, and the satin points sewn to a satin ribbon. The points are then fastened together as shown, and the muslin is trimmed with narrow satin ribbon.

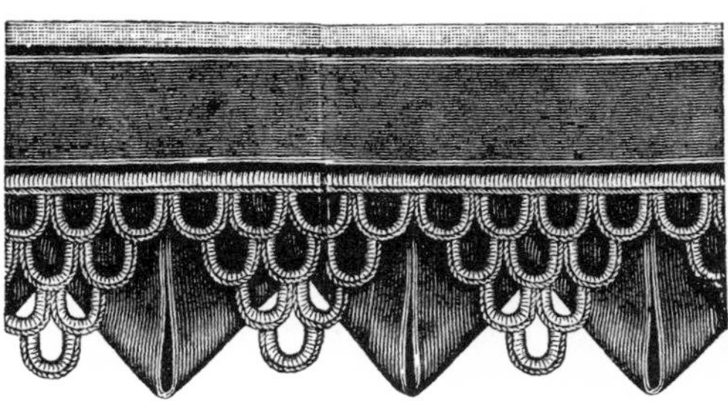

Figure 10. Pointed edging

Figure 11 shows a pointed edging. This also serves as trimming for chemises Russe, standing collars, cuffs, etc. It consists of points of muslin and lilac satin, and is formed of double material. Finish the muslin points with a Swiss muslin binding 1/3 inch wide, so that each point laps slightly over the next on the edge. The satin points are in like manner fastened to a lilac binding 2/3 inch wide. Then sew the two rows of points together, as shown, so the under edge of the lilac satin ribbon projects a little below the edge of the muslin.

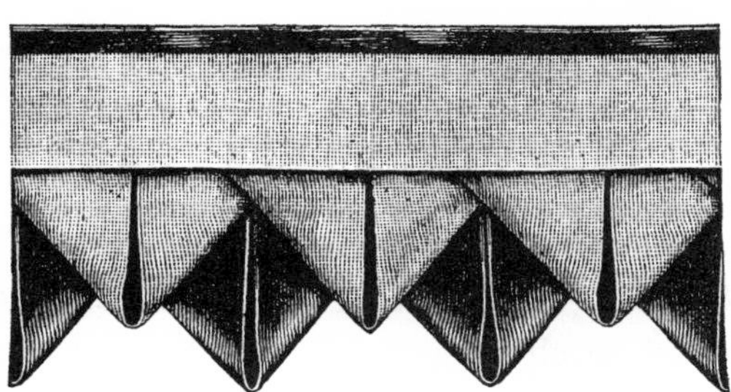

Figure 11. Pointed edging

Waist with Simulated Braid Trimming

This waist, or chemise Russe, is of Swiss muslin. It is trimmed with a simulated braid, or rouleau of pink satin ribbon 1 inch wide, and Valenciennes insertion and edging, each 2/3 inch wide. For the manner of making the trimming, see Figure 4 above and the appended description.

Cut both fronts, allowing 1 1/2 inches for the front hem. Cut the back in one piece. Cut the sleeves.

Hem the fronts. Finish them with small buttons and buttonholes. Take up the bosom pleats. Join the back and fronts according to the figures on the pattern. After the neck is finished, bind it with a straight piece of Swiss muslin 3/4 inch wide. Cover this band with pink satin ribbon, which is wound diagonally with the insertion. Gather in a frill of lace above the binding. Hem the under edge with a hem 1/5 inch wide. Gather the back. Finish the waist with a Swiss muslin belt 1 1/2 inches wide.

Join the sleeves according to the figures on the pattern. Turn down the material on the right side 1/3 inch on the bottom and sew on the trimming. Cord the armholes. Sew in the sleeves, bringing 26 on 26 of the waist front. Prepare the trimming, point the ends, and sew it on.

Waist with Simulated Braid

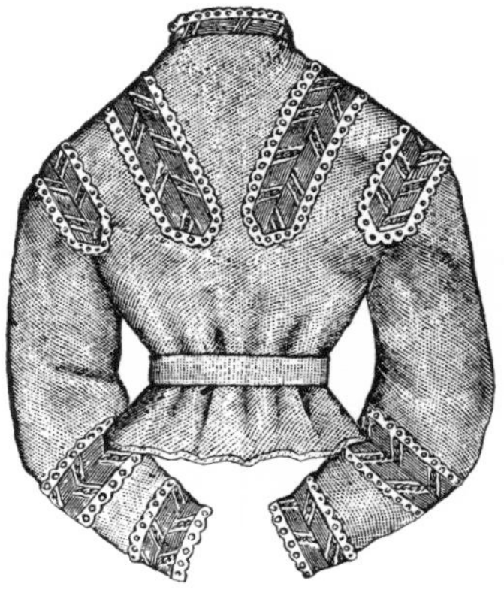

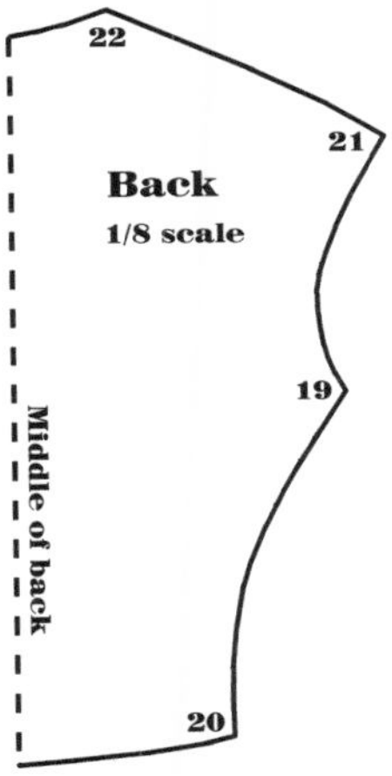

22
21
Back
1/8 scale
19
Middle of back
20

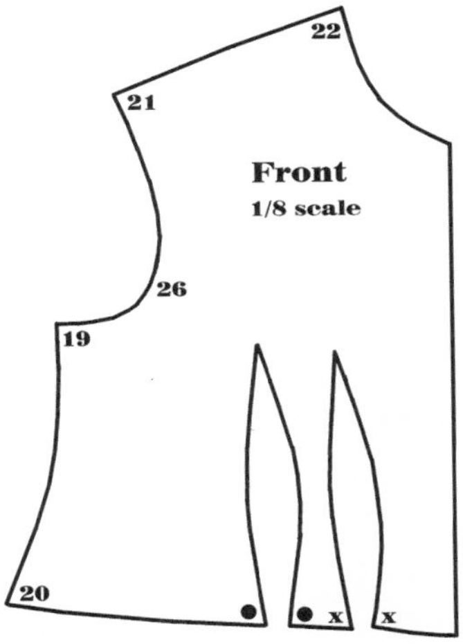

22
21
Front
1/8 scale
26
19
20
x
x

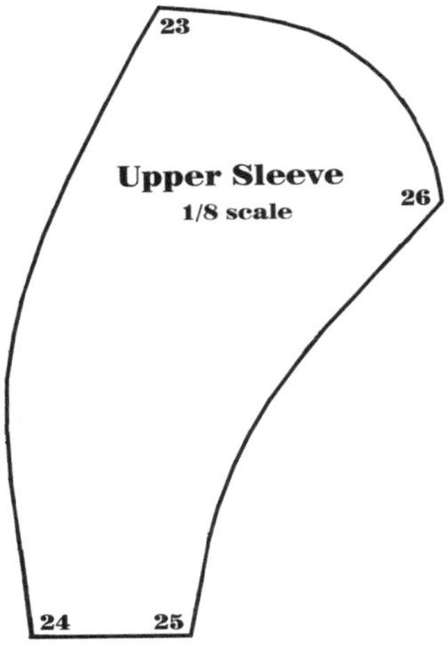

23
Upper Sleeve
1/8 scale
26
24 25

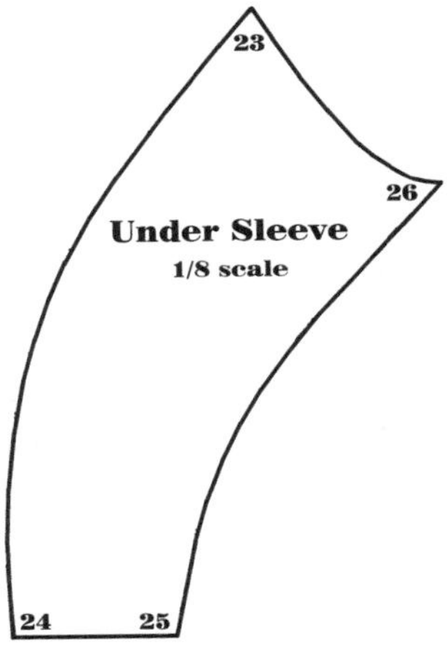

23
26
Under Sleeve
1/8 scale
24 25

Waist with Simulated Fichu

This Swiss muslin waist, or chemise Russe, is cut from the same pattern as the Waist with Simulated Braid Trimming. The trimming imitates a fichu. It consists of Valenciennes insertion sewn on in the form of tabs (with the muslin cut away underneath), lace 1/3 inch and 1 inch wide, worked figures in appliqué, and blue satin ribbon 1 inch wide. The insertion on the front of the right side is underlaid with the ribbon, which is also used for the points that finish the neck and the sleeves at the wrist. The neck is finished in front by a rosette of the blue satin ribbon. The manner of sewing on the trimming is shown by the illustrations.

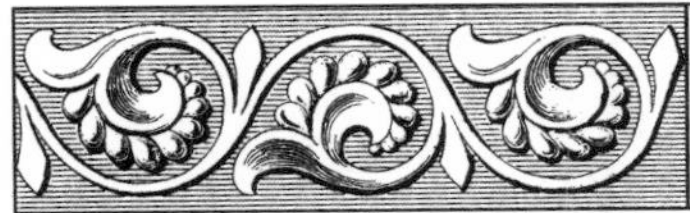

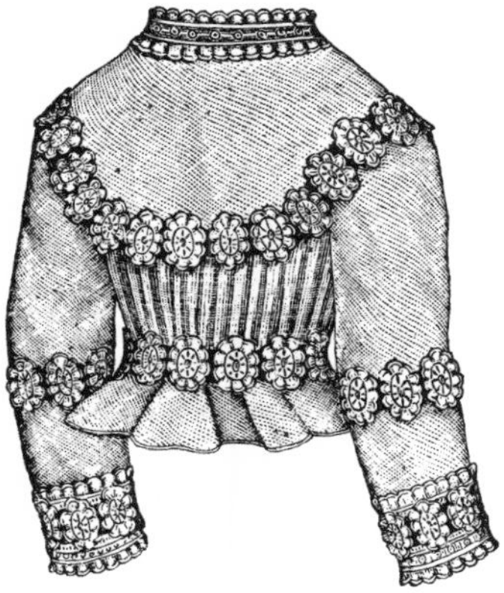

Waist with Simulated Bodice

Waist with Simulated Bodice

This Swiss muslin waist, or chemise Russe, is of plain muslin above, while the portion that imitates a bodice or peasant waist is of tucked muslin. If it be desired to make the waist tight, cut from the pattern for the Waist with Simulated Braid Trimming. If loose, cut from the pattern given for the Tucked Waist.

Trim the seam that joins the plain and tucked parts with lilac satin ribbon. This ribbon is trimmed with embroidered rosettes edged with Valenciennes, pleated on as illustrated. Figures 6 and 7 above give suitable rosettes. The trimming of the sleeves corresponds to that of the bodice. Finish the neck with a collar of Valenciennes insertion and lace, the ends of which are ornamented with an embroidered rosette. Finish the front with a bow composed of two cravat ends of muslin, lace, and embroidered rosettes. Cover the place where these ends are set on with a knot made of embroidery and lace. Loops and ends of lilac satin complete the bow. The belt is of satin ribbon ornamented with embroidered rosettes.

June 20, 1868

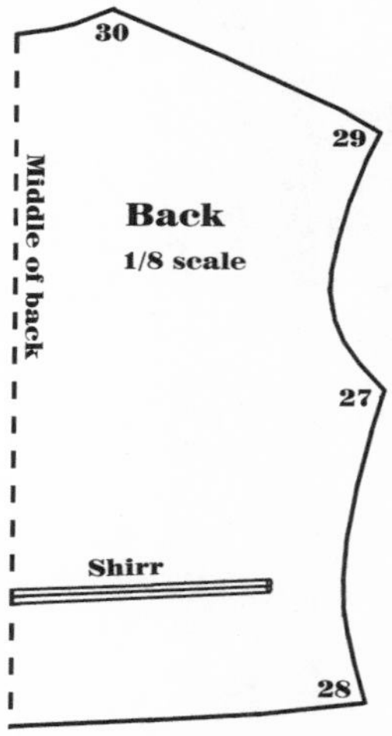

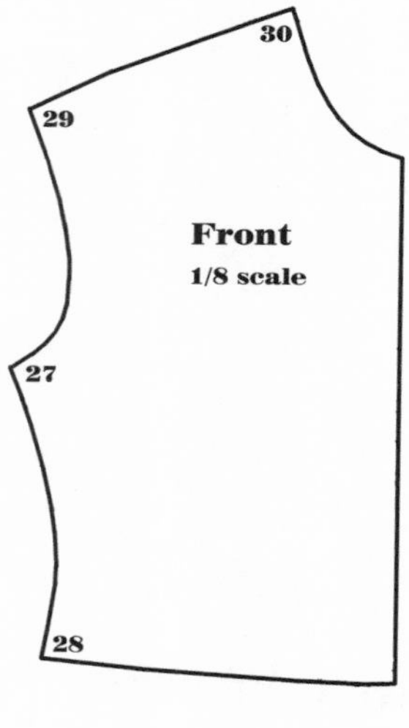

30
29
Back
1/8 scale
Middle of back
27
Shirr
28

30
29
Front
1/8 scale
27
28

Tucked Waist Trimmed with Bows

This Swiss muslin waist, or chemise Russe, is trimmed with bows of Valenciennes insertion, lace, and points of green satin ribbon. Cut the two fronts, and the back in one piece. Cut the sleeves of plain muslin from the sleeve pattern for the Waist with Simulated Braid Trimming.

Join the back and fronts according to the figures on the pattern. Finish the neck with a Swiss muslin binding 3/4 inch wide. Trim this binding with points of the green satin ribbon and lace, as illustrated. Finish the back with a shirr, as shown on the pattern. Then arrange the bows, as shown by Figure 1 above. Trim the sleeves with satin points, lace, and insertion. Sew them into the corded armholes. The belt is of green satin ribbon, ornamented with insertion and lace. It is finished on the front by one of the bows.

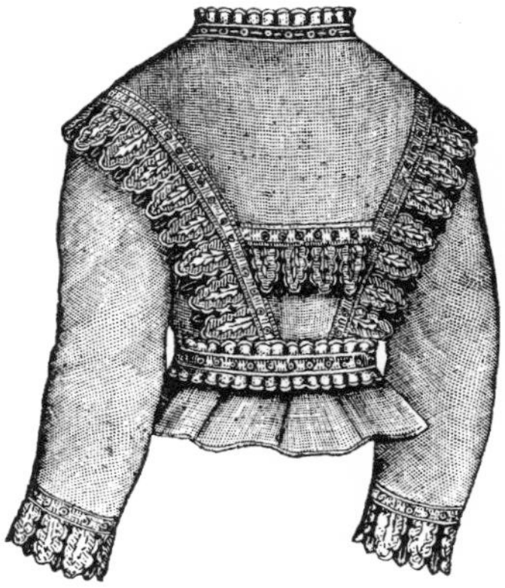

Waist with Bretelle Trimming

Waist with Bretelle Trimming

This Swiss muslin waist, or chemise Russe, is cut from the same pattern as the Tucked Waist. The trimming consists of needlework leaves edged with lace. These are set on to simulate bretelles, with loops of blue satin ribbon between, and surmounted with Valenciennes lace, which covers the seam. A Swiss muslin binding, trimmed with satin points and Valenciennes lace, is set on the neck. It is finished in front with a bow (see Figure 3 above). This bow is made of needlework leaves edged with lace, and loops of blue satin ribbon, to correspond with the bretelles. The sleeve trimming is shown in the illustration.

June 20, 1868

Waist with Bretelles

This waist, or chemise Russe, is cut from the pattern for the Tucked Waist. The bretelles of the front and back consist each of two Swiss muslin pieces, 2 inches wide on the shoulders, and sloping to 1 inch wide at the waist. These strips are laid in narrow cross pleats, and are joined with a guipure insertion about 1/2 inch wide. Cover the seams made by setting them on with guipure lace 1 inch wide, underlaid with pink ribbon. Cut the stuff away from under the bretelles. Finish the right front by a binding 1 inch wide. This is bordered with guipure lace, and ornamented with rosettes in embroidery. Finish the back with insertion in the middle, then cut away the Swiss muslin underneath. Hem the neck very narrow, and finish with lace. On the front set a bow of pink ribbon and lace, in the middle of which is an embroidered figure. The sleeve trimming corresponds to the waist trimming, and can be arranged from the illustration.

Chemise Russe

Chemise Russe with Embroidery

This chemise Russe is made of Swiss muslin, embroidered with black silk in point Russe. The pattern is the same as that for the Tucked Waist. The embroidery designs are given in four patterns.

Design for Upper Part of Sleeve
1/2 scale

Design for Lower Part of Sleeve
1/2 scale

June 20, 1868

Design for Back

1/2 scale

Design for Front

1/2 scale

Muslin Underskirt with Train

A muslin skirt with a train, and a flounce set on, should be worn with a trained dress. It supports the bottom of the dress, and causes it to hang gracefully.

Cut from the first side breadth, second side breadth, and back each two pieces. Cut from the front one piece. The pattern is not full length, so you must increase the length of all the pieces to the desired skirt length. On the first side breadth, second side breadth, and back also allow for the hem.

Join the breadths according to the figures on the pattern. From 13 to the top, in the back breadths, leave a slit and hem the edges. Hem the bottom of the skirt 2 inches wide. The flounce is about 10 inches wide, gathered on the top, and finished at the bottom by a hem 1 inch wide.

For the belt cut from the pattern four pieces. Join them in pairs, and run the upper edges together. Bind the skirt front with the double binding thus formed. Bind the back breadths with a narrow binding, the ends of which are joined to the belt. Through each side of the narrow binding run a string, which is fastened on the front binding and fastens the skirt.

June 20, 1868

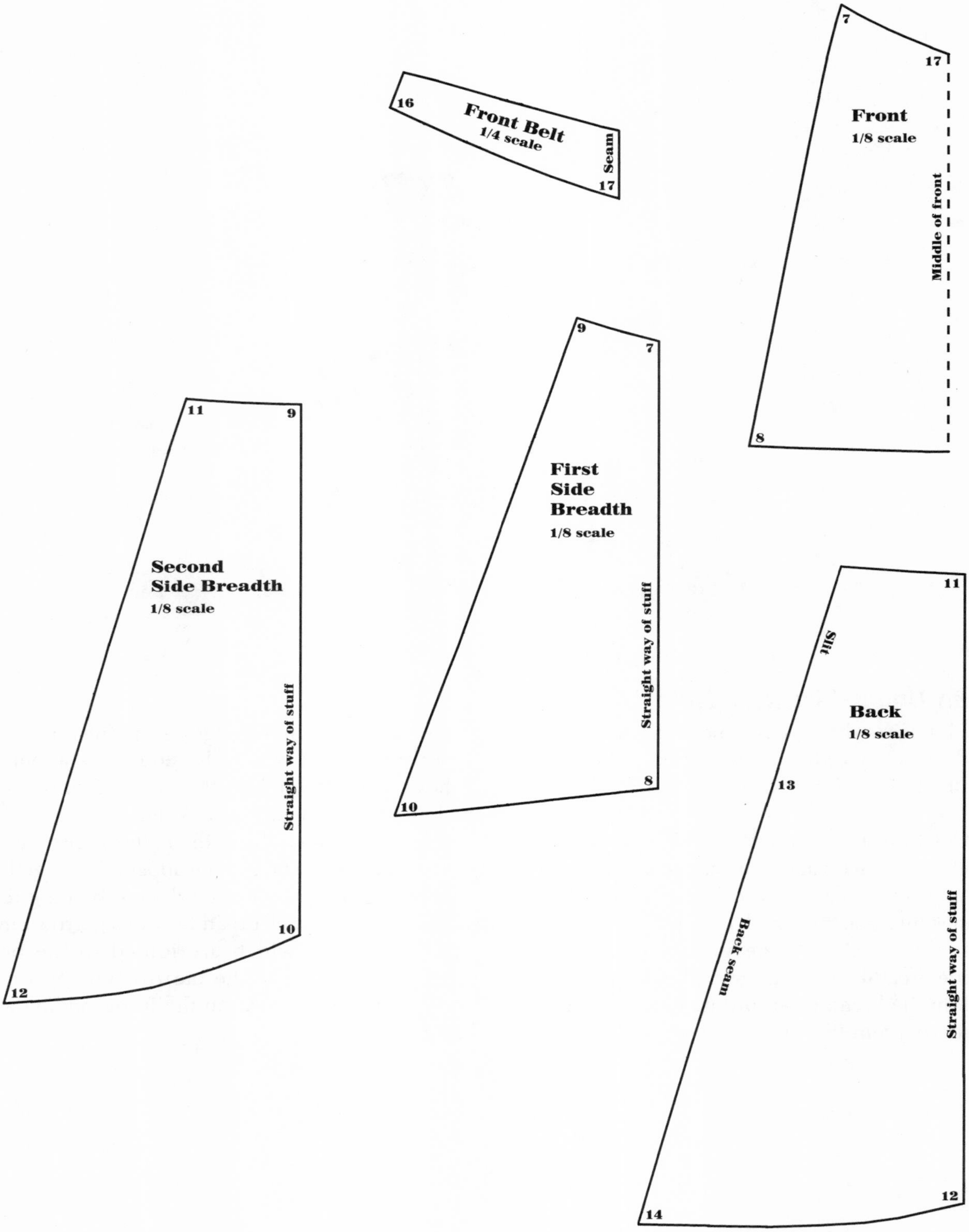

16
Front Belt
1/4 scale
Seam
17
7
17
Front
1/8 scale
Middle of front
8
9
7
First
Side
Breadth
1/8 scale
Straight way of stuff
8
10
11
9
Second
Side Breadth
1/8 scale
Straight way of stuff
10
12
11
Slit
Back
1/8 scale
13
Back seam
Straight way of stuff
12
14

Embroidered Lace Veil

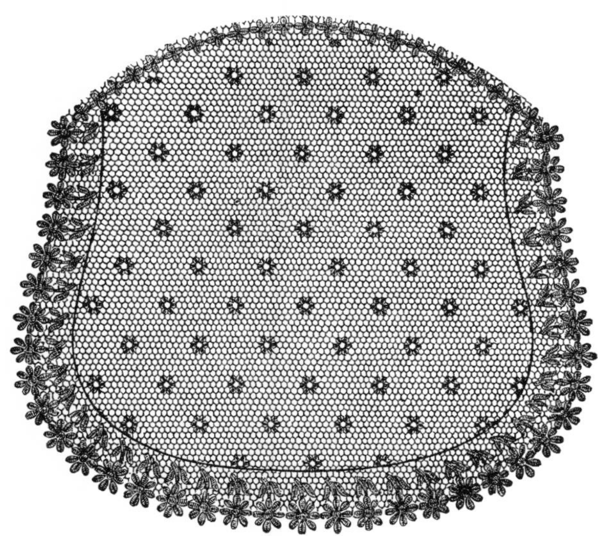

Embroidered Lace Veil

There are two favorite shapes for veils. One is the veil with tabs, which is fastened either over or under the chignon, or under the chin. The other is the short veil illustrated. The pattern of half the veil is given. The original is of black silk lace. The foundation is ornamented with small star figures, which are worked on the lace with black silk twist in the same manner as guipure on netting. The veil is bordered with wide edging, a section of which is shown full size. This is worked in the same manner as the figures. Above the lace may be worked the border illustrated. It is worked in point de minute. In working any of the embroidery, take care to hold the lace smooth and not draw it up with the stitches.

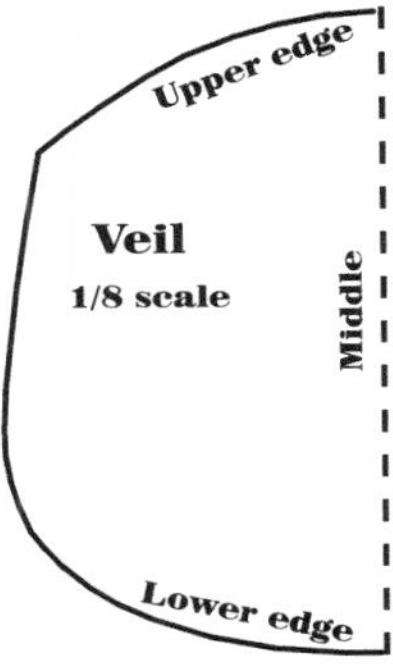

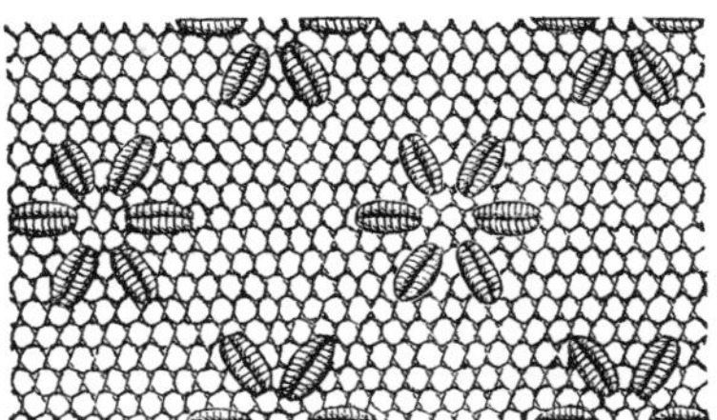

Figure 1. Figure in point de minute

Figure 2. Section of edging

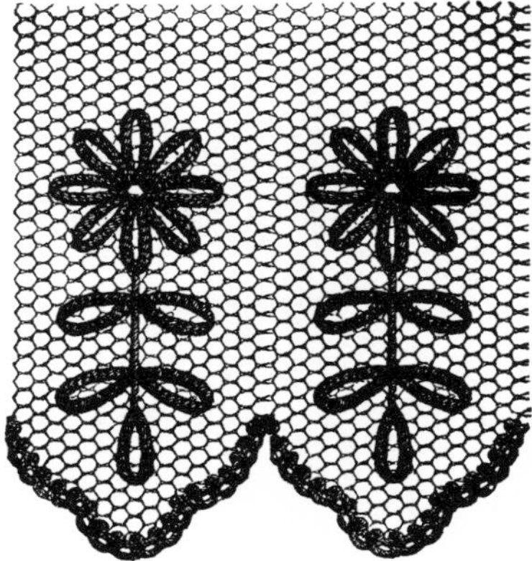

Figure 3. Section of edging

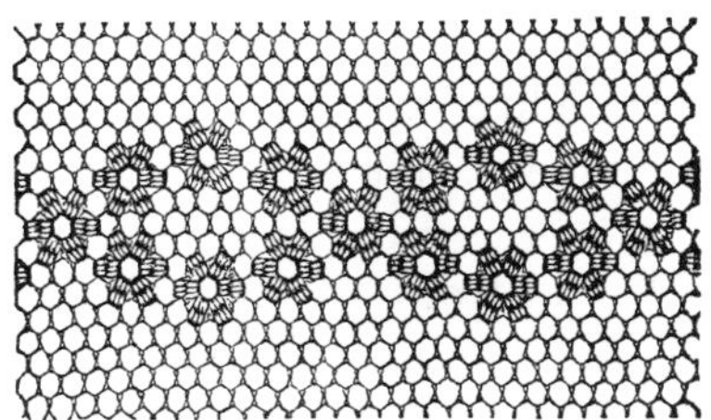

Figure 4. Border

June 27, 1868

Dress and Outer Wear Trimmings

These trimmings are for dresses, jackets, cloaks, etc. The materials requisite for making them are silk or satin, silk braid of different kinds, cord, silk twist, and beads. They are partly arranged on pasteboard and partly on wooden molds.

The trimming in Figure 1 is of fine silk braid. In making the upper part the braid is sewn on a pasteboard foundation previously covered with silk. The openwork parts are trimmed with beads. In the center of the upper part is set a small rosette of ribbon and beads.

Figure 1. Silk braid trimming

The rosette in Figure 2 is a beautiful trimming for stylish talmas and cloaks. The foundation, which forms part of an edge, is composed of pasteboard covered with silk. In the center is set a jet button, and around this is wound the silk braid, which is sewn fast to the foundation. A few cords of silk and beads join this rosette to the border.

Figure 2. Rosette trimming

The upper part of the fringe trimming in Figure 3 is of satin, bordered with fine braid and ornamented with braid and beads. The braid is then arranged in long ends, which are finished by tassels of silk twist and beads.

Figure 3. Fringe trimming

The wooden molds for the grelot tassel in Figure 4 are covered either by stretching threads of silk lengthwise and afterward weaving through them, or with crochet work. The stitch used for this is peculiar. It consists of slip stitches, which are worked from left to right, always putting the needle through the upper vein of a stitch of the last round. The under side of the work is the right side of the finished work.

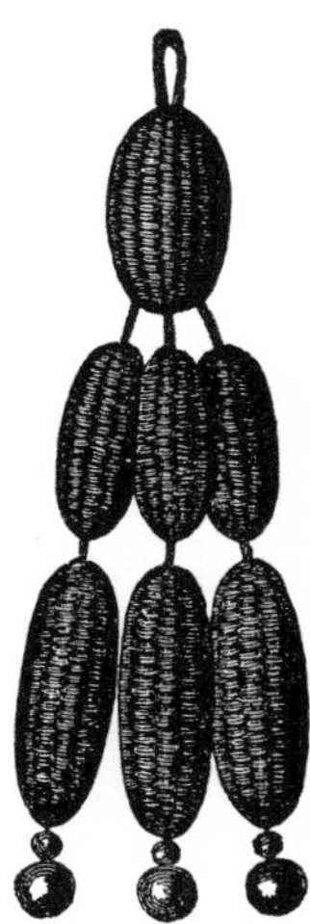

Figure 4. Grelot tassel

The trimming in Figure 5 is designed for the side and back seams of cloaks. The upper part consists of a pasteboard foundation, which is covered with silk, embroidered with cord, and bordered with beads. It is finished in the center with a jet button in the form of a star. The trellised portion is made of silk twist and beads. The fringe on the end is of bugles and beads strung on silk twist.

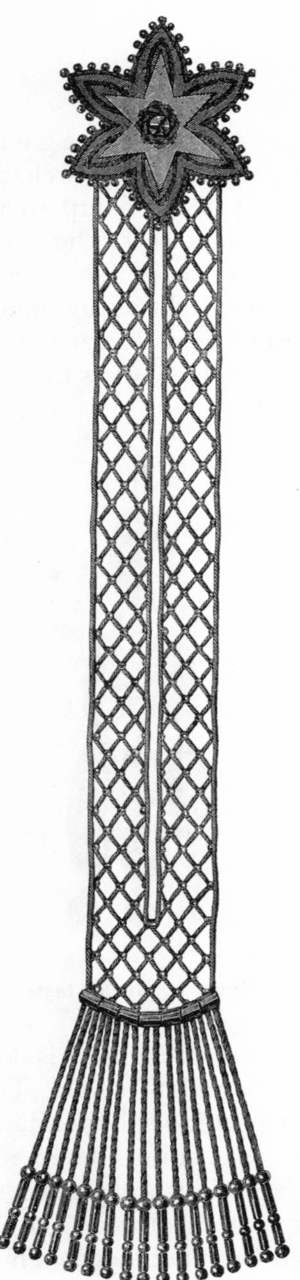

Figure 5. Beaded trimming–three-quarter size

The trimming in Figure 6 may be used as a heading for a tassel, or a clasp, or several of them may be arranged to form a border. It is composed of a pasteboard foundation, covered with satin. It is bordered with cord and beads, and embroidered with bugles and beads.

Figure 6. Heading or border

The upper part of the trimming in Figure 7 consists of two circular wooden molds, one within the other, covered with satin. It is embroidered with cord and braid, and bordered with the same cord arranged in loops. Two ends of braid or crochet work proceed from the center of the button. They terminate in silk tassels, which are surmounted with braid.

Figure 7. Tassel trimming

The head of the tassel in Figure 8 is composed of two flat and one round wooden molds, covered with woven silk twist. Braid may also be used for this covering. Bead cord and silk cord, with the ends raveled out, form the tassel.

Figure 8. Tassel trimming

The center of the rosette in Figure 9 is a star, formed of a pasteboard foundation, covered with satin, and embroidered with beads. The remainder is of silk cord and beads.

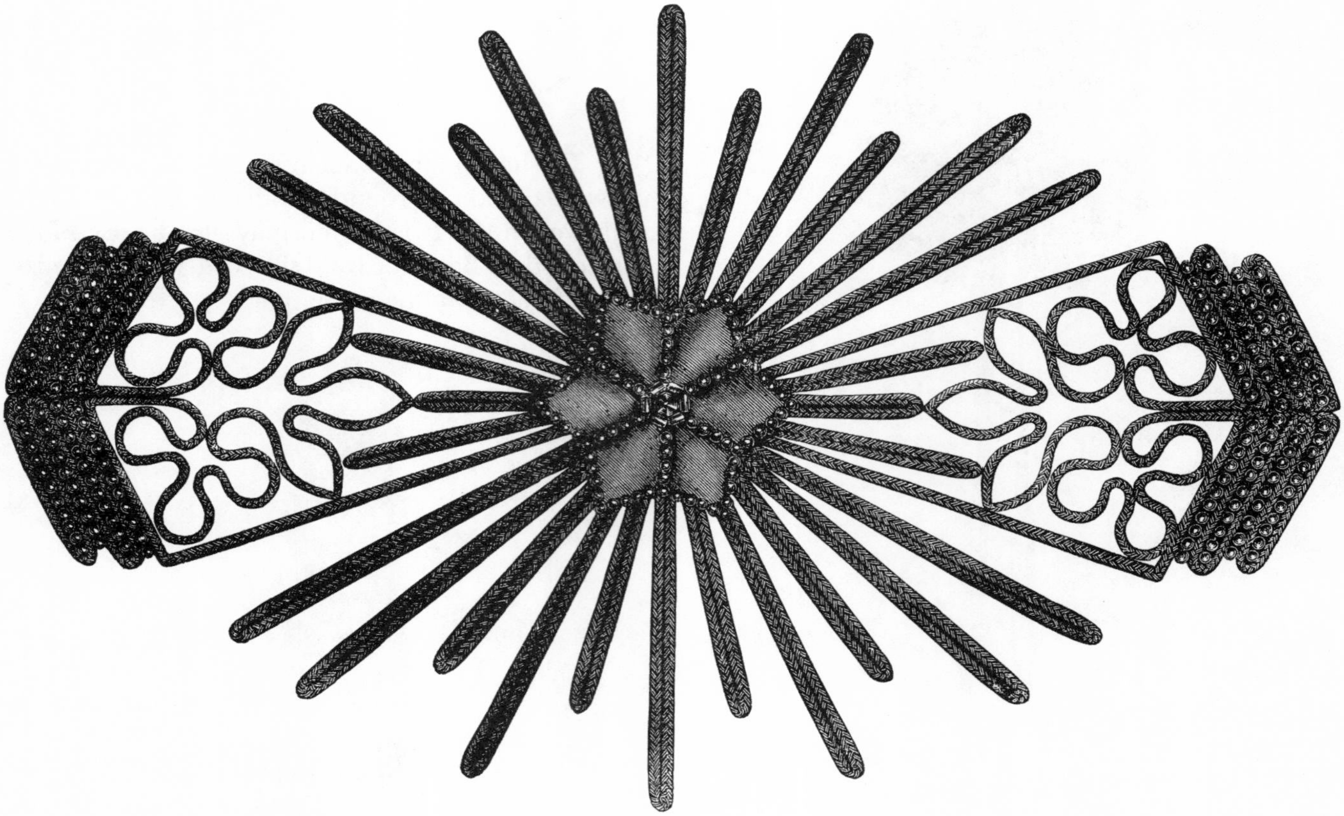

June 27, 1868

Figure 9. Rosette trimming

Figure 10 shows a clasp, in the form of an escutcheon, of silk and pasteboard. The application figure is worked in ribbed crochet stitch. The clasp is bordered with fine silk cord and beads. The fringe is formed of bugles and beads, strung on silk twist.

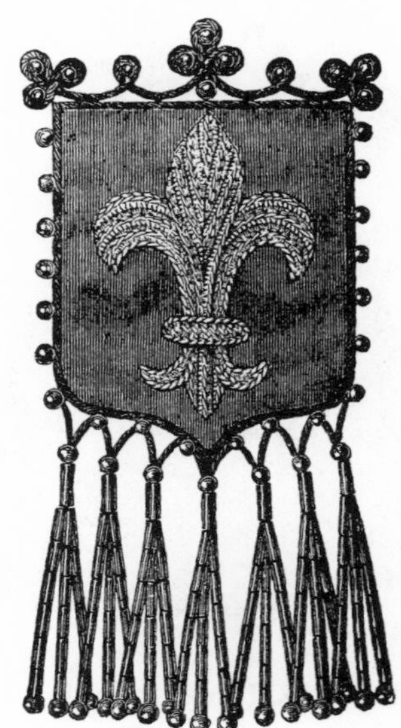

Figure 10. Clasp

July 4, 1868

Summer Bonnets

The picturesque mantilla bonnet is the most attractive of the summer styles, and is selected for evening drives, fêtes, and the watering places. The mantilla veil draping the head and shoulders is the principal feature of the bonnet, and gives its name to the coiffure. While this pretty caprice revives fading beauty, it is equally capable of heightening youthful charms.

This Spanish fashion has made black lace a universal favorite for summer bonnets. It was once thought that black lace was only suitable for elderly ladies. But gossamer tulle and Chantilly in fanciful puffs and flowing drapery, ornamented with field flowers, with metallic leaves, and real butterflies and insects, are gay enough for the most youthful belle of the season.

Among the flowers used are field blossoms of every hue, arranged in the same cluster. These are prettily made of feathers, imitating nature admirably. Dark crimson roses, and bright solferino shades are seen instead of the invariable scarlet rose so long worn. Diadems are made of dwarfed wheat, half ripe, or metallic leaves of a golden brown or yellowish green shade. Ivy and myrtle leaves of the deepest green, and trailing grasses, hang loosely over the chignon.

The prettiest straw bonnets are made of straw lace in guipure patterns over colored silk. Rows of the lace are sewn together, and finished with a straw fringe at the back.

Round Hats

Among round hats the Marie Antoinette is selected for the seaside and watering places. It has a high flat crown, with broad rim gracefully curved.

Another seaside and garden hat is appropriately called the Mandarin. It is broad and flat like the Chinese umbrellas, and serves at once for bonnet and parasol. It approaches almost to a point in the center. The only trimming is a cluster of lace, ribbon, and wheatears directly on the top. A veil of spotted tulle is fixed permanently to the hat beneath the trimming on the top, and falls below the rim all round. A row of black lace trims the rim inside.

A jaunty hat, designed for the races, is called the Nymph. A favorite model is of black crinoline. It is simply a high, round crown, encircled with parallel rows of black satin piping. A quilling of lace with a vine of jet leaves in the center forms the only rim or border. At the side is a cluster of field daisies, wild violets, and cornflowers. A mantilla veil of dotted blonde falls over the chignon, and is caught in front by a similar cluster of flowers.

Turbans are worn very high, and are broad enough to fit the head and reach slightly over the chignon. This is a more comfortable shape than the narrow-peaked hats of last season. The rim is curved outward, and turned up around the edge. A fall of lace, shaped like the mantilla veil, but narrower, is added to turbans, giving them very much the appearance of bonnets. They are surrounded by steel bands for trimming. Flowers and lace are sewn on the curved borders.

Traveling hats of piqué, linen, and shirred cambric, made on rattans and cords, are in favor.

Varieties in Dress

Short muslin dresses for evening may be made available for promenade and driving costumes by the addition of a fichu or polonaise.

Chambray gauze is the favorite material of the season for full dress. It has all the luster and light gossamer appearance of grenadine, but is more substantial, and does not so soon become limp and stringy. White is especially desirable for evening dress, trimmed with satin bands of a bright color piped with white. Stripes of buttercup color, of violet, wood color, or grass green alternating with white, are made with long skirts scalloped at the edge, and bound with satin of the same shade as the stripe. The scallops must be faced with white net to stiffen them and prevent curling up. The net facing is not hemmed at the upper edge, as it is held securely by the binding.

A novelty in dress goods is chambray gauze over satin of a contrasting color, producing the beautiful chameleon effect now so much in vogue. A dark rich combination, suitable for a brunette, is black gauze over cherry satin; for a blonde, transparent white over sea green, and blue over gold. Pearl gray and pink, lavender and buttercup color, and green over rose, are displayed together, blending with pleasing effect. These goods come in dress patterns, of which there are no duplicates. The gauze is arranged over the satin and folded with it as they are to be cut together.

A pale shade of buff just now in favor is described by fashion writers under several different names, such as sulfur, corn color, salmon, and lastly *couleur d'Isabelle*, suggestive to those versed in Spanish history of soiled linen.

Foulard suits in this new tint are selected for afternoon dresses. Dark brown and gray foulards, with skirts of different shades of the same color, were made up for the Jerome races. Mantillas and pelerine capes loosely tied behind are worn over the polonaise. When there are two skirts the mantilla is the only wrapping.

A unique addition to dressy toilettes is a kind of apron that almost forms a third skirt. It is cut long and rounding in front, sloping upward at the sides to the back, where it is held by a rosette or bow with sash ends. The upper skirt is raised at the sides and back in large puffs, and trimmed like the apron with crosscut bands of satin. The lower skirt is plain.

A black velvet waistband, resembling the peasant waists formerly worn, is beaded with jet. At the back and sides are cords and tassels for looping up the dress skirts.

The cardinal collar of linen, 2 inches wide all around, shaped to fit the slope of the neck, is selected for breakfast and street dress, instead of the standing collar. The Oxford or sailor's collar, deeply pointed on the shoulder, is worn by young ladies and blondes. Such breadth of plain linen is found to be very trying to dark complexions. A band of velvet, either black or colored, worn above the collar, is a relief to the glazed surface. We again remind our readers that dresses are cut very much lower at the throat, and simply corded without the standing binding lately worn.

Bathing suits of buff, blue, white, and scarlet serge are made with full blouses pleated into a square yoke. The sleeves are full and gathered into a band at the wrist. The trousers are buttoned at the sides and held full at the ankle. The trimming is wide braid of a contrasting color. Self-colored flannels and the shepherd's plaid, small black and white check, make neat and inexpensive suits trimmed with black braid. Serge is trimmed with appliqué of merino in fanciful designs.

Morning Dress

The cape on this dress is peculiar, but dressy. The sleeves at the wrist, and the upper part of the pocket, are gathered by an elastic cord. The original is of soft, light gray poplin, fastened in front with large covered buttons, and stitched on the outer edge with black silk.

Cut from the front and back each two pieces, leaving the length of the skirt as much longer than the pattern as may be desired. Cut two pieces from each pattern for the sleeves and pockets, allowing 1 1/2 inches for a hem on the upper part of the pockets. Cut from the upper cape, the under cape, and the collar each one piece; the collar double. Prepare the middle pieces, simulating capes. These are 4 inches wide, and must be the same length as the cape, and so sloped that the seam by which the first is sewn on falls on the line partly drawn in the under cape pattern.

Face the fronts. Sew the buttons on the left side, and work the buttonholes in the right side. Backstitch together the fronts and back. The skirt bottom is faced with a bias strip of the same material. Hem the upper part of the pockets. Run in an elastic cord next the lower part of the hem. Set the pockets on the skirt as shown by the figures on the pattern. Join the two sleeve pieces from 5 to 6 and from 7 to 8. Face the sleeves at the wrist. Run in an elastic cord 1/2 inch from the edge. Set the sleeves in the armholes according to the figures.

Next arrange the cape. Take up the shoulder seams in the under cape. Finish the lower and side edges of the under cape and upper cape, and the two pieces imitating middle capes, with a narrow bias facing. Sew the pieces along the designated lines on the under cape. Join the under cape and the upper cape at the neck. Fasten the cape to the dress. The neck is bound, and fastened with a hook and eye.

July 4, 1868

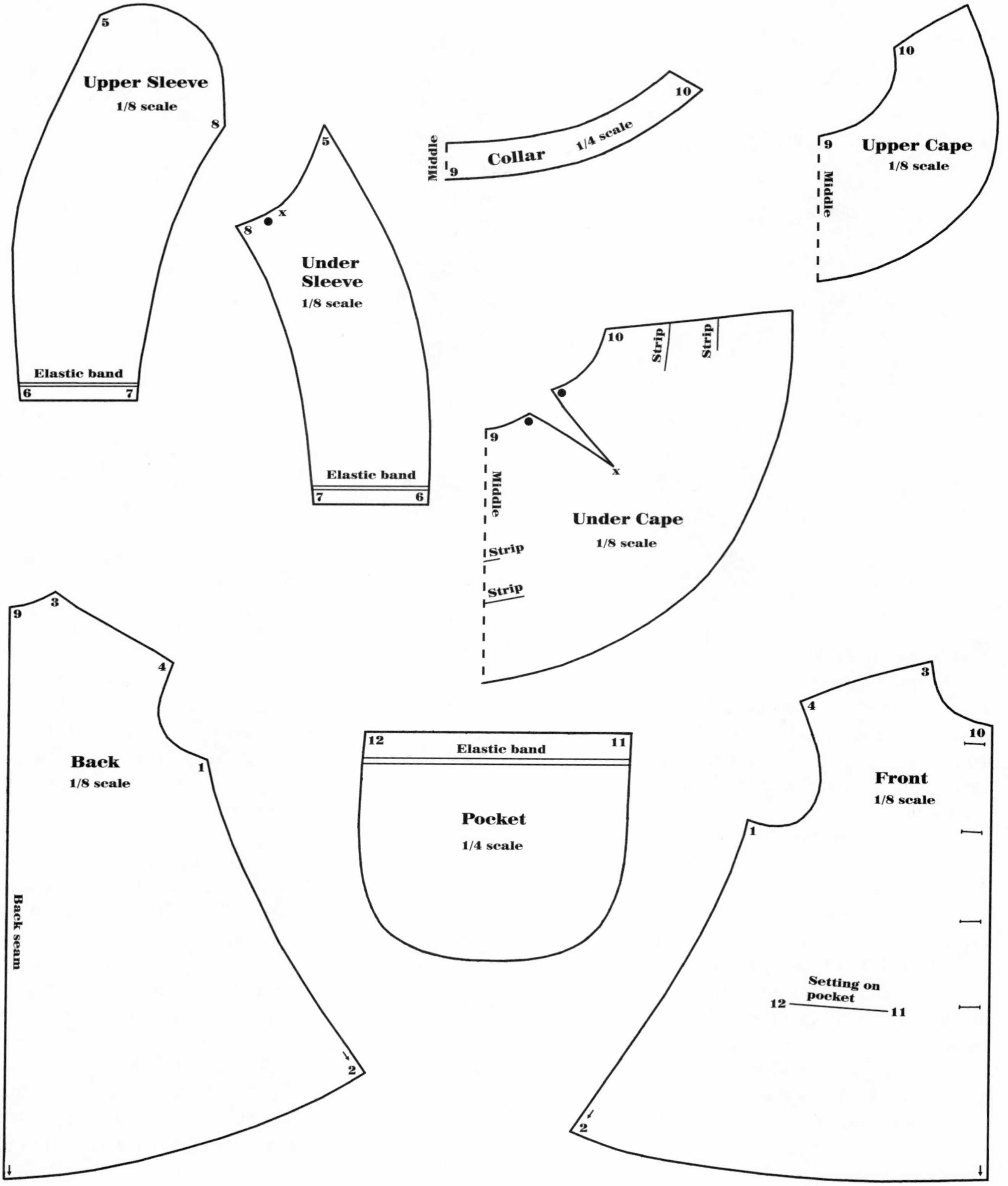
Upper Sleeve
1/8 scale
5
8
Elastic band
6
7
Under Sleeve
1/8 scale
5
8
x
Elastic band
7
6
Collar
1/4 scale
Middle
9
10
Upper Cape
1/8 scale
10
9
Middle
Under Cape
1/8 scale
10
9
x
Strip
Strip
Middle
Strip
Strip
Back
1/8 scale
9
3
4
1
2
Back seam
Pocket
1/4 scale
12
Elastic band
11
Front
1/8 scale
3
4
10
1
Setting on pocket
12
11
2

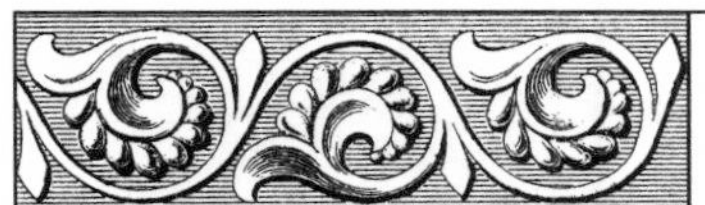

White Satin Ribbon Sash

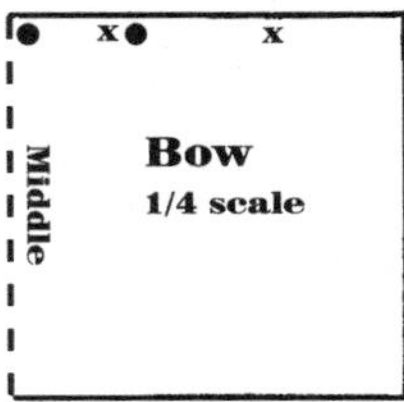

End
1/8 scale

White Satin Ribbon Sash

This sash is of white satin ribbon, 10 inches wide. The ends are finished with knotted fringe. The top is arranged in two or three pleats. For the bow, cut of the satin ribbon and stiff lace lining four pieces from the pattern. Baste the satin on the lining. Then trim one edge, and turn over both corners so the trimmed edge lies full in the middle of the triangle thus formed. Lay four pleats on each of these pieces, always bringing *x* on •. Sew the leaves thus formed on a foundation of the lining. Cover the place where they are sewn on with a satin loop. Having fastened the pleated sash ends under the bow, sew the whole to a belt made of satin folds.

Sash End
1/8 scale

Black Grosgrain Sash

This sash consists of two ends, for which a pattern is given. They are finished on the bottom with black silk knotted fringe, in one long loop 12 inches wide and two shorter ones, each 6 inches wide. The place where these are set on the belt, which is also of black grosgrain, is covered with a pleated piece of the same material.

Peasant Waist with Tunic and Sash

The original is of black grosgrain, trimmed with bias satin folds, black lace, and satin buttons.

For the waist cut of black grosgrain and muslin lining two pieces from the front, side front, side back, and back bretelle, and from the back one piece. Hem the fronts 1 1/2 inches wide. Work the buttonholes, and put on the buttons. Bind the upper and front edges with a narrow satin binding. Finish the upper edge with lace. Trim also the side front pieces with binding, lace, and buttons. Sew them to the fronts according to the figures on the pattern. Trim the back on the upper edge with binding and lace. Backstitch together all the parts of the waist according to the figures on the pattern. Trim the bretelles with satin binding and lace, and sew them on.

The tunic, which is sewn on the waist, has the form of a short gored skirt. It is open in front and rounded behind. It is trimmed on the edge with binding and lace, pleated at the sides, and fastened up with sashes, the edges of which are also bound and finished with lace. These sash ends are the continuation of the side front pieces. Similar sash ends are arranged on the back to appear to be a continuation of the bretelles.

The belt, which is made of satin and lined with some stiff material, covers the seam where the back sash ends are set on. This belt is fastened at the side.

Side Front
1/4 scale
38 37 31 33 34 32

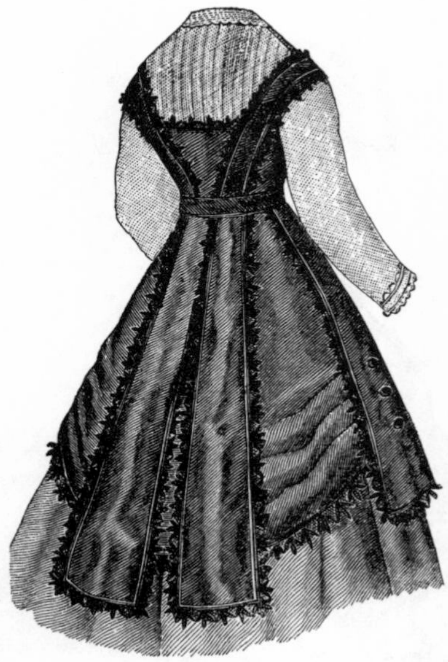

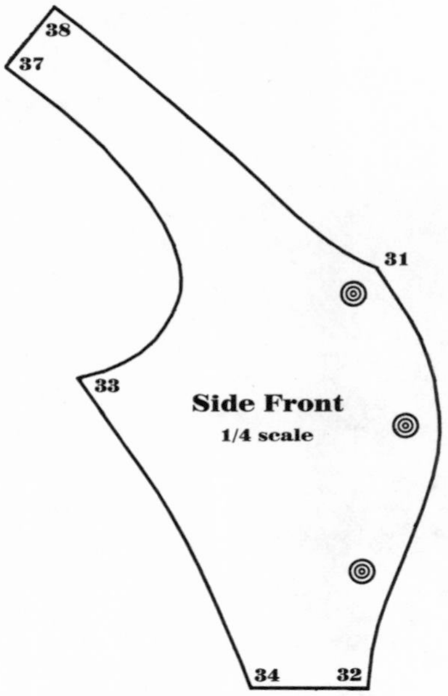

Front
1/4 scale
31 32

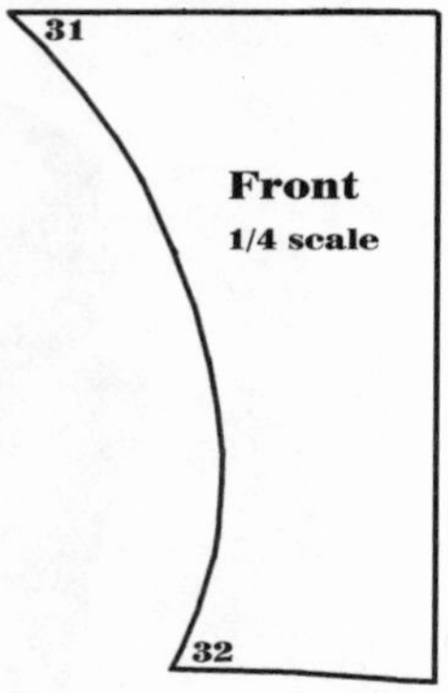

Back
1/4 scale
38 37 35 36
Middle of back

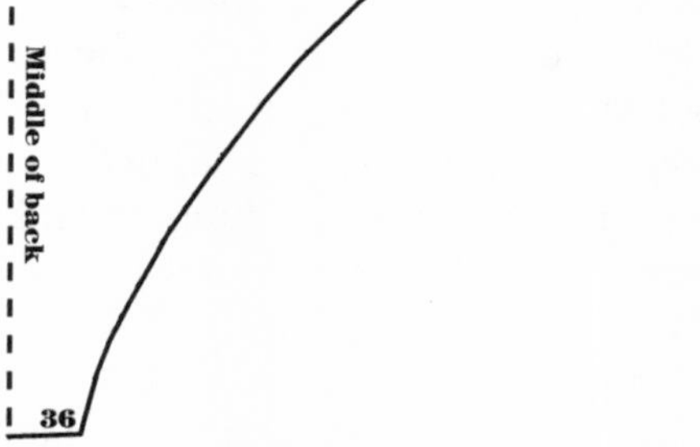

Back Bretelle
1/4 scale
38 37 39 36

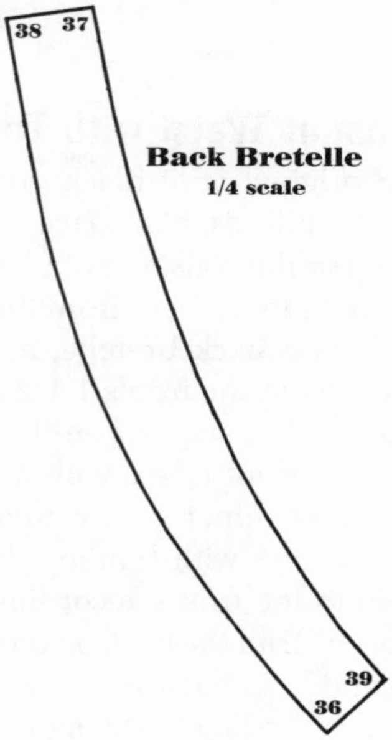

Side Back
1/4 scale
35 33 36 39 34

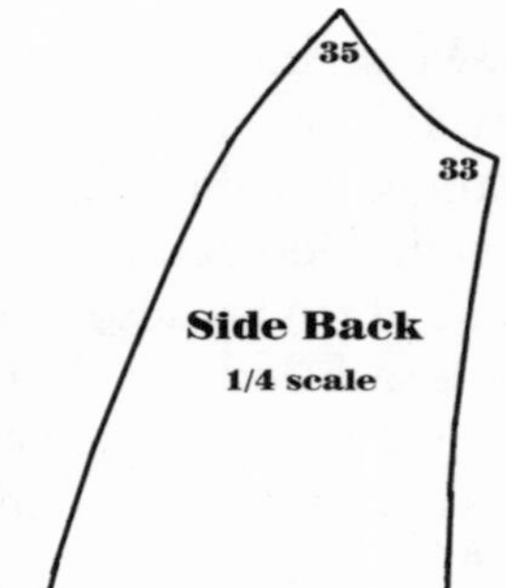

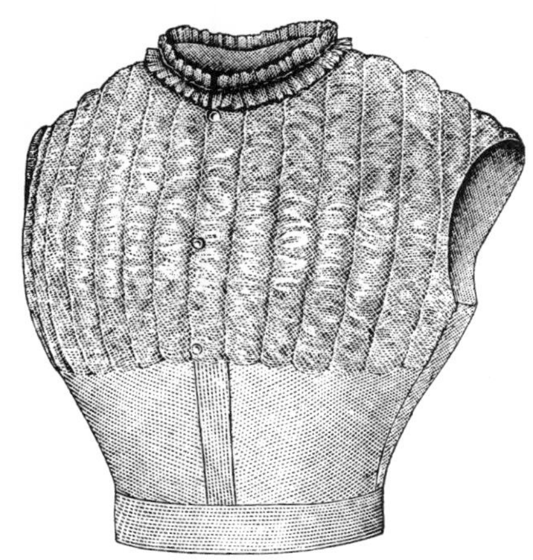

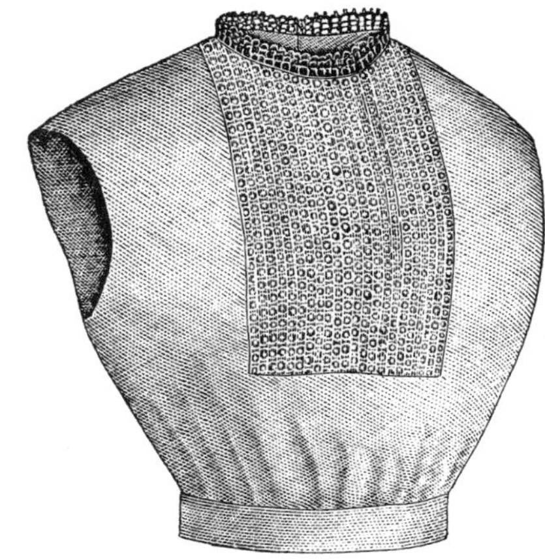

Illusion Chemisette

This chemisette may be worn with low-necked dresses or Swiss waists. It is puffed and finished around the neck with a narrow ruche.

Cut of thin muslin the fronts, allowing 1 inch for the front hems. Cut the back in one piece. Hem the fronts. Cover these and the back from the neck down to the narrow line on the pattern with puffs of illusion. For the puffs gather the illusion at regular distances of 1 1/2 inches, and sew to the waist loosely enough to form puffs. The hem of the right front must be covered by the puffing, and furnished with a few buttonhole loops. The hem of the left front remains loose and is furnished with little porcelain buttons.

Join the back and fronts according to the figures on the pattern. Hem the under edge. Face the neck and armholes with a narrow bias strip of thin muslin. Finish the neck by a ruche of illusion.

Muslin and Tatting Chemisette

This chemisette is designed to be worn with Pompadour dresses. It is made from the same pattern as the Illusion Chemisette, but opens behind instead of in front. It is made of Swiss muslin with a tatted bosom. The neck is also bordered with tatted edging.

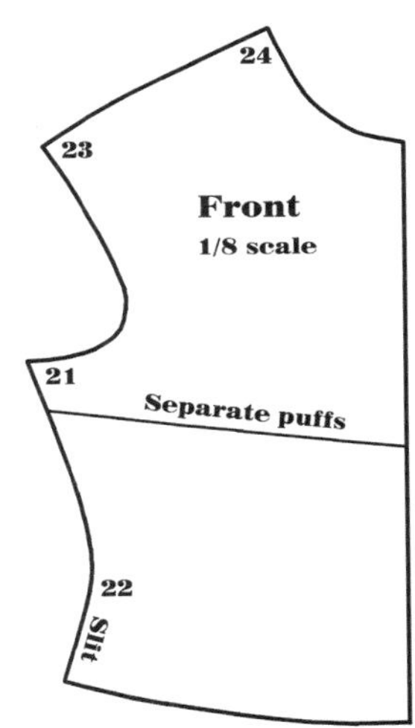

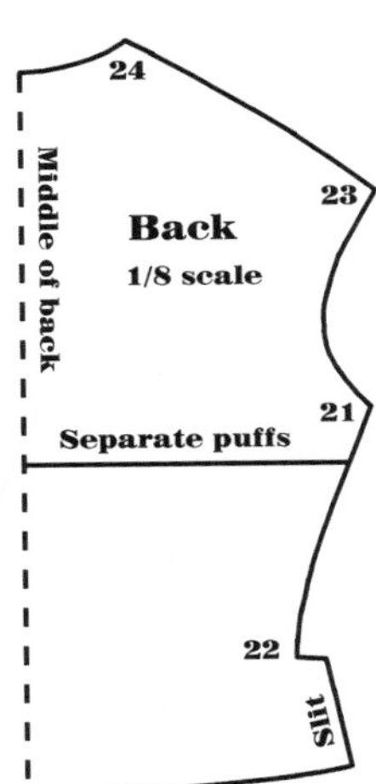

Black Silk Apron

Cut the middle breadth and side breadth. Sew them together according to the figures on the pattern. Hem the sides and under edge, or face with a strip of silk. Bind the upper edge with a belt of the material, lined with black silk. This belt is fastened at the side.

The middle part is trimmed on the bottom by a box-pleated flounce of the silk. Each pleat is again pleated in the middle. The upper edge of the flounce and the seams that join the middle and side pieces of the apron are trimmed with a row of puffs. For these puffs take a strip of the silk 3 inches wide. Hem both sides very narrow. Lay pleats at regular distances, so that they form a puff between each pleat. The pleating is hidden by small satin crossbands simulating clasps.

Black Silk Apron

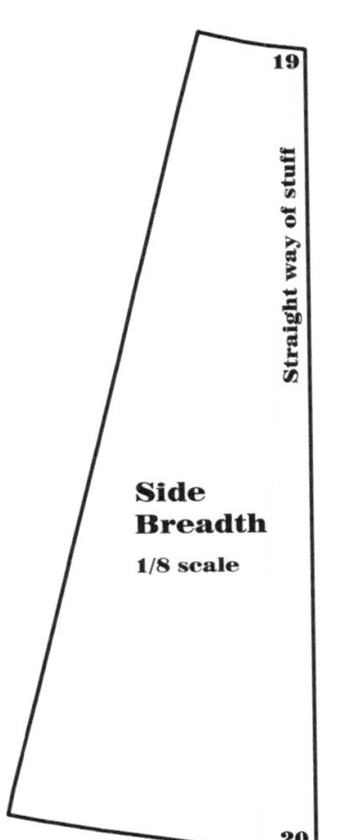

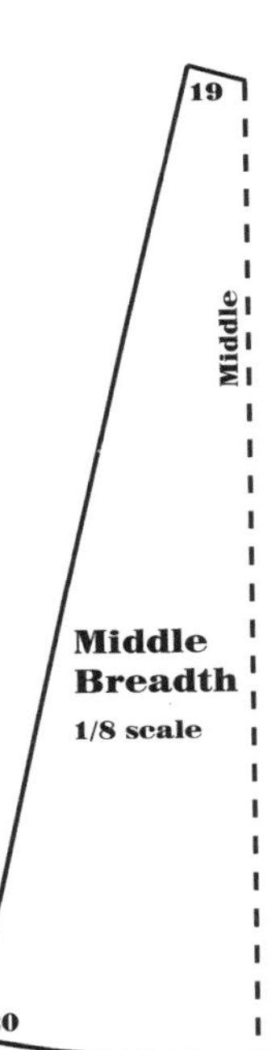

Black Silk Apron

This apron is cut from the same pattern as the Black Silk Apron above. The trimming consists of bands of bias silk. These are arranged at regular intervals and of a width varying to correspond with the sloping of the side pieces. Hold these bands loosely when sewing them on. Pleat each band in the middle. Cover the pleating with small loops of black satin. The remaining trimming consists of bias strips of silk 1 inch wide. These are lined with stiff muslin, and sewn on with a satin braid on both sides.

Helgolander Garden Hat

This garden hat completely protects the head and neck from the sun, and is, besides, easily made. The original is of colored linen, trimmed with a ruche of the same material.

Cut first the front. This is 32 inches long by 12 inches wide and of double material, straight on one side, but sloped from the middle each way on the other side till each end is only 9 inches wide. Backstitch the front across at regular distances of about 2 inches apart, forming spaces for the strips of pasteboard that are to be inserted. The edge of the front is bound with narrow ribbon. On the back lay a pleat between the middle strips of pasteboard.

Next cut one piece from the pattern. Hem the bottom narrow. Gather as shown by the pattern. Make two pleats on the upper edge, bringing *x* on •. Sew this to the back of the front piece. Finish by trimming the edge as well as the seam where the crown and cape are joined to the front with a linen ruche. The ruche is made by box pleating a double strip 1 1/2 inches wide.

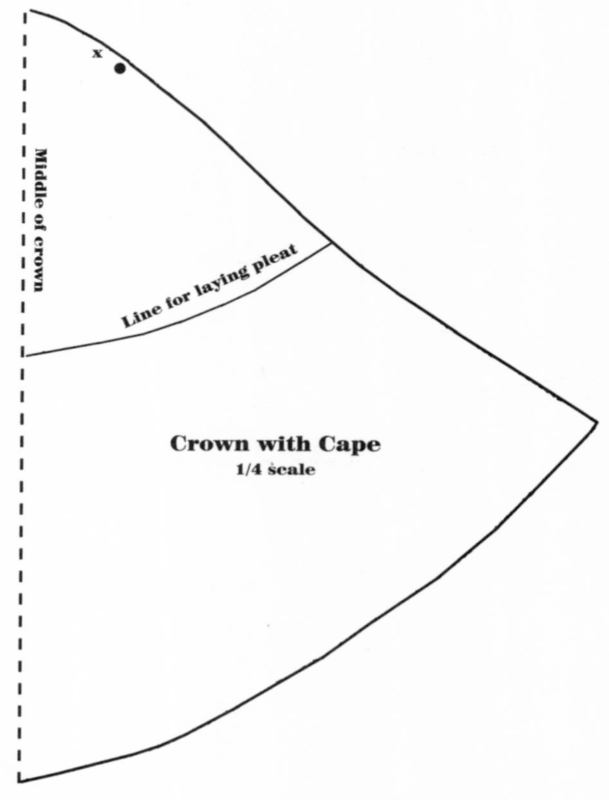

Talma with Sash Ends

Both dress and talma are of gray foulard. The talma is finished on the bottom with a crimped silk fringe, about 6 inches wide. It is afterward looped up in the middle of the back and fastened with a bow and ends of the same material. The knot of the bow is formed of a large leaf made in lacework of beads, cord, and gimp. The talma is fastened in front by a small bow with ends. This is also finished in the middle with a large leaf made in bead satin stitch on a stiff foundation.

July 4, 1868

Cut from the pattern two pieces, which are to be sewn together in the back. Take up the shoulder pleats. Face the edge with a piece of the material about 2 inches wide, also fastening the edges. In the middle of the back lay the stuff in pleats, always bringing *x* on •. Finish the edge with the fringe. Cover the place where the pleats are taken up with the bow.

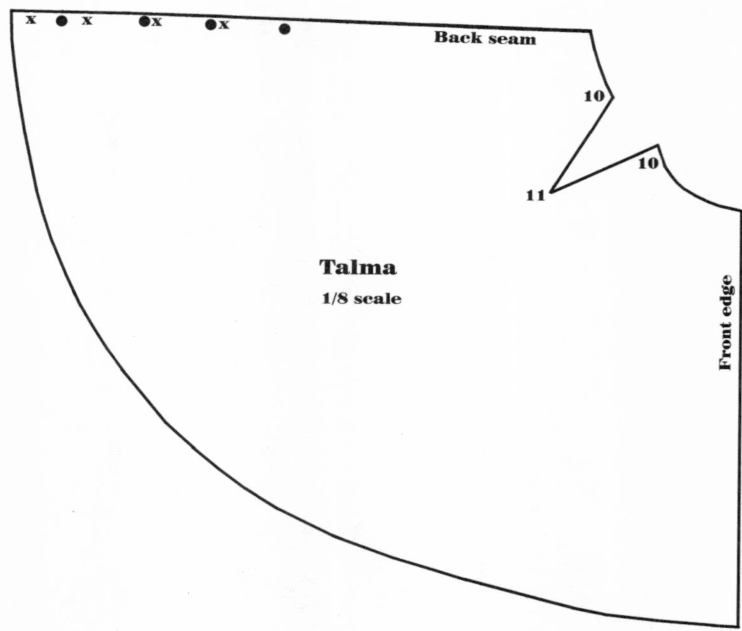

July 11, 1868

Wrappings

Notwithstanding the prevalent fashion of complete costumes for street dress, several new styles of mantles have been introduced this season. Outside garments for short suits are usually made with sleeves, as the polonaise and Watteau, or in fichus with sashes. Only a few scarf mantillas are made of the same material as the dress. Black wrappings, sold separately to be worn over any dress, are either scarf burnooses or of circular shape. Glossy faille and poult-de-soie are the materials for heavy mantles; a cashmere with crêpe finish is an intermediate article; and grenadine and net are the next grade below lace.

A stylish and peculiar mantle is called the Maintenon. The front and back shoulder pieces and sashes are of silk. The fall over the arms resembling sleeves, and the side bodies, are of guipure lace.

The most useful garment of the season is a polonaise or redingote of black silk, as it serves for an overdress to skirts of all the different colors. It is cut closer to the figure than those made in the winter, and is confined at the waist by a belt and short sash of four large loops, and wide fringed ends. The neck should be *en revers,* rolling almost to the belt. The front of the skirt should be fastened at the side seams so the full width may be rounded, and left without a row of buttons down the center, thus giving the appearance of an upper skirt. White bodies of tucked muslin, with turndown collars and cuffs, are worn with the colored skirt.

Fringe and lace are the most fashionable trimmings. Guipure lace is again very much used, and is imported in new designs of medieval patterns, and in leaves without flowers. A succession of small, narrow satin folds, ruches, quillings, or passementerie form the heading for fringe and lace. Buttons are large and flat. Tassels with square heads, long pendant cones, and flat grelots are used to ornament sleeves and revers.

Lace Garments

It is in lace wrappings that the greatest variety of shape is seen. These fanciful styles of mantles are not made in real lace. Chantilly, point, and fine thread mantles retain the standard shawl shape, with occasionally a circular garment. The burnooses, polonaises, and fanchonettes are considered only transitory fashions. They are made of the woven lama, or the new princesse lace. This closely imitates thread and has fine meshes. It is very soft, without that harsh wiriness peculiar to woven lace. The figures are shaded, woven thick and thin, producing a pretty effect when worn over colored silk.

Large lace points are not graceful with short dresses, nor are they now considered stylish with trained skirts when hanging plain from the shoulders. Ladies who possess valuable mantles are making them available by arranging a burnoose fold at the back, or by looping them in several folds at the neck, with a thread bow and barbe for ornament, or a rosette of lace or ribbon. The folds look careless and unstudied, but are arranged by the modiste with great care to prevent the lace from being injured.

Ladies who cannot afford to buy thread lace, and who object to lama, are advised that paletots and mantillas of guipure net can be made in good style at very small expense compared with the prices asked for imported mantles. The quaint, curious designs of guipure are particularly suitable for the present picturesque style of dress. Some pretty garments are formed of guipure insertion in lengthwise or diagonal rows, carefully sewn together. These jackets have the advantage over imported ones in being fitted to the figure for which they are designed. Bands of colored velvet are passed through the meshes of the lace to enliven the toilette when worn with a white dress.

Carriage Wrappings

The Bedouin style is repeated in all kinds of material for carriage and evening wrappings. Soft chiné crêpe, goat's hair, and woolen grenadine scarves, with the Arab fold in the back, are displayed in solid white, blue, or scarlet, and in stripes of color alternating with white.

The large round burnoose of fine cashmere, lined with soft Marseilles silk, is the favorite shape of the *sortie de bal.*

The Russian baschlik is in favor at the watering places. It is a hood meant to be worn on the head, and not merely for ornament. A cape, with long tasseled ends, covers the shoulders and crosses in front, affording the protection so necessary with low evening dresses after leaving a heated ballroom. It is an inexpensive and picturesque wrapping.

Seaside and Yachting Jackets

Seaside and yachting jackets of white serge are made short, close fitting, with nearly tight sleeves. They are buttoned with shell-shaped buttons of a color matching the silk with which they are trimmed. These jackets display a good figure to advantage, and are sought after during the boating season. The trimming is a fold of blue or scarlet grosgrain, with fluted shells of the same pendant as a border. A blue serge jacket, bordered with white, is made with pointed revers, disclosing a habit shirt.

The Moorish jacket is piquante and gay. It is made of black crêpe cloth, with sleeves, rounded in front to show a lace bodice. The back has pointed basques. The front and basques are braided with gilt, in arabesque patterns. Ball fringe of black and gilt on the edge.

Traveling Wrappings

The plaid Galway or Colleen Bawn circular of Scotch plaid is desirable for an extra covering in traveling. It has an upper cape, looped up in the back, with two rosettes. A burnoose of gray cloth, with bright plaid border, is reversible, being plaid on the under side, with a gray border. Waterproof blouses, with sleeves and cape, are confined by a belt, and reach to the edge of the dress. Gray linen overalls, similarly made, are preferred to the circular dusters.

Tatted and Crocheted Insertion

Tatted and Crocheted Insertion

This insertion is for chemises Russe, etc. It is worked with fine crochet cotton, the figures being first wrought. Each figure consists of four rings, and each ring of 9 ds. (double stitches), 1 picot (p.), 9 ds. Having worked four of these rings close together, tie the beginning and end threads, by means of which are formed the four-leaved figures.

These are joined by crochet stitches as follows. First round: Work 1 sl. (slip stitch), in a picot of a ring of a four-leaved figure, * 10 ch. (chain stitches), 1 sl. in the picot of the following ring, 10 ch., 1 sl. in the picot of the third ring, and at the same time in a picot of the new four-leaved figure. Repeat from *.

Second round: Work 1 tc. (treble crochet) in the 1st sl. of the former round. But, in completing this, a new tatted figure must be joined, which is done as follows. Just before the thread is brought through the last time, run the needle through a picot of the new figure. Then bring the thread through it and the loops already on the needle at the same time. Then 10 ch., 1 tc. in the next sl. of the former round. But, before completing the stitch, run the needle through the picot of the next ring of the figure just fastened on and also through a picot of a new figure. Draw the thread through both picots and the loops already on the needle at the same time. Then again 10 ch., 1 tc. in the next sl., fastening on the picot of the following ring. Repeat from *.

Third round: * Work 1 sl. in the picot of the lower ring of the first figure, 10 ch., 1 sl. in the 1st tc., 10 ch. Repeat from *. The remainder of the work can be easily executed from the illustration.

Having completed the requisite amount, run through it narrow ribbon or velvet.

July 18, 1868

Ladies' Hairdressing

The front hair, in order to be stylish, must be profusely crêpéd, and chignons increase in size in the same ratio that bonnets decrease. A quantity of false hair arranged in a variety of ways has become an important item in a lady's outfit. Its use is so universal that ladies no longer hesitate to acknowledge it. It can be removed at night; whereas an abundant suit of natural hair is uncomfortable to sleep in. Hairdressers say it is easier to arrange separate braids and switches that can be pinned on just when they are needed.

Light hair is at present so much the fashion that a yellowish powder, like the pollen of flowers, is used to make dark hair a regular blonde color. The antique powder and diamond dust are not so much used as during the winter.

"Boiled" Hair

Frizettes and braid puffs, over which chignons are arranged, are too warm and heavy for summer. A plan for dispensing with them and making a fine display of a small quantity of hair is called "boiling." It must be done by an experienced person.

The braid is plaited in innumerable tiny braids and put in a pot of boiling water. After it has been boiled for three or four hours it is dried by "baking" in an oven. When the small braids are taken out the hair will be crimped in the style now so fashionable, and the crimp will remain permanently, defying all moisture to make it limp. The crimps make the hair stand out so lightly that frizettes are not needed. It is then loosely plaited in a large "three plait" to form the chignon, and after being wound into shape is held securely by an invisible net. Such chignons weigh only two or three ounces, and may readily be put on without the aid of a hairdresser.

Hints About the Coiffure

The most stylishly arranged coiffures are those that appear to be dressed with the least care. This is, however, studied carelessness, and in it lies the perfection of the hairdresser's art. Long curls are only loosely curled at the ends and crimped. Chignons are loose and "fluffy," and puffs and frizzes are stuck about on the head in impossible places, where they never could have grown.

The chignon should be dressed close to the head, retaining something of the natural contour, instead of projecting from it as many ladies wear it, especially when puffs and frizettes are used. The object seems to be to cover the whole head with the chignon, as it is worn very far forward, often quite to the front crimps, and falls over the back of the head down to the growth of the hair on the neck.

Crimped chignons in large plaits and puffs are in favor for dressy occasions. The front hair is crêpéd, and a long curl is worn over the left shoulder. A succession of thin rolls, forming a coil, are preferred for morning and traveling coiffures. The Grecian twist, surrounded by a heavy plait, has been in favor for a long while and is still worn. A puffed center, with a crimped braid, is also very pretty, and easily arranged by the wearer.

Amazon Coiffure

A full-dress coiffure, called the Amazon, is admired for summer wear. It is formed of several rows of short curls, about 4 inches long, attached to a net foundation. The hair is exceedingly fine, and is not so heavy as the Grecian curls that are pulled out of curl by their own weight. On the crêpéd front hair is a diadem of hair, or of jewels, or it may be arranged in the Pompadour style over a cushion. Short water curls are fastened behind the cushion, and fall forward on the forehead.

Marie Antoinette Coiffure

The Marie Antoinette style is just now considered the highest fashion. The large chignon is crimped and braided in an oblong shape, being narrow and reaching far forward and low on the neck. To make this chignon the hair has to be mounted on a square frame with a comb attached. It is impossible to arrange it properly with a braid in which the hair is gathered into a single point. The front hair is brushed upward from the forehead and temples over a roll. A bow or rosette made of hair with a jeweled center or a small flower is placed on top of the head. Two curls on each side under the back hair are worn falling forward.

Headdresses

Wreaths and trailing garlands are more fashionable for full dress than the sprays and tufts of last season. Instead of a stereotyped row of the same flowers forming a crown we have diadems made of a variety of flowers, with fern leaves, metallic grasses, and golden-winged beetles and grasshoppers. Berries and fruit are also in vogue.

The Grand Duchesse headdress is a coquettish little hat made of small flowers. It is worn on the left side, and is scarcely large enough to conceal the crêpés. A long wreath encircles the head and is entwined in the chignon, falling almost to the waist.

For simple evening dress, sprays are used. Natural flowers are the best taste for home toilettes, but they soon fade and wither in the heated ballroom. The ingenious French stick them in quills filled with water to preserve their freshness.

For demitoilette narrow bands of ribbon, or of satin, the prevailing color of the dress, are worn over the front hair with long streamers beneath the chignon.

For middle-aged ladies who object to dressing their hair in elaborate styles, ribbon and flowers are mingled with lace barbes, and the tiny imported coiffures of Chantilly and point appliqué. Blonde lace in light patterns is preferred above all others for the hair. Real point is too heavy. Folds, and bars, and rosettes of satin, with a few small flowers, are arranged around the chignon, or brought slightly forward in front of it.

Caps

Small fancy caps for breakfast are eagerly adopted by newly married ladies, because they are universally becoming. They are made of muslin, with Valenciennes and guipure lace, interspersed with knots of ribbon. They are either square, or fanchons, or in the peasant shape, with a bag crown for the hair. When trimmed to match the white morning dress they are exceedingly pretty. Small muslin aprons trimmed en suite with the cap are worn with self-colored muslins.

For afternoon toilette ladies more advanced wear scarf coiffures of lace fastened beneath the chignon. A velvet rosette is on the brow. These may be economically made of tulle, tucked and edged with real blonde. In the fanchonette shape a puffed cap with wide blonde scarves is caught on the breast with a rose.

July 25, 1868

Fringes for Sashes and Paletots

These fringes may be made of silk, cotton, or fine cord. The upper edges of the fringes from Figures 2 and 3 are crocheted. The fringe in Figure 1 is knotted at the edge of the stuff. To make it, run through the edge of the stuff from six to eight threads, and tie them together. Then lay one strand diagonally to the right, and the other to the left, to form the crosslines illustrated. Arrange this on a pasteboard foundation. Stitch together the intersecting points as shown. Continue in this manner with the whole border, which may be wide or narrow, as desired. The remaining ends of the thread form the fringe.

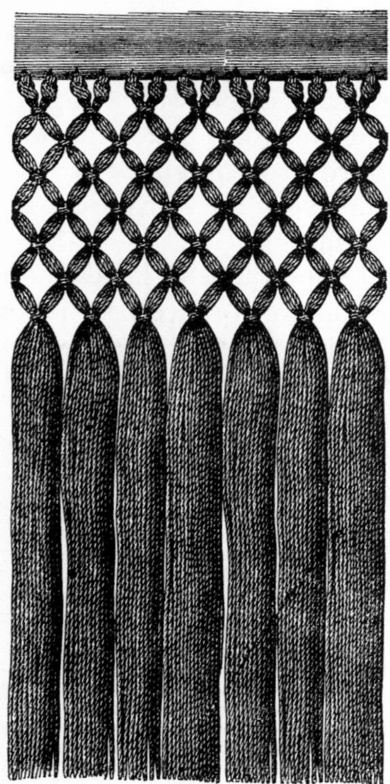

Figure 1. Fringe

To make the fringe in Figure 2, work first a foundation. Then on this, one round in single crochet and one round in double crochet. After this a round in slip stitch, crocheting after every 5th stitch 3 chain stitches, passing over 1 stitch of the last round.

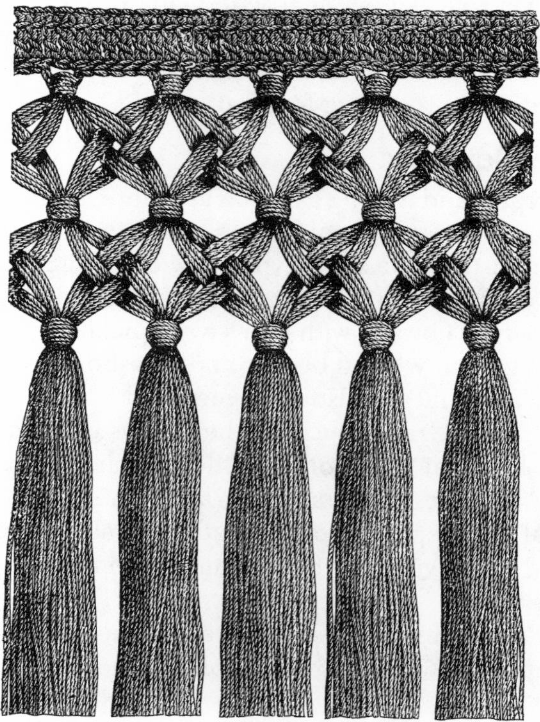

Figure 2. Fringe

Then tie in every one of these chain-stitch loops a strand 8 inches thick, which is laid together at half its length. Divide each of these sixteen-thread strands into four equal parts. Weave these, as shown, with the strands lying next. Then collect again sixteen threads, which fasten as shown. Divide again, and weave with the strands lying next. Finally, tie and even the ends of the fringe.

The border of the fringe in Figure 3 consists of a round in single crochet worked on the foundation, then a round in double crochet, after every 6 of which work 1 chain. The strands are divided, woven, and tied as shown.

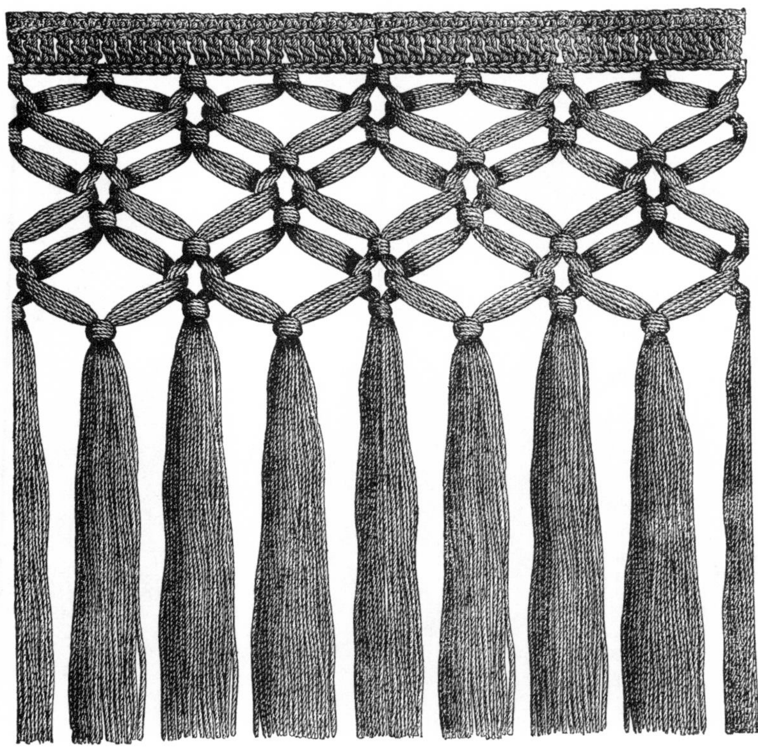

Figure 3. Fringe

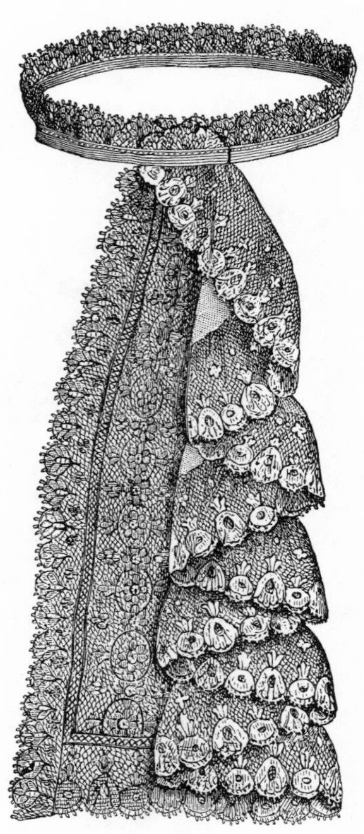

Collar with Bow and Revers

This collar, and the next two, are worn over high dresses, paletots, etc. They are made of Swiss muslin, lace, and colored ribbons.

This is a standing collar made of lace, with embroidered application figures and a muslin binding. The front is ornamented with a bow and revers. The bow consists of a three-cornered piece of Swiss muslin, the shorter side of which is 7 inches long. This strip is bordered with insertion 3/4 inch wide, which in turn is edged with lace 1 1/2 inches wide. The piece is then gathered up in pleats from the middle of the long bias side to the corner of the muslin, thus forming the ends. The upper corner is next turned over as shown. All the corners are trimmed with small bows of ribbon, which are ornamented with an embroidered figure in the center.

Collar with Frill

The standing collar consists of lace 1 1/4 inches wide, set on a muslin binding 1/2 inch wide. The front is finished with a frill, made of lace insertion 1 1/2 inches wide, which is bordered with a narrow row of hemstitch. One side of this insertion is edged with a strip of muslin, which is on one side cut into points 1 inch deep and 3/4 inch wide. On this is set a ruffle 1/2 inch wide, which is edged with lace 1 1/2 inches wide. The under edge of the insertion is bordered with the same lace. The other side is finished with lace 1 inch wide.

Collar with Chemisette Front

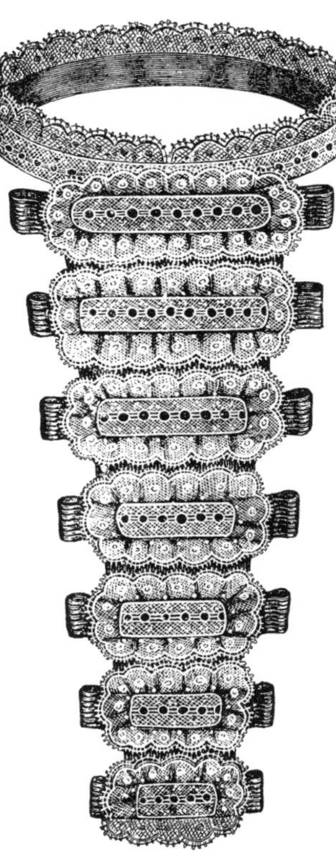

Collar with Chemisette Front

The standing collar is of Valenciennes lace 1 1/2 inches wide and lace insertion, under which is laid colored ribbon. This is fastened to a chemisette front made of insertion, underlaid with ribbon and bordered with lace. The single figures are set on a muslin piece that is 8 inches long, and 4 inches wide at the top and 2 at the bottom.

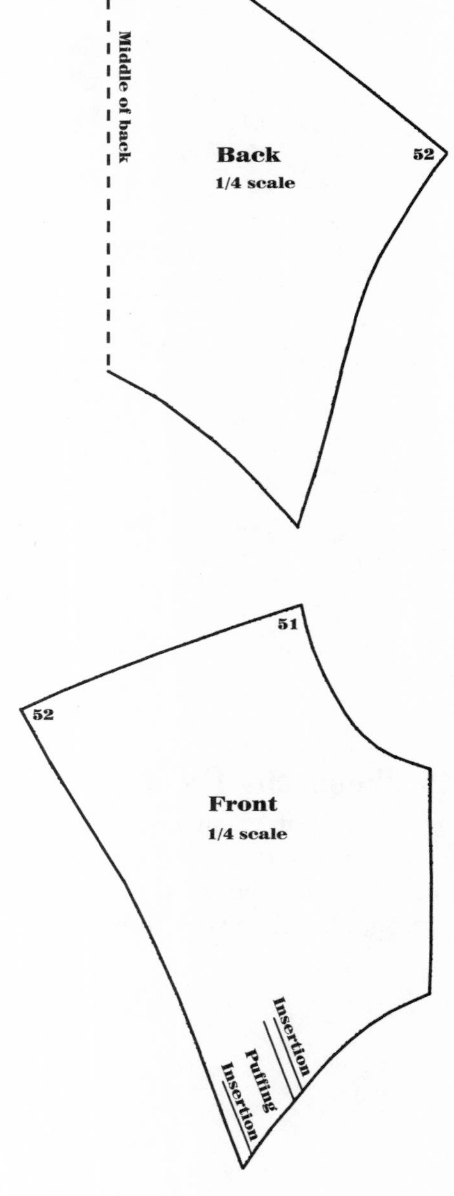

Pointed Fichu

This Swiss muslin fichu is bordered on the shoulders with a ruche 1 1/2 inches wide, edged with Swiss insertion and guipure lace. The bottom of the back and fronts and the neck binding are also trimmed with insertion and lace. The front is finished by a hem trimmed with insertion and with bows of green moiré ribbon 1 inch wide. Each point of the fronts and back is finished by a bow with ends. The fichu is fastened with buttons and buttonhole-stitch loops.

Chemise Russe

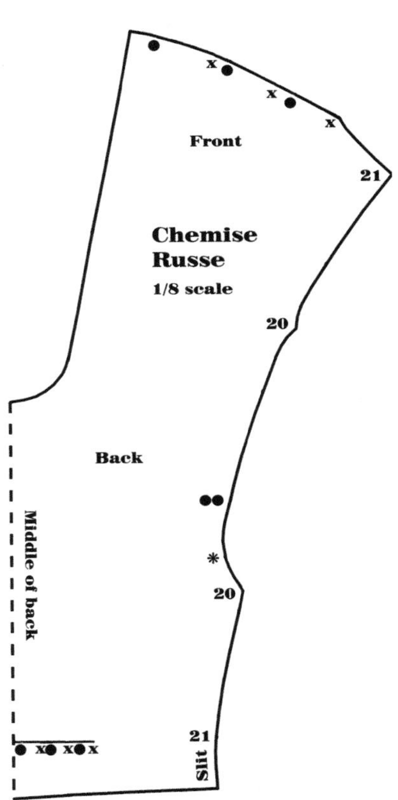

Chemise Russe with Linen Trimming

This Swiss muslin chemise Russe is cut without shoulder seams. The fronts are gathered at the waist, and are crossed diagonally. The trimming consists of one bias strip of fine linen 1/2 inch wide, and two strips each 1/3 inch wide. These strips are stitched down on both sides. The edge of the chemise Russe is trimmed with lace 1/3 inch wide.

Cut of Swiss muslin from the pattern one piece. Sew the side seams from 20 to 21. Then stitch on the neck and fronts, as shown in the illustration, the bias strips that hide the edge where the lace is sewn on. Pleat the under edge from *x* to •. Face the back under the row of pleats with a straight piece of Swiss muslin 1 inch wide. Hem the under edge with a narrow hem. The fronts are fastened to a band 1 inch wide, which is fastened with a button and buttonhole. A piece of Swiss muslin 3 inches wide and hemmed on the edge is gathered to the under part of this band.

The sleeves are cut from the pattern for the Foulard Écru Chemise Russe. Trim according to the illustration, and sew them into the armholes.

July 25, 1868

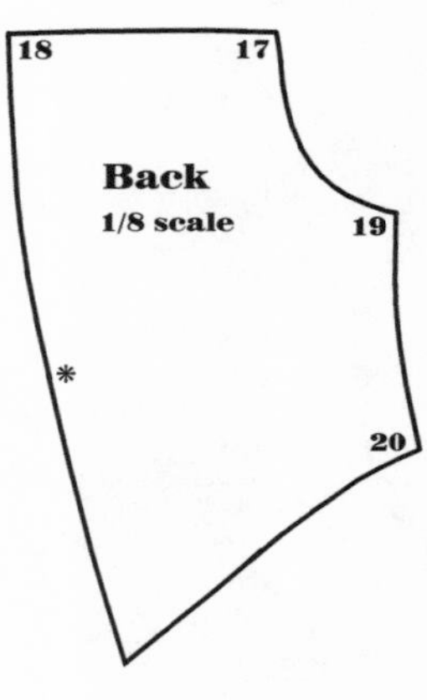

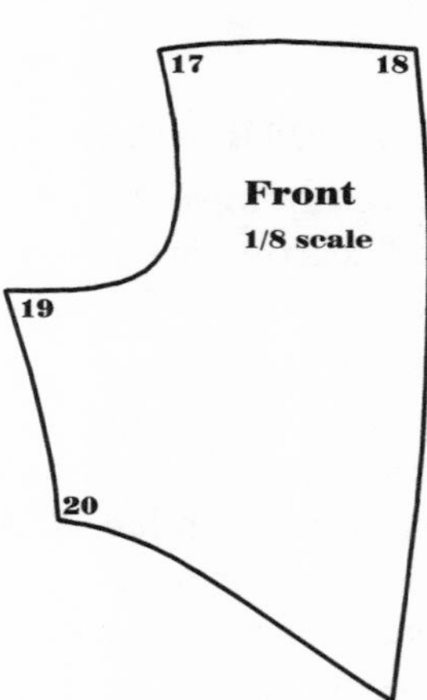

White Swiss Muslin Chemise Russe

Both fronts and backs of this pattern cross diagonally. The trimming consists of insertion 1/2 inch wide, underlaid with blue velvet ribbon, and edged on both sides with lace edging 1/4 inch wide. The armholes are trimmed with blue velvet ribbon 1 1/2 inches wide.

Arrange the fronts and backs of Swiss muslin according to the front and back patterns, laying them each in eight folds as illustrated. Join the backs so they cross each other as far as *. Then join the fronts according to the figures. Bind the bottom. Trim the shoulder seams with the insertion. The short sleeves are puffed and bound. The binding is trimmed with a Swiss muslin strip, laid in pleats and crossed four times with bands of the insertion. Sew in the sleeves and trim as illustrated.

Chemise Russe

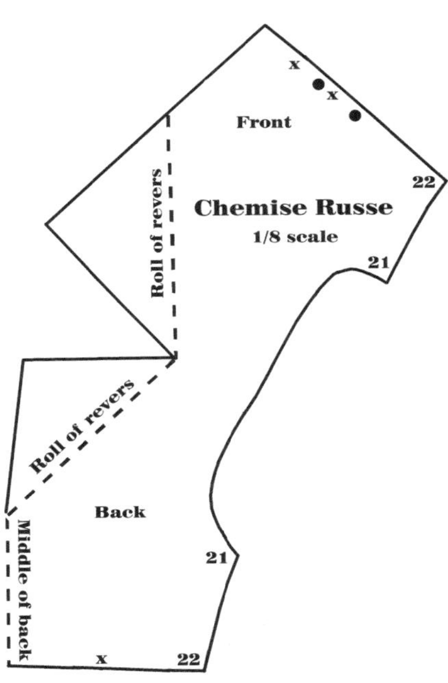

Chemise Russe with Long Sleeves

This low-necked chemise Russe with revers and long sleeves is made of muslin. It is trimmed with guipure insertion 1/2 inch wide, narrow guipure edging 1/3 inch wide, and wider guipure edging 1 1/2 inches wide. Narrow black velvet ribbon is run through the insertion. The belt is black velvet with a rosette in front.

Cut of Swiss muslin from the pattern one piece, allowing for front hems. Sew the side seams from 21 to 22. Trim the right front with insertion, bordered on both sides by the wide guipure lace. Work buttonhole-stitch loops corresponding to the size of the small buttons on the left front. In trimming the revers lay the edge over on the right side as shown by the dotted line. Cover with the insertion. The insertion is bordered on one side with the wide, and on the other with the narrow lace. Gather the back. Pleat the front, bringing *x* on •, and bind. Cover the binding with a belt of velvet ribbon finished with a rosette in front. Trim this belt with two rows of the narrow lace sewn together on the straight side.

Cut the sleeves from the pattern for the Foulard Écru Chemise Russe. At the back of the wrist cut a slit about 3 inches long. Lay the corners over on the right side. Trim as illustrated with insertion, wide and narrow edging, and velvet ribbon. Sew in the sleeves and trim the armholes.

Chemise Russe with Short Sleeves

This low-necked chemise Russe with revers and short sleeves is of Swiss muslin. The revers is lined with lilac silk. It is bordered on the outer edge with two rows of Valenciennes lace, arranged so the straight sides lie together. The belt is covered with a bias strip of lilac silk. This is laid in two folds and finished in front with a lilac bow.

Cut the chemise Russe from the pattern for the Chemise Russe with Long Sleeves. On the upper border allow the material to extend only to the dotted line. The revers is of muslin arranged as illustrated. It is lined with silk, which must extend 1/4 inch beyond the muslin on the outer edge. Finish the edge with lace. Sew the revers on the chemise in such a manner as to conceal the seam.

The short puffed sleeves are made of a piece of muslin 15 inches long by 5 wide in the middle. The ends are sloped till they are only 2 inches wide. Sew this piece together on the ends. Gather the under edge. Join it with a revers, which is cut and arranged as illustrated. On the upper edge gather according to the armhole size. Sew into the chemise.

Black Guipure Chemise Russe

This chemise Russe is made of black guipure net. It is trimmed with black lace insertion 1 inch wide and lace edging 1/3 inch and 1 inch wide. Both insertion and lace are embroidered with black beads and bugles. The insertion is put on over black satin ribbon, and bows of the same ribbon ornament the front.

Cut of guipure or tulle from the front two pieces. Cut from the back one piece. Cut the sleeves. Join the fronts and back according to the figures on the pattern. Bind the fronts with a straight strip of lace 1 inch wide. Face the neck with a strip of lace 3/4 inch wide. Lay two pleats in the bottom of each front, bringing *x* on •. Then bind with a strip of lace 2 inches wide. Arrange the insertion with the ribbon underneath, and edged by the narrow lace, as illustrated. The wider lace is pleated on the neck and sleeves.

Sew up the sleeves from 26 to 27. Set on the trimming. Sew the sleeves into the armholes, which are trimmed with ribbon, covered with insertion, and edged with lace on both sides.

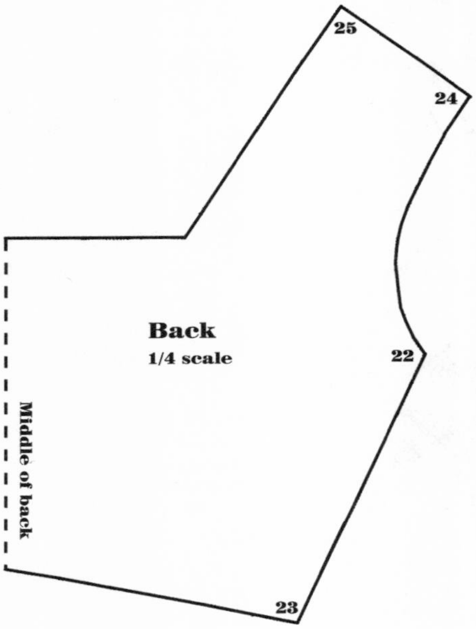

July 25, 1868

25
24
Back
1/4 scale
22
Middle of back
23
24 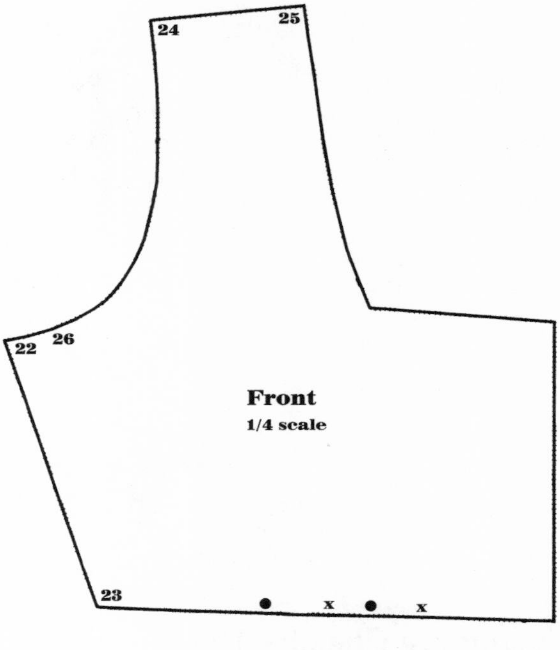
25
22
26
Front
1/4 scale
23
x
x 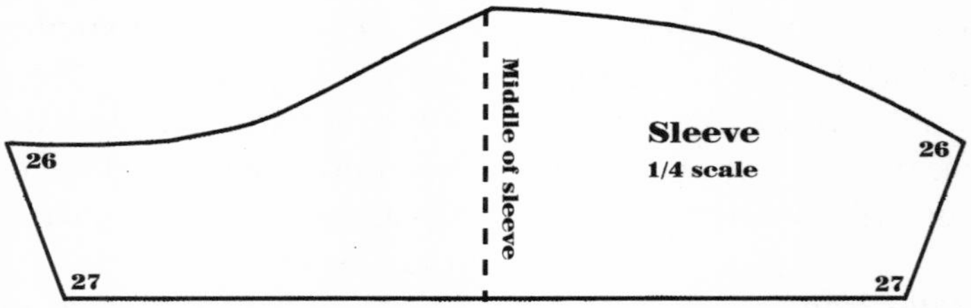
26
Middle of sleeve
Sleeve
1/4 scale
26
27
27

Chemise Russe with Pleated Trimming

This low-necked chemise Russe with pleated trimming is especially suited to young girls. It is cut from the same pattern as the Black Guipure Chemise Russe. It is made of white Swiss muslin, and is ornamented front and back with a pleated piece of muslin that is set in. The seam is covered with a pleated bias strip of Swiss muslin. In the middle of the front and back, at the point where the pleated strips cross, is placed a knot of the pleated muslin.

The neck is finished with a row of guipure insertion, through which velvet ribbon is drawn. This insertion is 1/2 inch wide, and is edged with guipure lace 1/3 inch wide. The sleeves are also of pleated muslin. The upper and lower edges are bordered with insertion, and the under edge also with lace.

Foulard Écru Chemise Russe

This chemise Russe is fastened diagonally in front. The trimming consists of brown satin ribbon 1/3 inch wide, white lace insertion 1 inch wide, and edging 3/4 inch wide.

Cut the two fronts. Cut the back. Cut both parts of the sleeves. Join the parts, cording the shoulder seams. Face the left front and set on small buttons for fastening. Around the neck and on the right front turn the edge over on the right side about 1/6 inch. Cover it with satin ribbon, then sew on the lace edging. The buttonholes on the right side are covered by the ribbon. Hem the lower edge.

Join the sleeves from 5 to 6 and from 7 to 8. Turn the edge over on the right side at the wrist and cover it with satin ribbon and lace. Put on the remaining sleeve trimming. Sew the sleeves into the corded armholes, making the figures correspond; hold the edge as loosely as necessary. Finish with the rest of the trimming according to the illustration.

Foulard Écru Chemise Russe

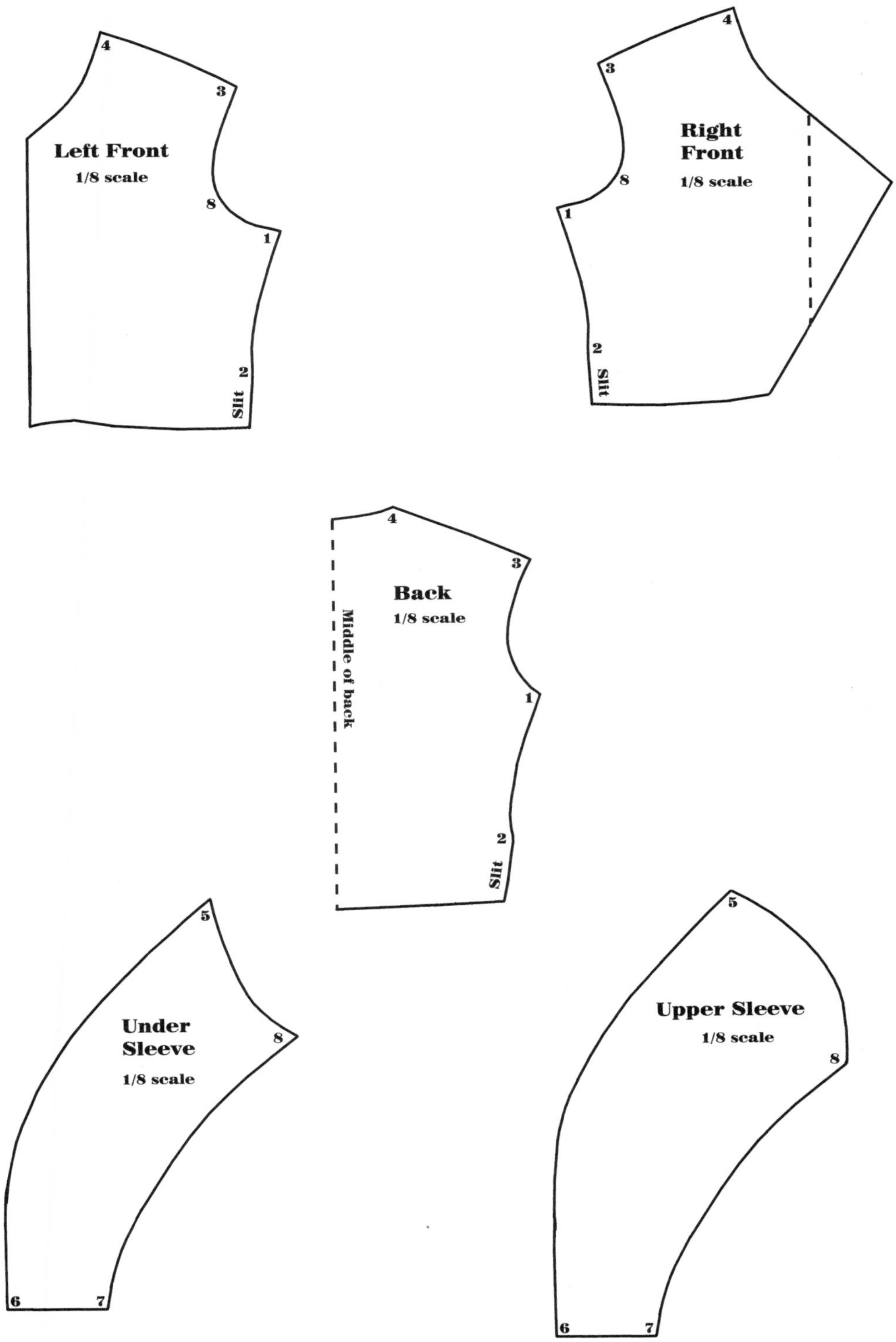

Left Front
1/8 scale

4 3 8 1 2 Slit

Right Front
1/8 scale

4 3 8 1 2 Slit

Back
1/8 scale

Middle of back

4 3 1 2 Slit

Under Sleeve
1/8 scale

5 8 6 7

Upper Sleeve
1/8 scale

5 8 6 7

July 25, 1868

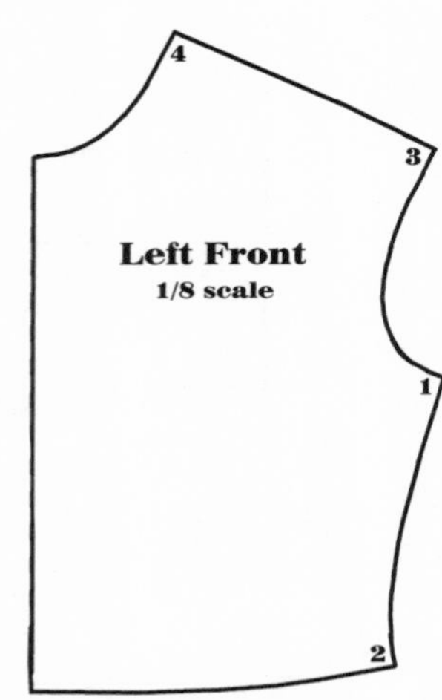

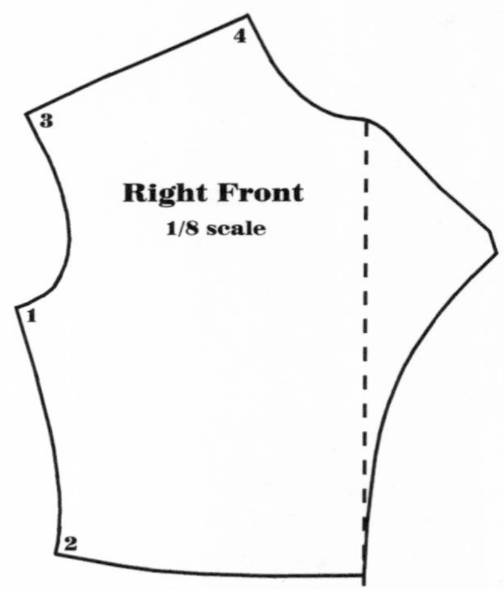

White Alpaca Chemise Russe

This chemise Russe is made of white alpaca, trimmed with bias folds of the same material 1 inch wide. These folds are corded with blue on the edges, and cover the place where the small blue ribbon points are set on. The latter are arranged as illustrated, the corners being turned down and laid in two pleats, *x* on •.

Cut both fronts (seen reversed in the illustration). The back and sleeves are cut from the pattern for the Foulard Écru Chemise Russe. Join the back and fronts, cording the shoulder seams. Hem the left front. Turn the edge over 1/6 inch on the right side around the neck and on the right front. Cover with the trimming. Fasten with buttonholes and small blue satin buttons. Hem the bottom. Three inches from the under edge sew a straight strip on the under side. Run two narrow white ribbons through the shirr thus formed. Sew in the sleeves with blue cord and trim as illustrated.

Point

Full scale

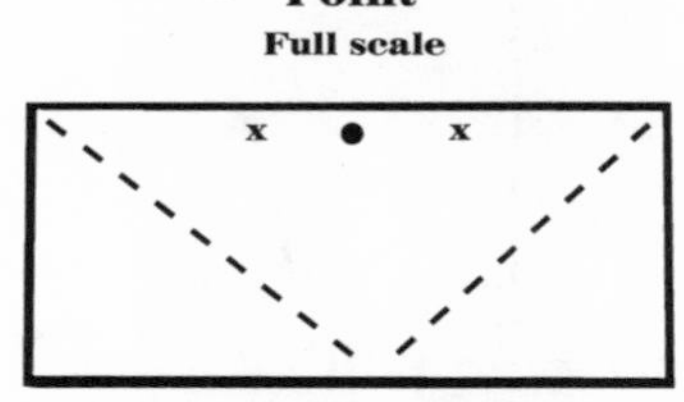

Walking Suit with Fichu

This walking dress with Marie Antoinette fichu is of changeable green and white cretonne. The fichu trimming consists of bias folds and quilling of the same material. The skirt is cut from the pattern for the Norderney Walking Dress in the May 23 issue.

Cut from the waist front two pieces, allowing 1 1/4 inches for the front hems. Cut from the waist back one piece. Cut the sleeves from the pattern for the Foulard Écru Chemise Russe.

Hem the fronts. Work the buttonholes in the right front, and sew the buttons on the left. Join the fronts and back according to the figures on the pattern. Hem the under edge of the waist. Lay the pleats, bringing *x* on •, as shown on the front and back. Face the sleeves at the wrists. Trim them with three double bias folds, surmounted with fluting 1 1/4 inches wide. Set the sleeves in the armholes. Cord the neck and set on small corded scallops. Each scallop is cut singly of the material. The front of the waist is finished with two double bias folds.

For the fichu cut from the back one piece, and from the front two pieces. Join the fronts and back according to the figures on the pattern. Hem the fichu. Lay the back in pleats from *x* to •. Then trim the under part with a fluting 2 inches wide, surmounted with three double bias folds. The fluting around the neck is only 1 inch wide. The fichu is fastened to a belt of the material 1 1/2 inches wide, which is fastened in front over the tabs. The sash consists of one short and two long ends. The ends are all finished with a fluting surmounted with double bias folds. They are pleated at the top and held together with a pleated knot.

The skirt is trimmed with five flounces. Each flounce consists of a strip of the material 3 inches wide. This is gathered to half its width on one side, and remains free on the under side. The gathers all lie in the same direction, and are about 1/4 inch wide. The upper edge of each flounce is finished with a double bias fold of the same material. The flounces are set on about 1 inch apart.

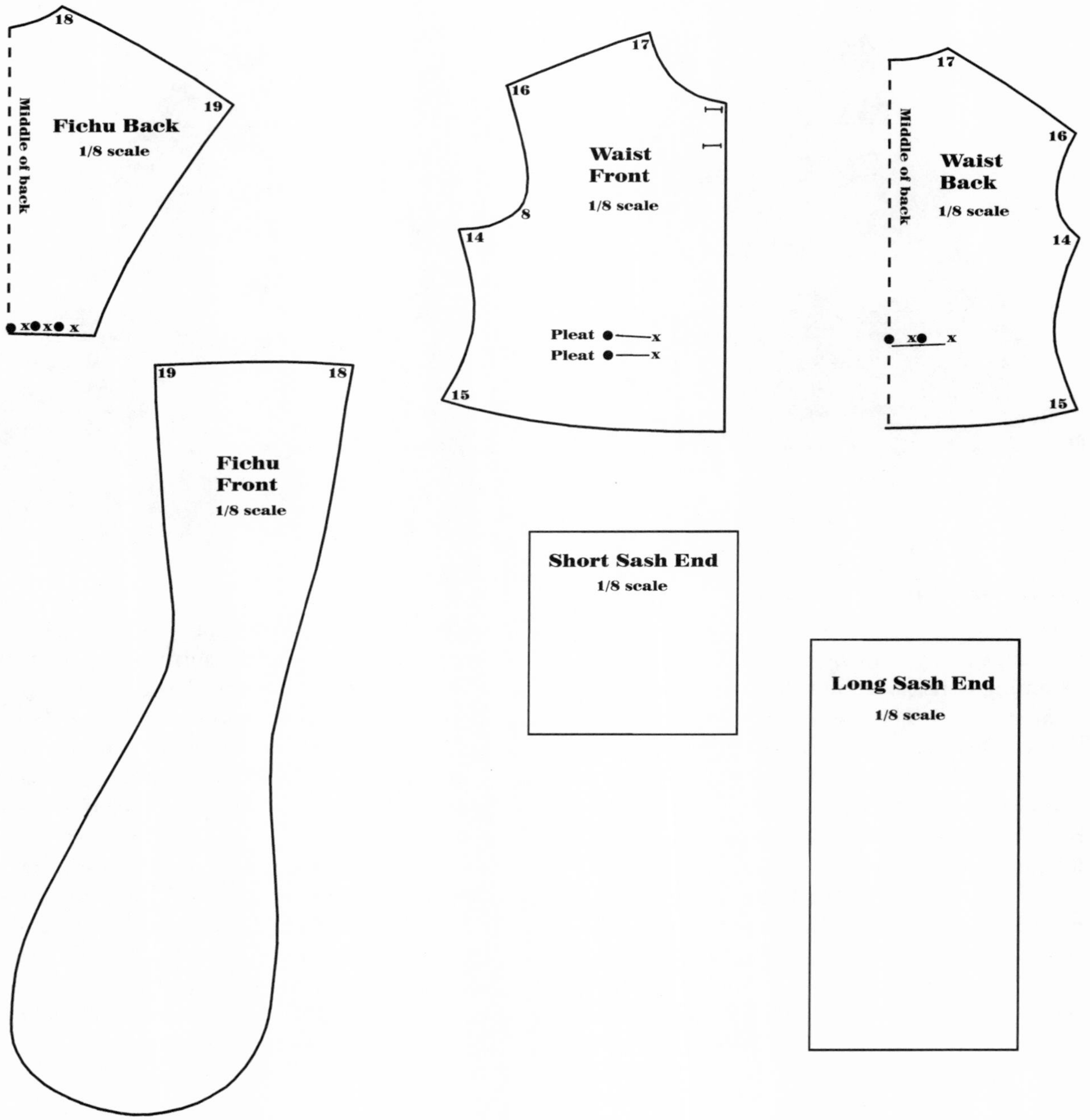

Riding Habit

Riding Habit

This habit is of black cloth. The waist is made with a rounded revers. The sleeves are finished with the cuffs turned back. The trimming consists of passementerie braid 1 inch wide.

From the material and lining cut from the front and side back each two equal pieces. Cut from the back and revers each one piece. Cut two pieces for each sleeve. Cut the cuffs.

Baste the outside on the lining. Take up the bosom pleats in the fronts. Face with a piece of the outside. Work the buttonholes and sew on the buttons. Join the side backs and backs according to the figures on the pattern. Bind the neck with the double material of the revers, which is rolled over along the line designated on the pattern.

Sew both pieces of the sleeve together from 7 to 8 and from 9 to 10. Then set on the cuffs according to the figures on the pattern. Face the under part of the sleeves with a bias strip of cloth. Lay two pleats in the upper edge. Sew in with a cord, bringing 10 to 10 on the front of the waist.

Cord the under edge of the waist. Trim as illustrated.

The gored skirt, which is gathered behind, is 135 inches wide and 65 inches long all the way around.

Side Back
1/8 scale
3
1
4
2
Back
1/8 scale
13
6
5
3
4
Middle of back
Front
1/8 scale
6
5
10
1
12
2
Middle
13
Roll of revers
Setting on of revers
Revers
1/4 scale
12
Under Sleeve
1/8 scale
7
x
x
10
11
8
9
Upper Sleeve
1/8 scale
7
10
11
8
9
Cuff
1/4 scale
11
Middle of cuff
8
9

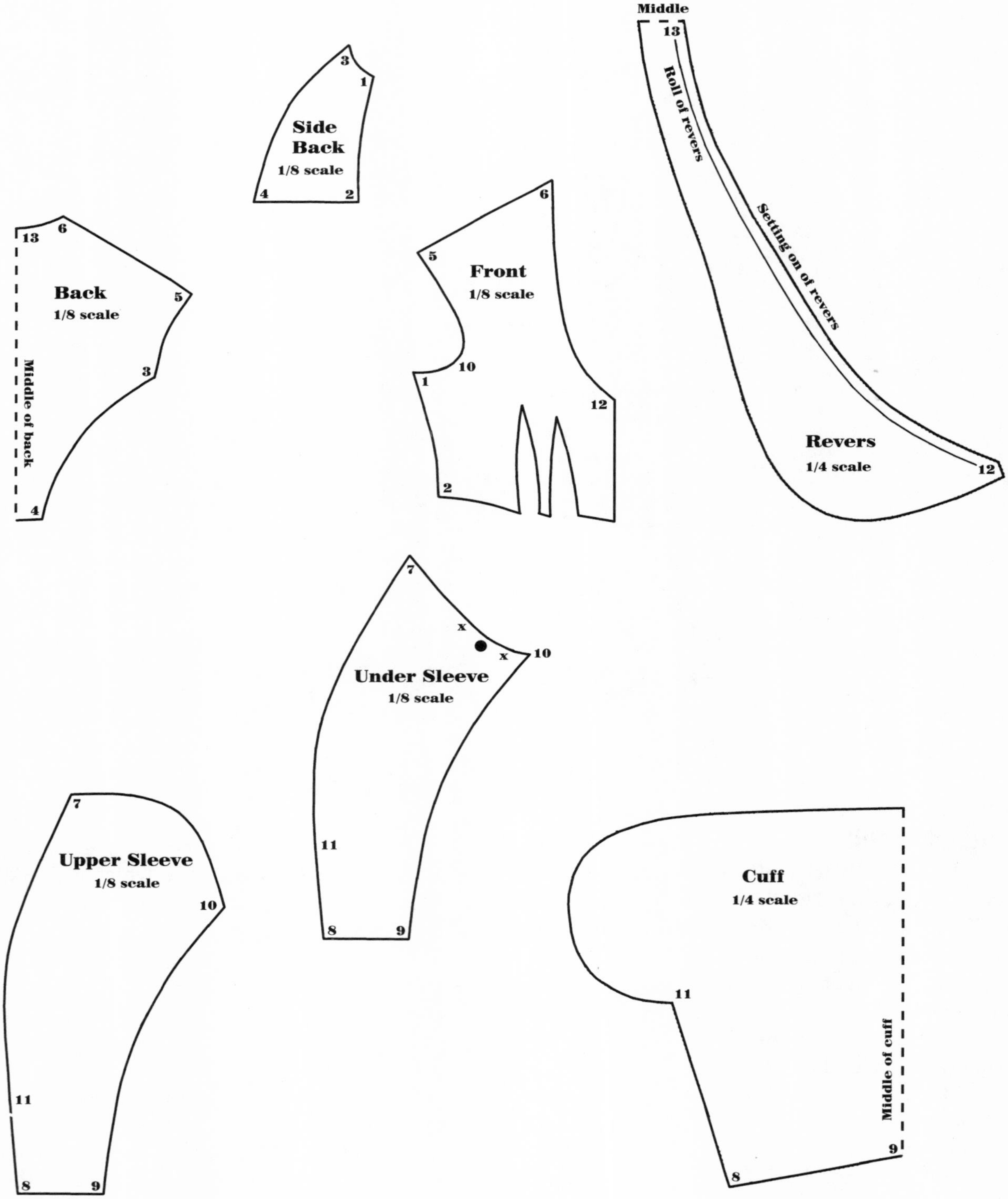

August 8, 1868

India Goods

A fancy for India goods is one of the caprices of the summer. These quaint antique goods, so long out of use, are now as anxiously sought after as if they were the last novel emanations from the looms of Lyons. At present the supply is short, and it is necessary to go to the India stores to find a variety.

The real India mull is of the soiled-looking, yellowish shade of white that is thought to enhance the beauty of fine lace. It is entirely without starch, and is as sheer as linen cambric, which it very much resembles. Among the white dresses universally worn this summer, India mull and French nainsook are the materials most in favor. They should be trimmed with Valenciennes lace and worn over dresses of glacé silk. India mull is 7/8 yard wide.

Corah silk is a glossy India foulard, of wiry material that is not easily crushed. It is of the pale nankeen shade now in vogue, and called by the French "écru," or unbleached. It is 1 1/4 yards wide. A dress pattern contains 8 yards.

The name "pongee" is given to various poplin mixtures of silk and linen, or lisle thread. But the real Delhi pongee is all silk, a light material, as cool as muslin, and pleasant to the touch. It is a bright buff color. Twenty yards are required for a dress, as it is only 1/2 yard wide. It makes very stylish traveling dresses, and is in favor for watering-place and seaside suits, as the moisture does not affect it. The umbrella is of the same silk as the dress, and should have a bamboo stick.

Tussore silk is a heavy foulard silk of a pretty fawn color. It is brought out in 10-yard pieces.

One of the pleasantest fabrics for summer wear is the genuine India foulard. It has none of the disagreeable harshness of the Japanese foulard, but is soft, smooth, and cool, and falls into graceful folds. There is a great variety of patterns this season. It is shown in stripes, dots, chintz patterns, and in solid colors. Foreign correspondents speak of the bridal white foulard and of shot or chameleon foulards. Pistache green and straw color are seen together, and pearl gray with blue. Foulards will wash, but should only be entrusted to a skillful laundress.

The checked and "thousand stripe" India silks cannot be too highly recommended. They wash like muslin, and the wear is endless. The genuine article is shown rolled over a stick, and is very light and cool. For morning dresses and demitoilettes they are very pretty, with the addition of a black lace apron or a white organdy fichu.

Pineapple cloth is made from the fibers of the pineapple, and is exceedingly durable. There is no more desirable goods for midsummer dresses. It was formerly objected to because the colors are not very decided. But vivid colors are not fashionable at present. The delicate shades of green, and lavender, and rose color on white, so often seen in this beautiful gauze, are especially stylish.

White Dresses

During the heated term white dresses are chosen for all occasions. There are piqués, muslins, grenadines, chambray, sultanes, and goat's-hair, made into morning dresses, promenade suits, dancing dresses, and trained robes, all of the universally worn white. Muslins are trimmed with tucks, puffs, ruffles, and Valenciennes worn over colored silk. Bunched-up tunics are made over short skirts and with trains. Infant's waists and fichus, Watteau paletots, and Marie Antoinette mantles of sheer muslin are ornamented with ribbon rosettes and fringed sashes. Frills and flounces of every quality of muslin may be bought ready made and fluted. The fluting shears are scarcely thicker than a knitting needle, and the effect is similar to old-fashioned crimping. Thin muslin flounces are also arranged in box pleats.

August 8, 1868

Piqué is prettily ornamented with guipure medallions, or clusters of lace representing flowers, truelove knots, and stars, lined with colored silk or chambray.

Short Muslin Dresses

Instead of the ponderous style of long, flowing dresses for morning, short gored skirts and sacques are adopted. These are convenient, as they are suitable for breakfast and for morning promenades. Exchanging a fancy slipper for a walking boot is the only alteration necessary. Muslins, lawns, linens, cambric, and chambray are made in this way, trimmed with ruffles of the same. The sacque should not be full, but must have a cool, negligée appearance. The seams under the arms are all that is necessary to give it proper shape. The under waist should be prettily trimmed, and belted with a ribbon belt the color of the skirt.

Hints About Sleeves

The two pieces of a coat sleeve should not be cut together. Many ladies who make their own dresses spoil the sleeve by shaping the upper and under parts precisely alike. The upper part should be 1 1/2 inches broader than the under part. It should also be longer, and held next the sewer, that it may be slightly fulled into the under part as it is sewn. At the armhole the front should be a convex curve, while the under part is concave. The sleeve should not be straight, but rounded to fit smoothly on the arm when half bent, as that is the position most frequently assumed.

The sleeves of wash dresses are now shaped like the ordinary linen undersleeve so much worn. Cut an ample coat sleeve long enough to reach halfway between the elbow and wrist, and finish out the length with a deep, loose cuff. The cuff must be interlined to make it hold starch. It is fastened with two buttons on the outside seam, or closed to run the hand through.

Bathing Costumes

Morocco boots with cork soles and linings are made for bathers. Those of moccasin shape, without heels, are preferred. A black oilcloth cap with a visor to protect the face from the sun, and turn the water, and a bag net for the hair, is the best waterproof arrangement for the head. Bathing suits made with trousers and blouse waist without skirt are objected to by many ladies as masculine and fast. But experience proves they do not expose the figure more than a wet clinging robe, and are much more comfortable in the water, where all superfluous drapery should be dispensed with. For this reason the fancy costumes with double skirts are clumsy and unbecoming. Trousers should be full and gathered into a band at the ankle. All-wool serge and flannel are the materials that cling least to the figure. Cotton and linen are penetrable at once by moisture, and are therefore objectionable.

Net Breakfast Cap with Cape

The crown and cape of this morning cap are cut in one piece of muslin. The trimming is lace insertion and lace edging, both 1 inch wide, and blue satin ribbon 3/4 inch wide. A bow of blue satin ribbon 2 1/2 inches wide is set on top of the head.

Cut of bias muslin from the pattern one piece. Hem the edge narrow. Set on the insertion, following the double line which designates a shirr. Trim the edge with lace. Run through this shirr a blue satin ribbon 30 inches long, which gathers the cap. Set the bow on the front.

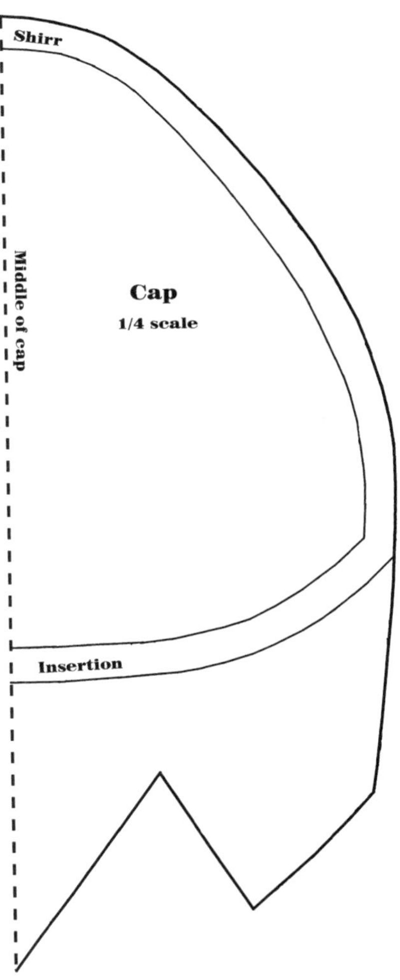

August 8, 1868

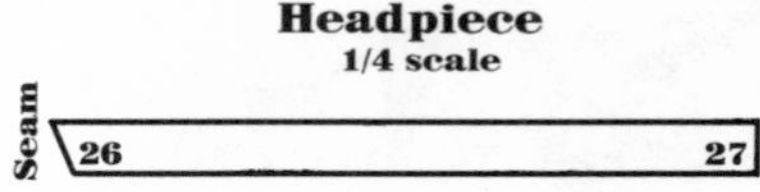

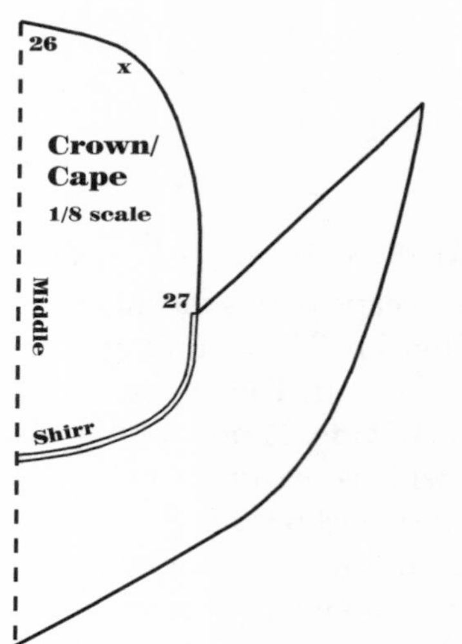

Breakfast Cap with Ribbon Trimming

This muslin breakfast cap is trimmed with Valenciennes insertion 3/4 inch wide, edging 1/2 inch wide, and bows of pink ribbon 1 inch wide.

Cut of bias muslin the crown and cape in one piece. Cut the headpiece of double material folded along the front. Gather the crown/cape piece on both sides from 27 to *x*. Join it to the headpiece. Set a bias strip of muslin on the under side of the crown/cape, where the double line designates the shirr.

Finish the front with a frill 1 1/2 inches wide, which is trimmed with lace. Sew ruches 1/2 inch wide and edged with lace on the front of the sides, from the ends of the headpiece to 1 inch above *x*. Edge the cape with insertion and lace. Run a rubber cord 9 inches long through the shirr. Finish with ribbon bows.

Fichu with Revers

Fichu with Revers

This fichu is of Swiss muslin and insertion 1 1/2 inches wide. It is cut from the pattern, and arranged according to the marked lines. Cut first one piece of muslin according to the pattern. Sew in the insertion as indicated by the lines, laying a pleat in the middle of the back at each corner. Cut away the muslin from under the insertion, and fell down the seams on each side. Cover the edges with a strip of embroidery 1/4 inch wide. Hem the edge narrow, and the fronts 1 inch wide as far up as the line for the revers. On the under edge, border with a fluting 3/4 inch wide. Finish the edge with lace 1 1/2 inches wide. Arrange a fluting of pink satin ribbon so the lace lies over it.

Turn the revers back as shown by the dotted lines. Trim the fichu on the edge of the revers and around the neck with lace 3/4 inch wide. This lace must be held a little full around the neck and the corners of the revers. Its upper edge is covered with a fluting of pink ribbon which is trimmed with a strip of embroidery. A bow of pink ribbon finishes the back and front. Fasten with buttons and buttonhole loops.

August 8, 1868

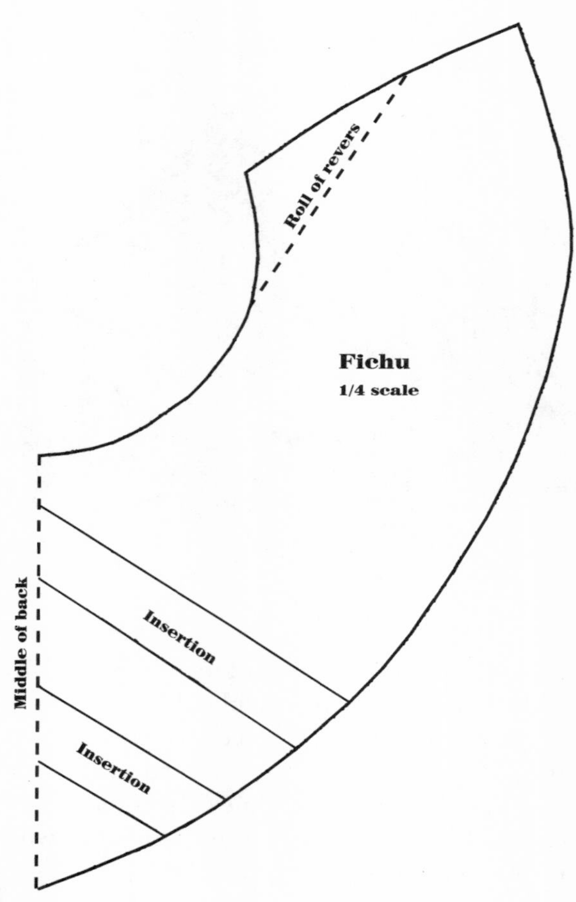

Bretelle Bodice

This bodice is made of Swiss muslin. It is trimmed with pink ribbon 1 inch wide, and lace edging 3/4 inch and 1 inch wide.

Cut of Swiss muslin from the pattern two pieces. Arrange on these pieces the ribbon and insertion over it as shown by the pattern and illustration. Form the bretelles each of a bias strip of muslin pointed at the ends, and lay each in four pleats graduating in width from the shoulder to the waist. Put on the bretelles. Join the pieces on the shoulder from 35 to 36. Border the neck with the narrow, and the rest of the edges with the wide, lace. Cover the shoulder seams with loops of pink ribbon.

August 8, 1868

Set on the back of the waist two sash ends of Swiss muslin, 32 inches long by 10 inches wide at the bottom, and sloping to the top. Trim the edges with insertion underlaid with ribbon and edged with lace. Pleat the upper ends and fasten under the fichu. Finish with a bow on the back of the fichu.

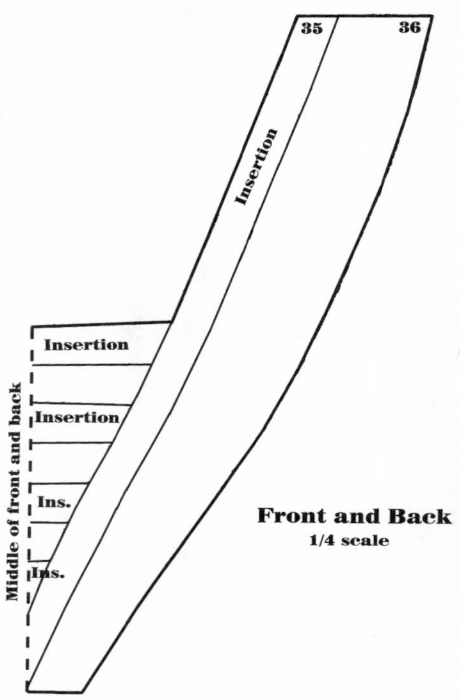

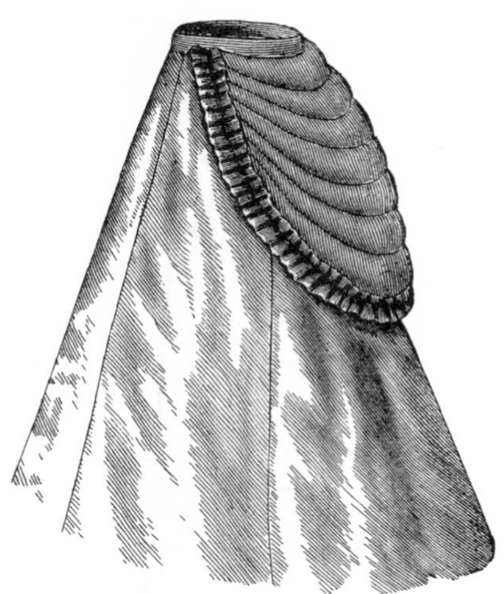

Bustle

As dresses are now worn gathered very full behind they are supported by a bustle, to give them a still fuller appearance. The bustle is worn above the crinoline.

Cut of muslin from the pattern one piece. Arrange on this the plain puffs, which are filled with feathers. Except for the upper edge, the bustle is bound and finished with a box-pleated trimming, which tends to conceal the outline of the bustle. Bind the upper edge. Fasten with a button and buttonhole.

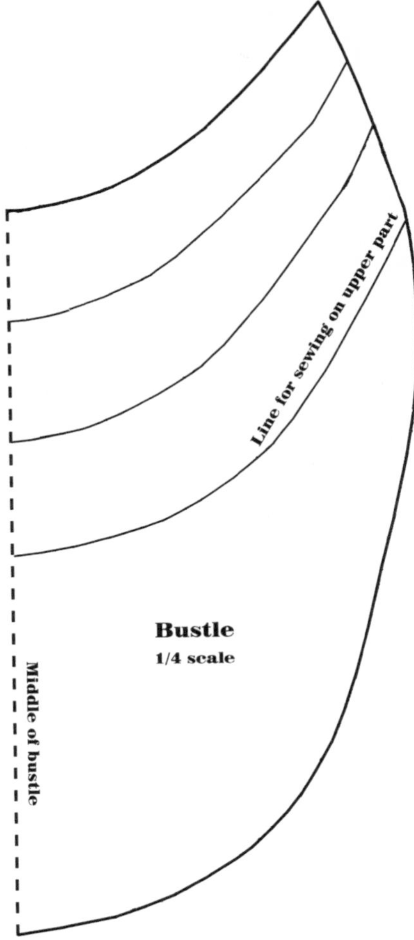

Bathing Cloak

Bathing cloak with cape of white flannel bound with red flannel. It can be worn either with or without a belt.

For the cloak cut both fronts and the back, adapting the length to the wearer. For the cape cut from the front two pieces and from the back one piece. For each sleeve cut two pieces.

Join the back and fronts of the cloak and cape according to the corresponding figures on the pattern. Bind the edges of both, except the upper edge, with red flannel 1 1/2 inches wide. Join the neck with a narrow binding. Sew together the fronts from the skirt bottom to *. Join the sleeves from 11 to 12 and from 13 to 14. Bind the bottom and sew them into the armholes, bringing 14 on 14.

Bathing Cloak

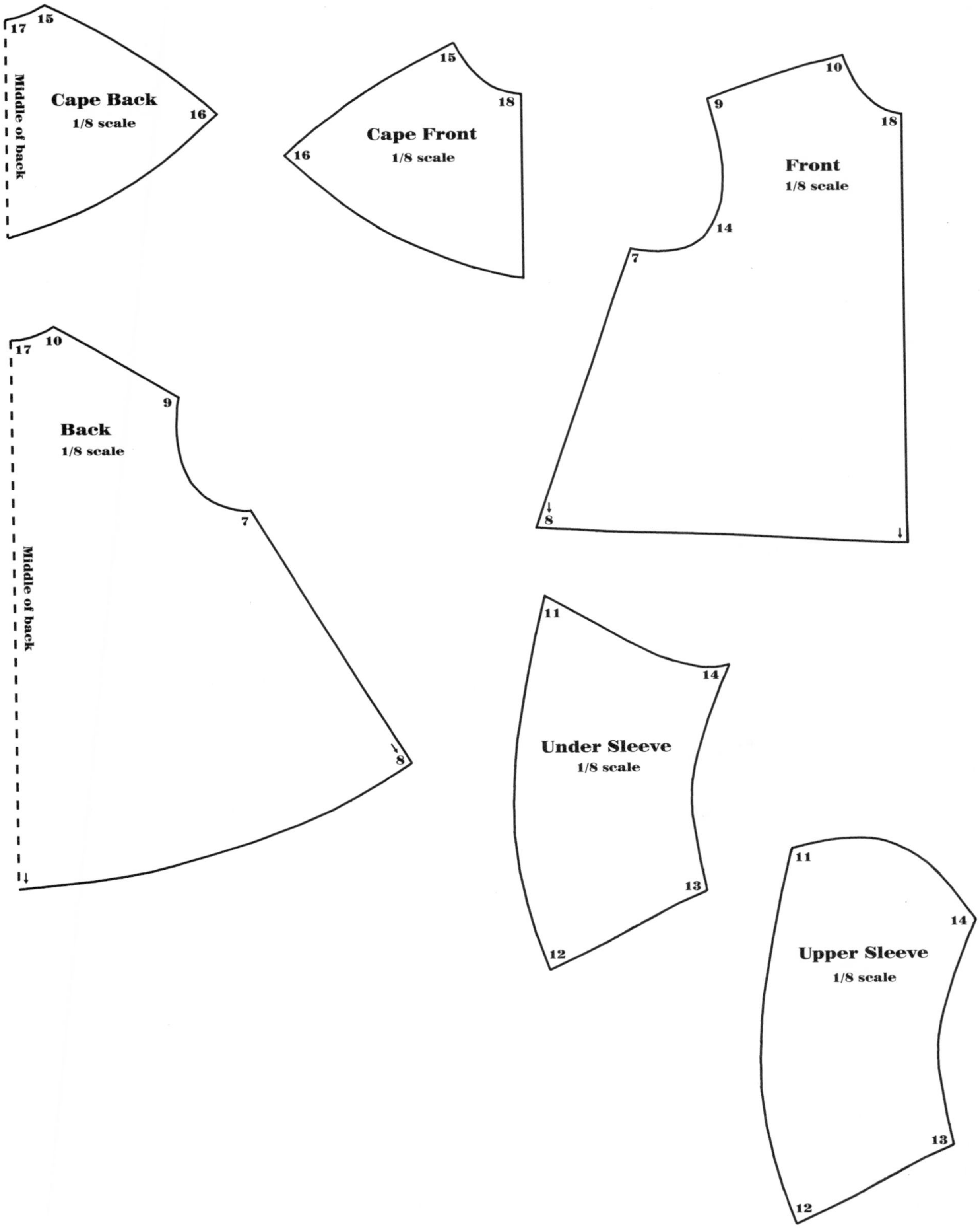

17 15

Cape Back
1/8 scale

16

Middle of back

15

18

16

Cape Front
1/8 scale

10

9

18

Front
1/8 scale

14

7

8

17 10

9

Back
1/8 scale

7

Middle of back

8

11

14

Under Sleeve
1/8 scale

13

12

11

14

Upper Sleeve
1/8 scale

13

12

Bathing Cap

The cap on the left of the previously given illustration is made in one piece without a seam. Cut of oiled silk from the pattern one piece. Bind this with narrow ribbon or worsted braid, and border with pleated red worsted braid 3/4 inch wide. Put two ribbons on the corners, and 3 inches above sew two longer ribbons. The first are to be tied under the chin. The others are brought back and crossed, then tied in a bow on top of the head. The rounded back of the hood forms a sort of cape.

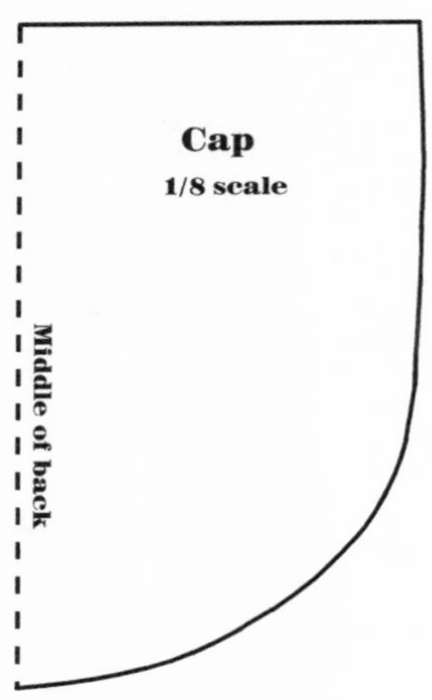

Bathing Cap

The cap shown on the right is of oiled silk with an edge of red worsted braid. Cut from the pattern one piece. Sew this together from 19 to 20. Bind with narrow ribbon. Set a ribbon on the back, through which run a piece of the braid, thus forming a shirr which makes the cape. On the back set a bow of red worsted braid about 1 inch wide. The strings are 25 inches long. Place them under the bow, and again fasten them on the front corner. The braid is made of the same ribbon, and is put on as shown by the pattern. In sewing this on hold the hood a little full from the middle on both sides to *x*. The tassel on the back is made of zephyr wool.

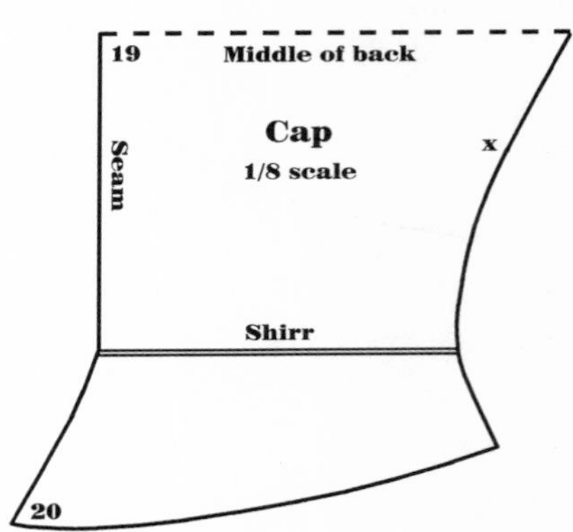

August 15, 1868

Netting Work

The materials required are a netting needle, meshes of different sizes, and yarn. The needle is brass, steel, bone, or wood. A needle of the size shown in Figure 1 is suitable for cord, crochet cotton, or fine woolen yarn. For heavier yarn, such as knitting cotton or worsted, the needle must be longer and heavier. For twine, thicker wool, etc. select a needle of bone or wood.

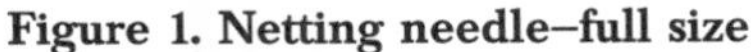

Figure 1. Netting needle–full size

In this case the corresponding mesh must be so large that the needle can be easily pushed through the stitches. The size, that is the circumference of the mesh, must correspond to the thread. In selecting a mesh it must be remembered that the holes of the network will be as large again as the circumference of the mesh. For example, a mesh 1/2 inch in circumference gives a hole 1/4 inch on one side of the square. The mesh must be smooth and of equal size throughout the length, so that the stitches are even and easily slipped off. The best meshes are round, and are made of horn, ivory, whalebone, polished wood, or steel. For fringe or long, fringelike stitches, flat meshes are required.

Select the material according to the design of the work. The thread must be smooth and without knots, so the stitches are smooth and even. An unequal thread makes the work difficult.

For beginning the work, first wind the thread on the needle. This is done by winding through the split ends, but care must be taken not to wind on too much, as it would render it difficult to draw through the stitches. Make of strong thread a large loop, and fasten it to a heavy sewing cushion. To this loop tie the end of the working thread. Now take the mesh in the left hand. Lay it between the thumb and forefinger. Then lay the working thread over the mesh and over the inner side of second, third, and fourth fingers of the left hand inward. Run it up behind these fingers, and lay the thread to the left so that it can be held fast with the thumb. Figure 2 shows the position of the mesh, as well as that of the working thread.

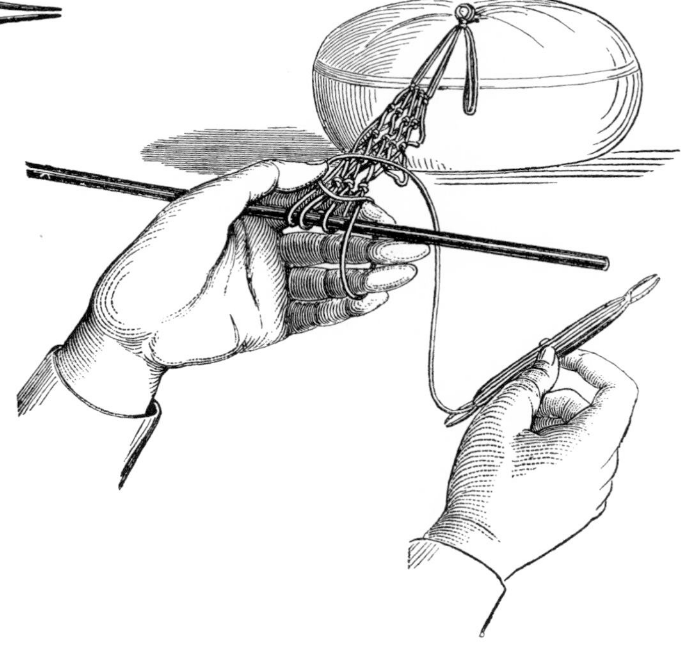

Figure 2. Making of knot

Then run the thread in between the second, third, fourth, and fifth fingers (see Figure 2). Push the needle (see Figure 3) through the loop on the fingers and behind the netting mesh through the loop on which the working thread is fastened (see Figure 5) so that a second loop is formed. This must be held by the little finger of the left hand. Now draw in the working thread by degrees, by which the loop held by the thumb becomes loosened. Also draw the second, third, and fourth fingers out of the loop marked *a* in Figure 4, still holding the loop marked *b* in that figure upon the little finger. Finally, drop the loop *b* from the little finger, and fasten the knot by drawing the thread firmly. This completes 1 stitch.

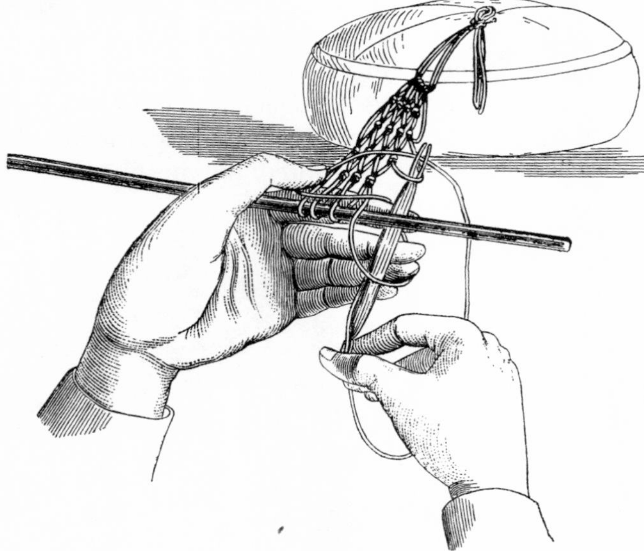

Figure 3. Making of knot

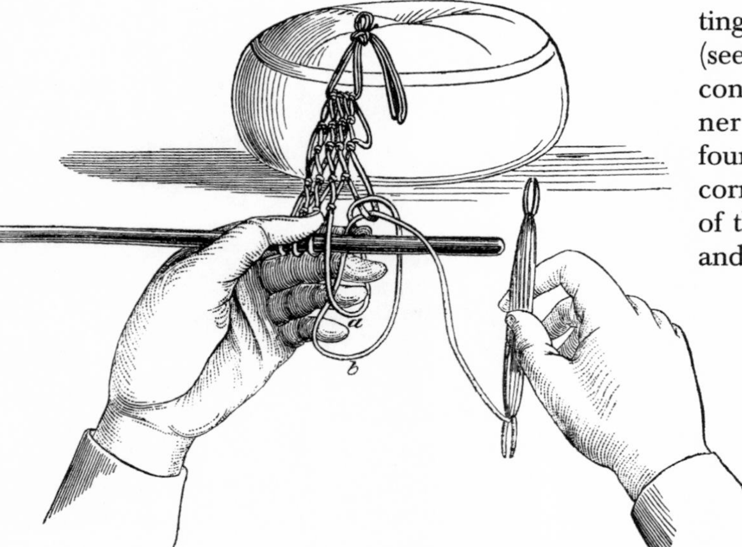

Figure 4. Making of knot

The remaining stitches that form the foundation are worked in the same manner. Figure 5 shows a row of foundation stitches, which are knotted on the loop.

Figure 5. Foundation stitches

Having worked the requisite number of foundation stitches, draw the mesh out of them. At the beginning of the next round turn the work, as netting is worked backward and forward, so that the last foundation stitch becomes now the first stitch of the following round. Make the knot as already described. However, put the needle through a foundation stitch instead of around the loop. Continue to work, turning the work, and without cutting the thread.

In this manner is worked the diamond netting, so called because the meshes take this form (see Figure 6). The knots for the plain netting, which consists of squares, are worked in the same manner (see Figures 7 and 8). For a four-cornered foundation in diamond netting, make a foundation corresponding to either the length or the breadth of the work. Work over all the stitches backward and forward till the foundation has reached the size desired. The foundation stitches are cut away afterward, as they will be somewhat longer than the other stitches. Or, instead, the foundation may be worked over a somewhat finer mesh.

Figure 6. Diamond netting

The plain netting, whether it be intended for a square or quadrilateral, is begun on one corner with 2 foundation stitches. On these work in rounds, turning the work, and add a stitch at the end of every round by working always 2 stitches over the last (see Figure 7).

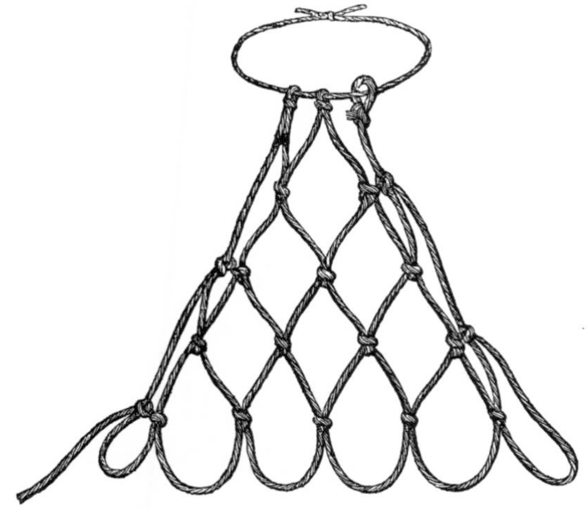

Figure 7. Making of plain netting

When the work has reached the requisite width, if a square is wanted, work one round without widening, and narrow 1 stitch in every following round. The is done by working together the last 2 stitches in every round, in doing which run the netting needle through the last 2 stitches of the round at the same time. Figure 8 gives the last knot somewhat loosened, which plainly shows the manner of working. When only 2 stitches remain, work these together by a knot without laying the thread over the mesh.

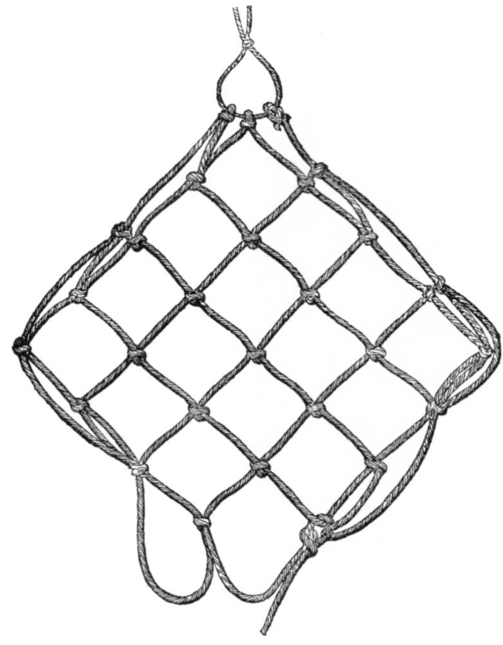

Figure 8. Making of plain netting

If a quadrilateral is desired, work in the completed portion, after having finished widening, a section as long as the long side of the figure. In doing this widen at the end of one round and narrow at the end of the next (as already described). Then narrow off the end precisely as when working a square.

Rosettes or small circular foundations are worked in two ways. Either make a foundation, the number of stitches corresponding to that of the outer row (see Figure 23). Tie the foundation thread and work around till it has reach the requisite size (see Figure 9). Or begin the same with a foundation of 6, 7, or 8 stitches, and work in the round, always making 2 stitches in 1. The widening is repeated in every round, and the 2 loops are always taken in the added (little) stitches of the former round (see

Figure 10). Triangular pieces are thus formed, which are regularly divided from each other by the added stitches, and are widened 1 stitch in every round.

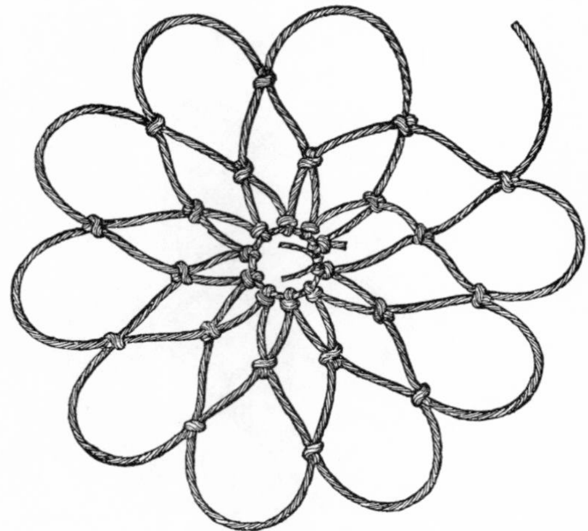

Figure 9. Circular foundation without widening

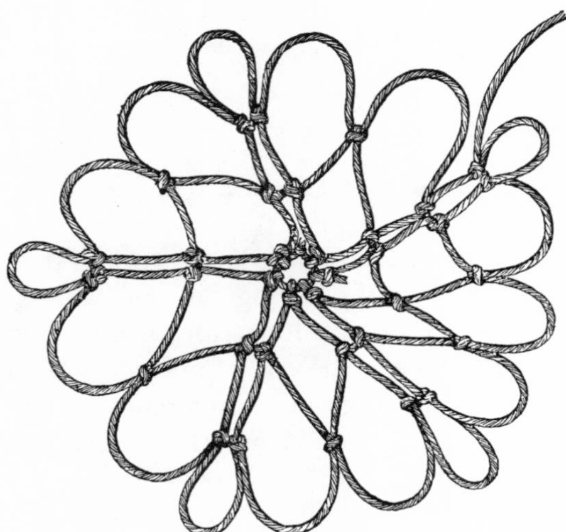

Figure 10. Circular foundation of triangular loops

Figure 11 shows another kind of diamond netting, called rose netting. It is worked over two meshes of different sizes. The one mesh must be half larger than the other. The knots are worked in the usual manner. The design is formed by weaving together 2 stitches. Draw the 1st of every 2 of the stitches worked over the larger mesh through the 2nd stitch, and work a knot in the stitch drawn through. Then with the point of the needle draw the thread of the 2nd stitch out in the direction of the arrow. Work a knot in this stitch also. Figure 11 shows one figure not yet finished; the others show the direction of the stitches. The round in which the stitches are woven together is always worked over the fine mesh. Work alternately also one round over the larger mesh, the next over the smaller. Figure 12 shows the rose netting worked with fine thread.

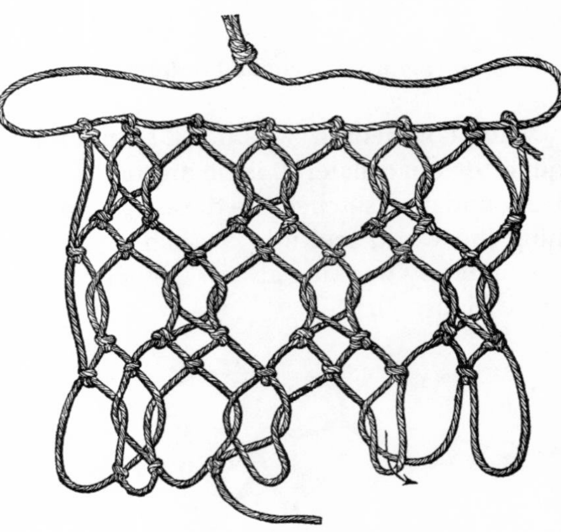

Figure 11. Making of rose netting

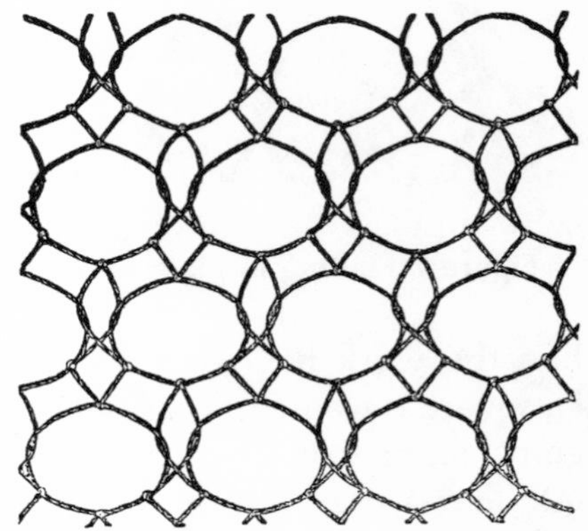

Figure 12. Rose netting of fine cotton

The fastening on of a new thread is done as shown in Figures 13 to 16. These are the cross knots used in netting and knotted work. Figure 13 shows the simple cross knot. Take the working thread about 1 1/2 inches from the end between the thumb and forefinger of the left hand. This is the end marked *a* in Figure 14. Then take the thread that is to be spliced on also between the thumb and forefinger of the left hand under the first thread, so that both ends of the threads cross. Wind the end *a* with the other thread marked *b*. Finally, draw the end *a* in the direction of the dotted line and of the arrow through the loop. Take the ends of the threads between the thumb and forefinger of the right hand, and with the left hand draw closely the thread *b*.

Figure 13. Finished single cross knot

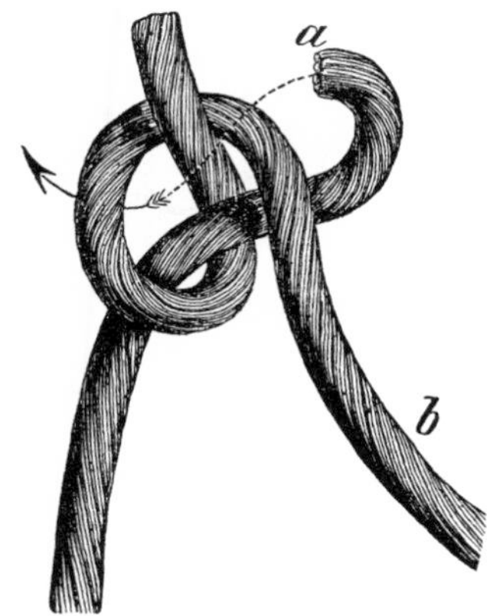

Figure 14. Tying of single cross knot

Figure 15 teaches the manner of tying the double cross knot. Figure 16 shows another kind of cross knot. Both are tied similarly to the last, and may be done by reference to the illustration. In tying the knot in Figure 15, it must be observed that the under end of the thread *a* is to be drawn.

Figure 15. Tying of double cross knot

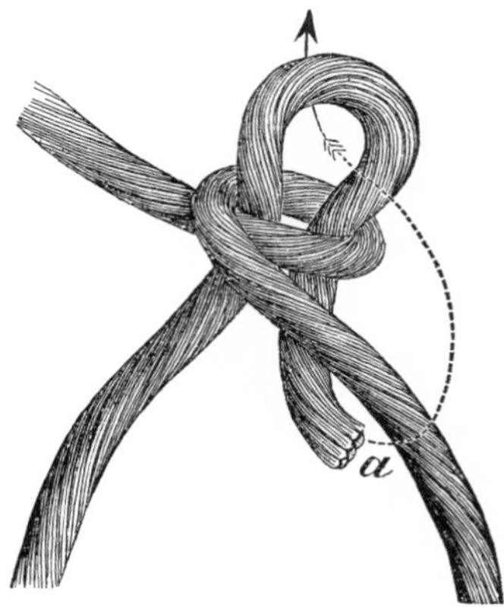

Figure 16. Tying of cross knot

Figure 17 is a kind of diamond netting. The design is formed by alternating two meshes of different sizes. The illustration shows where the meshes must be changed.

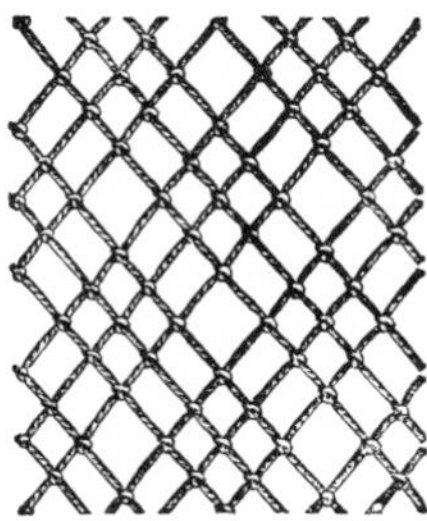

Figure 17. Diamond netting

August 15, 1868

Figures 18 to 21 show different manners of working the netting. This is done, according to the design of the work and the texture of the foundation, with coarse or fine yarn, coarse thread, or other materials. There are different styles of working.

The simplest is point de reprise (darning stitch) shown in Figure 18. Fill the holes (squares) of the netting with the yarn by taking a thread of the foundation on the needle, letting the next lie under the needle, and running the thread through in this manner. In the next (backward) row take on the needle those threads that before lay under it. Point de reprise must always be worked in the same direction. Large spaces worked in the same design should always be worked together, as the joining of a new section would render the work irregular.

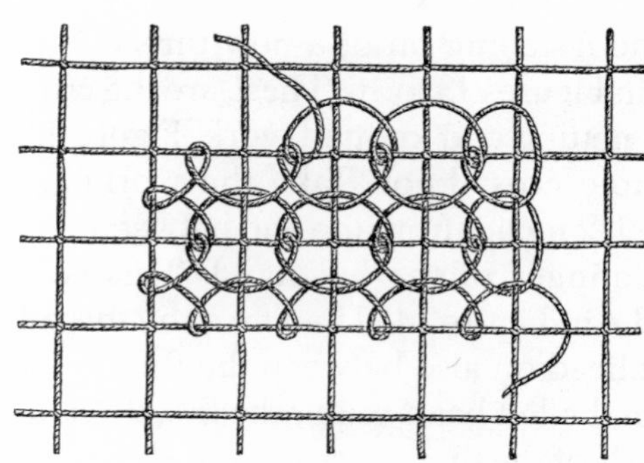

Figure 19. Point d'esprit on netted foundation

Figure 20 shows the point de toile stitch, also much used in netted guipure. This is really a double point de reprise, being worked both ways in the same manner.

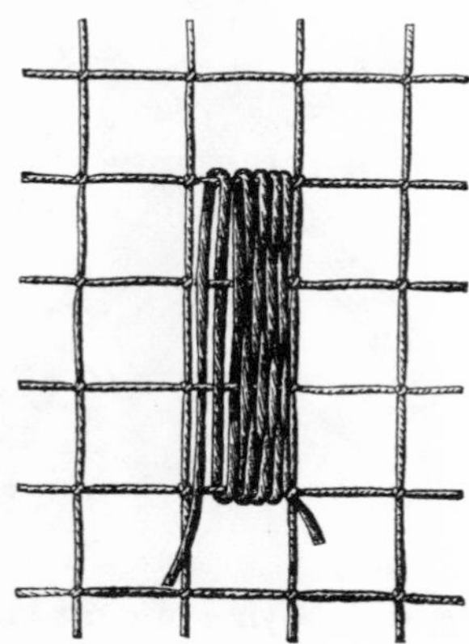

Figure 18. Point de reprise on netted foundation

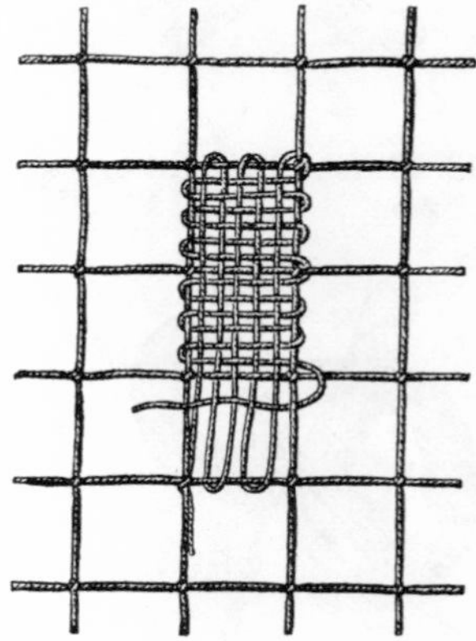

Figure 20. Point de toile on netted foundation

Figure 19 shows the point d'esprit stitch, which is especially used in netted guipure. This consists of buttonhole-stitch loops, worked around the netted squares as shown.

Figure 21 shows a foundation in rose netting, which is worked in point de reprise. This kind of pattern may be used for covers, curtains, etc.

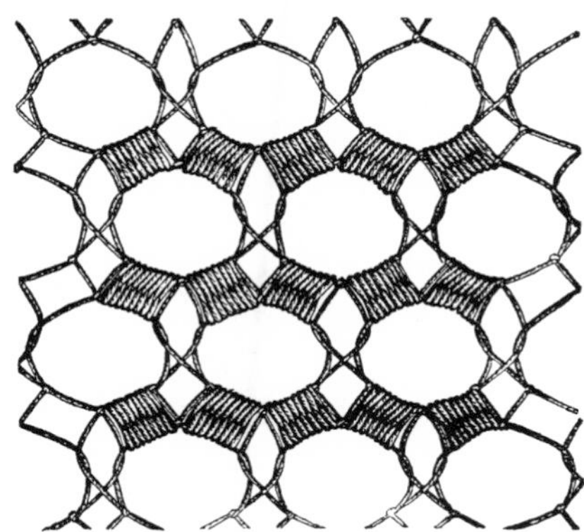

Figure 21. Point de reprise on rose netting

Shell netting (see Figure 22) may be used for the same purposes. For working, two meshes of different sizes are needed. Over the smaller mesh make a foundation of the requisite length. Then work one round over the same mesh. Now take the larger mesh and work over this alternately in the first 7 stitches each a knot, then in the following stitch 7 knots. In the next round, which is worked over the fine mesh, make in the 7 single stitches taken together 1 knot, but 1 knot in each of the 7 stitches that were taken from 1 stitch. After one plain round over the same mesh follows a round over the larger mesh, by which the design is continued as shown.

Figure 22. Shell netting

The little rosette in Figure 23 may be used for trimming collars, cuffs, cravats, etc. Begin with a foundation of 25 stitches over a mesh 3/4 inch in circumference. Work three rounds over a fine knitting needle. Join the middle stitches closely with single crochet worked in the foundation stitches.

Figure 23. Small netted rosette

The rosette in Figure 24 may be worked with fine or coarse yarn. Several may be set together to form covers, etc. Begin the rosette in the center by a foundation of 12 stitches. The rosette may be worked by reference to the illustration.

Figure 24. Netted rosette

Figures 25 to 27 show insertions that may be used for trimming underclothing and bed linen. They are worked with fine and coarse yarn, which lends a very pretty effect. They are all worked in diamond netting.

For Figure 25 make with fine yarn a foundation of the requisite size. Then work a round with coarse cotton and over a mesh about 1 1/2 inches in circumference. Then again two rounds with fine yarn and over a fine mesh. In doing so, in the first of these two rounds, twist every stitch of the preceding round from left to right as illustrated before working the knot. Now draw a thread through the stitches of the last round, and cut away the foundation stitches. Loose with a needle the knots out of the stitches worked with coarse yarn. Work now on this side of the insertion also two rounds with fine yarn and over the fine mesh, twisting every stitch as before. After this crochet a border on each side, consisting of single crochet worked in the netted stitches of the last round.

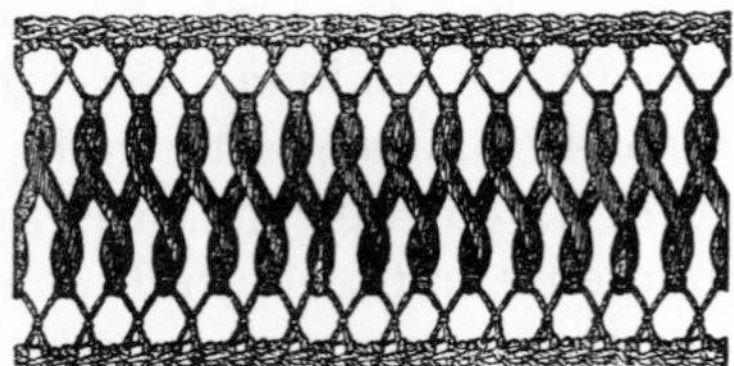

Figure 25. Netted insertion

The insertion in Figure 26 is worked similarly to Figure 25, and may be done by reference to the illustration.

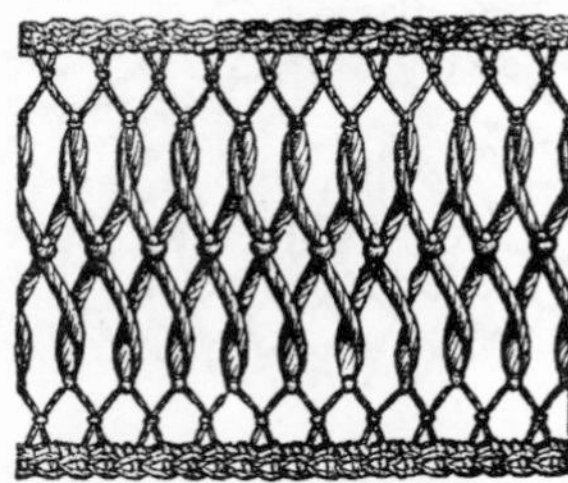

Figure 26. Netted insertion

By the aid of the illustration may also be worked Figure 27, the middle rounds of which are formed by rose netting.

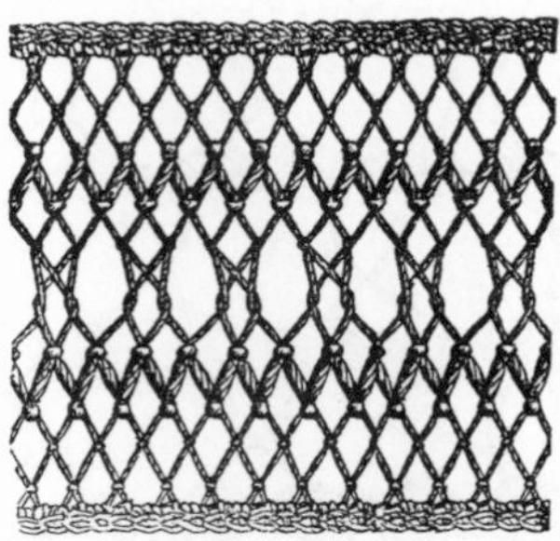

Figure 27. Netted insertion

Figures 28 to 30 show three netted edgings. These are worked similarly to the insertion. Take fine and coarse yarn. For Figure 30 twist the stitches twice before tying the knots. On the upper edge fasten the netted stitches by a round of chain stitch, in doing which work in also the stitches of the netting.

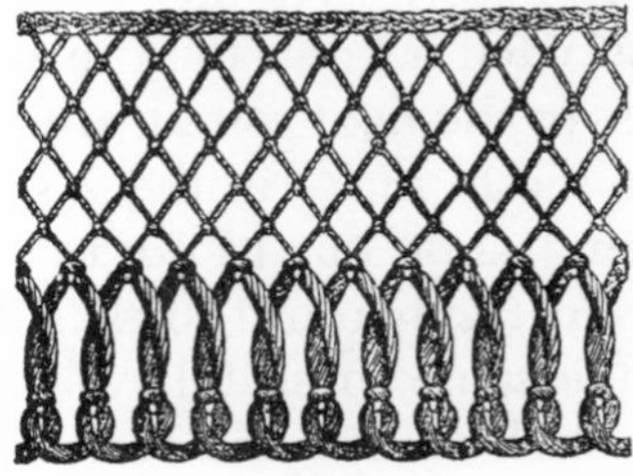

Figure 28. Netted edging

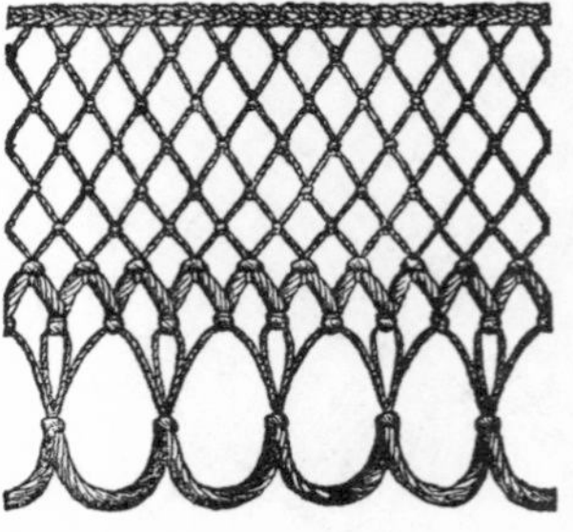

Figure 29. Netted edging

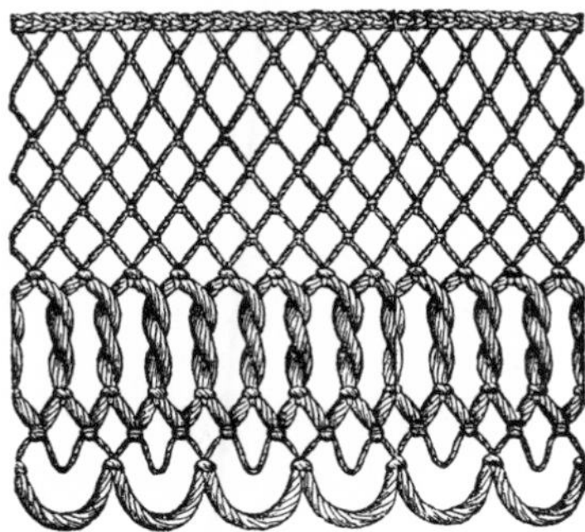

Figure 30. Netted edging

Figures 31 to 36 show different edgings worked in diamond netting. They are embroidered as shown, in point de toile, point d'esprit, and point de reprise. The under edges of Figures 31 to 33 are worked in buttonhole stitch.

Figure 31. Netted edging, embroidered

Figure 32. Netted edging, embroidered

Figure 33. Netted edging, embroidered

On Figure 34 the under edge is only wound with a thread. The design figures are worked backward and forward like a row of cross-stitch.

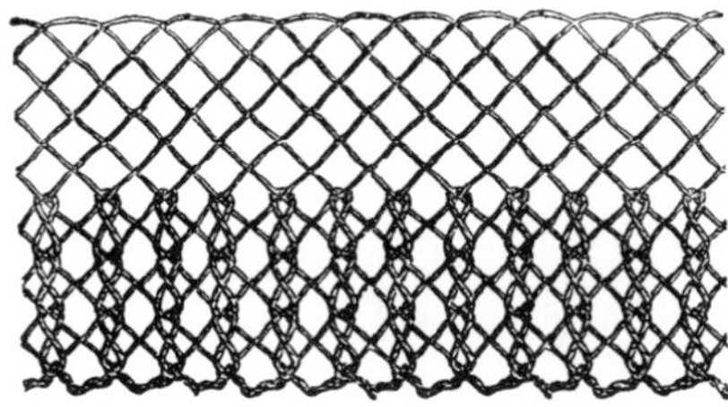

Figure 34. Netted edging

The edging in Figure 35 is an imitation of Valenciennes lace. It is worked in fine thread over a fine steel knitting needle. The under edge is worked in scallops with fine thread. Just above this is a row of coarser thread, in working which fasten together several threads of the netting, which forms the scallops. These scallops are bordered with fine picots. For making fine netting of this sort take a long sewing or embroidery needle, as a netting needle would be too fine to push through the holes.

Figure 35. Netted edging

The lace in Figure 36 is worked lengthwise. Take an embroidery needle, and work over a fine knitting needle 5 foundation stitches. Then work * five rounds, widening by 1 stitch at the end of the first, third, and fifth rounds. Then follow three plain rounds, and after this six rounds, in which work together as 1 stitch the last 2 stitches in the first, third, and fifth rounds. Repeat from * till the edging has reached the length desired. Work the edge with knitting cotton in buttonhole stitch. Work the figures shown in the illustration.

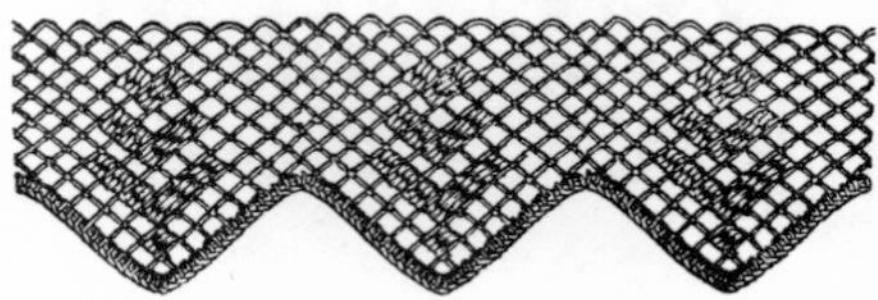

Figure 36. Netted edging

August 22, 1868

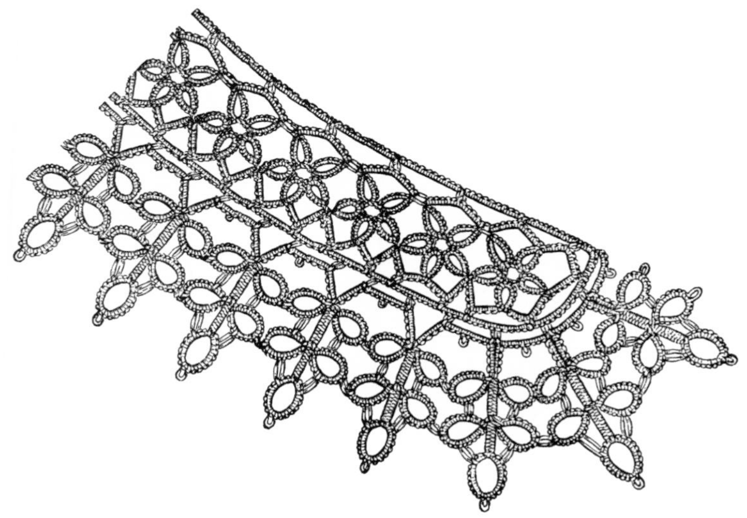

Tatted Collar

This collar is worked in fine tatting cotton with two threads (shuttles).

Begin with the insertionlike part of the collar; work first the upper and then the under part. To make the upper half of this part tie together the two working threads. Work * only with one thread for one leaf of the five-leaved figures 7 ds. (double stitches), 1 p. (picot), 1/6 inch long, 7 ds. At the end of this leaf work over the foundation thread a scallop composed of 5 ds., 1 p., 5 ds. Then a leaf like the former, which must, however, be fastened to a picot of the former leaf instead of working a new picot. Repeat from * till the row is long enough to make the collar.

On each end of the row work over the foundation thread a scallop of 5 ds., 1 p., 5 ds., 1 p., 5 ds., then * a leaf of 7 ds. Fasten to the picot that joins the first two leaves of the upper row, again 7 ds. Then work over the foundation thread a scallop of 4 ds., 1 p., 4 ds. Work after this a leaf, which must be fastened to the same picot of the former row to which the former leaves were fastened, a scallop of 4 ds., 1 p., 4 ds., and another leaf, which must also be fastened to the same picot. This completes one of the five-leaved figures. Now repeat from * till the insertionlike part of the collar is finished, then fasten the threads.

Border this with an edge, which is worked over a foundation thread. Fasten the threads on the 1st picot of the corner scallop (see illustration). Work 5 ds., 1 p., 5 ds., fasten to the following picot of the same scallop. Work 2 ds., 1 p., 7 ds., 1 p., 2 ds. * Fasten to the picot of the next scallop (on the under part of the insertionlike part). Work 5 ds., 1 p., 5 ds.; fasten to the picot of the next scallop; 2 ds., 1 p., 2 ds. Repeat from * till the round is completed.

The other edge is worked in the same manner. On the upper edge the number of stitches between every 2 picots of the insertionlike part must count 10.

Next border the ends and under edge with the following lace, which is worked with two threads. Fasten the working thread to the upper part of the end of the collar on the 1st picot (see illustration). Work over the foundation thread a scallop of 5 ds., 1 p., 5 ds., fasten to the next picot, then again over the foundation thread 4 ds. Close on that work with only one thread a ring composed of 10 ds., 1 p., 5 ds., 1 p., 5 ds. Then, after 3/10 inch space, a ring of 2 ds.; fasten to the last picot of the former ring. Work 8 ds., 1 p., 5 ds., 1 p., 5 ds.; after 3/10 inch space, a ring of 2 ds.; fasten to the last picot of the former ring. Work 8 ds., 1 p., 8 ds., 1 p., 2 ds.; then again, after 3/10 inch space, a ring of 5 ds.; fasten to the last picot of the former ring. Work 5 ds., 1 p., 8 ds., 1 p., 2 ds.; and after 3/10 inch space, a fifth ring of 5 ds. Fasten the last picot of the former ring, 5 ds., 1 p., 10 ds.; then over the foundation thread 4 ds.; fasten to the picot the working threads were fastened to before working the first 4 ds., before the first four rings. This completes a leaf of the lace.

The remaining leaves are worked in the same manner. They are joined to each other and to the collar as illustrated. Work also between every two leaves 4 ds., 1 p., 4 ds. over the foundation thread. The threads that join the five rings of each leaf are worked in point de reprise as shown.

Crocheted Collar

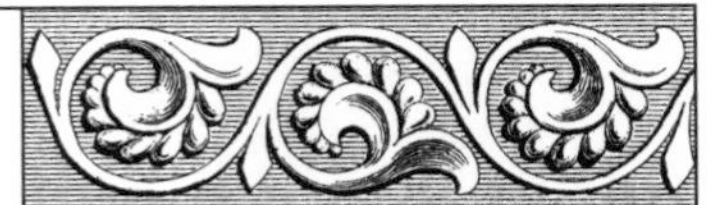

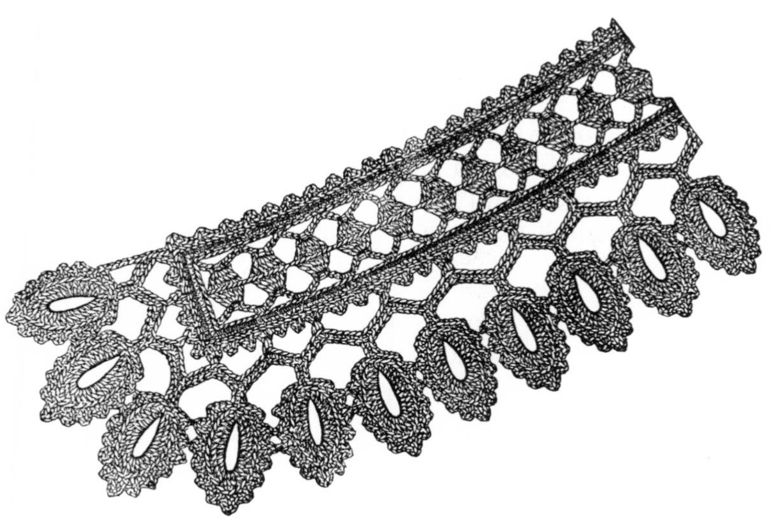

Crocheted Collar

This collar is worked with very fine crochet cotton. Begin on the upper edge of the collar with a foundation of 254 stitches. On this work backward as follows.

First round: Passing over the last stitch in every foundation stitch 1 sc. (single crochet). Turn the work. Crochet 1 ch. (chain stitch).

Then, going back on the first round, work the second round: Alternately 2 sc., 5 ch., passing over 4 stitches of the previous round.

Third round: Fastening on a new thread at the beginning of the second round, work in the middle stitch of every chain-stitch scallop 6 dc. (double crochet), after this always 2 ch.

Fourth round: Laying on a new thread, 3 ch., * 6 dc. in the dc. of the former round; these are not worked singly but together by drawing the thread through all at once, 6 ch.; from * repeat.

Fifth round: Fastening on the thread at the beginning of the second round, crochet 1 sl. (slip stitch) in the 1st sc. of this round, then 3 ch., 1 sl., in the 1st dc. of the third round, 3 ch., 1 sl., in the 1st ch. of the fourth round, then always alternating 5 ch., 2 sc. in the next chain-stitch scallop of the fourth round to the end of the same. On the other end work as in the beginning of the fifth round.

Sixth round: Fastening the thread on anew, in each stitch of the fifth round 1 sc.

Seventh round: Work 1 ch. Now turn the work and crochet back on the former round, so the stitches on the right side of the work appear wrong side out. Around the so far finished part except the foundation stitches, in every stitch 1 sc. On the corner a few stitches must of course be added, and the threads on the ends must be worked in.

Eighth round: Again work 1 ch. and turn and work, going back over the entire edge, always alternately 2 sc. in the next 2 stitches, 1 p. (picot); that is to say, 2 sc. separated by 2 ch. in the 3rd following stitch.

Ninth round: From this time leave the foundation stitches of the collar alone.

Tenth round: Work 1 sc. in the 1st p. on one end of the collar. Then three times alternately, 9 ch. 1 sc. in the 2nd following p. Then to the other end always alternately 9 ch. 1 sc. in the 3rd following p. Then again as on the previous end, passing over only 1 p. with the last 3 chain-stitch scallops.

The leaves that form the outer edge of the collar are worked together in one round as follows. Work 5 sc. in the first 5 stitches of the former round, * 18 ch. Join these in a round by working 1 sc. in the 6th ch. (in the upper vein). Then in this chain-stitch ring a round composed of 1 sdc. (short double crochet), 12 dc., 3 stc. (short treble), 12 dc., 1 sdc., 1 sc.

August 22, 1868

On this work a second round as follows. Work 2 sc. in the first 2 stitches of the former round. Then always alternately 1 p., that is 2 sc. separated by 2 ch. in the next stitch, 1 sc. in the following stitch. The picot that comes on the stc. on the point of the leaf must count 3 ch. At the end of the round 2 sc. in the last 2 stitches of the former round; 1 sl. in the 1st stitch of this round, then 2 sc. in the 1st 2 of the 18 chain. Working the 2nd sc. fasten at the same time the next ch. of the tenth round.

After this crochet 9 sc. in the next 9 stitches of the tenth round and repeat from *. In working do not forget to fasten the leaves together as shown with the picots.

August 29, 1868

Trimmings for Blouses and Waists

Figure 1 shows a trimming of batiste and French embroidery. The center of each rosette is a worked wheel.

The border in Figure 3 is on white piqué, worked in herringbone stitch and point Russe.

Figure 1. Trimming of batiste and French needlework

The trimming in Figure 2 consists of a double strip of white alpaca 1 1/4 inches wide, laid in box pleats 1/2 inch wide. The upper edge of each pleat is turned back and fastened with a few stitches exactly in the middle of the pleat. In doing this fasten only the upper layer of the material, to prevent the stitches from showing on the right side. The place where the pleated strip is set on is covered by a double bias fold of blue silk 1/3 inch wide, arranged as shown.

Figure 2. Blouse trimming

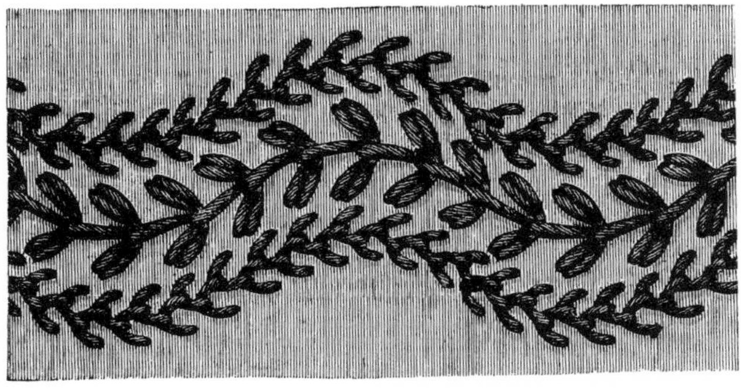

Figure 3. Point Russe border

Figure 4 shows a trimming of batiste and French embroidery. Work the edges with fine black silk in buttonhole stitch, leaving some distance between each stitch. Then buttonhole stitch the edges over this again with shorter and closer stitches. A black ribbon run through completes this trimming.

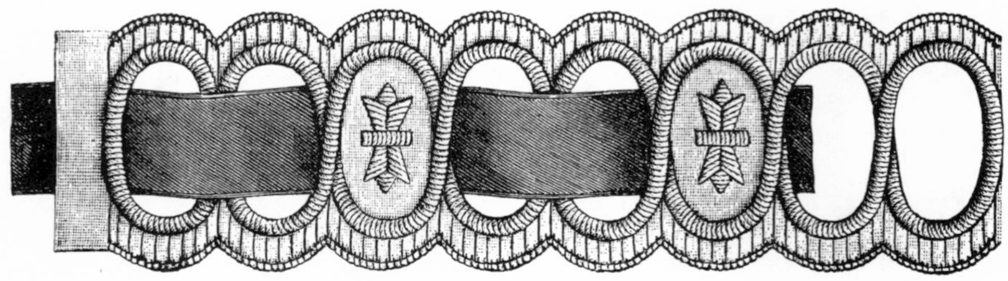

Figure 4. Trimming of batiste and French needlework

The trimming in Figure 5 consists of small rounded leaves of cherry silk, bordered with a piping of white alpaca. The back of each leaf is lined with linen. The folds that head the leaves consist each of a bias strip of cherry silk 1 1/4 inches wide. On one side of this sew a narrow double strip of white alpaca so that it stands out like a cord. Then lay the silk strip over so the cord lies along the middle of the strip, as shown, and sew the edges down.

Figure 5. Blouse trimming

The simple trimming in Figure 6 is worked on piqué. First sew on mignardise cord, and fasten the picots with herringbone stitch of fine black silk. The figures are worked with black silk in the same manner. Border the outer edge with a lace that consists of fine scalloped braid, in which has been crocheted two rounds of openwork in double crochet stitch.

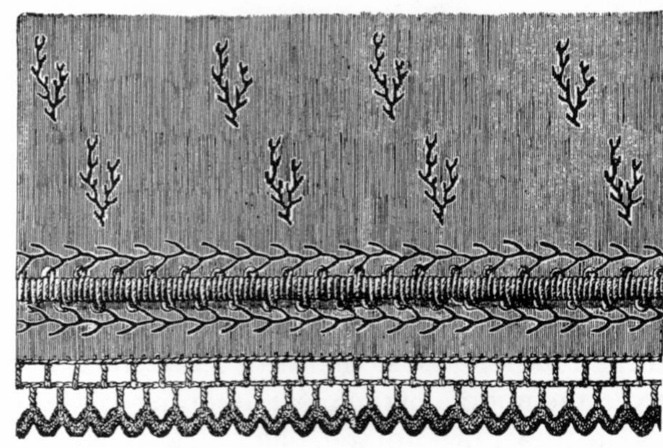

Figure 6. Trimming of piqué, mignardise, and point Russe needlework

The trimming in Figure 7 is also used for antimacassars. It is worked on lace in mull application. The edges of the application leaves are partly worked in buttonhole stitch and partly in straight half-polka stitch. The veins of the leaves are worked in the same manner.

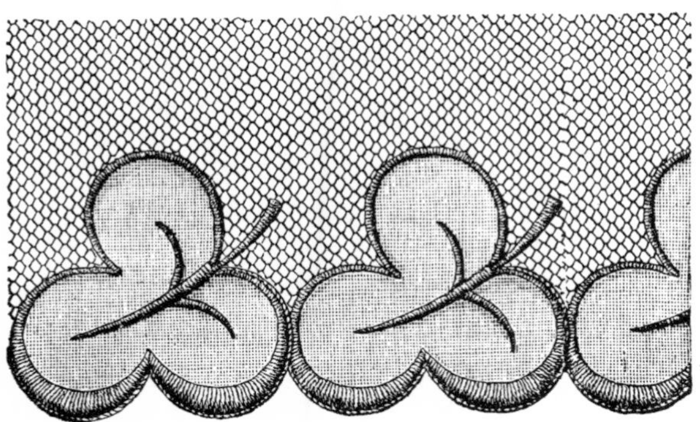

Figure 7. Lace border with mull application

The insertion in Figure 8 is worked of fine tatting cotton as follows. Work a ring of 6 ds. (double stitches), 1 p. (picot), five times alternately 2 ds., 1 p., then 6 ds. Turning this ring downward, work, at the distance of 1/3 inch, a similar ring. Continue till the insertion is long enough. The rings must, however, be fastened together by picots as shown. To form the pointed contour, two rings must follow each other on the same side after every nine rings.

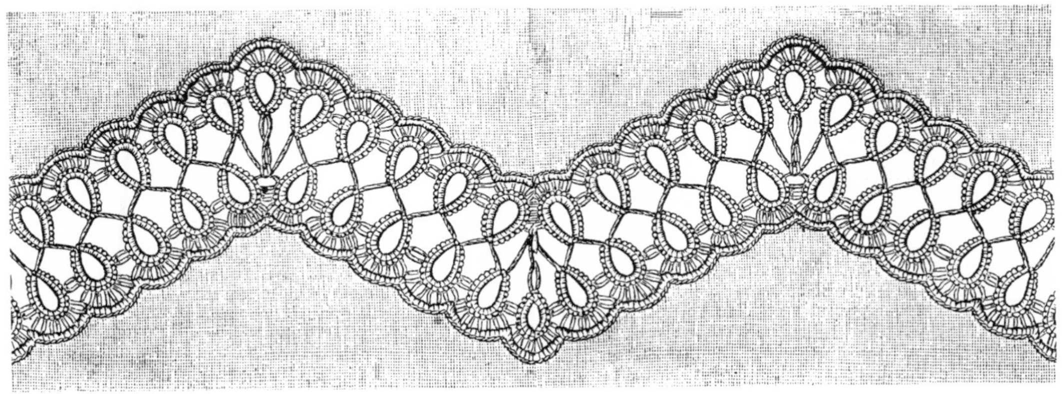

Figure 8. Tatted insertion set in the stuff

September 5, 1868

Crinolines

The shape to be introduced for the next season is admirable. In the first place, it is slightly larger than the shape worn during the summer. The heavy materials of winter clothing make this necessary. The pannier fullness at the back is made to curve gracefully, instead of bulging out suddenly. The front of the skirt is perfectly straight, fitting smoothly over the figure. In the back is a gradually sloping train, flaring out at the edge just enough to avoid coming into contact with the heels.

Promenade skirts, to be worn with short dresses, will be from 2 1/4 to 2 1/2 yards in circumference, for ladies of medium height. Skirts worn with trains on full-dress occasions measure 3 1/2 yards.

Open Fronts

The new open fronts, or "winged" skirts, are the novelty of the season. They give complete freedom for every motion, walking, sitting, dancing, or stepping in and out of a carriage. The upper part of the skirt is laced together, then comes a few hoops, and below them is the open winged front. It is an impossibility for the feet to become entangled in this skirt, as the limbs are free from the hoops in front from the knee down. A spiral spring has been invented to hold the steels securely around the curved opening. This open front may be applied to any hoop, but the one with which we were especially pleased is called the Winged Lace skirt. The net or lace is similar to that used in the Imperial Lace skirt, but of closer mesh. There are eighteen pliable hoops. The tournure is graceful. The skirt slopes toward the bottom, measuring 85 inches in circumference. This skirt may be put in the tub and washed thoroughly.

The Zephyrina Empress is a round skirt, slightly trained, and especially adapted to the short walking dress. There are twenty-five exceedingly light hoops. The broad tapes are woven to receive the springs, which are of flexible, well-tempered steel. Two rivets in each tape hold the steel securely. The lower part of the skirt is lined or covered with muslin. The Winged Zephyr is larger, and has a more decided train, to be worn with full dress. A patented eyelet fastening penetrates the tape and the steel spring, holding them more securely than a rivet. A walking skirt *à panier,* called the New Era, has a closed front. The pannier curve is simply but perfectly formed by several springs almost contiguous to each other in front, but expanded to 6 or 7 inches behind. The Twin Spring, or indestructible skirt, derives its name from having two springs woven together in each hoop. In the fifteen hoops there are thirty springs.

The Duplex Elliptic skirt comes next on our list. The name Duplex is given because the steels in each hoop are double. The title Elliptic refers to the shape. We also saw a new walking skirt made after the French model, with but few hoops at the hip and a great many at the bottom, or exposed portions of the skirt. This skirt may be bought with the pannier shape very full at the back and beginning to enlarge just back of the point of the hip. Or it may be plainly sloped, and supplied with a spiral pannier to support the hoop and give the pannier effect.

An excellent skirt, known as the Self-Adjusting, or Colby, has vertical wires, fastened by hinges to the lower hoop. This skirt is remarkably pliable, conforming as readily to the position of the wearer as an ordinary muslin skirt. It is very light, made of well-tempered steel, and is said to be very durable.

French Hoops

French skirts are always made of muslin, and contain only from five to ten hoops. A pannier bustle is a part of each skirt, the hips are merely covered by muslin without springs, and the greater number of hoops, seldom more than ten, are between the hip and knee. There is usually an arrangement to lace the whole skirt back of the figure, leaving the front straight and plain. One skirt is covered with net, in which the springs are woven. Another, of muslin, has a gored cover, trimmed with fluted ruffles. The cover may be buttoned on below, and will serve as a petticoat. This is an excellent idea for stout ladies with large hips, as the bulk is not increased by petticoats. Another Parisian skirt, of very graceful shape, is covered with cambric around the outer edges. The waist and hips have only tapes, with straps and buckles, by which the skirt may be shortened or lengthened for street dresses or for trains. An American skirt has the front width without springs, and buttoned down the center.

Muslin skirts, or those covered with net, are to be commended above the skeleton hoops, so productive of accident. Covers of muslin buttoned on the lower part of the skirt are absolutely necessary with the skeleton skirt. These covers do not fit every skirt, and are very clumsy looking if badly fitted. Consequently a set of covers must be made for each skirt. Net and muslin skirts are free from this objection.

Panniers

Panniers will certainly continue in vogue. There are at least twenty different patterns from which to choose. We advise our readers to buy a pannier skirt with the tournure forming part of the skirt, as this is less complicated, and does away with the necessity of having two belts about the waist. If a separate pannier is worn, we think those made of puffed haircloth give the most natural contour to the figure. They are soft, round, and yielding, and by enlarging the appearance of the hips make the waist look much smaller. As haircloth is expensive, an excellent pannier is made of muslin with flexible whalebones running from the waist downward, held in position by tapes underneath. Spiral-spring bustles are used beneath the hoop to support it, and give the pannier effect to old-style skirts. A variety of other panniers are made with steel springs, to be worn outside the crinoline. The Bon-Ton, one of the best of these, is very full at the back, with the necessary graduated slope on the sides.

Corsets

Ladies should make it a rule to have their corsets made to order, instead of purchasing those ready-made. The ordinary cheap corset has neither beauty of contour nor compactness of construction. The steel busks are too narrow to support the figure or form a proper foundation for the front of the corsage, and are often made of steel of so low a quality that it breaks easily.

In giving an order for corsets it is necessary to send the measure around the chest below the arms, from beneath the arm to the hip, the circumference of the hips, and the waist measure. There can never be a prescribed size for the waist, since fashion changes the length and position of it. The pannier as now worn produces the appearance of a small waist. A line drawn halfway between the hip and the lowest rib gives the point at which the tapering waist reaches its smallest dimensions. The corset should be large enough to meet in back.

The material of the corset should be very firm and strong. Flimsy and elastic materials soon stretch out of shape. Fine coutil is expensive, but it is economy to buy it as it wears well.

Frenchwomen, who are very particular about their figures, have their corsets made in three pieces, laced at the sides as well as the back. The busks and whalebones at the back are very long.

The popular glove-fitting corset is worthy of commendation. It is made without gores, and is cut on a correct principle, by which a perfect fit is obtained. It consists of three pieces; the bust, waist, and hips are cut separately. The spring-latch fastening is a great improvement on the old-fashioned clasps. The lower hook is constructed with a spring, which is pressed on the latch opposite, adjusting the other hooks and studs in a moment. The busks, of flexible steel, adjust themselves to every undulation of the figure.

An imported corset, that took a prize at the Paris Exposition, has a hundred whalebones. A French corset, called the Bride's Own, is made of glossy coutil that looks like satin. It is edged with Cluny lace and insertion. Others are embroidered with white and with scarlet. Imported corsets are also made of kid and morocco. Perfumed corsets are also made in London; these are molded by steam, and are very flexible. Gauze corsets for ladies in hot climates are also made.

Miscellaneous

A new spiral bosom pad is a good design, but is objectionable on account of being partly made of rubber. Very natural-looking busts are made of wire netting, in a solid piece covering the front from armpit to armpit. A muslin cover conceals the wire. It is held in place by elastic shoulder straps and belt.

Garters impede circulation and injure the shape of the limb, especially when worn below the knee. An excellent stocking supporter consists of an elastic waistband with two long tapes on each limb connected with an elastic strap at the knee that is buttoned to the stocking.

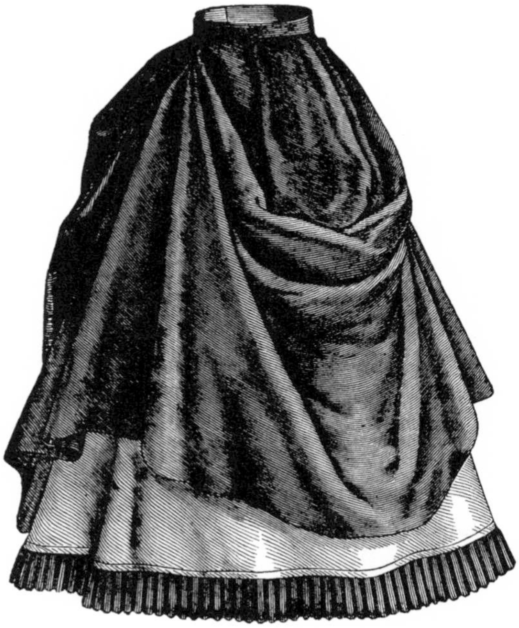

Looping Up Dresses

This new arrangement for looping up dresses is very simple and convenient. Sew three buttons on the skirt just below the belt, one in the middle of the back and one at each side. Make three loops worked of silk of the dress color, each about 1 1/2 inches long, to hold the buttons when the dress is looped up. Sew them on about 22 inches below the belt behind, and 16 inches below it at the sides. However, the distance of the loops below the buttons depends on the skirt length. The illustrations show the dress before looping up, the front of the dress looped up, and the back.

Making Corsets

To know whether a corset pattern must be enlarged or reduced, measure in the same manner as for a dress waist. The upper width of the corset must be at least 1 inch wider, and the dress 1 inch narrower than is given by the measure. The length of the corset is best determined by that usually worn. Enlarge or reduce the pattern till its measurements are correct.

To understand how to make a corset the proper size for any figure, see the pattern for the Brown Drilling Corset. The contour of the figures (the heavy line) gives the original size. The finer lines outside the contour on the front, second hip gore, third hip gore, and back show on which side and in what manner the pattern may be enlarged. The pattern may be made smaller on the same side. The front gores may also be made smaller, as shown by the lines on the first and second front gores. If, however, the corset needs to be very much widened, leave a surplus in addition on the front and back edges. If the pattern be too long or too short, shorten or lengthen it on the upper edge.

In cutting attention must be given to the rows of small lines on the pieces, which are marked "thread runs lengthwise." The backs must be cut straight on the back edges. On each piece from 1/2 to 1 inch must be allowed for the seams, as the pieces run over and under each other when set together. Cut the upper, under, and front edges according to the pattern.

The edges of the back may also be cut according to the contour of the pattern, or allowance may be made for a hem. In the former case linen tape of the requisite width is set under. In the latter case the hem may be stitched through, as shown by the narrow lines, to make a sheath for the whalebones and eyelets.

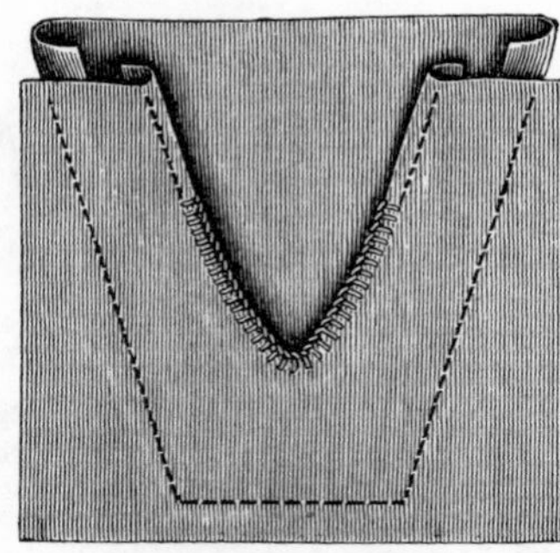

Figure 1. Setting on front gore–right side

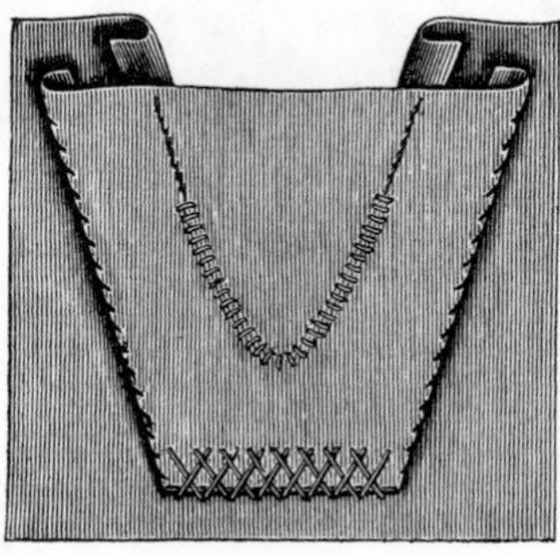

Figure 2. Setting on front gore–wrong side

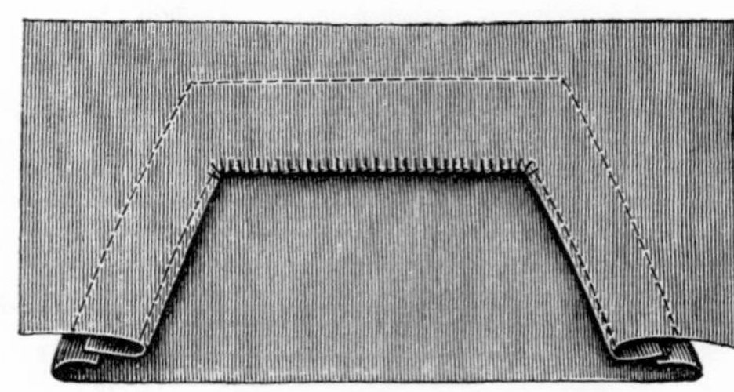

Figure 3. Setting on hip gore–right side

For running in the busk or steel spring, and the whalebones which are not brought under the seam, set on the under side of the corset, along the narrow line, linen tape of the requisite width. Stitch it down from the right side. The tape sewn on for the steel fastening remains loose on the front edge, and after the busk is run in is fastened with overcast stitches. For the buttons of the busk work buttonholes in the outside material in the proper place.

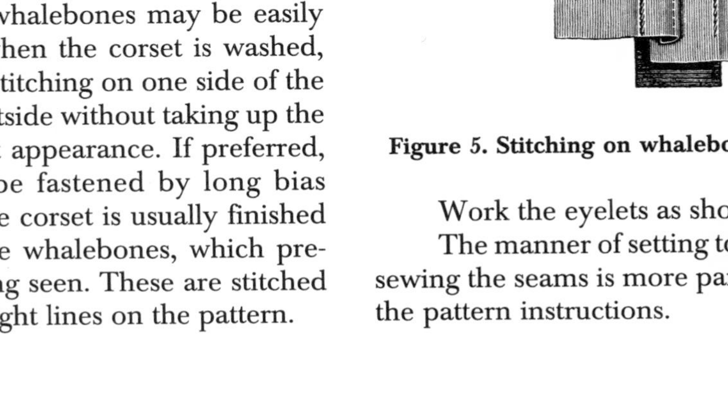

In order that the whalebones may be easily run in and taken out when the corset is washed, leave 1/2 inch without stitching on one side of the lower end. Stitch the outside without taking up the tape, to preserve a neat appearance. If preferred, the whalebones may be fastened by long bias stitches. The back of the corset is usually finished by cord ends above the whalebones, which prevent the ends from being seen. These are stitched in as shown by the straight lines on the pattern.

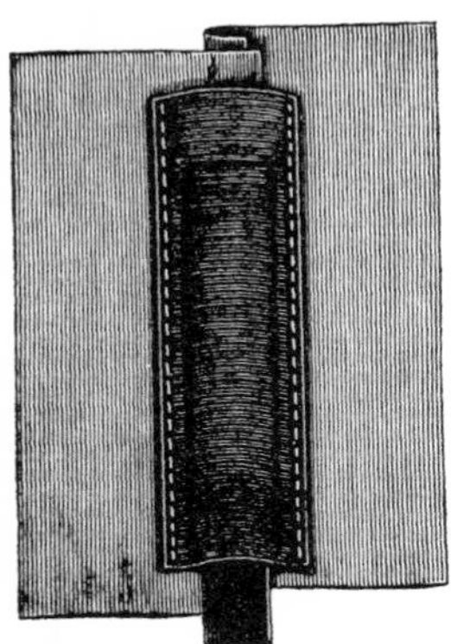

Figure 4. Stitching on whalebone sheath–right side

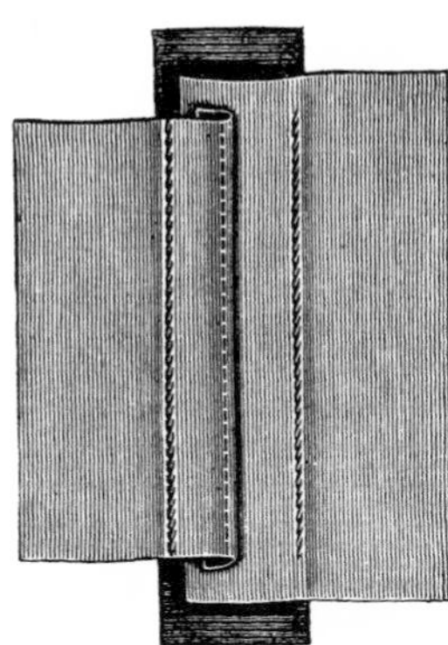

Figure 5. Stitching on whalebone sheath–wrong side

Work the eyelets as shown by the pattern.

The manner of setting together the pieces and sewing the seams is more particularly described in the pattern instructions.

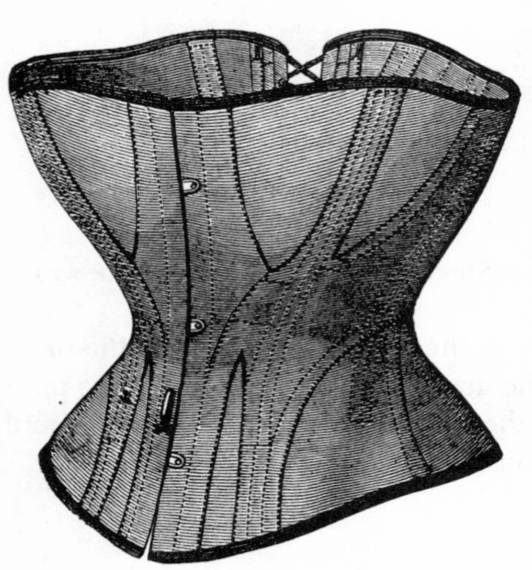

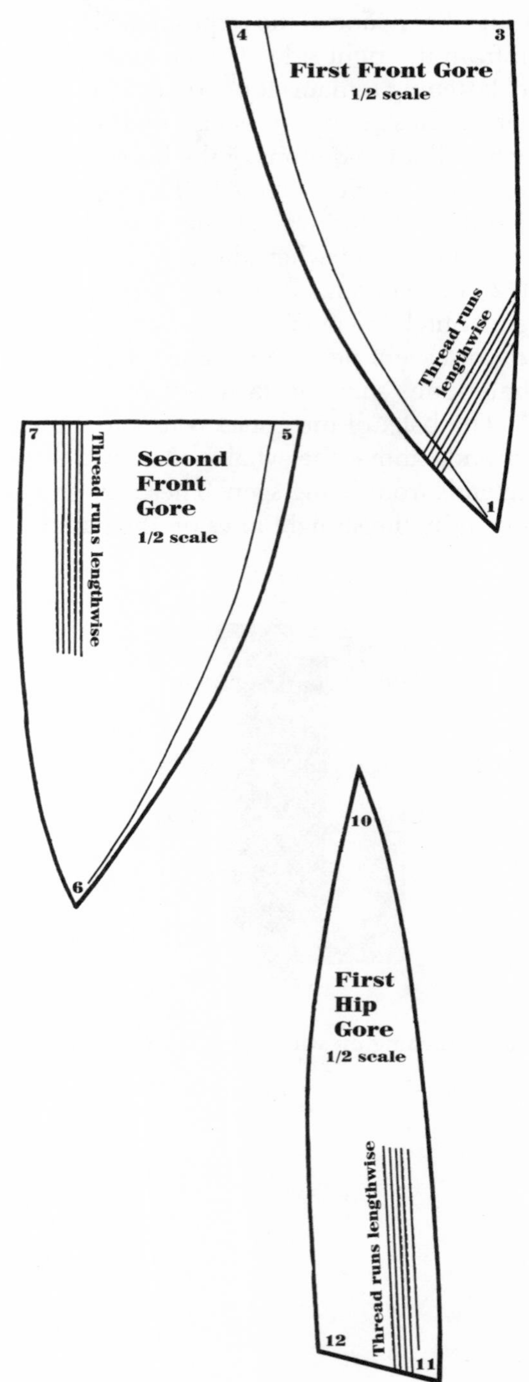

Brown Drilling Corset

Cut from the front, first front gore, second front gore, first hip gore, second hip gore, third hip gore, and back each two pieces. Take up the bosom pleat in each front, bringing 1 on 1 and 2 on 2 as shown. Set the gores in the front and back. Then join each front from 8 to 9 with the second hip gore. The seam is made with two rows of stitching, as also are the seams that join the fronts and backs from 17 to 18. Set on tape along the narrow line for the reception of the whalebones and busk. Stitch in the cords on the back. Bind the upper and under edges with linen braid. Finish it with a hook as illustrated. The eyelets are made as shown.

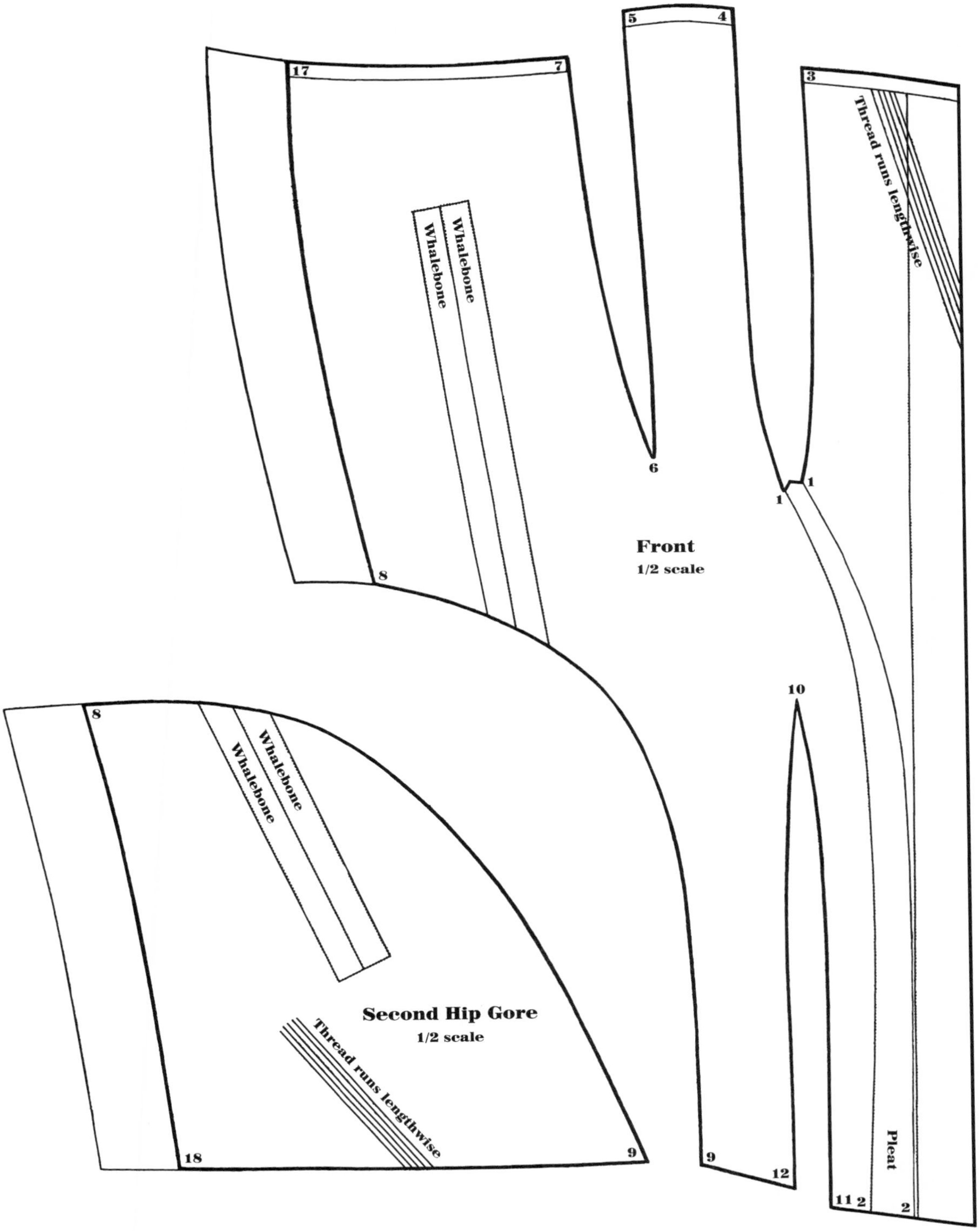

Brown Drilling Corset

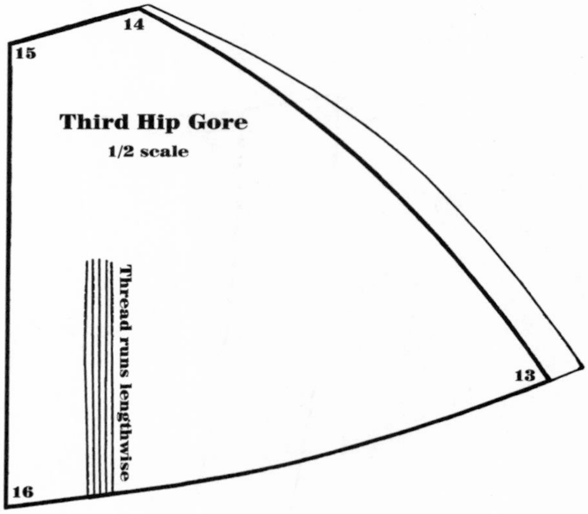

September 5, 1868

Third Hip Gore

1/2 scale

15 14 13 16

Thread runs lengthwise

Back

1/2 scale

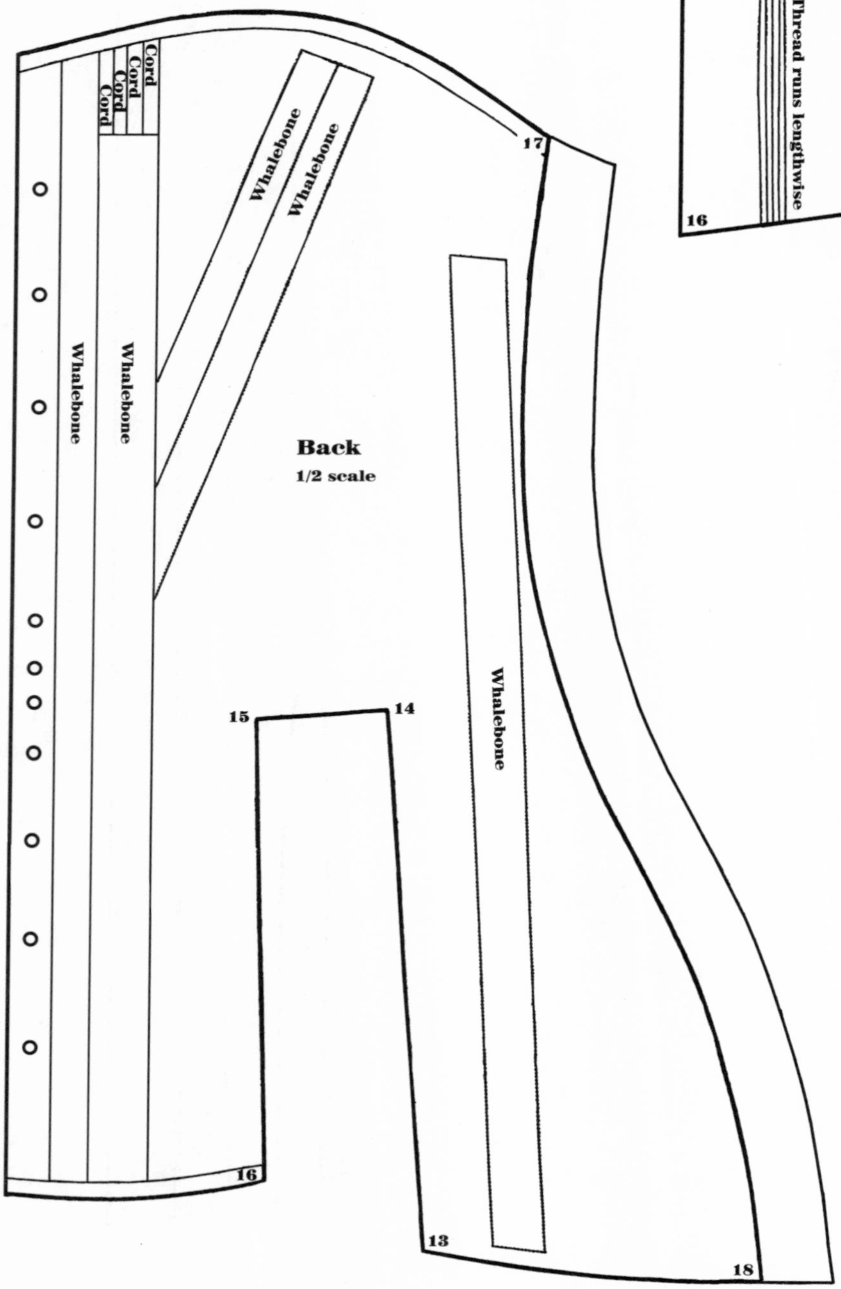

Cord
Cord
Cord
Cord

Whalebone
Whalebone
Whalebone
Whalebone
Whalebone

17 15 14 16 13 18

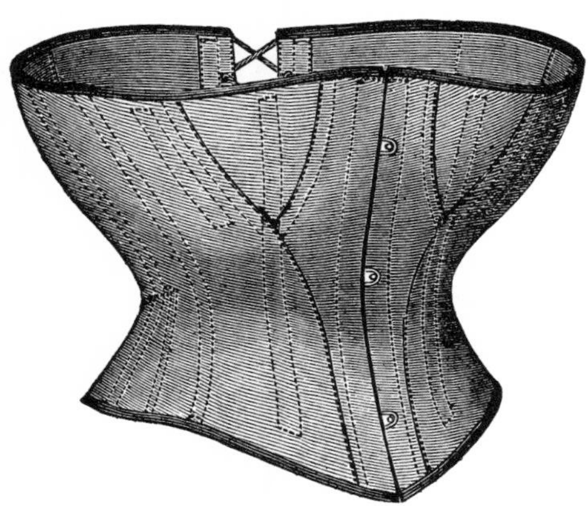

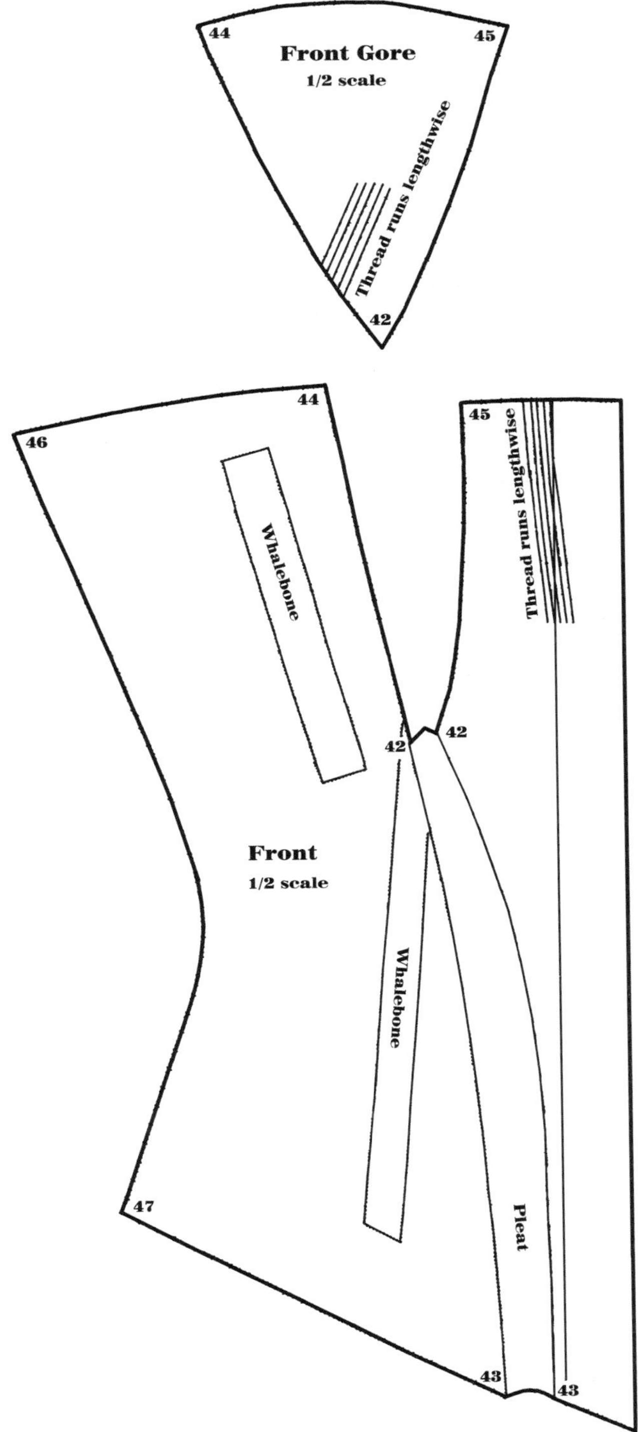

White Drilling Corset

This corset is of white drilling sewn with red silk. Cut from the front, front gore, side piece, hip gore, and back each two pieces. Take up the bosom pleats in the fronts, bringing 42 on 42 and 43 on 43. Set the front gore in the front and the hip gore in the side piece, according to the corresponding figures on the pattern. In setting in the gores the edge of the material must be laid over on the under side and stitched down as illustrated above. On the point of the front gore and along the upper edge of the hip gore, however, the material is not laid under but closely buttonhole-stitched down as illustrated. On the under side of the corset the gores are hemmed and cross-stitched down.

Join the front, side, and back pieces according to the figures on the pattern. In doing this lay together the pieces that are to be joined, lapping over 1/3 inch, lay the edges under, and make rows of stitching. Then set on the tape to form sheaths for the whalebones and busk. Run in the whalebones and work the eyelets. Bind the edges with red worsted braid.

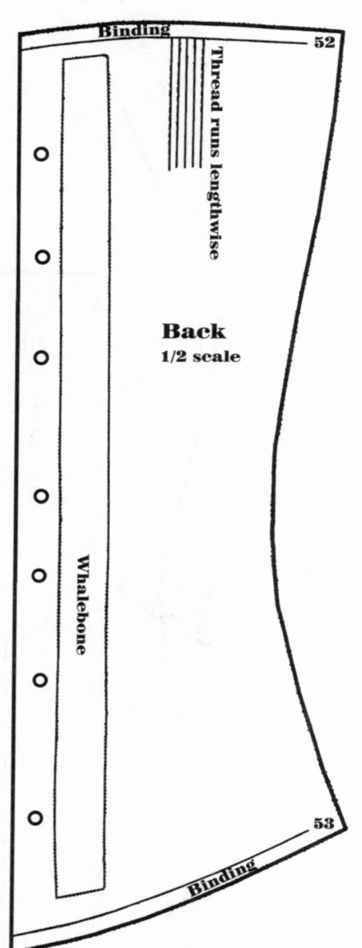
Binding
52
Thread runs lengthwise
Back
1/2 scale
Whalebone
53
Binding

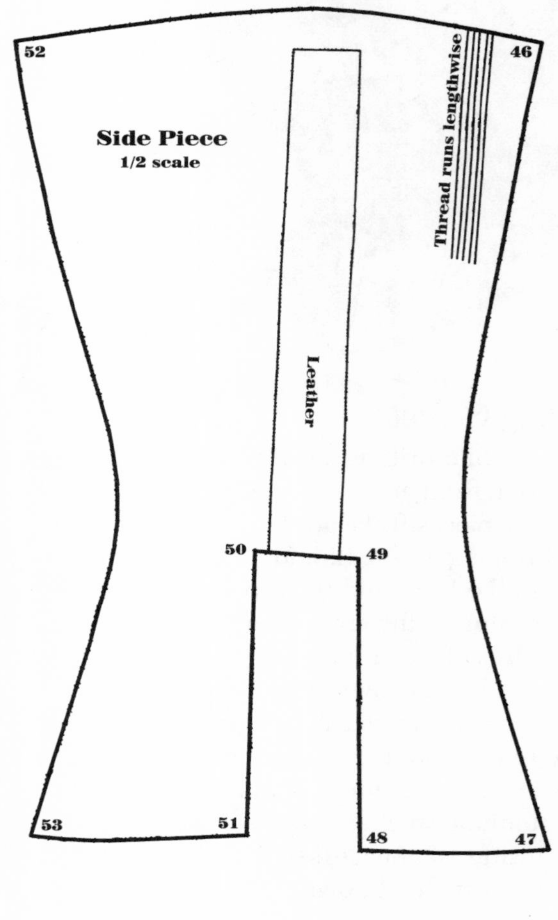
52
46
Side Piece
1/2 scale
Thread runs lengthwise
Leather
50
49
53
51
48
47

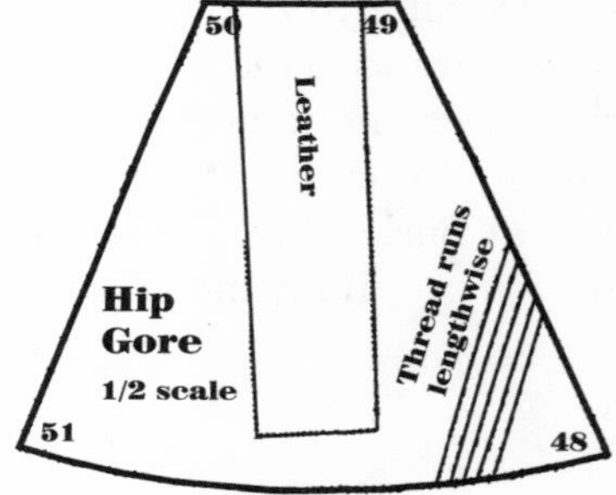
50
49
Leather
Hip
Gore
1/2 scale
Thread runs lengthwise
51
48

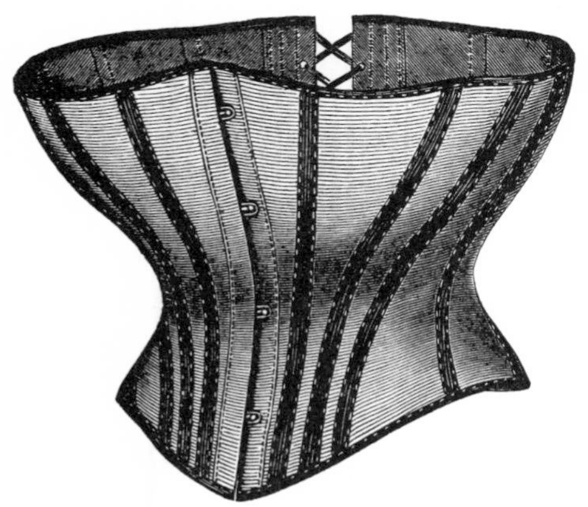

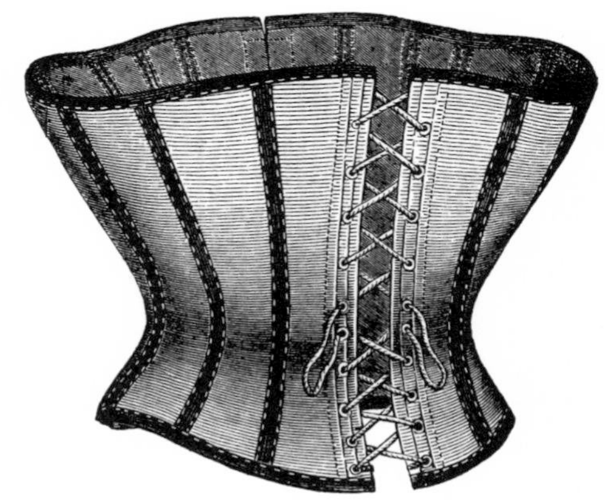

Corset Without Gores

This corset is made of white English leather. It is entirely without gores. To make the corset larger or smaller, allow or take off sufficient material on the back edge of each piece. The seams are covered on the right side with striped red ribbon 1/2 inch wide, which forms a pretty trimming.

Cut from the front, first front side piece, second front side piece, first side piece, second side piece, back side piece, and back each two pieces. Allow 1 1/2 inches on the back for a hem. This serves for the reception of the whalebone and eyelets, and is turned down and stitched as shown. The seams are sewn by a row of stitching on the wrong side. The edges are laid over each other as shown. The seams are covered on the right side with the ribbon, which is stitched down on both sides. Between the seam and the ribbon run in a thin whalebone. For the busk or steel spring stitch under a piece of English leather of the requisite width. Lastly, bind the upper and under edges.

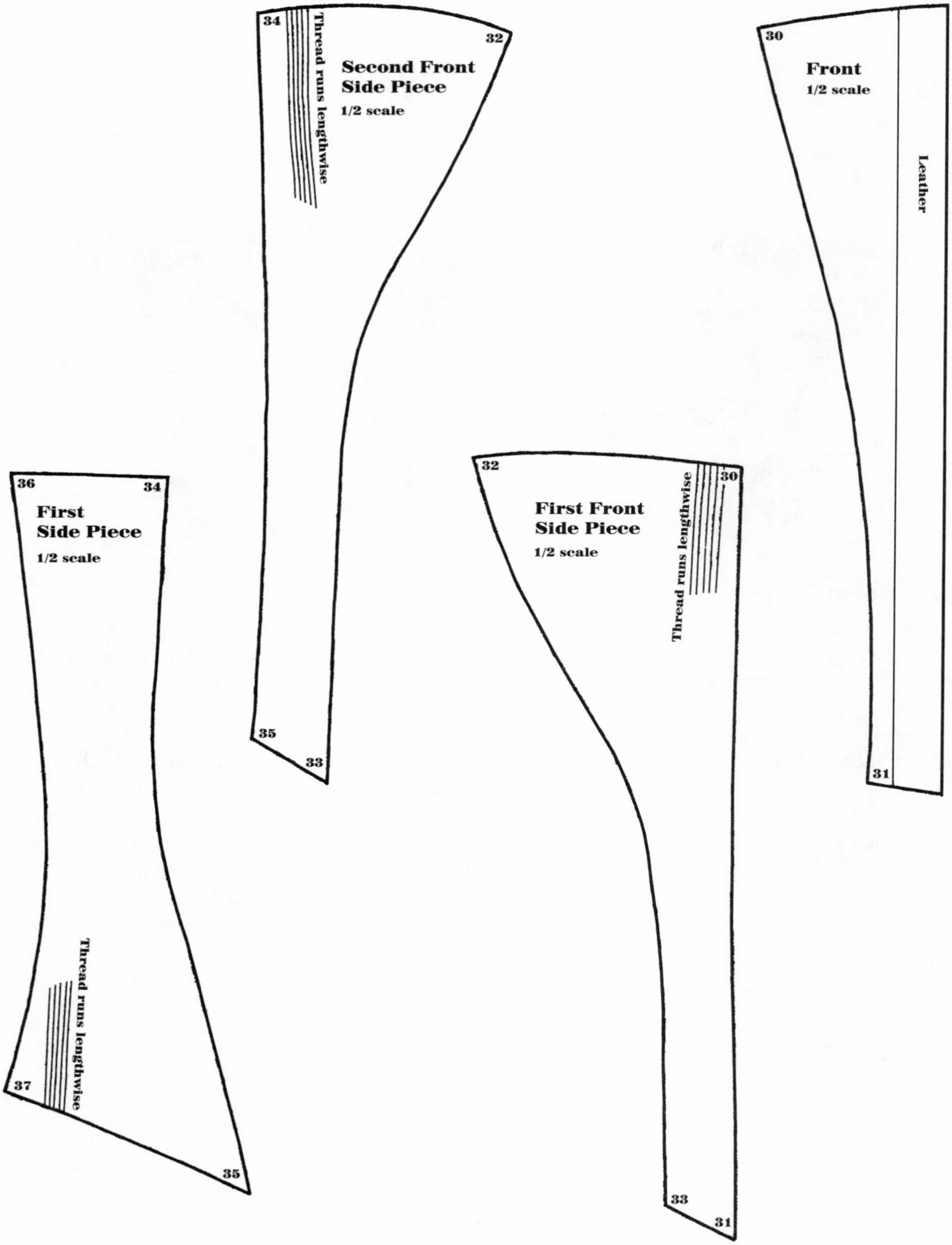

34
Thread runs lengthwise
32
Second Front Side Piece
1/2 scale
35
33

30
Front
1/2 scale
Leather
31

36
34
First Side Piece
1/2 scale
Thread runs lengthwise
37
35

32
30
First Front Side Piece
1/2 scale
Thread runs lengthwise
33
31

Corset Without Gores

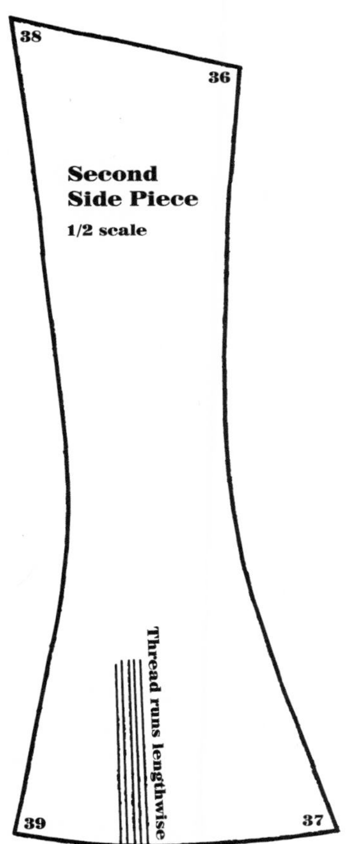

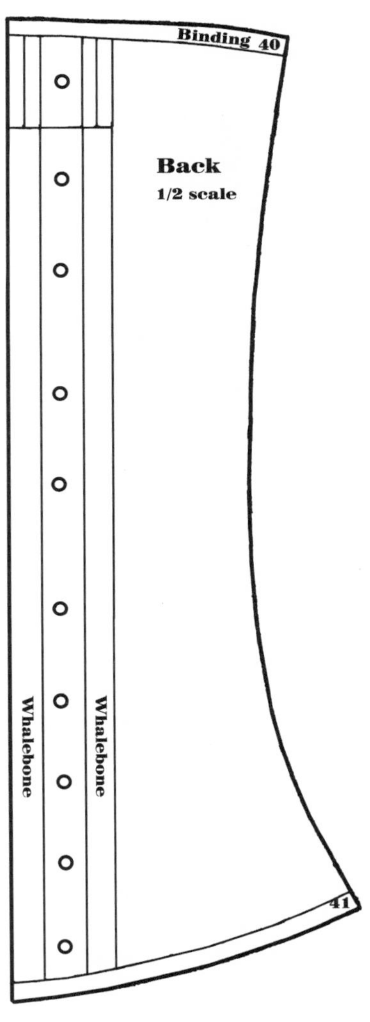

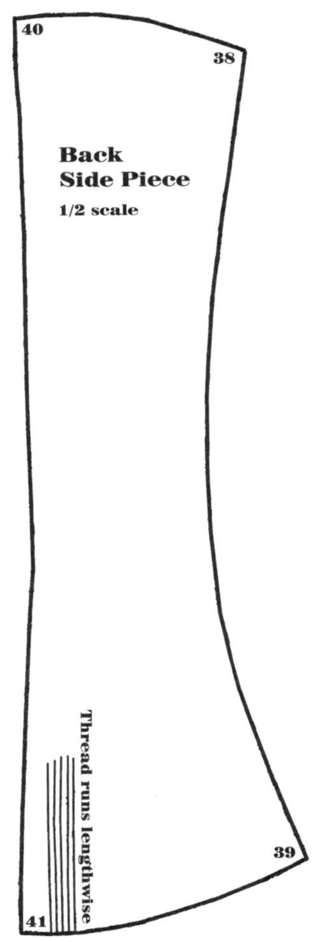

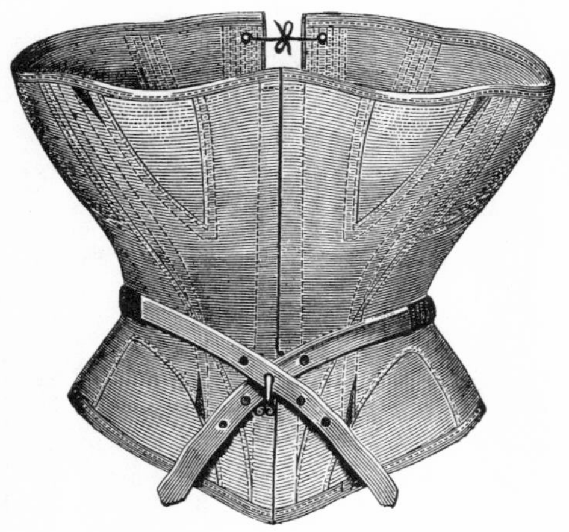

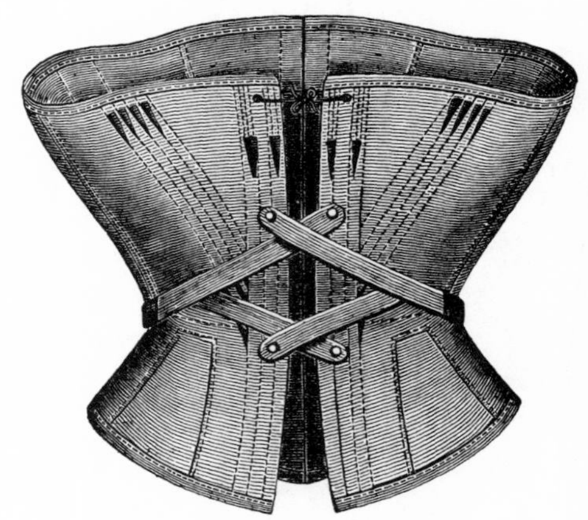

English Leather Corset

This corset is very easily fastened. Four bands, each 1 1/4 inches wide, are arranged on the back. Of these two are continued as a sort of strap, furnished with an elastic in the middle and on the front with several eyelets, by means of which the corset can be made tighter or looser. In arranging this the bands are crossed behind and fastened in front by looping the eyelets over a hook that is fastened on the corset. The original is of double light gray English leather. All the seams are sewn with cherry silk, the front and hip gores being set in between the double material of the corset.

Cut from the front two pieces. Cut from the first front gore, the second front gore, the first hip gore, the second hip gore, and the back each four pieces. Sew up the bosom pleats in each front, 14 on 14, and 15 on 15. This is done by laying the material over along the narrow line and stitching it down, fastening the threefold material along the plain line. Then cut linings for the fronts. These are without bosom pleats. Lay the lining and outside together.

Sew in the gores according to the corresponding figures on the pattern. First set the gores under the upper material of the corsets. Sew them down with two rows of stitching for the front, and one row for the hip gores, on which the material must be laid under in a narrow fold. On the points of the gores, however, the material need not be laid under, as the corset is sewn down to the gore with close buttonhole stitch. The hip gores may be slightly held in on the upper edge. The lining is hemmed down on the gores.

Now join the fronts and backs from 24 to 25. This is done by laying over the edge of the outside of the front and stitching it down to the back with two rows of stitching. Then the lining must be hemmed down so the stitches are not visible on the right side. Turn in the edges of the fronts and stitch them down. Arrange the double material of the backs.

Stitch the corset along the narrow lines of the front and back. Stitch also the corded ends of the back. Run in the whalebones and fasten them as shown. Set under a piece of linen tape as shown on the back. Bind the upper and under edges with gray ribbon.

Sew on the upper corners of the backs two pieces of linen tape, each 5 inches long, for fastening the corset. Sew on the four bands at the points designated by * and ••. Cover the stitches with buttons. The longer bands are 20 inches long including the elastic. The shorter bands which are fastened to the longer are each 8 inches long. Arrange the hook on the front as shown.

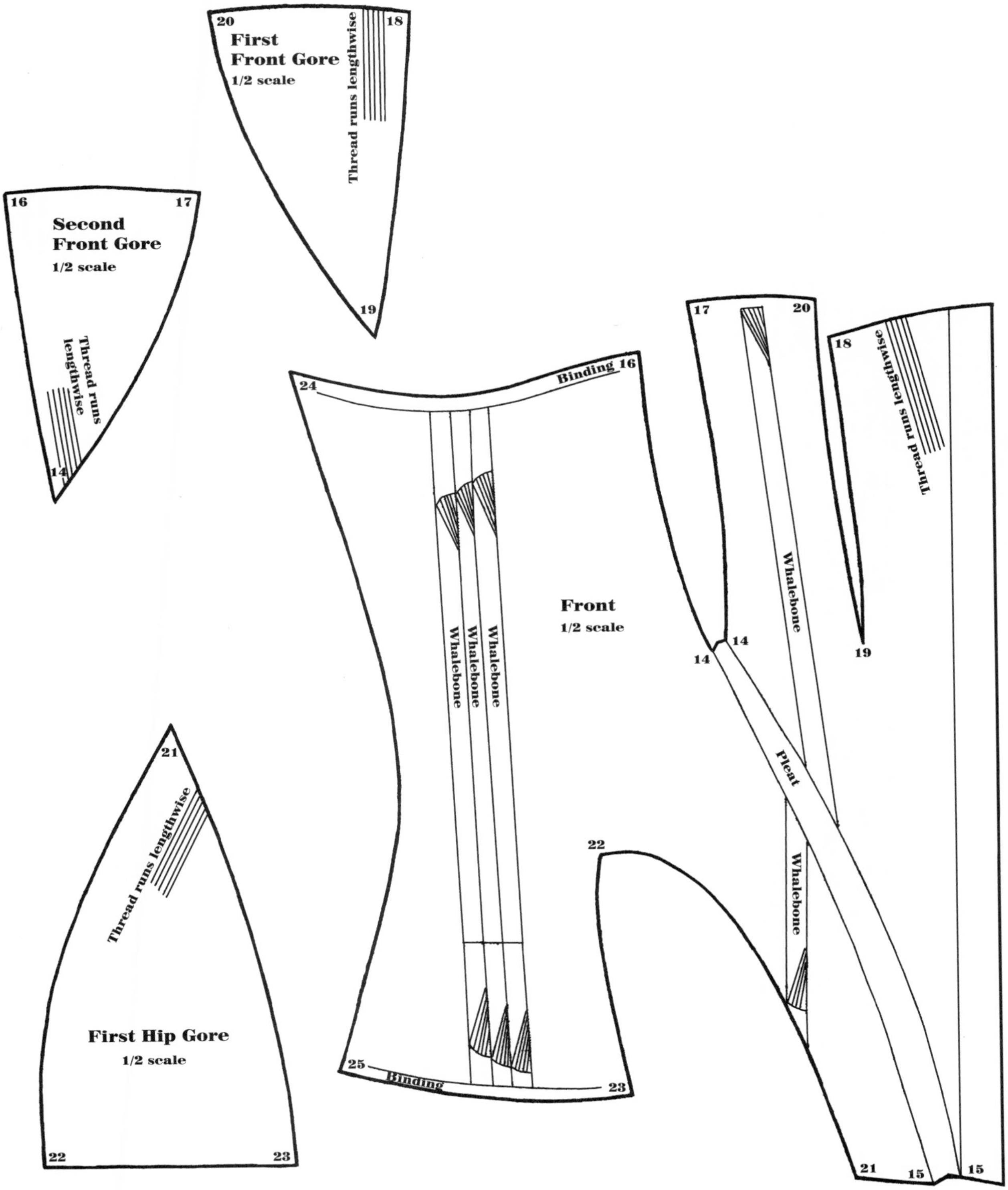

20
First
Front Gore
1/2 scale
Thread runs lengthwise
18
19
16
17
Second
Front Gore
1/2 scale
Thread runs lengthwise
14
24
Binding
16
Whalebone
Whalebone
Whalebone
Front
1/2 scale
25
Binding
23
22
17
20
18
Thread runs lengthwise
Whalebone
14
14
19
Pleat
Whalebone
21
15
15
21
Thread runs lengthwise
First Hip Gore
1/2 scale
22
23

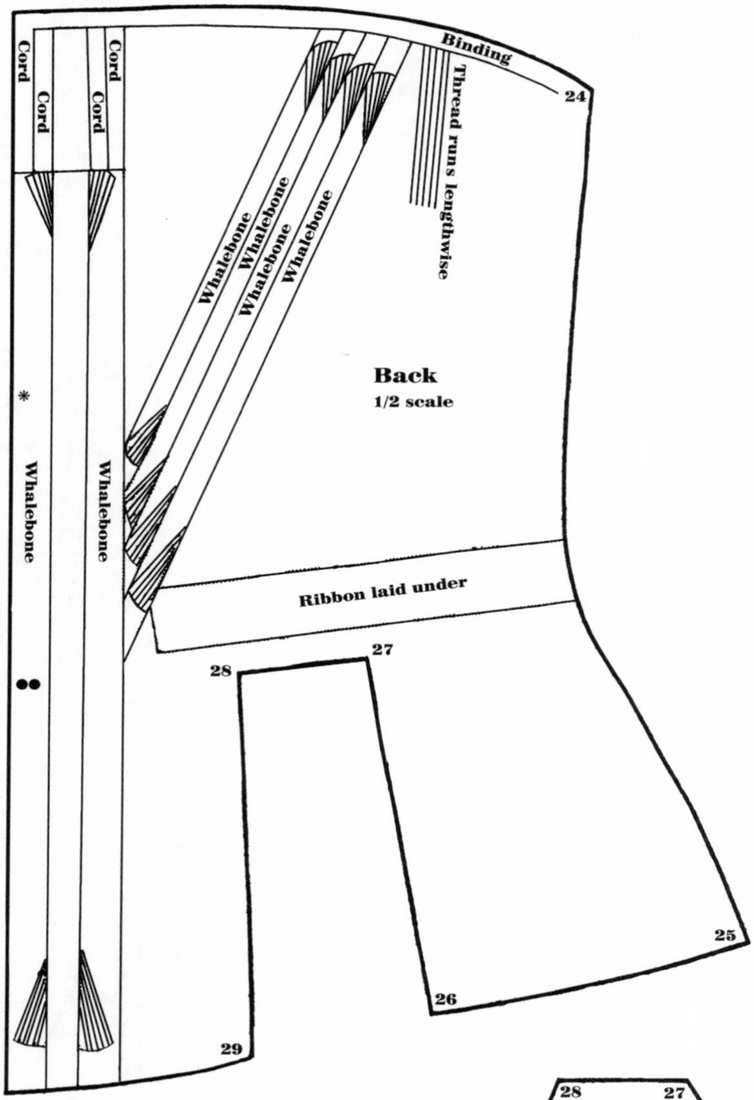

Binding
24
Thread runs lengthwise
Cord
Cord
Cord
Cord
Whalebone
Whalebone
Whalebone
Whalebone
Back
1/2 scale
*
Whalebone
Whalebone
Ribbon laid under
27
28
25
26
29
28 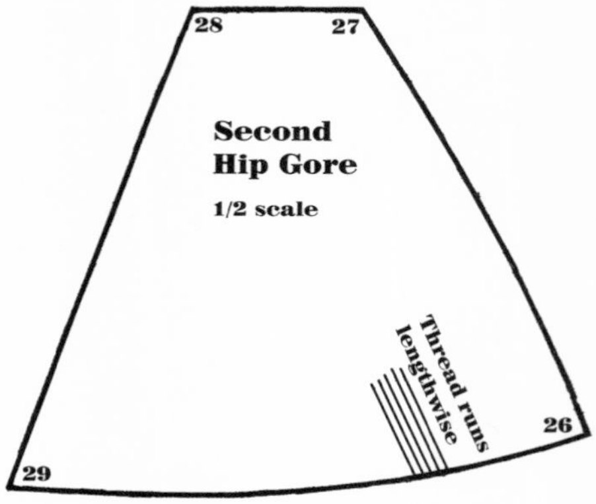
27
Second
Hip Gore
1/2 scale
Thread runs lengthwise
26
29

Cap of Ribbon and Lace Rosettes

The foundation of this cap consists of a straight piece of white buckram 8 inches long by 5 inches wide. This is rounded off on one end to the width of 2 inches for the front, and bound with narrow blue ribbon. The back is finished with three ends of blue ribbon 1 1/2 inches wide. These are ornamented with guipure rosettes as illustrated, though tatted, crocheted, or netted rosettes may be used instead. The lower ends hang loose and are notched.

The front of this cap is ornamented with a large rosette composed of loops of narrow blue ribbon each 1 1/2 inches long. This is arranged over a plain muslin foundation 4 inches long and 2 inches wide. The front of this is finished with a pleated frill of guipure lace 1 1/2 inches wide. On each side of the foundation, as illustrated, are strings of blue ribbon 4 inches wide and 23 inches long, which are fastened under the chignon.

September 5, 1868

Guipure Lace Cap

The original is of white guipure lace 1 1/4 inches wide, and green satin ribbon 1 inch wide. For the headpiece cut from the pattern two pieces of double material. Cut from the foundation pattern one piece of white muslin.

Hem the edge of the headpiece with a piece of white covered wire in the hem. Join this with the foundation according to the corresponding figures on the pattern. Bind the back edge.

The scarf ends are two ends of satin ribbon each 23 inches long; the edges are bordered with guipure lace. Fasten them to the cap and on the end of the headpiece. Border the back edge of the foundation with pleated guipure lace. Arrange two ends of the ribbon, each 12 inches long, which hang loose over the chignon. Sew to the edge of the headpiece a border of pleated lace that covers the place where the scarf ends were set on and extends to the back edge of the foundation. Make leaves of the satin ribbon by gathering up the ends over one side and leaving the other side pointed in each. Set them between the box pleats of the lace. The center of the cap is covered with three other rows arranged in the same manner. The center is finished with a clasp of the ribbon. The scarf ends are fastened under the chignon with a rubber cord.

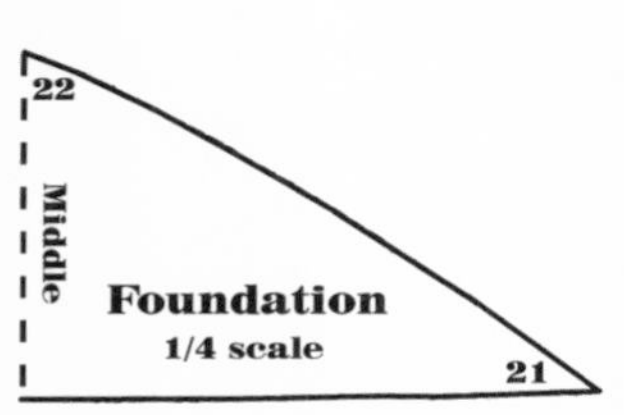

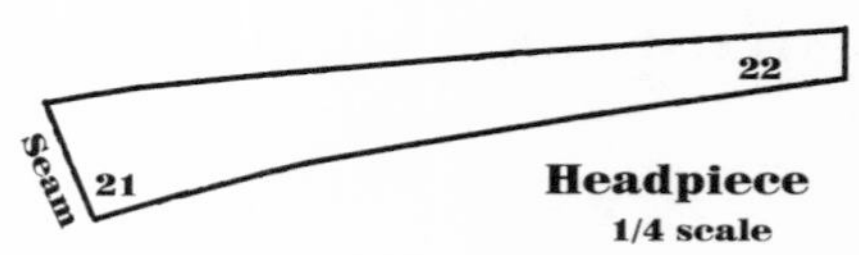

Lace Cap with Ribbon

Lace Cap Trimmed with Ribbon

This cap is made of lace edging and blue satin ribbon 1 inch and 1 1/3 inches wide. First cut the foundation of white muslin, extending the sash ends to the length desired. Take up the pleats and cover them with pleated lace. Bind the edges with narrow bias strips of the same material. In doing so lay in wire and make a pleat, bringing *x* on • at each side of the middle of the front. Trim the middle of the cap with a plain band of the wider satin ribbon. Then arrange the ribbon and lace as illustrated. The scarf ends are fastened in front with a rosette.

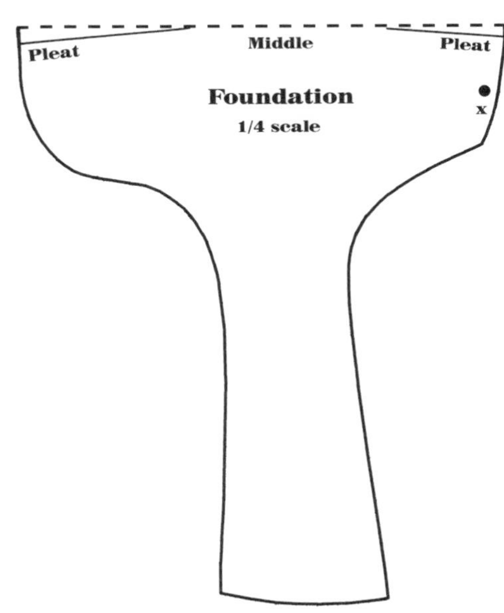

Pompadour Fichu

This fichu is very stylish, and is especially suited to young ladies. It is designed to be worn with a low-necked blouse or dress, whose sleeves are made to correspond with the fichu. The fichu is made of black lace, bordered with white blonde 1 1/2 inches wide.

Cut the two fronts and the back. Join on the shoulder from 72 to 73. Lay the ends in pleats, *x* on •. Sew these to the sash ends. These are 22 inches long, the width of the ends of the front on the upper ends, and 10 inches wide at the bottom. Hem the edges on the right side and sew on the blonde. The front is ornamented with a bow of green ribbon. The ends are fastened outside the belt.

Pompadour Fichu

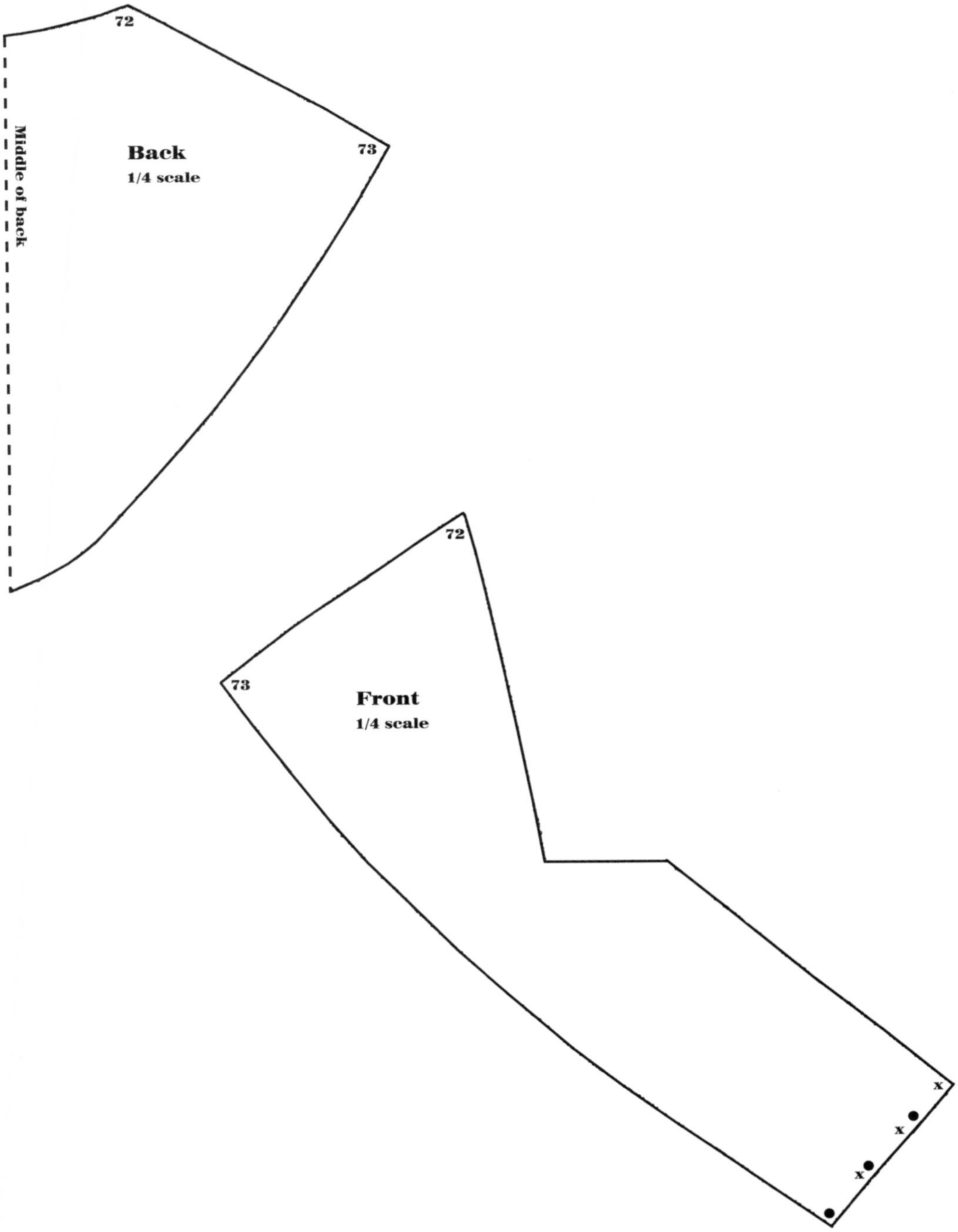

72

73

Middle of back

Back

1/4 scale

72

73

Front

1/4 scale

x

x

x

Baschlik Mantilla

This mantilla is new and peculiar. The fronts, which are crossed, are finished by long, broad scarf ends that are fastened together by a bow behind, where they gather up the skirt as illustrated. The original is of black grosgrain. It is trimmed on the edge with a pleated flounce of the same material, which is headed with a narrow bias fold.

From the pattern cut of the material two equal pieces. Sew them from 68 to 69, from 69 to 70, and from 70 to 71. Set the flounce under the edge of the mantilla with the bias folds. Cord the latter on the upper edge and sew them to a strip of lutestring. The point of the hood is finished with a heavy silk tassel. The bow that joins the ends is of heavy silk ribbon 3 inches wide.

Baschlik Mantilla

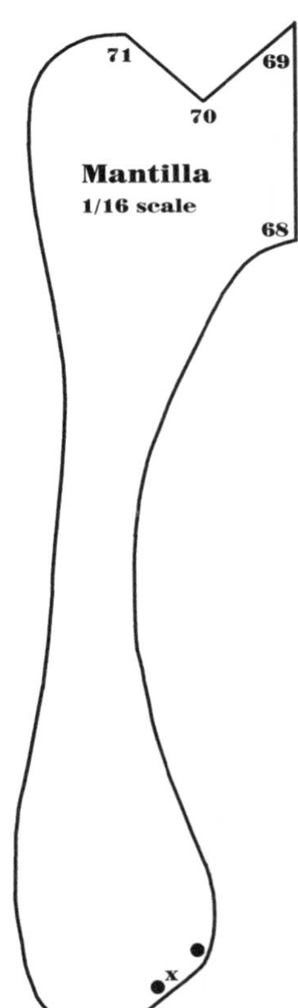

September 12, 1868

Colors

The shade that is to replace the conspicuous colors of last season is a brown garnet. This is not the purple garnet of two years ago, or the cranberry color of last winter, but a soft dark shade, such as is sometimes seen in sealskin. It is distinguished as *oreille dours,* or bear's ear. This color is shown in velvets, satins, silk, and cloth, with feathers and fringes of the same hue for trimming. A deeper tint, called "cachou," has more of the dead-leaf brown in it.

Gold-yellow and black promises to be a favorite combination for the autumn.

The feature of the season above everything else is the ever-changing chameleons. In the lavish abundance of color, three or four contrasting shades are reflected where once all was uniform. We have not only changeable silks and grosgrains, but poplin and woolen serges are made to reflect different colors. Gold and garnet are combined with every shade.

Woolen Goods

Serge is still in favor. All rough-surfaced goods are called serge. The diagonal reps is no longer its distinguishing feature. Changeable serge is sold. Gold, with blue, green, or purple; Bismarck and blue; garnet and gray are the colorings most frequently seen.

All-wool poplins, with narrow stripes of a bright color, with black, are shown for petticoats, or for the lower skirts of suits worn under a polonaise of changeable serge. Glossy poplins of high colors in large plaids are sold.

Waterproof tweed, a lighter gray and finer material than that now in use, is imported for fall. Suits of this new tweed, with short paletot and gored skirt, are sold. Material for the waist is furnished. The trimming is crosscut bands of silk.

Bonnets

The conspicuous feature of the new styles is the quantity of trimming heaped high on the top. Feathers, flowers, lace, and jet all appear on one bonnet.

We are sorry to say that the fanchon is passing away. The new shapes have the fanchon effect; they frame the forehead, leaving the ear exposed; but are radically different from the triangular bonnet so long worn.

It would puzzle a conjurer to say precisely what this new shape is, so completely is it concealed by the puffed and shirred material that covers it. Imagine a round bonnet with high double front, or rolling diadem, and a broad half-crown. The frame fits the top of the head closely, and is worn far forward. A large ornament, such as a jet star, a full-blown rose, or a hummingbird, is placed directly over the forehead in the center of a ruche of quilled lace. Back of this, and above it higher still, is the trimming, usually an erect aigrette of white heron's feathers, or short tufts of curled ostrich plumes.

A new color called "Florence" partakes of the tints of Metternich green, but is lighter, with yellow predominating instead of green. This light maize color shot with green is the fashionable chameleon for bonnets. The many shades of yellow from the light Prussian to the dark capucine are so conspicuously shown in the milliners' rooms that they arrest the eye at once.

Trimmings

Feathers are employed without stint. Short curled tufts of ostrich are used instead of a long feather. Four tufts of different shades of a primary color appear in the same cluster. Aigrettes of stiff white heron's feathers are stuck on the bonnets in erect positions, *à la Marie Antoinette.* Peafowl's feathers; the slender graceful plumage of the lophophore of dark changing hues; pheasant's tails of golden, red, and silver; the Argus feather dotted with a hundred eyes; and green and gold tufts from the breast of the colibri are a few of the varied importations.

The heads of small birds with long bills and breasts are seen on many hats, and sometimes the whole bird nestles amidst laces and flowers.

Instead of the tiny flowerets in vogue during the summer, we have now large flowers, full-blown roses, pansies of the largest species, and marguerites of rare size. Shaded metallic leaves and flowers are brought to perfection. Grapes and the brown foliage of autumn are imitated to life. The crystallized flowers are especially beautiful. Crystallized dragonflies, beetles, and cockchafers are among the ornaments.

Branches of pink coral can scarcely be told from the real Neapolitan. Jet in large flowers and leaves for bandeaux is worn again. Gilt and steel have disappeared.

Spanish lace, although a woven lace, has irregular meshes like real lace. The edges being woven instead of cut, it has the appearance of valuable lace. It is of the thinnest mesh with set figures of diamonds and flowers that resemble embroidery. Mixed laces are also shown, black embroidered with green, blue, or maroon. The colored blondes of the summer are passé.

Round Hats

The novelty in round hats is the Sultan. It is merely a high, bell-shaped crown without rim or visor, and is not unlike the Nymph hat of last season. Ribbon strings, instead of elastic, are used to tie it under the chignon.

Another hat peculiarly appropriate to the picturesque costumes now in vogue is called the Deauville. It is a triangular shape, pointed over the forehead, rising in the center, and receding again on the chignon.

Hats with rims have tall, sloping crowns, while others are flat and square. There is the Valois; the Bourbon; and the Louis Quatorze, Quinze, and Seize. The rims are caught up to show a lining of pleated satin or velvet of bright color.

Miscellaneous Items

The Carrick, or coachman's cloak of many capes, consists of but three capes or of several, as the fancy of the wearer dictates. White cashmere circulars trimmed with black lace are worn at the foreign spas. As the weather grows colder those of embroidered black cashmere, lined and wadded, will be substituted.

Small loose Turkish jackets of French cloth are worn for breakfast and indoor toilettes. They are black, white, and red, and have borders of embroidery in seed stitch, representing flowers of gay hues. They are buttoned in front, square at the belt or vandyked.

Pinked ruches of silk, crosscut bands elaborately stitched with the machine, pleated frills, and fringe are the trimmings for dresses.

Fichus are no longer worn with ends. Wide sashes with large bows made so that they stand upright replace the fichu ends. The newest shape is the Ninon de l'Enclos, combining the paletot and fichu, a sacque front with sash panniers behind. The trimming is gimp and fringe.

Many ladies of fashion have abandoned sashes as common, wearing instead a narrow waistband fastened at the side with sharp pointed ends, the bow at the side being called a sword bow.

High-backed tortoiseshell combs surmount the large chignons.

September 19, 1868

Silks

The glossy taffeta silk, a plain surface without cords, will be again worn. This is less expensive than grosgrain and poult-de-soie.

Changeable silks are promiscuously called glacé, shot silk, or chameleons. Instead of the plain black silk so generally worn, for street dresses we have a variety of dark shades blended with black, such as invisible green, blue, or purple. Bismarck is only seen in unison with blue or green; garnet and green combine; and a strange blending of colors forms the antique "frog" shades of last winter. These are heavy grosgrains, 7/8 yard wide. Light silks for evening are the "sunset" purple and gold; "moonlight gray," over which the colors flit like shadows on the water; and the beautiful "opal," reflecting pink, white, and blue.

Striped silks are to be used as the foundation skirts of the elaborate costumes to be worn this winter. A changeable stripe alternates with one of solid color. Striped satins of gorgeous colors are shown for petticoats. Good taste suggests a black overdress for these gay skirts. A bias border, 12 inches wide, of striped satin sewn on a black silk skirt makes a rich dress.

Serge and French Chintz

The silk-faced serge that proved so perishable during the summer is not seen this season. A plain all-wool serge takes its place, and promises to be the standard woolen material. It is shown in solid colors of every shade, in changeable hues, and newer still in stripes.

The gay plaids always seen in profusion in the early winter months are in smaller blocks, often merely checks, and of fewer colors.

French chintzes are in the usual small figures of bright colors on dark grounds.

Costumes

The wide Marie Antoinette flounce still remains. Sleeves are the straight coat shape, with very little trimming. Overskirts are puffed and looped in a variety of ways. The regular pannier overskirt, a large puff behind made by a drawstring extending from the side seams across the back, is not so popular as the reversed tunic, long in front and tied loosely at the waist behind, or the Camargo skirt, which is looped at the back and sides by a bow or rosette. It is all-important that the skirt be flat in front, only slightly full at the sides, and very full at the back.

Striped costumes will be worn in all materials, woolen, silk, satin, and velvet. The petticoat is in wider stripes than the overdress. The upper skirt and mantle are made of the same material, in narrow stripes, or a changeable goods in which the colors of the petticoat are blended.

Mantles and Cloaks

Fall wrappings are mantles of various scarf shapes, round at the back and looped with rosettes. The ends are square, or if crossed under a belt, long and pointed.

The cloak of the season has evidently been designed to form a complete costume, with merely the addition of a striped petticoat. The polonaise with a round cape, a Watteau fold, or pelerine ends, is the standard shape for cloth and velvet cloaks. The narrow coat sleeve still prevails. The material is necessarily so thick that the garment must be cut almost tight fitting to prevent a dumpy appearance at the waist. If the body of the garment is full it should be separate from the skirt, and pleated into a belt. Skirts are long, and puffed out as in costumes. The fall cloaks are of purple, dark brown, and black cloth.

Trimmings

The trimming most used is fringe with rich headings, so elaborately made that the expense is equal to that of valuable lace. One piece on a velvet cloak has a netted heading 4 inches wide. Plain tassel fringes are very handsome, especially those of camel's hair. Loops of ribbon, squares of velvet, feathers, quill shavings, chenille, and buttons are in the headings.

A great deal of guipure lace will be worn on velvet with a passementerie heading of leaves and vines formed of tiny buttons. Passementerie rosettes, with long pendant tassels, are newer than sashes. Buttons are very large, sometimes 3 inches in diameter. Bows of faille, bunches, knots, and shells of ribbon are seen among the trimming and folds in great profusion. Crosscut bands of velvet are edged with narrow satin. Faille and satin folds are placed alternately, or velvet and faille. Jet, which still remains on bonnets, has disappeared entirely from cloaks and dresses.

Bonnets and Hats

Strings of Syrian net, beaded with crystal, are placed over satin, in square set shapes. The advantage claimed is that they do not become limp and stringy as plain lace falls are apt to do. Garnet is prettily used in conjunction with gray and brown.

In round hats we have the Deauville in black and white felt, and a startling novelty that we think rather *prononcée*–garnet and green felt. The Ophelia, with crown and rim in one, like an inverted basin, fits the head closely. A new variety of the Sultan cap has the upper crown of bright green or blue velvet, with a band of black Astrakhan. A coquettish cap of black velvet, called the Robert, has a soft crown of two careless puffs. The Yelva is similar to the Deauville but smaller, and round at the center. This hat is the favorite with the leading milliners. Quilled silk linings are desirable.

The jauntiest hat shown us, and one we predict will be in favor with skaters, is the Polonaise–a cap with stiff sloping sides, and sunken tip or crown. It is brought out in black Astrakhan trimmed with jet aigrettes and chains. This Polish cap should be worn far back on the head, tipped slightly to the right.

The Figaro resembles a gentleman's smoking cap. It is a turban of Astrakhan with a network crown of chenille falling into a pouch at the side with tasseled ends. Colored silk may be placed beneath the open netting of chenille.

Tatted Cravat End

This cravat end and the next two, shown full size, are of Swiss muslin trimmed with tatted medallions.

We remark in the beginning that the work must always be turned when a downward ring follows an upward one, and vice versa. Begin the medallion for this cravat with the two rows of rings worked in one round that lie next the central lace stitch part. Work with one thread, in fine yarn, as follows. * First a ring of the inner row composed of 6 ds. (double stitches), 1 p. (picot) 1/8 inch long, 6 ds. Turn this ring downward, and work after 1/8 inch space a ring of the second row composed of five times alternating 2 ds., 1 p., then 2 ds. Turn the work anew, and after 1/8 inch space work again a ring like the first. But, instead of forming the picot, fasten to the picot of the similar ring. Again turning the work, make another ring of the second round as before, in which fasten to the last picot of the previous ring instead of working the 1st picot. From * repeat nine times. At the end of the rows join in a circle by fastening to the 1st picot of the first ring of the second row instead of working the last picot of the last ring of this row.

At the end of the rings of the second row work the outer row as follows. Tie together two threads. * Work with one thread a ring composed of 6 ds., fasten to the middle picot of a ring of the outer row, then 6 ds., close on this a similar ring, which must be fastened to the middle picot of the next ring of the outer circle. At the end of this ring work over the second thread (foundation thread) 9 ds., fasten to 2 corresponding picots of two rings at the same time, then again 9 ds. over the foundation thread. Repeat from * nine times. The first of two rings, however, must always be fastened to the next free middle picot.

Having completed the last row, fasten the working thread to the foundation thread under the first two rings of the row. Finish the center of the medallion with lace stitch as illustrated. In working this fasten also the picots of the inner round. Sew the finished medallion to the cravat with buttonhole stitches and cut away the material underneath.

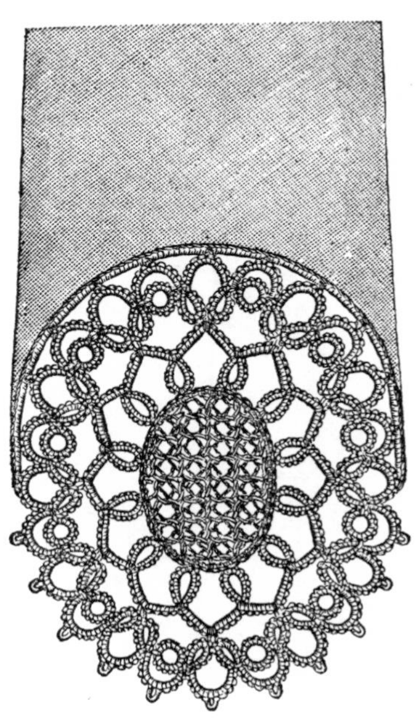

Tatted Cravat End

In making this medallion begin with the inner circle with two threads. Fasten them together. * Work next, with only one thread, a ring composed of 8 ds., 1 p., 8 ds., then close to this, over a foundation thread, a scallop composed of 5 ds., 1 p., 5 ds. Repeat from * eleven times. Having completed the last scallop, join the row in a circle by fastening the working thread to the first ring and then cutting it off.

For the outer row of the medallion work next, with only one thread, a ring by working 3 ds., fasten to a picot of a scallop of the finished round, and work again 5 ds., * a scallop (over the foundation thread) composed of 5 ds., 1 p., 5 ds., close on this a ring of 5 ds., fasten to the former ring 5 ds., then again a ring as before, which must be fastened to the picot of the next scallop of the former round. Make again a scallop and a ring as before, this last being fastened to the same picot to which the former ring was fastened. From * repeat ten times. Then work another ring, and close on this a ring which must be fastened to the former ring, then again a ring which must be fastened to the same picot to which the first ring of this round is fastened, and finally another scallop. Fasten the working thread to the first ring.

The inner part of the medallion consists of fine tulle, closely worked in buttonhole stitch with fine cord on the outer edge, on which the finished tatted edge is fastened. Work the tulle foundation in point d'esprit. This is done in the same manner as a netted foundation. The finished medallion is buttonhole stitched to the end of the cravat.

Tatted Cravat End

For making this medallion two threads are required. Fasten these together. * Then work, first, with one thread one of the three-leaved figures of the inner circle, which must be fastened to the middle part of the lace stitch. For every leaflet work 3 ds., 1 p., 5 ds., 1 p., 3 ds. But in working the second and third of the three leaflets fasten to the last picot of the former leaflet instead of working the 1st picot. Having completed the third leaflet, fasten the working thread to the middle leaflet where the row is fastened. Work over the foundation thread a scallop composed of 5 ds., 1 p., 5 ds., fasten the working thread to the picot on the point of the third leaf, work a scallop as before, and continue repeating from * yet six times; but the three-leaved figures must be fastened to each other as illustrated. At the end of the round fasten the working threads to the first leaflet of the first three-leaved figure and cut them off.

For the next round tie together again the two working threads. Work next a ring with only one thread, in doing which work 7 ds., fasten to a picot of a scallop of the former round, and work again 7 ds. * Then, over the foundation thread, work a scallop composed of 6 ds., 1 p., 6 ds., then a ring as before, which must be fastened to the same picot of the former round to which the former ring was fastened, then a ring as before, which must be fastened to the picot of the next scallop of the former round. Repeat from * twelve times more. Work again a scallop, then a ring, which last must be fastened to the same picot to which the former ring was fastened. Then fasten the working threads to the first ring of this round.

The figure in the middle of the medallion is worked with fine thread in buttonhole stitch and point de reprise as follows. Fasten the working thread to the picot of the middle leaflet of a three-leaved figure. Run it through the like picots of the remaining three-leaved figures back again to the picot where it was fastened. Then wind the threads between the picots several times as shown. In a similar manner run a thread through both double knots beneath the mentioned picot of each middle leaflet, and wind these also. Then work the inner part in point de reprise and buttonhole stitch as illustrated. The completed medallion is worked on the end of the cravat with buttonhole stitch.

Medallions for Cravats

These medallions, if worked in fine material, may serve as the centers for the rosettes given for cravat ends, and also as trimmings for blouses, collars, etc. The foundation of the medallions in Figures 1 and 2 is fine netting, worked over a very fine knitting needle, and then worked in the patterns illustrated with very fine thread.

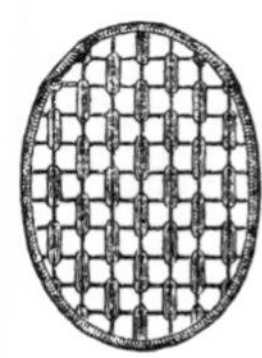

Figure 1. Net guipure medallion

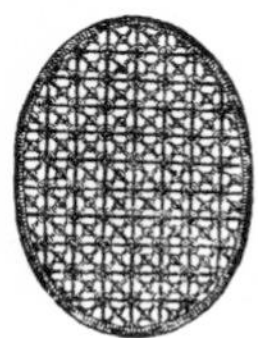

Figure 2. Net guipure medallion

The medallions in Figures 3 and 4 are worked on tulle, the first with double and the latter with single thread.

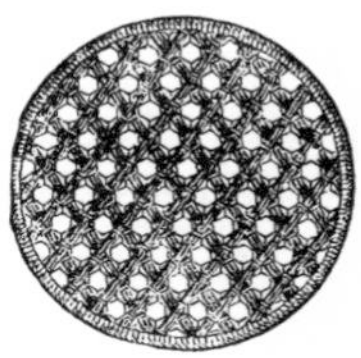

Figure 3. Medallion in lace stitch on tulle

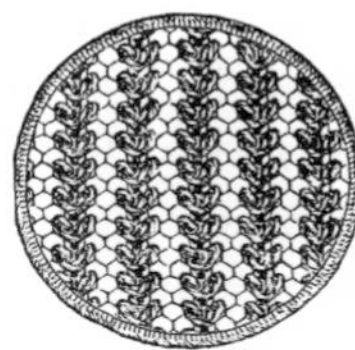

Figure 4. Medallion in lace stitch on tulle

September 26, 1868

Dress Goods

We have been especially pleased with a superior black silk called cashmere-de-soie. This is a corded silk, rich and heavy, yet as soft and pliant as cashmere. It has a fine luster and an intense blackness. It is in two widths, 27 inches wide and 32 inches.

Parisian taffeta of beautiful luster, and all pure silk, is largely imported. The revival of this goods, so long out of use, will be a cause of congratulation to all who have worn it. It will outwear the best grosgrain, and always looks fresh and new, as there are no cords to fray or catch the dust.

Black poult-de-soie is heavily brocaded. This is suitable for elderly ladies. The styles do not differ from last season, except that the brocaded figures are smaller. A thick black satin is brocaded with shaded autumn leaves, with the leaf shadow reflected beside it.

Striped satins of the gay Roman colors, like the scarves worn by gentlemen, scarlet, yellow, and black, or blue, green, and gold together, are imported for petticoats. Stripes of two colors, something bright with black or white, are sold.

Changeable and striped silks are shown in profusion. Soft rich ponsons in single shades are in the whole range of dark colors.

Evening Dresses

A line of ponsons in delicate tints, turquoise blue, pearl color, and Florence green, that require gaslight to develop their beauty, are displayed for evening dresses. The variations of color in the light, changeable silks are marvelous. Maize and scarlet enter into almost every combination. Black and a purple shade called "marguerite" combine with gay hues.

White will continue in favor for evening. White tarlatan robes are the newest thin dresses. These are in good taste and inexpensive. There are floral designs on the front widths of embroidery in one color–green, blue, or purple–with rouleaux of crêpe on the side seams and bordering the skirt. Garniture of embroidery and crêpe for the waist and sleeves. Another pattern has wheatears of crêpe, while on a third are folds of maize-colored silk worked with a feathered edge in black, and finished with black lace.

Poplins, Etc.

While the chameleon hues are most novel, single shades in the new bright garnet and green are stylish and desirable. Pongee poplin, a light fall material of silk and wool, heavier than that worn in summer, may be had in grave colors or gay combinations. Glacé poplin is suitable for midwinter. Striped poplin, with both sides alike, is chosen for petticoats.

Heavy Russian skirting in broad stripes of black with gold or purple, 5 quarters wide, is a stylish and serviceable material. Epingleine and crêpe Eugenie, rough-surfaced goods no longer new, are imported in stripes and changing colors.

Velours are ribbed diagonally, and instead of one solid color, four are combined, producing a beautiful glacé effect. On a green and gold ground are broad bias reps of green and scarlet. Gold and black is especially handsome in this elegant fabric.

A cheap article of serge, in striped and changeable patterns, is mixed linen and wool. At a little distance it would be mistaken for silk. A new silk-finished winsey resembles poplin, but is not so perishable. The all-wool plaids are very reasonable this season.

Morning Robes

Cashmere robes de chambre are in bright, warm grounds, poppy red, garnet, green, or black, with gay cashmere borders in which yellow predominates. The border extends around the skirt and up the front widths. The robe is worn flowing loosely from the shoulders, unconfined by a belt. Flowing sleeves are represented on the diagrams that accompany each pattern, with narrow borders for trimming. Cashmeres sold by the yard have white or scarlet grounds with wide-spreading figures and palm leaves.

Cloakings

Silk plush will be worn again for fancy sacques. It is imported in every shade of color. The fancy plushes are 1 1/2 yards wide. Purple, gray, and white are blended together; the pile gray and black, giving a changeable effect. Worsted plush is sold. White Astrakhan cloth, an excellent imitation of the real lambskin, is almost 2 yards wide. A soft white plush, worsted back with silk pile, is sold. Ermine cloth, white plush spotted with black, is handsome for evening wrappings. Among the darker goods is a cut Astrakhan, smooth instead of curled pile, of the new bear's-ear garnet. A frosted beaver of rare thickness is a golden brown shade. Plaid cloakings are sold for fall wrappings.

The prevailing styles of cloaks are longer than those of last season. From 4 to 6 inches is the added length. They are nearly tight fitting. Sashes are abandoned abroad, but will probably be worn here during another season. Wide-spreading fan-shaped bows and knots are arranged in an ingenious manner.

Underlinen

Yoked gowns with three widths of muslin slightly gored are the favorite shape, as they conceal the figure, and yet are not full enough to be clumsy. These are embroidered and ruffled around the neck and sleeves. Short peignoirs have the fronts tucked perpendicularly or in yokes, with cambric ruffles very narrow and fluted, or strong Valenciennes borders. The loose coat sleeve with deep cuff is appropriate. Standing collar, or the all-around turndown shape.

Buttonholes for Underclothing

These buttonholes are pretty, and especially commendable for their durability. Each stitch is described in detail. The barring is done before cutting or working. It may be done either by running around the buttonhole, as shown by Figure 1, or with chain stitch, as shown by Figure 2.

Figure 1. Barring of buttonhole

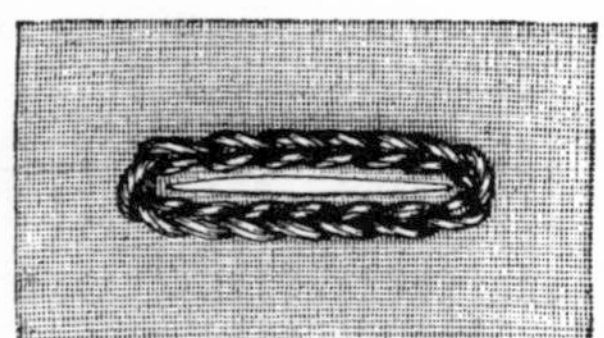

Figure 2. Barring of buttonhole

The buttonhole in Figure 3 is worked with long buttonhole stitches, each of which is fastened by a shorter stitch. Work, first, a long stitch (see Figure 4). Then from left to right take a short stitch as indicated by the needle in Figure 4.

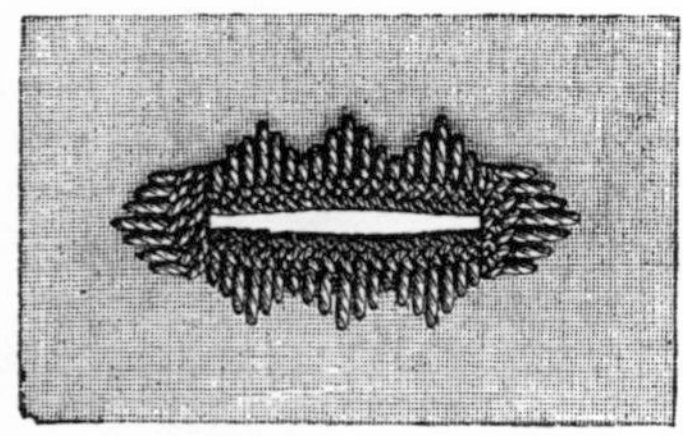

Figure 3. Buttonhole in pointed buttonhole stitch

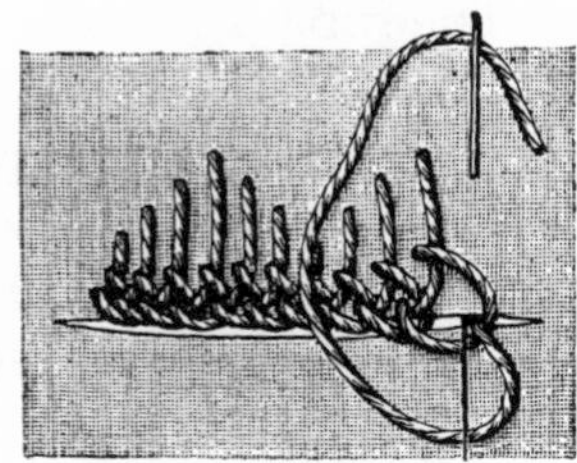

Figure 4. Making of pointed buttonhole stitch—enlarged

Figures 5 and 6 show a herringbone stitch buttonhole. Make a cross chain stitch, and one stitch putting the needle downward, the other in the opposite direction or upward, taking in the edge of the material. Having completed the herringbone stitch row, work inside of it a row in common buttonhole stitch.

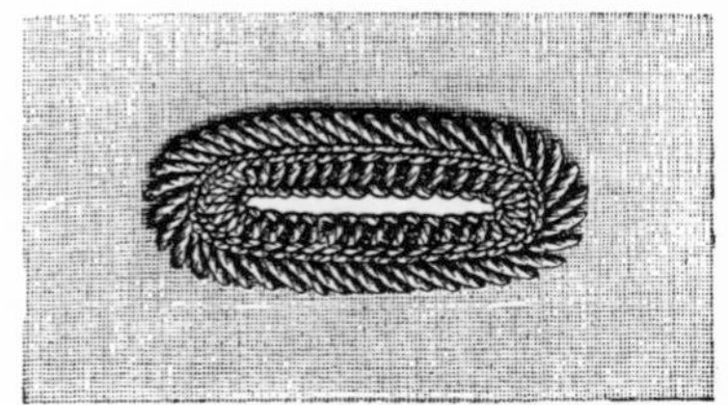

Figure 5. Buttonhole in herringbone stitch

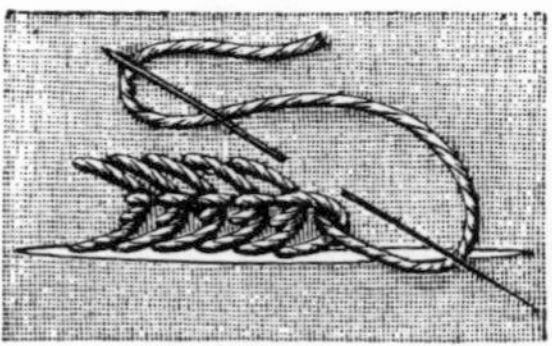

Figure 6. Making of herringbone buttonhole stitch—enlarged

The buttonhole with knotted finish is shown in Figure 7. Make, first, an ordinary buttonhole stitch. Then lay the thread outward and bring it again through the loop as shown by Figure 8. The finished round is ornamented with a row of knots, which are worked as shown by Figure 9.

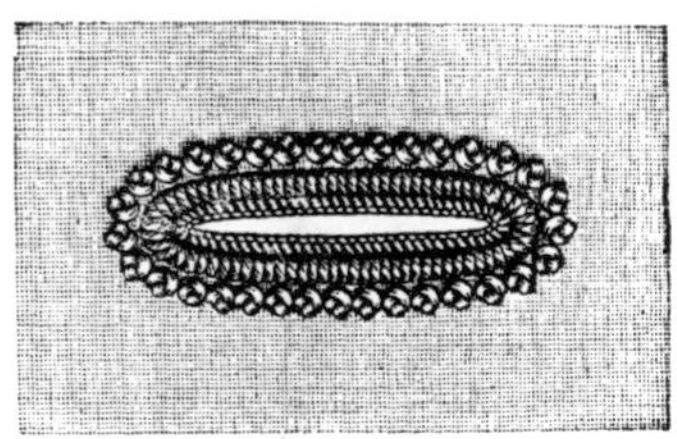

Figure 7. Buttonhole in knotted stitch

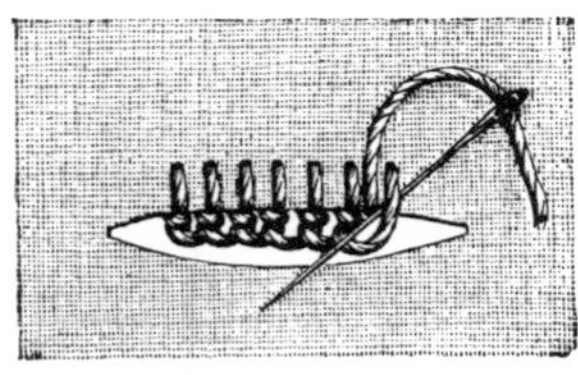

Figure 8. Making of knotted buttonhole stitch–enlarged

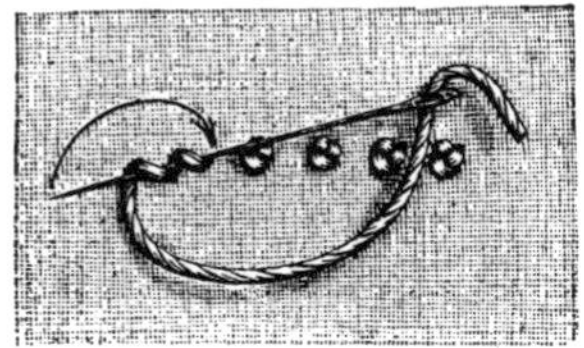

Figure 9. Making of knot for buttonhole

Figures 10 gives a buttonhole worked in double buttonhole stitch. Work, first, a common long buttonhole stitch. On this work a shorter stitch sideways from left to right (see Figure 11).

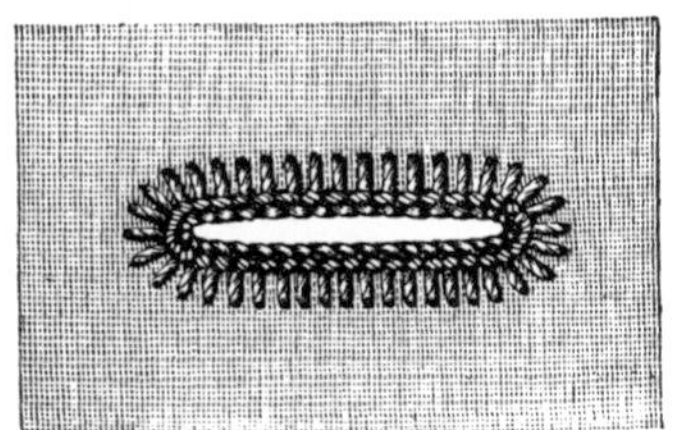

Figure 10. Buttonhole in double buttonhole stitch

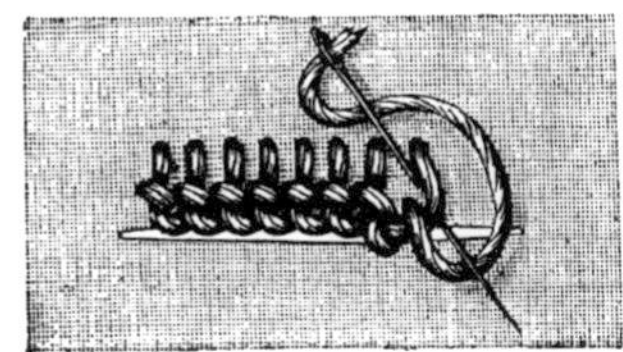

Figure 11. Making of double buttonhole stitch–enlarged

For the buttonhole in Figure 12, which is worked in tatted buttonhole stitch, lay a cord under instead of barring. Having cut the buttonhole, overseam this cord to the edge. Work the stitch after Figure 13 (which does not show the cord), being very careful to follow the thread of the material.

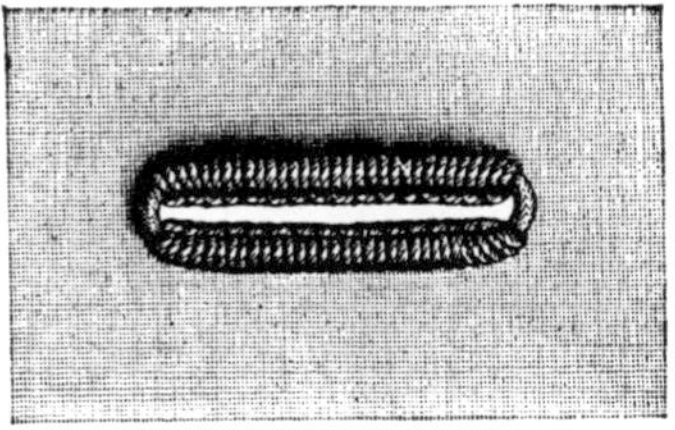

Figure 12. Buttonhole in tatted buttonhole stitch

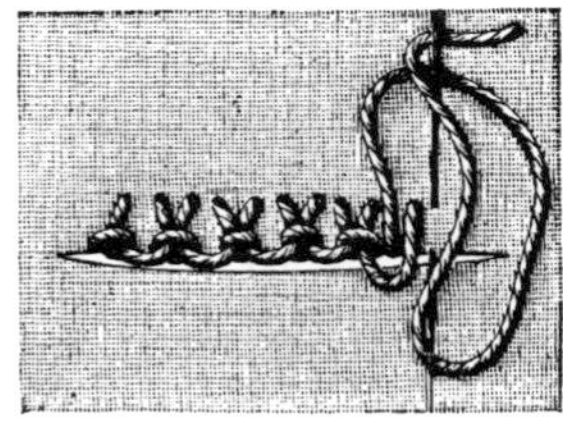

Figure 13. Making of tatted buttonhole stitch–enlarged

Figure 14 gives a buttonhole in twisted stitch. Having run the needle through, as shown by Figure 15, wind it from seven to eight times with the thread. Then draw the needle and thread through, pressing the twisted thread down on the right side. Run the needle back through the same place through which the stitch was taken preparatory to taking the next stitch.

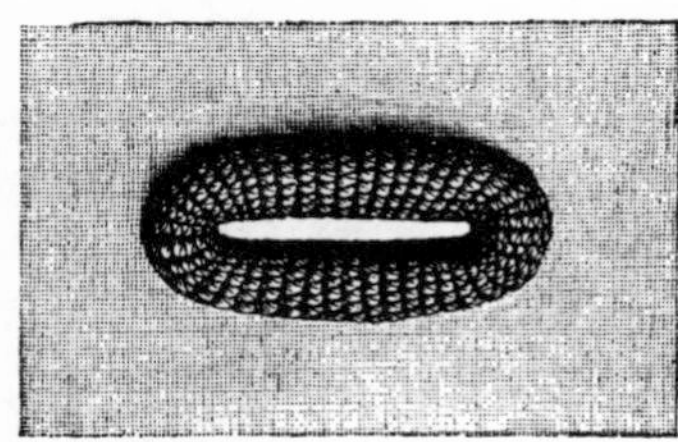

Figure 14. Buttonhole in twisted stitch

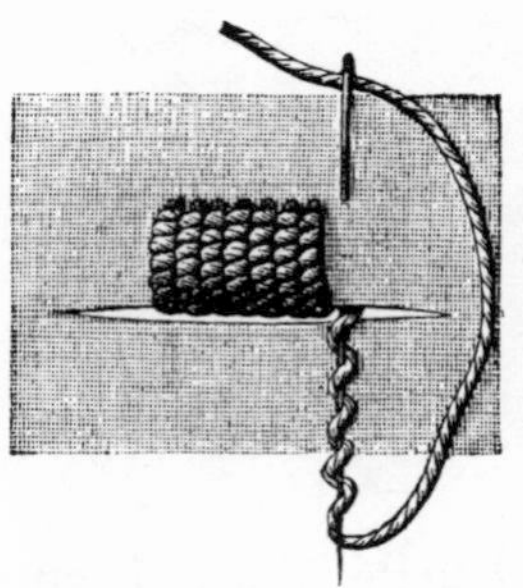

Figure 15. Making of twisted buttonhole stitch–enlarged

Buttons for Underclothing

These buttons are prettier and much more durable than purchased ones. They are all worked with fine thread.

Figure 1 shows a flat crocheted button. Beginning at the middle, work seven rounds in single crochet in the round, crocheting from left to right (see Figure 2). In the second round crochet always 2 stitches in 1 of the former round. The eighth round is also worked in single crochet, but a brass ring of the requisite thickness must be covered by it. In working this work 2 stitches in every 2nd following stitch of the former round. The under side of the work is the right side of the button.

Figure 1. Flat crocheted button

Figure 2. Making of crocheted button cover—enlarged

Figures 3 and 4 show how to re-cover the foundation of a worn-out button. Take the ring, lay it between two circular pieces of linen of equal size, and fasten the outer edge with a few overcast stitches. Then work as shown by Figure 4.

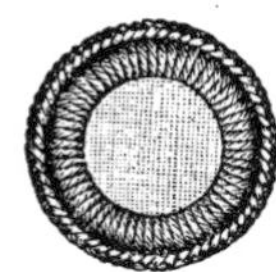

Figure 3. Button covered with linen

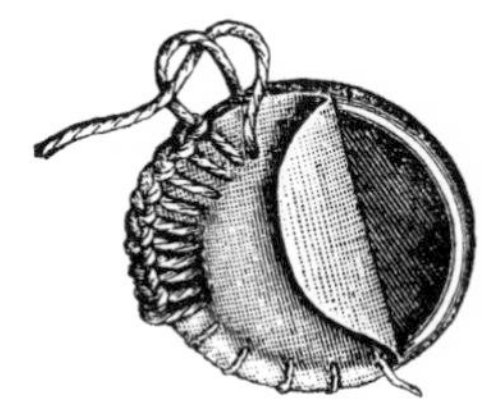

Figure 4. Covering of worn-out button—enlarged

The button shown by Figures 5 (upper side) and 6 (under side) is worked in single crochet. Work from the center outward three rounds over a foundation of cord, adding a few stitches in every round. Then crochet without cord and with the requisite widening two rounds. Then crochet two rounds with the same number of stitches, and finally the fifth and sixth rounds, in which narrow sufficiently.

Figure 5. Button with crocheted cover

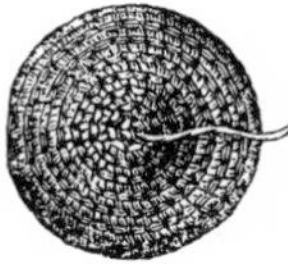

Figure 6. Button with crocheted cover

September 26, 1868

Trimmings for Underclothing

Some of these trimmings are designed for blouses, collars, pocket handkerchiefs, etc. Others are for underclothing, children's clothing, etc.

The edging in Figure 1 is worked on fine linen, partly in overcast and partly in buttonhole stitch. The center of each figure is a wheel in lace stitch.

Figure 1. Trimming for lingerie and underclothing

Figure 2 consists of two rows of open cross-stitch that join two rolls of cloth together, and connect these with a double collar, cuff, etc.

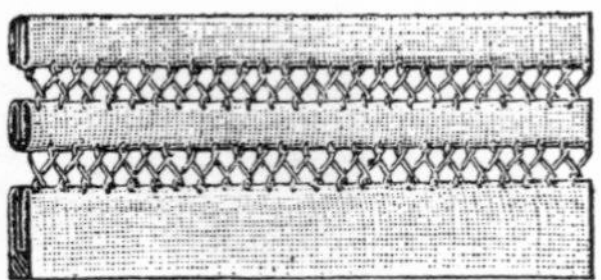

Figure 2. Trimming for lingerie and underclothing

The insertion in Figure 3 may also be used as embroidery for a pocket handkerchief above the seam. It is worked on muslin. The edges of the material, which are left in crossbars, are corded. The portions cut out are filled with lace stitch.

The trimming in Figure 4 is made of linen or muslin. It serves as the binding and sleeves of the Chemise with Small Sleeves. The material is laid at regular distances in very narrow tucks, which are joined to a pointed band.

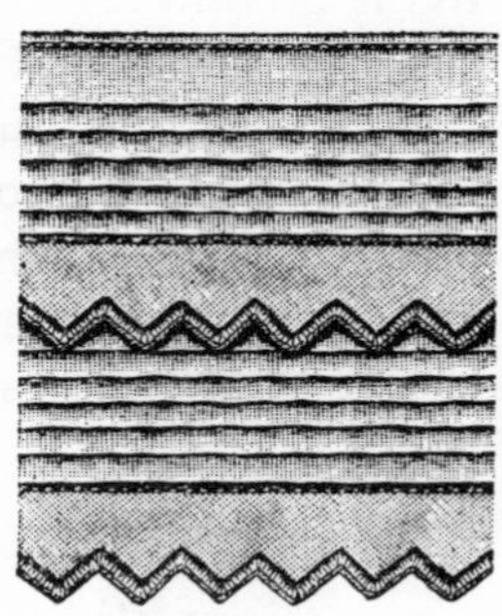

Figure 4. Trimming for lingerie and underclothing

The trimming in Figure 5 consists of strips of muslin 2 inches long and 1 inch wide, arranged in a box pleat 1/3 inch wide. These strips are joined by cross-stitches to very narrow strips worked with a row of herringbone stitch. Each side is completed by a strip of muslin stitched down.

Figure 3. Trimming for lingerie and underclothing

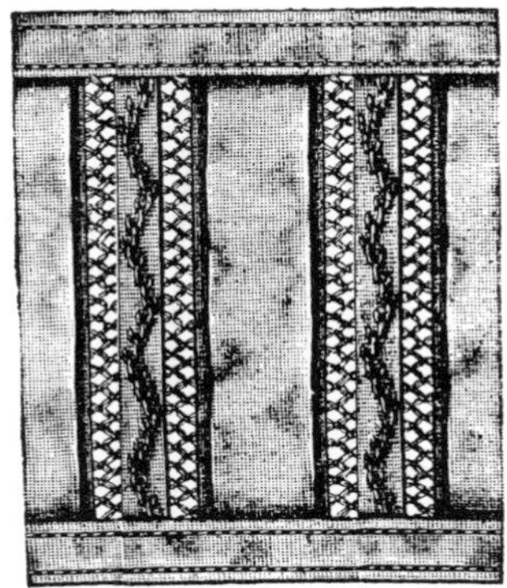

Figure 5. Trimming for lingerie and underclothing

The middle part of the trimming in Figure 6 consists of a strip of muslin 2 inches wide, which is set underneath pointed strips on each side. The edges are stitched down.

Figure 6. Trimming for lingerie and underclothing

The trimming in Figure 7 is made on Swiss muslin. The edges of the twisted strips are corded, the material is cut away between, and the space filled with lace stitch. This embroidered strip is pointed on both sides and stitched down on a strip of muslin.

Figure 7. Trimming for lingerie and underclothing

Crocheted Edgings for Underclothing

Both these edgings are crocheted on a hemmed edge.

For Figure 1, the seam is joined to the cloth by an openwork seam composed of three rows of buttonhole stitch. The edging consists of four rows of small picots.

First round: * Work 1 sc. (single crochet), in the hem, 5 ch. (chain stitches), 1 dc. (double crochet), in the 1st of these, passing over a sufficient space. Repeat from *. The remaining rounds are made in the same manner, taking care to work the sc. around the picot of the former round.

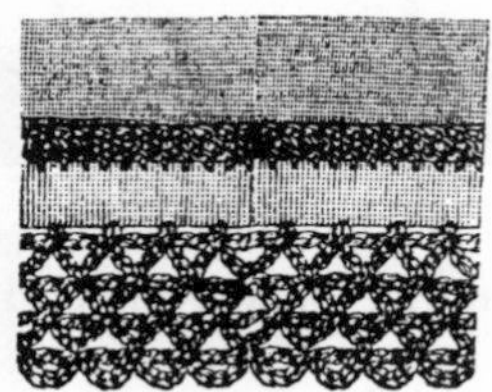

Figure 1. Crocheted edging for lingerie

The hem in Figure 2 is worked with a row of herringbone stitch. The edging consists of three pointed rows, worked in three rounds.

First round: Work 1 sc. in the hem, * 4 ch., pass over the last of these. Going back on the remaining, 1 sc., 1 short treble crochet, 1 dc. Passing over the requisite space, repeat from *. Work two more rounds in the same manner, taking care always to work the sc. in the point of the preceding round.

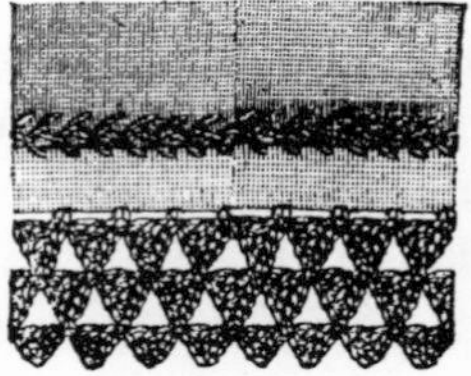

Figure 2. Crocheted edging for lingerie

Needleworked Figures For Lingerie and Underclothing

These figures are embroidered on muslin, Swiss muslin, piqué, etc. They are suitable for blouses, collars, cuffs, and pincushion covers, as well as underclothing.

The lightest parts of each design are in appliqué. The black stitches are worked with black silk as shown. The stitches used are straight and diagonal half-polka stitch, buttonhole stitch, knotted stitch, satin stitch, lace stitch, and common back stitch.

Figure 1. Needleworked figure

Figure 2. Needleworked figure

Figure 3. Needleworked figure

Figure 4. Needleworked figure

Figure 5. Needleworked figure

Figure 6. Needleworked figure

Figure 7. Needleworked figure

Chemise Yoke

The straight front of this yoke, which is 2 1/2 inches wide, the straight back, which is 1 1/4 inches wide, and the shoulders of the same width are all worked together.

Having cut the yoke of linen in this manner, draw out threads at regular distances each way, to form small squares (see Figure 1). Now fasten the corners and spaces between as shown, and work in the center of each square four knots. Scallop the outer edges and work with buttonhole stitch; as a heading for which work a straight row in buttonhole stitch.

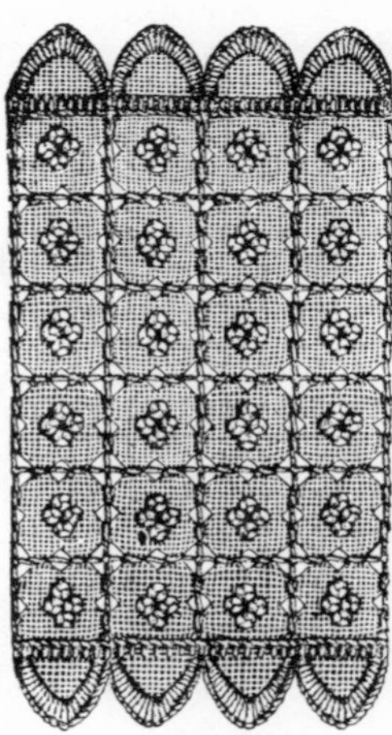

Figure 1. Section of chemise yoke–full size

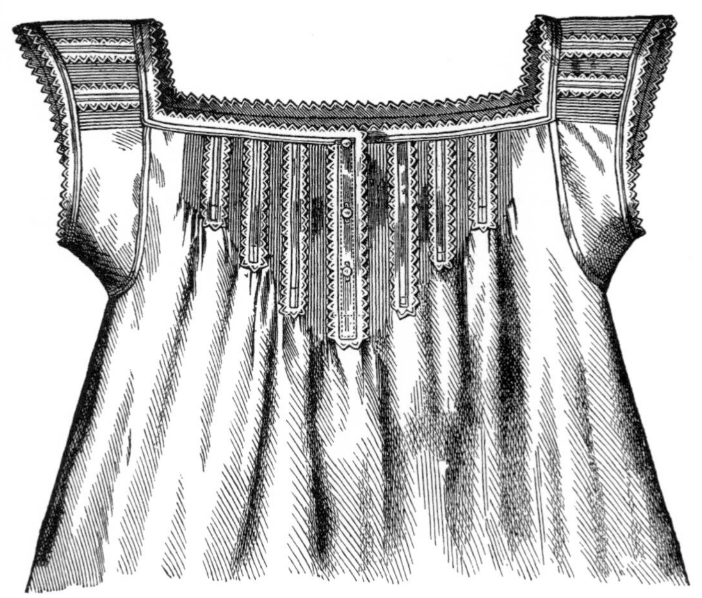

Pompadour Chemise

The front of this chemise is arranged in clusters of ten pleats 1 inch apart, every five in one direction, and loose at the under edge. Between the clusters are arranged two rows of embroidered edging. These are sewn on with a strip of muslin 1/8 inch wide, which forms a heading. The upper part of the sleeves is arranged in the same manner.

From the back pattern cut the front and back of the requisite length. Pleat the upper part of one of these pieces so it takes the form of the front pattern. Set on the trimming. Cut a slit for the front. Face the left side underneath, and the right on the outside. On the left put the buttons, and on the right work the buttonholes and trimming. Sew up the sides from the armhole to the bottom. Hem the latter.

For the sleeve arrange a piece of material of the requisite size as shown by the pattern. Then cut out the sleeves in the given form. Sew them together from 35 to 36. Finish the sleeve with a needlework edging. This is set under the sleeve and stitched down from the right side, in doing which stitch down the sleeve edge.

Bind the neck and trim with needlework edging.

September 26, 1868

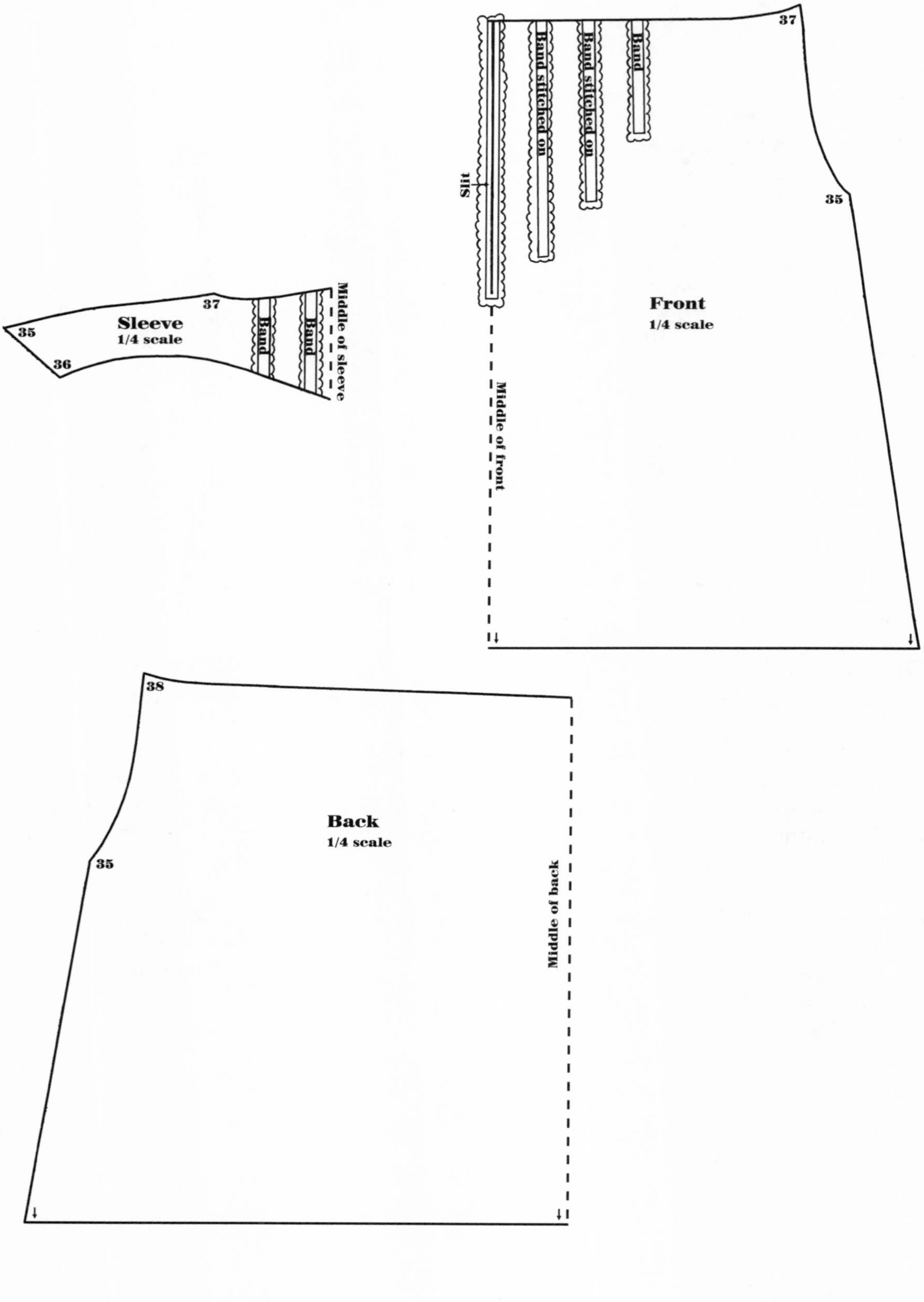
Sleeve
1/4 scale
35
36
37
Band
Band
Middle of sleeve
Front
1/4 scale
37
35
Band stitched on
Band stitched on
Band
Slit
Middle of front
Back
1/4 scale
38
35
Middle of back

Chemise with Small Sleeves

This chemise is especially suitable for wearing with low-necked dresses. The yoke and sleeves consist of strips of very narrow pleats and needlework edging.

From the main pattern cut the front and back, lengthening the chemise as much as required in the direction of the arrow. Each sleeve consists of a strip of muslin laid in twelve very narrow pleats, six in a cluster, and between the clusters a row of the narrow needlework edging, which also finishes the edge. The pleated strip must be shaped according to the sleeve pattern, which gives half the sleeve. The yoke is arranged in the same manner as the sleeves. Lay a few very small pleats in it when sewing on the embroidery to give it the desired rounding.

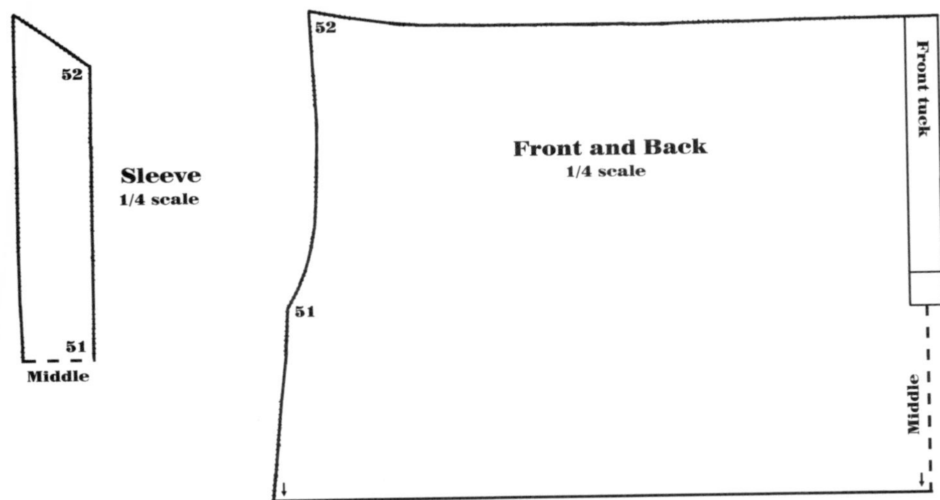

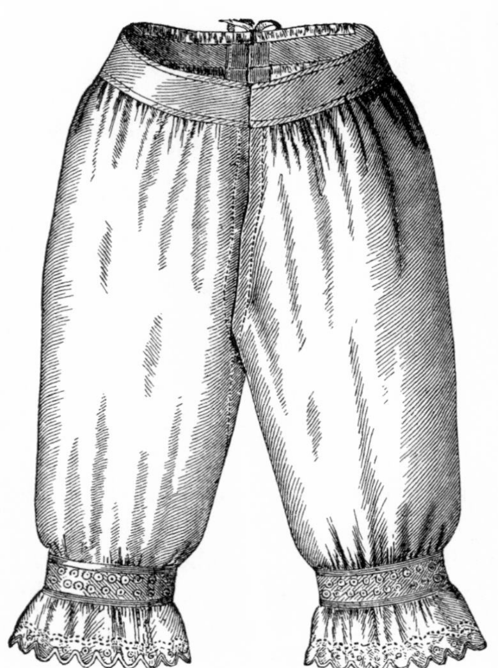

Drawers with Round Belt

These drawers are trimmed with an embroidered band 1 1/2 inches wide, and an embroidered frill 2 inches wide. From the leg pattern cut two pieces. Join each piece from 1 to 2. Face the edge of the backs with a bias strip of muslin 1 inch wide. Gather the under edge and fasten to the band. On the upper part sew together the two pieces in the front from 4 to 5. Gather the upper edge and sew it into the binding, which is cut of double material and furnished with a shirr.

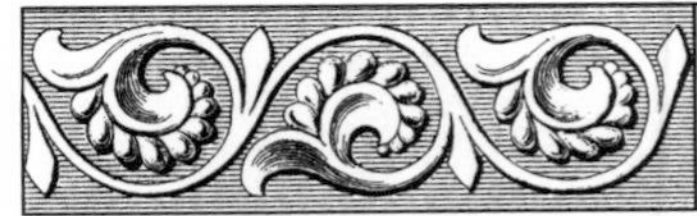

Drawers with Round Belt

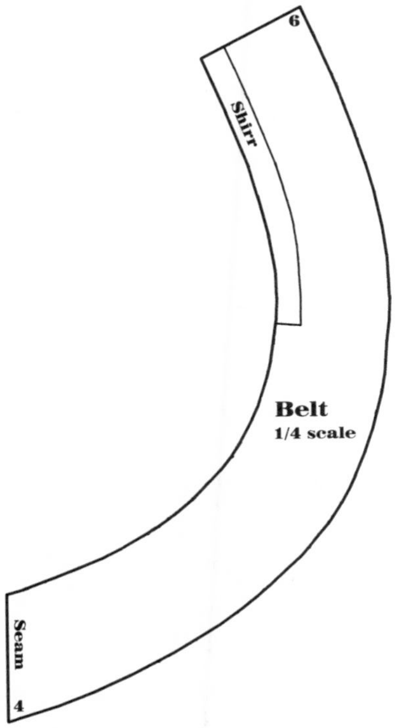

6
Shirr

Belt
1/4 scale

Seam
4

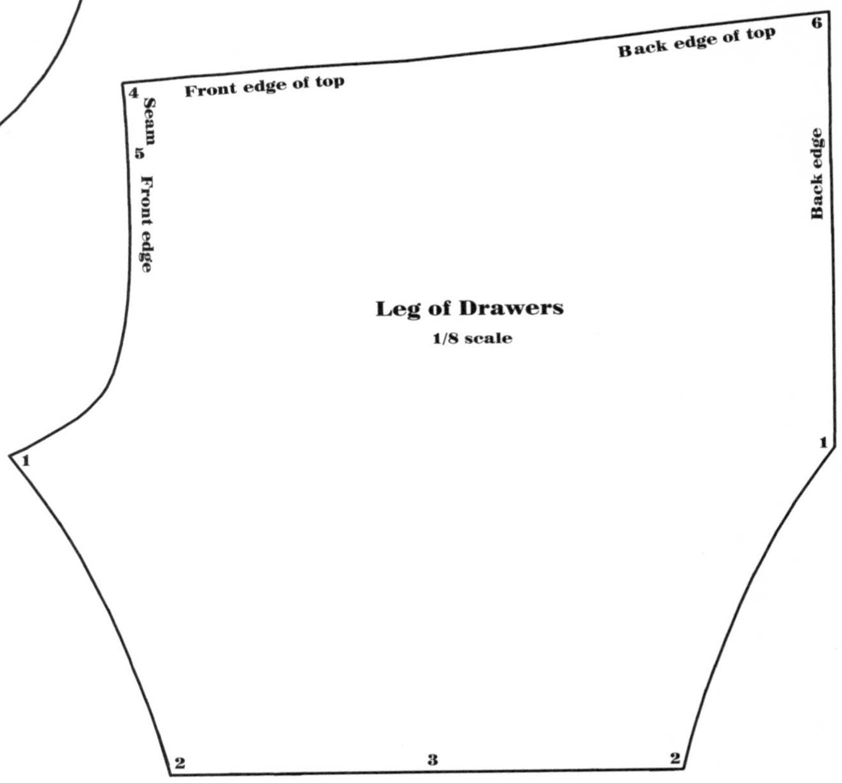

4 Front edge of top
Seam
5
Front edge

Back edge of top 6
Back edge

Leg of Drawers
1/8 scale

1
1

2 3 2

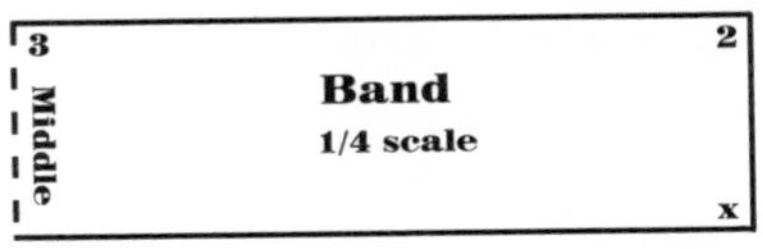

3 2
Middle
Band
1/4 scale
x

Nightdress with Revers

This nightdress is of white dimity. The revers cut with the collar is its peculiar feature. The collar is pointed behind.

Cut from the front, collar, and both cuff patterns each two pieces, allowing 1 inch on the left front for a hem. Cut the back and the sleeves.

Stitch the shoulders and fell the side seams. Trim the revers with needlework 1/2 inch wide. Set it on the fronts according to the corresponding figures on the pattern. The revers is sewn on the front with the seams. The seam on the left front is stitched down on the right side, fastening in the edge of the revers at the same time. On the right front set a band 1 1/2 inches wide, which also fastens the revers. Put on the buttons and buttonholes. Join the neck to the collar with a cord. Stitch the hem on the under edge 1/2 inch wide.

Sew the sleeves from 8 to 9 and from 10 to 11. Trim the cuffs with the needlework and lay the pieces over and under each other from 9 to *x* and from 9 to •. Join the under edge to the cuffs. Sew the sleeves into the armholes, bringing 11 on 11 of the fronts.

Belted Nightdress

This nightdress is cut from the pattern for the Nightdress with Revers. It is of fine muslin. The fronts are arranged in small pleats. They are trimmed with narrow bias folds and edging 1 inch wide as illustrated.

Nightdress with Revers

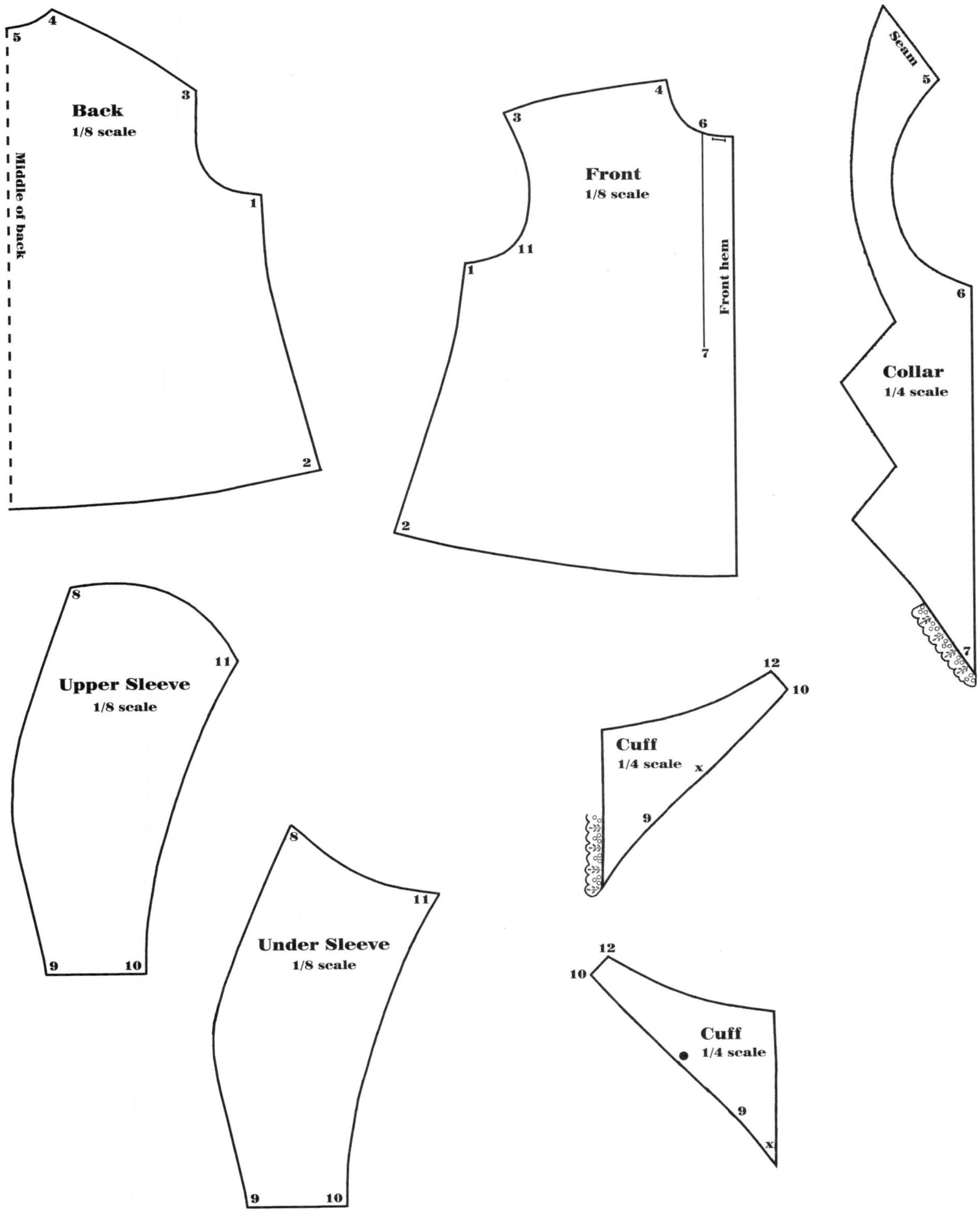
Back
1/8 scale
Middle of back
5
4
3
1
2
Front
1/8 scale
Front hem
3
4
6
11
1
7
2
Collar
1/4 scale
Seam
5
6
7
Upper Sleeve
1/8 scale
8
11
9
10
Under Sleeve
1/8 scale
8
11
9
10
Cuff
1/4 scale
12
10
x
9
Cuff
1/4 scale
12
10
9
x

Muslin Peignoir

This muslin peignoir is trimmed with embroidered insertion 1 1/2 inches wide and narrow embroidered edging. Cut both fronts and the back. Lengthen the under parts as much as desired, following the direction of the arrows. Cut the sleeves.

Arrange the fronts between the two lines designated on the front pattern by an *x*, in pleats 1/4 inch wide, so the form fits on the front shape. Lay over on the right side the front edges of both fronts, following the narrow line so that 27 is on 27. Stitch it down together with an embroidered edging 1 inch wide. Gather the back from the middle to * on each side. Join with the yoke according to the figures on the pattern.

Join the back and fronts. Hem the bottom. Bind the neck. Arrange for the collar a piece of embroidered insertion edged with embroidery. Sew up the sleeve from 33 to 34, set a strip under the lower edge, and sew into the corded armhole.

Muslin Peignoir

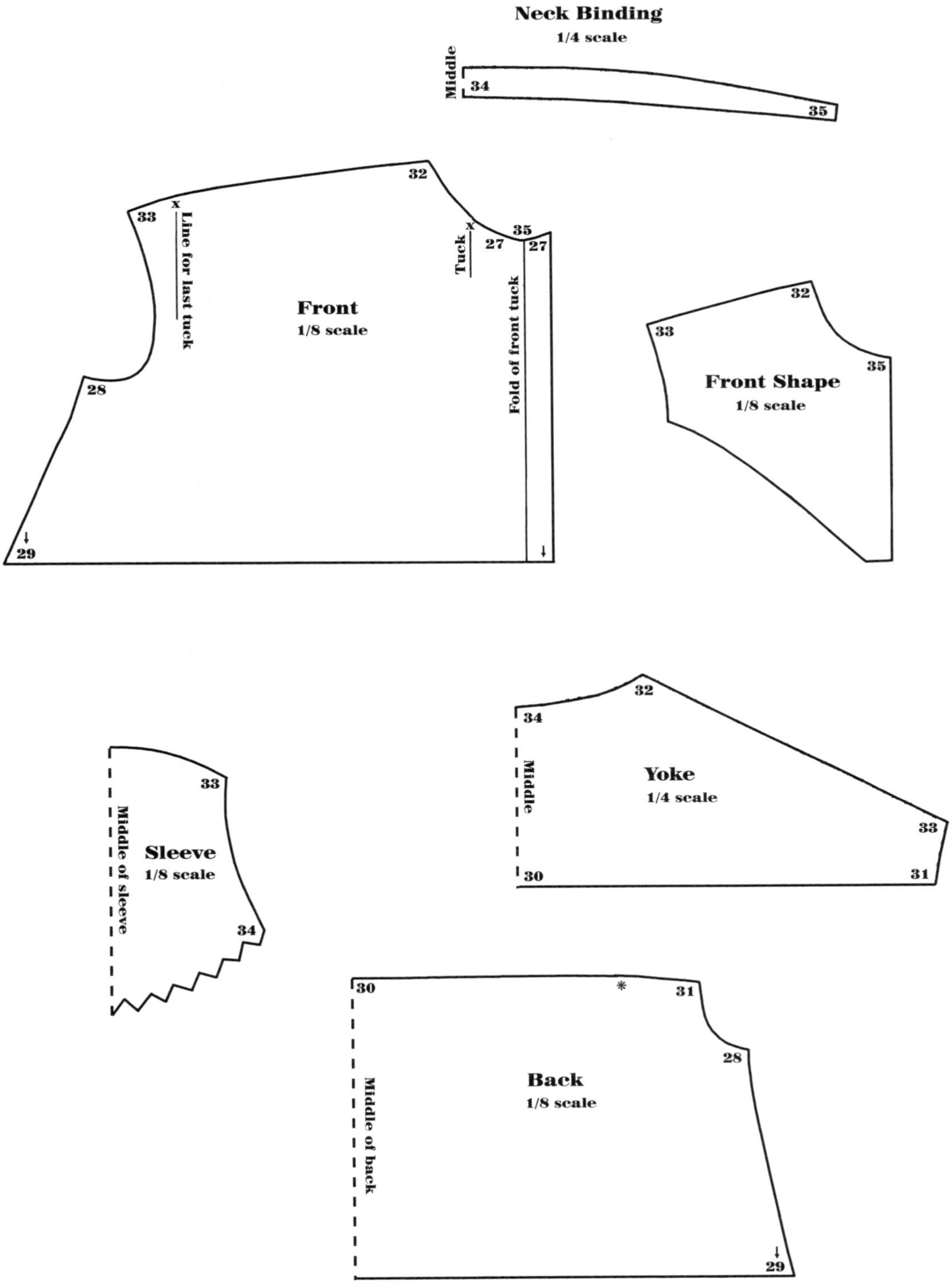

October 3, 1868

Chignons

"Additional hair" is now universally worn, and indispensable for full dress. Plaited chignons and coils of crimped hair are worn for morning toilettes, and light short curls, in the Diana Vernon style, for evening. Two long locks are worn over the left shoulder, partly crimped and partly curled. Newer than this is a short, crimped fall extending around the lower edge of the chignon, concealing the back of the neck. The ends are in ringlets. It is made of boiled hair, in which the crimp is permanent. Crêpés for the front hair are arranged to represent natural waves, and are put on in a way that defies detection; a harmless deception, much better than destroying natural hair with crimping pins. The chignon is still worn very high and large. Tortoiseshell combs are in favor again. All fancy combs are to give place to the plain straight band of tortoiseshell, engraved with gold.

A simple chignon for morning is made of hair 16 inches long, plaited over crêpés. These are made into three wide plaits, each of three strands. The two outer ones form a curve with the center plait between. Plain shell comb at the top. Another, very stylish, is formed of two puffs placed crosswise above a shell comb. Several short ringlets below fall on the neck. A dressy chignon for evening has only two plaits, with curls of different lengths between, and falling from the sides. The front hair is drawn back over a high Pompadour roll, with short frizzed curls on the forehead.

Evening headdresses are coronets of flowers, high and prominent on the forehead; large carnation or rose in the center, with buds and shaded leaves at the side. A bridal wreath has full-blown orange flowers in the center of the diadem, with branching vine and buds.

Kid Gloves

The fashionable colors for kid gloves this winter will be Vesuvius, flame color, bear's ear garnet, and the glowing sultan red. A forest of colors in the wood browns and bright capucine are in unquestionable taste, as are all the shades of gray and purple, from the dark Humboldt, more red than blue, to the delicate pearl color. A box of gloves shows fine gradations of color, the difference between the shades scarcely perceptible; but it is necessary to keep this variety to match silks of all shades.

The most popular glove is that with two buttons or studs on the wrist. A shorter glove has the center stitching extending to the top of the wrist between studs of gilt or silver. The silk tirettes with crimped tassels are the exact shade of the kid. Useful black kids are enlivened by stitching of purple, magenta, green, or white between silver eyelets laced by a cord and tassel of the same bright hue. The wristband is also bound and welted with a color. An improved glove fastening is a moveable chain adjusted with studs at either side of the wrist, and caught by a hook when drawn together.

All the light tints of cream, salmon, flesh color, and white are made in long gloves for evening, with three, four, or six buttons extending above the wrist, and sloped to fit a tapering arm. Many of these are stitched in contrasting colors with beautiful effect. The substantial undressed kid for demitoilette is made in the very best style. The castor gloves of light doeskin, for walking and driving, are soft and pliant, and fit as neatly as kid.

Veils

New veils of real lace are larger than the mask veils, are square cornered, and long enough to fall below the chin, instead of cutting the face in two like the shallow veils of the summer. The dots are small, and the border not very deep. Some have 1-inch bands of insertion to tie across the chignon. Fancy veils for round hats are round and short with long tabs. They are of Spanish net in diamond and polka spots, with embroidered borders. Modistes affirm that colored embroidery on veils is too pronounced to please the fastidious. Gauze and grenadine veils are 1 yard long, with a string in one end, worn around the crown of the hat.

Collars and Neckties

Embroidery on Swiss muslin and linen cambric is revived this season for collars and chemisettes. The collars are not very wide, and are turned down and slightly pointed in front, or with a square revers. The edges are scalloped and bordered with narrow Valenciennes. A few standing collars, a style becoming to long necks, are straight behind with points turned down in front. A knot or bow of lace is worn in front. Muslin chemisettes for surplice waists are embroidered in a point to the belt, and cut low in the neck with a standing frill of Valenciennes.

Collars of French cambric in stripes or figures are being generally adopted for morning toilettes and traveling. Black and cherry stripes are in favor, but require to be carefully worn, especially on the street, where they look best with black costume. Deep cuffs are made of cambric of the same pattern as the collar. If in stripes a belt is sometimes added, fastened with a jet buckle.

The necktie has become an important feature of feminine dress. It is not really a necktie but a bow that takes the place of the breastpin. Broad ribbons, shaded, striped, or self-colored, are tied into loose bows and knots, with a studied carelessness that is the perfection of art. Rich sultan red, matching the feathers so fashionable on hats, is most often used. A half yard is all that is required for a knot with fringed ends.

Velvet dog-collar necklaces, with lockets attached, or fastened with an ornamental slide, are becomingly worn above turndown collars. If the neck is long the band may be 1 inch wide. On short necks narrower velvet is tied behind with long loops and ends.

Shoes

The half Polish boot of the summer will give place in cold weather to the full Polish fitting high up on the calf of the leg. Toes are medium round; the shank is very narrow; and the heel high, slender, and curved. The fashionable buttoned boot for walking has the uppers of glove kid or, if preferred, glazed kid, the lower of pebbled morocco. Very dressy boots are stitched with white, and buttoned with imitation pearl buttons. Models of English shoes are much lower on the ankle than those worn here, with heels of the broad military shape. These are comfortable for walking, but are not so showy as the French shape now in favor, with Louis XV heels.

Tassels and satin bows no longer decorate the top of the boot, but are removed to the instep. A new rosette of kid, bound with silk, extends high up on the instep. It transforms the plainest slipper into the stylish Pompadour shape.

Miscellaneous

An economical suggestion is a black silk tunic or overskirt, with a small cape reaching to the waist, to be worn over short silk dresses that have become defaced. A small cape of black silk, composed of successive collars like the Carrick, is trimmed with satin folds, and, with the addition of a tunic, gives variety to costumes.

October 10, 1868

Fall Mantles

The universal adoption of short costumes for the street is rapidly doing away with extra overgarments. A lady no longer finds it necessary to provide herself each season with a separate wrapping, since her suits are complete in themselves, each with its own wrapping, made of heavy or light material, as the weather requires. Instead of the variety of silk and faille wrappings usually imported at this season, only a few new patterns are brought out.

These are scarf shaped with baschlik hoods, Watteau casaques with a broad pleat in the back, or the long polonaise with capes. The trimming is pleatings of the material in frills, or the flat marquise ruche sewn at top and bottom. Cashmere is more stylish than silk. It is made in baschlik mantles and in large circulars with capes, trimmed with lace or fringe. Braiding embroidery, and a little jet, may be used on cashmere.

Plush Jackets

Some very dressy plush jackets are made in the bright Alexandra blue, garnet, and French gray. They are short and jaunty, fitting the figure closely, are slightly wadded, and trimmed with satin piping or silk cord. A hood cut in two points from which long tassels are pendant is a stylish addition. White buttons of velvet or pearl.

Cloth Cloaks

Cloth cloaks are gored pelisses or tight-fitting basquines with capes or a hood, and are to be used as the upper garment of suits. As the prices are high, but few persons will care to buy more than one during the season.

It is therefore best to be content with a black cloak that may be worn with petticoats of every color. The gay, warm-looking garnet cloth, a novelty this winter, the rich Humboldt purple, the dead-leaf brown, and the soft violet-gray are very alluring in their beauty. But they will neither combine nor contrast well with other colors, and are too conspicuous to be worn all winter.

Trimmings

Scarcely a cloak is shown without fringe on some part of it. A new fringe has slender, pear-shaped pendants. Wide netted heading is suitable for velvet, and is in favor with old ladies. Bullion cords and tassel fringe are more dressy.

Faille and satin are pleated in a variety of ways for frills and ruches, and as a heading for fringe. Six or eight bands of satin the color of the cloth, crosscut, 1/2 inch wide, are stitched on at both edges. Wider bands have several rows of stitching, done with accuracy, in straight lines. Flat satin braid of different widths is newer than folds. Wide serge or military braid is serviceable on plain garments. Velvet bands cut bias from the piece are piped with faille or satin. Tassels of unusual length and grelots of passementerie adorn the hoods and capes. Rosettes and triple bows of satin or faille, or both together, are features of the Watteau casaque. Buttons, both small and large, are used in profusion.

Carriage Wrappings and Shawls

Heavy plaid flannels, 1 1/2 yards wide, are made up into extra carriage cloaks. These are serviceable for traveling, and are worn over suits on cool mornings on the promenade. The Royal Stuart plaid, the McGregor, the McFarlane, the Rob Roy, and plaids of every clan are in favor. Ladies of quiet tastes choose large blocks of black and white, or the irregular blue and green plaid. Gay young misses wear the bright colors in which Highlanders delight.

The shape is a gored circular, pointed behind and at the sides, with armholes concealed by a large cape with pointed fold forming a hood. Folds of satin and fringe of the several colors of the plaid form the trimming.

Woolen shawls, soft as merino but very heavy, are in stripes and plaids. The stripes are wide and regular bars of black, scarlet, and gold together, or the broken Roman stripe with all the hues of the rainbow. The chlamys, a cashmere circular laden with colored embroidery and appliqué, is a gorgeous opera cloak to be worn later in the winter. Shawl-shaped garments with an Arab fold are trimmed with fringe and black lace. White plush with pink or blue stripes, having the effect of fringe, is sold for evening wrappings.

Plaids

It is probable we will have at least a short reign of this gay attire for demitoilette. It can never be full dress. Modistes report importations of Highland costumes for morning promenades and traveling. They are also using plaid poplins, silks, and velvet as trimming, but very carefully, not broad bands of plaid, but narrow braids, piping, and binding.

The heavy poplin reps, with thick raised cords, silk and wool together, are the handsomest plaids. They are 1 yard wide. Smooth poplins are in plaids of all the clans. All-wool flannels in large plaids are sold for cloaks.

Striped Dresses and Petticoats

Zebra-striped dresses are growing into favor. Handsome striped poplins, woolen and satin together, blue, gold, green, and garnet, with black, are 1 yard wide. Excellent all-wool poplins are shown in 1-inch stripes for skirts, and narrower stripes of the same color and material for the overdress. Striped velvets are the climax of extravagance in petticoats. The velvet skirts are trimmed with bias folds of the silk of the overdress, and the dress with folds of the velvet petticoat.

Seamless boulevard skirts are in new colors, softer material, with new borders like appliqué. Balmorals have broad Roman stripes, and a new pattern in imitation of the borders on camel's-hair shawls.

Corsets

New corsets of good shape and make are of strong yet thin coutil, less clumsy than the thick corset jeans. The whalebones are in cases stitched on the outside, leaving a smooth surface next the body, a great comfort to corset wearers. A novel feature in these new stays is a perfume in the whalebone cases that counteracts the disagreeable odor emitted by whalebone when warmed by the natural heat of the body.

Another novelty is the crinoline corset for dancing. It is of crinoline or canvas, manufactured for the purpose, thin, cool, and comfortable for crowded receptions. It is made in three horizontal pieces, clasping the waist tightly, with graceful slope on the hips and bust.

Swiss Aprons

Imported Swiss aprons are trimmed with tiny tucks or appliqué folds, stitched or in braid patterns, medallions of Valenciennes, and lace borders. Bands and pockets are lined with ribbon to display the work on them. Bretelles of lace and ribbon pass over the shoulders.

Tortoiseshell and Jet

Instead of tawdry French gilt and wooden jewelry for morning toilette, we will have a return of plain jet and tortoiseshell in massive blocks, cubical pendants, bars, and crescent shapes. Combs, brooch, earrings, buttons, and bracelets are made en suite, and engraved with gold in Greek patterns, initials, or monograms.

Handkerchief Border

Both this border and the next are worked above the hem of the pocket handkerchief. The openwork stripe on this border is formed of Valenciennes lace, which is worked fast to the muslin on each side with satin stitch points. At regular distances work flower twigs in satin and straight half-polka stitch. The center of the flower is composed of lace stitch. Having completed the embroidery, cut away the material from under the insertion.

Handkerchief Border

This border consists of insertion of netted guipure and single embroidered flower twigs. Work the insertion with fine thread over a fine steel knitting needle. Then work the strip in point de toile. Buttonhole stitch the strip on the muslin, work the embroidered figures, and cut away the muslin under the insertion. The embroidered twigs may also be in application.

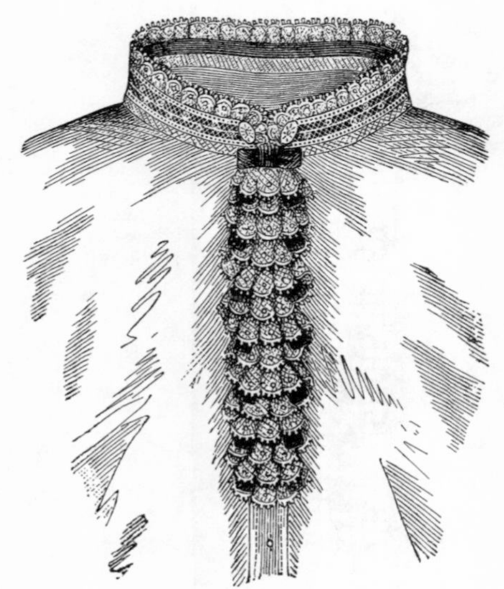

Hortense Collar

This collar is made of Valenciennes insertion 1/2 inch wide, bordered on each side with embroidered insertion 1/5 inch wide, and trimmed with an embroidered figure on the ends. The under edge is bound with a strip of muslin 1/3 inch wide. The upper one is bordered with Valenciennes lace 1/2 inch wide.

For the jabot, which is arranged on the front, prepare a strip of double muslin 10 inches long and 1 inch wide. Trim this with Valenciennes lace 1 inch wide. Between the rows of lace set loops of green satin ribbon 1/2 inch wide. The same ribbon is also laid under the collar.

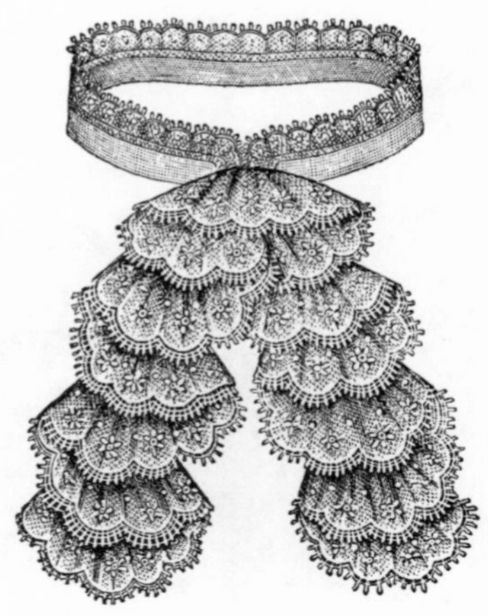

Marquise Collar

The collar is arranged in the same manner as the Hortense collar. For the foundation of the jabot prepare two pieces of double muslin 8 inches long and 1 inch wide. Sew them together at the upper ends. Finish with gathered lace 2 inches wide.

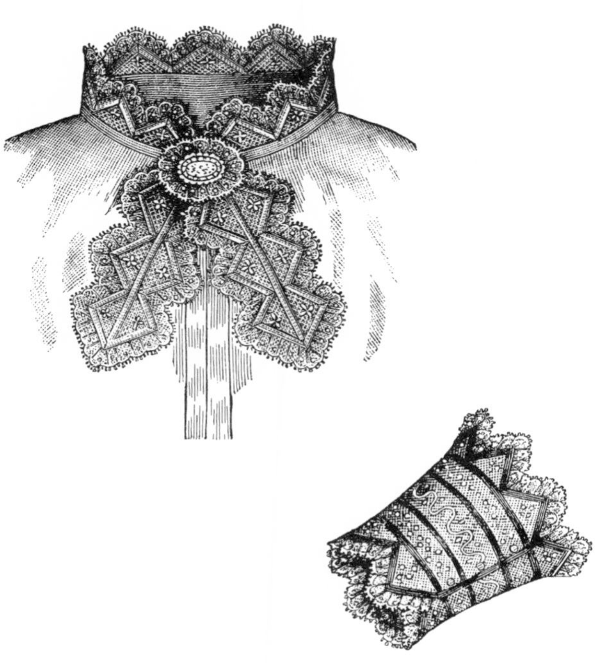

Pointed Collar with Cuffs

This pointed collar is of figured Valenciennes edged with gathered Valenciennes lace 1/2 inch wide. The seam on the edges is covered with a very narrow bias strip of muslin, which is set on with a double row of stitching. The collar is joined to the chemisette with a muslin binding 1/2 inch wide.

The ends match the collar. They consist of two pointed strips sewn together in the middle, the seam being covered with a very narrow bias strip of muslin stitched down twice. Join the two ends as shown. Finish with a rosette edged with the lace. The cuffs may be made corresponding to the collar.

Standing Collars

Both these collars, full-size sections of which are shown, are made of very narrow white cotton braid and lace stitch. The edging alone of Figure 1 is crocheted.

To make the collar in Figure 1, first draw the lines for the braid on stiff paper. Fasten the braid on them. Join with buttonhole stitch of fine white thread.

Then crochet the lace on the edge of the collar. This consists of two rows of chain-stitch scallops, in which each scallop counts 5 chain stitches. The last round is worked in picots as follows. One single crochet in the 1st chain-stitch scallop of the former round, 7 chain stitches, 1 slip stitch in the 2nd of these, 1 chain stitch, and continue in this manner.

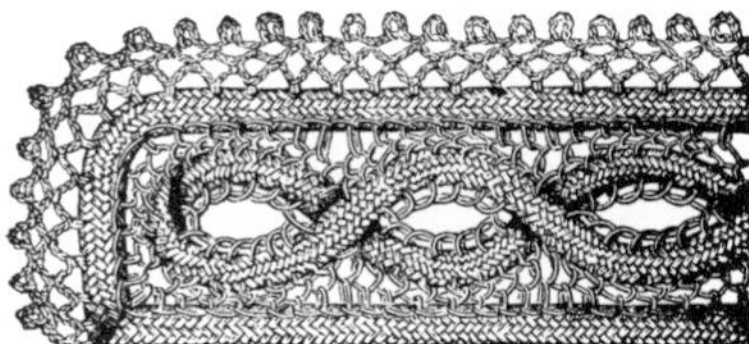

Figure 1. Section of braid and lace standing collar

The collar in Figure 2 is worked in a similar manner. In this case join the braid with a kind of cross-stitching of thread, which is again wound as shown.

The lace on the outer edge is formed of three rows of buttonhole-stitch loops. But each row must be worked by the winding of the thread before working the following row, the stitches of which must be worked in the loops made by this winding. By this means the three rows of buttonhole stitch follow each other so as to bring the stitches perpendicularly over each other.

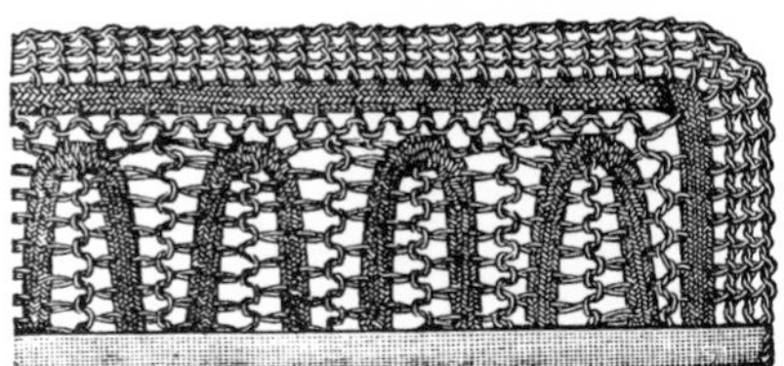

Figure 2. Section of braid and lace standing collar

October 10, 1868

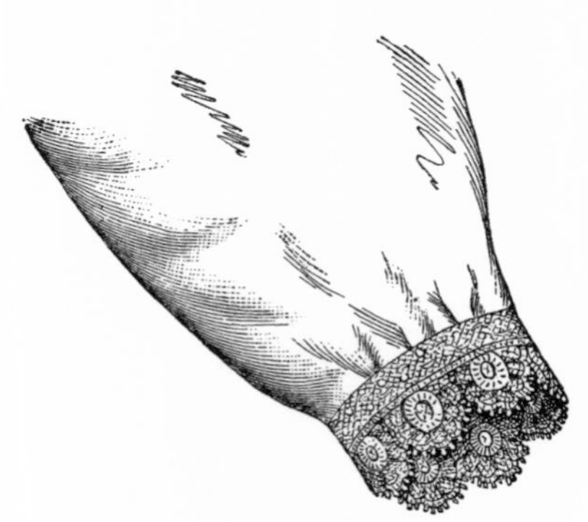

Adeline Collar

This collar consists of small rounded figures. Each is made of an embroidered rosette, with Valenciennes lace 1/2 inch wide gathered around it. These figures are fastened first to very narrow insertion (see full-size illustration) and then to the muslin binding on the neck. The front consists of two pieces of fine muslin each 3 inches wide and of different lengths. Both ends are trimmed with the figures, and the sides only with the narrow insertion and lace. Both the upper ends are gathered up in a wickel seam to the width of 1 inch and sewn to very narrow insertion. The cuff matches the collar.

Duchesse Collar

This collar corresponds to the Hortense collar, but is without the embroidered figures and the ribbon laid underneath.

The jabot is of Valenciennes lace, but it may also be made of Valenciennes net and edged with lace. Cut from the pattern two pieces. Lay them over along the narrow line on the wrong side. Lay the pleats *x* on • in each part. Sew both parts together along the pleated edge. Cover the seam with an oblong rosette of lace.

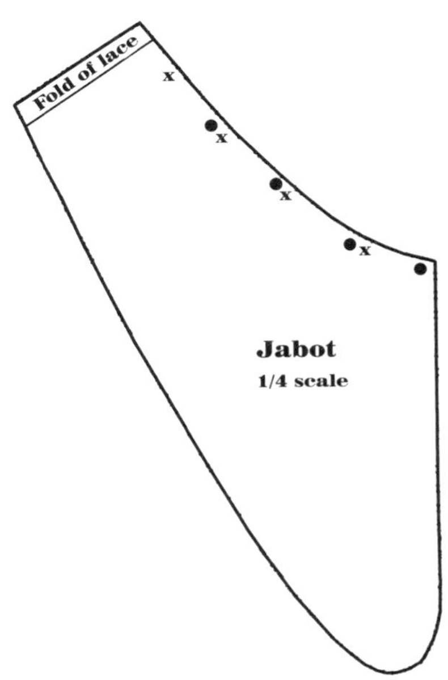

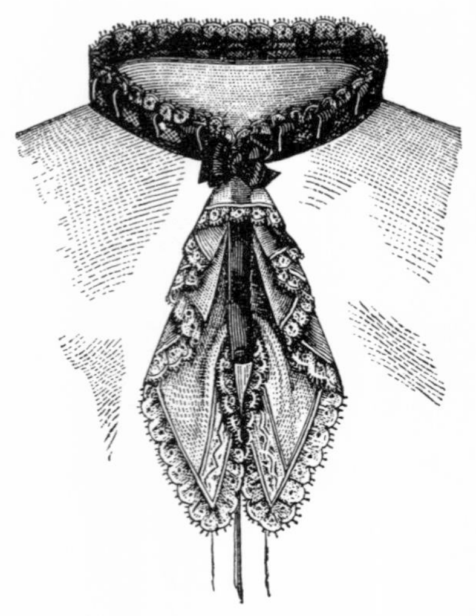

Louise Collar

This collar is made of Valenciennes insertion 1/3 inch wide, and embroidered insertion 1/6 inch wide.

For the jabot on the front of the collar, cut a piece of muslin and Valenciennes insertion from the pattern. Sew together the edges of the stuff from 35 to 36 and from 36 to 37. Set on a piece of Valenciennes insertion so that the middle comes on the middle line. Cut away the muslin under the insertion. Then border the jabot with embroidered insertion 1/6 inch wide, and Valenciennes insertion 2/3 inch wide.

Lay the pleats in the jabot, bringing *x* on •. Make a box pleat in the middle, the outer sides of which are indicated by the dotted line. Under this box pleat set a loop of satin ribbon. Fasten the jabot on the collar. Cover the place where it is set on with a small lilac bow.

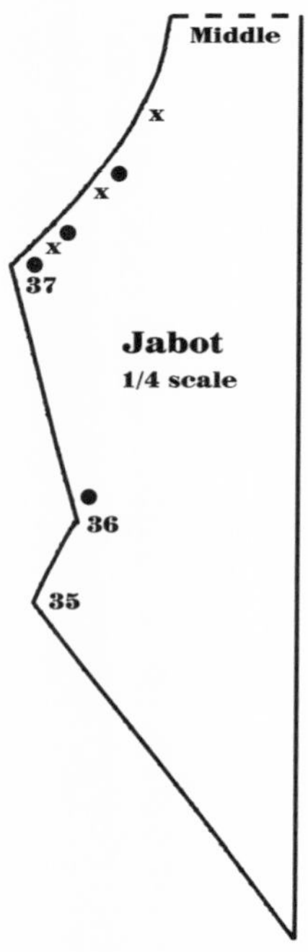

Collar with Rounded Bavettes

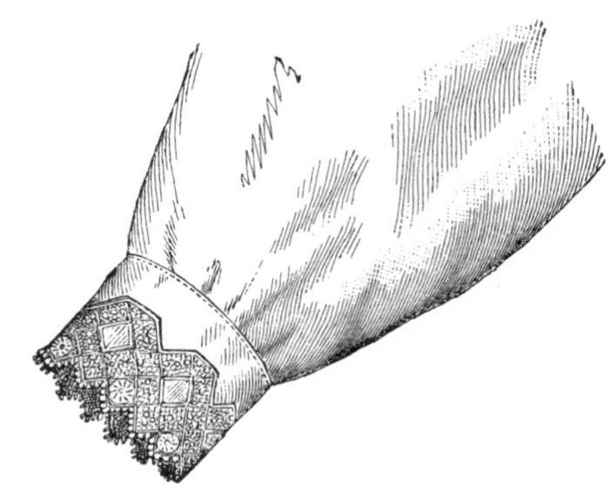

Collar with Rounded Bavettes

This collar, with matching cuffs, is made from fine double linen, Valenciennes insertion 1/3 inch wide, and small embroidered squares. The insertion must be laid in pleats between the points, to form the insertion points. The design for the squares is also given on the pattern. The insertion is loosely overseamed on the linen. The outer edge of the collar is bordered with Valenciennes edging 1/2 inch wide.

For the bavettes arrange from the pattern two pieces of muslin, Valenciennes insertion, and embroidered squares. Border each part with narrow Valenciennes lace. Join the pieces which have previously been pleated, bringing *x* on •, by referring to the pattern.

Half the cuff is given.

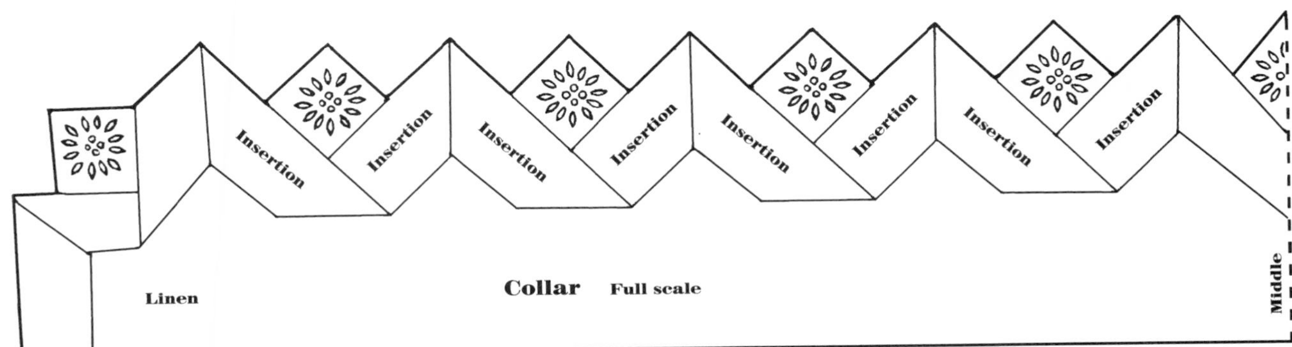

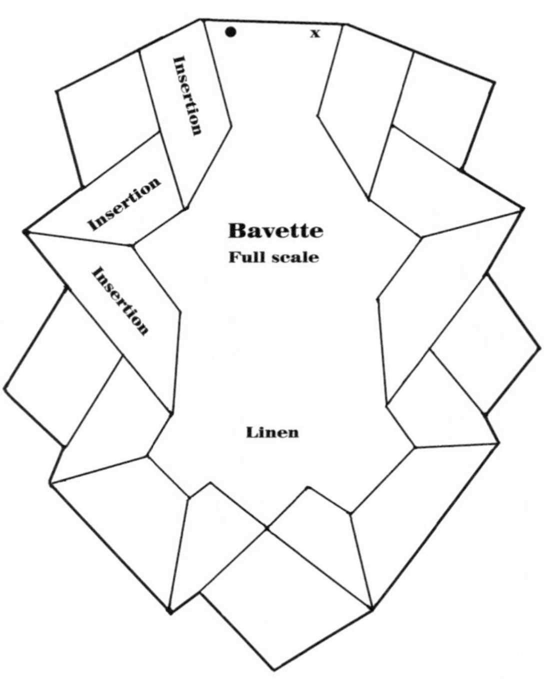
x
Insertion
Insertion
Bavette
Full scale
Insertion
Linen

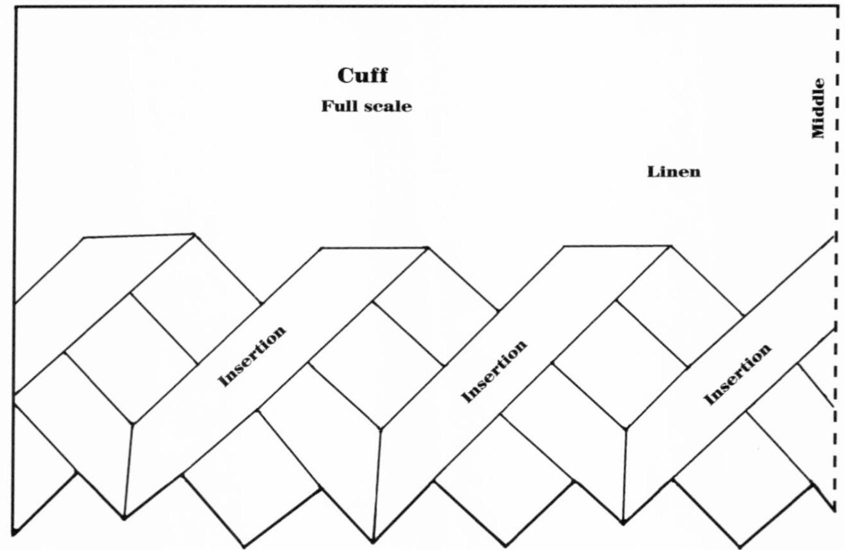
Cuff
Full scale
Middle
Linen
Insertion
Insertion
Insertion

Jabot and Cap

Jabot and Cap

This jabot is made of a piece of Valenciennes lace 28 inches long and 1 1/2 inches wide, arranged on a small tulle foundation, and ornamented with bows of red satin ribbon 1 inch wide.

Gather the lace with wickel or overstitch. Cut the tulle foundation. Hem the outer edges and sew on the lace. Begin at ••, and sew the lace on the edge, following the direction of the arrow as far as *x*. Then lay the lace so the scalloped edge points downward. Next arrange the upper part in an oblong rosette, and again proceed to the point marked *x*. From *x* to *, where the end of the lace must reach, sew it to the foundation under the upper row of lace. The ends are easily hidden under the overlapping lace. Arrange the bows as illustrated.

In arranging the jabot on a bodice, turn down the upper edge at about half the width of the lace. Arrange a narrow piece of similar lace on the bodice neck as a standing collar. If it be desired to wear the jabot as a cap, set two long strings of satin ribbon on the sides.

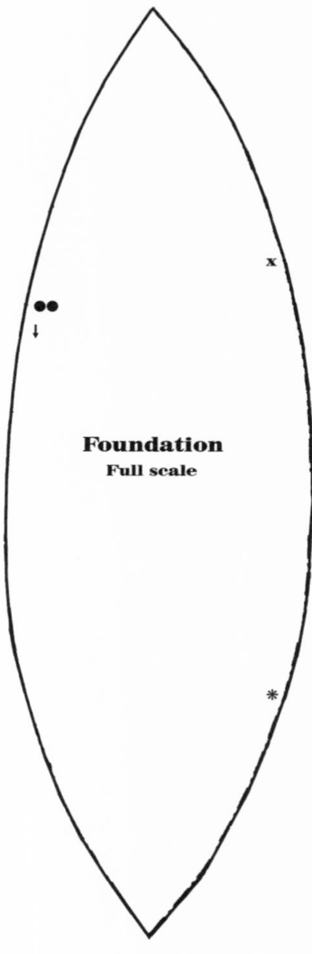
x
●●
↓
Foundation
Full scale
*

Nilsson Hat

Two long black ostrich feathers, a tuft of violets, and a few sprigs of mignonette form the tasteful and stylish trimming of this hat. The foundation (shown reduced size) is made of black foundation lace and figured tulle.

Cut of foundation lace from the pattern one piece. Cover this with gathered tulle. Bind the foundation with a strip of black silk 1 1/2 inches wide, in which a layer of stiffening has been placed. Lay a wire on both sides of the binding. Bend the foundation into the desired shape. Trim with feathers and flowers as illustrated. A sash of tulle edged with lace may replace the feathers (see second illustration).

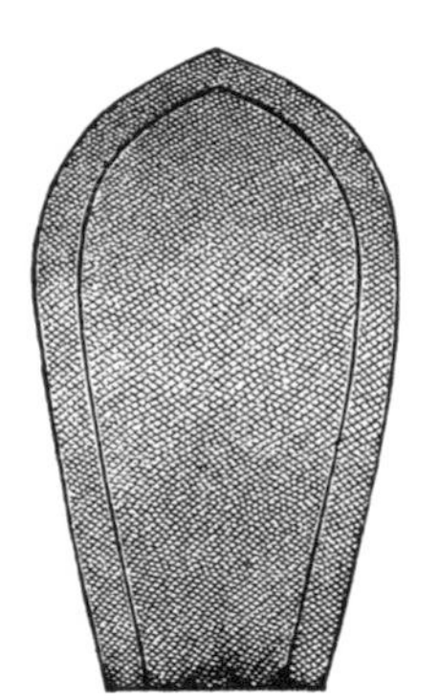

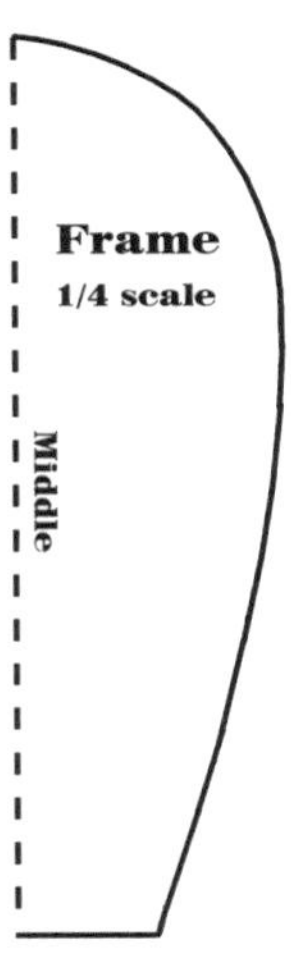

Low-Necked Pleated Waist

This waist is very stylish, and especially suitable for young girls' dresses of thin material.

Cut of fine muslin from the front, side back, and sleeve each two pieces. Cut from the back one piece. Allow 1 inch on the right front and 2 inches on the left for hems. These are furnished with buttons and buttonholes. Take up the bosom pleats in the fronts.

Arrange the outside material, the back and fronts of which are pleated and the sides plain. For the front take a piece of the material of the requisite size. Make a narrow hem on the front edge. Gather the under edge closely, leaving enough material to cover the sides. Baste this gathered material on the lining, slightly gathering the upper part of the front, and bringing the greater part of the gathers on the shoulders to lie over the waist in the form of bretelles. Arrange the back in a similar manner. Join the waist according to the figures on the pattern. Run limber whalebones in the seams and bosom pleats. Cord the neck and bottom.

Sew up each sleeve according to the figures on the pattern. Hem the bottom. Set on the latter a pleated piece of the outside material. Over this put a flounce 20 inches long, which is sloped under the arm and edged with embroidery. Cord the armholes. Sew in the sleeves according to the figures on the pattern.

Edge the neck with embroidery. Sew in a Russian chemisette, formed of a pleated piece of the outside material of the requisite width.

Low-Necked Pleated Waist

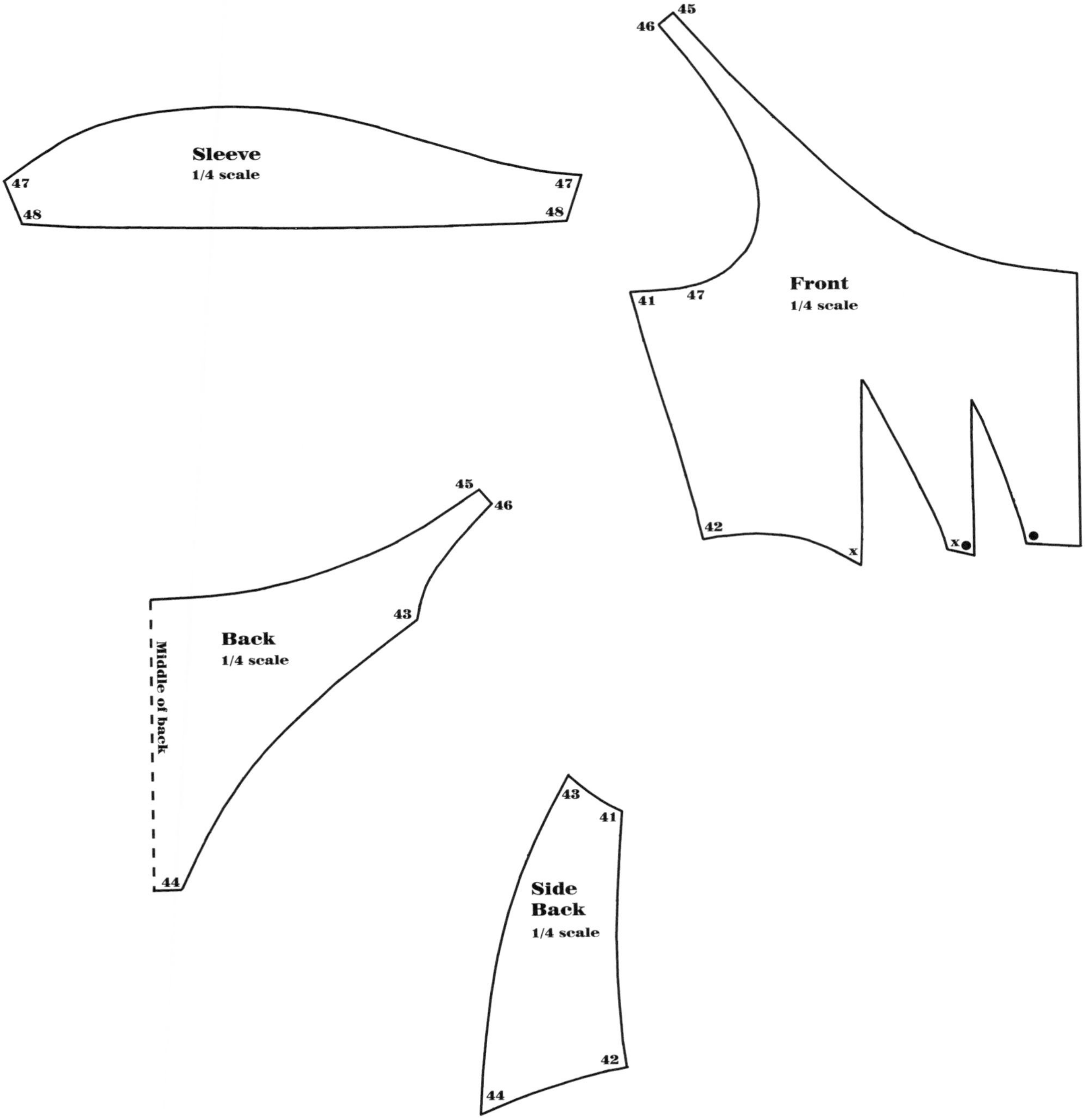

October 10, 1868

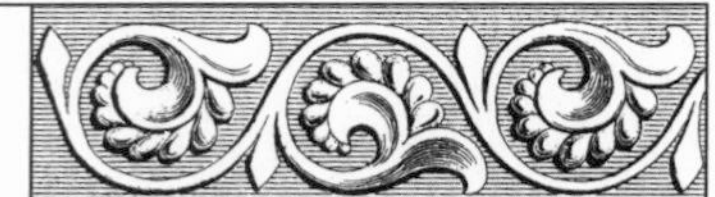

Walking Dress with Watteau Paletot

This suit is of brown poplin, cut bias. Dress without trail and long paletot, looped up on the back and sides, with belt and sash. The skirt is finished with two flounces each 3 inches wide. These are laid in very narrow plain pleats and set on with a brown silk piping, leaving a heading above the latter. The paletot is bordered in the same manner. The remaining trimming of the paletot consists of bias folds edged with brown silk, part of which are 2/3 inch and part 1 inch wide; fluting 1 1/4 inches wide; small rounded pieces of the material bound with silk, which at the same time form the standing collar; buttons covered with the stuff, with fine cord drawn over; and lastly, loops of heavy silk cord, which fasten the paletot as illustrated.

Cut from the front and back each two pieces. Cut both parts of the sleeves. Sew the two backs together from 3 to 4 and from 3 to 5. Lay a pleat on each side of the seam, bringing *xc* on *•c* and 3 on 3. The sides of this pleat are left without fastening on the under side. Next join the back and fronts according to the figures on the pattern. Turn the edges of the fronts over on the right side and fasten them down with a bias fold 1 inch wide. Then face the under edge 1 inch wide and sew on the flounce. Cord the neck and set on the rounded pieces, covering the seam with a narrow bias fold of the silk. The fluting is arranged on the bodice in the form of a heart, as illustrated, and the seam is covered by a bias fold 2/3 inch wide.

Sew the sleeves together according to the figures on the pattern. Turn the under edge over on the right side. Set on the rounded pieces together with two bias folds 1 inch wide. Sew the sleeves into the armholes. The seam is taken on the right side and covered with a bias fold. This is narrower under the arm than on the shoulder, and finished with a narrow epaulet of fluting.

Set the buttons and loops along the fronts as illustrated. Gather up the paletot by tacking *xa* on *•a* on each side seam, and *xb* on *•b* on the back seam. On each pleat on the side seam set a large button with a cluster of tassels. On the back of the paletot, on the edges of the pleat in the middle, sew a belt 1 1/2 inches wide, the rest of which is left loose, and fastened in front under the paletot with hooks and eyes. On the upper side of the same pleat set a corded belt lined with buckram, which must be fastened on the side. The place where this belt is fastened, as well as where it is sewn on the back of the paletot, is covered with a bow and ends of the paletot material, double and lined, and arranged as illustrated.

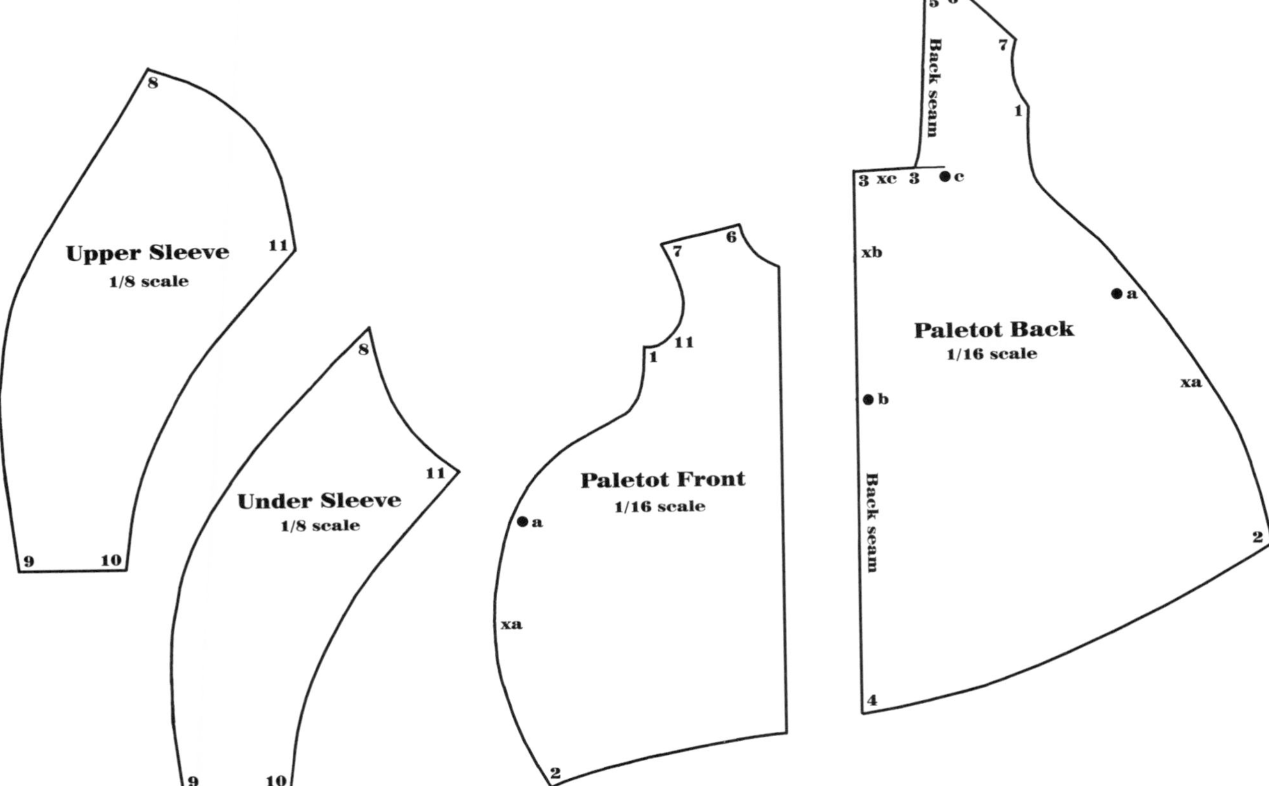

October 17, 1868

New Bonnets

At the millinery openings a great many fanchons and fanchonettes were displayed. This shape is universally becoming, and will continue to be worn throughout the season, perhaps longer. But it is no longer the only choice.

Milliners are making a high, round pouf bonnet that encircles the front of the head above the ears, sloping upward at the back to fit snugly on the edge of the high chignon. The diadem, a conspicuous feature this season, is better adapted to this round shape than to the fanchon with long ears. Puffs and erect aigrettes behind prevent the diadem from looking too high and prominent. When properly adjusted to the head, the new shape will be found to have the becoming effect that has kept the fanchon so long in favor.

All the different materials, satin, faille, velvet, lace, feathers, and flowers, enter into each bonnet. Diadems are of jet, flowers, feathers, and lace quillings, but most frequently of velvet lined with satin of another color, the lining showing at the edges like piping. On the body of the bonnet the material is shirred, puffed, or in reversed pleats, never plain on the frame. Narrow strings tied behind with falls of lace and velvet in front still prevail, but not to the exclusion of bows under the chin as during the summer. With the present fashion of cutting dresses low at the throat, the front bow is becoming and comfortable in cold weather.

Lace drapery falling low at the sides, and caught at the back of the chignon by a bow and ends, is a graceful feature of winter bonnets. A novelty in lace falls has a wide pleat behind, pointed like a hood, and trimmed with bows, *à la Renaissance,* down the center. The front of this drapery has revers fastened by a bow without ends.

Sultan red is a favorite color for bonnets, as it is becoming to dark and fair alike. Florence green, lighter than Metternich, and the royal pink, so long out of use, are selected for youthful faces. Garnet; rich, warm crimson; leaf brown; and gold-yellow with black, are chosen for those more mature. The light shades of French gray, drab, and brown are contrasted with Alexandra blue, with scarlet and cherry. Violet is trimmed with deeper purple. White still prevails for evening hats.

Straw bonnets are not largely imported at this season of the year. A few waved and plaited braids, gray, brown, and black, and the yellow Italian straws, are shown. Wreaths of scarlet berries, shaded autumn leaves, or pansies of different color, form the diadem. Loops and bows of velvet and short ostrich tufts complete the trimming. The diadem may be of pleated velvet, with a jet marguerite or hummingbird in the center.

Crpe bonnets for fresh mourning cover the frame smoothly, with a diadem of reversed pleats. Jet diadems of square blocks are designed especially for mourning. Black royal velvet and lusterless faille are used for more dressy mourning, trimmed with Brussels net and jet ornaments.

Hats

Round hats are almost universally worn at this transition season before new bonnets are purchased. A black straw hat, high crowned with turned-up rim, is the shape most generally adopted. It is called promiscuously the Valois, the Louis Quinze, and the Rupert. Small birds with long, graceful plumage ornament the left side.

The black velvet Deauville sloping from the middle, back, and front is the most elegant of the new styles. The trimming of quilled lace and flowers is massed over the forehead.

The Sultan's fez, a round crown like an inverted cup, is a piquant novelty. It is made by sewing successive rows of lace or puffs of satin around the frame. Clusters of flowers, feathers, and lace, or ribbon rosettes, are arranged on the top of this Turkish cap. Long strings of narrow ribbon tie under the chignon. Lace veils drooping at the side are sometimes added, but they detract from the character of the hat. Sultan red is the proper color for this hat, but all others are used.

The felt hats are of excellent material. High colors, such as garnet, are shown. Skating turbans have tops of colored velvet with sides of Astrakhan sealskin, or wreath of curled ostrich feathers.

Bonnet Frames and Lining

As many ladies make their own bonnets, we give a few hints about the materials. First, select the frame. The new pouf bonnets are complicated, requiring the skill of an experienced milliner; hence it is best to attempt only a simple fanchon with a high front. This should be narrow across the top, short at the ears, with a raised diadem. Milliners prefer wire frames with lace covers for silk and satin bonnets, buckram for velvet. Turbans and Deauville frames of light buckram are bought at the same price. An eighth of a yard of marseline silk, cut bias of the proper shape for lining, or muslin, is furnished. Silk is preferred, as it does not catch in the hair. A slip of argentine or oilpaper is placed inside to protect the bonnet from the oil of the hair.

Silk, Satin, and Velvet

Buy silks, satins, and velvets cut bias from the piece. Narrow silks, plain taffeta, and corded, cut on the bias, are sold. If shirred on the frame 1/2 yard is necessary. Three-eighths covers the frame plainly, and affords enough for folds. Satin is sold in all the fashionable shades. If only used for trimming, such as binding the frame, for piping or folds, the quantity required is from 1/8 to 1/4 cut bias. Half a yard makes a shirred or puffed bonnet. Scotch plaid satin in high colors is sold for trimming. Black velvet is sold. The drab shades are in great variety. A puffed fanchon with pleated diadem requires 1/2 yard of velvet, with some satin for trimming. There is a fine corded velvet called royale, but uncut velvet with coarser cords is less expensive. Silk plush is sold for round hats. This is much narrower and lighter than the cloak plush.

For mourning bonnets the best English crpe should be selected. It is heavier than the French crpe, with deeper crimps, and is worn for winter and summer. From 1/4 to 3/8 is the quantity for a plain bonnet; if made in folds, 1/2 yard is necessary.

Two yards of satin ribbon, 2 inches wide, for strings, are tied behind. There is corded ribbon for the same purpose.

Ornaments

A fashionable diadem for a lady of thirty is of black marguerites with yellow centers, or a coronet vine of crystallized autumn leaves. Large pansies, different colors in the same wreath, are bought of fair quality. A diadem of scarlet berries is suitable for a young girl. Sprays of the wild rose made of velvet and satin adorn the black velvet hats of blondes. Scarlet pomegranate clusters, mountain ash berries, rose geranium, and yellow buttercups are selected for brunettes.

Tiny hummingbirds, with long bills and outspread wings, nestle amidst laces in the center of the coronet, or are poised on the left side of the bonnet with long plumage attached. A variety of small birds is sold. Stylish feathers are white and colored. The prettiest aigrettes are of curled ostrich feathers with heron's feathers erect in the center. Breasts of peacocks and gulls are sold for round hats. Short ostrich tufts are inexpensive and very fashionable. Four tufts, different shades of one color, adorn a hat. Long white ostrich plumes are sold. Pretty wreaths, made of the tips of peacock's feathers, encircle a round hat, trimming it completely.

We have spoken of jet ornaments in a previous number. We have said nothing about lace, because it is most frequently used for elaborate bonnets that require the artistic hands of a milliner.

Tirettes for Looping Up Skirts

The illustrations show an easy and simple manner of making tirettes, by means of which a trained dress may be looped up in a puff behind in the Watteau or Camargo style (see first illustration).

Sew small brass rings on the wrong side of the skirt, about 5 or 6 inches from each other, as shown by the second illustration. The ring in the center back is about 20 inches from the belt, and the rings at the sides about 4 inches. However, if the train is very long the rings must be sewn further down.

Through these rings run two long silk cords of the dress color. Sew one end of these cords fast inside the belt. Run the other end through a small buttonhole between the front and side breadths of the skirt. Finish the ends on this side with a button covered with the dress material, which prevents them from slipping through.

When is it desired to loop up the dress draw the cord, thereby puffing the skirt as shown. In letting it down pull the skirt slightly behind, whereupon it falls easily.

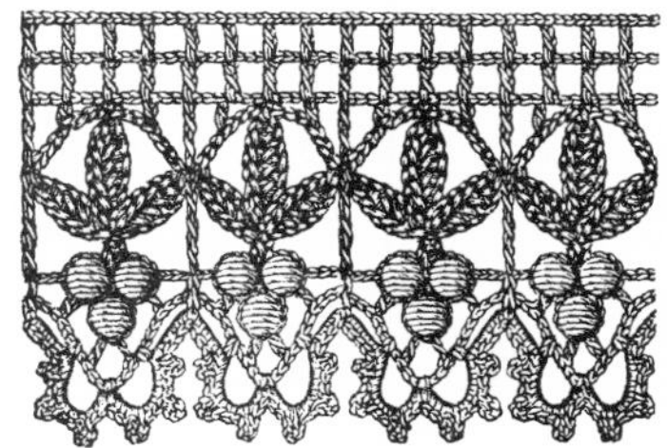

Needlework and Crocheted Edging

To make this edging, work first the three small berries together on muslin with medium knitting cotton. Sew around the berries in half-polka stitch. Cut away the material close.

The crochet work is done with fine cord. Work together the three leaflets as follows. Work 8 ch. (chain stitches), passing over the last of these back on the next 6, 1 sc. (single crochet), 1 sdc. (short double crochet), 2 dc. (double crochet), 1 sdc., 1 sc. After this two leaves worked in a similar manner and 1 sc. in the 1st stitch of the first 8 ch. and in the first berry, on which fasten the thread.

Having finished the requisite number of these leaf-twigs and berries, join them, first, with one round of crochet. Crochet 1 sc. in the outside edge of a berry, putting the needle through from the left side. Work 5 ch., 1 sl. (slip stitch) in the edge of the opposite berry of the same twig, 7 ch., 1 sl. in the outer edge of a new twig, etc.

Then work for the scallops on the outer edge of the lace three rounds as follows. First round: Work 1 sl. in the middle of the chain stitches that join two twigs, * 3 ch., 1 dc. in the next berry, 4 ch., 2 dc. separated by 5 ch. in the middle berry, 4 ch., 1 dc. in the next berry, 3 ch., 1 sl. in the middle of the chain stitches that join the next two twigs. Repeat from *.

Second round: Work 1 sl. in the 1st sl. of the former round, * 4 ch., 1 sc. in the next scallop of 4 ch., 6 ch., 1 sc. in the following chain-stitch scallop, 6 ch., 1 sc. in the next chain-stitch scallop, 4 ch., 1 sc. in the next joining stitch. Repeat from *.

Third round: * Work 4 sc. on the 1st chain-stitch scallop, 1 p. (picot), 2 sc., 1 p., 2 sc., 1 p., 2 sc. around each of the 2 following chain-stitch scallops, 4 sc. in the next chain-stitch scallops. Repeat from *.

Four rows now follow, which form the upper edge of the lace and are crocheted on the other side. First round: * Work 1 tc. (treble crochet) in the joining stitch between two twigs, 1 sc. in the point of the next leaf, 7 ch., 1 sc. in the point of the following leaf, 7 ch., 1 sc. in the point of the following leaf. Repeat from *.

Second round: * Work 1 sdc. in the tc. of the former round, 2 ch., 1 sdc. in the 5th of the next 7 ch., 2 ch., 1 sc. in the sc. at the point of the next leaf, 2 ch., 1 sdc. in the 3rd of the next 7 ch., 2 ch. Repeat from *.

The two following rounds consist of openwork double crochet stitches as shown.

October 17, 1868

Needlework and Crocheted Edging

For this lace, which is very pretty worked with fine material, work first the figures that imitate a pansy. These are embroidered singly on fine lace in buttonhole stitch and point de reprise.

Then with fine thread work the part between the figures, crocheting first the leaf twigs together with the stems which are continued to the upper edge of the lace. Crochet, beginning with the stem, 6 ch. (chain stitches), 1 dc. (double crochet) in one of the two side leaves of a flower which was worked in buttonhole stitch, putting the needle through from the leaf side, 7 ch., 1 dc. in the same leaf, 4 ch., passing over the last of these work back on the next 3 ch. 1 sc. (single crochet), 1 sdc. (short double crochet), 1 dc., 1 dc. in the next dc., 1 sdc., 1 sc., 1 sl. (slip stitch) in the next 3 ch. This forms one leaflet of the twig.

After this crochet 6 ch., 1 dc. in the former leaf, 4 ch., passing over the last of these work back on the remaining stitches 1 sc., 1 sdc., 4 dc., 1 sdc., 1 sc., 1 sl. in the same stitch that took up the sc. This completes the second leaf.

Crochet now 5 ch., 1 dc. in the former leaflet, then 6 ch.; passing over the last of these work back on the remainder 1 sc., 1 sdc., 5 dc., 1 sdc., 3 sc.

Now follow two leaves, worked in the same manner as the first two, and joined to each preceding leaflet with a double crochet stitch, and to the opposite leaflet with a slip stitch. In working the last leaflet fasten on a new flower as shown, putting the needle through from the under side. On the chain stitches between the leaflets, as also the ones on the stem, work single crochet, fastening with a double crochet stitch to the same leaflet of the new flower.

Having worked the requisite number of twigs for the length of the lace, work the scallops on the outer edge in two rounds as follows. First round: * Work 1 sdc. in the buttonhole-stitch edge of the middle lace leaflet of a flower, 1 ch., 1 sdc. close to the former sdc., 1 dc. in the point of the next crocheted leaflet, 2 ch., 1 tc. in the next joining stitch between two leaflets, 3 ch., 1 dc. in the point of the next leaflet, 3 ch., 1 tc. in the following joining dc., 5 ch., 1 sdc. in the point of the middle leaflet. Then crochet around the other side of the leaf twig in the same manner as far as the next flower. Repeat from *.

Second round: * Work 1 sc. in the ch. between the 2 sdc., 3 sc. in the next 2 ch., 2 sc., 1 p. (picot, composed of 4 ch. and 1 sl. in the 1st of the 4), 1 sc. around the following 3 ch., 1 sc., 1 p., 2 sc. around the next 3 ch., 1 sc., 1 p., 3 sc., 1 p., 1 sc. around the following 5 ch. Work in the same manner on the other side of the scallop. Repeat from *.

Crochet now two rounds for the upper edge of the lace. First round: Work 1 sc. in the stem of a leaf twig, 1 tc. in the next buttonhole-stitch leaf of a flower, * 4 ch., 2 sdc. each separated by 2 ch., in the next point de reprise leaf of a flower, 3 ch., 2 sdc. each separated by 2 ch., in the following leaf, 4 ch., 1 sdc. in the next lace leaflet of the flower, 1 sc. in the stem of the next leaf twig, 1 tc. in the side leaflet of the following flower. Repeat from *.

The next round consists of dc. each separated by 3 ch. and 3 stitches space.

Trimmings for Dresses and Skirts

The prettiest dress trimmings this season are ruffled or pleated flounces of different widths, joined with various kinds of ruches and frills. The trimmings in Figures 1 to 6 are shown quarter size.

In Figure 1, a strip of cloth 6 inches wide and pointed on one side is made into a flounce by box pleating. This is surmounted with a pleated bias fold. The fold is corded on both sides and edged with a narrow box-pleated frill.

Figure 1. Flounce

Figure 2 shows a melon trimming. This consists of a strip of cloth 7 inches wide, which is cut into deep points on one side and gathered as shown. A strip 3 inches wide is cut into smaller points and set opposite. The place where these are set on is covered with a fold, which is gathered up crosswise.

Figure 2. Melon trimming

The trimming in Figure 3 is made of a strip of cloth 8 inches wide, which is doubled down 2 inches on the upper edge and laid in double box pleats. The upper fold of each pleat is laid back on the right side and fastened with a stitch. About 1 inch above the flounce is set a ruche 2 1/2 inches wide, pleated in the same manner.

Figure 3. Trimming with double box pleats

The simple trimming in Figure 4 consists of pleated frills 2 inches wide pointing upward, and a similarly pleated flounce 9 inches wide, the heading of which covers the seam where the narrower ones are sewn on.

Figure 4. Pleated flounce

The lower part of the trimming in Figure 5 is formed of a gathered flounce 6 inches wide. Six inches above this is set a pleated frill 2 inches wide, each pleat of which is laid back on the right side and fastened with a stitch. A pleated strip of trimming 5 inches wide covers the place where this frill and the flounce are set on.

Figure 5. Flounce

The rich trimming in Figure 6 consists of a pleated flounce 8 inches wide. The lower edge is finished with a narrower pleated strip and the upper with a close pleating. In addition the upper edge of the flounce is finished with a double bias fold, on which is set, at regular distances, bows of the trimming material.

Figure 6. Pleated flounce

October 24, 1868

Dress Waists

The shape of closed corsages is not materially altered from the styles given in the spring. French models are round waists of medium length with narrow belts. Points will be introduced later in the season for full dress. Shoulder seams are short and high, defining the outline of the shoulder–a fashion that makes the figure look square. To prevent this the corsage is cut very full at the bust by means of short bosom pleats placed near together. Some French dresses have three bosom pleats on each side to give the required fullness. The back is broad at the shoulders, has well-curved side bodies, and is tapered down to measure only 1/3 of the belt length.

The bodice is higher at the throat than the styles worn in warm weather. All imported dresses retain the 1/2-inch standing band. If cut low at all it must be only in front, as dresses sloping at the sides and back are generally unbecoming.

Buttons and buttonholes are indispensable. Half-a-dozen hooks and eyes sewn on the belt and above it relieve the buttonholes from the strain at the waist. A narrow facing of the dress material is sewn beside the buttons to prevent the white underclothes showing through the buttonholes.

The trimming begins at the belt, extending up the front near the buttons, forms a square in the back, and is brought down again to the belt. Pompadour squares and round berthas are designed on plain waists. Several rows of piping, with fringe on the last row, form a round collar.

Open Waists

Open waists with chemisettes are very much worn. The Maria Theresa waist, square with an inside fichu of folds, is suitable for handsome materials. It should always be accompanied by the open sleeve, tight to the elbow, and ruffled. The rolling collar, or revers, is a revival of an old fashion familiar to all. It is fashionable for demitoilette, both for house and street, with a chemisette of muslin or cambric. When used for more dressy attire a lace chemisette is necessary. The heart-shaped waist opens very low, and will not admit of lace alone. Young ladies with plump figures wear two narrow puffs of muslin edged with lace, or net, extending up the front of the corsage and around the neck. The surplice or shawl waist has deep pleats on each shoulder falling in folds to the belt and crossed like a fichu. This is becoming to slender figures. The back is slightly fulled into a belt, or shaped over the hips, and held in place by a drawstring.

French modistes make all waists and skirts separate. This is a bad plan for any but slight persons, as it requires several thicknesses at the belt, making the waist large and clumsy.

Low Corsages

Evening corsages are very low and square and filled out to the proper height with tulle folds *à la Greque,* and lace. When made entirely of the dress material they are not cut so indecorously low as were many dresses last season. Lace is to be the favorite garniture. Wedding toilettes this winter will be conspicuous for their elegant simplicity.

Sleeves

Coat sleeves still prevail for street dresses, but with additional trimming. They are small at the wrist and trimmed to simulate a wide pointed cuff. A bias puff at the top gives the appearance of broad shoulders. A new idea is to add 3 or 4 inches to the length of the front half of the coat sleeve and hold it slightly full from the elbow to the armhole. A broad pleated puff at the elbow is gaining favor. A pointed cap put on in box pleats is a good style.

There is greater variety in sleeves for house dress. The styles called Cavalier and Marie

Antoinette are similar to the Maria Theresa sleeve. A French sleeve is half long, straight, and nearly tight. It is cut off square at the elbow, and the lower part of the arm is covered by a puffed undersleeve.

Trained Skirts

Trains are more moderate and graceful than the extreme styles worn of late. With the exception of the pannier puff the general effect of the skirt is similar to those of last season, though made with fewer gores. To particularize, a trained skirt should measure from 5 yards to 5 1/2 in width to prevent hooping. It should be flatly gored in front and at the sides, but very full and bouffant behind. The front width is gored closely. Stout figures require two gored side widths, slender persons only one. New skirts are not made with three side gores unless the material is so narrow as to compel it.

A word of advice here: Never piece gored breadths at the bottom. Design the shape and number of gores with reference to the width of the material. Two full widths are placed behind, and some French dresses have three full back widths. The front and first gored widths are sewn to the belt without fullness. The back widths are gathered or arranged in small pleats all turned one way. A thick silk cord is used around the skirt instead of binding braid.

Panniers and Tunics

The pannier puff is generally adopted on long dresses. It is very becoming to tall, slender forms, but should be worn with moderation by the short and stout.

To form a pannier puff, 1/4 or 1/2 yard extra length is added to the top of the full back widths and gathered into the side seams. The fullness extends 1/4 or 3/8 yard below the belt. A drawstring or row of trimming is then extended across the back widths, drawing them in to fit closely over the crinoline. The full material then falls over the drawstring and forms a puff. The sash is fastened at the side seams under the belt, and tied in a large bow below the center of the pannier.

A closely gored skirt may be modernized by the addition of a double pannier puff. This consists of two lengthwise puffs attached to a belt. A band 2 inches wide and 1/2 yard long extends down the back. Into this is gathered on each side a width of the dress material 3/4 yard long. The front is rounded at the lower corners and held slightly full beneath the trimming, which consists of folds and fringe or a ruffle. Bows or buttons on the band in the back. The puffs should be lined with thin crinoline or stiff muslin. This pannier may be made of black silk, with a small square apron and bretelles, and worn over colored dresses that have become defaced.

Tunics are worn reversed, fastening behind like an apron. They are long in front, rounding to the belt in back, disclosing a pannier puff on the trained skirt. A good plan, designed for a lady too stout to wear a double skirt, is to simulate a tunic on the front and adjacent side widths, adding a crescent-shaped extra width at the second side seam, on which the trimming is extended up to the belt. On a heavy black silk the tunic is simulated with a pleated flounce of satin. This is an economical arrangement, and has all the effect of a full tunic.

Belts with fan-shaped bows are more worn than sashes. If a sash is preferred it must be double of the dress material, tied in a large bow with short fringed ends.

Short Dresses

Short dresses are adopted for breakfast, for the promenade, for church, for dancing, and on all occasions but those of great ceremony, such as bridal calls and wedding receptions.

Street suits are made with two skirts, or a polonaise with added fullness behind that produces the appearance of a double skirt. The lower skirt barely escapes the floor, is quite narrow, hanging almost straight from the waist, and seems to cling to the figure. It is worn over a very small crinoline, without steels in front. The upper skirt has an apron front, with pannier puffs behind made in the manner already described. If the upper skirt is looped at the sides and back instead of puffed, do not be afraid of looping it too high. It is only necessary that the edges do not hoop. Over this is a short loose basque confined by a belt. A round cape, caught up in the back and shoulders, completes the suit.

The baschlik mantle is in great favor. Mantles and basquines are lined with flannel or wadded to make them comfortable in cold weather. Flannel is preferred as it is most pliable.

Cloth suits are sufficiently heavy for the coldest weather. Six yards and 1/2 of double-width cloth makes a suit. The trimming is bands of faille edged with satin. Thirteen yards of empress cloth of stripes of two sizes, are sold for suits. There is no trimming necessary. Modistes require from 15 to 20 yards of material for a flounced suit.

Trimmings

Gathered flounces are obsolete. All kinds of trimmings are pleated. The last novelty is a ruche of diagonal pleats. The lower skirt of suits is trimmed with one flounce, 2/8 or 3/8 wide, in pleats all turned one way and secured at both edges. A lining of stiff muslin makes the flounce set better. The pleats at the top are sometimes reversed to form a marquise ruche. The upper skirt has a pleated ruche and fringe.

A cheaper trimming is serge braid, all wool and coarsely woven. Another simple garniture is three rows of rich wide velvet ribbon on which are set buttons the color of the dress at intervals of 1 inch. Black ruffles are bound with plaid. Gay plaids are scalloped and bound with black silk sewn on with a cord of scarlet merino.

Grosgrains and satins are trimmed with lace and fringe. Rich passementerie ornaments, tassels, and bows are placed between groups of pleats on flounces.

Morning Dresses

Morning dresses are worn loose and flowing from a round yoke like a collar. They are lined throughout with white mohair or alpaca, and are slightly wadded in front. The Watteau wrapper has a broad fold in the front and back. Trimming extends down the center of the fold. Serge braid is a serviceable trimming for cashmere. Another wrapper is short at the sides to disclose a striped petticoat. Lavender and cherry is a pretty contrast for robes de chambre. Pale blue cashmere is trimmed with white serge braid.

Figure 1. Satin trimming

Trimmings for Blouses and Jackets

Both these trimmings are formed of rolls made of satin strips 3/4 inch wide. For trimming a thin black blouse, use black satin; for a white blouse, colored satin. Cut strips of the requisite length and breadth. Make rolls of the size shown in the illustration. Arrange them to one of the styles shown and sew them to a bias strip.

Figure 2. Satin trimming

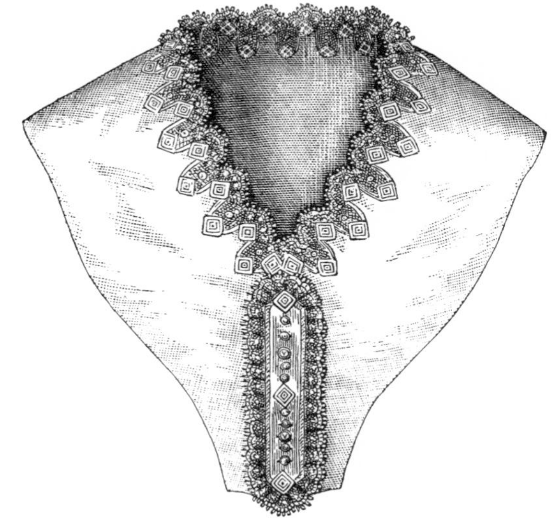

Pleated Mull Chemisette

This chemisette with crossed fronts is to be worn with the Maria Theresa Dress. It is made of muslin, and is trimmed on the edge with lace 1 inch wide. The fronts are arranged in pleats 2/3 inch wide, bias of the material. Face the back on the neck with a bias strip of the material 2/3 inch wide. Sew together the back and fronts, cording the shoulder seams. Bind the bottom, and hem the remainder narrow, after which sew on the lace.

Embroidered Chemisette

This chemisette is to be worn with the Maria Theresa Dress. It is cut from the same pattern as the Pleated Mull Chemisette, except the fronts are straight from the edges where they lap over. It is of fine nainsook, scalloped around the neck and edged with lace and embroidered. The right front is finished with a straight piece of the material 3/4 inch wide, trimmed with lace and embroidery. The chemisette is fastened with small linen buttons.

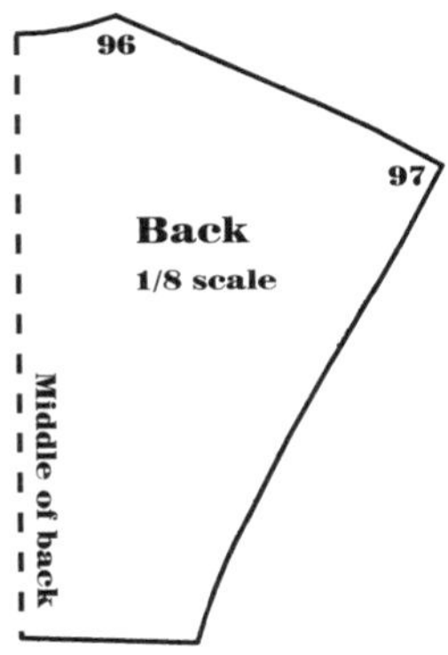

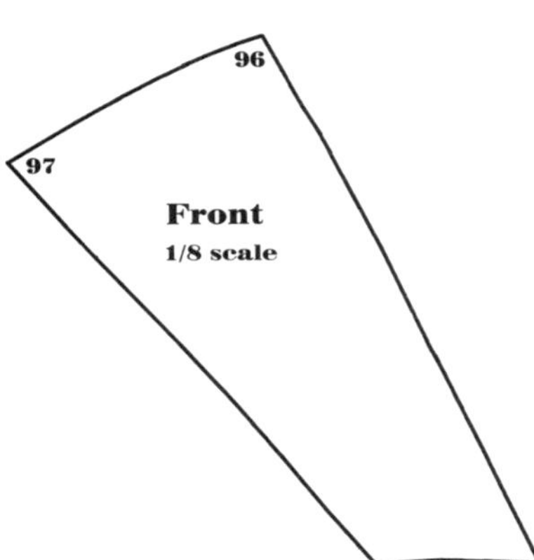

October 24, 1868

Maria Theresa Dress Waist

This dress is of black poult-de-soie. The waist has a rounded piece cut out in front. Being more graceful than square corners, this style has entirely supplanted the Marie Antoinette waist. The sleeves are half long and finished with a frill on the under edge. The dress trimming consists of black satin piping and lace 1 1/2 inches wide. The dress is completed by a three-cornered kerchief of fine Brussels lace, bordered with lace edging. This is laid in a few pleats on the back of the neck and the ends are crossed in front. The undersleeves are of lace edged with wide lace edging.

Make the waist from the front, side back, back, and sleeve. Cord the top and bottom. Finish the sleeves with a frill 6 inches wide in the middle, sloping to 4 inches wide at the ends. Arrange the trimming as shown by the pattern. The belt with sash is of the dress material, and finished with a rosette.

Maria Theresa Dress Waist

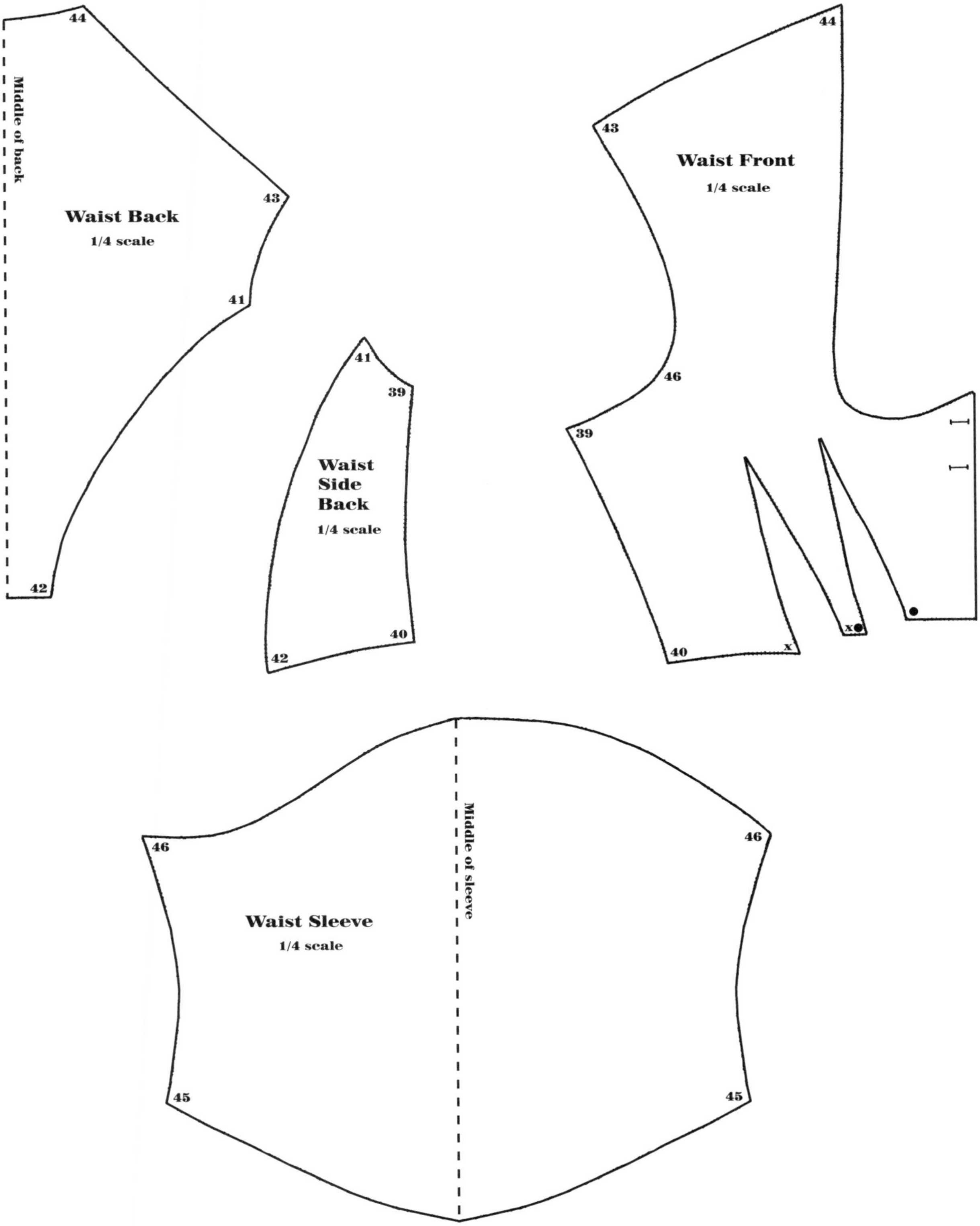

October 31, 1868

Edgings and Insertions

The edgings given are different widths, and are worked partly with fine and partly with coarse thread.

The lace in Figure 1 is worked lengthwise. On a foundation of the requisite length, crochet one round sc. (single crochet), then one round crossed dc. (double crochet), after each crossed dc. 2 ch. (chain stitches), passing over 2 stitches of the former round, and after this another round sc.

Now work on the other side of the foundation stitches the fourth round as follows. Work 12 sl. (slip stitches) on the first 12 foundation stitches, always putting the needle around the back veins of the stitches, * 9 ch., passing over 5 stitches, 24 sl. in the following 24 stitches of the foundation. Repeat from *. It is unnecessary to mention the repeating from * in the remainder of this or the following descriptions. Reference to the illustrations will render it sufficiently clear.

Fifth round: Work 9 sl. in the first 9 sl. (putting the needle around the entire stitch), * passing over 3 sl. of the former round, work 19 dc. in the next chain-stitch scallop, pass over the next 3 sl. of the former round, and work 18 sl. in the following 18 stitches of the former round.

Sixth round: Work 4 sc. on the first 4 stitches, * passing over the following 5 stitches of the preceding round, + 1 tc. (treble crochet) in the 1st dc., crocheted in the chain-stitch scallop, 10 ch., 1 sl. in the 3rd of these (counting from the beginning), 2 ch., passing over 1 dc. From + repeat eight times. Then work 1 tc. in the last dc. of those worked in the scallop, passing over the next 5 stitches of the former round, 4 sc. on the following 4 stitches, 7 ch., 4 sc. in the next 4 stitches.

Seventh round: Work 1 sc. in the 1st sc. of the preceding round, 2 ch., 1 sc. in the next chain-stitch ring, then * seven times alternately, 7 ch., 1 sc. in the next chain-stitch ring, then 7 ch., 1 sc. in each of the 3 following chain-stitch rings.

Eighth round: * Seven times alternately 1 sc. in the middle stitch of the next chain-stitch scallop, 3 ch., 1 picot of 5 ch. and 1 sl. in the 1st of the 5 ch., then 3 ch., 1 sc. in the middle stitch of each of the next 2 chain-stitch scallops.

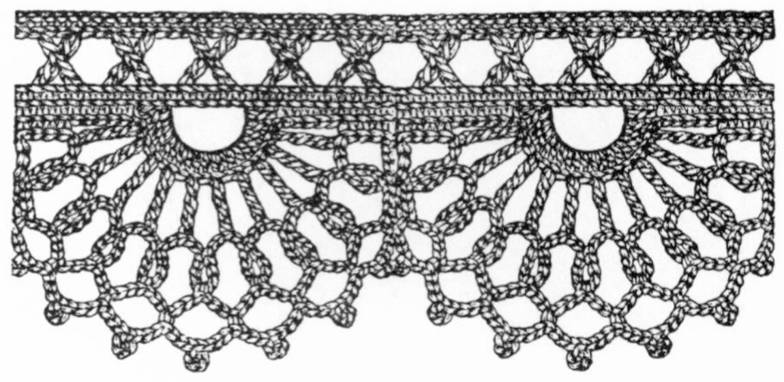

Figure 1. Crocheted edging

The lace in Figure 2 is also worked lengthwise. Make a foundation of the requisite length. Crochet, returning on this a row of leaves as follows. Work 5 ch., in the 2nd of these 1 tc., which must not, however, be entirely worked off. Work 1 tc. in the 1st of the 5 ch., work this stitch off with the remaining stitches on the needle. This completes a leaf. Close on this work a second leaf. With these two leaves pass over 5 foundation stitches, and crochet 1 sl. in the following foundation stitch.

The second to sixth rounds are worked like the first round, but in these the slip stitches must always come between two leaves.

Seventh round: * Work 1 sl. between the first two leaves of the former round, one leaflet, then three picots, each composed of 5 ch., and 1 sl. in the 1st of the 5 ch., 1 s1. in the point of the last leaflet, again a leaf.

Figure 2. Crocheted edging

The lace in Figure 3 is also crocheted lengthwise. Work on a foundation of the requisite length three rounds of chain-stitch scallops, each consisting of 7 ch. In working the first round always pass over 3 foundation stitches. In the following rounds work the sc. stitches in the chain-stitch scallops of the former round.

Fourth round: * Work 1 sc. in the 1st chain-stitch scallop of the former round, 7 ch., 1 sc. in the next chain-stitch scallop, 4 ch., 1 leaflet (worked as in Figure 2), 1 sc. in the following sc. of the former round, 1 leaflet. Then drop the loop from the needle, run the needle through the 1st of the 5 ch. of the first leaflet, and draw through the dropped loop of the second leaflet, so the two leaflets are joined, then 4 ch.

The fifth to eighth rounds may be worked by reference to the illustration and to the description already given.

Figure 3. Crocheted edging

The lace in Figure 4 is crocheted crosswise as follows. Work 12 ch., join these in a ring with 1 sl., and work 13 sc. in the following 8 stitches of the ring (the remaining 4 ch. remain free). Then crochet close on this a second ring composed of 12 ch., work 6 sc. in the 1st 4 of these, then 8 ch., and returning, 1 sl. in the middle stitch of the first scallop. Then crochet 13 sc. in the next 8 ch., after this 7 sc. in the next 4 ch. of the second scallop. Close on this work another ring composed of 12 ch., work 6 sc. in the following 4 ch. of these, then 8 ch., and returning, 1 sl. in the middle stitch of the next scallop to the right. Then passing over 12 sc. work 6 sc. in the following 4 of the 8 ch., again 8 ch., and returning, 1 sl. in the middle stitch of the scallop at the right. After this work 13 sc. in the next 8 ch., 7 sc. in the 4 ch., still free of the following scallop, 6 sc. in the next 4 ch. of the next scallop. The edging has now reached its full width, and is continued in the same manner.

Figure 4. Edging crocheted crosswise

The edging in Figure 5 consists of alternated cross treble stitches which are crocheted crosswise. The edge is finished by a picot row.

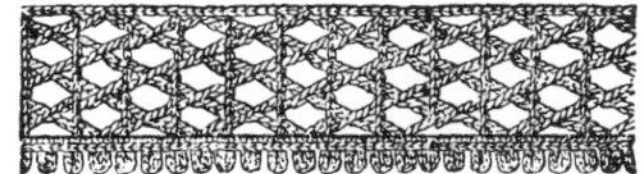

Figure 5. Edging crocheted crosswise

The edging in Figure 6 is worked lengthwise in two rounds as follows. First round: * Work 14 ch., passing over the last 2 of these, work in the 12 following each 1 dc. But each of these dc. stitches is only half crocheted, retaining the last loop on the needle, and finally finish the loops on the needle by working them off, drawing the thread through all at once; draw it tightly. Crochet 2 ch., then 1 sl. in the stitch before the last of the 2 stitches that were passed over of the 14, putting the needle through from the back of the stitch. Repeat from *. On the straight side of this round crochet an openwork round of dc., referring to the illustration.

Figure 6. Crocheted edging

For the first round of the lace in Figure 7, on a foundation of the requisite length work alternately 1 dc., 1 ch., passing over 1 foundation stitch.

Second round: Work 1 dc. in the following dc. of the former round, * 5 picots, each composed of 5 ch and 1 sl. in the 1st of the 5, 1 dc. in the previously worked dc. of this round, 2 dc. separated by 2 ch., in the 3rd following dc. of the former round.

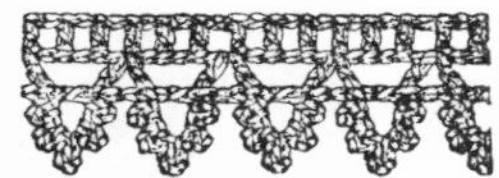

Figure 7. Crocheted edging

For the lace in Figure 8, make a foundation of the requisite length. Crochet on this, for the first round: * Work 2 sc. in the following 2 foundation stitches, 2 ch. passing over 2 foundation stitches.

Second round: Work 1 stc. in the 2nd of the next 2 sc. of the former round, * 2 ch., 2 stc. in the same stitch in which was worked the preceding stc., 1 stc. in the 2nd of the following 2 stc. of the former round.

Third round: Work 1 sc. in the 1st stc. of the former round, 2 ch., * 2 sc. in the next 2 stc., 2 ch., passing over 2 stitches. The fourth round is like the third, but the sc. stitches fall on the sc. stitches of the former round.

Fifth round: Work 1 sc. in the 1st sc. of the former round, 2 ch., pass over 2 stitches, work 2 stitches in the next 2 sc. of the former round, 3 ch., * 1 sc. in the following sc., 5 ch., 1 stc. in the next sc. of the former round, pass over 2 stitches, 1 stc. in the following sc., 5 ch., 1 sc. in the next sc., 3 ch., passing over 2 stitches, 2 sc. in the following 2 sc. Then for the twig in a point work 7 ch., 1 stc. in the 3rd of the 7 ch., 5 ch., 1 sc. again in the 3rd of the 7 ch., then 6 ch., 1 dc. in the 2nd of the 6 ch., 4 ch., 1 sc. also in the 2nd of the 6 ch., 8 ch., 1 sc. again in the 2nd of the 6 ch., 4 ch., 1 dc. in the 2nd of the 6 ch., 4 ch., 1 sl. also in the 2nd of the 6 ch., then 2 ch., 1 sc. in the 3rd of the 7 ch., at the beginning of the twig, 5 ch., 1 stc. again in the 3rd of the 7 ch., then 2 ch. This completes a twig. Crochet still 2 sc. in the next 2 sc. of the former round, and 3 ch., passing over 2 stitches.

Sixth round: * Work 3 sc. in the dc. figure before the first twig of the former round, and the 1st of these 3 sc. in the first scallop composed of 5 ch., the 2nd between the 2 dc., and the 3rd in the following scallop of 5 ch., then 3 ch., 1 dc. in the stc. of the first leaf of the next twig, 2 ch., 1 dc. in the next chain-stitch scallop of the second leaflet, 1 ch., 1 dc. in the following chain-stitch scallop of same leaflet, 2 ch., 2 dc. separated by a ch. in the little leaflet at the point of the twig, 4 ch., 2 dc. separated by a ch. in the same leaf, 2 ch., 1 dc. in the next chain-stitch scallop of the following leaflet, 1 ch., 1 dc. in the following chain-stitch scallop of the same leaflet, 2 ch., 1 dc. in the stc. of the following leaflet, 3 ch.

Seventh round: Work 1 sc. in each stitch of the former round, after every 3 sc. crochet 3 ch. Widen at the point; in the inside of the points the picot of 3 ch. is omitted. Finally, crochet another round like the seventh on the other side of the foundation stitches.

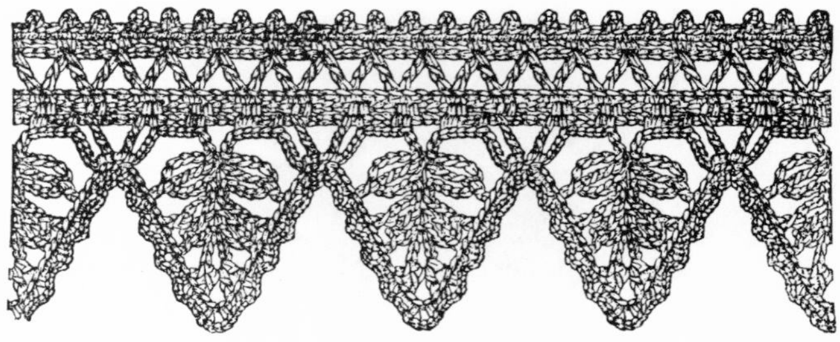

Figure 8. Crocheted edging

The edging in Figure 9 is worked partly crosswise and partly lengthwise. Begin with a foundation of 6 stitches. Work a scallop composed of 6 ch., and crochet on the foundation stitches 6 dc., 1 ch.

Then turn the work, crochet 6 sc. on the 6 dc., then again a scallop of 6 ch., and 6 dc. on the 6 sc. Continue in this manner. Lastly, crochet in each chain-stitch scallop 4 dc. separated by 1 ch., and then the last round of ch. as shown by the illustration.

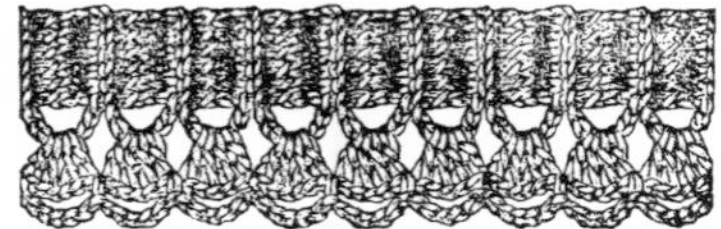

Figure 9. Crocheted edging

The edging in Figure 10 is worked lengthwise. On a foundation of the requisite length crochet a round as follows. Work 1 dc. in the 1st foundation stitch, * 2 ch., 1 dc. in the same foundation stitch, work this stitch off with the following dc., which is worked in the 3rd following foundation stitch.

Second round: Work 1 sc. in the 1st stitch of the former round, * 2 leaflets separated by 3 ch. (worked like the ones in Figure 2), passing over 5 stitches of the former round, 1 sc. in the following stitch.

Third round: * Work 1 stc. in the 1st sc. of the former round, 2 ch., 3 sl. in the 3 ch. between two leaflets, 2 ch.

Fourth round: * Work 1 sc. in the 1st stc. of the former round, 3 ch., 1 dc. in the next sl., 10 ch., 1 dc. in the dc. just worked, 1 dc. in the 3rd sl., 3 ch.

Figure 10. Crocheted edging

The lace in Figure 11 is worked lengthwise of fine white thread, and is worked in lace stitch. On a foundation of the requisite length crochet, for the first round: * Work 3 dc. in the first 3 foundation stitches, 3 ch., passing over 2 stitches, 1 sdc. in the following foundation stitch, 3 ch., passing over 2 stitches.

Second round: In every stitch of the former round work 1 sc.

Third round: Work 4 sl. in the 1st 4 sc., * 9 ch., passing over 5 stitches, 5 sl. in the following 5 stitches.

Fourth round: Work 7 ch., * 3 dc. in the next chain-stitch scallop, 11 ch.

Fifth round: Work 1 sl. in the 1st of the 7 ch. at the beginning of the round, 5 ch., 1 sc. in the 2nd following ch., 5 ch., * 1 sc. in the middle stitch of the next 3 dc., 5 ch., 1 sc. in the 5th of the 11 ch., 5 ch., 1 sc. in the 2nd following ch., 5 ch.

Sixth round: * Work 1 sc. in the 1st sc. of the former round, around the next chain-stitch scallop, 1 sc., 1 sdc., 1 dc., 1 picot of 4 ch. and 1 sl. in the 1st of these, 3 dc., 1 p. as before, 1 dc., 1 sdc., 1 sc., then 1 sc. in the next sc. of the former round. After this, on the next chain-stitch scallop, 1 sc., 1 dc., 1 p. as before, 1 dc., 1 sdc., 3 sc., 1 sl. in the next sc. of the former round. Then on the following chain-stitch scallop, 3 sc., 1 sdc., 1 dc., in working which fasten to the corresponding dc. of the former round. Then on the following chain-stitch scallop 3 sc., 1 sdc., 1 dc., in working which fasten to the corresponding dc. of the former scallop, 1 p., 1 dc., 1 sc.

Finally, work the lace stitch as shown.

Figure 11. Crocheted edging with lace stitch

The edging in Figure 12 is worked crosswise. Begin with a foundation of 13 stitches. Crochet, returning on these, 3 ch., 1 dc. in the 2nd following foundation stitch, then three times alternately 1 ch., passing over 1 stitch, 1 dc., then 7 ch., 1 sc. in the last foundation stitch. This completes a round.

Now turn the work, crochet 7 ch., then 11 dc. in the chain-stitch scallop of the former round, 1 ch., three times alternating 1 dc., 1 ch. The dc. are always crocheted in the next single ch. between 2 dc. of the former round. 1 dc. in the 3rd of the 3 ch. at the beginning of the first round. This completes the second round.

Repeat both rounds till the edging has reached the length desired.

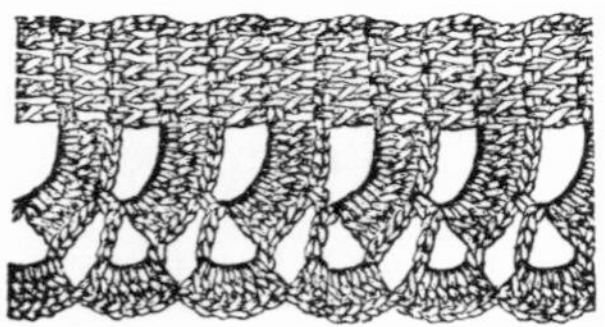

Figure 12. Edging crocheted crosswise

Work, first, the middle part of the edging in Figure 13 crosswise, as follows. Work 11 ch. as foundation, then 7 ch. Returning on the foundation 1 dc. in the 1st foundation stitch, then three times alternating, 1 ch., passing over a foundation stitch, 1 dc., then 6 ch., 1 dc. in the last foundation stitch. * Now turn the work, crochet 3 ch., then 9 dc. in the scallop of 6 ch. Again turn the work, crochet 7 ch., 1 dc. in the 2nd following of the 9 dc., then three times more alternately 1 ch., passing over 1 stitch, 1 dc., then 6 ch., 1 dc. in the 3rd of the 3 ch *before* the 9 dc.

On the straight side of the edging crochet an openwork round of dc. Work 9 dc. in each chain-stitch scallop on the under edge.

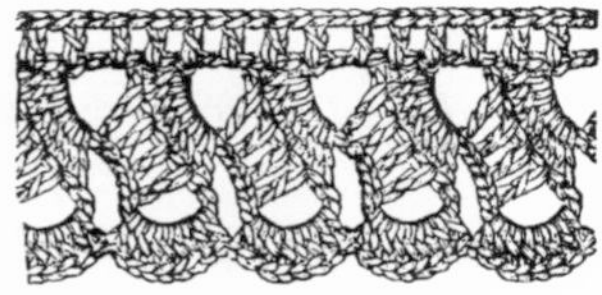

Figure 13. Edging crocheted crosswise

To make the insertion in Figure 14, on a foundation of the requisite length crochet, for the first round, alternately 6 ch., 1 sl., always in the 3rd following stitch of the foundation.

Second round: Always 2 dc. in the 2 middle ch. stitches of each scallop of the former round, and after this always 5 ch.

Third round: Work 1 sl. in the middle stitch of each chain-stitch scallop of the former round, after each of these 2 ch.

Fourth round: Always 2 sl. in each 2 ch. of the former round, and between these 4 ch. Then crochet on the other side of the foundation a round like the one just described.

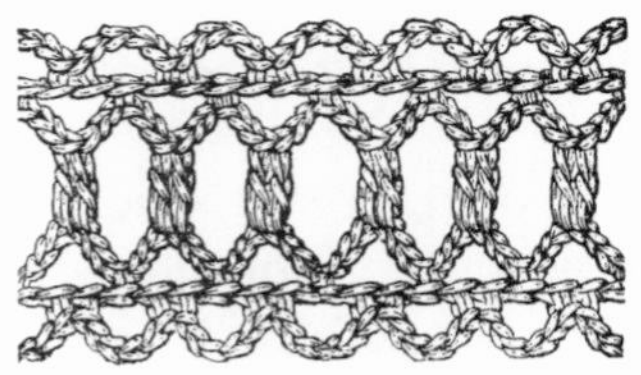

Figure 14. Crocheted insertion

To make the insertion in Figure 15, on a foundation of the requisite length work as the first round: In the next foundation stitch 1 dc., which is, however, not entirely worked off, * 1 dc. in the 3rd following foundation stitch, work off both stitches together; 2 ch., 1 dc. in the stitch in which the last stitch was taken up. This is, however, not entirely worked off. Repeat from *.

Second round: Always 2 sc. in the 2 ch. and 1 sc. in the dc. of the former round.

Crochet a similar round on the foundation, and after this a round as follows. Work 1 sc. in a stitch of the former round; 1 leaflet (5 ch., 1 dc. in the 2nd, 1 stc. in the 1st of the 5 ch., work off the dc. and stc. stitch together), then 4 ch., with which pass over 4 stitches of the former round.

Crochet another piece precisely like this; but in working, always fasten to the finished part after every 4th ch. of the 4 ch. stitches.

Figure 15. Crocheted insertion

The pretty edging in Figure 16 is knitted with fine thread. The thick parts are of alternate embroidered figures and imitation leaflets. It is worked in backward and forward rounds with a foundation of 11 stitches.

Knit for the first round: Slip 1, knit 2, make 1, knit 2 together twisted, make 1, knit 2 together, make 1, knit 2 together, knit 2.

Second round: Slip 1, knit 1, purl the remaining stitches.

Third round: Slip 1, knit 1, make 1, knit 2 together, make 1, knit 2 together, make 1, knit 2 together, knit 2, widen 1, knit 1.

Fourth round: Slip 1, knit 3, purl the remaining stitches.

Fifth round: Slip 1, knit 2, make 1, knit 2 together, make 1, knit 2 together, knit 4, widen 1, knit 1.

Sixth round: Slip 1, knit 5, purl the remaining stitches.

Seventh round: Slip 1, knit 1, make 1, knit 2 together, make 1, knit 2 together, knit 6, widen 1, knit 1.

Eighth round: Slip 1, knit 7, purl the remaining stitches.

Ninth round: Slip 1, knit 2, make 1, knit 2 together, make 1, knit 2 together, knit 5, knit 2 together.

Tenth round: Slip 1, knit 5, purl the remaining stitches.

Eleventh round: Slip 1, knit 1, make 1, knit 2 together, make 1, knit 2 together, make 1, knit 2 together, knit 3, knit 2 together.

Twelfth round: Slip 1, knit 3, purl the remaining stitches.

Thirteenth round: Slip 1, knit 2, make 1, knit 2 together, make 1, knit 2 together, make 1, knit 2 together, make 1, knit 2 together.

Fourteenth round: Slip 1, knit 1, purl the remaining stitches.

Fifteenth round: Slip 1, knit 1, make 1, knit 2 together, make 1, knit 2 together, make 1, knit 2 together, make 1, knit 2 together, knit 1.

Sixteenth round: Slip 1, purl the remaining stitches.

Now repeat from the first round till the edging has reached the length desired. The little figures are worked on nainsook in buttonhole stitch, cut out, and sewn to the edging. The leaflets are worked with enameled cotton as illustrated.

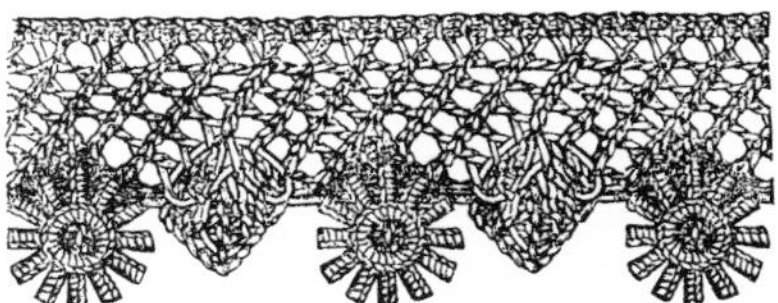

Figure 16. Knitted edging

Embroidered Purse

This elegant purse is made of white silk reps with embroidery in fine colored silk twist. It is shown full size. The embroidered rays of the central rosette, which is the same on both sides of the purse, are worked in close buttonhole stitch with silk in various bright colors. The knots between are worked alternately with yellow and black silk. The feathered circle that encloses the rosette is worked in one color (violet in the original), either with fine silk in half-polka stitch, or with coarse silk in point Russe. It may also be worked with gold tinsel, which must be cut into small pieces of a suitable length, and sewn on as illustrated.

The two pieces of silk are joined around the edges with close buttonhole stitch of violet silk; with every second stitch sew on a gold bead. Line the inside with white leather. Join the top to a bronze clasp with stitches in violet silk. These stitches are covered by sewing on gold beads.

The grelot fringe on the edge of this purse is especially beautiful. The loops of the fringe, which are interwoven, are crocheted in white silk, and afterward embroidered with knots in different colors of silk. The grelots are worked in single crochet over a round piece of wood or a large bead. The darker ones are worked in violet silk, and the smaller ones in white. All are ornamented with brightly colored knots.

November 7, 1868

Furs

Small collars, boas, and sacques are the fashionable choice in shape. Two styles of collars are shown. The most dressy shape is the Imperial collarine, very small, only 8 inches deep behind, with short, square fronts trimmed with the tails of the animals. Ladies who consider comfort the first essential prefer the new pelerine cape, slightly pointed back and front, and sufficiently large to afford protection to the chest and shoulders. The half-cape with long, square ends is entirely out of fashion. The Princesse boa introduced this season is a graceful style, short in front, and shaped to fit the neck. A short, straight boa tied at the throat, or fastened by passing the head of the animal through a loop, is in favor with young ladies; but the long bertha boa is more distingué.

The fur cloaks are gracefully shaped sacques, made 34 inches long, with coat sleeves, standing collar, and pockets. Large, clumsy capes are not in keeping with the present style of street dress, and have entirely disappeared. Sacques are more comfortable, as they fit closer to the figure.

Muffs are smaller even than last season. The round shape is preferred for full dress; the flat pocket muff, suspended by a cord around the neck, for shopping and skating. Three, four, and sometimes five dark stripes adorn mink muffs. The ends are trimmed with a single tassel of brown bullion attached to a diamond-shaped head, or with the tails of the animal pendant from a passementerie acorn. Changeable silk linings are not used. Snuff-brown satin, or Turkish serge of the shade of the fur, are in better taste and more durable. Sables have a soft lining of eiderdown.

Breitschwanz is a peculiarly fine skin taken from stillborn lambs, or those very young. It is as lustrous as satin, with smooth surface in large crinkled waves natural to the fur but resembling appliqué. It is lighter than the Russian lamb, yet very warm as it is soft and pliable, clinging closely to the figure.

Chinchilla, the softest of all furs and most fragile, is more highly appreciated abroad than here, where we have so many imitations. The best quality is soft as down and in delicate shades of gray.

The royal ermine is of immaculate whiteness, without that yellow tinge erroneously believed to enhance its value. The black tails with which it is spotted should be marked and distinct. It is no longer called opera fur, as it is worn with full day dress.

Fur Hats and Trimmings

Jaunty hats of fur seal, of krimmer, and of breitschwanz are made for the promenade and for skating. Heavier furs with long pile are too clumsy for hats. The crowns are high and sloping. Brims narrow. The only trimming is slender plumes directly in front, extending over the crown, without destroying its well-defined outline. The lining is of quilted satin. Another style has a rolled brim. Turbans are out of fashion.

Traveling hoods are made of velvet or plush, bordered with beaver.

Fur borders on cloaks and dresses are the height of style. We were shown a border of sable tips, 2 inches wide. Chinchilla is a favorite fur trimming on velvet. A mink border, 2 inches wide, costs according to quality. Astrakhan, krimmer, and Russian lamb are cut for trimming in different widths. Astrakhan will be popular for trimming skating suits.

Tatted Fanchon

This fanchon, tatted in worsted, is new and serviceable. The pattern is of white zephyr worsted, and consists chiefly of a simulated band of insertion with a violet ribbon drawn through. This forms the foundation and extends to form the strings. It is completed with rosettes and small figures. Instead of white wool the fanchon may be worked in lilac, gray, or red. Black wool is especially suitable for elderly ladies.

Begin with the simulated insertion, which is worked lengthwise in two rounds. Work first, * a ring composed of 5 ds. (double stitches), four times alternately 2 ds., 1 p. (picot), then 5 ds. Turn this ring downward, and work at the distance of 1/5 inch space on the thread a small ring composed of 7 ds., 1 p., 7 ds. Turn the work so that the first ring points upward. Work at the same distance another ring like the first; but, instead of working the 1st picot, fasten it to the last picot of the similar ring. Turn the work. Work at the distance of 1/5 inch a ring of 7 ds., 1 p., 7 ds. Repeat from * forty times. The picot of the last small ring must be 1/5 inch long.

Now work for the end of the foundation six times alternately, and always after 1/5 inch space, a large and small ring in the same manner as the former. But each of these six rings must be fastened to the long picot of the last small ring of the band instead of working picots. This completes one side of the band and one end. Work, now, the second side and the other end. In working the other side join each small ring to a corresponding ring on the other side.

Tatted Fanchon

Work next two three-leaved figures from Figure 1, then eight two-leaved figures and two single rings. Join these by reference to the large illustration, and fasten to the finished band by the picots.

Figure 1. Trefoil for fanchon

Outside of these arrange the rosettes. Of the four large rosettes which count each twelve rings (see Figure 2), three are arranged on the back of the fanchon and one on the front. The small rosettes (see the large illustration) number but eight rings each around the edge.

Figure 2. Large rosette for fanchon

November 14, 1868

Winter Cloaks

The patterns given in this issue for stylish winter cloaks can be economically made by anyone with ordinary ingenuity. Tight-fitting paletots are preferred, although the sack is still worn. Sacks are often arranged in the Watteau fashion by setting a belt under the back, bringing it outside at the side seams, and fastening it in front, thus forming a wide pleat at the back. For elderly ladies we recommend the burnoose shape, with hood or cape, the latter being pleated very high.

Two leading styles are the polonaise, or paletot, with a belt, and the basquine with loose fronts and tight corsage back, the fullness of the pannier skirt added at the belt. Coat sleeves, small at the wrist, are universal. Capes of various shapes and depths, usually to the elbows, are worn with both styles. Narrow-shouldered persons seek the appearance of breadth given by the small pelerine cape of the cloak material, while the broad-shouldered wear pointed hoods on cloth, or lace overcapes on velvet.

An ingenious modiste makes a pretty hood of the round-cornered thread lace veils, now out of fashion, by fastening the top to the neck of the cloak, and gathering the edges toward the center by an elastic cord run through the border. When ornamented with Renaissance bows of satin, this forms an elegant and economical finish for a velvet cloak.

The pannier puff is seen on many velvet cloaks. Cloth is more frequently caught up with pleats in the Camargo style. Immense bows, pleated loops, like fans, and puffed ends hanging from the back of the belt, give the Grecian bend tournure. Long broad sashes make any cloak look old fashioned and dowdy.

The Watteau polonaise is largely imported. It is a most stylish garment for a tall, erect figure, but the round-shouldered should beware of it, as the broad fold in the back increases this in appearance.

The Louis XV basquine, more youthful and dressy, differs from the Watteau only in having the fold begin lower in the back, and being caught up in a pannier puff. The Camargo is the best choice for stout figures. Mantillas of satin, velvet, and cashmere, with round backs and long square fronts, are worn by elderly ladies. The scarf baschlik is more youthful.

A style to be commended is a talma, slightly shaped to the figure, held at the waist by a belt under the cape. The front continues in long ends that are fastened low down behind like a sash. The skirt of a long dress may be drawn out in a puff over these ends, thus forming a pannier, and adapting a house dress for the street.

The added length prophesied for cloaks is not evident. A very long garment would appear clumsy with a short dress.

Materials

The materials most used for cloaks are velvet, Astrakhan, beaver of different kinds, and cashmere. Heretofore the choice was limited to velvet, cloth, and fur. This season lighter materials, such as satin, faille, and cashmere, thickly wadded and interlined with flannel, are shown as novelties. A sleeved bodice made of thin silk, wadded and quilted, is worn under these cloaks–a comfortable device for people who suffer with cold, but designed by the French to give that embonpoint they consider so desirable.

Blue-black velvet is more fashionable than dead black. In buying velvet for a cloak, remember that the 28-inch width cuts to greatest advantage.

The serviceable tricot beaver is not a new cloth, but it retains its popularity. It has a ribbed surface, which is scarcely perceptible in the finer qualities, becoming merely a waved thread, but is plainly defined in coarser goods. It is 1 1/2 yards wide. Two yards and 3/8 are required for a paletot with cape. Heavy castor beaver is smooth, glossy, and more expensive than tricot, but it is stiff and unyielding, and consequently cold. Many French cloaks are of the thick Eskimo beaver, weighty and warm, a smooth outer surface with rough nap inside. Soft pliable chinchilla beaver, with short, curled fleece, and the velvet meltons are shown in high colors–garnet, mulberry, purple, and green. A black velvet cloth without luster is desirable for mourning cloaks.

Excellent imitations of fur, seal, and Astrakhan can scarcely be told from the genuine article, but we do not advise their purchase because we deprecate all imitations. The same money is better spent in a tricot beaver, which is all that it professes to be. Moreover, these shaggy cloths are not desirable. The long fleece is woven into a coarse, sleazy fabric, and with very little wear the fleece falls out, leaving a threadbare surface. The same thing is true of plush with very long pile.

White velvet cloth, 1/2 inch thick, soft and pliable, is sold for opera cloaks. An article called racket cloth, like a heavy opera flannel, is sold for breakfast jackets. Heavy corduroys, 3/4 wide, are sold for the same purpose.

Trimmings

Trimmings are principally of satin and grosgrain. They may be of different colors, but must always be in harmony with the cloak color. They consist of flutings, flounces, cords, pipings, etc. Trimmings that imitate scallops or squares are particularly stylish. Revers, tabs, and bows are also in favor. Tight-fitting paletots are finished with sashes.

A simple and elegant trimming is a diagonal pleating made of satin edged with velvet. Another good style is a box-pleated frill of faille 4 inches wide, cut straight, and raveled 1/2 inch on each edge. This is around the wrist and elbow. A ruche of same is on the neck, with large bows on the shoulder sides of the skirt, and the back of the belt. Thick ruches of satin, faille, and velvet about the neck of French cloaks are worn in lieu of furs.

Fringe and faille are the favorite trimmings for cloth. Satin is restricted to velvet. Fringes include handsome netted fringe, very full, with heavy trellised heading; chenille fringe, each strand tipped with satin; wide tassel fringe, each tassel long and full but distinct; and the novel fringe made of quill shavings, solid black or in well-blended shades.

Leaves and vines of passementerie for heading lace and fringe are made of satin braids or cords without jet. Pointed serge braid is shown for cloth cloaks. Rosettes of passementerie, with long tassels pendant in the center, are looped with cords for fastening cloaks. Similar ornaments are on the shoulders and sides of skirts. Buttons and buttonholes on a faced slip are concealed in front.

Russian lamb, Astrakhan, and angora fringe are used to trim cloth and cashmere. A pinked ruche of cashmere is in good taste.

The handsomest velvet cloaks are almost covered with thread lace, or are bordered with sable or chinchilla. Velvet muffs trimmed to match accompany these. Berthas, Watteau drapery, bretelles, and rosettes with looped ends at the throat and back are of the finest Chantilly. Lower priced velvets are trimmed with satin bows, chenille or netted fringe, leaf passementerie, a row of alternate loops of satin and faille, or a pleated faille frill, raveled at the edge to form fringe.

Carriage Wrappings and Opera Cloaks

The carriage wrappings in general use are plaid circulars and burnooses. Four and 1/4 yards of double-width plaid make a double circular with hood. This appears to be a large quantity, but even more is sometimes necessary to make the plaids fit when joined together. The graceful burnoose requires 1 3/8 yards of double-width goods. This is cut in two down the center fold and sewn together at the ends. The seam is concealed in the Arab fold at the back. White plush striped with scarlet or orange is made in the same way, trimmed with llama tassels and fringe.

November 14, 1868

A few sacques with wide sleeves, or with full sabot sleeves, held by a band near the wrist, are shown for opera. But these are troublesome to get on and off at an entertainment, and circulars and burnooses are preferred.

Shawls

India shawls have new waving designs in the border, and gorgeous colors rather than the quiet subdued hues hitherto considered essential. In real India cashmere magenta, white, and Metternich green are blended with fine effect. They are not thought too striking and pronounced because the material is fine, and the black and dark brown dresses with which such shawls are worn admit a gay wrapping.

Scarlet centers are most fashionable for square shawls with borders, black for the long shawls when filled up. Striped India shawls are sold for extra carriage wrappings, shopping, and traveling. They make very comfortable afghans, and endure any amount of wear.

Cloak Trimmings

In cloaks of heavy material the buttonholes are bound with silk or satin instead of being worked in the ordinary manner. Figure 1 shows the buttonhole completed, and Figure 2 shows how this is done. For each edge take a bias strip about 1 inch wide and of the requisite length. Sew it along the edge. Then turn it over, putting the stuff through the buttonhole. Sew it down on the wrong side without allowing the stitches to show on the right side. Finish the ends with a few buttonhole stitches.

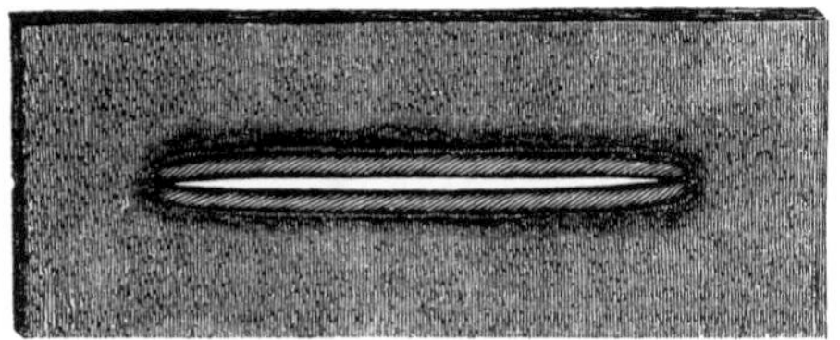

Figure 1. Buttonhole bound with satin

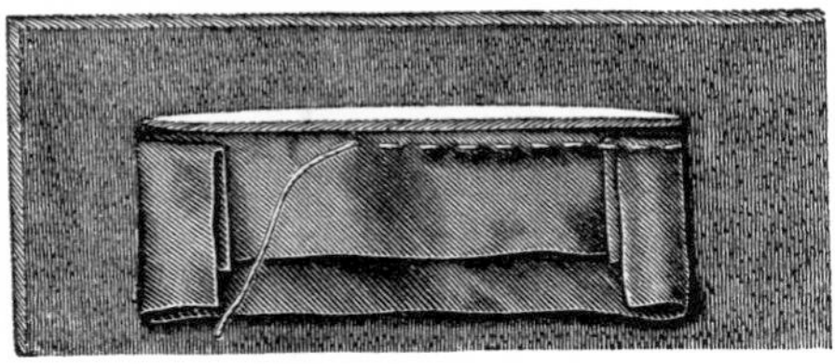

Figure 2. Binding of buttonhole

Many cloaks are so fastened that the buttons and buttonholes are not visible. To do this a buttonhole strip is sewn on the under side. Figure 3 shows the strip reduced in size. Make the buttonhole strip of a piece of silk double and lined with some heavy material. Work the buttonholes, and sew the strip to the cloak along the ends and the inner side. The front edge is left loose, but the strip is fastened with a band between each buttonhole. The buttons are either sewn on the left front or on a piece of the material set on underneath for that purpose.

Figure 4 shows a bias fold arranged to serve at the same time for binding and trimming a cloak or jacket. Lay the edges over as shown and stitch it down on the cloak. Then turn the other side over the edge and hem it down on the under side. If it be desired for trimming alone, stitch down only the upper side.

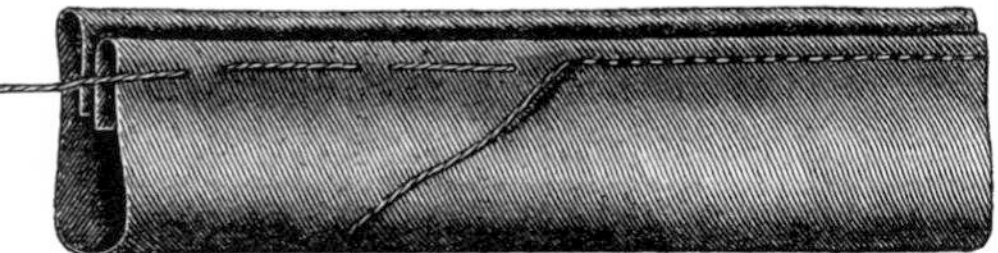

Figure 4. Bias fold for binding and trimming

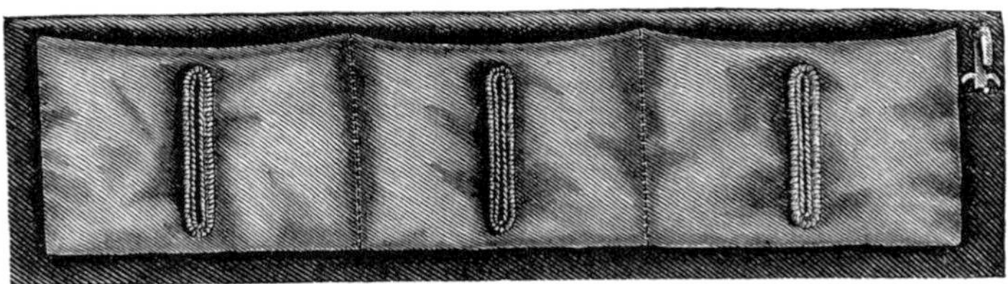

Figure 3. Buttonhole strip set on wrong side of cloak

Figure 5 shows the section of a cloak trimming. This consists of a satin strip, which is stitched on with four cords, and forms the binding at the same time.

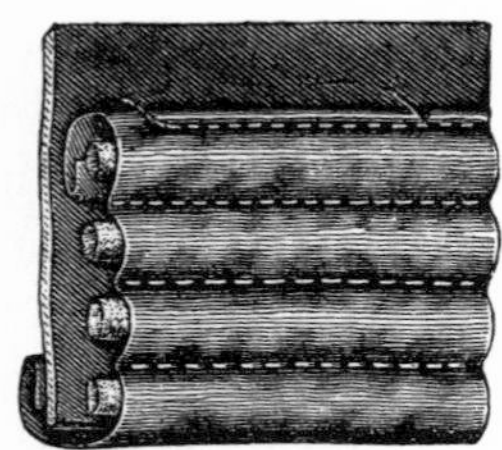

Figure 5. Satin cording

Figure 6 shows how to sew in a double cord, which is much used for the edge of cloaks. It requires a bias strip about 1 1/2 inches wide, in which are sewn two cords. The edge of the cloak is stitched over the edges of the cord.

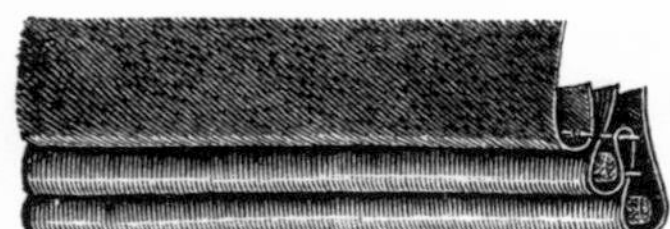

Figure 6. Double cording

The trimming in Figure 7 consists of a bias strip arranged to form a double piping on each side of a cord.

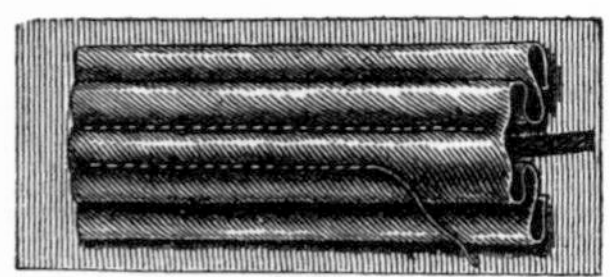

Figure 7. Bias cording

Figures 8 and 9 show how to arrange piping of different colored satin. Double the first bias strip through the middle. Sew fast to this one edge of the second bias strip. Hem down the other edge. Figure 8 shows the right side, and Figure 9 the wrong side.

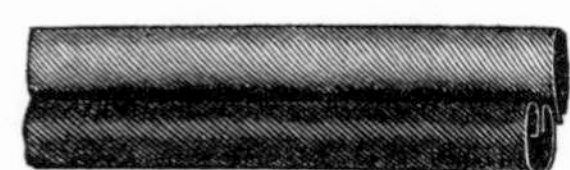

Figure 8. Satin piping of two colors

Figure 9. Satin piping of two colors

Figure 10 shows a loop made of two colors as in Figures 8 and 9. The loop is fastened to the cloak with a satin-covered button.

Figure 10. Satin loop of two colors

Figure 11 shows a section of a pleated belt, and how to arrange the material.

Figure 11. Section of pleated belt

Figure 12 is made of satin with lutestring lining. The strips are cut straight of the same material as the cloak. They are stitched on each side, pleated, and finished with a narrow bias fold along the middle.

Figure 12. Pleated ruche

Figure 13 shows a trimming made of a strip 3 inches wide pleated diagonally, and another one pleated straight. The two strips are fastened together with a bias fold.

Figure 13. Pleated trimming

Camargo Paletot

This paletot is of dark blue beaver. Two and 1/2 yards of material 1 3/8 yards wide are required. It is trimmed with wide and narrow fluting of black grosgrain. A bias fold of black grosgrain covers the place where the fluting is set on. The back is finished with a double lappet of pleated grosgrain. The belt is of pleated grosgrain finished in the front and back with a bow of the same.

Cut from the front and side piece each two pieces. Cut from the back, skirt back, and collar each one piece. Cut both parts of the sleeves.

Backstitch together the back, side, and front pieces according to the corresponding figures on the pattern. Leave the seam on the side of the skirt unsewn. Lay the seams open, sewing them down

carefully so the stitches are not visible on the right side.

Backstitch the seams in the under part of the fronts from 27 to 28 on 28. Join the fronts with the skirt back from 25 to 26. Pleat each front, bringing *xa* on •*a*. Bind the edge of the pleat with a narrow strip of silk. Hem it down on the wrong side. Overseam the front and side pieces from 32 to 30. Pleat the upper part of the skirt, so that 35 falls on 35 of the back. Backstitch these pleats to the back of the waist. Face the fronts. Finish the right front with a few hooks and the left with eyes. Cover the heavy facing with a black silk facing.

Sew on the collar according to the corresponding figures on the pattern. Pleat up the paletot, bringing *xb* on •*b* of each front. The pleats may be fastened up with hooks and eyes so as to wear the paletot either with or without them. Sew on the trimming as illustrated. A half-size section and directions for making the trimming are given above. Trim the collar with a narrow quilling of grosgrain. Cover the seam where it is sewn on with a bias fold.

Sew up the sleeves from 38 to 39 and from 40 to 41. Finish the inside of the wrist with a narrow grosgrain quilling, letting half the width extend beyond the edge. Cover the place where this is set on with a facing 2 inches wide. Finish the outside of the wrist with a quilling 3 inches wide, headed with a bias fold. A similar bias fold is sewn on the edge of the wrist. Lay two pleats in the sleeve, *x* on •. Sew the sleeves into the armhole according to the corresponding figures on the pattern.

The double lappet in back is formed of two strips of grosgrain each 7 inches wide. These are hemmed narrow on the outer edge and then pleated. The under one of these strips is sewn to a plain piece of grosgrain. This must be previously pleated, with all the pleats running the same way. The upper strip laps 1 inch over the under one. Set a narrow binding on the upper edge and sew it to the waist. The belt covers the seam made by sewing on the skirt.

November 14, 1868

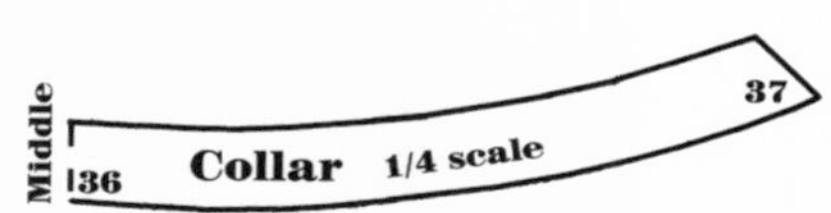

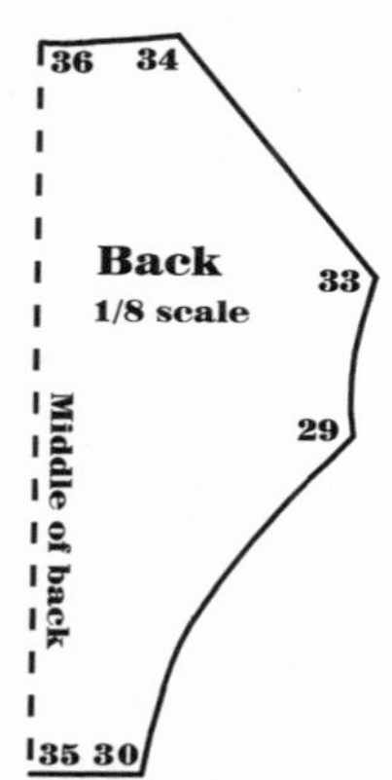

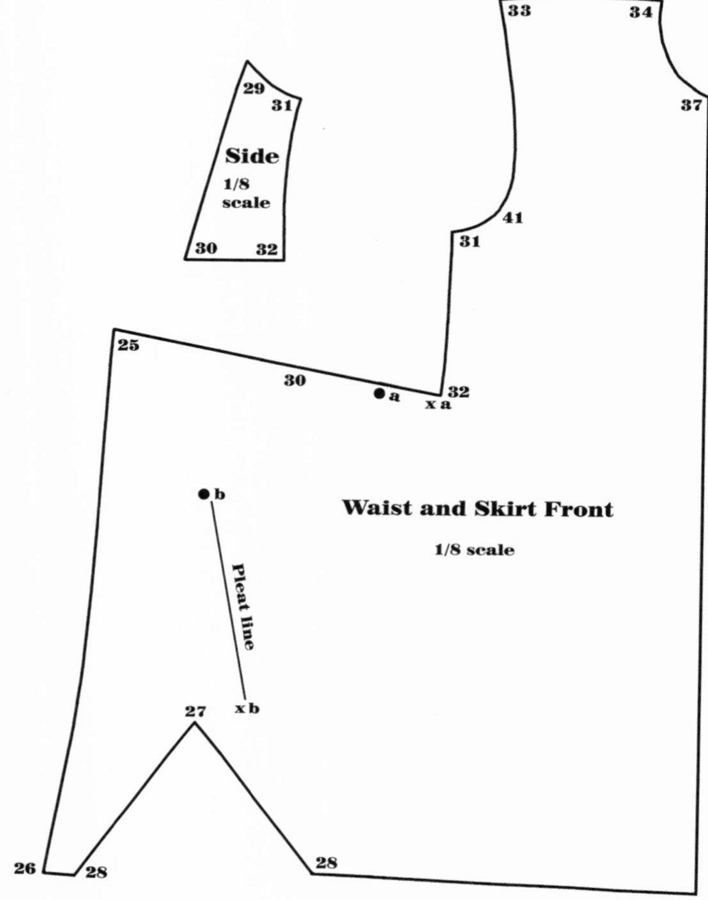

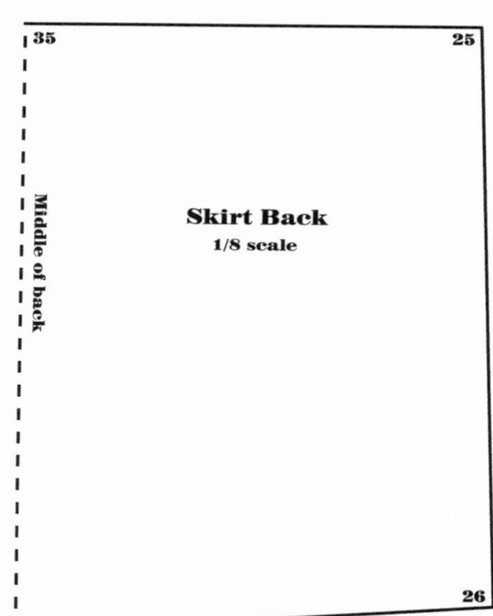

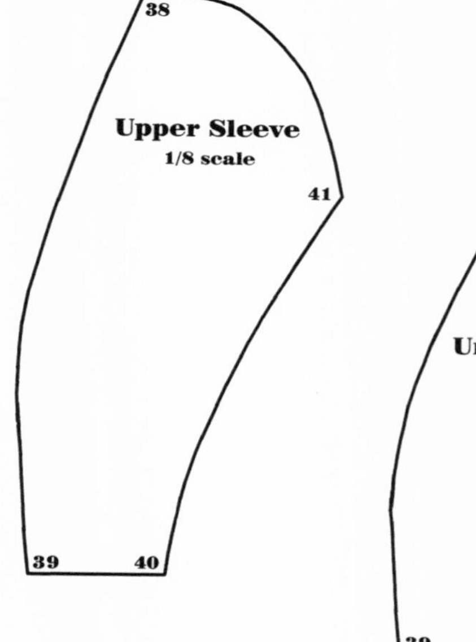

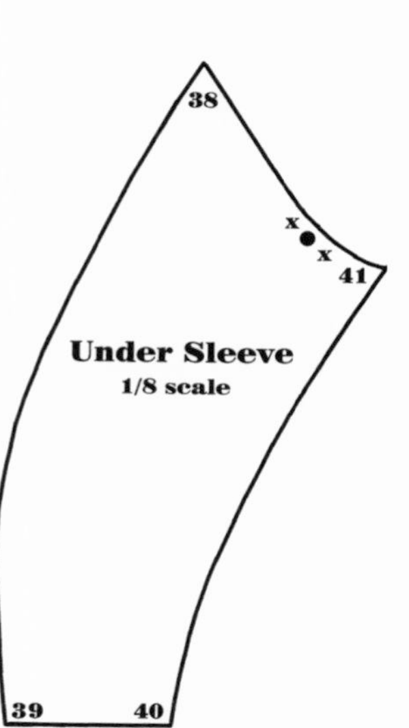

Watteau Paletot

This paletot is of black velvet, lined with silk and a thin layer of wadding. It requires 4 1/2 yards of yard-wide velvet. The trimming consists of bias folds of black satin, two widths of black lace, and large passementerie buttons with tassels.

Cut of the lining, outside, and wadding from the front two pieces, and from the back one piece. Cut the sleeves.

Cover one side of the wadding with footing. Lay the silk on this, and quilt in squares. Put the finished lining on the outside.

Lay each front in three pleats, *x* on •. Backstitch the seams from 3 to 4*a* on 4*a*. In each seam leave one part of the silk, and hem it down afterward to cover the seam (cut the wadding out first).

In the back, backstitch the seams from 1 on 1 to 2 on 2. Then lay it over along the narrow line on each side, so that x*a* comes on •*a*, *xb* on •*b*, and the narrow line on the wider line. Lay the sides of the back in three pleats, *x* on •.

Sew the back and fronts together on the shoulder from 7 to 8, and on the sides from 5 to 4. Next lay the side, which is arranged with the front, in a box pleat so the corners marked 4 and 4 lie under the middle marked 4. Sew up the seam from 4 to 6. Stitch the sides of the box pleats to the back and fronts of the paletot.

Sew the lining down along the edges. Arrange the trimming as illustrated. The sleeves match the paletot and are trimmed as illustrated.

Watteau Paletot

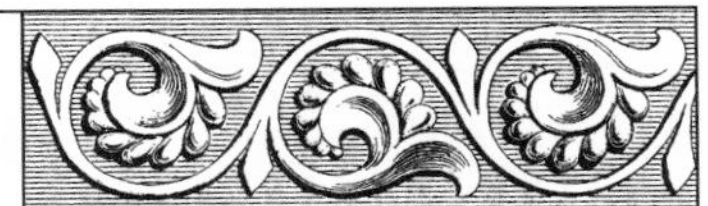

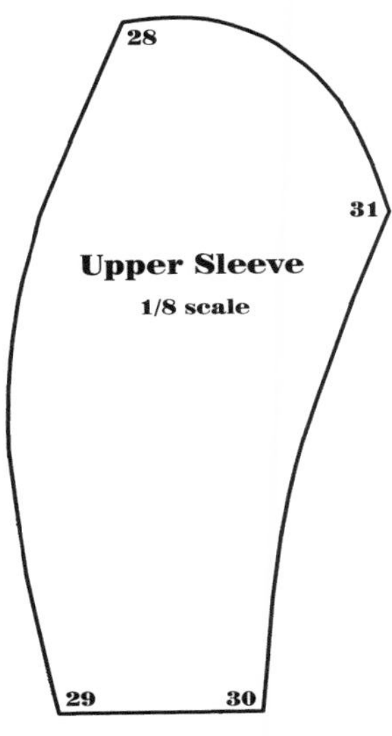

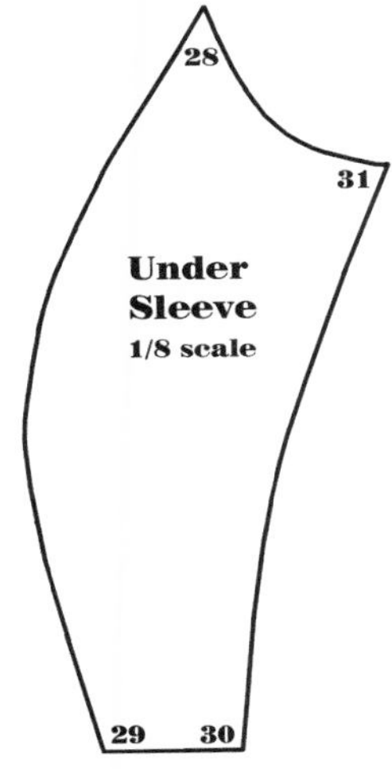

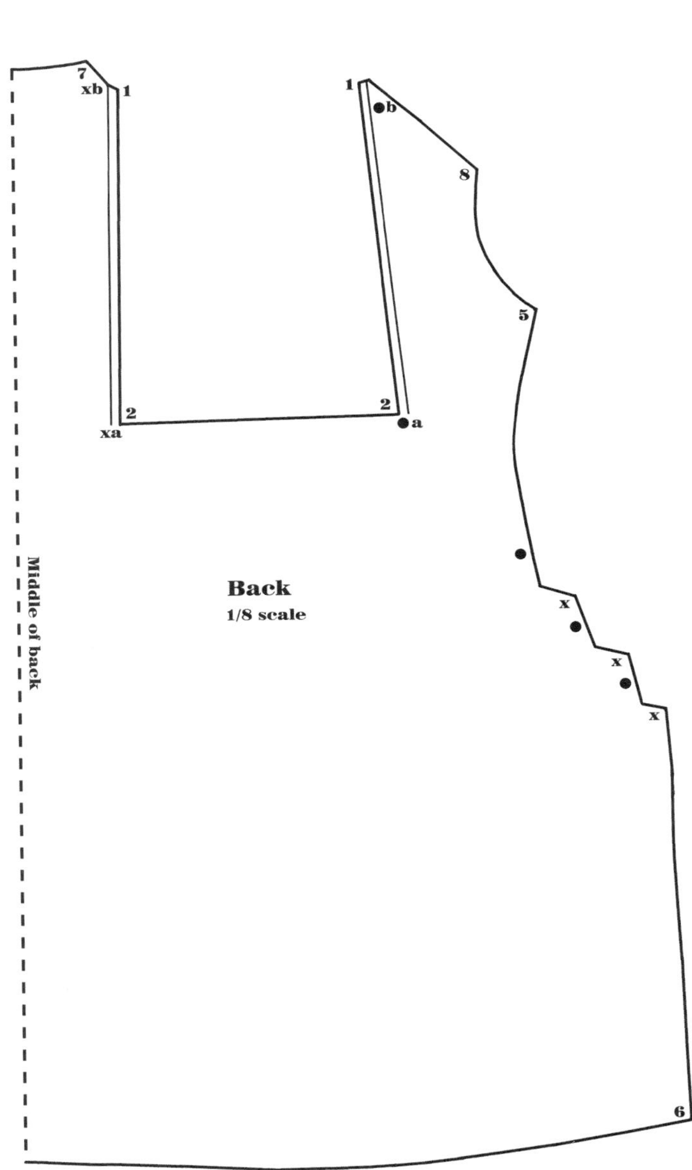

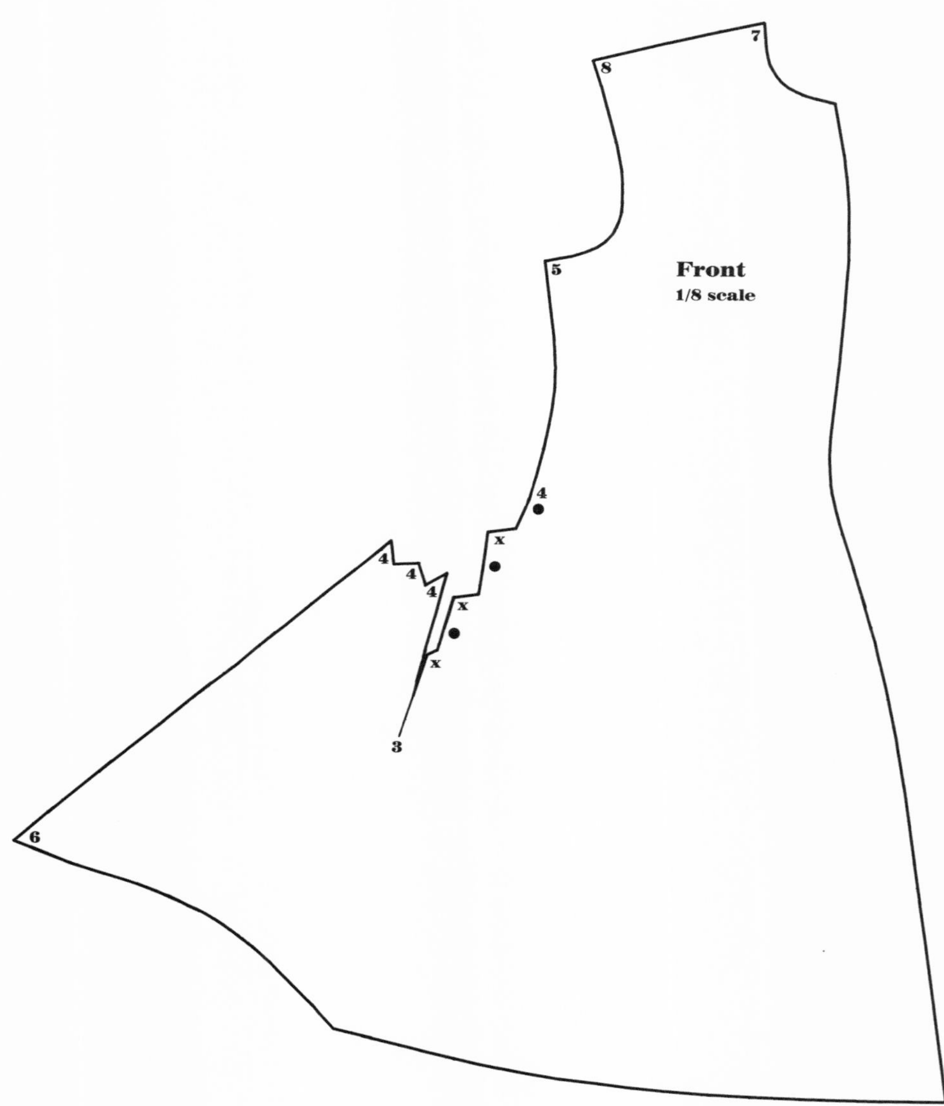
Front
1/8 scale
7
8
5
4
x
4
4
4
x
x
3
6

Adeline Paletot

This is a tight-fitting paletot of dark brown beaver. Two yards of velour 1 3/8 yard wide are required. It is richly trimmed with bows and broad bias folds of black grosgrain; the trimming imitates over-pieces. The belt and bows are also of black grosgrain.

Cut from the front, side front, and side back each two equal pieces. Cut from the back one piece. Cut the sleeves from the pattern for the Watteau Paletot.

Join the front, side front, side back, and back according to the corresponding figures on the pattern. Backstitch the seams and carefully fasten them open. Cord the edges and face them with a strip of silk 3 inches wide. Face the bottom of the sleeves and trim them as illustrated. Set them into the corded armholes.

The bows are made of a strip of grosgrain 5 inches long and 3 inches wide. They are set on so that each one covers the place where the next below is fastened. The sash ends are fastened with a bow on the side of the paletot. They are 6 inches wide, and are lined. The belt is made in the same manner.

Back
1/8 scale

68 67 65 66

Middle of back

Front
1/8 scale

68 67 61 62

Side Back
1/8 scale

65 63 66 64

Side Front
1/8 scale

63 61 62 64

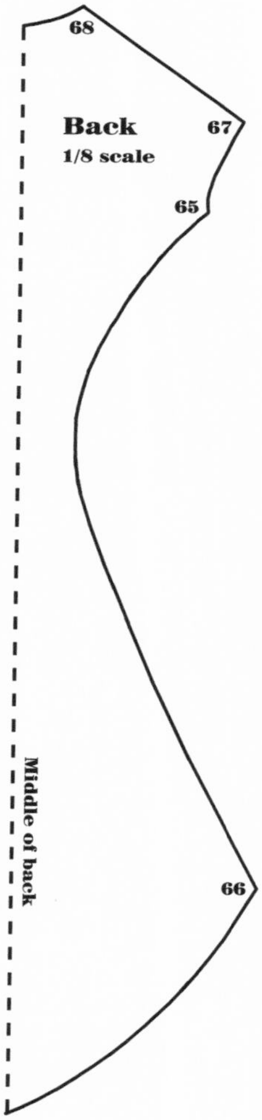

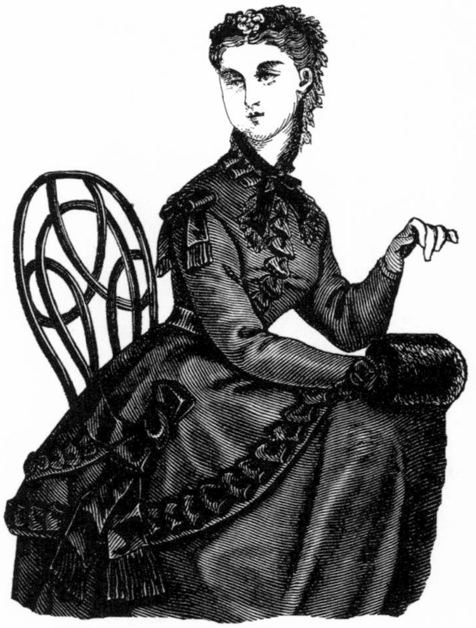

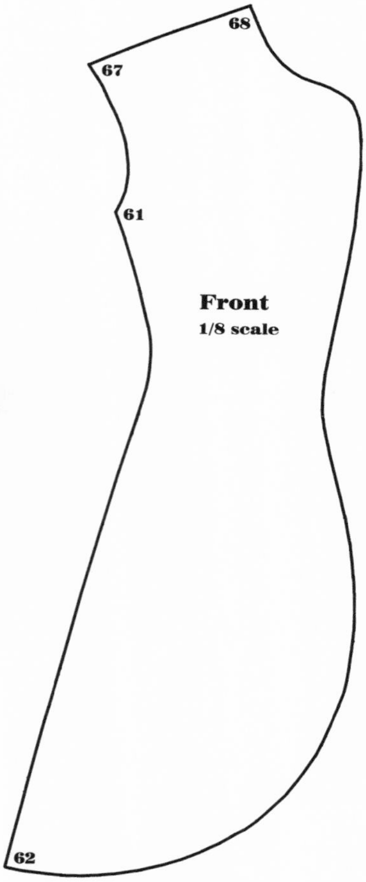

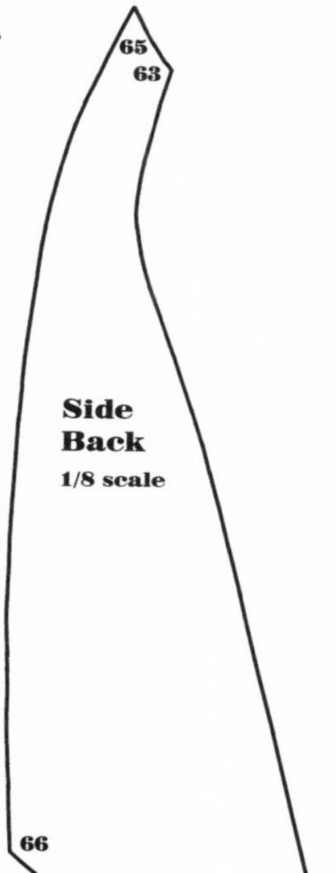

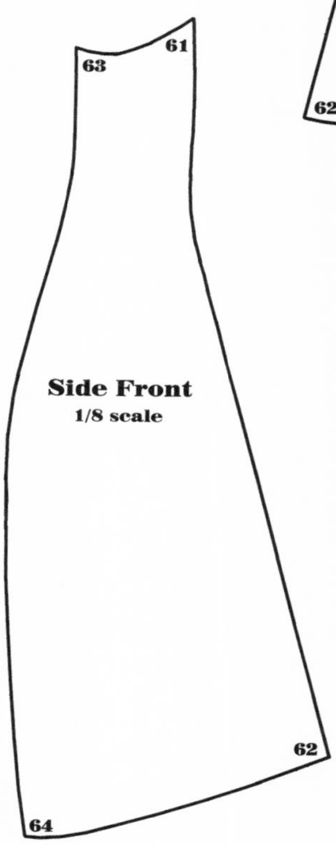

Mousquetaire Paletot

Mousquetaire Paletot

This paletot is of garnet velour. Two yards of material 1 3/8 yards wide are required. The fronts, which lap over above, are sloped below, and therefore do not lap over. The trimming is put on both fronts. It consists of bias folds of black satin, black silk cord, black silk fringe 3 inches wide, and large passementerie buttons. The edges are bound with a bias fold.

Cut both fronts. Cut one piece each from the back and collar. Cut the sleeves.

Join the back and fronts according to the corresponding figures on the pattern. Backstitch the seams, press them out, and cover them with a bias strip of black silk. Sew on the collar, and bind the edges. The binding consists of a bias fold. This is blindstitched on the right side, and the double material is hemmed down on the under side like ordinary binding. Cut the buttonholes and bind with satin. Sew them together on the under side all but the upper three, thus making the lower ones merely simulated buttonholes. Face the fronts with silk. Line the collar also with silk. Arrange the trimming as illustrated. Make a button of the cord on one side of each buttonhole by sewing it on wound around.

Sew up the sleeves according to the figures on the pattern. Bind them at the wrist. Face and sew on the trimming. Sew them into the armholes, bringing 78 on 78 of the front. Cover the seam with a bias fold.

November 14, 1868

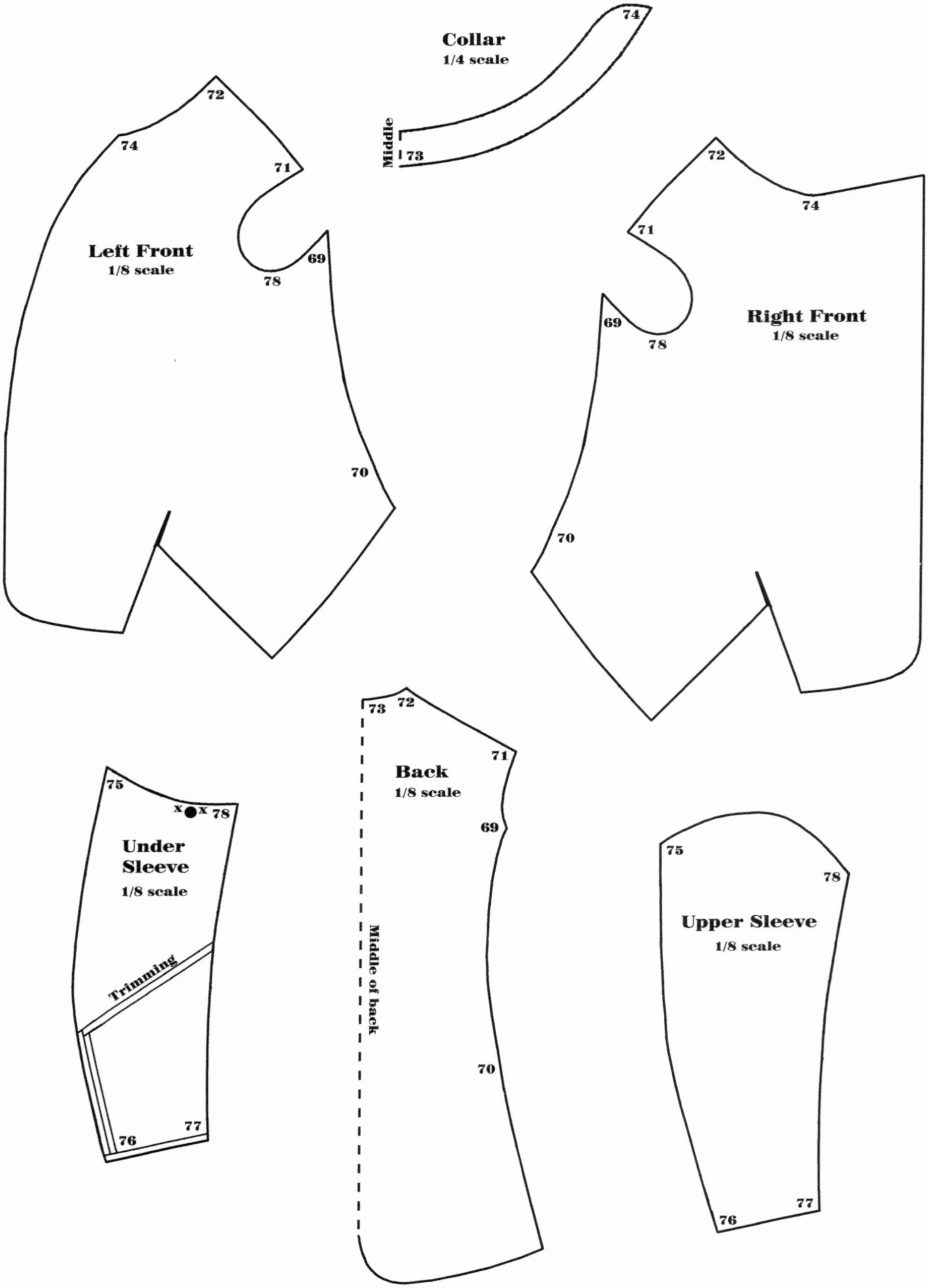
Collar
1/4 scale
74
Middle
73
Left Front
1/8 scale
72
74
71
69
78
70
Right Front
1/8 scale
72
74
71
69
78
70
Back
1/8 scale
73
72
71
69
70
Middle of back
Under
Sleeve
1/8 scale
75
x x 78
Trimming
76
77
Upper Sleeve
1/8 scale
75
78
76
77

Burnoose for Elderly Lady

This burnoose is especially designed for elderly ladies. It is made with a cape, which is also arranged in a pleat behind. It is of black cashmere, with very thin wadding and silk lining, and requires 3 1/2 yards of yard-wide goods. The simple trimming consists of black satin bias folds, silk tassels, and black lace buttons.

Cut of outside material, wadding, and lining from the front, back, and cape front each two pieces. Cut from the cape back one piece.

Quilt the wadding and lining together. Baste on the outside. Sew together the back from 9 to 10 and from 11 to 12. Lay a pleat in the middle of the back by fastening *x* on •, and stitching the edges down on the burnoose. Then join the back to the fronts from 13 to 14. Sew one side of the lining with the seam, and hem the other down over the seam afterward. Cut the wadding away from the seams so that they are not too thick.

Join the fronts and back of the cape. Cord the outer edges and sew on the trimming as illustrated. Lay the upper part of the cape in a box pleat, fastening *x* on •. Sew the inner edges of the pleat along the dotted line on the cape back. Sew the cape on

November 14, 1868

the burnoose according to the corresponding figures.

The standing collar is made of lined and corded pieces. These must be arranged on a straight piece of silk as illustrated, then sewn to the burnoose on the under side.

Sew a large round button on the cape pleat. Fasten with buttons and loops of cord. Trim the corners with silk tassels.

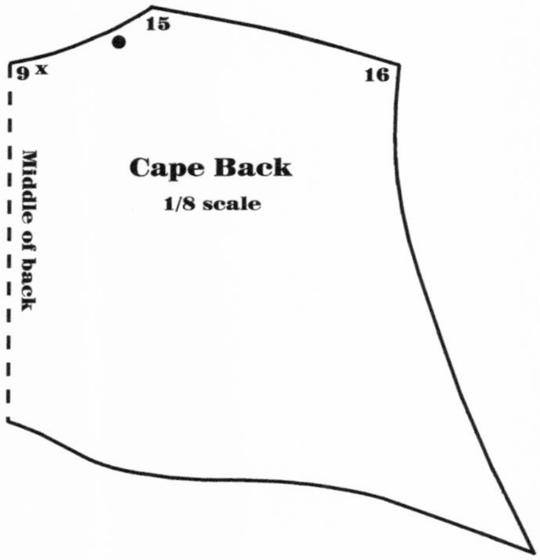

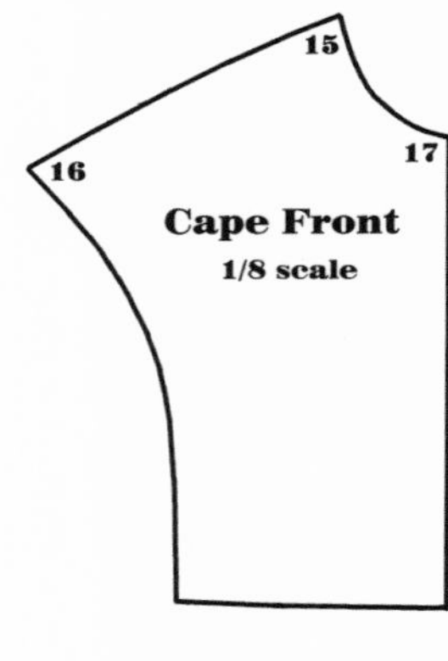

15
9 x
16
Middle of back
Cape Back
1/8 scale

Burnoose for Elderly Lady

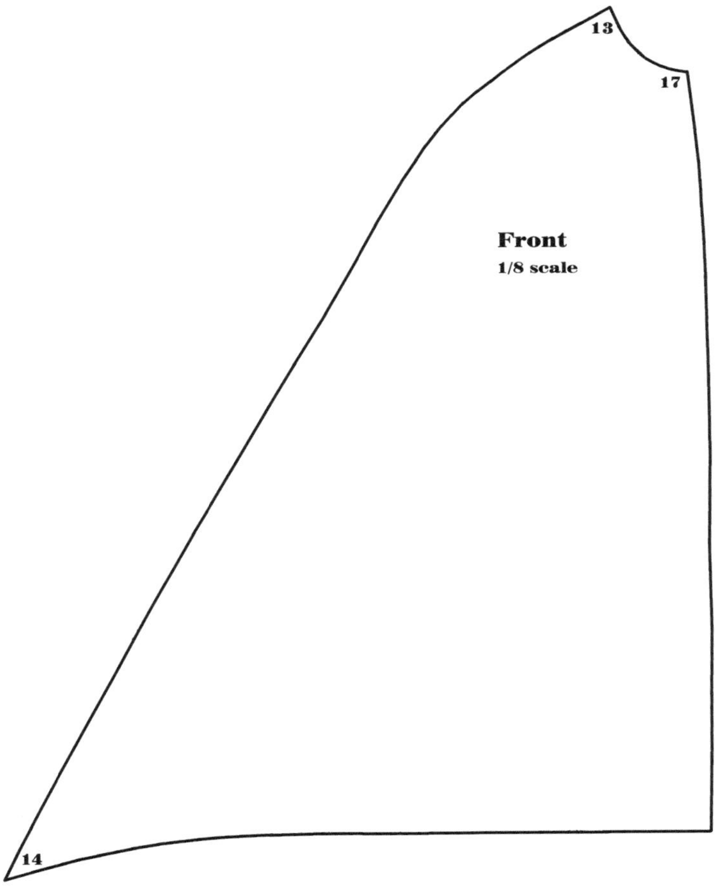

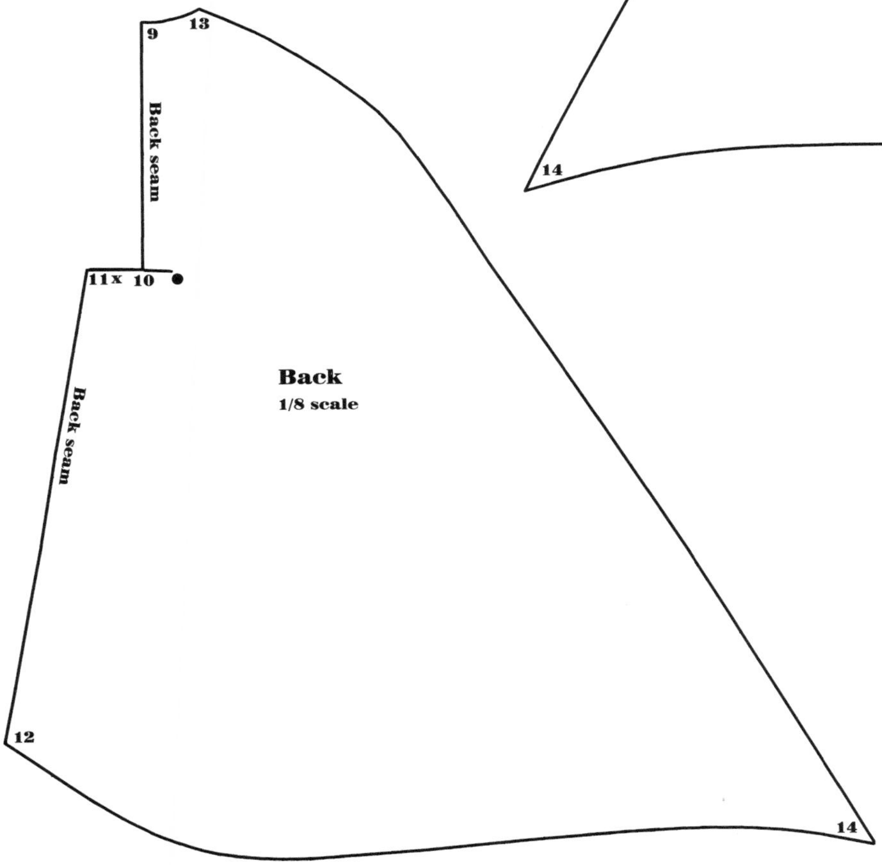

November 21, 1868

Winter Bonnets

A new and improved Marie Antoinette has a flaring front pointed over the forehead, and a sharp half crown edged with a cape or curtain of bias velvet 2 inches wide, forming two waved scallops and also pointed in the center. A stylish feature of its trimming is a satin rosette of numerous loops placed on the point of the crown. For elderly ladies this bonnet is made in black velvet, purple, or brown, trimmed with rich black lace and satin. For younger ladies the flaring fronts of black velvet Marie Antoinettes are shirred and lined with green satin, or gold, or royal pink.

Another shape admired by young and petite ladies has a narrow, rolling front that frames the face, then curves away from it. High diadems are not becoming to diminutive faces. The crown, or headpiece, is deeply indented in the center, displaying the chignon to advantage.

A novel fastening for velvet strings is a slipknot made to resemble the sailor's tie. It confines the strings at the throat, or can be moved lower down, as the wearer chooses. It is prettily made of carelessly folded satin, or of velvet in narrow pleats. Many bonnets have long satin strings fringed at the ends, one slightly longer than the other, so that they may be tied at the side. Strings entirely of lace are easily crushed, and are too light for street use in winter, hence they are confined to full-dress bonnets. Velvet strings lined with satin and bordered with lace are more suitable for promenade hats.

A pretty diadem is formed by ostrich tips arranged against the front of the bonnet, to fall on the forehead with that becoming effect ladies seek when permitting frizzed curls to escape from the front of the coiffure. Long ostrich feathers are curled by the application of heat, giving them a downy, light, and wavy appearance. These are used as diadems and as fringe, taking the place of the lace fall at the back of the bonnet.

La Seville, a peculiarly Spanish bonnet, black, without an atom of color, is something between a hat and a bonnet. It is straight and high over the forehead, made of black velvet in careless puffs over a half crown, with a bandeau of jet marguerites. A mantilla veil of black embroidered blonde, 1/2 yard deep, covers the shoulders like a round pelerine, and is fastened in front by a jet ornament. An aigrette and pompon of feathers at the side.

We commend these black hats on the score of economy, as they are suitable for every costume, and all black is no longer restricted to mourning, or all white to brides. Jet, lace, and the spirited little aigrettes relieve the hat of the accusation of somberness.

A stylish little fanchonette does not even require a frame. Two box-pleated quillings, or ruches of black velvet lined with orange satin, the lining showing at the edges, are mounted on cap wire, and extended across the head from ear to ear. The ruches are 2 1/2 inches wide in the center, narrowing toward the cheeks. Narrow black lace edges the back and front of the bonnet. A black ostrich tuft curls at the side from beneath a large tea rose. Strings of poult-de-soie ribbon, thickly ribbed, tie either front or back. This simple little fancy is easily imitated by ladies who make their own bonnets, as many must do now that a bonnet of a bright color can only be worn with a suit of that color, or with black.

Lapis lazuli velvet, the deepest blue imaginable, is faced with white satin, or with pale amber. Evening bonnets are of white royal velvet, the golden-green Florence, rose-pink, or lavender, with satin linings of self-color or white. Shaded satin roses with autumnal foliage, feather tufts, aigrettes, and blonde lace complete the trimming.

The few straws shown are trimmed with a toisade, or twist of velvet, over the front, a many-looped rosette of thickly ribbed ribbon on the back, and an erect ostrich tuft at the side. Sultan red ribbon, with black feathers, trims the black straws tastefully. Gray and the yellowish Italian straws are trimmed in the same manner, with green or lapis blue.

Mourning bonnets are of pleated crêpe, arranged in the styles we have described for colors, and trimmed with a little dull jet.

Round hats are more worn than ever. High-crowned hats of velvet and felt, with turned-up side rims, are most in favor. The round fez in scarlet or black, and the Louis XVI toque, made of dark crimson velvet, are trimmed with black lace and small green hummingbirds. Gray felt is trimmed with maroon velvet and ostrich feathers, or with the brown garnet.

Headdresses

Evening headdresses are full garlands across the front hair with trailing vines over the chignon. The same flower in different colors is in each coiffure. Sweet-pea wreaths and small honeysuckles, pink, white, and scarlet on the same vine, are large and full in front with a long spray at the side. Mossy vines and tendrils have large half-opened roses over the forehead, with small buds on trailing branches at the side or back.

A stylish ornament for the hair is a feather and gilt aigrette, the gilt tipped with turquoise. This is attached by a hairpin to the chignon. In others each strand of gilt is tipped with stones of a different color. Real hummingbirds with gold beaks and gilded wings are beside aigrettes of heron feathers tipped with colored stones. Butterflies, with pins to fasten them on, are made of transparent mother-of-pearl.

Tortoiseshell combs, the top held on by hinges, form a short bandeau in front of the chignon. Plain tortoiseshell bands large enough to clasp under the chignon are also worn. Jet vines for surrounding the chignon, made of balls, leaves, and the favorite marguerite pattern, are large in the center, smaller toward the sides.

November 28, 1868

Knitted Fichu Mantilla

This mantilla is provided with a hood that may be drawn over the head. The ends are crossed in front and fastened behind. The pattern is of white zephyr, knitted in an openwork design, edged with a scalloped edging and bordered under this with a knitted lace of black wool.

The pattern of the stitch is shown in Figure 1 and knitted as follows. First round: Slip the 1st stitch,

Knitted Fichu Mantilla

* narrow 1 crossed, then slip 1 again, narrow 1, throw the thread around twice. From * repeat.

Second round: In every thread that was thrown around knit 1 and purl 1. The remainder must be purled. In the next round repeat this alternating. Also, after the 1st slip stitch, knit 1, then throw the thread around, and take up 2 stitches in succession.

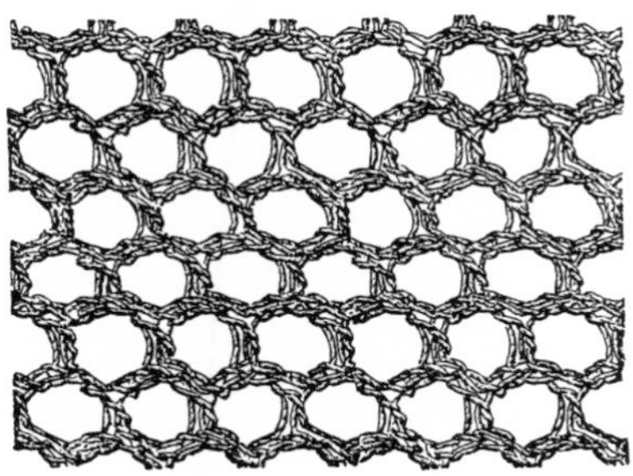

Figure 1. Stitch for mantilla

Cut the pattern of paper muslin, lengthening the ends in the direction of the arrows. Begin the mantilla on the bottom with a foundation of 20 stitches. Knit in the above design, widening or narrowing as the pattern requires.

For the hood knit a square piece, the foundation of which must count 60 stitches. Crochet around three sides of this two rounds as follows. First round: Always 1 sc. (single crochet) in an edge stitch, 3 ch., passing over sufficient space.

Second round: Alternately 5 dc. (double crochet) in a chain-stitch scallop, 1 ch. (chain), 1 sc. in the next chain-stitch scallop, 1 ch. Sew the edges of the middle side together under the scallops. Join the opposite side to the neck of the mantilla from *x* to •. Crochet the edge from * to • with black, and from * on with white wool in the manner given above.

For the lace, which begins at the point marked * on the pattern, make a foundation of chain stitches of black wool as long as the entire outer edge of the mantilla. Knit these stitches off on the wooden knitting needle designed for the work (this is done as the first round in Tunisian stitch). Work as follows. First round: Alternately make 1, narrow 1. Second round: Knit plain. Third round: * Knit 1, make 1, knit 1, make 1, narrow four times in succession, make 1, knit 1, make 1.

Now repeat the second and third rounds till the lace has reached the desired width. On the mantilla this is 6 inches, and on the sash 3 inches wide. After the last round cast off loosely. Sew the lace on under the white scallops. Two bows of black velvet ribbon are arranged on the back of the hood.

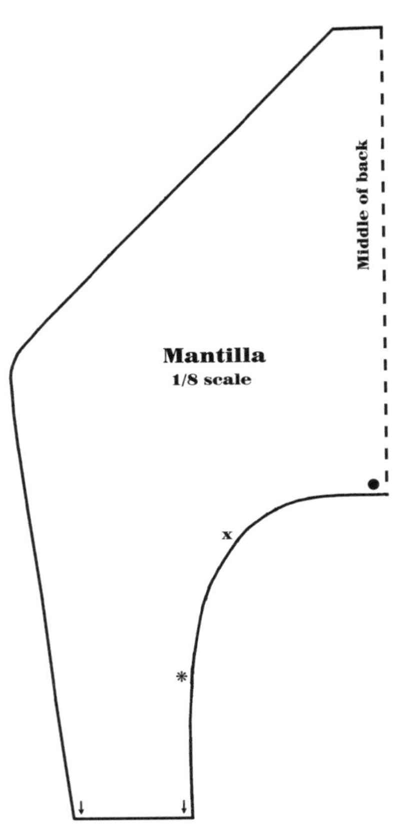

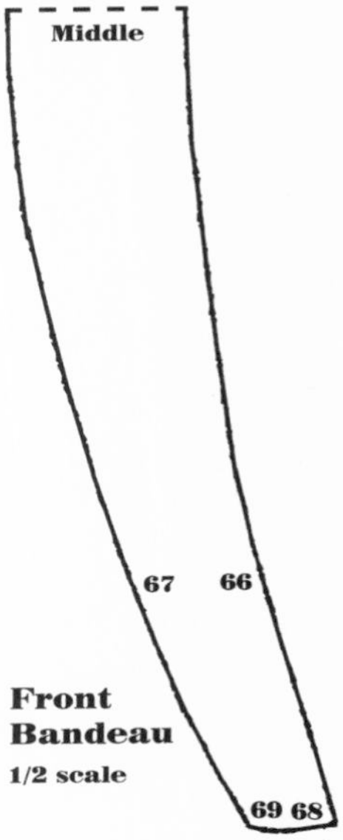

November 28, 1868

Middle

67 66

Front
Bandeau
1/2 scale

69 68

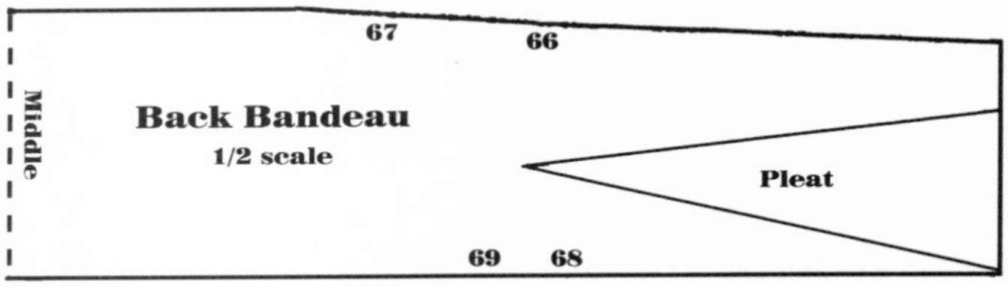

67 66

Middle

Back Bandeau
1/2 scale

Pleat

69 68

Ophelia Bonnet

This bonnet is of black velvet, trimmed on the left side with a spray of leaves and a bunch of long fine grasses.

For making the frame cut one each of the front bandeau and the back bandeau, from double black foundation. Lay a pleat in the back bandeau and bind the edges with narrow black velvet over a wire. Cover the front bandeau with a velvet puff, on each side of which blindstitch a little black satin roll. Now join the two bandeaux according to the corresponding figures on the pattern. Set on this a second large puff, which is sewn to the back edge of the frame, and reaches to the upper edge of the front bandeau, where it is sewn fast. Cover the remaining ends of the back bandeau smoothly with velvet and bind the back with narrow velvet.

Sew on the black satin ribbons, which are 1 1/4 inches wide and 10 inches long. The strings are of lace 7 inches wide. One is 30 inches long and the other 25. Both are edged with lace 2 inches wide. Gather the upper ends of both strings. Fasten the shorter piece to the middle of the back of the bonnet, allowing the longer piece to reach over this to the left side, where the end is hidden by the spray. Fasten the lace ends again on the ends of the back bandeau. Finish the front with a rosette of black satin ribbon with long loops and ends.

Madelon Bonnet

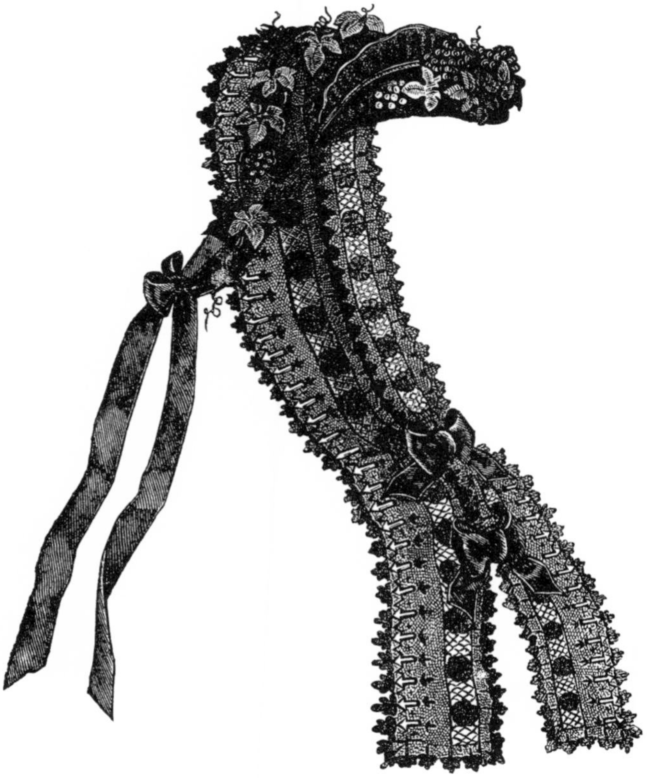

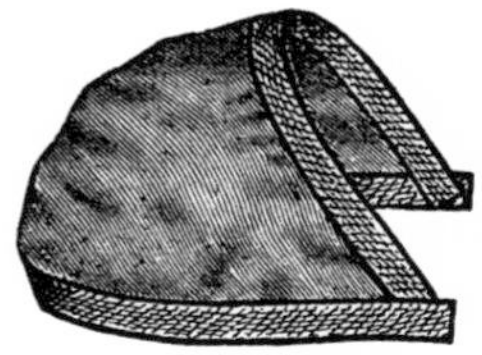

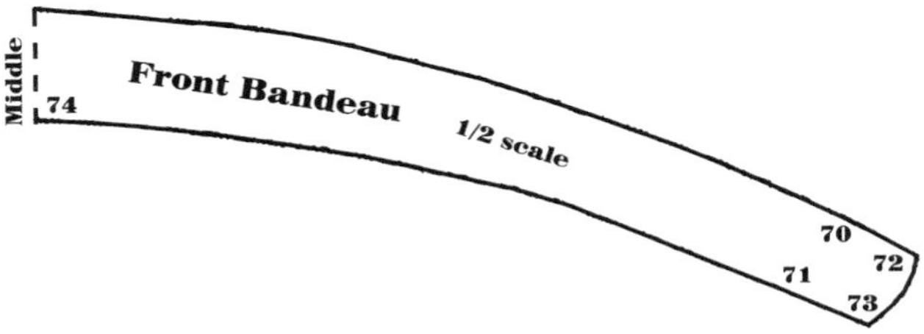

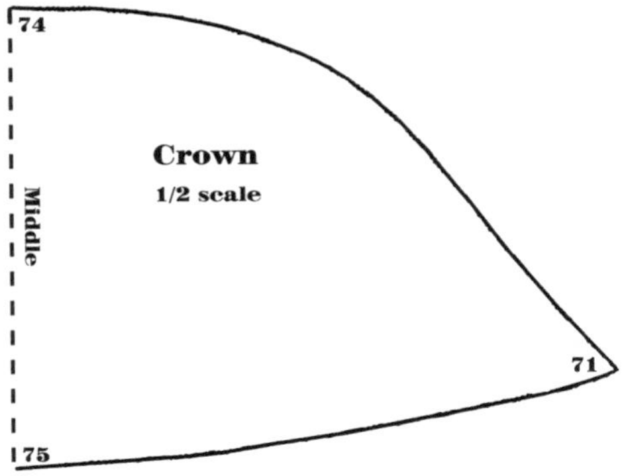

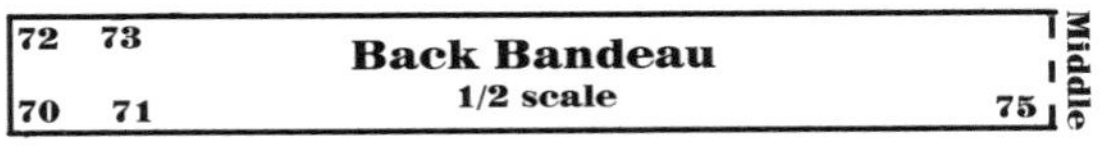

Front Bandeau
1/2 scale
Middle
74 70 71 72 73

Crown
1/2 scale
Middle
74 71 75

Back Bandeau
1/2 scale
72 73 70 71 75
Middle

Madelon Bonnet

This bonnet is of garnet velvet, trimmed with garnet satin, a wreath of garnet velvet leaves and black berries, and black lace strings. Cut one each of the crown, front bandeau, and back bandeau from double black foundation. Sew a wire on each side of the bandeaux. Then sew them to the foundation, in doing which the latter must be slightly fulled. Sew on the front a wire coil. This is formed by rolling a fine wire around a fine tatting mesh or large lead pencil, and afterward flattening out the coil. Next cover the frame with a velvet puff, the front edge of which is sewn inside the bonnet edge and covered there with lace edging. The wire serves to hold out the puff. About 1 inch from the front edge sew an upright bandeau. This is composed of a strip of bias satin 2 inches wide. This strip is doubled, with a fine wire inserted in the doubled edge, and is pleated on the under edge. The place where this is set on is covered by a satin piping 1/3 inch wide.

The satin ribbons are 1 1/4 inches wide and 35 inches long. The strings are 30 inches long. They consist of lace insertion 1 inch wide, on the front side of which sew edging 1 inch wide and on the back 3 inches. These are sewn on the back of the bonnet. Then the wreath is arranged as shown.

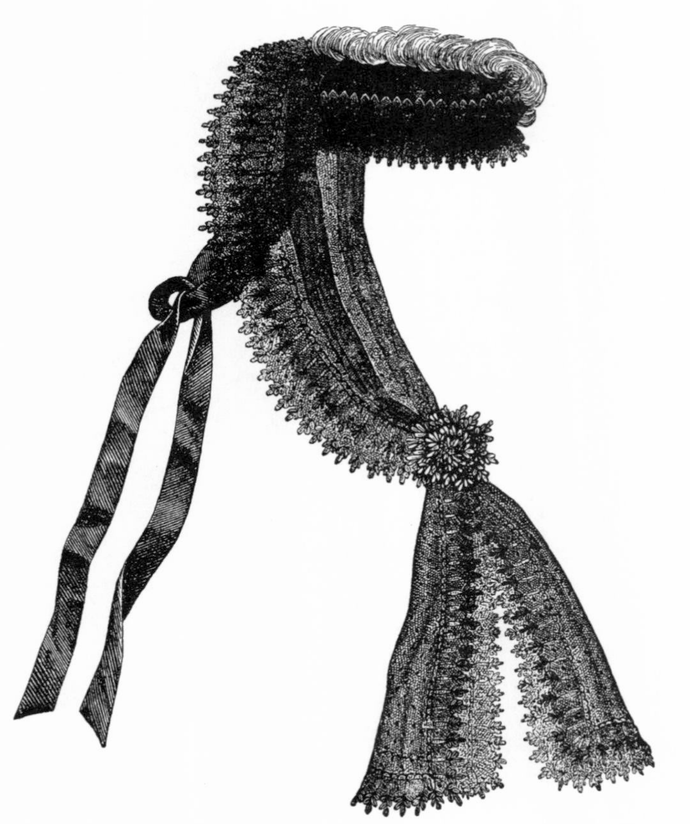

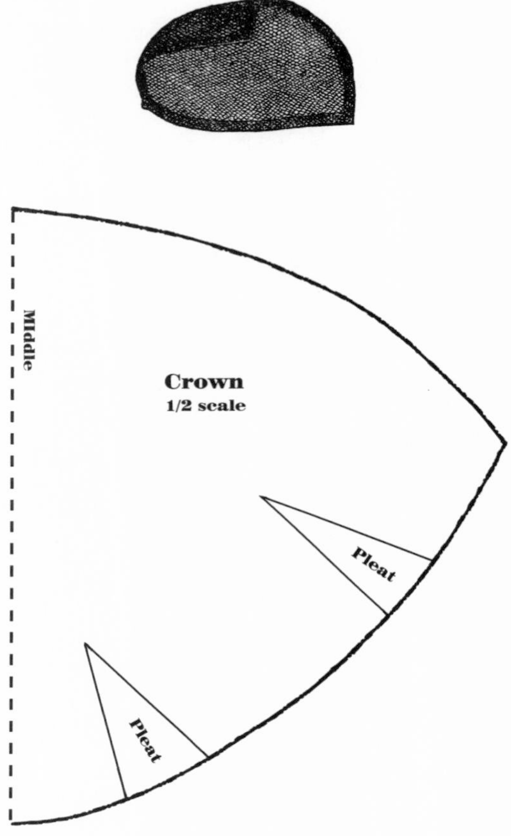

Stuart Bonnet

This bonnet is of black silk rep. It is trimmed with a violet feather, lace 1 1/2 inches wide, and black lace strings 50 inches long and 6 inches wide, which are edged with lace.

For the frame, cut one of the pattern from double black foundation. Take up the pleats on the front. Sew on the outer edges a strong wire, the ends of which must lap over 3/4 inch.

On this frame arrange the silk, which has been laid crosswise in three box pleats, leaving a space half the width of the pleat between each. Border the front edge of the bonnet with gathered lace. Sew in a lining. Bind the outside and lining together with a narrow bias strip of lutestring.

Sew on the front edge of the bonnet a bandeau of foundation and wire 1 inch wide, the upper side of which is edged with lace. Cover this bandeau with a puff consisting of a bias strip of rep 4 inches wide. This is arranged on the upper side in box pleats in a diadem, and sewn to the bandeau so that the diadem stands up free. On its under side gather the strip, sew it fast inside the edge of the bonnet, and cover the seam with gathered lace.

Lastly arrange the feather, the ribbons, which are 1 1/4 inches wide and 25 inches long, and the strings, which are pleated on the back edge of the bonnet. A lace rosette fastens the ends in front.

Galotti Bonnet

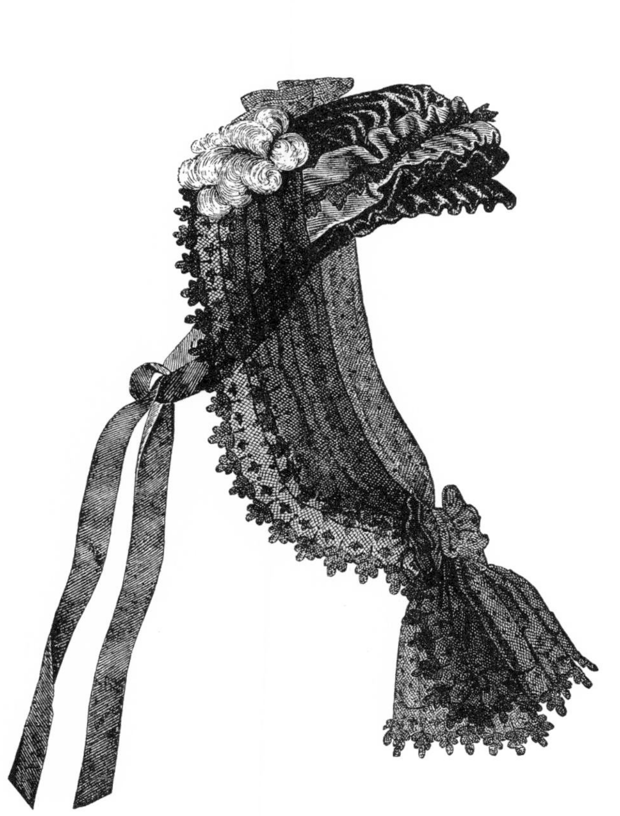

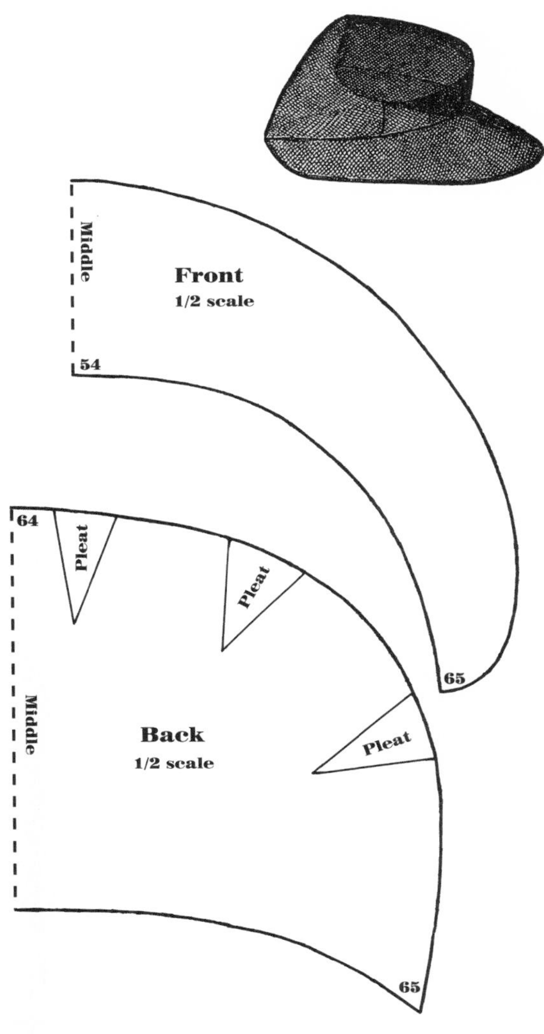

Galotti Bonnet

This bonnet is of violet velvet and violet satin. It is trimmed with a small violet feather, black lace 2 inches wide, and plain black lace strings 20 inches long and 8 inches wide, dotted with beads.

To make the frame, cut one each of the back and front from double black foundation. Sew in wire all around the front and on the back. Lay the back in pleats and sew it to the front, according to the corresponding figures on the pattern.

Cover the back with a puff of velvet and the front with another of satin. This last is arranged on the back edge in a box-pleated diadem 1 inch high. Then gather the front and sew it down on the inside of the bonnet. Between the diadem and the front puff sew gathered lace. Put in a lutestring lining. Bind the back with a narrow strip of velvet or satin. On the inner edge of the front of the bonnet, cover the edges of the lining and front puff with lace. In the inner front arrange a narrow band of foundation, which is covered with a bias strip of velvet 2 1/2 inches wide and pleated along the middle.

Border the strings with edging. Lay a few pleats on the upper edge and sew them on the back of the bonnet. The place where the feather is set on is covered with a lace bow similar to the one that fastens the ends in front. The violet satin ribbons are 1 1/4 inches wide and 25 inches long.

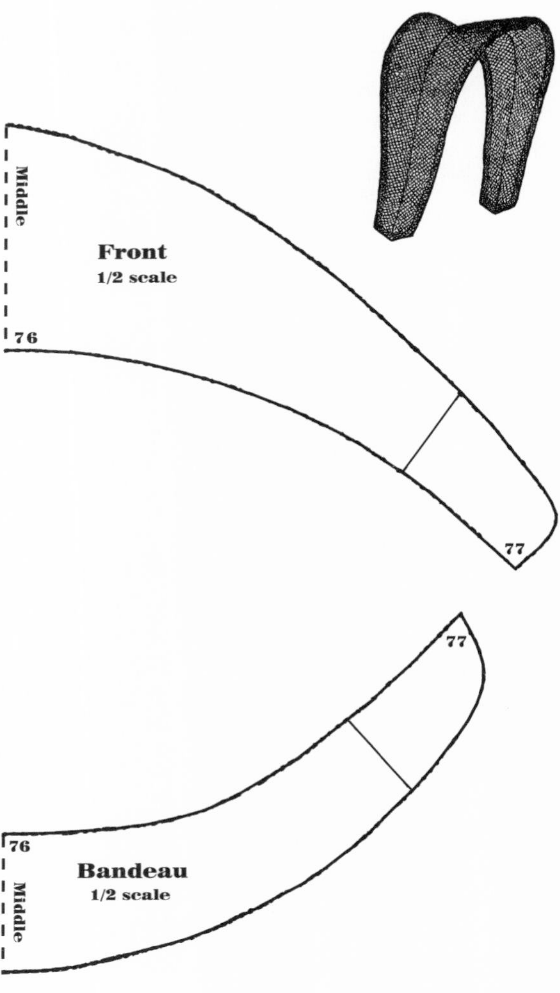

Lucretia Bonnet

This bonnet is of black velvet, trimmed with lace rosettes and a garnet flower spray.

To make the frame, cut one each of the front and bandeau from double foundation. Join the two pieces according to the corresponding figures on the pattern. In doing so, full the front. Sew a wire along the seam, and also a few other rows of wire, and wire the outer edges.

Cover the frame with a velvet puff, which is sewn down on the outer edge and pleated and sewn down along the seam. The seam is covered with gathered lace 2 inches wide. Now put in a black lutestring lining. Bind it with black velvet or lutestring. Fasten inside on the under corners of the bonnet a bandeau of double foundation 1/3 inch wide. To this sew two rows of lace gathered, with the gathered parts together. Set between these little lace rosettes as shown.

Set on the back of the bonnet a veil of figured lace 8 inches long and 16 inches wide. On the under edges set the satin ribbons, which are 20 inches long and 1 1/4 inches wide, and also the 20-inch-long strings. These strings are of black satin ribbon 2 inches wide, laid in threefold box pleats in every 2 inches. The upper edges are fastened with a few stitches. Between the box pleats lay the ribbon in little plain pleats. Trim with rosettes of lace 1 1/4 inches wide. The same lace is sewn on the back of the bonnet and ends. Lastly, arrange the flower-twig as shown.

December 5, 1868

Dress Goods for Mourning

Imperial serge is taking the place of bombazine for handsome street suits worn in deep mourning. This is the same material as bombazine, a mixture of silk and wool, but with better body and more distinct twill. It is as soft and full to the touch as Tibet merino. It is slightly more than 1 yard wide. The coarser English serge, all wool with a very broad twill, is durable and lusterless, and makes a serviceable winter suit for traveling and shopping.

Biarritz cloth, an all-wool fabric resembling corded delaine, is even more desirable than serge for street wear, as the straight longitudinal cords are more readily cleaned than a bias twill. It is about 40 inches wide. The well-known empress cloths, and the thick poplin alpacas with demiluster, are the best goods for ordinary street suits.

Henrietta cloth, which is really a silk-warped cashmere, retains its dead-black color as long as a thread of it remains. It makes a more elegant house dress than bombazine. Ladies who retain their partiality for bombazine are reminded that the English bombazine will give greater satisfaction in wearing than the light, frail fabric made by the French. Black cashmere with double twill is in demand for both house and street dresses. The glossy alpacas are not considered suitable for morning, but a demiluster alpaca of firm texture will be found serviceable and inexpensive for house dresses. A variety of velours and ottoman reps are shown, but are generally too lustrous. Only the woolen reps is suitable for deep mourning.

The Bonnét and Ponsons silks with half luster are serviceable for mourning silks, but should be worn only in the house. A grosgrain with but little gloss and of excellent quality is sold in the 3/4 width. The lusterless faille and the cashmere-de-soie with thicker threads than grosgrain are the richest materials for full dress. Heavy, dowagerlike Antwerp silk falling into rich folds has a broad reps. It is sold in 1-yard-wide goods, and a rare article is 1 1/2 yards wide. A thick silk for younger ladies in slight mourning has a satin stripe 2 inches wide.

Half Mourning

Dresses of solid purple and gray are not now used for half mourning. The black materials mentioned are chosen, and are also trimmed with black–not crêpe or plain folds, as in deep mourning, but pleated frills, quillings, and ruches of thick silk. A purple bow at the throat and the trimming of the hat is the only color introduced. In suits the petticoat is sometimes purple, and the kid gloves are stitched with the same shade.

Cloaks and Suits

Paletots of the different Astrakhan furs, trimmed with angora fringe, are the handsomest cloaks for mourning. Astrakhan cloth is also greatly used. The dead-black beaver cloths are made into half-fitted basquines, with cape and belt, trimmed with bands of silk, or bordered with Astrakhan.

Serge and Biarritz cloth suits are heavily lined or wadded, and the outer garment is used as a cloak with other dresses. The pelisse is worn with a belt and small cape. The trimming is several narrow folds overlapping each other. Five folds, each 1 inch wide, in a cluster, headed with piping, trim the skirt; three folds the cape and pelisse.

Heavy worsted fringes and the serge braid, so strong that it is called Hercules braid, are used for plain suits. Crêpe quillings are soon destroyed. The dress material is the best trimming for handsome suits. With the addition of an Astrakhan collar and muff, a flannel-lined suit can be worn all winter.

Puffs, panniers, and gathered ruffles are incongruous with mourning attire, as they look gay and dressy. Pleated trimmings and festooned drapery are more in keeping, such as box-pleated ruches and flounces, and small capes looped with rosettes. There is also the Camargo looped upper skirt over a petticoat bordered with a pleated flounce. Arrange the flounce in groups of box pleats, three in a cluster. It should be bound at the lower edge, and headed with a pleated ruche of the same, or a bias band 2 inches wide. The Camargo upper skirt has six breadths; the side widths are narrow and gored. The skirt is quite long and caught up in pleats at the sides and back.

Tibet merino and cashmere long shawls are worn in the burnoose style, a fold arranged in the back, and the long end thrown over the left shoulder.

Bonnets and Veils

English crêpe doubled over a high frame, with a pleated crêpe diadem, is the favorite bonnet for winter. Bombazine is not used as it is too heavy. Narrow ribbons tie under the chin, and long crêpe folds are left hanging in front, caught together by a bow or slipknot. The white ruche of tarlatan is only worn by widows. It extends merely across the forehead in the diadem style. White tarlatan bows at the throat are not used. The veil of English crêpe is worn, tied over the bonnet. It is usually 1 1/2 yards long, but the length is varied according to the degree of relationship.

Collars and Handkerchiefs

Standing collars with wide lapped ends are the best for mourning, as the corsage is usually made high and close. The 2-inch hem of cambric handkerchiefs is deep black, a better style than a border above them. Jet and onyx jewelry is in massive styles, like cameos and coral. The watch chain should also be of jet.

December 12, 1868

Wedding Dresses

Bridal toilettes are remarkable for their elegant simplicity. The richest materials plainly made embody the correct idea of a dress for a bride. The more girlish attire she has hitherto worn is abandoned to her bridesmaids, and something of the new wifely dignity is foreshadowed.

White satin and lace are, as they must ever be, the first choice for the wedding dress. Thirteen yards of bridal satin is required in the popular 3/4 width. Simple tulle trimmings and flowers add but little to the expense. It is the rich laces that increase the bills. A lace tunic with garniture for corsage, a combination of round point and point appliqué, is sold. Lace trousseaux contain a flounce, shawl, barbe, handkerchief, trimming lace, and covers for fan and parasol. More costly sets with a bridal veil of corresponding pattern are only imported to order.

But such extravagance requires a full purse. We write for brides-expectant less lavish of expenditure, who will be content with a grosgrain or poult-de-soie, or else a lustrous taffeta or faille. If a still lower price is desired we commend an Irish poplin, rather than a flimsy, cheaper silk. The texture is the best of its kind, and when selected with fine luster and even, heavy cords is almost as handsome as grosgrain. Alpaca and other woolen goods are better suited for shrouds than wedding dresses, and the white crpe sometimes worn by brides in mourning is too sadly suggestive. Economy and poetry combine in the traditional bridal dress of soft, flowing muslin. Fine organdy adorned with filmy Valenciennes is at present the fashionable acceptation of the poetic idea.

Panniers are not popular for wedding dresses, though occasionally worn. Long trained skirts, gored closely at the sides and very full behind, trimmed with a wide flounce of tulle or satin, are the prevalent style. High bodice and close sleeves are most frequently worn when the ceremony is performed at church. Low corsage with pannier skirt for home weddings. Tulle tunics are in favor, edged with a ruche of the same. Grecian folds are in vogue for low corsages, and lace epaulets and cuffs, with flowers in the center, for high waists.

Bridesmaid's dresses are of tulle and tarlatan in successive puffs, with a tulle overskirt looped with flowers. A different flower and a becoming color of trimming is assigned to each bridesmaid.

Flowers, Veil, Etc.

Orange blossoms are losing prestige for bridal flowers. The buds are stiff, and the full-blown flowers large and coarse looking. They are prettiest and least unbecoming when mingled with other small flowers, such as clematis, jasmine, or the bridal spirae. In Europe myrtle blossoms are worn by young girls, and orange flowers only by widows.

A flower set consists of a diadem, with long sprays falling on each shoulder, a corsage bouquet with a chatelaine attached for looping the tunic, and sprays for the shoulder. Simpler sets are merely a wreath and bouquet; a brooch and earrings may be added.

The veil is a large half circle of tulle, the width of the tulle forming the length of the veil. It is placed over the diadem, the front falling over the face. Or else a short veil is added, and this is thrown back by the first bridesmaid when the ceremony is ended. A wide hem or pleated ruche may border the veil, but the soft gossamer tulle is prettiest without trimming, the undefined edge losing itself in the rich folds of the dress. The shorter veils sometimes worn by bridesmaids are in the same shape, but merely drape the back of the figure. A widow marrying again does not wear a veil.

December 12, 1868

The front hair is crpéd. Soft, light, airy curls float at the back over small finger puffs formed of the natural hair.

The bridal fan is of white silk or satin under lace, with pearl sticks. Handkerchief trimmed with lace of the kind used in the dress. Gloves of softest kid, and boots of the dress material buttoned with Roman pearls and trimmed with blonde lace.

Jewelry

Pearls are always the accepted bridal jewelry, and a prominence is given them in wedding parures even when associated with diamonds. The fancy at present is for the Moorish styles, large pearls in a knife-edge setting of polished gold.

The engagement ring is a solitaire diamond or pearl in crown setting without enamel. The wedding ring is a plain hoop not very wide, made of twenty-four-karat gold.

Outdoor Toilettes

The bridal bonnet worn when returning calls, and on occasions of ceremony, is usually white, though many prefer a bonnet matching the dress in color. If white it should be of royal velvet and misty blonde lace, a diadem of ostrich tufts or marabou, and a cluster of wild roses or clematis, but never an orange flower.

The carriage dress of poult-de-soie or satin, either mauve or violet, has a full train flounced with black lace. A velvet basque a darker shade than the dress. Light kid gloves. Lace collar and diamonds. A MacFarlane of striped plush for a carriage wrapping.

A less wealthy bride should select a silk or an Irish poplin of becoming shade, with bonnet to match, and a black velvet polonaise that will serve with other dresses. Pink coral jewelry or Byzantine mosaics.

A handsome short suit is indispensable for the street and for church, where a train should never enter. There is no prescribed color. A woman of taste does not wish to proclaim her brideship to the passing crowd. An economist will select a skirt of rich material to be worn with her velvet polonaise, and a velvet pouf of blue or other becoming shade in harmony with the skirt. Wood-brown kid gloves or dark maroon suffice for almost any suit. French kid boots buttoned at the side.

In the spring a bride selects a gray poplin for her traveling dress. A golden brown or the dead-leaf shade is preferred for autumn. Cloth rivals poplin this season. Fine woolen serge or cashmere is less expensive. Fur is the best trimming for cloth; satin quillings for poplin; serge, braid, and bullion fringe for twilled goods.

The outer garment is flannel, lined or wadded. A MacFarlane of Scotch tartan serves for additional wrapping. The velvet bonnet or the round hat of felt, and the undressed kid gloves match the dress in color.

Morning and Afternoon Dresses

The prettiest inexpensive morning dresses are of white alpaca or merino in the Watteau style, bordered with colored ruches. The tiny breakfast cap is a mere rosette of Valenciennes with ribbon, leaves, and strings. Short plaid dresses, or merino of self-color, made with gored skirt and wide bias flounce and a small pelerine cape, are homelike and serviceable. Crosscut bands of silk for trimming.

Afternoon dresses of colored poplin or of black are made with demitrain and trimmed with plaid velvet bands and sashes. Surplice and Pompadour waists, with muslin chemisette. A black silk overskirt looped or puffed, and a small bodice or bib back and front is worn over colored dresses to give variety to a small wardrobe. A velvet bodice, a sleeveless jacket of black satin and lace, plaid sashes, and bretelles are all graceful additions to home dress.

The hair is arranged in a braided chignon with a flowing crimped tress. A velvet band surrounds the chignon and is tied with a bow on top.

Evening Dresses

The wedding dress without the veil is worn to parties as a compliment to the hostess. Lavender, pearl, a delicate gray, and the light Pompadour fawn are trousseau colors. The skirts have the demitrain, fashionable for all but wedding dresses, low round corsages filled out with lace and tulle, or else high square corsage and sleeves ruffled at the elbow. Neither sashes nor panniers adorn the skirts, which are very full at the back.

White kid boots serve with almost any dress. A light glove faintly tinged with color is preferred to pure white.

Hoopskirt

To the under part of this hoopskirt, which is made of red cashmere, are fastened bands of the same material, fastened on buckles. By means of this arrangement the skirt may be made longer or shorter as desired.

Cut from the front and bustle each one piece (for the last a muslin lining at the same time). Cut from the side piece and back each two pieces.

Backstitch together the front, side piece, and back according to the corresponding figures on the pattern, as well as both back parts of the skirt. Sew tapes on the under side for the hoops as partly shown on the pattern.

Arrange the bands of cashmere and lining. Each of these is 25 inches long, 2 1/2 inches wide on the under edge, and sloped to 1 inch wide on the upper edge. Sew these bands to the skirt on the under, wider ends. Furnish with crossbands on the under side 4 inches from the upper edge.

Stitch the pieces of the bustle together from the right side and simultaneously fasten in the bands for the buckles. These bands are each 3 inches long. Having pushed on the buckles, double the bands together in the middle and stitch them down above the buckles. Through the double material of the bustle run steel springs of suitable length so as to slightly stretch the stuff. Bind the bustle between the double material of a straight belt. The long bands are fastened in the buckles, and the surplus ends run through the crossbands on the under side.

Hoopskirt

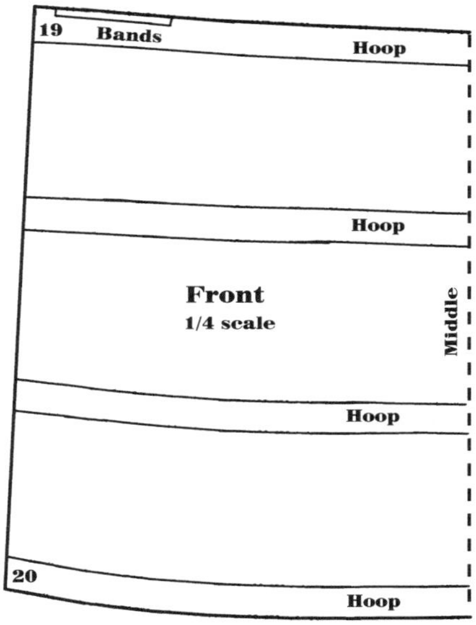

19 Bands Hoop

Hoop

Front
1/4 scale

Middle

Hoop

20 Hoop

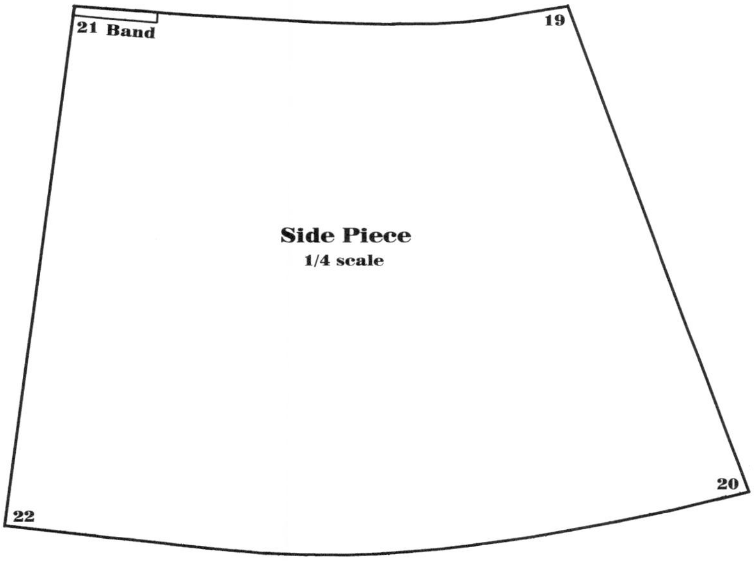

21 Band 19

Side Piece
1/4 scale

22 20

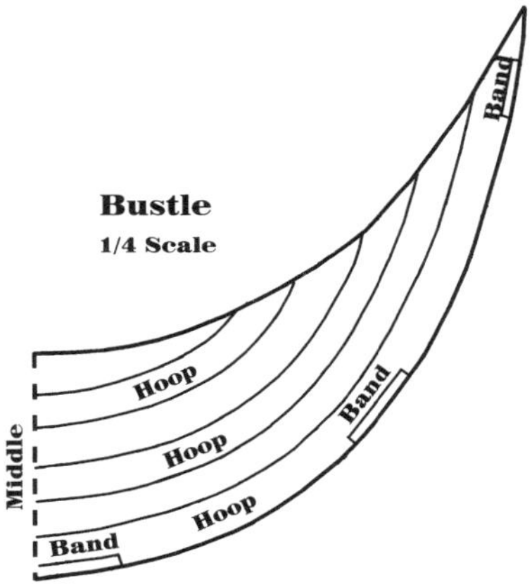

Bustle
1/4 Scale

Band

Hoop

Band

Hoop

Middle

Hoop

Band

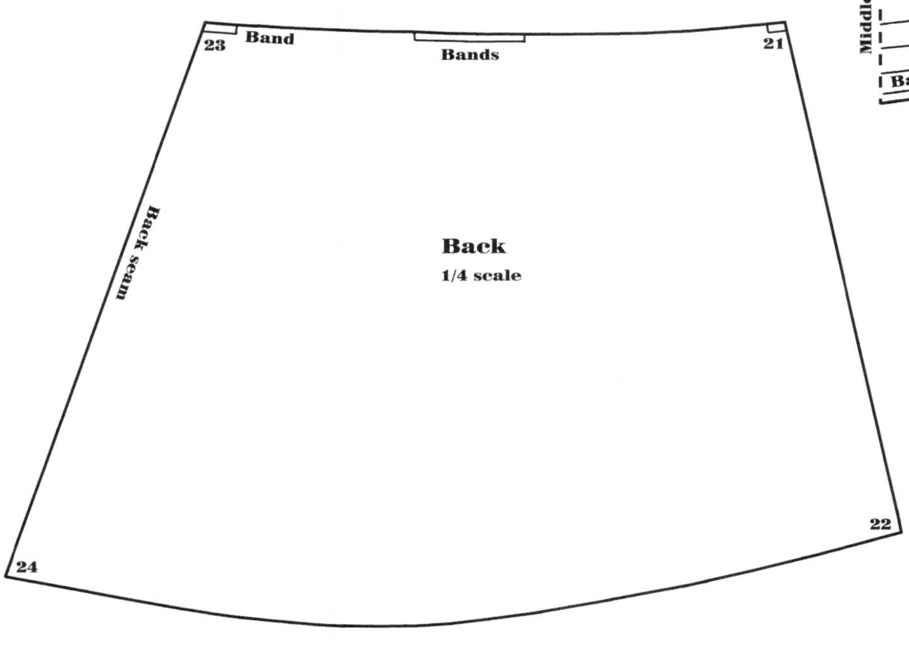

23 Band Bands 21

Back seam

Back
1/4 scale

24 22

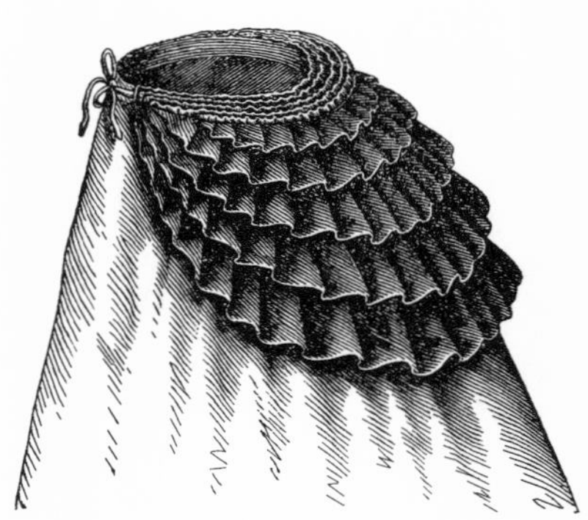

Horsehair Bustle

This bustle is of white horsehair. It consists of five sloping pieces of stuff which are pleated and overlap each other. The under (larger) piece is 20 inches long and 30 inches wide. Each following piece is 4 inches shorter, so that the upper one is only 4 inches long and 16 inches wide. Each piece of stuff is rounded on the under edge and hemmed and pleated on the upper edge, so the hem stands out. The remaining edges are corded with a heavy cord.

Having arranged the pieces in this manner, join them so the heading of each pleated part stands out over and below the preceding one. Through the hem of the under (larger) piece run a cord. This serves for tying on the bustle, and can also draw it up into a closer shirr, rendering the pannier thicker.

Pannier Bustle

This bustle is simple and easily made. It is of white cashmere with muslin lining, scalloped on the outer edge and furnished with steel springs that give it the shape illustrated.

Cut of muslin and cashmere each one piece from the pattern. Lay the pieces together. On the upper edge face with linen tape 1 inch wide. Stitch on along the narrow lines, on the right side, worsted braid for the steels. Bind the scalloped edges with narrow red worsted braid. Bend the steel springs into the proper shape. Bind the ends with linen tape, and run them in. Fasten the upper ends with a few stitches. Bind the upper edge of the pannier with braid. On the under side of the pannier, along the curved line, run in a steel. Fasten the ends with a few stitches. On each end sew a piece of linen tape 14 inches long. When putting on the pannier, run these strings back through an eyelet hole designated by a * and tie. Draw these strings tighter or looser to make the pannier round more or less. On the front corners sew strings 16 inches long for tying.

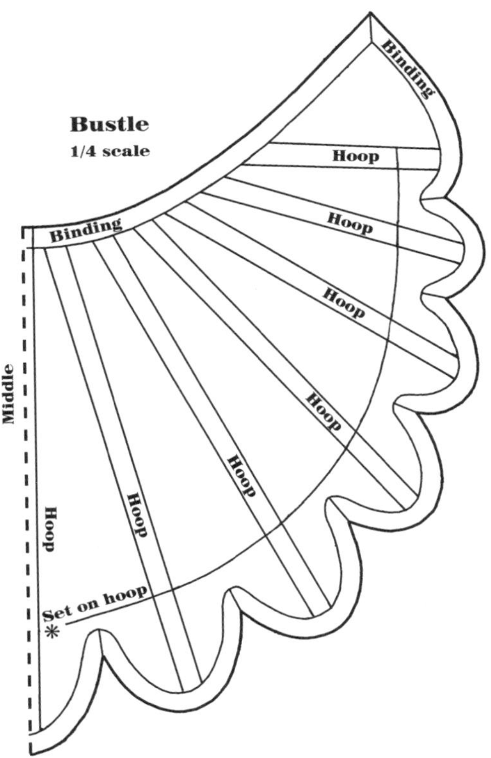

Trimmings for Underskirts

These trimmings are made partly of bias strips of the skirt material, and partly of bias strips of bright-colored silk or velvet.

The trimming in Figure 1 consists of two pleated strips and two clusters of bias folds, all of the skirt material. The pleated strips are each 4 inches wide, and are hemmed on the under edge. The pleats are narrow, and all run the same way. Above each of these arrange the bias folds. The lower one of each cluster hides the seam where the pleated strip is set on.

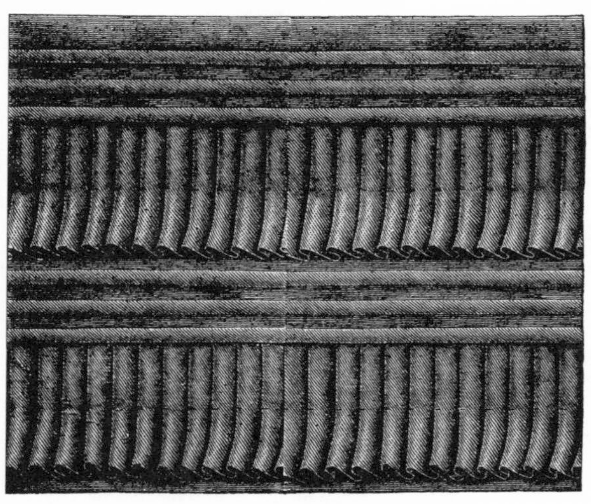

Figure 1. Trimming for colored underskirt

The underskirt for which the trimming in Figure 2 is designed must be scalloped on the under edge as shown. The edge of the scallops is then bound with colored silk. It is edged with a fluting of the skirt material 1 1/4 inches wide, which is set on underneath. Under this lay a strip of silk like the binding, and sew the scallops down on it.

Next cut a strip of the underskirt material 2 1/2 inches wide and as long as the skirt width. Cut one side in scallops the same size as those on the bottom of the underskirt. Trim with binding and fluting. Sew this on the under edge of the silk part as shown. The facing of the underskirt must be wider than the trimming and must reach above it.

Figure 2. Trimming for colored underskirt

The trimming in Figure 3 consists of a flounce 3 inches wide. The under edge is bound with colored silk. Above this flounce arrange a piece of the skirt material 1 3/4 inches wide which has been scalloped and bound, also with colored silk, on one side. Above this scalloped piece set bias folds of the skirt material edged with silk piping.

Figure 3. Trimming for colored underskirt

Underskirt with Train and Bustle

This is an elegantly trimmed white underskirt with train and bustle. The under edge of the skirt is trimmed with a fluting 3 1/2 inches wide, stitched on with a bias fold. Above this is arranged a row of points cut singly, trimmed with embroidered edging, and headed with edging and narrow insertion.

Cut the front and the side pieces, cutting the under part longer than the pattern in the direction of the arrows. Cut the back in one piece. Cut the belt.

Join the parts and hem the under edge. Fasten the upper edge between the double material of the belt, which is corded. From 30 put on a very narrow binding. Run narrow tape through this, which must be drawn up and tied in front as illustrated. Sew tape 3/4 inch wide on the back pieces as shown on the side piece. Run tape through and tie it in front to form the bustle. Finally, sew the trimming on the bottom.

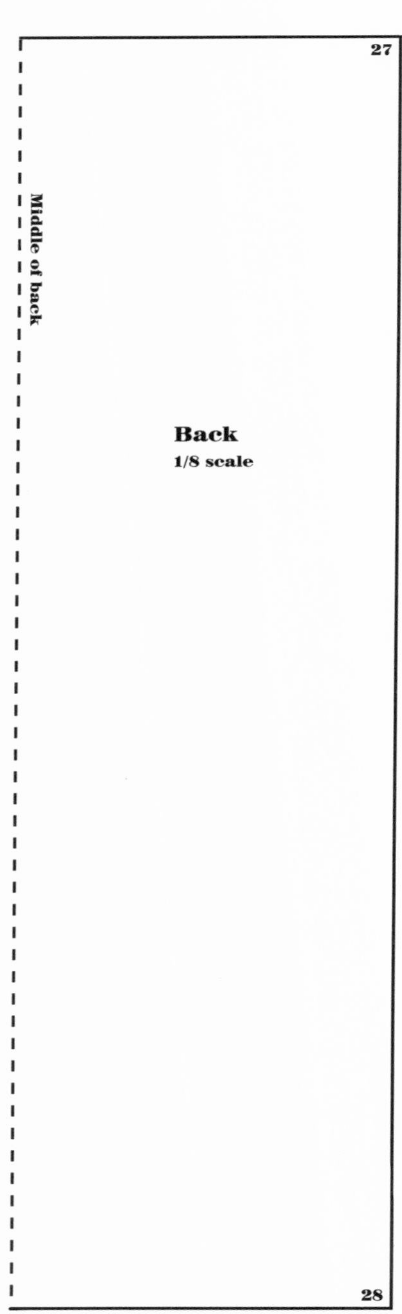
27
Middle of back
Back
1/8 scale
28

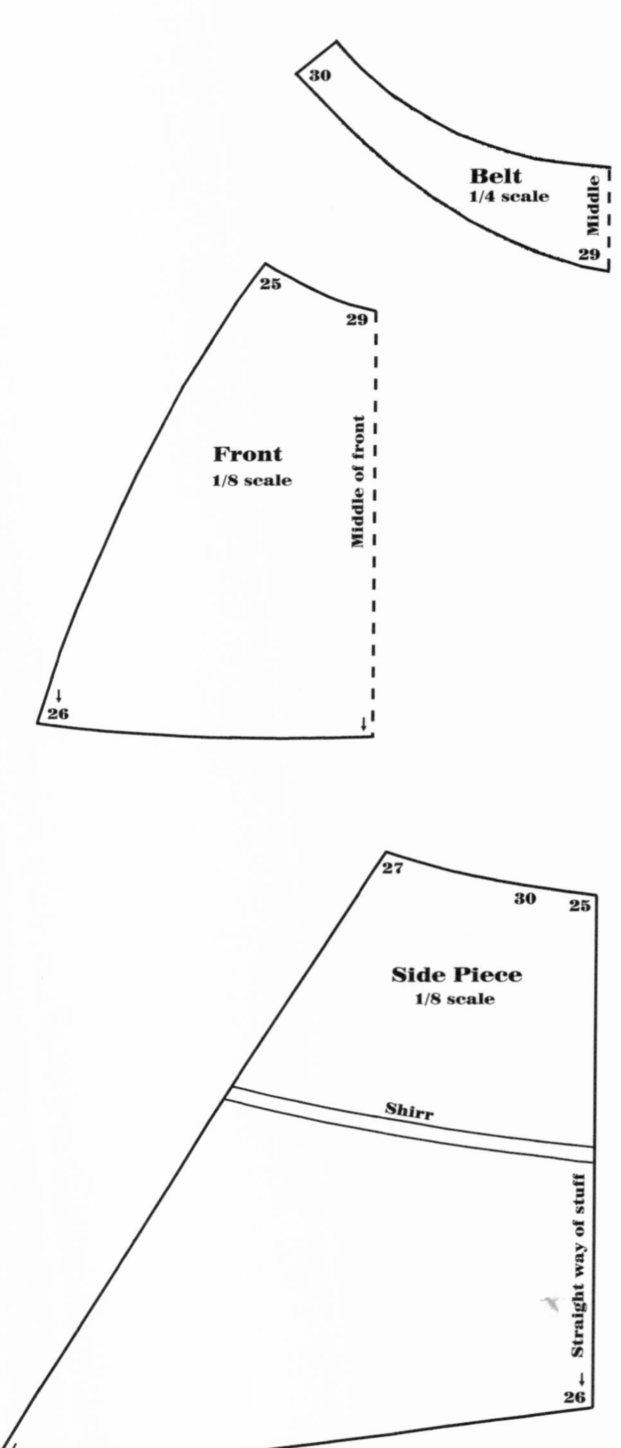
30
Belt
1/4 scale
Middle
29
25
29
Front
1/8 scale
Middle of front
26
27
30
25
Side Piece
1/8 scale
Shirr
Straight way of stuff
26
28

Underskirt Trimmed with Satin

This skirt is of black alpaca. The under part is covered 15 inches deep with striped red and black satin. Face with alpaca, and sew a black worsted cord inside the lower edge.

The skirt may be cut from the pattern for the Underskirt with Train and Bustle. However, since this skirt is without any train, the back must be cut but little longer than the front.

December 12, 1868

Bridal Toilettes

These bridal toilettes are partly for young girls and partly for widows. Those for young girls require a veil. The dresses are of white grosgrain or satin, or they may be of fine India or Swiss muslin. The skirts are gored and with trains. The waists are mostly worn high, though they are sometimes cut very low in front and finished with a high chemisette. Or a blouse may be worn instead of the waist, in which case it is cut out in front. Sashes are always of the same material as the dress.

The first figure shows a bridal toilette for a widow. The dress and sash are of white satin trimmed with wide silk fringe. The wreath and bouquet are of myrtle. Cut the skirt from the pattern for the Norderney Walking Dress in the May 23 issue. However, make allowance for the train. Cut the waist from the pattern in this issue. The illustration shows the manner of arranging the trimming.

To make the waist cut of satin, and muslin as lining, from the front and side back each two pieces. Cut from the back one piece. Cut both parts of the sleeves.

Take up the bosom pleats and face the fronts. Put on the buttons and make buttonholes. Join the back, front, and side pieces according to the corresponding figures on the pattern. Run whalebones into the side seams and bosom pleats. Cord the neck and waist.

Sew up the sleeves according to the corresponding figures on the pattern. Face the wrists. Sew the sleeves into the corded armholes. Arrange the trimming as illustrated.

The second figure shows a bridal toilette for a young girl. The wreath and bouquet are of orange flowers. The veil is of plain silk lace. The dress is of Swiss muslin, and the waist is lined with silk. The waist is cut from the pattern in this issue. It is cut out in front along the narrow line. The neck, wrists, and shoulder seams are trimmed with a narrow muslin ruche. The high chemisette is of guipure. The skirt is gored and trimmed with four muslin flounces as shown.

The third figure shows a bridal toilette for a widow. It is of white grosgrain with a high waist, cut from the pattern in this issue. The Marie Antoinette fichu is of white Valenciennes. Myrtle flowers in the hair.

The fourth figure shows a bridal toilette for a young girl. It is white satin with a high waist (cut from the pattern in this issue) and sash. The trimming is wreaths and sprays of orange blossoms, arranged as illustrated. Orange flowers form the wreath on the head. The veil is of silk lace.

The fifth figure shows a bridal toilette for a young girl. It is of white grosgrain. The polonaise is trimmed with Valenciennes insertion and edging as shown. Wreath of orange flowers. Veil of plain white silk lace.

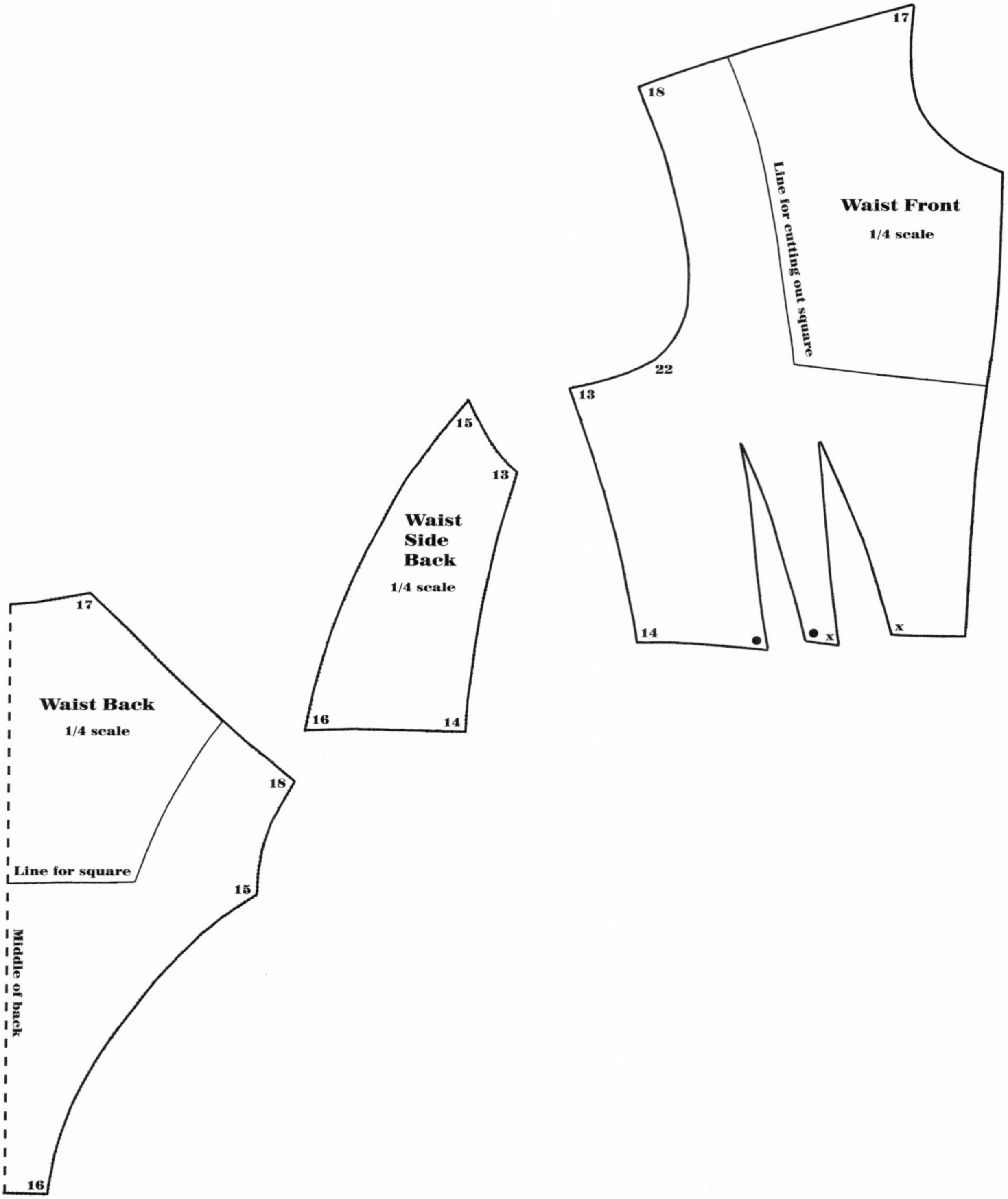

Waist Front
1/4 scale
Line for cutting out square
17
18
22
13
14
x

Waist Side Back
1/4 scale
15
13
16
14

Waist Back
1/4 scale
17
18
Line for square
15
Middle of back
16

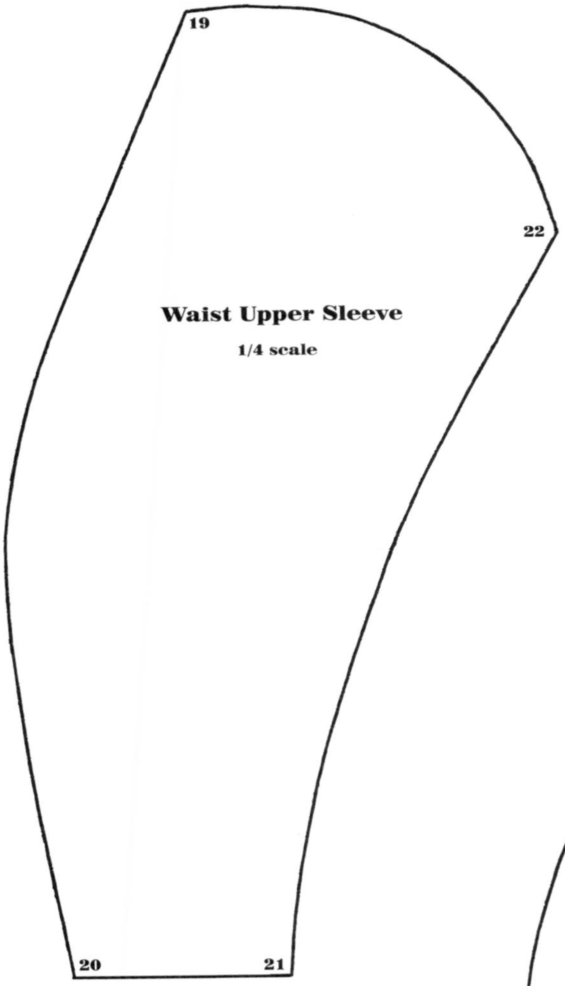

19
22
Waist Upper Sleeve
1/4 scale
20
21

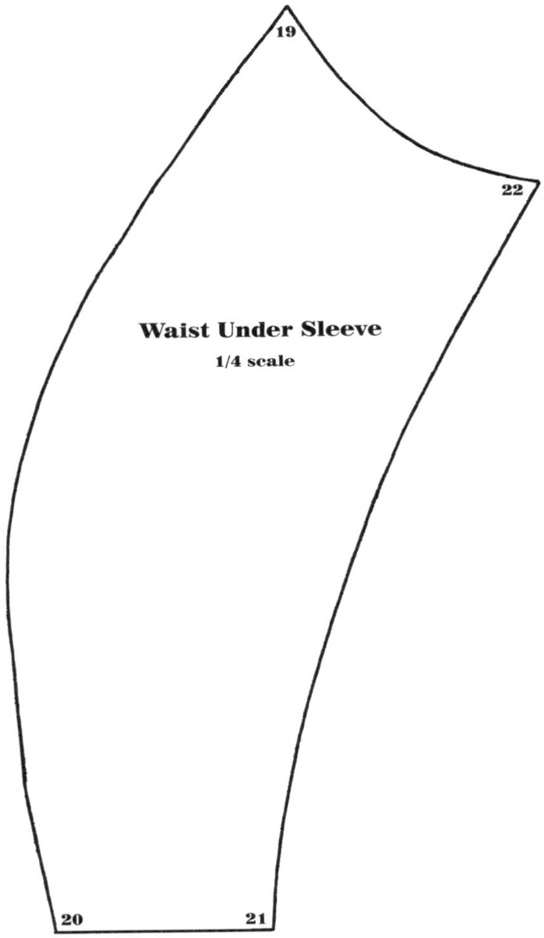

19
22
Waist Under Sleeve
1/4 scale
20
21

High Waist with Fichu and Peplum

This dress is of dark blue serge, and is completed by a fichu and peplum of the same material. Cut the waist from the same pattern as the waist for Bridal Toilettes.

For the fichu and peplum cut from the front and peplum each two equal pieces, and from the back one piece.

Backstitch together the back and front on the shoulders from 1 to 2. Lay the edges of the fichu material over on the right side. Cover with a pleated ruche 2 inches wide of the bias material. Trim the upper edge of the fichu with a pleated ruche 1 1/4 inches wide.

Cord the edges of the peplum and trim like the fichu. Finish the trimming of the fichu and peplum with a ruffle of the same width as the ruche, as illustrated.

Make a belt of the same material and finish it on the back with a rosette, also of the same material.

High Waist with Fichu

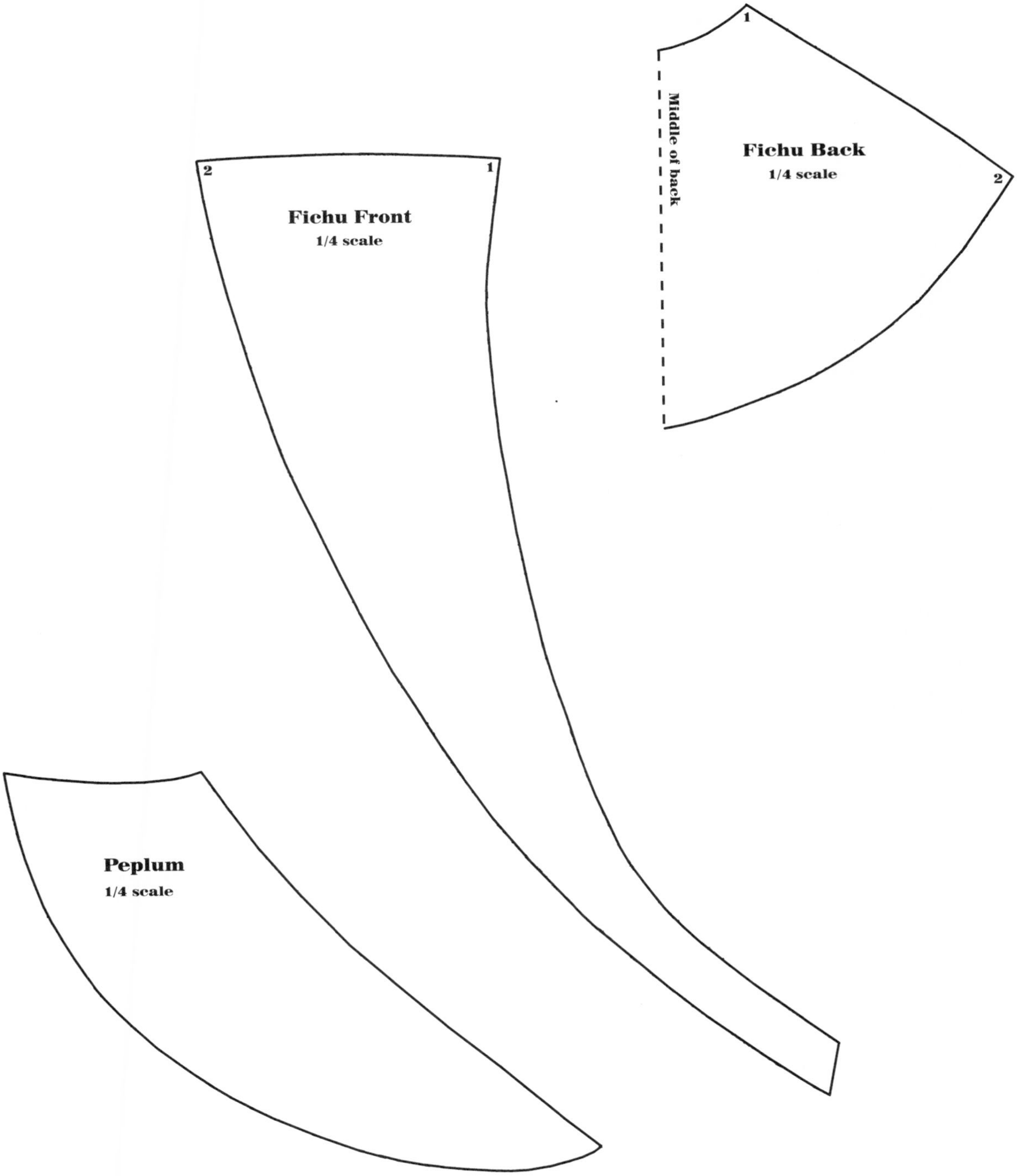

Fichu Back
1/4 scale
1
2
Middle of back

Fichu Front
1/4 scale
2
1

Peplum
1/4 scale

High Waist with Fichu and Peplum

This dress is of garnet reps with a high plain waist. The pattern given for the waist for Bridal Toilettes is suitable. The fichu and peplum are made of the dress material. They are trimmed with a cretonne fluting and bias folds of satin of the same color.

Cut the fichu and both parts of the peplum. Cord the upper edge of the fichu with satin. On the outer edges set a cretonne fluting 1 1/4 inches wide, headed with a bias satin fold. Trim the peplum with a fluting 2 1/2 inches wide and two bias folds.

The belt is of the same material 2 inches wide and edged with satin cord. Arrange the sash as illustrated.

High Waist with Fichu

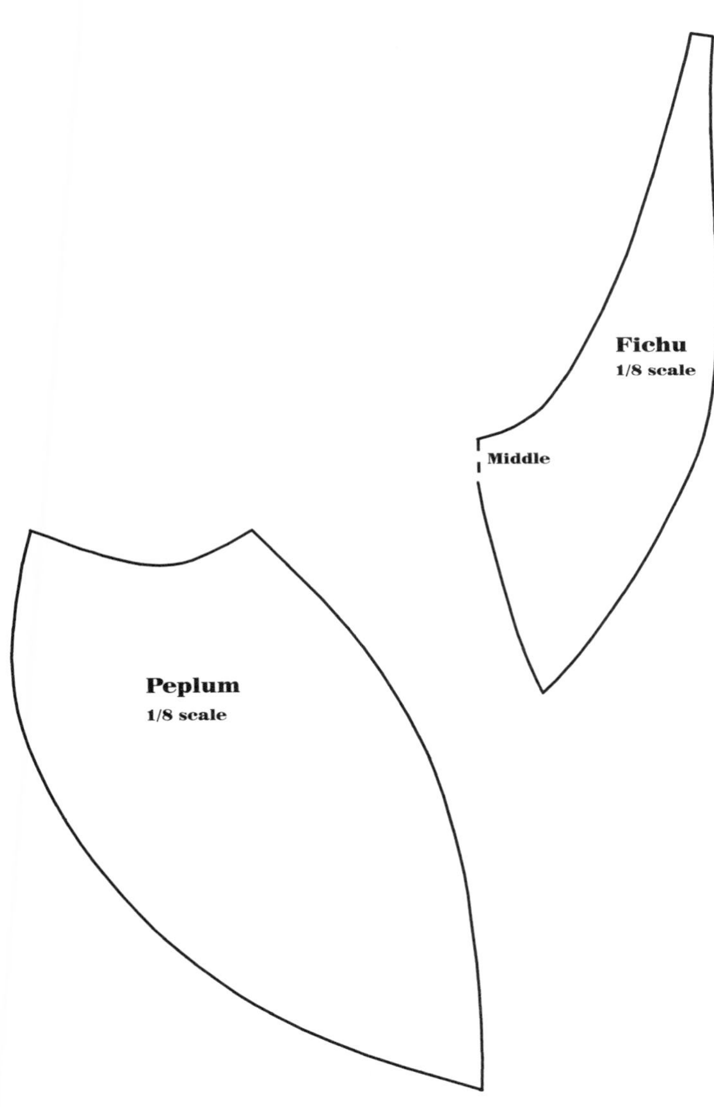

Designs for Embroidering Lace

The two designs given here serve for covers, curtains, or veils.

The stripes of the design in Figure 1 are embroidered on coarse lace, one with twist and the other with untwisted knitting cotton. The manner of working is shown at the ends of the two unfinished strips. The hole through which the needle is put for the next stitch is designated by a •, and the one through which it is drawn back on the upper side of the work by an *x*.

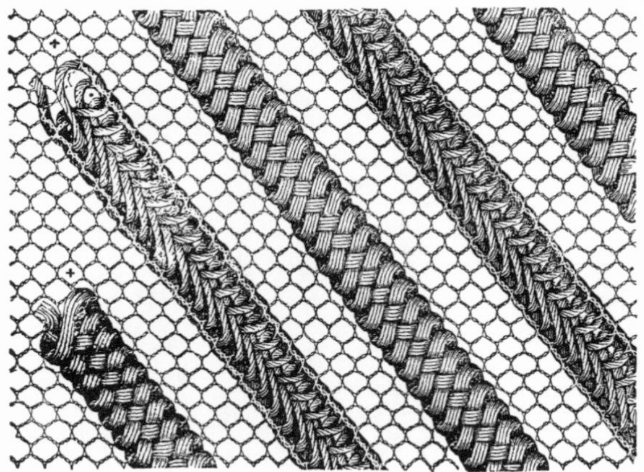

Figure 1. Design for embroidering lace

Figure 2. Design for embroidering lace

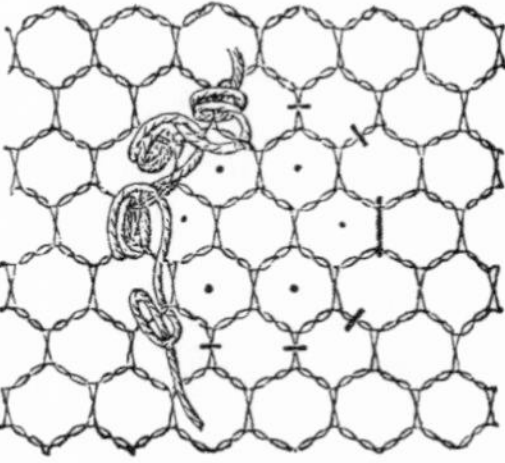

Figure 3. Manner of embroidering lace

The figures of the design in Figure 2 are worked with loose cotton or coarse filoselle silk in a kind of quilting stitch, shown in Figure 3. Always run the thread twice around the designated threads of the lace. But in the second stitch do not bring the thread out where the working of the next thread is commenced, but first in the next hole designated by a • in Figure 3. The stitches to be worked are shown by a short line.

Figured Lace Veil

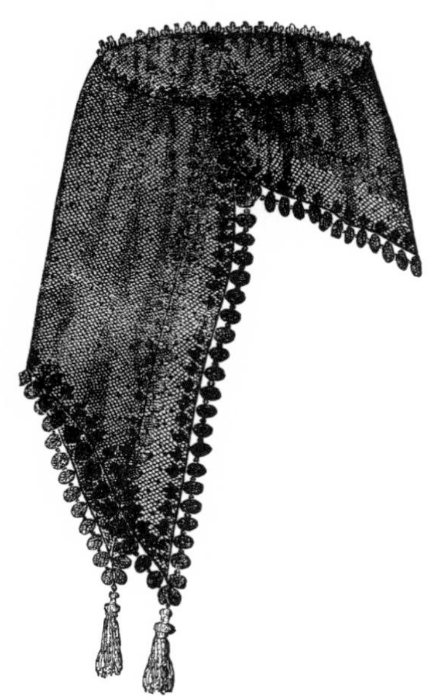

Figured Lace Veil

This veil may be worn either with round hats or bonnets. It consists of two parts, joined together with an elastic cord drawn through the top, which fastens it to the hat. It is of figured silk lace.

Cut of lace from the front and back each one piece. Border these pieces on the outer edges, except the upper edges (the front with the additional exception of the edges between 5 and 6) with lace 1 1/4 inches wide. Join the front and back according to the figures on the pattern so the lace of the back piece laps over the front. Finish the upper edges with narrow lace. Run through an elastic cord, the edges of which are tied together.

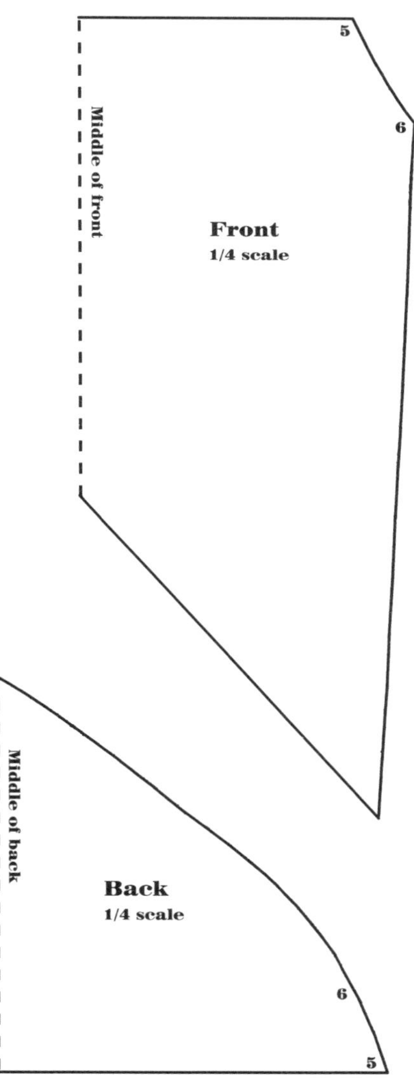

December 19, 1868

Evening Dresses

High-colored silks are in favor for evening dresses. Red in its various shades is the leading color. There is the caroubier, sultan, ruby, grenade, garnet, and a dull deep hue called "antique" red, all of which are sought after by brunettes. The brilliant poppy red, so beautiful by gaslight, is selected by blondes. Satin of the same shade trims silks of these colors for very young ladies. Black lace softens their brightness for those more advanced. Gold, yellow, and capucine are gorgeous hues in vogue this season, entirely covered with black illusion. Blue and green together appear among eccentric French toilettes. For instance a blue silk is trimmed with puffings of green tulle, or a gauze overdress of the Forty-Second plaid is worn over white silk.

Chameleon grosgrains in delicate shades of mauve, pink, and blue, shot with white, make beautiful dresses for gaslight wear. Green was too much worn last winter to remain popular this season. Glossy taffeta is used as transparents beneath chambray gauze and tulle, producing chameleon effects. The French employ foulards for this purpose.

Tarlatan and crêpe are preferred for Watteau drapery and panniers over silk, as tulle is so thin that it is scarcely perceptible. The chambray gauzes are in beautiful variety. White muslin dresses are more popular than ever, and are laden with ruffles, puffs, tucks, and lace. Organdy appears best when first made; but it is very frail, and does not wash well. The best white muslin is called French-Swiss, a paradoxical name for a more substantial yet finer material than that commonly called Swiss.

These dresses are simply worn over white lingerie, or are made very gay by wearing a colored silk evening dress beneath them—a soiled or faded dress of a previous season being made useful in this way.

Trains and Crinolines

Trains are reported to have been increased in length, but we have not seen a model that measured more than 80 inches from the waist to the floor. Three-quarters of a yard added to the length of the figure is advised by the best modistes.

Trains appear to have grown longer because they are worn over very small hoops, or without any. A skirt of haircloth, gored and trained, with three deep flounces on all but the front width, is the fashionable substitute for a steel spring skirt.

Styles of Making Dresses

The Watteau bodice of colored satin over a white silk or muslin dress is the novelty of the season. This bodice is becoming to slender, tall figures. It is a low-necked basque with added drapery fastened in a broad pleat at the top of the back, falling loosely below the waist and caught up to form a pannier puff. This drapery in thin materials over silk is also very pretty, and should have more fullness than when made of satin. It is sometimes made with high corsage like the Watteau cloak, with a square front filled in with tulle.

The Louis XV corsage, high and round, with long narrow opening in front for a chemisette, is in vogue for full-dress dinner parties. The chemisette reaches almost to the belt, and is only about 4 inches wide. Sleeves to such dresses are nearly tight, with a Pompadour bow by way of epaulet, and a deep pleated ruffle at the elbow headed by ruches. The Maria Theresa style has a wide folded chemisette and half-long sleeve flowing from the elbow.

A gathered flounce from 10 to 20 inches wide, with a heading of puffs and ruches, is the most prevalent mode of trimming trained skirts. Tablier designs of lace and ruches on the front width, with large butterfly bows at each end, are in vogue. The three full back widths are lined at the top with stiff muslin, and box pleated, to form a pannier. A sash from the belt supports the pannier, and is knotted beneath it.

Few evening dresses are made without a pannier, or tunic, except for stout people. Then the trimming is made to simulate a tunic, and a short sash with several loops is added, to give a full tournure.

Colored silk or satin pannier skirts, with apron fronts and peasant waists, are worn over white silk, and are especially pretty with short dancing dresses. Sometimes they are worn with dresses of contrasting hue, such as fawn color with cerise, blue over salmon, and, in the Pompadour colors, pink with drab or blue. These are gay and striking, and people of more quiet taste prefer the dress and pannier of two shades of the same color. This is a convenient way of concealing the soiled parts of last season's dresses, as they are usually most defaced on the front width and under the arms. A piece of chamois leather sewn in the armhole is the most efficient dress protector.

Lace tunics, with a flounce to match, are more used than ever. A lace point is draped to form a reversed tunic by putting the center in front, looping it with flowers at the side, and interlapping the ends high at the back. If lace cannot be afforded, billowy puffs of tulle, divided by satin pipings, form pretty overskirts.

Sashes are fastened at the left side near the front when the skirt has a pannier; otherwise they are placed behind to give a bulky tournure. Fan-shaped ornaments of pleated satin, bows with triple loops, and the fluted Renaissance bows are in better style than sashes.

Varieties

Round pelerine capes of lace or puffed tulle are newer than fichus crossed on the bosom. Another style is square in front, the back simulating a long pointed hood behind, with a ladder of bows in the center. Grecian folds of Lyons tulle, with a knot of satin or a bouquet on the breast, puffed bretelles, and berthas of blonde and lace, ornament low corsages. The short sleeve is puffed usually, and is longer than last winter. The extreme décolleté styles lately worn are very much moderated. Wide black velvet bretelles, embroidered with white marguerites, adorn many dresses.

Short dresses will come into very general use during the holiday gaieties. They are made with two skirts, flounced and panniered precisely like street suits, without the outer garment.

Long gloves, with four or six buttons on the wrist, are most used for evening wear. Flesh tints are preferred to pure white.

The Marie Antoinette slipper, with a point behind, a curved heel, and a rosette covering the instep, is frequently worn. But a gaiter matching the dress, or else white, is the popular shoe for parties.

Headdresses are full diadems, with side sprays and jeweled butterflies and aigrettes. Pink and white eglantine are in great favor this season; and there can be nothing more beautiful than the simple wild rose.

The Marie Antoinette fan of white or buff silk, or lapis and emerald satin, is painted in gay designs after Watteau and Lancret. The sticks are opal-tinted pearl, with a point lace border at the top barred with pearl. A pretty fan is of pink or blue satin with Valenciennes edge and carved sticks of imitation ivory.

Powdered hair in the antique style is greatly in favor, especially with married ladies. Natural blonde hair is highly prized when of a yellowish golden hue. When nature has not supplied this fashionable tint art is resorted to. High crimped chignon, with a row of puffs above the forehead and frizzed curls falling low on the face, is the best style for dinner coiffure. Soft flowing curls for evening entertainments.

Opera Bonnets and Wrappings

A pouf of white royal velvet or rose-pink or China blue in corrugated folds is the most elegant round hat for evening wear. A marabou cluster, or a spray of flowers with an aigrette of white heron's feathers is in front, and a double bow of thick satin on top. Bonnets are high diadems of velvet with two or three velvet bars across the head, displaying the elaborately dressed hair between. A deep pelerine of Spanish blonde edged with lace covers the chignon, and is fastened in front with a bouquet.

The MacFarlane cloak, a circular with a cape in front concealing the arms and a hood behind, is the handsomest evening wrapping. It is made in velvet cloth striped with satin, trimmed with chenille fringe.

Cravat End in Braid and Lace Stitch

This cravat is 32 inches long. The end is shown full size.

First draw the design for the braid on stiff paper. Sew the narrow white cotton braid on this. The braid is joined together by buttonhole stitch as shown. Work two rows; buttonhole stitch on the outer edges.

To make this cravat more quickly, sew the braid on fine lace, which takes the place of the lace stitch.

Cravat End in Mignardise and Crochet

This cravat is 32 inches long. The end is shown full size.

Crochet with fine cotton as follows the loops on one side of the mignardise. First round: * Work 1 sc. (single crochet) in the first loop, six times alternately 3 ch. (chain), 1 sc. in the following loop of the mignardise, and pass over the following six loops. Repeat from * till the work is double the desired length of the cravat. Then cut off the mignardise and working thread.

Second round: Work 1 sc. in the middle stitch of each of the following 5 chain-stitch scallops, after every sc. 4 ch., then * 1 sl. (slip stitch) in the middle stitches of the 2 chain-stitch scallops in the deep hollow between two scallops of the mignardise 4 ch., 1 sc. in each of the next 4 chain-stitch scallops, after every sc. 4 ch. From * repeat.

Then crochet also in the loops on the other side of the mignardise a round like the first round, and after this a round like the second round. The last is, however, worked only to the middle of the strip. In continuing the second round double the strip together at half its length. In working every middle 1 of the successive 5 chain-stitch scallops, fasten to the middle 1 of the opposite 5 chain-stitch scallops of the finished half.

The ends of the cravat are made as shown. Through the middle run green velvet ribbon.

December 26, 1868

Jewelry

The fashion is to imitate antique models, classic and barbaric, such as were copied last year.

Pendants in the shape of gold fringes and lockets swing from every article of jewelry. Brooches are arranged to be worn as pendants from necklaces. Earrings are long and slender, or else large hoops. Bracelets are narrow 1/2-inch bands, with the long marquise medallion in the center, or the ribbon bracelet of innumerable links of gold as pliable as ribbon. Rings are small hoops of gold with a long oval medallion of enamel or a setting of stones.

Diamonds and Pearls

The knife-edge setting, as jewelers term a slender threadlike border of gold, is the best style for brilliant stones. The gold is scarcely visible, and is only employed to hold the diamonds securely. If a color must be associated with diamonds select one of the dark rich stones, such as the velvetlike blue sapphire, darkest green emeralds, or rubies. A superb ring shown us has a square medallion bordered by diamonds, and in the center a large sapphire.

Pearls in unison with pale blue turquoise are greatly in favor. Strung seed pearls are usually chosen for brides. For general use rose pearls in Etruscan gold, or in the new perforated setting of gold with a reddish tinge. Three different races of pearls are represented in one bracelet, a glossy black pearl, a rose pink, and a milk-white pearl.

Turquoise, Coral, Etc.

Turquoise is more in favor just now than any colored stone for evening dress. A dark shade of scarlet coral is handsomest when mounted with diamonds, and there is then no danger of mistaking it for the coralline imitation. Emeralds begin to find a rival in the sea green chrysoprase which is now cut in cameos and set in diamonds. Amethysts have had their day for the present.

Malachite is a popular stone for morning and evening wear, but it necessitates a black, white, or green dress. A handsome set includes brooch, earrings, and sleeve buttons. Dark lapis lazuli is chosen in polished flat surfaces with pendant drops. Pretty sets of crystal are engraved on the reverse side in floral designs, such as lily of the valley, and painted in vivid colors.

Perforated Gold and Enamel

Perforated gold jewelry is the novelty of the season. It is made of red gold pierced in intricate patterns like lace. The workmanship is elaborate and very difficult to execute. Pale Roman gold in Pompeian designs continues in favor.

Unpolished enamel on gold is the most artistic jewelry worn. Floral designs are in better taste than sacred subjects. A new fancy is for Japanese designs.

Byzantine Mosaics and Cameos

Byzantine mosaics in Egyptian designs are greatly worn, and are suitable for a larger variety of dresses than any other jewels. A full parure has infinitesimal stones of most brilliant colors.

Among a rare collection of historic cameos is the profile of Marie de' Medici, the head of Isabella of Castile, and the full face of Gabrielle d'Estrées on black onyx mounted in perforated gold with pearls and diamonds. A bright green chrysoprase represents Castor and Pollux.

Lockets and Necklaces

A pretty Christmas gift is a locket now universally worn, pendant from a gold necklace or a velvet ribbon. Roman gold in massive Egyptian design, with a monogram or an inscription in turquoises or brilliants, is one of the handsomest styles. More delicate ones are of fine red gold in a perforated pattern. A pretty oval locket is of blue enamel studded with pearl. A locket shaped like a jockey cap has a watch with a face as small as a ten-cent piece. The self-winding key is at the side, and the movement is very fine. A Byzantine cross is worn as a pendant.

The Genoese ropework necklaces are very beautiful, and newer than the spiral chains.

Slipper Design in Application

In the illustration the slipper is of gray cloth; of course any other color may be chosen. The design is in various bright colors of cloth and black, worked on and embroidered with different colored silk twist using the stitches shown.

Appendix A Dressmaking and Pattern Alterations

This material is drawn from articles in the September 4, 1869 *Harpers Bazar*.

Dressmaking

The sewing machine is invaluable for making dress corsages. With the proper tension, every seam can be sewn more neatly and substantially than it could possibly be done by the fingers.

Fashionably made corsages show the figure in its natural and beautiful proportions. The seams follow as closely as may be the outlines of the figure. For instance, shoulder seams are placed on the shoulder, not back of it, as was formerly the case. There is no attempt to make the back look narrow by placing the side seam behind the arm instead of under it. The shoulders do not extend over the arm, but are short enough to make the armhole in its appropriate place. Armholes should be ample enough for comfort.

The inner seam of a sleeve should fall over the center of the arm. When the sleeve is being sewn in the armhole it should be held above, so that its slight fullness may be gradually gathered into the armhole. The sleeve will then stand out properly around the armhole.

The waist is of natural length, neither immoderately short nor long, but terminates at the natural taper just above the hips; nor is it compressed by tight lacing. Easy-fitting corsets, with but few whalebones, are worn to support the figure, but not to make it smaller.

Many ladies prefer to have the dress skirt separate from the waist and attached to a belt. To prevent the two portions of the dress from parting, it is well to extend the waist over the hips in loose, easy flaps, to be thrust under the skirt. The whalebones do not extend over the hips, but stop at the narrowest taper of the corsage.

Shoulder seams are no longer corded. A cord is not required around the neck if a standing band is used. If the dress is cut away low at the throat, according to the summer fashion, it is corded without a band. Armholes are always corded. Many modistes object to cording the waist at the belt, as the cord is apt to draw. They use instead a bias facing stitched on to give it sufficient strength.

Blouse waists may be made from the patterns for tight waists. Merely omit to seam up the bosom pleats, allowing the fullness to form gathers to be attached to a belt.

Satin jean and ordinary twilled cotton are the materials most used for dress linings. They are durable and firm. Consequently they wear well, and do not stretch out of shape. Linen is also used. But it is elastic, soon shows soil, and is objectionable on account of the chilled feeling it gives the wearer when it is first put on. Modistes prefer silk linings as they fit to the figure more smoothly, and give the garment a more tasteful appearance. Thick substantial taffeta is used for this purpose.

White lining is used for all dresses with light grounds. Dark drab and gray are used for thick colored materials. One yard and 1/8 is the quantity required. Gray silk is usually selected for dark dresses, but brighter colors are often chosen by way of variety.

Waists of grenadine dresses, when cut high in the neck, are lined throughout with substantial silk and fitted to the figure by bosom pleats. It is the exception to the rule this season to make thin dresses with blouse waists over low linings. If it is desired to display the neck and arms, the whole corsage is cut low and worn with a lace chemisette or fichu.

Low corsages for full-dress occasions are buttoned in front when the waist is partly concealed

Appendix A

Figure 1. Taking the measure–front

by a bertha or other elaborate trimming. If the low bodice is but little trimmed, it is fastened behind by eyelets and a silk cord for lacing. Buttons should not be set on a dress waist merely for ornament. They are for use, not show, and require button-holes opposite to make them effective. Fancy bows on the front of the corsage are much used at present. Hooks and eyes beneath them fasten the waist securely.

Underskirts of short suits are lined throughout with paper muslin. They are faced with haircloth or foundation muslin, to give them proper stiffness. Wigging is no longer used. Trained dresses of thick material are too heavy and burdensome to require lining. A deep facing of haircloth, covered at the bottom with silk or alpaca in the dress color, is preferred for trained skirts.

Taking the Measures

The patterns given in the *Bazar* are of one form, and of course cannot fit everybody. To alter them to be useful to all our subscribers, the measurements

Taking the Measures

Figure 2. Taking the measure–back

must first be taken by the following rules. They must be very exact, to make the pattern fit well.

The tape measure is laid on the waist as shown by Figures 1 and 2. Note the measurements; but in the widths only half the measurement must be allowed.

Begin with the most important measurement, the width under the arms. Lay the tape measure across the back, run it under the arms, and join the ends in the middle of the front, letting it lie rather loose all the time. For the width across the bust, measure from one arm to the other; the measure must lie loosely.

In taking the under measure round the lower part of the waist, lay the tape measure around to fit. Then take off from 1/2 to 1 inch if it be desired to make it tighter. The length of the waist is measured from under the arm.

Take the length of the sleeve by measuring along the inside seam from the top of the sleeve to the wrist.

Take the measures for the length and width of the back, as well as the length of the shoulder seams, as shown in Figure 2. For the skirt measure the length on the front, back, and sides.

For a tight paletot or jacket, measure in the same manner as for a dress waist, except all the measures must be somewhat wider. Measure lengths as for a dress waist. For a sacque paletot, measure only the back and bust widths and the length of the shoulder.

Increasing or Diminishing the Pattern

Decide before cutting the pattern whether it needs to be enlarged or diminished. By altering as shown, the size is changed but the form remains the same, by which means a perfect fit of waist will be ensured. Patterns for jackets, paletots, mantillas, etc. may be altered in the same manner.

Compare the measurements you have taken with the pattern by laying them on (see Figure 3). If the pattern does not correspond to them, it must be altered as shown. The heavy line shows the contour of the pattern given. The narrow line shows at what points and in what proportion it must be enlarged. The dotted line shows at what points and in what proportion it must be diminished.

Shorten or lengthen the sleeve on the upper and under edges so the elbow remains in the proper position. The upper edge of the sleeve should be about 3/4 inch wider than the armhole, and should

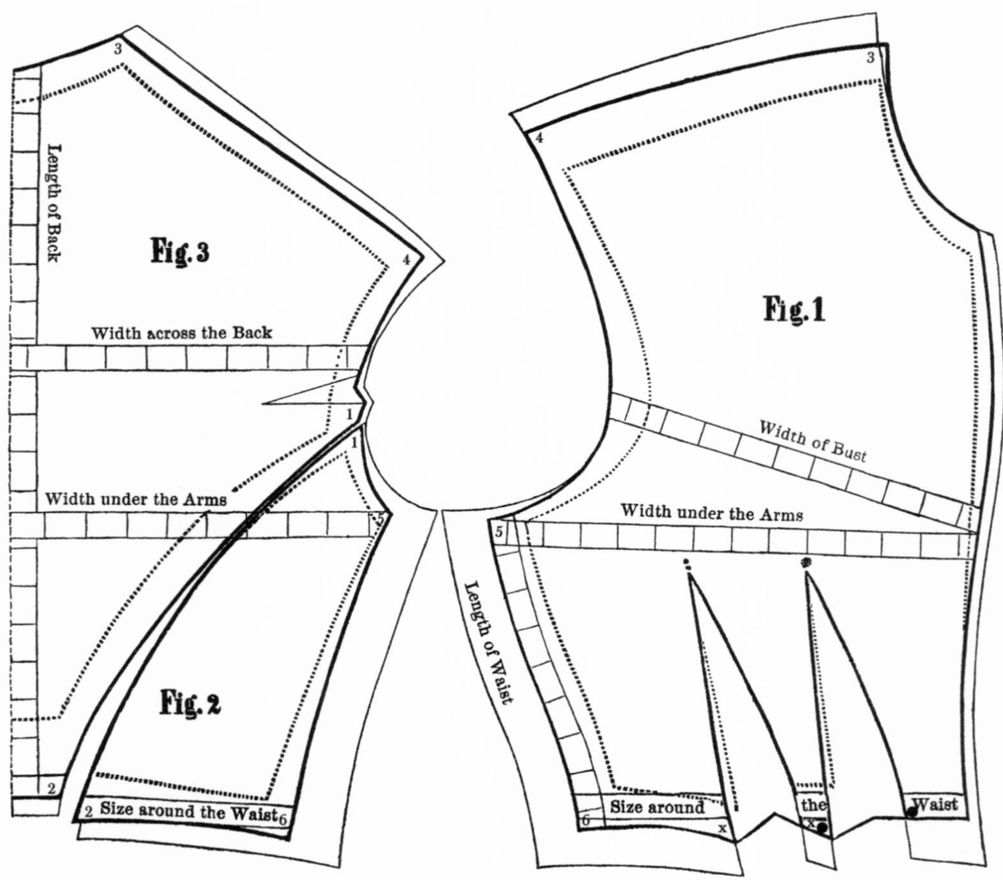

Figure 3. Enlarging and diminishing the pattern

be held in when sewing in the sleeve. If it is still wider, lay a little pleat in the under side.

Cutting the Waist and Skirt

For a waist cut first the linings of fine muslin or drilling. Double the material at half its width, and fasten the patterns with pins smoothly on the material. The back, which is always cut in one piece for a dress fastening in front, is laid along the middle on the straight edge of the material, which is folded over. Along the contours of the patterns stick a coarse needle through the material, to mark them with a row of holes. Then cut the waist, allowing 3/4 inch for the seams and 1/4 inch on the neck and waist. Allow 1 inch on both fronts for the hems.

Take up the bosom pleats marked on the patterns. If small pleats are designated on the fronts and back, take these up next. Set along the middle of the under part of the back a piece of linen tape 4 inches long and 2/5 inch wide. Sew together the pieces along the dotted contours, and according to the corresponding figures on the pattern.

Now try on the waist wrong side out. Make what alterations seem necessary. This is easily done by taking up or letting out the seams. The positions of the seams must now be carefully marked, and the bosom pleats taken higher or lower, as the arm or shoulder requires. Rip the pieces apart again and take out the bosom pleats. Baste the lining carefully on the outside, which must be cut exactly to correspond to the lining.

Figure 4 gives instructions for cutting a gored skirt. The straight lines indicate the straight edge of the material, and give half the front and back breadths. The dashed lines give the sloping of the breadths on the upper and under edges and sides. Make the length of the skirt from the measurements already taken. For a trailing skirt cut the back breadths from 8 to 20 inches longer (according to the desired length) than the side breadths. In figured materials the figures must run the same way in all the breadths.

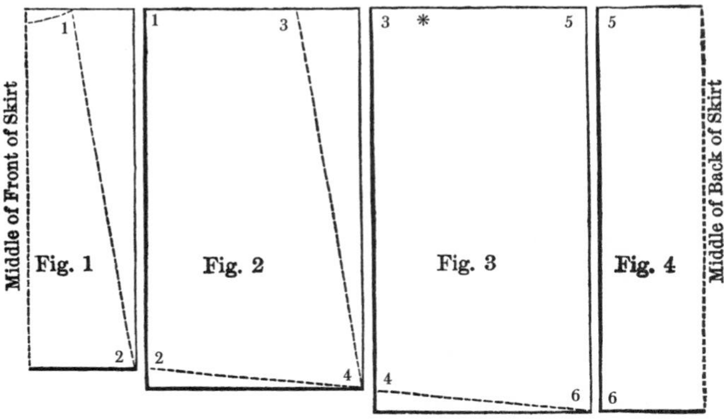

Figure 4. Cutting the skirt

Making the Waist

If the waist is to be buttoned, hem the fronts 1 inch wide before sewing the parts together. Work the buttonholes on the right front, and sew the buttons on the left. Figure 5 shows how to work the buttonholes. First run a thread around the edge of each, after which cut the buttonhole. Work the edges loosely with overcast stitches. Work the buttonhole by bringing the needle through close above the threads, then winding the thread again around the needle, etc. The ends are worked in the same manner, but not till both sides are completed.

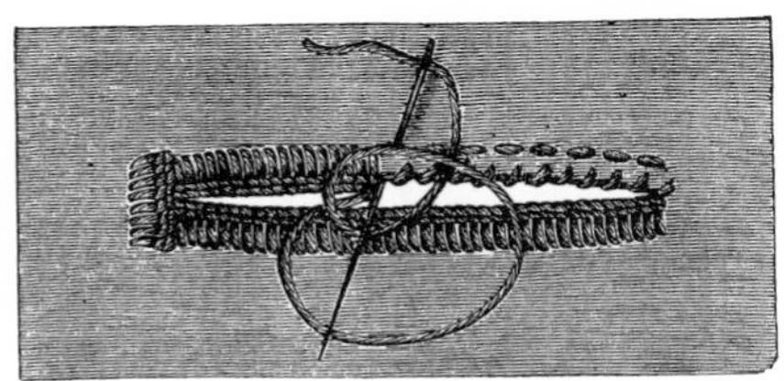

Figure 5. Making buttonhole

Figures 6 and 7 show the manner of sewing on buttons. Lay the button on the designated place, and sew it on from the under side with coarse thread. The button is sewn only in the middle of the under part. The stitches must take up as little space as possible so as not to stretch the buttonhole apart. Then run the needle out on the right side, wind the stitches six or eight times with the thread, and fasten the thread on the under side.

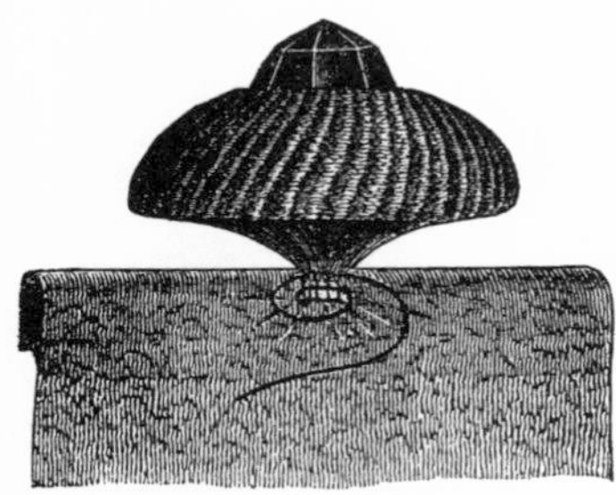

Figure 6. Sewing on button

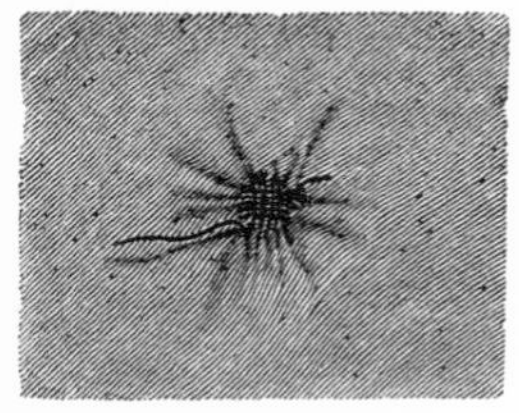

Figure 7. Sewing on button–wrong side

Instead of buttons, the waist may be fastened with hooks and eyes. Sew the eyes to an under strip (made of outside and lining). Stitch the strip on the left front, covering the place where the eye was set on. Sew the hooks on the hem of the right front as shown by Figure 8. In doing so fasten both layers of the lining, but leave the outside material alone. Then hem down the outside, and run the points of the hooks through it.

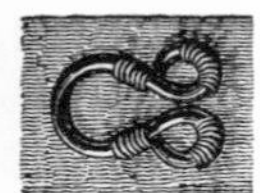

Figure 8. Sewing on hook and eye

Low-necked waists are of late fastened again behind. The backs are arranged for a cord. Turn down the outside material 1 1/2 inches on the under side. Prepare the double material for two round slender whalebones, as shown by Figure 9. Then work the intervening space with eyelets, after which run in the whalebones as below.

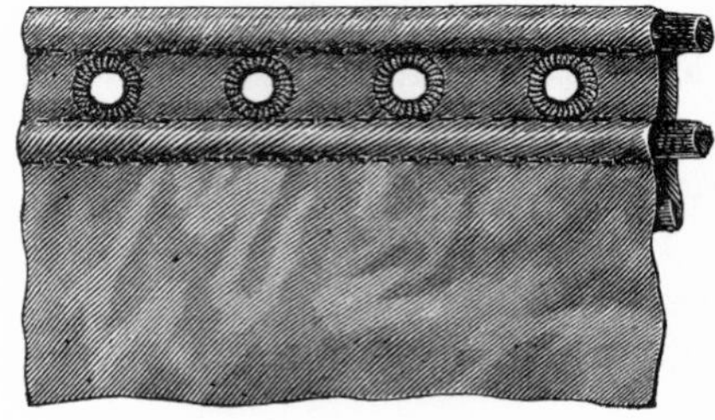

Figure 9. Sewing in whalebones and making eyelets

Take up the bosom pleats, and backstitch together the different parts of the waist. Cut away the front edges of the seams of the side pieces and the front edge of the seam of the fronts, to the width of 2/5 inch. Then run a line of stitching about 2/5 inch from the back edges of these seams, taking care not to put the needle through the outside material. In the space thus formed, and in the spaces which must be made in like manner in the bosom pleats, and also in that formed by the tape on the back, run in whalebones. Run holes in the ends of the whalebones and fasten them carefully to the waist lining. The stitches must not show on the right side. Figure 12 gives the wrong side of a waist with the shoulder seams not yet sewn up, and shows distinctly how far the whalebones must reach.

Making the Waist

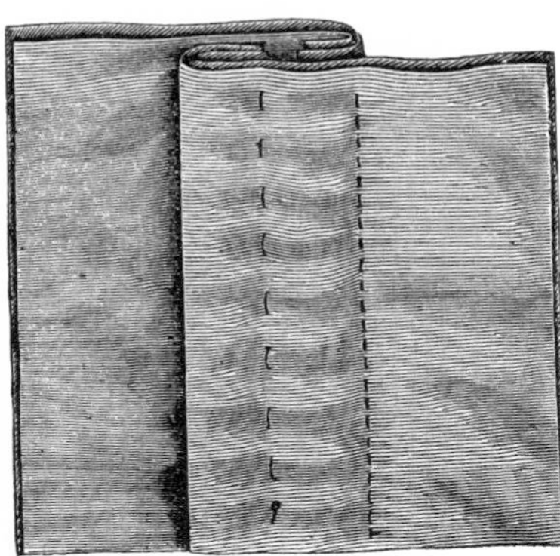

Figure 10. Sewing seam of waist

The neck and bottom of the waist are corded. The cord is run in a bias strip of the material 1 inch wide, or in silk that corresponds to it. Sew this cord on the right side of the waist, backstitching close to the cord so that its edge extends about 2/5 inch beyond the edge of the waist (see Figure 13). This is then hemmed down on the wrong side (see Figure 14) so the cord forms the edge of the waist, and the stitches are not visible on the right side.

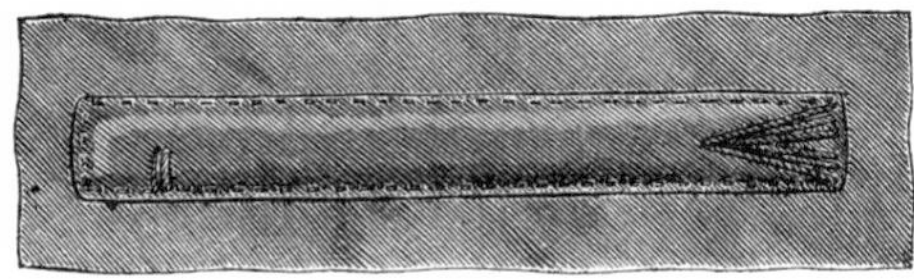

Figure 11. Fastening whalebone

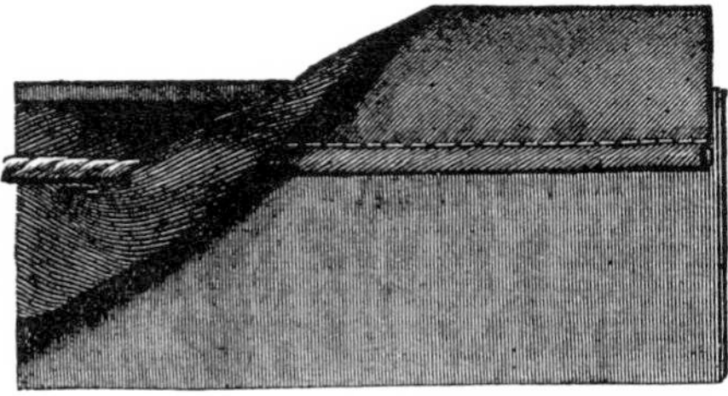

Figure 13. Sewing on cord

Figure 12. Wrong side of high waist

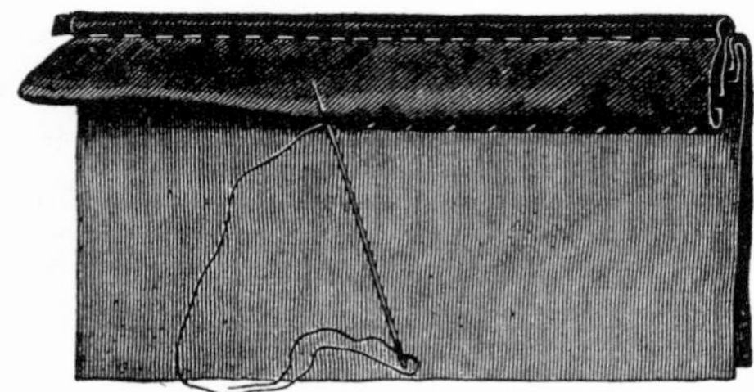

Figure 14. Hemming down cord

Cord the armhole around the dotted line in Figure 12. The edge of this cord must lie along the edge of the waist material, and the ends must extend about 1/4 inch over each other on the waist side seam. Sew in the sleeve, and overcast the armhole seams.

Finally, sew to the armholes loops for hanging up the dress. Double a strip of bias material 1 inch wide, and of the requisite length. Lay a cord along the middle, and hem the edges together as shown by Figure 15. Then turn the ends over 1/6 inch and sew the loop on the garment as shown by Figure 16.

Figure 15. Loop inlaid with cord

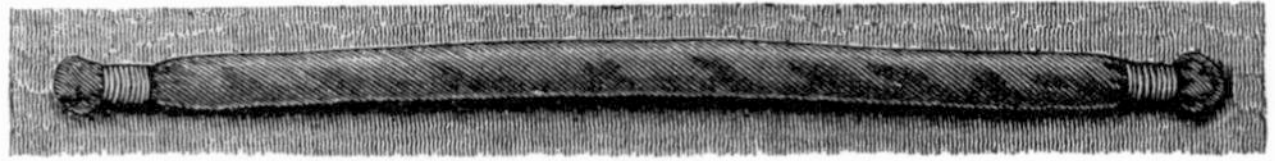

Figure 16. Sewing on loop

Making the Skirt

The skirt breadths are backstitched together and the seams overcast, or they are joined with a double seam. In sewing a bias and straight edge together the bias edge must lie above. In silk stuffs, which are generally very firmly woven, it is advisable to cut little slits in the selvage 3 or 4 inches apart to prevent the seams from drawing. The slit of the skirt is about 14 inches long, and is left open on the left side. The slit for the pocket is on the right side between the front and side breadths.

Having sewn the breadths together, face the bottom with a strip of foundation muslin 12 inches wide, to stiffen the skirt and keep the bottom clean. Then sew a piece of the outside material, 4 inches wide, to the foundation on the wrong side. Turn so the seam lies inside (see Figure 17) and the under edges come together.

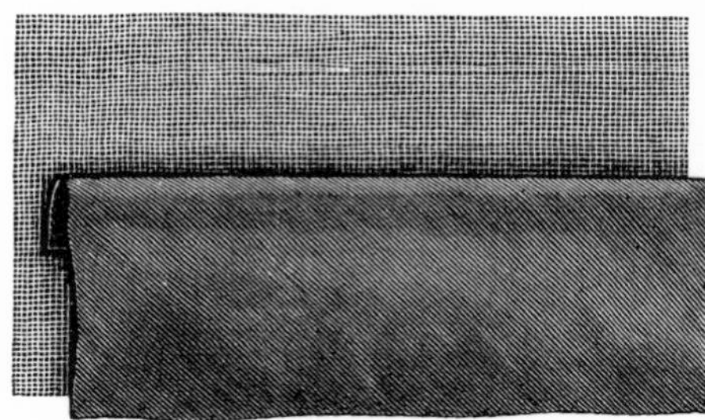

Figure 17. Sewing on facing with foundation muslin

Run this facing on the skirt, in doing which the right sides must come together. Then turn so that the seams lie inside, as shown by Figure 18. Lay the skirt on a table, and turn up the foundation smoothly on the inside. As the skirt is smaller above than below, the foundation must be sloped off at the seams and the ends joined. The foundation may also be cut in separate pieces from the skirt pattern, and sewn up like the skirt. In sewing on the foundation run the needle from right to left horizontally through the stuff, but work from left to right.

Making the Skirt

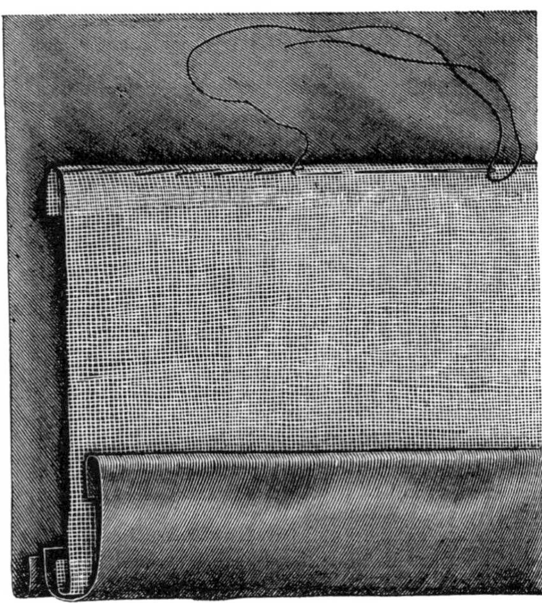

Figure 18. Sewing on foundation muslin facing

Bind the bottom with woolen or silk braid, which must be stitched down along the right side (see Figure 19) and then hemmed down on the wrong side (see Figure 20). The skirt may also be edged with cord, sewn on with overcast stitches.

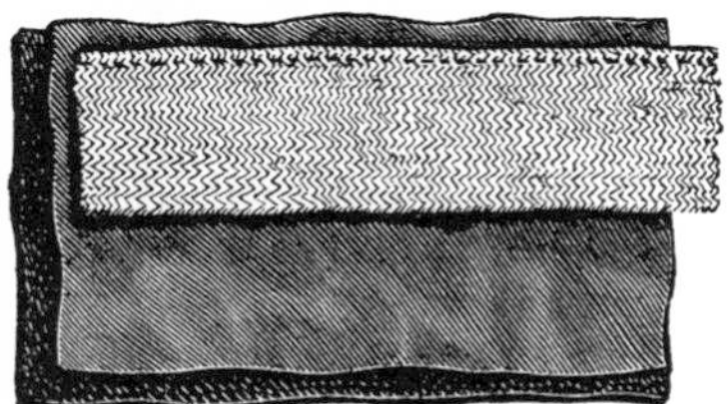

Figure 19. Sewing on braid–right side

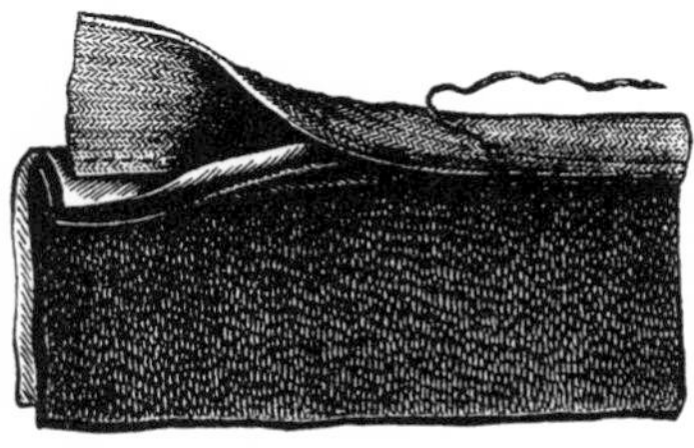

Figure 20. Sewing on braid–wrong side

On the left side of the slit set an under piece 1 1/2 inches wide. Hem the right side, and lay it over 1 inch on the under side. Or a piece may also be set on the side breadth, in which case an under piece is set on the back breadth, and the edge is not laid over on the under side.

The upper edge of the skirt is pleated and gathered. Lay each side breadth in a few pleats, running toward the front. The front breadth may also be laid in a pleat on each side. Then bind the skirt on the double material of a belt 1 inch wide, of the outside and lining. In doing so gather the back of the skirt from the middle to * on Figure 4, as shown in Figure 21. The pleats are again sewn together 1 inch from the upper edge. To make the back fuller a piece of lining 12 inches long, and of the requisite width, may be gathered in with the skirt. In sewing on the belt let the left side breadth lap 2 1/2 inches under the back breadth, so the slit will not be visible.

Figure 21. Arranging and sewing pleats

The ends of the belt are provided with hooks and eyes. In fastening the skirt first hook the single hook into the eye on the left end of the belt, and then the two hooks into the two corresponding eyes. The skirt, which must not be sewn to the waist, must be furnished with several hooks on the inside of the belt, for which corresponding eyes must be sewn on the bottom of the waist on the outside. For hanging up the skirt finish the back of the belt with two loops.

Sewing Seams

These seams are for heavy woolen materials. The invisible seam shown in Figure 22 is used for piecing. It is worked from the wrong side, similar to overcast stitch. But the needle must be run through but half the thickness of the edge of the material, so the seam is invisible on the right side.

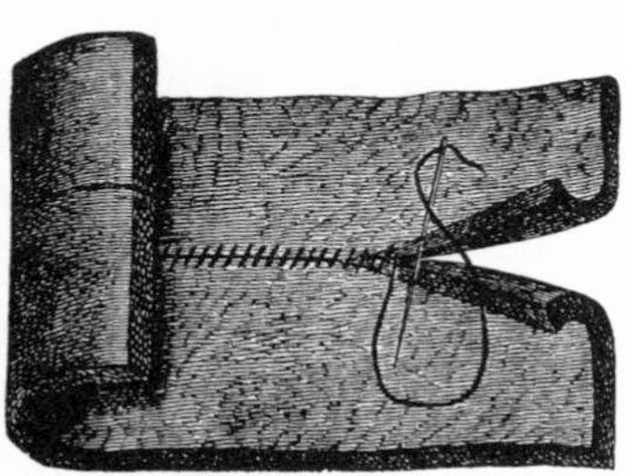

Figure 22. Invisible seam

Figures 23 and 24 show a flat seam. Backstitch the edges of the material together from the wrong side. Press the seam out with the fingers or a flatiron. Hem the edges down on the inside without putting the needle through on the right side.

Figure 23. Flat seam–right side

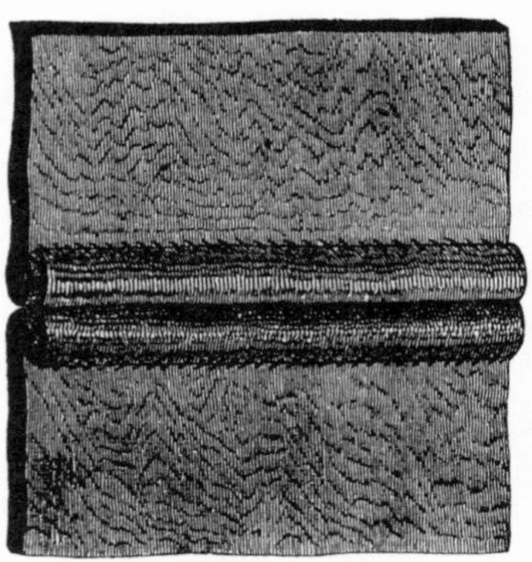

Figure 24. Flat seam–wrong side

To sew the double seam in Figure 25, lay the upper edge of the material 1/5 inch from the edge of the under piece so both right sides lie together. Lay the upper piece over and stitch it down where the seam needs to be stitched, through only two thicknesses of the material.

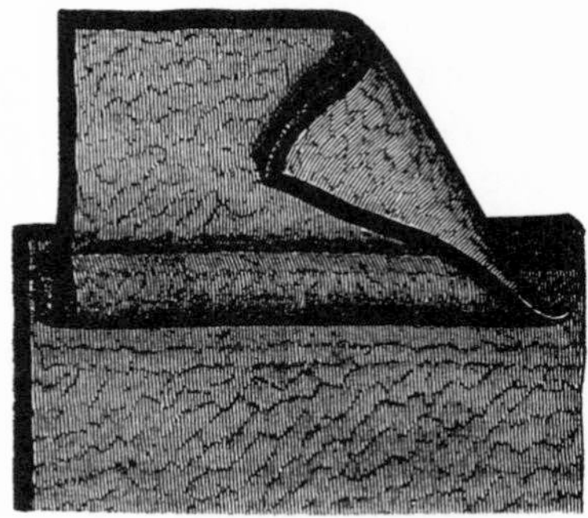

Figure 25. Double seam

The cord seam shown in Figures 26 and 27 not only sews the different pieces of material together but forms a pretty trimming, as the edge of the upper piece stands out in relief, like a cord. Lay the edge of the upper piece 1/5 inch over on the under side. Stitch it down on the under piece a hair's breadth from the edge.

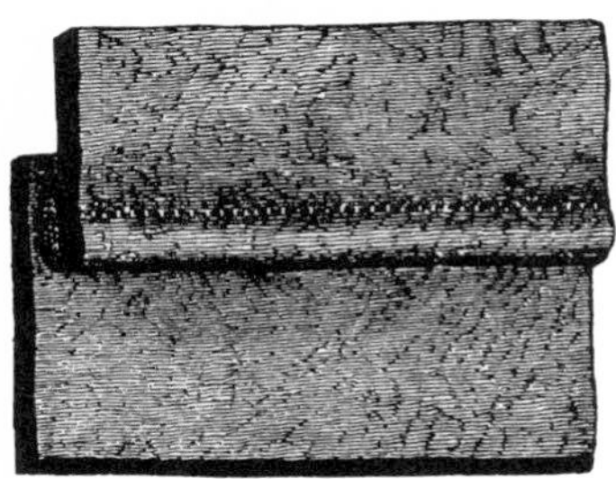

Figure 26. Cord seam

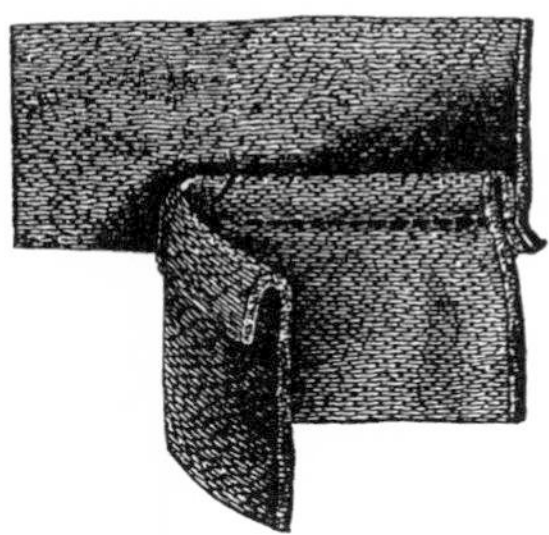

Figure 27. Making cord seam

We will call this the invisible hem. Figures 28 and 29 show the manner of binding. The strip that forms the binding is laid on the outside of the material and run down as far from the edge as the binding should be wide. Then lay it over on the under side, and sew it down so the stitches are not visible. For making this hem take a few threads of the material on the needle, and then run it through the strip. The points through which the needle is run are designated by • and *x*.

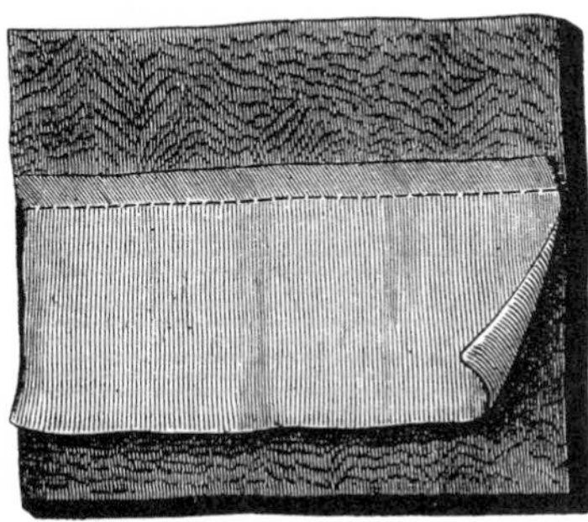

Figure 28. Binding–right side

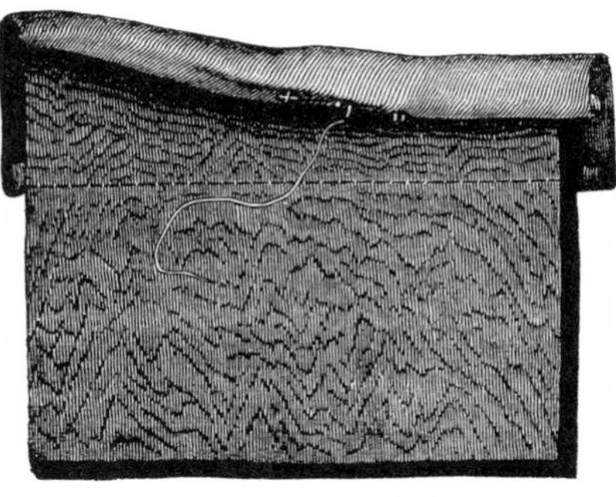

Figure 29. Binding–wrong side

For the stitched hem in Figure 30 lay the material 1/2 inch over on the under side. Stitch it down on the right side.

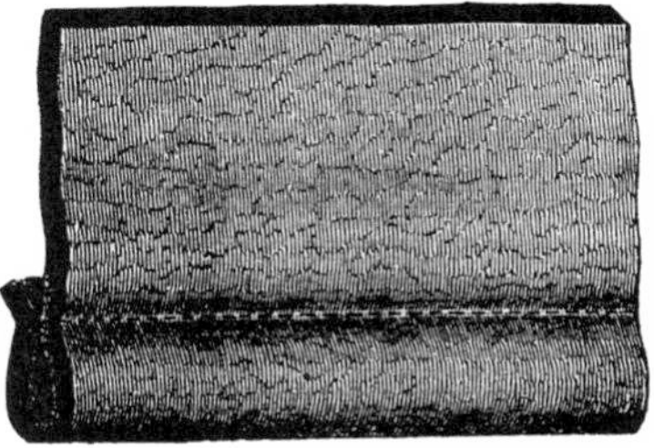

Figure 30. Stitched hem

Making Pocket Slits

Make the pocket slit, for vests, jackets, etc., of the requisite length, as shown by Figure 31. Cut small slits at the ends.

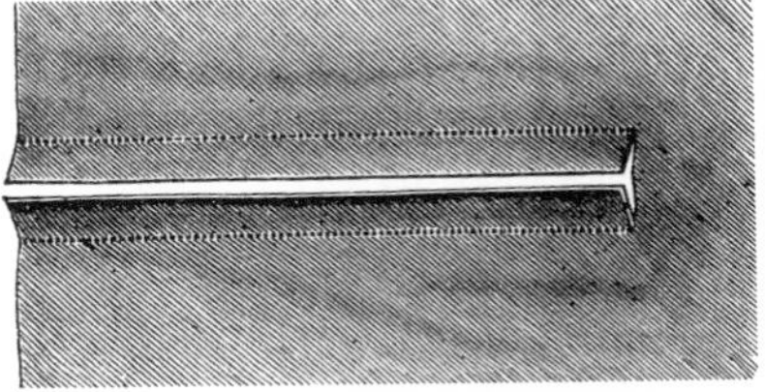

Figure 31. Pocket slit

If you wish to finish it as in Figure 32, sew the edge of the material along the dotted line on Figure 31 from the under side to the upper edge of the pocket. Stitch it down from the right side so the edges of the material lie together. On the right side of the under slit run a bias strip of the material, which must then be laid over on the under side and stitched down from the right side. Sew the ends of the slit down on the pocket as shown.

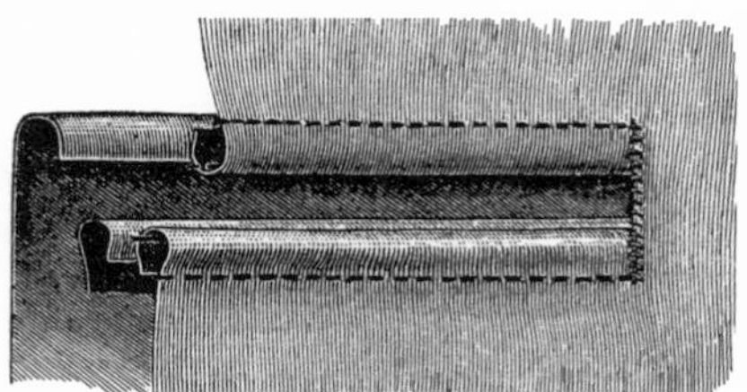

Figure 32. Binding pocket slit

The pocket slit in Figure 33 is arranged similarly, except the sides must first be corded. Sew the pocket piece on from the under side.

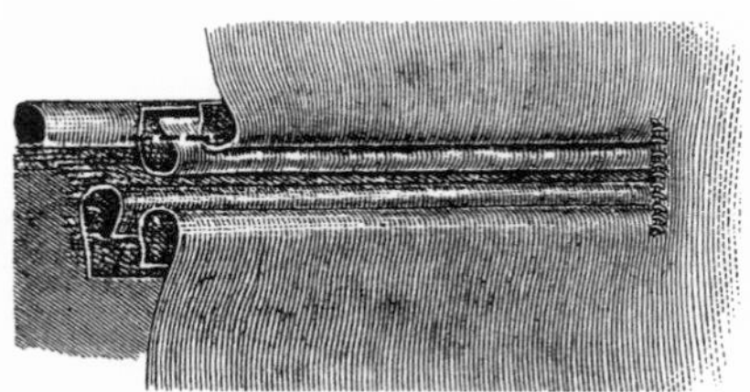

Figure 33. Cording pocket slit

Covering Buttons

These buttons serve for dresses, paletots, etc.

Figures 34 and 35 show how to cover buttons with cloth. Cut the cloth 2/5 inch larger than the button. Run a thread around the edge, by which the material is drawn into close gathers after a little wadding has been laid on the upper surface. Then sew a cross of thread on the under side as shown in Figure 35. Run the needle through this cross when sewing on the button.

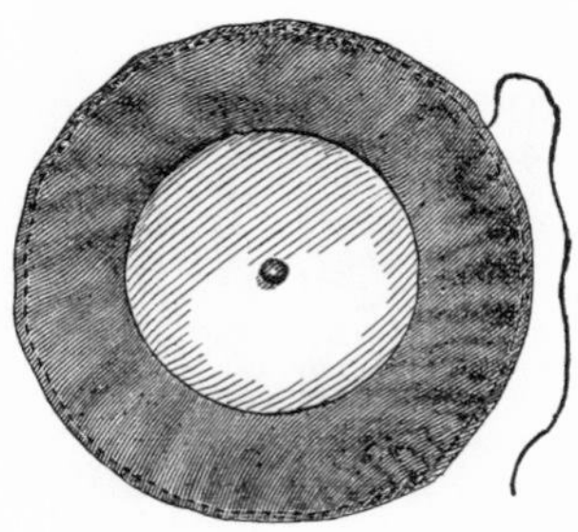

Figure 34. Covering button with silk

Figure 35. Button covered with silk–under side

Figure 36 shows a button the cover of which is crocheted of black silk and sewn on a foundation covered with cloth. The crocheting consists of slip stitches. They are not worked as ordinarily from right to left, but from left to right, in a sort of coiled design. This stitch is particularly recommended for passementerie.

Figure 36. Crocheted button cover

For making this cover wind a mesh 1 inch in diameter seven or eight times with the silk thread. Draw the threads off, and crochet them over closely with single crochet to form a firm ring. Then take the needle out of the work. Turn the work. Crochet on the under side slip stitches from left to right, always putting the needle in the forward vein of the stitch, as shown by Figure 37. In the following rounds always put the needle through the back vein of a stitch. Work altogether seven rounds without widening or narrowing.

Figure 37. Crocheting button cover

Now stretch the cover over the button so the under part of the work comes outside. The center of the button is covered with a jet bead.

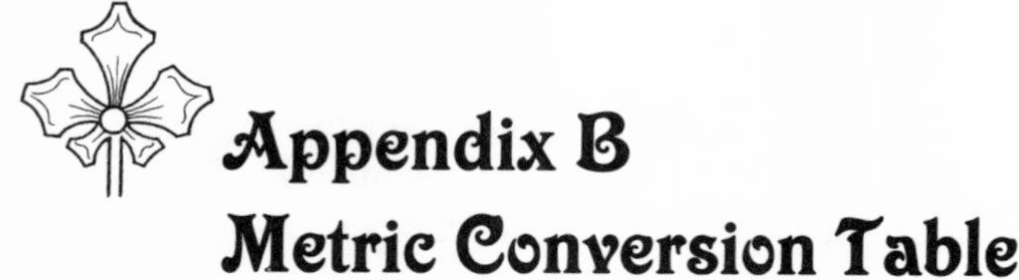

Appendix B
Metric Conversion Table

This table contains the English and metric equivalents of measurements often used in sewing. In addition it contains the metric equivalents of period measurements (5ths, 10ths, 3rds, and 6ths of inches) used in *Harpers Bazar*. Numbers running to several decimal places and (most) fractions under 1/16 inch have been rounded for easy use.

English Measurement	Metric Equivalent	Metric Measurement	English Equivalent
1/10 in.	2.5 mm	1 mm	1/32 in.
1/8 in.	3.2 mm	2 mm	1/16 in.
1/6 in.	4.2 mm	3 mm	1/8 in.
1/5 in.	5.1 mm	4 mm	5/32 in.
1/4 in.	6.4 mm	5 mm	7/32 in.
3/10 in.	7.6 mm	6 mm	1/4 in.
1/3 in.	8.5 mm	7 mm	9/32 in.
3/8 in.	9.5 mm	8 mm	5/16 in.
2/5 in.	1.0 cm	9 mm	11/32 in.
1/2 in.	1.3 cm	10 mm (1 cm)	13/32 in.
3/5 in.	1.5 cm	2 cm	3/4 in.
5/8 in.	1.6 cm	3 cm	1 3/16 in.
2/3 in.	1.7 cm	4 cm	1 9/16 in.
7/10 in.	1.8 cm	5 cm	2 in.
3/4 in.	1.9 cm	6 cm	2 3/8 in.
4/5 in.	2.0 cm	7 cm	2 3/4 in.
5/6 in.	2.1 cm	8 cm	3 1/8 in.
7/8 in.	2.2 cm	9 cm	3 1/2 in.
9/10 in.	2.3 cm	10 cm	3 15/16 in.
1 in.	2.5 cm	15 cm	5 7/8 in.
1 1/4 in.	3.2 cm	20 cm	7 7/8 in.
1 1/2 in.	3.8 cm	25 cm	9 13/16 in.
1 3/4 in.	4.4 cm	30 cm	11 13/16 in.
2 in.	5.1 cm	35 cm	13 3/4 in.

Metric Conversion Table

English Measurement	Metric Equivalent	Metric Measurement	English Equivalent
2 1/4 in.	5.7 cm	40 cm	15 3/4 in.
2 1/2 in.	6.4 cm	45 cm	17 11/16 in.
2 3/4 in.	7.0 cm	50 cm	19 11/16 in.
3 in.	7.6 cm	55 cm	21 5/8 in.
3 1/4 in.	8.3 cm	60 cm	23 5/8 in.
3 1/2 in.	8.9 cm	65 cm	25 9/16 in.
3 3/4 in.	9.5 cm	70 cm	27 9/16 in.
4 in.	10.2 cm	75 cm	29 1/2 in.
4 1/2 in.	11.4 cm	80 cm	31 1/2 in.
5 in.	12.7 cm	85 cm	33 7/16 in.
5 1/2 in.	14.0 cm	90 cm	35 7/16 in.
6 in.	15.2 cm	95 cm	37 3/8 in.
6 1/2 in.	16.5 cm	100 cm (1 m)	39 3/8 in.
7 in.	17.8 cm	1.25 m	1 yd. 13 3/16 in.
7 1/2 in.	19.1 cm	1.50 m	1 yd. 23 1/16 in.
8 in.	20.3 cm	1.75 m	1 yd. 32 7/8 in.
8 1/2 in.	21.6 cm	2.00 m	2 yd. 6 3/4 in.
9 in. (1/4 yd.)	22.9 cm	2.50 m	2 yd. 26 7/16 in.
9 1/2 in.	24.1 cm	3.00 m	3 yd. 10 1/8 in.
10 in.	25.4 cm	3.50 m	3 yd. 29 13/16 in.
10 1/2 in.	26.7 cm	4.00 m	4 yd. 13 1/2 in.
11 in.	27.9 cm	4.50 m	4 yd. 33 3/16 in.
11 1/2 in.	29.2 cm	5.00 m	5 yd. 16 7/8 in.
12 in. (1 ft.)	30.5 cm	5.50 m	6 yd. 9/16 in.
1/2 yd. (18 in.)	45.7 cm	6.00 m	6 yd. 20 1/4 in.
3/4 yd. (27 in.)	68.6 cm	6.50 m	7 yd. 3 7/8 in.
1 yd. (36 in.)	91.4 cm	7.00 m	7 yd. 23 9/16 in.
1 1/4 yd.	1.14 m	7.50 m	8 yd. 7 1/4 in.
1 1/2 yd.	1.37 m	8.00 m	8 yd. 26 15/16 in.
1 3/4 yd.	1.60 m	8.50 m	9 yd. 10 5/8 in.
2 yd.	1.83 m	9.00 m	9 yd. 30 5/16 in.
2 1/2 yd.	2.29 m	9.50 m	10 yd. 14 in.
3 yd.	2.74 m	10.00 m	10 yd. 33 11/16 in.

Appendix C
Resources

Blum, Stella, ed. *Fashions and Costumes from Godey's Lady's Book*. Mineola: Dover Publications, 1985.

Black-and-white plates showing the evolution of fashion from 1837 to 1869.

Blum, Stella, ed. *Victorian Fashions and Costumes from Harper's Bazar: 1867–1898*. New York: Dover Publications, 1974.

Black-and-white plates chosen from almost the entire Victorian run of *Harper's Bazar*.

Buck, Anne. *Victorian Costume and Costume Accessories*. Carlton: Ruth Bean, 1984.

A concise history of fashion. Mostly women's clothes, with a chapter each on men and children.

Byrde, Penelope. *Nineteenth-Century Fashion*. London: B. T. Batsford, 1992.

A history of fashion; equally devoted to men's and women's clothes.

Caulfeild, S. F. A. and Blanche C. Saward. *Encyclopedia of Victorian Needlework*. New York: Dover Publications, 1972.

Reprint of an 1887 work. It includes definitions of terms, descriptions of tools and materials, and instructions for the stitches of many types of needlework.

Ginsburg, Madeleine, ed. *Victorian Dress in Photographs*. New York: Holmes & Meier, 1983.

Photos of men, women, and children with substantial captions, including some from the late 1860s.

Grimble, Frances. *After a Fashion: How to Reproduce, Restore, and Wear Vintage Styles*. San Francisco: Lavolta Press, 1998.

Covers medieval through Art Deco styles for women and men. Guides readers through each stage of a reproduction project and advises them on all aspects of collecting vintage clothes.

Marquis, Philippe. Graph Paper Printer. http://perso.easynet.fr/~philimar/graphpapeng.htm.

A freeware program that enables you to easily define and print your own graph paper.

Olian, JoAnne, ed. *80 Godey's Full-Color Fashion Plates 1838–1880*. Mineola: Dover Publications, 1998.

Color plates with descriptive captions in a section up front. Includes a brief history of *Godey's Lady's Book* and its fashion coverage.

Picken, Mary Brooks. *A Dictionary of Costume and Fashion Historic and Modern*. Mineola: Dover Publications, 1999.

A useful guide to costume and textile terms.

Rothstein, Natalie, ed. *Four Hundred Years of Fashion*. London: Victoria and Albert Museum, 1984.

Includes photos of a few late 1860s garments in the Victoria and Albert collection.

Thieme, Otto Charles, ed. *With Grace and Favour: Victorian and Edwardian Fashion in America*. Cincinnati: Cincinnati Art Museum, 1993.

A museum catalog that contains color photos of several surviving late 1860s garments.

Index A
Patterns and Instructions by Garment Type

This index organizes the patterns and instructions by garment type. Some garments belong to, and are listed under, more than one type. In some cases the original source does not make it clear whether a garment is for day or evening, or whether a dress waist is separate or attached; so the categorization of these garments is tentative. Most articles on trimmings for specific garment types are under "trimmings and decorations." Individual trimmings contained within these articles are listed in the index by construction technique.

Index A

Garment Types

Index A

Garment Types

Index B
Patterns and Instructions by Construction Technique

This index organizes the patterns and instructions (including those for individual trimmings) by construction technique. Some patterns are listed under more than one technique. The distinction between "heirloom sewing" and "sewing" is somewhat arbitrary. If you are looking for sewing patterns you may wish to browse both categories.

Embroidery

Index B

Construction Techniques

Knitting

Lace Making

Millinery

Index B

Construction Techniques

Sewing

Index B

Tailoring

Tatting

Index C
Fashion Columns

This index includes the descriptions of styles, fabrics, trims, colors, and all instructions in the fashion columns. It does not include patterns or instructions from other articles.

A

B

C

Index C

Books by Lavolta Press

After a Fashion: How to Reproduce, Restore, and Wear Vintage Styles, by Frances Grimble

Covers medieval through Art Deco styles for women and men. Guides readers through each stage of a reproduction project and advises them on all aspects of collecting vintage clothes.

356 pages, 147 illustrations, $38

Reconstruction Era Fashions: 350 Sewing, Needlework, and Millinery Patterns 1867–1868, by Frances Grimble

Women's patterns and instructions from the first 14 months of *Harper's Bazar.* Includes articles on needlework techniques and fashion trends.

529 pages, 609 illustrations, $45

The Voice of Fashion: 79 Turn-of-the-Century Patterns with Instructions and Fashion Plates, by Frances Grimble

Women's patterns for 1900 through 1906, selected from *The Voice of Fashion.* Includes rulers for the Diamond Cutting System.

463 pages, 93 illustrations, $42

The Edwardian Modiste: 85 Authentic Patterns with Instructions, Fashion Plates, and Period Sewing Techniques, by Frances Grimble

Women's patterns for 1905 through 1909, selected from *The American Garment Cutter Instruction and Diagram Book* and *The American Modiste.* Includes chapters of a 1907 dressmaking manual and rulers for the American System of Cutting.

430 pages, 112 illustrations, $42

Further information is available on our web site, http://www.lavoltapress.com.

Our books can be purchased in bookstores or ordered from Lavolta Press at 20 Meadowbrook Drive, San Francisco, CA 94132. If mail ordered, shipping is $4 for the first book and $2 for each additional book (for book post within the US). California purchasers must add sales tax. Prices subject to change without notice.